Windows® 7
Secrets®

Windows® 7
Secrets®

Paul Thurrott
Rafael Rivera

Wiley Publishing, Inc.

Windows® 7 Secrets®

Published by
Wiley Publishing, Inc.
10475 Crosspoint Boulevard
Indianapolis, IN 46256
www.wiley.com

Copyright © 2009 by Wiley Publishing, Inc., Indianapolis, Indiana
Published simultaneously in Canada

ISBN: 978-0-470-50841-1

Manufactured in the United States of America

10 9 8 7 6 5 4 3 2

For general information on our other products and services please contact our Customer Care Department within the United States at (877) 762-2974, outside the United States at (317) 572-3993 or fax (317) 572-4002.

Wiley also publishes its books in a variety of electronic formats. Some content that appears in print may not be available in electronic books.

Library of Congress Control Number: 2009931755

To Stephanie, Mark, and Kelly—Paul

To my father, who started me on my wonderful Windows journey—Rafael

About the Technical Editors

Todd Meister has been developing using Microsoft technologies for over 15 years. He's been a Technical Editor on over 50 titles ranging from SQL Server to the .NET Framework. Besides technical editing titles, he is an Assistant Director for Computing Services at Ball State University in Muncie, Indiana. He lives in central Indiana with his wife, Kimberly, and their four children.

Joli Ballew is a Microsoft MVP and holds several Microsoft certifications including MCSE, MCDST, and MCTS. Joli has written over 30 books, teaches at two local junior colleges, manages the network and Web site for North Texas Graphics, and regularly writes for several Web sites. In her spare time, Joli enjoys gardening, golfing, and traveling.

About the Authors

The author of over 20 books, **Paul Thurrott** is a technology analyst for Windows IT Pro and the majordomo of the SuperSite for Windows (www.winsupersite.com). He writes a weekly editorial for Windows IT Pro UPDATE (www.windowsitpro.com/email), a daily Windows news and information e-mail newsletter called "WinInfo Daily News" (www.wininformant.com), and a monthly column called "Need to Know" in *Windows IT Pro Magazine*. He also blogs daily via the SuperSite Blog (community.winsupersite.com/blogs/paul), posts regularly on Twitter (www.twitter.com/thurrott), and appears weekly in the highly rated and hugely popular Windows Weekly podcast with Leo Laporte (www.twit.tv/ww).

Rafael Rivera is a software developer for a VAR 500 company, Telos Corporation, where he works on mission critical systems. He is a Certified Reverse Engineering Analyst (CREA) and takes Windows apart on his blog Within Windows (www.withinwindows.com). He also regularly "tweets" (www.twitter.com/withinrafael). Rafael was born on the same day as Windows 1.0—November 20, 1985—which many believe is no coincidence.

Credits

Acquisitions Editor
Jenny Watson

Executive Editor
Carol Long

Senior Project Editor
Kevin Kent

Development Editor
Jeff Riley

Technical Editors
Todd Meister
Joli Ballew

Production Editor
Kathleen Wisor

Copy Editor
Luann Rouff

Editorial Director
Robyn B. Siesky

Editorial Manager
Mary Beth Wakefield

Production Manager
Tim Tate

**Vice President and
Executive Group Publisher**
Richard Swadley

**Vice President and
Executive Publisher**
Barry Pruett

Associate Publisher
Jim Minatel

Project Coordinator, Cover
Lynsey Stanford

Compositors
Craig Johnson and
Maureen Forys,
Happenstance Type-O-Rama

Proofreader
Dr. Nate Pritts, Word One

Indexer
Robert Swanson

Cover Designer
Ryan Sneed

Acknowledgments

I don't even know where to start, so I'll start at the beginning.

Thanks Mom and Dad, for pushing me to pursue my passions.

Thanks Gary, for starting me down this path in 1993. I miss you.

Thanks Adam, for having big ideas and taking a chance on me.

Thanks to everyone at *Windows IT Pro Magazine*—past and present—for an amazing decade of growth and change.

Thanks to Jeff, Aimee, and Brittany at Lenovo. You are the best.

Thanks to Allen, Glen, and Marco at HP. My infrastructure is built on your stuff, and I appreciate all your help.

Thanks, Stephanie, for believing in me and for giving me the time and space I need to get this kind of thing completed. As always, you are the glue that makes our family work.

Thanks to Mark and Kelly for understanding about the missed baseball and softball games. You both make me smile every day.

Thanks to Rafael for joining me on this confusing, busy, and stressful adventure. It's nice to have a true co-author for a change, one I can trust with anything, bounce ideas off, and truly collaborate with. Welcome aboard.

Thanks to Kevin and Jen at Wiley for all your help. Hey, we finally got one done on time! Also, thanks to Katie, who has moved on to bigger and better things, and to all the editors who worked on this title. Thanks, too, to Carol for your invaluable help. You know why.

Thanks to Lucas for always being ready to find the answer. Thanks, too, to all my friends and acquaintances at Microsoft and Wagged who helped me along the way.

Finally, thanks to my readers and listeners from around the world. I've enjoyed the conversations and hope they continue well into the future. It's been a fantastic ride, but what makes this fun isn't so much the products as it is the relationships you make along the way.

—Paul

A very special thanks to my parents, for letting me consume their food and electricity while working on this title night and day. I love you both!

A gut punch for Paul, for giving me the opportunity to contribute to his series of books built by users for users. I look up to him. So should you.

A hug and a kiss to my girlfriend, Jenny, for being a proud and incredibly supportive super-nerd, and for making me the happiest guy alive.

A special shout out to my friends Morgan and Jimmy, in ice cream heaven Vermont! Chunky Monkey, baby!

A salute to Kevin, Jen, and all the folks at Wiley for tolerating our delays and helping us push the book out on time. Without them, you wouldn't be reading this. Seriously.

And finally, a thumbs up to all my readers around the world. I enjoy writing for you all!

To the people that spam me. I hate you.

—Rafael

Contents at a Glance

Contents

Part IV: Digital Media and Entertainment 357

Chapter 11: Digital Music and Audio 359

Chapter 12: Organizing, Fixing, and Sharing Digital Photos 419

Preface

Welcome to *Windows 7 Secrets*. We hope you enjoy combing through this book as much as we enjoyed digging deep into Windows 7 to find the most valuable information for you. Ultimately, Windows isn't just about the pieces that Microsoft ships on a disc; it also includes the satellite products and services that support the base OS. This book reflects that fact and, as a result, we hope you will find it more valuable and useful. Thanks for reading.

—Paul Thurrott
paul.thurrott@penton.com

—Rafael Rivera
rafael@withinwindows.com

July 2009

Web Site Supporting the Book

This book is only the beginning: more secrets can be found online. For updates, errata, new information, and an ongoing blog with interactive discussions, please visit the SuperSite for Windows (www.winsupersite.com) and WithinWindows (www.withinwindows.com). The official site for the book can be found at www.winsupersite.com/book.

Icons Used in This Book

The following icons are used in this book to help draw your attention to some of the most important or most useful information in the book.

Secret   The Secret icon marks little-known facts that are not obvious to most Windows users. This information is rarely documented by Microsoft, and when it is, it's done so in a way that's not easy for users to find.

tip   The Tip icon indicates a helpful trick.

note   The Note icon points out items of importance.

cross ref

The Cross-Reference icon points to chapters where additional information can be found.

caution

The Caution icon warns you about possible negative side-effects or precautions you should take before making a change.

Read This First

◆ ◆

In This Chapter

Discovering that, yes, Windows 7 really is that good

Taking a quick tour of new and improved Windows 7 features

Looking at the products and services that complete the Windows 7 experience

Continuing your exploration of Windows 7 on the Web

◆ ◆

Well, it's here. Windows 7 is Microsoft's latest desktop operating system, and while that's notable on its own, this time around Microsoft appears to have really gotten it right. With Windows Vista, those in the know fought an uphill battle trying to convince people that it wasn't as horrible as pundits and know-nothing bloggers claimed. But Windows 7 is different. This time around, Microsoft has tweaked, prodded, and improved virtually every single aspect of the OS, and as a result the Windows Vista goose has evolved into the Windows 7 swan. Despite sharing common underpinnings, Windows 7 is perceived to be dramatically superior to Windows Vista. And that opinion is nearly universal: all those clowns that were falling over each other to out-criticize Windows Vista now can't compliment Windows 7 enough. For once, they may be on to something: Windows 7 is the best OS to come out of Redmond in a long, long time. And in this initial chapter, we'll try to explain why that is so.

Believe the Hype

Virtually everywhere you look, the reviews are positive. With Windows 7, Microsoft has finally provided a technically excellent and lust-worthy desktop OS. It's "Vista done right." It's an apology for the mistakes of its predecessor, a technological mea culpa that tries to right the wrongs. Okay, maybe. But we think of it like this. Windows 7 is the finest desktop OS Microsoft has ever released. It benefits from the work that came before, in Windows Vista, and from a strict adherence to principles of simplicity, elegance, and clarity. Microsoft didn't bite off more than it could chew, and instead of the mess of weird bundled applications and capabilities that muddled Windows Vista, Windows 7 presents a much clearer picture. In fact, the more time you spend with Windows 7, the more you realize that Microsoft went over this product with a fine-toothed comb. No code, no bit, no pixel was left untouched. If something could be simplified, cleaned up, tweaked, or made better in some way, it was.

All that said—Windows 7 isn't perfect. Heresy, we know. But consider the following.

While Windows 7 performs better than Windows Vista, it's still slower than XP on the same hardware and less compatible with existing hardware and software, even with the Windows XP Mode solution. We think that's just fine. After all, Windows XP is almost a decade old. More important, the differences are minimal and negligible on newer hardware.

Some Windows 7 features will be confusing. The new Windows 7 taskbar hides windows, and the improved notification area hides icons, obscuring the fact that applications are autoloading during boot-time, increasing the amount of time that it takes to boot and killing off value system resources.

Finally, if you're coming to Windows 7 from Windows Vista, the change won't seem as dramatic as it will if you stuck with XP. That's because Windows 7 is really just an evolution of Windows Vista. So you can expect more of the same, even though it's a "better same"—if that makes sense.

Taken in context, Windows 7 is something special. But just as it's important to understand how to take advantage of its best new features, it's equally important to know where it falls flat so you find workarounds. And when you think about it, that's exactly what this book is all about. We document the good, the bad, and the ugly. Fortunately, with Windows 7, it's mostly good.

Windows 7 in 15 Minutes

This entire book is, of course, dedicated to Windows 7 and, to a lesser extent, the ecosystem of products and services that complete the Windows experience. But if you're looking for a quick rundown of some of the most important new changes and features in Windows, you don't have to read the whole book, at least not yet. Instead, we present here a crash course on Windows 7. Read on and you can learn about the most important new features of Windows 7 in the time it takes to sip a perfectly made latte. And we'll point you to where you can find out more about these features, when applicable: *Windows 7 Secrets* wasn't designed to be read from cover to cover. Instead, you should feel free to jump around and explore those topics that are the most confusing or interesting first.

Better "Itties"

Compared to its predecessors, Windows 7 offers better reliability, compatibility, security, and, um, "performity," or what we jokingly call the "itties." These improvements are pervasive to Windows 7 and appear at every level of the experience, from low-level tweaks that make the system run better to major end-user features that are so fun and useful they'll literally bring a smile to your face.

On the reliability front, Windows 7 is engineered to withstand problems, proactively seek out issues that might otherwise undermine system integrity, and then help you solve problems that do manage to get through Windows 7's defenses using the new Windows Troubleshooting infrastructure (see Figure 1). And unlike with Windows Vista, most Backup and Restore features are available in all Windows 7 product versions.

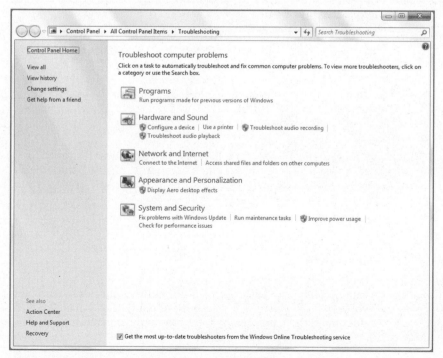

Figure 1: Windows Troubleshooting helps you solve problems.

cross ref

You can find out more about Windows 7's repair and recovery tools in Chapter 25. We discuss Backup and Restore in Chapter 24.

Windows 7 also builds off of the hardware and software compatibility improvements that Microsoft engineered over the first 3 years of Windows Vista's lifetime. If Vista compatibility isn't good enough, a new feature called Windows XP Mode provides the capability to run many Windows XP applications in a special virtualized environment, side-by-side with native Windows 7 applications. Windows XP Mode is shown in Figure 2.

Figure 2: Windows XP Mode enables you to run XP applications side by side with Windows 7 applications.

cross ref

We discuss Windows XP Mode in Chapter 3.

Microsoft made huge security gains in Windows Vista, and Windows 7 builds on that foundation by making the controversial User Account Control (UAC) feature less annoying, adding new security and privacy controls to Internet Explorer 8 (see Figure 3), and adding important new monitoring capabilities to Action Center, the replacement for Vista's Security Center.

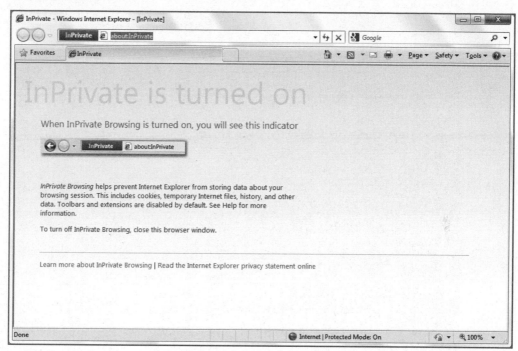

Figure 3: Internet Explorer 8 InPrivate Browsing lets you cover your tracks online.

> **cross ref**   We look at security in Chapter 7.

On the performance front, Windows 7 marks the first time since, oh, the early 1990s that a new version of Windows actually substantially outperforms its predecessor on the same hardware. Windows 7 runs so well that it will tame everything from a 3-year-old Ultra Mobile PC (UMPC) to a modern if otherwise underpowered netbook.

Simpler Setup

Thanks to improvements in the componentization of the underlying operating system, Windows 7 Setup, shown in Figure 4, is simpler and faster than ever. So whether you're doing a clean install of the OS, upgrading from Windows Vista, migrating from Windows XP or Vista, or upgrading a version of Windows 7 to a better version of Windows 7, Microsoft has you covered. And using tools like Windows Easy Transfer, it's possible to ensure that all your old settings and data make it from your old PC to Windows 7 no matter how you upgrade.

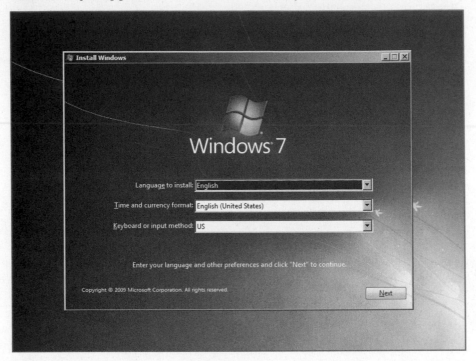

Figure 4: Windows 7 Setup is simpler and faster than previous versions and has fewer steps for you to babysit.

cross ref   We cover all installation eventualities in Chapter 2.

New Aero Desktop Capabilities

When Windows Vista debuted in 2006, the glasslike Windows Aero user interface was the biggest usability news. But in Windows 7, Microsoft takes Aero to the next level with a wide range of new desktop effects. These include such things as Aero Peek, shown in Figure 5, Aero Shake, Aero Themes, and Aero Snaps. But the Windows desktop isn't just about desktop effects. Windows 7 also makes it easier than ever to modify other aspects of the user experience, including the use of desktop gadgets and support for high-DPI displays and multiple monitors.

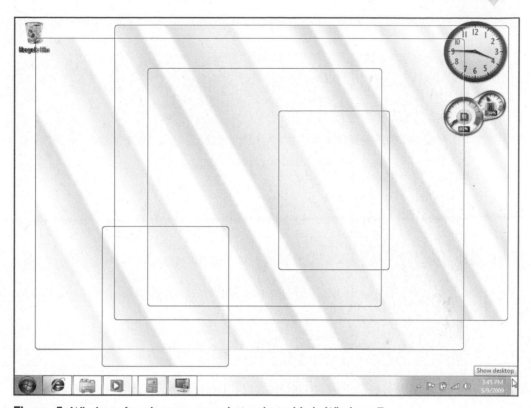

Figure 5: Windows Aero is more pervasive and capable in Windows 7.

cross ref   We examine the Aero desktop effects and Windows desktop gadgets in Chapter 4.

Enhanced Taskbar

In one of the more controversial changes in Windows 7, Microsoft has dramatically enhanced the capabilities of the taskbar, essentially combining the capabilities of the Quick Launch toolbar and taskbar from Windows Vista into a single user experience. Now, you can pin shortcuts to the taskbar, rearrange buttons on the taskbar as you see fit, and manage running and nonrunning applications from this single location. The new Windows 7 taskbar is shown in Figure 6.

Figure 6: The new Windows 7 taskbar is indeed super.

cross ref   The Windows 7 taskbar is also covered in Chapter 4.

Jump Lists

In addition to the new taskbar, Microsoft has enhanced shortcuts in the Windows 7 taskbar and Start menu with a new feature called Jump Lists. These context-sensitive "Mini Start Menus" appear when you right-click, providing access to customized task and recent document lists for the underlying applications. While all applications get a standard Jump List, developers are free to customize these lists in interesting ways, and of course, built-in Windows 7 applications often come with customized Jump Lists, like the Media Player Jump List shown in Figure 7.

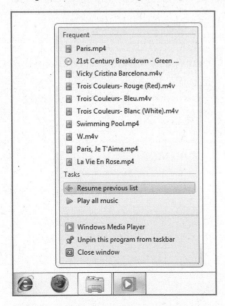

Figure 7: Windows Media Player sports a customized Jump List.

⬦ cross
  ref
In Chapter 4, we introduce Jump Lists.

Windows Touch

While Apple popularized multi-touch capabilities in the smartphone space with the iPhone, Microsoft can be credited with doing so on the PC. Building on the Tablet PC and touch capabilities in previous versions of Windows, Windows 7 is the first to offer pervasive multi-touch functionality courtesy of Windows Touch, shown in Figure 8.

Figure 8: Windows Touch lets you control a PC entirely with your fingers…or just finger paint.

⬦ cross
  ref
Windows Touch is, ahem, touched on in Chapter 4 and Chapter 18.

Libraries

In a new bid to end the organizational nightmares that dog many Windows users, Windows 7 combines the virtualization technology it introduced in Windows 7 with the special shell folder concepts it has been evolving since Windows 95. The result is Libraries, special saved searches that aggregate content from around the PC file system and present them in a single cohesive view. Windows 7 includes built-in Libraries such as Documents, Music, Pictures (shown in Figure 9), and Videos, but you're welcome to make your own as well.

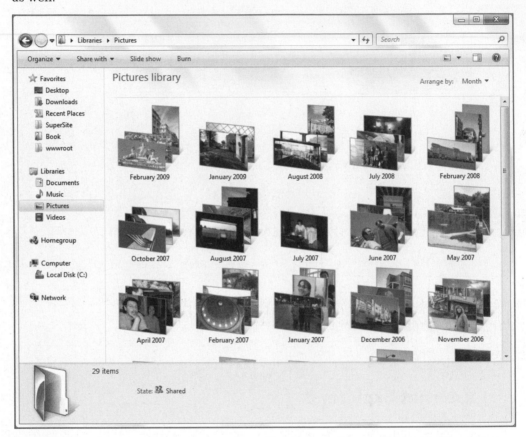

Figure 9: Libraries aggregate content and provide unique and attractive organizational view styles.

cross ref
     We explain Libraries in Chapter 5.

HomeGroup Sharing

While Windows has included increasingly easier network-based sharing capabilities over the years, Windows 7 is the simplest yet. Thanks to a new feature called HomeGroup, shown in Figure 10, you can easily share documents, music, pictures, videos, and printers on your home network and do so without mucking around with user names and permissions.

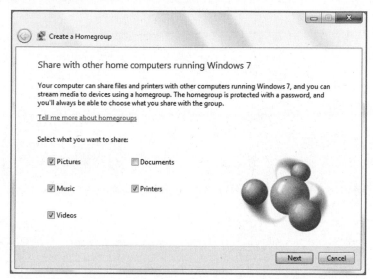

Figure 10: The Windows 7 HomeGroup feature makes it easier than ever to share media, documents, and printers on your home network.

cross ref   HomeGroup sharing is covered in Chapter 9.

Internet Explorer 8

Windows 7 includes the latest version of Microsoft's popular browser, Internet Explorer 8, shown in Figure 11. This browser builds on the important usability and security foundation of its predecessor and adds such features as Web Slices, Accelerators, Compatibility View Updates, InPrivate Browsing, and more.

Figure 11: Internet Explorer 8

**cross
ref**

We look at Internet Explorer 8 in Chapter 20. IE8's security features are covered in Chapter 7.

New and Improved Applets

While legacy Windows applets got short shrift in Windows Vista, they've all been enhanced and updated in Windows 7. And there are some new applets, too. All Windows 7 users will be able to utilize dramatically updated versions of Paint, WordPad, and Calculator, as well as a few new bundled apps like Sticky Notes and XPS Viewer, shown in Figure 12.

**cross
ref**

We look at Windows 7 applets in Chapter 4.

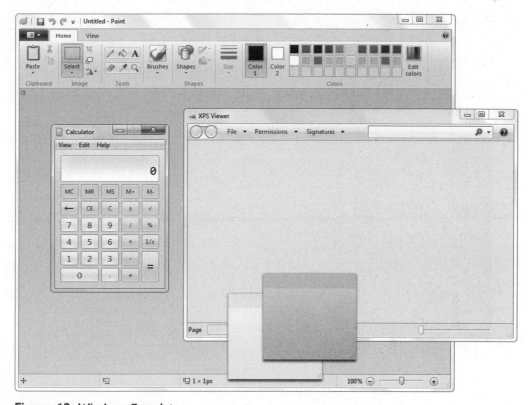

Figure 12: Windows 7 applets

But Wait, There's More

You want more? Oh, there's more. In addition to the hundreds of other features and changes that are included in Windows 7, Microsoft is also busy expanding the Windows ecosystem to include products and services that extend Windows 7's capabilities or, in some cases, fall outside of the traditional PC desktop. We cover a number of these technologies in the book because they do indeed complete the Windows 7 experience.

Windows Live Essentials and Windows Live Services

A few years before Microsoft shipped Windows 7, it began separately reevaluating the relationship between its PC operating system and the various online products and services it was then offering through its MSN brand. Executives at the company determined that they wanted to bring the company's Windows, online, and mobile experiences together in ways that were seamless but wouldn't run into any of the antitrust issues presented by previous integration strategies regarding Internet Explorer and Windows Media Player.

The result was Windows Live, a set of online products and services that extend the Windows user experience in exciting and unique ways. The sheer number of Windows Live services is somewhat daunting, and complicating matters is the fact that there are other Microsoft Live services, including Office Live, Games for Windows Live, Xbox Live, Live Mesh, and more.

And of course, Microsoft has removed several applications from Windows 7 and now ships them as part of the Windows Live Essentials suite (see Figure 13). This way, they can be updated more frequently—and Microsoft can stave off the antitrust regulators.

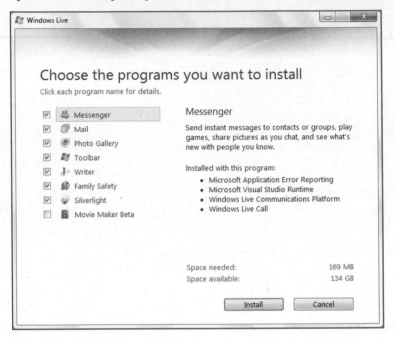

Figure 13: Windows Live Essentials

---

cross ref   Microsoft's Live services are discussed in detail in Chapter 23, and we cover the various applications in the Windows Live Essentials suite throughout the book.

Zune

While Microsoft continues to evolve its Windows Media platform and includes an impressive new Windows Media Player in Windows 7, the company seems to realize that the future lies elsewhere. For this reason, it has been pushing its Zune digital media platform on the side as well; and from what we can tell, the Zune—shown in Figure 14—has enough important unique features that it's a viable Windows Media replacement. Heck, it may even offer the iPod serious competition—someday.

Figure 14: Microsoft Zune

cross ref   The Zune is so important it gets its own chapter, Chapter 14.

Windows Mobile

Microsoft has been plying the PDA and smartphone market for almost 15 years, but recent versions of Windows Mobile are finally starting to get interesting. Looking at running a version of Windows that can fit in your pocket? Windows Mobile might be exactly what you're looking for. Windows Mobile 6.5 is shown in Figure 15.

Figure 15: Windows Mobile 6.5

cross ref   We provide a short overview of Windows Mobile in Chapter 19.

Windows Home Server

While Windows 7 offers seamless network-based sharing, it doesn't really offer any central-ized management of your PCs, media, documents, and other data. That's where Windows Home Server comes in. And despite the name, Windows Home Server is as simple to use as it is powerful. The Windows Home Server admin console can be seen in Figure 16.

Figure 16: Windows Home Server helps you consolidate your media and data to a central location on your home network.

cross ref   Windows Home Server is the subject of Chapter 10.

Our Promise to You

We've barely scratched the surface of the changes you'll find in Windows 7 and covered throughout this book. But as noted previously, Microsoft—and Windows 7—isn't standing still. For this reason, no book, even one as comprehensive as we've tried to make this one, can cover it all. So join us online, at Paul Thurrott's SuperSite for Windows (www.winsupersite.com) and Rafael Rivera's Within Windows (www.withinwindows .com). In this way, *Windows 7 Secrets* is a living document, one that will be updated on an ongoing basis online. And if you're looking for an even more direct relationship, follow us on Twitter. Paul can be found at @thurrott, and Rafael is at @WithinRafael. See you online!

Part I

Surviving Setup

Selecting the Right Windows 7 Edition

Chapter
1

♦ ♦

In This Chapter

Basic differences between the Windows 7 product editions

Which Windows 7 product editions you can safely avoid

Differences between the 32-bit and 64-bit versions of Windows 7

Determining the best Windows 7 for you

Choosing between the home and business versions

Choosing between Windows 7 Home Premium and Professional

Features available in all Windows 7 versions

Choosing Windows 7 Ultimate

♦ ♦

If you haven't purchased Windows 7 yet—or you'd like to know whether or not it's worth upgrading from the version you do have to a more capable version—this chapter is for you. Here, we'll explain the differences between the many Windows 7 product editions and help you pick the version that makes the most sense for you.

The Way We Were: XP and Vista Product Editions

Back in 2001, life was easy: Microsoft released Windows XP in just two product editions, Windows XP Home Edition and Windows XP Professional Edition. The difference between the products was fairly obvious, and with its enhanced feature set, XP Pro was the more expensive and desirable version, as one might expect.

Over time, however, Microsoft muddied the waters with a wealth of new XP product editions. Three major product editions were added: Windows XP Media Center Edition (which received three major releases and one minor update between 2002 and 2005), Windows XP Tablet PC Edition (which received two major releases between 2002 and 2005), and Windows XP Professional x64 Edition, which took most of XP Pro's feature set and brought it to the x64 hardware platform. Other XP versions, such as XP Embedded and XP Starter Edition, can't really be considered mainstream products, because they targeted specific usage scenarios and were never made broadly available to consumers.

Secret

Most PCs sold during Windows XP's lifetime were 32-bit computers based on Intel's x86 platform. While the industry was widely expected to make the jump to 64-bit computing at some point, that leap came from an unexpected place: Intel's tiny competitor AMD developed the so-called x64 platform, which is essentially a 64-bit version of the aging x86 platform. The x64-based PCs are completely compatible with x86 software, and though all PCs sold today are, in fact, x64-compatible, most PC operating systems to date (including Windows Vista) were sold in 32-bit versions for compatibility reasons. (Even Intel is on board: though the x64 platform was created by AMD, all of Intel's PC-compatible chips are now x64 compatible as well.)

Though not as technically elegant as so-called "native" 64-bit platforms like the ill-fated Itanium, the x64 platform does provide all of the benefits of true 64-bit computing, including most importantly a flat 64-bit memory address space that obliterates the 4GB memory "ceiling" in the 32-bit world. For the purposes of this book, when we refer to 64-bit computing, we mean x64. And as we look ahead to the generation of PCs that will ship during Windows 7's lifetime, what we're going to see, predominantly, are x64 versions of the OS. That said, Windows 7 comes in both x86 and x64 variants, as we'll discuss later in this chapter.

tip You may occasionally hear Windows 7's product editions referred to as *SKUs*. This term stands for *stock keeping unit*. While we typically use the more common terms *product edition, version,* and *product versions* throughout this book instead, these terms are all pretty much interchangeable.

Following is a list of the major Windows XP versions that Microsoft shipped between 2001 and 2006. In a moment, we'll compare these products with their corresponding Vista versions:

> Windows XP Starter Edition (underdeveloped countries only)
>
> Windows XP Embedded (sold in embedded devices only)
>
> Windows XP Home Edition
>
> Windows XP Home Edition N (European Union only)
>
> Windows XP Media Center Edition
>
> Windows XP Tablet Edition
>
> Windows XP Professional Edition
>
> Windows XP Professional Edition N (European Union only)
>
> Windows XP Professional Edition K (South Korea only)
>
> Windows XP Professional x64 Edition
>
> Windows XP for Itanium-based systems

All Windows XP product versions, except Windows XP Professional x64 Edition, and Windows XP for Itanium-based systems, were available only in 32-bit versions.

note The N and K versions of Windows exist because of antitrust-related actions against Microsoft around the world. These versions are each limited in some way and have proven unpopular with customers. Obviously, Microsoft wouldn't even make them unless they were so required.

For Windows Vista, Microsoft surveyed the market and came away with two observations. First, its experiment splitting the Windows XP (and Microsoft Office) product lines into multiple product editions had proven enormously successful for the company. Second, customers appeared willing to pay a bit more for premium product SKUs, such as XP Media Center Edition, that offered extra features. It doesn't take a rocket scientist to see that Microsoft's experiences over the past few years led directly to the situation we had with Windows Vista: the company created six core Vista product editions, two of which were considered premium versions. Or, if you include the so-called N and K editions (for the European Union and South Korea, respectively), there were actually nine product editions. Or, if you count the 32-bit and x64 (64-bit) versions separately, since they are in fact sold separately for the most part, there were 17 product editions. Add the (RED) version of

Windows Vista Ultimate—which was originally available only with select new PCs from Dell and, eventually, at retail—and you've got 18. Or something. Here's the list:

Windows Vista Starter

Windows Vista Home Basic

Windows Vista Home Basic (x64)

Windows Vista Home Premium

Windows Vista Home Premium N (European Union only)

Windows Vista Home Premium (x64)

Windows Vista Home Premium N (x64) (European Union only)

Windows Vista Business

Windows Vista Business K (South Korea only)

Windows Vista Business N (European Union only)

Windows Vista Business (x64)

Windows Vista Business K (x64) (South Korea only)

Windows Vista Business N (x64) (European Union only)

Windows Vista Enterprise

Windows Vista Enterprise (x64)

Windows Vista Ultimate

Windows Vista Ultimate (x64)

Windows Vista Ultimate Product (RED) Edition

Secret   Microsoft originally planned an Itanium version of Windows Vista, which would have run on high-end workstations, but the company cancelled this project during the beta process due to a lack of customer interest. Thus, the mainstream PC platform of the future is now secure: it will be 64-bit, and it will be x64, not Itanium.

In addition to spamming the market with an unbelievable number of product editions, Microsoft also increased the number of ways in which customers could acquire Windows Vista. As always, most individuals simply got Vista with a new PC, and some continued to purchase retail boxed copies of Windows Vista. Then there were the not-quite-retail versions of the software, called *OEM versions*, which were technically supposed to be sold only to PC makers, but were widely available online; and a new option called Windows Anytime Upgrade that enabled you to upgrade from one version of Vista to another. It was confusing. And it's still that confusing, because these purchase options are all available with Windows 7 as well. But then that's why you're reading this chapter, right?

Here's our advice: don't get bogged down in semantics or complicated counting exercises. With a little bit of knowledge about how these product editions break down and are sold, you can whittle the list down quite a bit very quickly and easily. Then, you can evaluate which features are available in which editions and choose the one that's right for you based on your needs.

Windows 7 Product Editions: Only a Little Bit Simpler

As with Windows Vista, Windows 7 will ship in many different product editions. On the surface, this seems confusing—just as confusing, in fact, as the Vista product line. But this time, Microsoft made a few commonsense changes to the product lineup that should make things easier on most people. So assume the Lotus position, breathe deeply, and relax. It's not as bad as it sounds.

For starters, though there are, in fact, almost as many Windows 7 product editions as there were for Windows Vista, most individuals will only need to consider a handful of commonsense product editions. And with Windows 7, unlike with Vista, these product editions are all true supersets of each other, so there are no overlapping feature sets, as there were with some of the Vista product editions. That's good news, both for those migrating to Windows 7 and for those Windows 7 users who think they might want a more powerful product edition.

Consider a typical issue with the Windows Vista product editions. In that version of Windows, the Windows Vista Business edition didn't include Windows Media Center, a fun digital media application that was part of the Home Premium product. But business users enjoy digital media too, especially when traveling, and they told Microsoft that this division in the feature set didn't make sense.

Okay, here's what Microsoft is offering with Windows 7:

Windows 7 Home Basic (developing markets only)

Windows 7 Starter

Windows 7 Starter x64

Windows 7 Home Premium

Windows 7 Home Premium (x64)

Windows 7 Home Premium N (European Union only)

Windows 7 Professional

Windows 7 Professional (x64)

Windows 7 Enterprise

Windows 7 Enterprise (x64)

Windows 7 Ultimate

Windows 7 Ultimate (x64)

Secret

See the big change? That's right: the Starter and Home Basic versions have switched places this time around. In Windows Vista, Starter edition was aimed at developing markets only and wasn't available to mainstream Windows customers, while Home Basic was broadly available worldwide on budget PCs. In Windows 7, this is no longer the case. Now, Windows 7 Home Basic is made available only with new PC purchases in emerging markets, while Windows 7 Starter will be sold worldwide, primarily on netbooks and other very low end, budget PCs.

Why not just have one or two product editions, as we did back when Windows XP first shipped? Microsoft says that it has over one billion Windows users worldwide and that their needs are diverse and cannot all be met with a single product. So it has instead moved to a "Russian nesting doll" model, where as you increment up the list of Windows 7 product editions, features or capabilities are simply adopted from the previous editions. They are true supersets of each other, and additive, not arbitrarily different.

Secret

Because of antitrust regulations in the European Union (EU), Microsoft created special "E" versions of the various Windows 7 versions that do not include Internet Explorer. Unlike other versions of Windows 7, these Windows 7 versions don't allow you to add or remove Internet Explorer via the normal Control Panel-based mechanism. But Microsoft is making Internet Explorer available to users of these products separately, and of course, PC makers in the EU will always include a Web browser with their Windows 7 E-based machines. Aside from the absence of Internet Explorer, the Windows 7 E versions are functionally identical to their U.S.-based counterparts. Note, too, that the Windows 7 N Editions, also sold only in Europe, do not include IE 8 either.

Understanding the Differences and Choosing the Right Version

The first step is to understand the differences between each Windows 7 product edition. Then, you need to understand the various ways in which you can acquire Windows 7, either as a standalone product or as an upgrade to an existing version of Windows (including, confusingly, Windows 7 itself). After that, you can weigh the various trade-offs of each option—features, price, and so on—and act accordingly.

Let's do it.

Step 1: Whittling Down the Product Editions List

While the clinically sarcastic will dryly complain that there is precious real-world difference between Vista's 18 product editions and Windows 7's 12, that's just a smoke screen. In the real world, most people will have to choose only between two Windows 7 product editions. To get to this number, we need to temporarily forget about the differences between 32-bit and 64-bit versions (don't worry, we'll get to that) and just skip over the versions that really don't matter. Once we do this, the following list emerges:

> Windows 7 Starter (32-bit or x64)
>
> Windows 7 Home Premium (x64)
>
> Windows 7 Professional (x64)
>
> Windows 7 Ultimate (x64)

Okay, this is four options, not two, but it's still a much more manageable list than what we started with. Before we whittle this down to just two options, let's take a closer look at the four options now in front of us. After all, there were 12 product editions in the original list. How did we cut it down this far so quickly?

Here's how.

Windows 7 Home Basic

You don't need or want Windows 7 Home Basic. But it's even simpler than that: you can't get it anyway. That's because Windows 7 Home Basic is available only with new PCs in emerging markets. You can't get it in the U.S., Europe, or any other developed area.

So unless you're buying a PC in one of the few countries in which you can acquire Windows 7 Home Basic, you probably won't hear much more about this product. And if you are buying such a PC, your computing needs are pretty basic, so it's unlikely that you're ready for this book just yet.

The K and N Editions Aren't for You, Either

Whatever Windows 7 versions are being offered in Korea (with a K moniker) or in Europe (with an N moniker), they're designed to satisfy the antitrust regulations and rulings in those locales, and you should also ignore them. Why? Because these versions are more limited than the non-K and non-N Windows 7 versions that are sold in South Korea and the EU, respectively. And they don't cost any less, so there's no reason to even consider them, even if you do live in these areas.

Consider the Windows 7 N edition, which is sold only in EU markets. This product came about because of a 2004 EU ruling that required Microsoft to offer versions of Windows without the Windows Media Player included. The requirement for a separate version of Windows was intended to enhance competition in the market for media players, such as the downloadable RealPlayer application.

But because Microsoft sells its N versions for the same price as its full-featured Windows versions, demand for the N versions never materialized. Until there's a big price difference, consumers will continue to interpret N to mean Not Interested. Ditto for the K versions, though we're having trouble coming up with a witty K-related word to help you remember why. All you need to remember is that you should forget these versions ever existed.

You're Not the Enterprise

Windows 7 Enterprise is a special version of Windows 7 that is aimed at Microsoft's largest corporate customers. It is functionally identical to Windows 7 Ultimate, but there is one difference between the two products: whereas Windows 7 Ultimate is available at retail (both with new PCs and as stand-alone software), Windows 7 Enterprise is available only through Microsoft's corporate volume licensing subscription programs. Because of the unique way in which you must acquire this version, chances are good you won't be hunting around for Windows 7 Enterprise. That said, if you do get a PC from work with Windows 7 Enterprise on it, you're using the functional equivalent of Windows 7 Ultimate.

32-bit Versions of Windows 7

The differences between 32-bit (x86) versions of Windows 7 and 64-bit (x64) versions are more complex, but here's the weird bit: though virtually every single PC sold over the past several years was x64 compatible, virtually every single copy of Windows that went out the door before Windows 7 was, in fact, a 32-bit version.

No more. With Windows 7, it's time to leave the 32-bit world behind for good, and the first step is to run a 64-bit version of Windows 7. These versions of Windows 7 are fully compatible with most of the 32-bit software that runs on 32-bit versions of the OS, and they are likewise just about as compatible with the wide number of hardware devices that are available on the market.

The biggest reason to go 64-bit is RAM: after all, 64-bit versions of Windows 7 can access far more RAM than 32-bit versions (up to 192GB, depending on which version of Windows 7 you're talking about, compared to less than 4GB of RAM in 32-bit versions).

Folks, with one minor exception, it's time to say good-bye to 32-bit versions of Windows. So with Windows 7, almost universally, we recommend that you seek out 64-bit (x64) versions instead.

What is the one exception? Many netbook computers come with a version of Intel's Atom microprocessor that is incompatible with the x64 instruction set, and thus with x64 versions of Windows 7. On such a PC, you will need to use a 32-bit version of Windows 7 instead. And that's just fine: given the limited usage scenarios for these computing lightweights, that's perfectly acceptable. It's also the exception to the rule.

Secret   Contrary to the conventional wisdom, 64-bit software isn't magically faster than 32-bit software. That said, 64-bit PCs running a 64-bit version of Windows 7 and native 64-bit software can often outperform 32-bit alternatives. But that's because you can stick far more RAM in the 64-bit machine: systems with massive amounts of memory just aren't as constrained and can operate to their full potential.

Step 2: Whittling a Little Further

Rationale aside, you may be looking back over the preceding list and thinking, well, hold on a second there: that's still four product editions. Is Microsoft really simplifying anything? Yes, because the vast majority of Windows 7 users will really have to consider only two of these product editions:

> Windows 7 Home Premium
>
> Windows 7 Professional

Microsoft and its partners will focus most of their efforts selling Windows 7 Home Premium and Professional to the retail and consumer markets (and Enterprise to volume licensing business customers). That means most consumers will simply have two options when it comes to Windows 7: Home Premium and Pro—just like with XP when that OS first shipped.

Meanwhile, Ultimate and Starter are, by definition, niche products that are available only to address low-volume but important markets. But what really makes this work is the previously mentioned "Russian stacking doll" structure whereby each version is a true superset of the one below it. This is a huge and important change.

Step 3: Understanding the Differences Between the Product Editions

Once you've whittled the list down to two or four contenders, it's time to evaluate them and understand which features are available in each product edition. There are various ways to present this kind of information, but we find that tables, logically divided by category, are easy on the eyes and mind. Tables 1-1 through 1-9 summarize how the product editions stack up.

Table 1-1: User Interface Features

	Starter	Home Premium	Professional	Ultimate/ Enterprise
Windows Basic UI	Yes	Yes	Yes	Yes
Windows Aero UI	—	Yes	Yes	Yes
Windows Aero Glass effects	—	Yes	Yes	Yes
Aero Peek	—	Yes	Yes	Yes
Aero Snaps	Yes	Yes	Yes	Yes
Aero Shake	—	Yes	Yes	Yes
Aero Background	—	Yes	Yes	Yes
Windows Flip	Yes	Yes	Yes	Yes
Windows Flip 3D	—	Yes	Yes	Yes
Live Taskbar Previews	—	Yes	Yes	Yes
Live Preview (Explorer)	—	Yes	Yes	Yes
Jump Lists	Yes	Yes	Yes	Yes
Windows Search	Yes	Yes	Yes	Yes

Table 1-2: Security Features

	Starter	Home Premium	Professional	Ultimate/ Enterprise
More granular UAC	Yes	Yes	Yes	Yes
Action Center	Yes	Yes	Yes	Yes
Windows Defender	Yes	Yes	Yes	Yes
Windows Firewall	Yes	Yes	Yes	Yes
IE8 Protected Mode and DEP support	Yes	Yes	Yes	Yes
Windows Update (can access Microsoft Update)	Yes	Yes	Yes	Yes
Fast User Switching	Yes	Yes	Yes	Yes
Parental Controls	Yes	Yes	Yes	Yes

Table 1-3: Performance Features

	Starter	Home Premium	Professional	Ultimate/ Enterprise
Windows ReadyDrive	Yes	Yes	Yes	Yes
Windows ReadyBoost	Yes	Yes	Yes	Yes
SuperFetch	Yes	Yes	Yes	Yes
64-bit processor support	Yes	Yes	Yes	Yes
Physical processor support	1	2	2	2
Processor core support	Unlimited	Unlimited	Unlimited	Unlimited
Max RAM (32-bit)	4GB	4GB	4GB	4GB
Max RAM (64-bit)	8GB	16GB	192GB	192GB

Table 1-4: Reliability Features

	Starter	Home Premium	Professional	Ultimate/ Enterprise
Windows Backup	Yes	Yes	Yes	Yes
System image	Yes	Yes	Yes	Yes
Backup to network	—	—	Yes	Yes
Encrypting File System (EFS)	—	—	Yes	Yes
BitLocker	—	—	—	Yes
BitLocker To Go	—	—	—	Yes
Automatic hard disk defragmentation	Yes	Yes	Yes	Yes
Previous Versions	Yes	Yes	Yes	Yes
Create and attach (mount) VHD	Yes	Yes	Yes	Yes

Table 1-5: Bundled Applications

	Starter	Home Premium	Professional	Ultimate/ Enterprise
Internet Explorer 8	Yes	Yes	Yes	Yes
Windows Gadgets and Gallery	Yes	Yes	Yes	Yes
Games Explorer with basic games (FreeCell, Hearts, Minesweeper, Purble Place, Solitaire, Spider Solitaire)	Yes	Yes	Yes	Yes
Premium games (Internet Backgammon, Internet Checkers, Internet Spades, Mahjong Titans)	—	Yes	Yes	Yes
Calculator	Yes	Yes	Yes	Yes
Paint	Yes	Yes	Yes	Yes
Snipping Tool	—	Yes	Yes	Yes
Sticky Notes	—	Yes	Yes	Yes
Windows Journal	—	Yes	Yes	Yes
Windows Fax and Scan	Yes	Yes	Yes	Yes
Windows PowerShell and ISE	Yes	Yes	Yes	Yes
WordPad	Yes	Yes	Yes	Yes
XPS Viewer	Yes	Yes	Yes	Yes
Windows Anytime Upgrade	Yes	Yes	Yes	—

Table 1-6: Digital Media and Devices

	Starter	Home Premium	Professional	Ultimate/ Enterprise
Windows Photo Viewer	Yes	Yes	Yes	Yes
Basic photo slide shows	Yes	Yes	Yes	Yes
Windows Media Player 12 with Play To	Yes	Yes	Yes	Yes
Windows Media Player Remote Media Experience	—	Yes	Yes	Yes
MPEG-2 decoding	—	Yes	Yes	Yes

continues

Table 1-6: Digital Media and Devices (continued)

	Starter	Home Premium	Professional	Ultimate/ Enterprise
Dolby Digital compatibility	—	Yes	Yes	Yes
AAC and H.264 decoding	Yes	Yes	Yes	Yes
DVD playback	—	Yes	Yes	Yes
Can install MPEG-2 (DVD playback) add-in	Yes	n/a	n/a	n/a
Windows Media Center	—	Yes	Yes	Yes
Windows DVD Maker	—	Yes	Yes	Yes
Device Stage	Yes	Yes	Yes	Yes
Sync Center	Yes	Yes	Yes	Yes

Table 1-7: Networking Features

	Starter	Home Premium	Professional	Ultimate/ Enterprise
SMB connections	20	20	20	20
Network and Sharing Center	Yes	Yes	Yes	Yes
HomeGroup sharing	Join only	Yes	Yes	Yes
Improved power management	Yes	Yes	Yes	Yes
Connect to a Projector	Yes	Yes	Yes	Yes
Remote Desktop	Yes	Yes	Yes	Yes
Remote Desktop Host	—	—	Yes	Yes
IIS Web Server	—	Yes	Yes	Yes
RSS support	Yes	Yes	Yes	Yes
Internet Connection Sharing	—	Yes	Yes	Yes
Network Bridge	—	Yes	Yes	Yes
Offline files	—	—	Yes	Yes

Table 1-8: Mobility Features

	Starter	*Home Premium*	*Professional*	*Ultimate/ Enterprise*
Windows Mobility Center	—	Yes (No Presentation Mode)	Yes	Yes
Windows Sideshow (Auxiliary display)	—	Yes	Yes	Yes
Sync Center	Yes	Yes	Yes	Yes
Tablet PC functionality	—	Yes	Yes	Yes
Multi-Touch support	—	Yes	Yes	Yes

Table 1-9: Enterprise Features

	Starter	*Home Premium*	*Professional*	*Ultimate/ Enterprise*
Domain join (Windows Server)	—	—	Yes	Yes
XP Mode licensed	—	—	Yes	Yes
AppLocker	—	—	—	Yes
Boot from VHD	—	—	—	Yes
BranchCache	—	—	—	Yes
DirectAccess	—	—	—	Yes
Federated Search (Enterprise Search Scopes)	—	—	—	Yes
Multilingual User Interface (MUI) Language Packs	—	—	—	Yes
Location-aware printing	—	—	Yes	Yes
Subsystem for UNIX-based Applications	—	—	—	Yes

Though 32-bit versions of Windows 7 "support" 4GB of RAM, they can only access about 3.1GB of RAM, even when a full 4GB of RAM is installed in the PC. This is because of a limitation in the way that 32-bit versions of Windows handle memory access. If you were to install an x64 version of Windows 7 on the same system, you would have access to the entire 4GB of RAM. The 64-bit Windows 7 versions have dramatically improved memory capacity, as noted in the preceding tables.

The most amazing thing about that 192GB address space on Windows 7 Professional, Enterprise, and Ultimate is that it's a moving target and could, in fact, increase in the years ahead. In fact, it's increased since Windows Vista. On that system, the maximum amount of RAM was a relatively paltry 128GB. Ah, progress.

Step 4: Making the Right Product Edition Choice

Armed with the information in the preceding tables, we can think of Windows 7 as being divided into four basic product categories, each of which is neatly covered by a single product edition.

First up is Windows 7 Starter, which covers the bare-bones end of the market (netbooks and other very low-end PCs). Starter edition offers basic functionality, but has some serious limitations, not the least of which is that it can run only three applications at a time.

Then we have the two mainstream Windows 7 versions, Home Premium and Professional. Home Premium is a superset of Starter: it has no application limitations, comes with the snazzy Aero Glass effects, and includes numerous digital media features. Professional is a superset of Home Premium, adding network backup, EFS, offline file access, and other power user features.

At the top end of the market is Windows 7 Ultimate. This is the full meal deal, and it includes BitLocker, multi-language capabilities, and everything else Windows 7 has to offer.

Let's see how these options break down.

tip   Obviously, there is one other consideration to make here: price. For example, while Windows 7 Ultimate may seem like a best of both worlds type product, it also comes with premium pricing. We'll examine the various ways in which you can purchase Windows 7, and the cost of each option, later in this chapter.

Choosing Between Windows 7 Starter and Home Premium

Table 1-10 shows some of the features that differ between the Starter and Home Premium versions of Windows 7 for home users. If you've decided that a consumer-oriented version of Windows 7 is what you need, Table 1-10 will help you decide which of the two available versions will best suit you.

- ♦ **Choose Starter** if cost is the primary issue and you don't need fancy Aero Glass effects or features like Media Center, the ability to burn DVDs, or any of the other features that come with Home Premium.
- ♦ **Choose Home Premium** if you have a Tablet PC or if you want the more extensive multimedia features of the Home Premium version.

Table 1-10: Comparing Windows 7 Starter and Home Premium

	Starter	*Home Premium*
Aero Glass effects	—	Yes
Aero Peek	—	Yes
Aero Shake	—	Yes
Aero Background	—	Yes
Windows Flip 3D	—	Yes
Live Taskbar Previews	—	Yes
Live Preview (Explorer)	—	Yes
Physical processor support	1	2
Max RAM (64-bit)	8GB	16GB
Premium Games	—	Yes
Snipping Tool, Sticky Notes, Windows Journal	—	Yes
Windows Media Player Remote Media Experience	—	Yes
DVD playback	—	Yes
Windows Media Center	—	Yes
Windows DVD Maker	—	Yes
IIS Web Server	—	Yes
Tablet PC and Multi-Touch support	—	Yes

Choosing Between Windows 7 Home Premium and Professional

Table 1-11 compares the features that are present in the Home Premium and Professional versions of Windows 7.

◆ Windows 7 Professional, unlike Home Premium, supports domain networking. This enables users to log on to a network server using Microsoft's Active Directory (AD) technology and share centrally managed resources.

◆ Windows 7 Professional, also unlike Home Premium, includes support for XP Mode and Windows Virtual PC, which enables you to run XP-compatible applications virtually under Windows 7. This means that Windows 7 Professional (and Enterprise and Ultimate) are much more compatible with legacy applications than is Windows 7 Home Premium.

Table 1-11: Comparing Windows 7 Home Premium and Professional

	Home Premium	*Professional*
Max RAM (64-bit)	16GB	192GB
Backup to network	—	Yes
Encrypting File System (EFS)	—	Yes
Remote Desktop Host	—	Yes
Offline Files	—	Yes
Windows Mobility Center	Yes (No Presentation Mode)	Yes
Domain joining (Windows Server)	—	Yes
Windows XP Mode/Windows Virtual PC	—	Yes
Location-aware printing	—	Yes

Secret

While Windows XP Mode and Windows Virtual PC are new to Windows 7, this isn't the first time Microsoft has attempted to include this technology in Windows. Back during the Windows Vista beta, Windows Vista Enterprise was originally going to include a feature called Virtual PC Express. However, before Windows Vista was finalized, Microsoft decided to make its entire Virtual PC product line—which enables you to run operating systems and applications in virtualized environments under a host OS—available for free. Windows Virtual PC is the new version of Virtual PC, and the big new feature this time around is that Windows 7 Professional, Enterprise, and Ultimate customers can get an entire virtualized Windows XP environment for free with the download. See www.microsoft .com/virtualpc for more information.

Choosing Windows 7 Ultimate

Windows 7 Ultimate combines all of the features that are available in all of the other Windows 7 versions, adds some unique features of its own, and comes with a premium price tag. In fact, Windows 7 Ultimate is so expensive compared to Windows 7 Home Premium and Professional that the only serious reason to get it is if you absolutely must have two drive encryption features, BitLocker and BitLocker To Go. Frankly, it's not worth it for most people.

Secret   The cheapest way to get Windows 7 Ultimate will be with a new PC, and when PC makers have occasional special offers that make it cheaper than usual. Keep your eyes open for such offers: if you can get Ultimate edition for little additional cost, it will absolutely be worth having, since it's the full meal deal.

Purchasing Windows 7

There are almost as many ways to purchase Windows 7 as there are Windows 7 product editions. This can make acquiring Windows 7 somewhat complex, especially if all you want to do is purchase a Setup disc and install the operating system on your own PC. Here are the ways in which you can acquire Microsoft's latest operating system.

With a New PC

The single best way to acquire Windows 7 is with a new PC from a major PC maker such as Dell, HP, or Lenovo. That's because Windows is cheaper when bundled with a new PC, and PC makers spend huge amounts of time testing every hardware device that they sell in order to ensure that customers have the best possible experience.

One thing that has sullied this market, of course, is *crapware*, a practice in the PC market where PC makers include useless or unwanted preinstalled applications on their preconfigured PCs. The good news is that this practice is slowly going away: Dell and other PC makers now offer new PCs without crapware, either for free or for a small fee.

The cost of Windows on a new PC varies from PC maker to PC maker and from machine to machine. Generally speaking, a copy of some version of Windows 7 will be included in the price of virtually every PC sold today, and the actual cost to you will range from roughly $30 to $80. The cost of upgrading to more expensive Windows 7 versions will vary as well. Based on some informal research (OK, we simply browsed the sites of PC makers online) it looks like you can typically move from Windows 7 Starter to Home Premium for less than $30, which is an excellent deal. The upgrade to Windows 7 Professional will typically set you back a bit more, say $35 to $80. And the upgrade to Windows 7 Ultimate is about $125 to $150. (These additional costs are all based on a core system running Windows 7 Starter, and can, of course, change over time.)

As an example, Figure 1-1 shows Dell's "configurator" for a typical home PC.

Figure 1-1: When you're buying a new PC, be sure to get the Windows 7 version you really want.

As you'll see in a moment, the cost of upgrading to a better or more expensive Windows 7 version is almost always lower if you do it at the time of the PC purchase. But regardless of the cost, it will always be easier to upgrade during the purchase process because the PC maker will install and configure the OS for you.

Retail Boxed Copies

If you were to walk into an electronics superstore like Best Buy, the versions of Windows 7 you would see are what's known as *retail boxed copies* of the software. You will see both *Full* and *Upgrade* versions of the software, and you should see a version of each for Windows 7 Starter, Home Premium, Home Premium x64, Professional, Professional x64, Ultimate, and Ultimate x64. Disregarding the obvious differences between 32-bit and x64/64-bit versions, here's the difference between each:

✦ **Full version.** A full version of Windows 7 can be used to perform a *clean install* of Windows 7 only. That is, it cannot be used to upgrade an existing version of Windows to Windows 7. Full versions of Windows 7 are more expensive than Upgrade versions.

✦ **Upgrade version.** An upgrade version of Windows 7 can be used to perform a clean install of Windows 7 or upgrade an existing version of Windows to Windows 7. Upgrade versions of Windows 7 are less expensive than Full versions because you must be an existing Windows customer to qualify for Upgrade pricing.

And that's the rub. Understanding whether you qualify for an Upgrade version of Windows 7 can be somewhat confusing. And even then, it's not very clear when you can perform an in-place upgrade over an existing Windows version. Here are some guidelines.

Those Who Don't Qualify for an Upgrade Version of Windows 7

If you are currently running any MS-DOS-based version of Windows—including Windows 95, Windows 98, Windows 98 Second Edition, or Windows Millennium Edition (Me)—or any version of Windows NT (3.x and 4.0), including Windows 2000, you don't qualify for any Upgrade version of Windows 7. That means you will need to grab a more expensive Full version instead. Because the Full versions of Windows 7 cannot be used to perform an in-place upgrade to Windows 7, you'll need to back up all your documents and other data and your application settings, and find all your application install disks or executables so you can reinstall them after Windows 7 is up and running.

Those Who Do Qualify for an Upgrade Version of Windows 7

If you are running any mainstream desktop version of Windows XP—including Windows XP Home Edition, Professional Edition, Media Center Edition (any version), Tablet PC Edition (any version), or XP Professional x64 Edition—you qualify for an Upgrade version of Windows 7.

That said, there is one serious limitation when upgrading from XP: you will not be able to upgrade in-place but will need to perform a clean install instead and then migrate your settings and data over to the new Windows 7 install. (That is, you qualify for Upgrade pricing only.) We explain this process in Chapter 2.

Those Who Qualify for an Upgrade Version of Windows 7 and an In-Place Upgrade

If you're running any version of Windows Vista and you want to upgrade in-place to Windows 7, you can do so. The trick is understanding how different versions of Windows Vista map to different versions of Windows 7. For example, Microsoft will not let you upgrade from Windows Vista Home Premium to Windows 7 Professional. Likewise, you cannot upgrade from a 32-bit version of Vista to a 64-bit version of Windows 7, or vice versa. Table 1-12 clarifies the in-place upgrade story.

Table 1-12: Which Versions of Windows Vista Can Upgrade In-Place to Which Versions of Windows 7

Windows Version	Windows 7 Starter	Windows 7 Home Premium	Windows 7 Professional	Windows 7 Ultimate
Windows Vista Home Starter	No	No	No	No
Windows Vista Home Basic	No	No	No	No
Windows Vista Home Premium	No	Yes	No	No
Windows Vista Business	No	No	Yes	No
Windows Vista Ultimate	No	No	No	Yes

Your decision regarding which version to purchase will also be influenced by the cost difference of the more capable versions. Table 1-13 shows the current U.S. list prices for the different Windows 7 versions. These prices will almost certainly change over time.

Table 1-13: U.S. List Prices for Windows 7 Product Editions

Windows 7 Home Premium

Windows 7 Home Premium Full	$199.99
Windows 7 Home Premium Upgrade	$119.99

Windows 7 Professional

Windows 7 Professional Full	$299.99
Windows 7 Professional Upgrade	$199.99

Windows 7 Ultimate

Windows 7 Ultimate Full	$319.99
Windows 7 Ultimate Upgrade	$219.99

Secret   Adding to the complexity here is that all retail versions of Windows 7, except for Windows 7 Starter, are available in both 32-bit and 64-bit (x64) versions. Windows 7 Starter will not be made available as a retail product but will instead be sold with new PCs only.

Pricing in countries other than the United States will vary, but should adhere to the relative positioning shown in Table 1-13.

Secret   If you're buying a retail copy of Windows 7 and you already own a qualifying previous version of Windows, such as XP, don't buy a full version of Windows 7. Instead, find out what Microsoft's current requirements are to qualify for an upgrade version, which is much cheaper. To successfully load an upgrade version, you usually must be installing onto a machine that has the old version installed, or you must have the old version on a CD (which you insert briefly during the installation of the new OS as proof). Microsoft can change these requirements at any time, so confirm this before whipping out your plastic.

tip

Not sure what Windows XP or Vista product edition you have? In that OS, open the Start menu, right-click the My Computer (or, in Vista, Computer) icon, and choose Properties from the pop-up menu that appears. The window that appears will include your Windows product edition.

Secret

Users with multiple PCs who are interested in Windows 7 Home Premium might also consider the specially priced Windows 7 Family Pack. Available for $149.99 in the United States --though prices could vary wildly at retail—the Family Pack provides three Windows 7 Home Premium product keys, allowing you to install the OS on, yup, you guessed it, three different PCs, and at bargain pricing.

OEM Versions

One of the biggest secrets in the software world is that Microsoft's operating systems are available from online retailers in so-called OEM ("original equipment manufacturer") versions (which come in just the Full SKU) that are aimed at the PC builder market. These are the small "mom and pop"-type PC makers who build hand-crafted machines for local markets. OEM packaging is bare-bones and does not come with a retail box. Instead, you get the disc, a Product Key, and a slip of paper describing the product.

OEM versions of Windows 7 differ from retail versions in some important ways:

♦ **They are dramatically cheaper than retail versions.** As shown in Table 1-14, the OEM versions of Windows 7 are dramatically cheaper than comparable retail versions. Note, however, that OEM pricing fluctuates somewhat, so the prices you see online could be a bit different. Shop around for the best prices.

♦ **They do not come with any support from Microsoft.** Because PC makers support the products they sell directly, Microsoft doesn't offer any support for OEM versions of Windows 7. This explains the cost differential, by the way.

♦ **You are not really supposed to buy them unless you're building PCs that you will sell to others.** Technically speaking, OEM versions of Windows 7 are available only to those who intend to build PCs to sell to others. Furthermore, online retailers who sell OEM versions of Windows 7 are supposed to verify that you're a PC builder and/or sell the products with some kind of hardware. For this reason, you'll sometimes be asked to purchase a hardware tchotsky like a USB cable when you purchase OEM software.

♦ **There's no box.** This shouldn't matter too much, but you don't get the cool Windows 7 retail packaging when you buy OEM. Instead, you pretty much get an install disc shrink-wrapped to a piece of cardboard and a product key.

Table 1-14: U.S. List Prices for Windows 7 OEM Product Editions

Windows 7 Home Basic	
Windows 7 Starter OEM	$39.99
Windows 7 Home Premium	
Windows 7 Home Premium OEM	$73.99
Windows 7 Business	
Windows 7 Professional OEM	$139.99
Windows 7 Ultimate	
Windows 7 Ultimate OEM	$199.99

Depending on which version you're looking at, the savings are usually substantial. All of the OEM products (which are "Full" versions) are less expensive than the Upgrade retail versions of Windows 7. That said, OEM products cannot be used to upgrade an existing PC: they're for new installs only.

As with the retail versions, you also have to choose between both 32-bit and 64-bit OEM versions of Windows 7 online. However, you can't purchase Upgrade OEM software because OEM versions are only aimed at new PC installs.

OEM versions of Windows 7 are sometimes sold in multi-OS packs. So, for example, you can purchase a three-pack of Windows 7 Ultimate if you'd like. You know, because you're a PC maker.

Windows Anytime Upgrade

Windows 7 provides an integrated capability to upgrade from a less powerful product edition to a more capable version at any time. Once you've installed Windows 7, you simply run the Windows Anytime Upgrade applet, select a source to purchase an upgrade license from, and your PC is quickly enhanced with the more powerful version you've selected. Because of the way in which the Windows 7 product line is designed, however, Windows Anytime Upgrade is available only in the following product editions:

- ◆ **Windows 7 Starter** can be upgraded to Windows 7 Home Premium, Professional, or Ultimate via Windows Anytime Upgrade.
- ◆ **Windows 7 Home Premium** can be upgraded to Windows 7 Professional or Ultimate via Windows Anytime Upgrade.
- ◆ **Windows 7 Professional** can be upgraded to Windows 7 Ultimate via Windows Anytime Upgrade.

Windows Anytime Upgrade is shown in Figure 1-2.

We examine Windows Anytime Upgrade more closely in the next chapter.

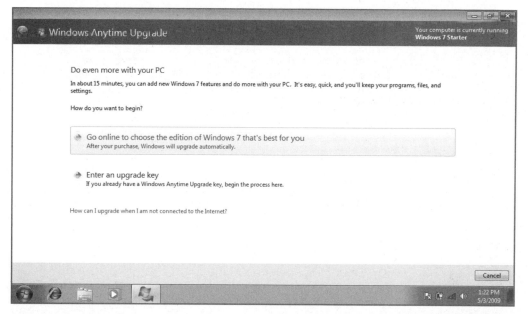

Figure 1-2: Windows Anytime Upgrade lets you upgrade from certain Windows 7 versions to other, more powerful versions.

Secret

There are other ways to acquire Windows 7, actually. We mentioned previously that Microsoft sells subscription-based software through its volume licensing programs, for example, and those users will typically get Windows 7 Enterprise. However, in this book we're focusing on the ways in which individuals can acquire Windows 7. If you do get a copy of Windows 7 Enterprise with a work PC, remember that this version of Windows 7 is functionally identical to Windows 7 Ultimate.

Summary

Windows 7 certainly offers a lot of options when it comes to picking a product version, but with a little know-how, you will be able to make the right choice, one that matches both your needs and your budget. In this chapter, we've given you what you need to know to match a Windows 7 version to your needs. Now you just need to figure out how much the upgrade is going to cost. Remember that it's often much cheaper to acquire a new Windows version with a new PC, so if you're going to be buying a new PC, be sure to get the right Windows 7 version at that time. Or, if you're more technically proficient, you can save big bucks with an OEM version. We will look at clean installs, upgrade installs, along with other ways to install and upgrade to Windows 7, in the next chapter. No matter how you choose to acquire Windows 7, we've got you covered.

Installing or Upgrading to Windows 7

Chapter
2

♦ ♦

In This Chapter

Acquiring Windows 7 with a new PC

Performing a clean install of Windows 7

Upgrading Windows XP to Windows 7

Upgrading Windows Vista to Windows 7

Windows Anytime Upgrade: Upgrading from one Windows 7 version to another

Performing a clean install with an Upgrade version of Windows 7

Delaying product activation

Installing Windows 7 on a Mac with Boot Camp and via software-based virtualization solutions

♦ ♦

So you want to install Windows 7? Well, in this chapter we'll walk you through the many ways you can acquire Windows 7, including a clean install, where Windows 7 is the only operating system on your PC; and an upgrade, where you upgrade an existing version of Windows to Windows 7, leaving all of your data, settings, and applications intact. You'll also learn about related topics, such as slipstreaming, delaying product activation, and—shocker—how to install Windows 7 on a Mac. Yes, Microsoft's latest operating system runs just great on those overpriced Apple machines too!

Taking the Easy Way Out: Acquiring Windows 7 with a New PC

The simplest way to get a working copy of Windows 7 is to buy a new PC. Stop laughing; we're serious: even though PC makers tend to fill their machines with oodles of useless utilities, add-on programs, and other sludge—called *crapware* for obvious reasons—the one thing you can always be sure of when you buy a new PC is that Windows 7 is going to work out of the box. That is, all of the hardware that comes as part of your new PC purchase will work without any additional effort on your part. In addition, you won't have to step through the various setup-related issues discussed later in this chapter. In fact, if you did purchase a PC with Windows 7 preinstalled, most of this chapter won't apply to you at all. You should be able to simply turn on your new PC and get to work.

 **Secret**
One thing PC purchasers should know about is how to *restore* their system, returning it to the state it was in when new. Virtually all new PCs sold today include a means by which you can do this. Most of the time you can restore your PC using a special hidden partition on the system's hard drive. Other PC makers actually include a restore disk, or restore DVD, with the system. Check your documentation to be sure that you know how to restore your system if necessary. And when you're removing all of that junk that the PC maker installed on your previously pristine Windows 7 installation, be sure you don't remove anything you'll need to recover your system.

Interactive Setup

If you purchased a copy of Windows 7 on DVD at a retailer or online store (or "e-tailer," as we like to call them), you can install Windows 7 using Microsoft's simpler new Interactive Setup Wizard, which guides you through a series of steps required to get Windows 7 up and running. There are three primary ways to install Windows 7 using Interactive Setup: a clean install, where Windows 7 will be the only operating system on the PC; an upgrade, where you upgrade an existing operating system to Windows 7, replacing the old with the new; and a dual-boot, where you install Windows 7 alongside your old operating system and use a boot menu to choose between them each time you reboot. You'll look at all three methods in this chapter, in addition to a fourth and related (but secret) installation method: a clean install using Upgrade media.

Clean Install

A *clean install* of the operating system is the preferred method for installing Windows 7. Although it's possible to upgrade to Windows 7 from certain previous Windows versions (see the next section), this path is perilous and can often result in a Frankenstein-like system in which only some of your applications work properly. In our experience, it's best to start with a clean slate when moving to a new operating system, especially a major release like Windows 7.

caution Be sure to back up your critical data before performing a clean install. Typically, you will wipe out your PC's entire hard drive during a clean install, so any documents, e-mail, and other data will be destroyed during the process. Also, make sure you have all the installation files for the applications and hardware drivers you'll need to reinstall after Windows 7 is up and running. We recommend copying them to a recordable disc, USB memory key or drive, network share, or other location.

Secret If you're worried about whether your PC can run Windows 7 effectively, be sure to check out Microsoft's Windows 7 Upgrade Advisor tool first. This tool will check the hardware (and, for upgraders, software) installed on your system and determine whether you will run into any issues. You can find the Upgrade Advisor on Microsoft's Web site at: www.microsoft.com/windows/windows-7/upgrade-advisor.aspx.

Step-by-Step: Windows 7 Interactive Setup

This section walks you through the entire Windows 7 setup process, using Microsoft's Interactive Setup Wizard. This application was completely overhauled for Windows Vista and then further streamlined for Windows 7, and it's now much simpler and faster-moving, especially when compared to the version used in Windows XP.

Follows these steps to install Windows 7 as a clean install:

1. Insert the Windows 7 DVD in your PC's optical drive and reboot the system. After the BIOS screen flashes by, you may see a message alerting you to press any key to boot from the CD or DVD. If so, press a key. Some systems, however, do not provide this warning and instead boot from the DVD by default.

   A black screen with a pulsating Windows logo and the text "Starting Windows" will appear, as shown in Figure 2-1.

Secret If your system does not boot from the DVD, you may need to change the system's boot order so that the optical drive is checked before the first hard drive. To do this, consult your PC's documentation, as each PC handles this process a little differently.

Figure 2-1: From inauspicious beginnings such as these come great things.

2. Eventually, the screen displays a colored background and the initial Setup window appears, as shown in Figure 2-2. Here, you can preconfigure the language, time and currency formats, and keyboard or input method you'll use during Setup.

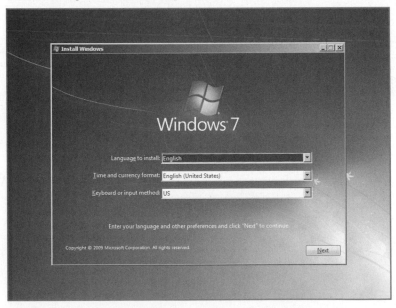

Figure 2-2: These settings apply only to Setup, not the eventual Windows 7 installation.

3. Click Next. A window titled Install Windows appears, as shown in Figure 2-3. To continue with Interactive Setup, click Install now.

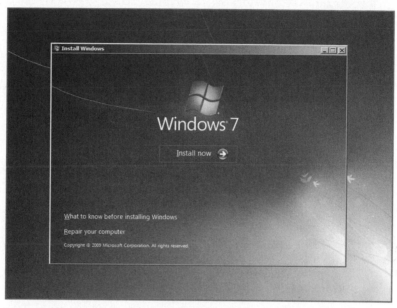

Figure 2-3: This window jump-starts Setup or, if you need them, the Windows 7 recovery tools.

This window also provides a way to access Windows 7's new recovery tools. If you run into a problem with Windows 7 later, such as not being able to boot into Windows for some reason, you can boot your system with the Setup DVD and use these tools to help fix the problem. Choose the link "Repair your computer" to access these tools.

Note how a single letter is underlined in the Install Windows window. If for some reason your mouse doesn't work, you can press Alt plus the related key on your keyboard to select the appropriate action. For example, pressing Alt+R on the keyboard will start the repair process.

4. In the next window (see Figure 2-4), you must agree to the End User License Agreement (EULA). Although very few people actually read this document, you should take the time to do so, as it outlines your legal rights regarding your usage of Windows 7. We're not lawyers, but we think it says that Microsoft exerts certain rights over your first born and your soul.

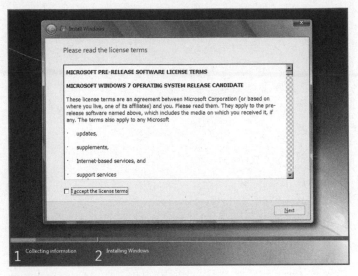

Figure 2-4: No, no one ever reads this.

5. In the next window, shown in Figure 2-5, select Custom (advanced) as the install type. You don't need to click the Next button here: just selecting an option will advance the wizard to the next step.

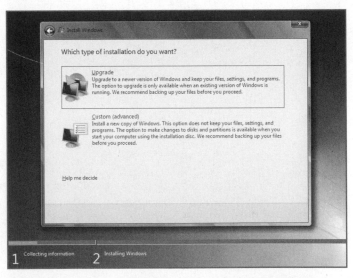

Figure 2-5: Here, you determine the install type. Upgrade is (go figure) for upgrades, while Custom is for clean installs.

6. In the next window, choose the disk, or partition, to which you will install Windows 7. On a clean install, typically you will be installing Windows 7 to the only disk available, as shown in Figure 2-6.

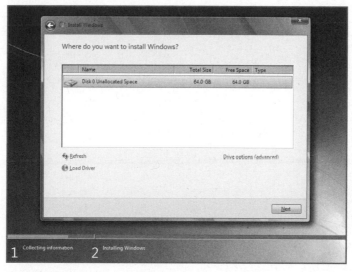

Figure 2-6: Pick the partition, but not any partition.

Secret

You can access the Setup routine's disk configuration tools by clicking the option "Drive options (advanced)" or by tapping Alt+A. These tools enable you to delete, create, and resize partitions if needed.

Note that you may see two or more partitions if your PC is configured with two or more physical hard disks or a single disk that is divided into two or more partitions (Figure 2-7).

Secret

If you are performing a clean install on a previously used machine, we advise you to format the disk during this step to ensure that none of the cruft from your previous Windows installation dirties up your new Windows 7 install. You don't actually need to format a new disk. If you attempt to install Windows 7 on an unformatted disk, setup will simply format the disk to its maximum capacity automatically.

Figure 2-7: You may see two or more partitions.

In addition to the partition on which Windows 7 is installed—what Microsoft calls the *system disk*—Setup also creates a second, hidden partition at the root of the drive. This partition, which takes up 100MB of space, is there for two reasons: it provides space for Windows 7's recovery tools, which, unlike in Vista, are installed to the hard drive by default so they're always there; and it provides space for BitLocker, an optional disk encryption technology.

7. After you've selected the disk and formatted it if necessary, you can walk away from your computer for 10 to 20 minutes, depending on your hardware. During this time, Setup will copy the various files it needs for installation to the hard drive, expand the Windows 7 image file from the DVD, install Windows 7 and any included software updates, and complete the installation by attempting to load drivers for your hardware. A screen like the one shown in Figure 2-8 will display during this entire process.

8. After a reboot or two, your PC will launch into the second, and final, interactive phase of Setup. You'll know something wonderful is about to happen because you'll see the screen in Figure 2-9 after Setup reboots for the final time.

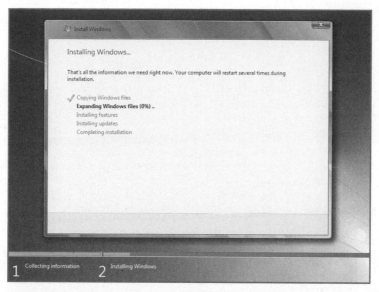

Figure 2-8: Grab a quick snack while setup installs Windows 7.

Figure 2-9: This looks promising.

tip During reboots, you may see the screen that says "Press any key to boot to the CD or DVD." Once you've started Setup, ignore that or installation will restart.

9. In the first screen after the reboot, shown in Figure 2-10, you are prompted for a user name and a computer name.

Secret

The values you enter here are important. For your user name, you can enter just your first name (*Paul* or *Rafael*) or your full name (*Paul Thurrott* or *Rafael Rivera*), but understand that whatever value you enter will be used throughout Windows to identify you as the owner. Typically, when you install a software application, for example, the setup routine for the application will pick up this information from the system, too. So be sure you enter the name you really want here. The computer name identifies your computer on your home network, and while it's easy to change after the fact, it's also a good idea to enter something meaningful within the confines of the naming restrictions: alphanumerics are just fine, as are dashes, but no underscores or other characters. Our advice is to go simple: *Den-PC, Home-computer,* or whatever.

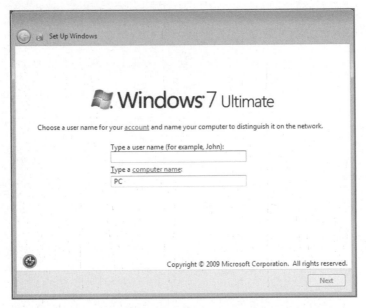

Figure 2-10: Specify the account you'll typically use in Windows 7.

Secret

A few notes about this initial user account. Unlike Windows XP (but like Windows Vista), Windows 7 does not create a visible administrator account automatically, for security reasons. Nor are you allowed to create up to five user accounts, as you were during XP Setup. Instead, you can create a single user account during setup. That user account will be given administrator privileges. Subsequent user accounts—created in Windows 7 using the User Accounts Control Panel—are given limited user privileges by default, but that's easy enough to change. You'll learn how to create and modify user accounts in Chapter 8.

10. Next, you will be prompted to enter a password and a password hint, as shown in Figure 2-11. Alarmingly, this step is optional.

Figure 2-11: Next up: password control.

caution

Be sure to use a password, please. It's unclear why Microsoft even makes this optional, as using a strong password is one of the most basic things you can do to keep your system more secure.

11. Enter your Windows product key (Figure 2-12). This is a 25-digit alphanumeric string—in blocks of five separated by dashes—that you will find on a bright yellow product-key sticker somewhere in your Windows 7 packaging. You can also choose to have Windows 7 automatically activate for you.

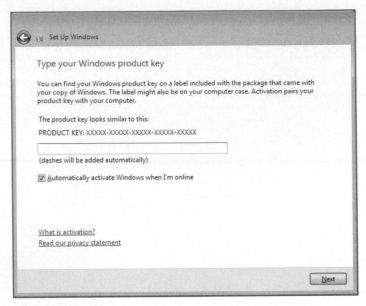

Figure 2-12: Spread 'em. This is where Microsoft ensures you're genuine.

As it turns out, you do not actually have to enter your product key here. If you don't, you have 30 days to evaluate Windows 7 before the system forces you to enter the key and activate.

Do not lose your Windows 7 product key or give it away to anyone. Each Windows 7 product key is valid for exactly one PC. After you've installed Windows 7 and activated it—which ties the product key to your hardware—you won't be able to use this number again on another PC, at least not easily. Note, however, that you can reinstall Windows 7 on the same PC using this same product key. If for some reason you are unable to electronically activate Windows later, Windows 7 will provide a phone number so you can do it manually.

12. Next, choose whether to enable Automatic Updates, as shown in Figure 2-13. You should use the recommended settings, in which Windows automatically downloads and installs all updates. Alternately, you can choose to install only important updates or be prompted later.

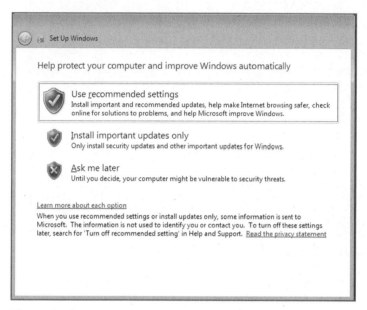

Figure 2-13: In this part of setup, you configure automatic updates.

This behavior is far more aggressive than the similar Setup screen that Microsoft added to Windows XP with Service Pack 2. Note that you can't choose to download but not install updates as before.

13. Configure the time zone, date, and time, as shown in Figure 2-14.

Even if you're not particularly careful about setting the time correctly here, Windows 7 will eventually adjust to the correct time automatically because it is configured out of the box to synchronize with an Internet time server. That said, you should at least make an effort to ensure that the time is reasonably correct to avoid problems with this process.

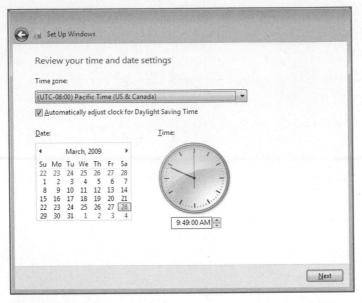

Figure 2-14: Curious that the time zone defaults to Pacific Time.

14. If you are in range of a wireless network, Windows 7 Setup will prompt you to connect to a wireless network, as shown in Figure 2-15.

15. If you are connected to a wired or wireless network, you'll see the current location screen shown in Figure 2-16. From here, you can choose whether the network you're accessing is a Home network (and thus private), a Work network (also private), or a Public network (such as a library, coffee shop, or airport). Windows configures networking appropriately in each case.

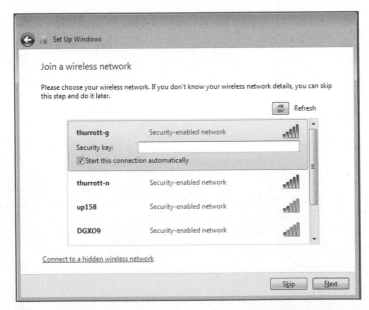

Figure 2-15: Using a wireless network? You'll see this screen, too.

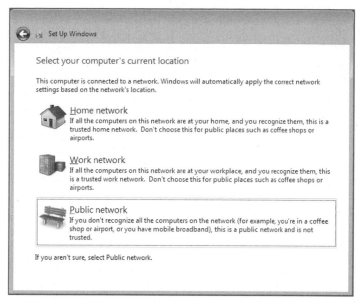

Figure 2-16: This handy window makes sure you are as secure
as you need to be, depending on which type of network you're using.

16. Next, you are asked to configure a new Windows 7 feature called HomeGroup.
    Simply click Skip here, as shown in Figure 2-17. We discuss the HomeGroup fea-
    ture, and how you can configure and use this feature, in Chapter 9.

Figure 2-17: You can safely skip HomeGroup configuration for now.

17. Now, Windows 7 finalizes your settings, prepares your desktop, and takes you to it, as shown in Figure 2-18. You're done! Well, not quite.

Figure 2-18: At last: your initial boot into the Windows 7 desktop.

Post-Setup Tasks

Now it's time to finish configuring Windows 7 so you can begin using it. The first step is to check out your hardware drivers: ideally, all of the hardware connected to your PC has been detected, and Setup has installed drivers for each of your devices. But first, let Automatic Updates run, an event that will occur automatically if the PC is connected to the Internet: this first update often installs a few final drivers that were missed during Setup, as shown in Figure 2-19.

Figure 2-19: After you boot into the desktop for the first time,
Automatic Updates will run, often installing and configuring some missing drivers.

To see whether all is well, you need to open a legacy Windows tool called Device Manager. (Windows 7 includes a newer way to access your hardware devices called Devices and Printers, but Device Manager is still the easiest way to ensure that all of your hardware is running properly.) There are a number of ways to access the Device Manager, but the quickest is to select Search from the Start menu, type **device man,** and press Enter. This causes the Device Manager window to appear (see Figure 2-20).

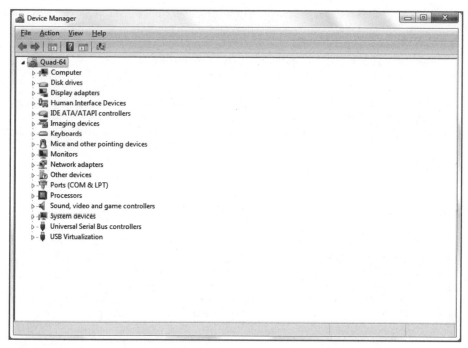

Figure 2-20: Device Manager tells you at a glance which hardware devices are connected and properly configured for your PC.

If any of the entries, or nodes, in the Device Manager tree view are open, displaying a device with a small yellow exclamation point, or *bang*, then you need to install some drivers. There are four basic ways to install drivers in Windows 7, listed here in reverse order of preference:

♦ **Automatically:** Right-click the unsupported device and choose Update Driver Software. Windows will search the local system, including any setup disks, to find the appropriate driver. In my experience this method almost never works, but it's worth trying.

♦ **Manually:** As before, you right-click the unsupported device and choose Update Driver Software. This time, however, you must supply the driver files via a setup disk or other means.

♦ **As an executable setup disk or download:** Many drivers come in self-contained executables whereby you run a setup routine just as you would for an application program. If possible, be sure to use a Windows 7–compatible setup application: these should work just fine. However, Windows XP drivers often work as well, albeit with a little grumbling on the part of Windows 7.

♦ **Using Windows Update:** This is the best way to install drivers, and it's the first place to visit if you discover that Windows 7 Setup didn't install all of your hardware. The hardware drivers found on Windows Update aren't always as up-to-date as those supplied directly from the hardware manufacturers. That said, Windows Update–based drivers have been tested extensively and should always be your first choice. Note that Windows 7 will likely connect to Windows Update automatically if you have a configured network adapter, grabbing any device drivers it can, within minutes of booting into the desktop for the first time.

tip   To manually find drivers on Windows Update, open the Start menu and choose All Programs ⇨ Windows Update. Click the Check for Updates link in the upper-left corner of the Windows Update application, as shown in Figure 2-21.

Repeat the preceding processes until all of your hardware devices are working. If you did run Windows Update during this time, you will likely have seen a number of Windows 7 product updates as well. You should install those updates before moving on to the next step.

Now it's time to install your applications. Install them one at a time and reboot if necessary after each install as requested. This process can often take a long time and is mindnumbingly boring, but you should only need to do it once.

With your applications installed, it's time to restore any data that you might have backed up from your previous Windows install; or, if you have installed Windows 7 to a brandnew PC, you can transfer user accounts, music, pictures, video files, documents, program settings, Internet settings and favorites, and e-mail messages and contacts from your old PC to Windows 7 using an excellent Windows 7 utility called Windows Easy Transfer. (From the Start menu, select Search, type **easy,** and then press Enter.) This utility is a full-screen wizard-like application (see Figure 2-22) that you can install and run on your previous OS as well. (We explore Windows Easy Transfer more in just a bit.)

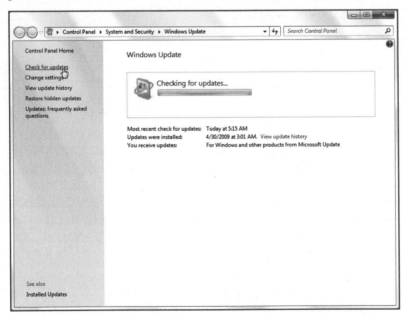

Figure 2-21: In Windows 7, Windows Update can update your operating system, hardware drivers, and many Microsoft applications.

Figure 2-22: Windows Easy Transfer makes short work of transferring your old data, documents, and custom settings from Windows Vista to Windows 7.

Upgrading

When most people talk about upgrading to a new version of Windows 7, they are typically referring to what's called an *in-place upgrade*. When you perform an in-place upgrade of Windows 7, you replace your existing version of Windows with Windows 7. An in-place upgrade, it is hoped, will bring with it all of your applications, documents, and custom settings. It is hoped.

The reality is that in-place upgrades often don't work as planned. For this reason, we don't recommend upgrading from your current Windows version to Windows 7. If you simply must perform such an upgrade, behave as if you were doing a clean install just in case, and back up all of your crucial documents and other data ahead of time. That way, if something does go wrong you won't be stranded.

Before even attempting an upgrade, you should understand what kinds of upgrades are possible. Windows 7 ships in a wide range of product editions, most of which have direct relations in Windows XP and Vista. That said, only Windows Vista can be used to perform an in-place upgrade to Windows 7. If you're using Windows XP, you will instead need to perform what's called a *migration*. In this type of upgrade, Windows 7 Setup backs up your Windows XP install, does a clean install of Windows 7, and then reapplies your settings, documents, and other data back to the new install. Because a migration and an in-place upgrade are very different in practice—though it is hoped that they have similar results—we cover them separately here.

note From a licensing perspective, only certain Windows versions are eligible for a Windows 7 upgrade. That is, you can't purchase and install an Upgrade version of Windows 7 unless you're using a supported Windows version now.

If you're running Windows 95, Windows 98 (or Windows 98 Second Edition), Windows Millennium Edition, Windows NT 4.0, or Windows 2000, you are out of luck. You cannot purchase an Upgrade version of Windows 7, and you cannot perform an in-place upgrade from your current operating system to any Windows 7 product edition. Instead, you must purchase the Full version of the Windows 7 product edition you want, and perform a clean install, as specified earlier in this chapter.

If you're running Windows XP, you are eligible to purchase an Upgrade version of the Windows 7 product edition you desire. However, you cannot perform an in-place upgrade. Instead, you need to perform a clean install, as discussed previously, using the Upgrade version.

The only Windows version that qualifies for a Windows 7 Upgrade version and can be upgraded in-place to Windows 7 is Windows Vista. However, within this set of operating systems there are still some restrictions. These include the following:

- Windows Vista Starter can only be upgraded to Windows 7 Starter.
- Windows Vista Home Basic can only be upgraded to Windows 7 Home Basic.
- Windows Vista Home Premium can only be upgraded to Windows 7 Home Premium.
- Windows Vista Business can only be upgraded to Windows 7 Professional.
- Windows Vista Ultimate can only be upgraded to Windows 7 Ultimate.
- 32-bit versions of Windows Vista can only be upgraded to 32-bit versions of Windows 7.
- 64-bit versions of Windows Vista can only be upgraded to 64-bit versions of Windows 7.

Okay, let's get upgrading.

Upgrading Windows XP to Windows 7

While Windows Vista allows you to perform an in-place upgrade to Windows 7, Windows XP does not, so you'll need to use a built-in utility on the Windows 7 Setup DVD called Windows Easy Transfer to transfer your documents and settings from your XP-based PC to a backup location first. (This backup location is typically an external hard drive, but you could also use network-based storage if you have such a thing.)

Secret

Windows Easy Transfer does not back up your applications, so you will need to reinstall those manually after Windows 7 is installed.

After this backup is completed, you perform a clean install of Windows 7 on the PC and then use Windows Easy Transfer again to transfer everything back. This may sound pretty simple, and it is, but it's a time consuming process. Here's how it works:

1. On your Windows XP PC, insert the Windows 7 Setup DVD. Cancel any auto-run window that may appear.

2. Open My Computer, right-click on the Windows 7 Setup DVD, and choose Open. Then, navigate to D:\support\migwiz (assuming D:\ is your optical drive).

3. Run *migsetup.exe*. The Windows Easy Transfer utility will start up, as shown in Figure 2-23. Click Next and Windows Easy Transfer will scan the user accounts on your PC for data to back up, as shown in Figure 2-24.

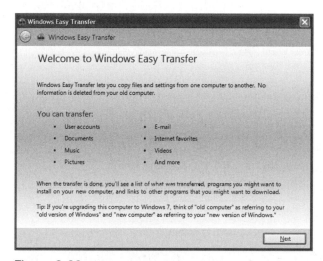

Figure 2-23: Windows Easy Transfer runs on your XP machine to back up important data before you install Windows 7.

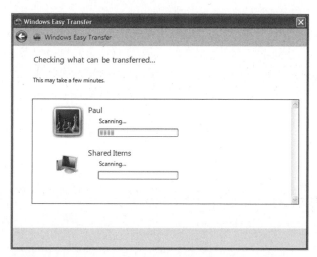

Figure 2-24: Before you can do anything, Windows Easy Transfer needs to see what it can back up.

4. When the scanning process is complete, the wizard will show you how much space the data from each user account will take up (see Figure 2-25). You can click the Customize link under each account to customize what will be backed up. As you can see from Figure 2-26, the resulting window, Modify your selections, provides you with an Explorer-like view of the PC, allowing you to dive in and manually select (or deselect) content that will be backed up. When you're done, click Next.

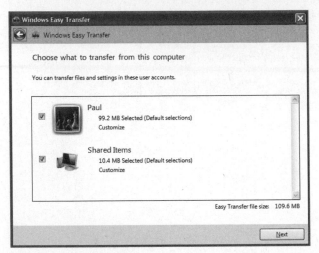

Figure 2-25: After some churning, the Easy Transfer wizard lets you know how much space it will need.

Figure 2-26: Not sure it found everything? You can use this tool to check.

5. In the next phase of the wizard, you are prompted to provide a password for the Easy Transfer file that will be created (see Figure 2-27). This step is *not* optional, so provide a password you know you'll remember later, or you'll have to start all over with the transfer process. Click Save to continue.

Figure 2-27: Your Easy Transfer file is password protected.

6. Now you are prompted to save your Easy Transfer file, typically onto a USB-attached external storage device. Click Save to continue. As shown in Figure 2-28, the Windows Easy Transfer wizard will now (slowly) save this file to your destination of choice. When the save is complete, click Next to complete the wizard.

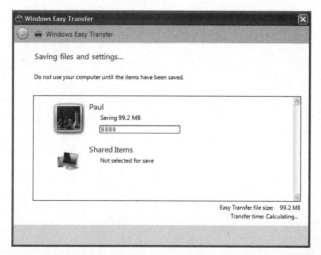

Figure 2-28: You will use the file that's being created here to rescue your data and settings after you migrate to Windows 7.

Secret

At this point, it's advisable to use whatever backup utility you have to back up your entire Windows XP PC if possible. If you do not have such a utility, consider copying the entire contents of the XP hard drive to an external storage device (like a USB hard drive), just in case. This manual backup will not allow you to get back to your XP install if all goes poorly, but it will provide you with access to some critical data that the Easy Transfer wizard may have missed. It's better to be safe than sorry.

7. Now, following the instructions in the previous section, perform a clean install of Windows 7 on your Windows XP–based PC by booting from the Windows 7 Setup DVD. You will most likely need to delete the hard drive's XP partition in order to do this, so be sure you've backed up everything first.

8. Once Windows 7 is installed and up-to-date, it's time to bring back your XP-based settings and data. To do so, connect the external storage to which you saved the Easy Transfer file, open it, and double-click on the file. Windows Easy Transfer will launch, open the file, and present you with the password entry screen shown in Figure 2-29. Enter your password and click Next.

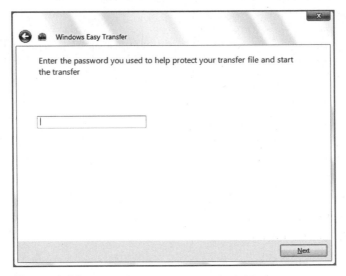

Figure 2-29: Once Windows 7 is installed, it's time to get your settings and data back.

9. Windows Easy Transfer will open the file and then display one or more users (see Figure 2-30), giving you the option to choose which data to transfer over. Note that you can click the Customize link as before and use this wizard to get at a very particular piece of data if you'd like. Make sure the appropriate user(s) are selected and then click Transfer.

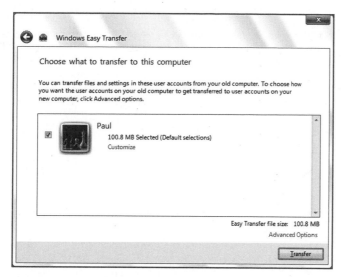

Figure 2-30: Choose the user(s) you want and proceed.

Secret

You could also click the Advanced Options link to display the window shown in Figure 2-31. This provides some very important functionality, including the ability to map a user account on the old XP-based PC with a differently named user account in Windows 7. Nice!

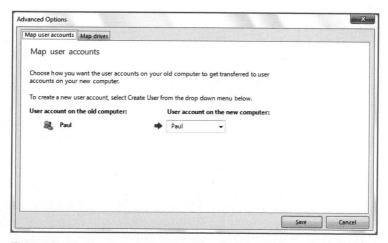

Figure 2-31: Here, you can determine which XP-based users' data goes to which Windows 7 accounts.

10. The data and settings will be transferred over as shown in Figure 2-32. The amount of time this takes will, of course, be determined by the size of the Easy Transfer file; but it takes a lot less time than creation of the file.

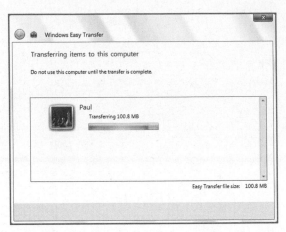

Figure 2-32: The contents of the Easy Transfer file are quickly migrated over to the new install.

11. Once the transfer is complete, the wizard will provide a list of data that was transferred, as well as a list of applications you may want to install in Windows 7. You might notice things like your old desktop and other changes as well, as shown in Figure 2-33.

12. After you close the wizard, you'll be prompted to restart your computer.

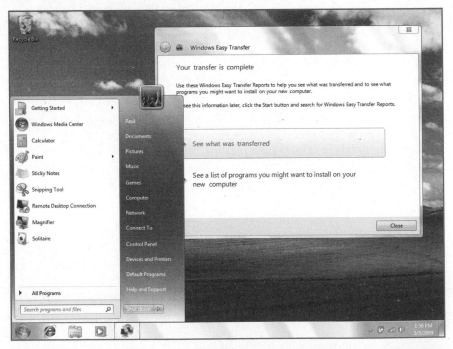

Figure 2-33: What's old is new again: Windows 7 now has all your old XP settings and data.

Secret

The information provided by Windows Easy Transfer here is quite valuable. If you click on either link, *See what was transferred* or *See a list of programs you might want to install on your new* computer, you'll be provided with a detailed transfer report and, more compellingly, a program report that explains which of your old Windows XP applications have more modern equivalents. The program report also lists applications that were installed on your old XP install, along with links so that you can re-download and install them under Windows 7 (see Figure 2-34).

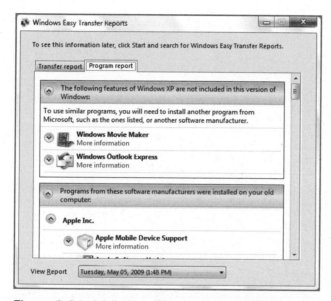

Figure 2-34: A Windows XP migration to Windows 7 does not include applications, but Microsoft does provide a few pointers so you can get up and running on your own.

Secret

In case it's not obvious, Windows Easy Transfer isn't just useful if you are installing Windows 7 on a PC that used to be used for Windows XP. You can also use it to migrate from an old XP-based computer to a new Windows 7–based computer. That way, you can have all your old settings and documents on your new PC too. In fact, you can do this with Windows Vista as well as XP.

Upgrading Windows Vista to Windows 7

If you're undaunted by the process of upgrading your copy of Windows Vista to Windows 7, in-place, then you've come to the right place. This section describes how it's done. Most of the process is virtually identical to the steps outlined for performing a clean install earlier in the chapter. The big difference is time: in our experience, upgrading from Windows Vista to Windows 7 can take several hours, especially if you're doing so on a well-worn PC.

Here's how it works:

1. Launch Windows 7 Setup from within Windows Vista. Simply insert the Windows 7 Setup DVD into your PC's optical drive, triggering the AutoPlay dialog. Click Run setup.exe and the Setup routine will run (after a UAC prompt), displaying the window shown in Figure 2-35.

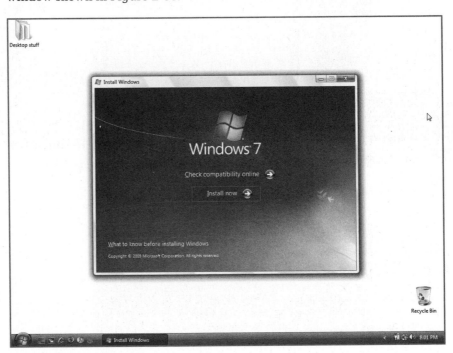

Figure 2-35: When upgrading from Windows Vista to Windows 7, you will typically run Setup from within Windows Vista.

2. Click Install now to continue. After some preparatory work, you'll be asked if you want to go online to get the latest updates for installation. Always do so, because Microsoft continues to improve Windows 7, and updates the Setup process specifically. Setup will search for and download any updates.

3. Setup then asks you to agree to the EULA. In the next step, shown in Figure 2-36, you are asked, "Which type of installation do you want?" It's time to step back a second and regroup. This is where we veer off into new territory.

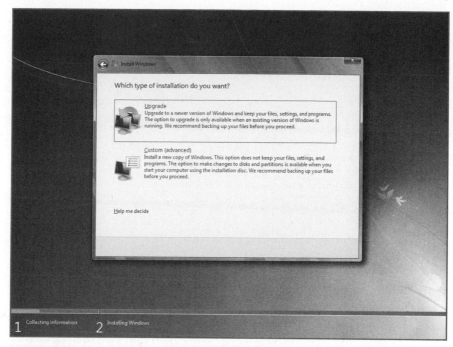

Figure 2-36: When upgrading—go figure—you must choose the Upgrade option.

4. Instead of choosing Custom, choose Upgrade. Setup first runs a compatibility check to determine whether any of your hardware or software needs to be reinstalled—or will work at all—after the upgrade is completed. After scanning your system, Setup presents you with a Compatibility Report (see Figure 2-37). What you see here depends on how old and weather-beaten your system is. The more stuff you've installed, the greater the chance problems will occur. A version is also saved to your desktop as an HTML file (see Figure 2-38).

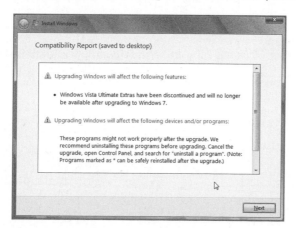

Figure 2-37: Cross your fingers: if you're lucky, nothing important will be unsupported in Windows 7.

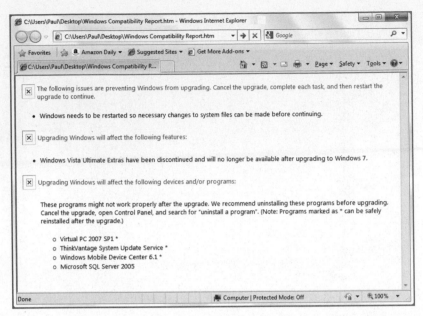

Figure 2-38: A Web page version of the Compatibility Report provides more information.

Sometimes the Setup wizard will find enough incompatible programs on your PC that it cannot continue. In other cases, it will list incompatible programs and recommend uninstalling them before continuing. In either case, you should uninstall any offending apps before proceeding, and then hunt for replacements after Windows 7 is installed.

Assuming you haven't found any show-stopping problems, Setup will continue similarly to how it does during a clean install. Unlike in previous Windows versions, Windows 7 Setup literally backs up your settings, data, and application information, performs a clean install of the operating system, and then copies everything back such that it should all work as it did before.

Setup could take several hours and reboot several times. When this is all done, it will step you through an abbreviated version of the post-Setup steps you see with a clean install: you'll be prompted to (optionally) enter your product key, configure Automatic Updates, review the time and date settings (which, unlike with a clean install, are already correctly configured in most cases), select the computer's current network location (Home, Work, or Public), and then optionally configure HomeGroup sharing. After that, Windows 7 Setup finalizes your settings, prepares your desktop, and then loads it.

If everything goes well, a desktop that looks reasonably like the one you configured for Windows Vista will appear (see Figure 2-39).

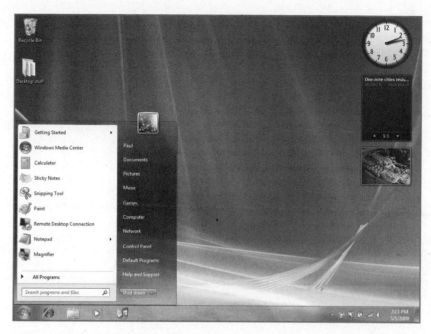

Figure 2-39: Look familiar? This desktop was upgraded from Windows Vista.

The big mystery, of course, is your data and applications. Spend some time testing each application to see if everything works. Figure 2-40 shows the Firefox Web browser, previously installed and configured in Windows Vista, up and running with a few weird add-on errors.

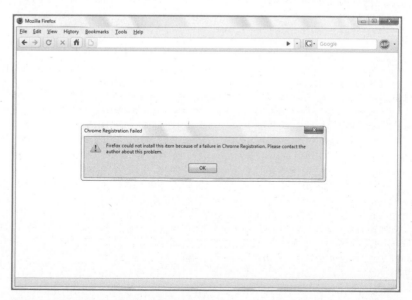

Figure 2-40: If all goes well, your previously installed applications should still work. If not, you may need to reinstall.

> **caution** Because of the potential for problems, we recommend backing up any crucial data and settings before performing any operating-system upgrade.

Upgrading from One Windows 7 Version to Another with Windows Anytime

Microsoft offers a bewildering number of options when it comes to purchasing Windows 7 versions and upgrades, but one of the nicest additions to this panoply of choices is *Windows Anytime Upgrade*, which is built into Windows 7 Starter, Home Premium, and Professional editions. Windows Anytime Upgrade enables you to upgrade from one of those versions to a higher-end Windows 7 version at a drastically reduced price. Which versions you can upgrade to and the cost of that upgrade depend on the version from which you're starting.

Secret Microsoft first offered this service in Windows Vista, but Windows Anytime Upgrade had a tortured history in that OS. For the first year or so that Windows Vista was on the market, Microsoft allowed users to electronically upgrade from one version of Windows Vista to another using Windows Anytime Upgrade. The company would send a product key to you via e-mail and you could use your existing Vista Setup DVD to perform the upgrade. This process, while convenient, proved too confusing for far too many users, so Microsoft discontinued electronic upgrades of Windows Vista in early 2008. Good news, however: the electronic upgrade capabilities of Windows Anytime Upgrade made a comeback in Windows 7!

Table 2-1 explains which Windows Anytime Upgrade options are available, along with current pricing (in U.S. dollars).

Table 2-1: Windows Anytime Upgrade Choices and Pricing

Upgrade from ...	... to Windows 7 Home Premium	... to Windows 7 Professional	... to Windows 7 Home Ultimate
Windows 7 Starter	Yes ($79.99)	Yes ($114.99)	Yes ($164.99)
Windows 7 Home Premium	—	Yes ($89.99)	Yes ($139.99)
Windows 7 Professional	—	—	Yes ($129.99)

Pricing, as you can see, is heavily discounted over the traditional retail Upgrade cost. If you're running Windows 7 Starter, Home Premium, or Professional, upgrading in this fashion is probably the way to go.

Here's how it works. You can access the Windows Anytime Upgrade application, shown in Figure 2-41, from the Control Panel (it's hidden in System and Security) or by typing **anytime** in Windows Start Menu Search. (It's also available from within the Start menu and the System window. Yes, Microsoft is very keen to get more of your money.)

There are two options in the main Windows Anytime Upgrade display: *Go online to choose the edition of Windows 7 that's best for you* and *Enter an upgrade key*. The first option launches IE and provides a Web site that enables you to compare the features and prices of different Windows 7 upgrades, as shown in Figure 2-42.

This Web site presents the various Anytime Upgrade prices, as noted in Table 2-1, and a rundown of the various features in each Windows 7 product edition.

Purchasing is straightforward: click the Buy button next to the Windows Anytime Upgrade option that's relevant to your situation (say, Business to Ultimate). IE will then navigate to a secure e-commerce site so you can make the purchase.

The second option, *Enter an upgrade key*, is used after you've already purchased an electronic upgrade. When you click this link, you're prompted to enter your new product key (see Figure 2-43).

After verifying the key and prompting you to accept the license terms, Windows Anytime Upgrade then performs the upgrade using code that's already installed on your PC (see Figure 2-44).

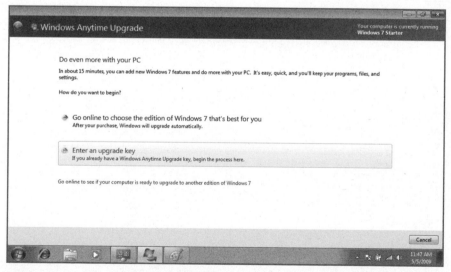

Figure 2-41: Windows Anytime Upgrade provides a way for you to upgrade from one version of Windows 7 to another for less money.

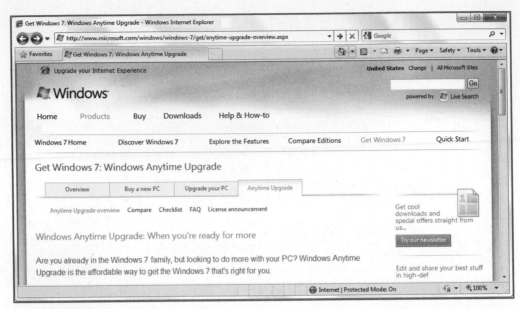

Figure 2-42: The Windows Anytime Upgrade Web site provides pricing and other information regarding your upgrade options.

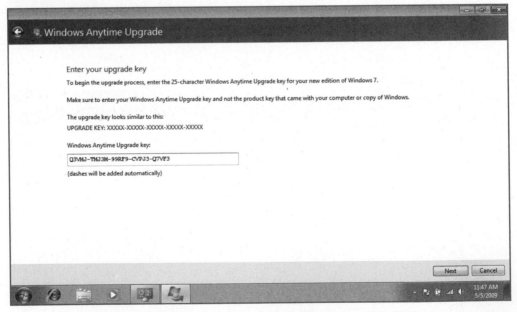

Figure 2-43: Ready to go? Just enter your new product key and you're off.

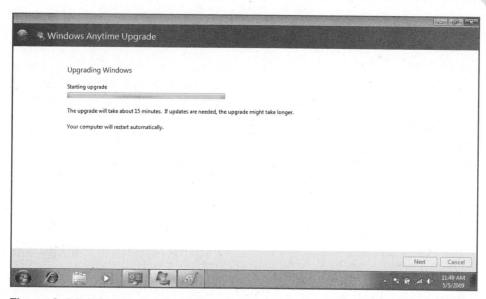

Figure 2-44: Windows Anytime Upgrade doesn't require a Setup DVD or other media.

note Amazingly, the Windows Anytime Upgrade process takes just 15 minutes to complete, though it does require a couple of reboots.

When the upgrade is complete, Windows Anytime Upgrade will display information about the new version of Windows 7 you've installed. Click Close to complete the upgrade (see Figure 2-45).

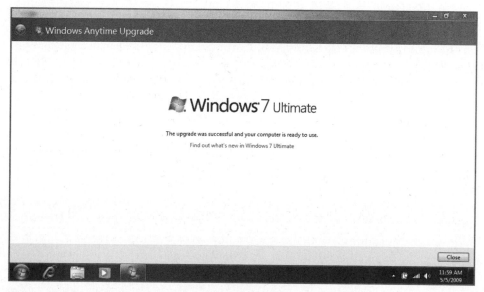

Figure 2-45: And you're done: the quickest Windows upgrade ever.

Performing a Clean Install with an Upgrade Version of Windows 7

While most Windows 7 product editions are available in both Full and Upgrade versions, the differences between each aren't widely understood. The more expensive and seemingly more capable Full versions are designed to be installed only in a so-called "clean" install, as documented earlier in this chapter. That is, when you purchase a Full version of Windows 7 Starter, Home Premium, Professional, or Ultimate, you're expected to install the software on a PC from scratch, and not upgrade an existing version of Windows to Windows 7.

The Upgrade versions of Windows 7, despite their apparently lower status, are in fact more powerful than the Full versions, because they can be used in different ways. Yes, you can use an Upgrade version of Windows 7 to upgrade an existing version of Windows to Windows 7, but you can also use an Upgrade version of Windows 7 to perform a clean install of the operating system.

The process for doing so, alas, is fairly convoluted. This wasn't always the case: in previous versions of Windows, you could boot a PC with the Upgrade Windows Setup disk and, at some point during setup, be prompted to insert the Setup disk from your then-older Windows version to prove that you qualified for Upgrade pricing. With that bit of legal maneuvering out of the way, you could then proceed with setup and complete a clean install using the Upgrade media.

Unfortunately, Microsoft disabled this upgrade compliance capability back in Windows Vista, leading some to believe that it was now impossible to use Windows Upgrade media to perform a clean install. Microsoft's own support documentation says as much. In Knowledge Base article 930985, the company notes that "you cannot use an upgrade key to perform a clean installation of Windows."

Fortunately, there are workarounds, including the method documented here, which should work for just about anyone, though the process is admittedly a bit time-consuming.

According to Microsoft, the only way to perform a clean install of Windows 7 using Upgrade media is to do so on a computer on which a previous version of Windows XP, Vista, or 7 is already installed. For this to work, you need to insert the Windows 7 Upgrade disk while running the previous operating system, run Setup, and then choose Custom (Advanced) at the appropriate place during setup (as documented previously in this chapter).

This method is perfectly acceptable for users who wish to install Windows 7 in a dual-boot setup, where two different operating systems reside on the hard drive simultaneously. But if you want a cleaner system that's free of previous OS detritus, there's a better way—a *secret* way.

Undocumented Method for a Clean Install of Windows 7 with Upgrade Media

Secret

To perform a clean install of Windows 7 with Upgrade media, you need to install Windows 7 once using the Upgrade Setup disk, but without entering your product key during Setup. Then, once you've loaded the Windows 7 desktop for the first time, you can run Setup again from within Windows 7 and choose Upgrade (even though you'll be "upgrading" to the exact same version of Windows 7). Allow Setup to complete a second time, and then you're good to go: you can enter your product key after the second Setup routine is completed and activate Windows 7 successfully.

Here are the complete instructions:

Step 1: Install Windows 7

Boot your PC with the Windows 7 Upgrade DVD. After the preliminary loading screen, install Windows 7 normally. When you are prompted to enter your product key, leave the product key field blank, deselect the option titled "Automatically activate Windows when I'm online," and then continue.

Setup will install Windows as documented in the "Clean Install" section earlier in this chapter. (Refer to that section for a complete rundown of the process.) Once Windows 7 is successfully installed and you are logged on, you'll be presented with your new Windows 7 desktop. Don't get too comfortable, however, as you're about to do it all again.

Step 2: Upgrade from Windows 7...to Windows 7

If you try to activate Windows now, it will fail because you've performed a clean install of Windows 7 and you have only an Upgrade product key. That means you have 30 days during which you can run this non-activated version of Windows 7. But why wait 30 days?

According to Microsoft, Upgrade versions of Windows 7 support upgrading from "a compliant version of Windows, such as Windows 7, Windows Vista, or Windows XP." Well, you just installed Windows 7, so why not just upgrade from that install? That's right: you're going to upgrade the non-activated clean install you just performed, which will provide you with a version of the OS that you can, in fact, activate.

To do this, just select Computer and double-click on the icon for the DVD drive that contains the Windows 7 Upgrade media. Run Setup again, this time from within Windows 7. When you get to the appropriate phase of Setup, choose the Upgrade option. Windows will install as before, though you might notice that it takes quite a bit longer this time. (Upgrade installs take up to 60 minutes, compared to 20 minutes or so with clean installs, and reboot at least one additional time.)

When Setup is completed, enter the username and password you created during the first install and log on to Windows.

Now that you've "upgraded" Windows 7, product activation will actually work. To activate Windows 7 manually and immediately (unless you told it to do so during setup), from the Start menu, type **activate** in Start Menu Search, launch Windows Activation, and click *Activate Windows online now*.

Is this process legal? After all, anyone could purchase an Upgrade version of Windows 7 (thereby saving a lot of money compared to a Full version) and use it to perform a clean install even if they don't own a previous, compliant Windows version.

If you own a previous version of Windows, yeah, it is legal. If not, no, it isn't legal. It's that simple. From a technical standpoint, Microsoft designed Windows 7 to support upgrading from a previously installed copy of Windows XP, Vista, or 7. It's not a hacker exploit, but rather a supported process that was deliberately programmed into the setup routine. It's perfectly okay…as you are indeed a licensed user of a previous version of Windows. So go forth and upgrade. Legally.

Delaying Product Activation

Retail versions of Windows 7 must be activated within 30 days. Otherwise, the system slips into an annoying state in which it notifies you, every 60 minutes, that the system must be activated. Still, the 30-day grace period is useful, especially if you're just testing some things and want to ensure that your new install is working properly before you lock things down and tie your one product key to this particular PC.

That said, sometimes 30 days isn't enough, and if you want to extend this grace period, we've got some good news: thanks to a barely documented feature aimed at Microsoft's corporate customers, it's actually possible to extend the activation grace period up to a total of 150 days. You just have to be a bit vigilant.

The key to extending the grace period is a command-line program in Windows 7 called Software Licensing Manager (SLMGR), which is actually a VBScript script named slmgr.vbs. (It can be found in c:\windows\system32 by default.) Using this script with the -rearm parameter, you can reset (or, in Software Licensing Manager lingo, "re-arm") Windows 7's 30-day activation grace period. This effectively resets the clock on the activation grace period back to a full 30 days whenever you run it.

Unfortunately, you can run this script successfully only four times, so it's theoretically possible to re-arm the product activation grace period to a total of 150 days (30 days of initial grace period plus four additional 30-day grace periods). That said, even the most careful of users will likely want to re-arm the grace period with a few days remaining each time, but you're still looking at over 100 days of non-activated Windows 7 usage.

You can view your current grace period in the System window. To do so, open the Start menu, right-click the Computer icon, and choose Properties. The bottom section of this window, Windows activation, displays how many days you have until the grace period ends, and provides a link to activate Windows immediately, as shown in Figure 2-46.

Windows activation
 22 days to activate. Activate Windows now
Product ID: 00447-015-8630506-70469   Change product key

Figure 2-46: Time to activate…or re-arm the grace period.

Here's how to re-arm the Windows 7 product-activation grace period:

1. Open the Start menu, select Search, and type **cmd**.
2. Right-click the cmd shortcut that appears and choose *Run as Administrator* from the pop-up menu that appears. Windows 7's command-line window appears.
3. Type the following text in the command-line window and press Enter when complete: **slmgr.vbs -rearm**.

   When the command is run successfully, the Windows Script Host window shown in Figure 2-47 appears, noting "Command completed successfully. Please restart the system for the changes to take effect."

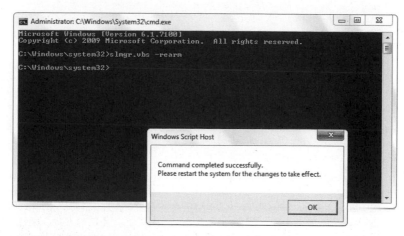

Figure 2-47: Happiness is a full 30-day grace period.

4. Click OK to close the Windows Script Host window and then restart the PC. When you reboot, reload the System window. The grace period has been reset to 30 days. Voila!

Secret

The Software Licensing Manager script wasn't designed solely to extend the Windows 7 grace period. If you run `slmgr.vbs` from a Windows 7 command-line window without any parameters, you'll eventually be presented with the dialog shown in Figure 2-48, displaying the many possible options (Note: Figure 2-48 shows the first and second dialog you see in succession).

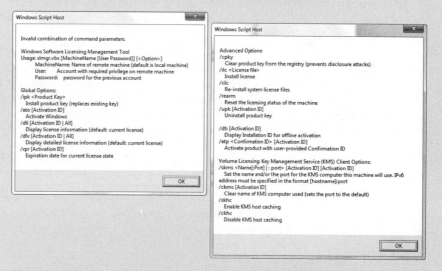

Figure 2-48: The Software Licensing Manager script performs a number of useful product activation–related services.

continues

continued

The most interesting of these include the following:

- `-ipk`: **Enables you to change the Windows product key**
- `-dlv`: **Displays a detailed list of license information about your PC, including the Windows 7 product version and type (e.g., retail)**
- `-ato`: **Activates Windows 7**
- `-dti`: **Activates Windows 7 offline, without an Internet connection**

Installing Windows 7 on a Mac

When Apple switched its desirable Macintosh computers from the aging Power PC architecture to Intel's PC-compatible x86 platform in 2006, the computing landscape was changed forever. No longer were PCs and Macs incompatible at a very low level. Indeed, Macs are now simply PCs running a different operating system. This fascinating change opened up the possibility of Mac users running Windows software natively on their machines, either in a dual-boot scenario or, perhaps, in a virtualized environment that would offer much better performance than the Power PC–based virtualized environments of the past.

These dreams quickly became reality. Apple created software called *Boot Camp* that now enables Mac users to dual-boot between Mac OS X (Leopard or higher) and Windows XP, Vista, or 7. And enterprising tech pioneers such as VMware and Parallels have created seamless virtualization environments for Mac OS X that enable Mac users to run popular Windows applications alongside Mac-only software such as iLife.

Now consumers can choose a best-of-both-worlds solution that combines Apple's highly regarded (if expensive) hardware with the compatibility and software-library depth of Windows. Indeed, Paul has been using an Apple notebook running Windows 7 ever since Microsoft's latest operating system shipped in early beta form.

Secret

The differences between these two types of Windows-on-Mac solutions are important to understand. If you choose to dual-boot between Mac OS X and Windows using Boot Camp, you have the advantage of running each system with the complete power of the underlying hardware. However, you can access only one OS at a time, and you need to reboot the Mac in order to access the other.

With a virtualized environment running under Mac OS X, you have the advantage of running Mac OS X and Windows applications side by side, but with a performance penalty. In this situation, Mac OS X is considered the *host* OS, and Windows is a *guest* OS running on top of Mac OS X. (This works much like Windows Virtual PC and XP Mode, which we document in Chapter 3.) Thus, Windows applications won't run at full speed. With enough RAM, you won't notice any huge performance issues while utilizing productivity applications, but you can't run Windows games effectively with such a setup. Note, too, that the Windows 7 Aero user experience is not available in today's virtualized environments, so you would have to settle for Windows 7 Basic instead.

Regardless of which method you use to install Windows 7, be aware of a final limitation: you need to *purchase* a copy of Windows 7, as no Mac ships with Microsoft's operating system. This is a not-so-fine point that Apple never seems to mention in their advertising.

Dual Boot with Mac: Using Boot Camp

Boot Camp is a feature of Mac OS X and is configured via that system's Boot Camp Assistant. As shown in Figure 2-49, Boot Camp Assistant is available from the Mac OS X Utilities folder (Applications ➪ Utilities) and provides a wizard-based configuration experience.

Boot Camp is available only in Mac OS X 10.5 "Leopard" or newer, and it supports only 32-bit versions of Windows XP, Vista, and 7.

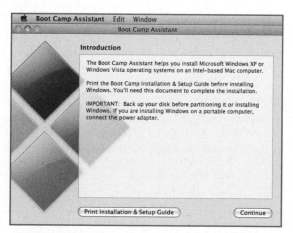

Figure 2-49: Boot Camp helps you configure a dual boot between Windows and Mac OS X.

The key to this wizard is the Create a Second Partition phase, where you can graphically resize the partition layout on the hard disk between Mac OS X and Windows, as shown in Figure 2-50. (Macs with multiple hard drives can be configured such that Mac OS X and Windows occupy different physical disks, if desired.)

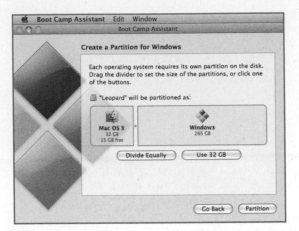

Figure 2-50: Drag the slider to resize the Mac and Windows partitions.

After that, Boot Camp prompts you to insert the Windows 7 Setup DVD and proceed with setup. From a Windows user's perspective, setup proceeds normally and Windows looks and acts as it should once installed. Be sure to keep your Mac OS X Setup DVD handy, however. It includes the necessary drivers that Windows needs to be compatible with the Mac's specific hardware.

Once you have Windows 7 up and running on the Mac, there are just a few Mac-specific issues you should be aware of:

◆ **Configuring Boot Camp:** When you install Windows 7 on a Mac using Boot Camp, Apple installs a Boot Camp Control Panel application, which you can access by selecting Start Menu Search and typing **boot camp**. This application helps you configure important functionality such as the default system to load at boot time (Mac or Windows).

There's also a system notification tray applet that enables you to access the Boot Camp Control Panel and Boot Camp Help and choose to reboot into Mac OS X.

◆ **Switching between operating systems at boot time:** While you can choose the default operating system at boot time via the Boot Camp Control Panel application, or choose to boot into Mac OS X from within Windows by using the Boot Camp tray applet, you can also choose an OS on-the-fly when you boot up the Mac. To do so, restart the Mac and then hold down the Option key until you see a screen with icons for both Mac OS X and Windows. Then, use the arrow keys on the keyboard to choose the system you want and press Enter to boot.

◆ **Understanding Mac keyboard and mouse differences:** While Macs are really just glorified PCs now, Apple continues to use unique keyboard layouts and, frequently, one-button mice. As a result, you may have to make some adjustments when running Windows on a Mac. Table 2-2 lists some commonly used keyboard commands and explains how to trigger equivalent actions on a Mac.

Table 2-2: Windows Keyboard Shortcuts on the Mac

Windows Keyboard Shortcut	Apple External Keyboard	Built-In Mac Keyboard
Ctrl+Alt+Delete	Ctrl+Option+Fwd Delete	Ctrl+Option+Delete
Alt	Option	Option
Backspace	Delete	Delete
Delete	Fwd Delete	Fn+Delete
Enter	Return	Return
Enter	Enter on numeric keypad	Enter
Insert	Help	Fn+Enter
Num Lock	Clear	F6
Pause/Break	F16	Fn+Esc
Print Screen	F14	F11
Print active window	Option+F14	Option+F11
Scroll/Lock	F15	F12
Windows	Command	Command

Windows on Mac: Virtualization Solutions

If you'd prefer to join the ever-increasing ranks of Mac switchers—you traitor, you—you can still run Windows and, more important, Windows applications, from within Mac OS X. You do so via a virtualized environment such as VMware Fusion or Parallels Desktop, both of which fool Windows into running inside of a software-based PC that itself runs as an application under Mac OS X.

In the past, virtualized environments presented a number of huge issues, especially on the Mac. First, performance was abysmal, owing mostly to the underlying architectural differences between the PowerPC and Intel x86 platforms and the difficulty in translating running code between them. Second, virtualized environments have typically presented Windows and its applications as a sort of thing-in-a-thing, whereby the entire Windows environment would run inside a closed-off window that was quite separate and distinct from the Mac environment in which it was running. Moving back and forth between the Mac and Windows environments was jarring and difficult.

Modern virtualized environments—such as VMware Fusion and Parallels Desktop—have mostly overcome these issues, just as Windows Virtual PC has on the Windows side. Thanks to the underlying Intel x86 platform now used by the Mac, virtualization offers better performance because there's no need to do on-the-fly code conversion. Yes, performance still suffers, but you might be surprised by how well Fusion and Parallels Desktop actually work.

More impressive, perhaps, both VMware Fusion and Parallels Desktop offer unique new usage modes that blur the line between the Mac and Windows desktops. VMware Fusion offers a feature called Unity that enables you to run a Windows application directly from the Mac Dock, switch between Windows and Mac applications using the Mac's Exposé window switcher, and drag and drop files between both systems.

Parallels Desktop offers a similar feature called Coherence, which also integrates Windows applications into the Mac desktop experience. Coherence even supports copy and paste between Mac and Windows applications, and many other integration features.

VMware Fusion also offers an impressive bit of integration with Apple's Boot Camp functionality. If you've already installed Windows 7 in a dual-boot setup with Mac OS X using Boot Camp, Fusion will detect that Windows install and automatically enable you to access it as a virtualized environment from within Mac OS X. This, truly, is the best of both worlds, as you can choose to access Windows 7 natively via Boot Camp or virtualized from within Mac OS X using Fusion, all on the same machine.

You can find out more about VMware Fusion from the VMware Web site at `www.vmware .com/products/fusion`. Likewise, you can find out more about Parallels Fusion online at `www.parallels.com/products/desktop`.

Summary

Although Windows 7 Setup is simpler and faster than the Setup routine used by Windows Vista and (even more noticeably) XP, there are still many options to understand and features you'll need to go back and configure manually after Setup is complete. Depending on which version of Windows 7 you purchased and your needs, you can clean-install Windows 7 as the sole OS on your PC, upgrade an existing Windows XP or Vista installation to Windows 7, use Windows Anytime Upgrade to upgrade from one version of Windows 7 to another, delay product activation from 30 days to 150 days, and use the Windows 7 Upgrade media to perform a secret Full install of the product. Users with a lot of money burning a hole in their pocket who are interested in getting the best of both worlds can even do the unthinkable: install Windows 7 on a Mac.

Hardware and Software Compatibility

Chapter

3

♦ ♦

In This Chapter

Choosing not to install Windows 7 over an older operating system

Recognizing when you may have to install Windows 7 over an older OS

Using the Windows 7 Upgrade Advisor to catch problems in advance

Taking action if the Windows 7 Upgrade Advisor indicates that an updated driver "isn't available"

Understanding Windows 7 compatibility issues

Using devices and printers

Achieving better backward compatibility with XP Mode and Windows Virtual PC

♦ ♦

One of the biggest issues you'll face when moving to a new version of Windows—any version, not just Windows 7—is compatibility. Whenever Microsoft changes the underpinnings of Windows, both hardware and software compatibility are going to suffer. That said, Microsoft claims that Windows 7 offers far better backward compatibility than did previous Windows versions, mostly because it is architecturally a minor upgrade when compared to Windows Vista and thus shares the same software and hardware compatibility prowess as its predecessor. However, all it takes is the loss of a single necessary hardware device or software application to turn any Windows upgrade into a disaster. In this chapter, we examine some of the compatibility issues you can run into when making the move to Windows 7, and how you can troubleshoot them.

Hidden Perils of the Windows 7 Upgrade

With all the new features and functionality provided by Windows 7, you might be tempted to buy a retail version of the operating system and install it over your existing copy of Windows Vista or, in the case of Windows XP, perform a migration-type upgrade. While we do cover upgrade scenarios fully in Chapter 2, we don't generally recommend upgrading an older PC to Microsoft's latest OS, for the following reasons (all of which are especially true for XP users):

◆ Your old PC may not be up to the challenge of running Windows 7. You may need substantial investments in additional RAM, a more capable video card, a larger hard drive, or all of the above to get adequate performance from Windows 7.

◆ Some of your hardware, such as printers and networking adapters, may not work at all after you install Windows 7—unless you update the drivers they need to versions that are Windows 7–compatible.

◆ Even if you find that one or more of your drivers need to be updated, the vendor of your hardware may not make a Windows 7–compatible version available for months, years, or ever. (It's happened before with previous versions of Windows.)

◆ Some of the software that's installed and running just fine in Windows XP may not work properly once you've performed the upgrade. (There are workarounds for this, however, as described later in this chapter.)

◆ Finally, some software or hardware may never work in Windows 7. Companies do go out of business, after all. Others simply stop supporting older models to entice you to upgrade to a new machine.

Avoid Installing Windows 7 over Windows Vista

Secret

We recommend that you get Windows 7 preinstalled with your next new PC. This is the best way to acquire Windows 7. Another reasonable option, assuming you know what you're doing and have recent hardware, is to purchase a retail version of Windows 7 and then perform a *clean install* of the OS on your existing PC. We *don't* recommend that you install Windows 7 over Windows Vista.

Here's why. Installing Windows 7 on top of Windows Vista may cause incompatibility problems that you might not be able to fix easily. When you buy a new PC with Windows 7 preinstalled, it's almost certain that the components in the PC will have been selected for their compatibility and will have the latest driver software. PC makers also support their products with Web sites that provide the latest known drivers. These sites aren't usually as up-to-date as they should be, but they will at least work.

In general, you shouldn't consider installing Windows 7 on a PC that previously ran Windows XP or Vista unless the following conditions are true:

- You need a feature of Windows 7 that you can't add to XP. (Much less likely with Vista.)
- You need an application that requires Windows 7.
- You can't afford even the least expensive new PC that comes with Windows 7 preinstalled.

Even if one of the preceding conditions is true, you may be better off backing up all of your old data to a CD/DVD or removable hard disk, formatting the old PC's hard drive, and doing a clean install of Windows 7. This avoids the possibility that some components of the old OS will hang around to cause conflicts. If you've never backed up and formatted a hard drive, however, don't try to learn how on any PC that's important to you.

If you do decide to install Windows 7 on an older PC, at least run Microsoft's Windows 7 Upgrade Advisor, described in this chapter, to determine which drivers you may need to update first; and regardless of how you need to install Windows 7, check out Chapter 2 first, which provides a thorough overview of the various ways in which you can get this system installed.

The Windows 7 Upgrade Advisor

To help you determine whether your current PC has the performance characteristics and hardware and software compatibility needed to avoid issues before upgrading or migrating to Windows 7, Microsoft provides a handy tool called the Windows 7 Upgrade Advisor.

The Upgrade Advisor performs an analysis of your PC and is partly designed as a marketing tool, as it will recommend which version of Windows 7 is right for your system. (Curiously, it almost always recommends one of the more expensive, premium versions.) The Upgrade Advisor also provides real-world benefit outside of Microsoft's needs: it will tell you which hardware devices and software applications need updates before they can work with Windows 7; and because the back end of the Upgrade Advisor application runs on Microsoft's servers, it always provides up-to-date information.

tip The Windows 7 Upgrade Advisor can be downloaded from the Microsoft Web site. See `www.microsoft.com/windows/windows-7/upgrade-advisor.aspx`.

Secret While the Windows 7 Upgrade Advisor is primarily designed to help users of previous Windows versions discover whether their PC can be upgraded successfully to Windows 7, it also has a secret second use: it can be run on Windows 7 and used to determine whether your PC is able to run a more capable (and more expensive) version of Windows 7.

Using the Upgrade Advisor

The Windows 7 Upgrade Advisor is a simple wizard-like application, as shown in Figure 3-1.

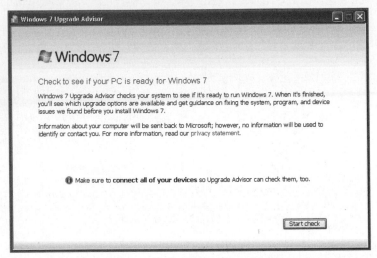

Figure 3-1: The Windows 7 Upgrade Advisor can be used to determine whether your PC has what it takes to compute in the 21st century.

The Upgrade Advisor is designed to test two different kinds of hardware compatibility:

♦ Whether your hardware is fast enough and modern enough to run Windows 7 satisfactorily

♦ Whether your device drivers are compatible with Windows 7

The Upgrade Advisor's initial screen suggests that you should plug in any devices you may want to use with Windows 7. It's easy to forget some, but this is absolutely the right time to have them checked out, so here's a short list to jog your memory about the various devices you want to ensure are plugged into your PC and powered on before you start the Upgrade Advisor's system scan:

♦ Printers and scanners (make sure they're powered on not just plugged in)

♦ External hard disk drives, backup devices, and USB drives of all kinds

♦ An extra USB hub that you seldom use—plug it in anyway to check it

♦ Spare USB keyboards and mice that you may have forgotten

♦ An iPod, Zune, or other MP3 player, even if you seldom synchronize it to your PC

♦ Headphones and other audio devices (they may require audio drivers that won't be tested unless the devices are jacked in to an audio port).

When you've checked for all of the preceding and you are satisfied that you've plugged in and turned on everything you might want to test, click the Start check button in the Upgrade Advisor to continue. Depending on the speed of your system, the scan (see Figure 3-2) can take anywhere from a minute or two to several minutes.

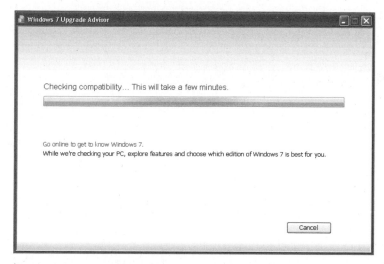

Figure 3-2: Hold your breath, as the moment of truth awaits.

Picking through the Results

The Upgrade Advisor tests three areas: the PC's hardware, to determine whether it meets the minimum Windows 7 requirements; the various hardware devices attached to the system, to ensure that they all have compatible drivers; and the software applications.

When the test is complete, you will see a display like the one shown in Figure 3-3. Almost invariably, the Upgrade Advisor will tell you that your system has received mostly passing grades.

Figure 3-3: How did you do? On most PCs built since 2006, the Upgrade Advisor will report that the system can easily handle the core Windows 7 experiences. If a PC fails the System Requirements test, don't even consider installing Windows 7 on the machine without some serious hardware upgrades.

Look below this message, however, and you may see some issues. As shown in Figure 3-4, many older XP-based PCs will have a number of problems to investigate. In some cases, the Upgrade Advisor will explain what's wrong and provide links for more information.

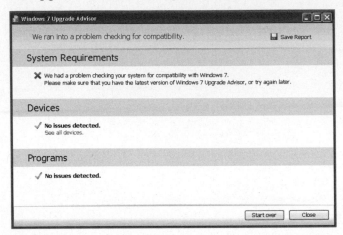

Figure 3-4: Many XP-era PCs will have a bit of upgrading ahead before they can be moved to Windows 7.

As shown in Figure 3-5, the Upgrade Advisor can provide information about how your system conforms to Windows 7's requirements.

Figure 3-5: The Upgrade Advisor will compare your PC to what it knows to be correctly working hardware and software.

If you decide at this point to install Windows 7 on your own PC, and that PC later proves to perform too slowly for you, you can always upgrade your RAM, video board, and disk drive—possibly even swap out your motherboard for a new model—to improve the situation after the fact. However, you should have a reasonable concept of acceptable minimum performance before performing the upgrade. We discuss our minimum hardware recommendations for Windows 7 in Chapter 2.

Drivers That Lack a Windows 7–Compatible Version

If the Upgrade Advisor reports that a particular driver you need may not exist, the first place to start your search is the site of the hardware vendor. New drivers are released every day, so the one you need may have just come out and it's likely that the hardware maker will make it available long before it shows up on Windows Update.

Smaller companies and those that no longer support a particular model of hardware may never spend the time to develop a Windows 7–ready driver. In that case, you may have no choice but to purchase newer hardware that does have a driver you can use in Windows 7.

Understanding Windows 7 Compatibility Issues

Any discussion of PC compatibility, of course, encompasses two very different but related topics: hardware and software. In order for a given hardware device—a printer, graphics card, or whatever—to work correctly with Windows 7, it needs a working driver. In many cases, drivers designed for older versions of Windows will actually work just fine in Windows 7. However, depending on the class (or type) of device, many hardware devices need a new Windows 7–specific driver to function properly on Microsoft's latest operating system.

Software offers similar challenges. While Windows 7 is largely compatible with the 32-bit software applications that Windows users have enjoyed for over a decade, some applications—and indeed, entire application classes, such as security software—simply won't work properly in Windows 7. Some applications can be made to work using Windows 7's built-in compatibility modes, as discussed below. Some can't. Those that can't—like legacy 16-bit software or custom software typically found in small businesses—might be able to find solace in the new XP Mode feature in Windows 7. We examine XP Mode at the end of this chapter.

A final compatibility issue that shouldn't be overlooked is one raised by the ongoing migration to 64-bit (x64) computing. Virtually every single PC sold today does, in fact, include a 64-bit x64-compatible microprocessor, which means it is capable of running 64-bit versions of Windows 7. However, until Windows 7, virtually all copies of Windows sold were the more mainstream 32-bit versions of the system. We'll explain why this is so and how the situation is now changing in favor of 64-bit with Windows 7.

Secret

From a functional standpoint, x64 and 32-bit versions of Windows 7 are almost identical. The biggest difference is RAM support: while 32-bit versions of Windows "support" up to 4GB of RAM, the truth is, they can't access much more than 3.1GB or 3.2GB of RAM because of the underlying architecture of Windows. 64-bit versions of Windows 7, meanwhile, can access up to a whopping 192GB of RAM, depending on which version you get.

Hardware Compatibility

One of the best things about Windows historically is that you could go into any electronics retailer, buy any hardware device in the store, bring it home, and know it would work. Conversely, one of the worst things about any new version of Windows is that the previous statement no longer applies. Paul (who, let's face it, is old) often tells the story about the time he was wandering down the aisles of a Best Buy in Phoenix, Arizona, over a decade ago when Windows NT 4.0 first shipped, with a printed copy of the Windows NT Hardware Compatibility List (HCL) in his hand. He needed a network adapter but had to be sure he got one of the few models that worked in the then new NT 4.0 system.

Windows 7 users face a similar problem today, though there are some differences. First, there's no HCL available anymore, at least not a public one, so you're a bit more on your own when it comes to discovering what's going to work. Second, Windows 7 is already far more compatible with existing hardware than NT was back in the mid 1990s. Indeed, thanks to a 3-year head start with Windows Vista—with which Windows 7 shares the same compatibility infrastructure—Microsoft claims that Windows 7 is actually far more compatible with today's hardware than Windows XP was when it first shipped back in 2001. Based on our extensive testing and evidence provided by Microsoft, this is clearly the case. But then, that was true with Windows Vista as well, though overblown tales of that system's compatibility issues burned up the blogosphere during virtually its entire time in the market.

We've tested Windows 7 for over a year on a wide variety of systems, including several desktops (most of which use dual- and quad-core x64-compatible CPUs), Media Center PCs, notebook computers, Tablet PCs, TouchSmart PCs, netbooks, and even an aging Ultra-Mobile PC. Windows 7's out-of-the-box (OOTB) compatibility with the built-in devices on each system we've tested has been stellar, even during the beta, and it only got better over time. (In this case, OOTB refers to both the drivers that actually ship on the Windows 7 DVD as well as the drivers that are automatically installed via Automatic Updating the first time you boot into your new Windows 7 desktop.) On almost all of these systems, Windows 7 has found and installed drivers for every single device in or attached to the system. So much for all the compatibility nightmares.

Myths about how the Windows Aero user interface requirements would require mass hardware upgrades also dissipated during the Vista time frame. And sure enough, by the time we got to Windows 7, we stopped seeing anything other than the Windows Aero UI on every single modern (2006 or newer) PC we've tested. (With the following exception: when you install Windows 7 Home Basic or Starter, you don't gain access to Windows Aero—but this is due to limitations of the OS, not the hardware.)

As always, you could still run into hardware issues with older scanners, printers, and similar peripherals, especially if you're coming from Windows XP. Paul's network-attached Dell laser printer wasn't supported by Windows 7–specific drivers at launch (though it was in Windows Vista with Service Pack 1 and newer). But because it's really a Lexmark printer in disguise, he was able to get it up and running just fine using Lexmark drivers.

If you're coming from Windows Vista, or are using Windows Vista-era hardware, you're in much better shape. For the most part, everything should just work. TV-tuner hardware? Yep. Zune? Done. Apple's iPods? They all work (even on x64 systems). Windows Media–compatible devices? Of course; they all connect seamlessly and even work with Windows 7's Sync Center interface.

Software Compatibility

We regularly use and otherwise test what we feel is a representative collection of mostly modern software. This includes standard software applications—productivity solutions and the like—as well as games.

We both run a standard set of applications across most of our desktop and mobile PCs. We've also tested numerous video games to see how they fare under Windows 7. (Hey, someone has to do it.) The results have been very positive: not only do most Windows XP-compatible applications and games work just fine under Windows 7, many pre-Windows 7 games also integrate automatically into Windows 7's new Games Explorer as well. Unless it's a very new game designed specifically for Windows 7, you won't get performance information as you do with built-in games, but the game's Entertainment Software Ratings Board (ESRB) rating is enough to enable parents to lock kids out of objectionable video games using Windows 7's parental-control features. It's a nice touch.

If you're coming from Windows Vista, the extra performance boost you get from simply migrating to Windows 7 is astonishing. No, Windows 7 doesn't offer the same raw performance as does Windows XP. But it's close. And it's much faster than Windows Vista. Much faster.

cross ref   See Chapter 16 for more information about gaming and Windows 7.

The biggest software-compatibility issues you're going to see in Windows 7 will involve very old applications that use 16-bit installers, and classes of applications—especially antivirus, antispyware, and other security solutions—that need to be rewritten to work within Windows 7's new security controls. Security vendors will fix their wares, no doubt about it. But what about 16-bit applications and other software that just won't run under Windows 7? Surprise. Microsoft has an answer. It's called XP Mode, and we examine this software later in the chapter.

x64: Is It Time?

The one dark horse in the Windows 7 compatibility story is x64, the 64-bit hardware platform that we're all using today (though few people realize it). The x64 platform is a miracle of sorts, at least from a technology standpoint, because it provides the best of both worlds: compatibility with virtually all of the 32-bit software that's been created over the past 15 years combined with the increased capacity and resources that only true 64-bit platforms can provide.

When Windows Vista first debuted back in late 2006, x64 compatibility was a mixed bag. Hardware compatibility, surprisingly, was excellent, and virtually any hardware device that worked on 32-bit versions of Windows Vista also worked fine on 64-bit versions. Software was another story. Too often, a critical software application simply wouldn't install or work properly on 64-bit versions of Windows, making these versions a nonstarter for most.

Time, however, truly heals all wounds. A huge number of compatibility issues were fixed over Windows Vista's first year on the market, and x64 versions of Windows Vista are now largely compatible, both from a hardware and software perspective, with anything that works with 32-bit versions of the system.

With Windows 7, the situation is even better. With this system, x64 is now the mainstream hardware and software computing architecture for the first time, and you will most likely obtain an x64 version of Windows 7, no matter how you acquire it. In our view, x64 is the way to go. So if you have a choice, open yourself up to the massive RAM improvements that accompany x64 versions of Windows 7.

Dealing with Software Incompatibility

Regardless of Windows 7's compatibility successes, compatibility issues can still bite you when you least expect it. Fear not: there are ways to get around most software incompatibility issues. You just have to know where to look.

Compatibility Mode

If you do run into an application that won't work properly in Windows 7, first try to run it within a special emulation mode called *compatibility mode*. This enables you to trick the application into thinking it is running on an older version of Windows. There are two ways to trigger this functionality: automatically via a wizard, or manually via the Explorer shell. There's also a third related function, the Program Compatibility Assistant, which appears automatically when Windows 7 detects you're having a problem installing or using an application.

Let's take a look at all three.

Using the Program Compatibility Wizard

The Program Compatibility Wizard is a simple application that detects issues on your PC and can automatically fix them for you. Or, if the wizard doesn't detect an issue, you can simply point it at the misbehaving application and have it do its thing, using recommended settings or a manual troubleshooting process.

You'd think that using a wizard would be easier than manually configuring compatibility mode; and that would true if you could just find the thing: unfortunately, the Program Compatibility Wizard isn't available from the Windows 7 user interface. Instead, you have to trigger it using this secret.

Open the Start menu and type **program compatibility** in Start Menu Search. One result will come up: *Run programs made for previous versions of Windows* (see Figure 3-6). You click that to start the Program Compatibility Wizard.

Yes, really.

The admittedly bare-bones-looking Program Compatibility Wizard (see Figure 3-7) steps you through the process of identifying the application to run in compatibility mode and which settings you'd like to configure.

When you click Next, the Program Compatibility Wizard will attempt to find any badly behaving applications. If it can't find any, you can choose the application from a list of applications or click Not Listed and manually show the wizard where to find the application in question.

Figure 3-6: It's well hidden, but the Program Compatibility Wizard might be just what you need to get that stubborn legacy application to run correctly in Windows 7.

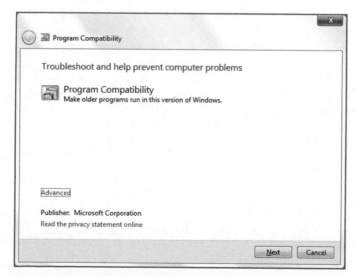

Figure 3-7: It ain't pretty, but the Program Compatibility Wizard usually gets the job done.

Once you've identified the program you'd like to fix, you can try the recommended settings, which is always a good idea. If this fixes things, you can simply go about your business. If it doesn't, the wizard will walk you through the process, asking a series of questions, as shown in Figure 3-8.

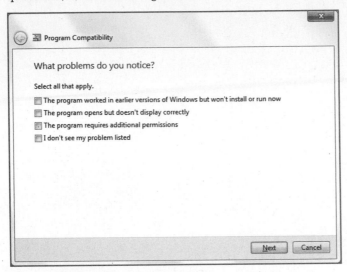

Figure 3-8: Still not working? Tell the wizard your troubles.

For example, if you know an application worked on a previous version of Windows, and it's not working now in Windows 7, you can pick from an extensive list of Windows versions to emulate, including Windows Vista, Windows Vista with Service Pack 1 (SP1), Windows Vista with Service Pack 2 (SP2), Windows Server 2003 with SP1, Windows XP with SP2, Windows XP with SP3, Windows 2000, Windows NT. 4.0 with SP5, Windows 98/Windows ME, or Windows 95.

Once you've answered a few questions, the wizard will apply the appropriate settings to the application and prompt you to test-run the application to see how things work out. You can then either accept the configuration, go back and make changes, or just quit the wizard.

Enabling Compatibility Mode Manually

You don't actually have to hunt around for the Program Compatibility Wizard if you want to run an application in compatibility mode. Instead, find the executable (or, better yet, a shortcut to the executable, such as the ones you'll find in the Start menu), right-click, and choose Properties. Then, navigate to the Compatibility tab, shown in Figure 3-9.

As you can see, this tab provides all of the options found in the wizard, but in a handier, more easily contained location. Just pick the options you'd like, click Apply, and test the application. Once it's working correctly, you can click OK and never bother with this interface again.

Compatibility mode is a great (if hidden) feature, but it's no panacea. Some applications will simply never run on Windows 7, no matter what you do.

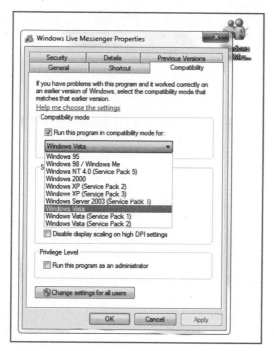

Figure 3-9: Any application can be run in compatibility mode.

Secret

Compatibility mode should not be used to enable older security applications such as antivirus software. These types of applications should be run only on the operating systems for which they were designed.

Understanding the Program Compatibility Assistant

When Windows 7 detects that you're installing an application with a known compatibility problem or suspects that a just-completed application installation has not concluded successfully, it will offer to fix the problem. This functionality, called the Program Compatibility Assistant, occurs automatically, as shown in Figure 3-10. You're free to decline the offer if you believe the application ran correctly. There is no way to trigger it manually, as you can with program-compatibility mode. Like any good neighbor, it will simply appear when needed.

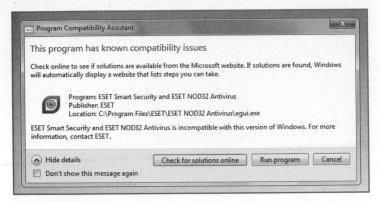

Figure 3-10: The Program Compatibility Assistant will pop up whenever it thinks you need help.

Windows Virtual PC and XP Mode

When all else fails, a new Windows 7 feature can come to the rescue. Actually, there are two features involved:

◆ **Windows Virtual PC** is a software solution that provides a virtual machine environment in which *guest* operating systems, with their own applications and services, can run separately and independently from the *host* environment, or physical PC.

◆ **XP Mode** provides a virtual version of Windows XP in which you can configure virtualized, XP-based applications to run side by side with native Windows 7 applications. This effect is shown in Figure 3-11.

Figure 3-11: It's crazy but it's true: Windows XP and Windows 7 applications can now run side by side.

Secret Windows Virtual PC is free for all Windows 7 users, but Windows XP Mode is a perk of the Professional, Enterprise, and Ultimate versions of the operating system. You can download both from www.microsoft.com/windows/virtual-pc/download.aspx.

The next sections take a look at both of these new Windows 7 components.

tip Windows Virtual PC is the latest version of Microsoft's venerable Virtual PC product line. Previously, this environment was made available as a standalone application to users of various Windows versions. With Windows Virtual PC, however, this product is now a Windows 7 feature. And though it doesn't ship on the disc with Windows 7, it can only be installed on Windows 7.

Understanding Windows Virtual PC

To the operating system and applications running in a virtual environment like Windows Virtual PC, the virtual machine appears to be a real PC, with its own hardware resources and attributes. These virtualized systems have no knowledge or understanding of the host machine at all.

Though virtual machines cannot rival the performance of real PCs for interactive use—they're useless for graphically challenging activities such as modern, action-oriented games, for example—they are perfect for many uses. In fact, virtual machines are often used to test software in different environments, or test Web sites and Web applications with different browser versions.

Secret Looking for a way to play old DOS-based games under Windows 7? Forget Windows Virtual PC. Instead, check out DOSBox. It's awesome, and if you're looking for a Duke Nukem fix this is the place to be (see www.dosbox.com).

In Windows 7, the Windows Virtual PC virtualized environment—shown in Figure 3-12—plays a special role. Because new versions of Windows are often incompatible with legacy applications, a virtual machine environment running an older version of Windows and those incompatible legacy applications can be quite valuable. Best of all, in such cases, users are often less apt to notice any performance issue because older operating systems tend to require fewer resources anyway.

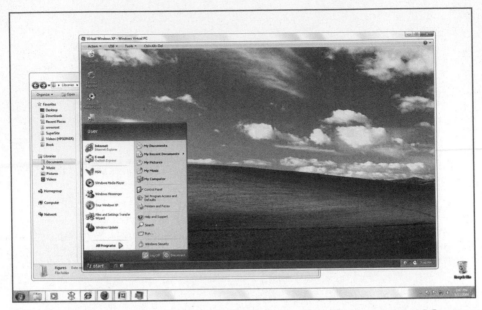

Figure 3-12: Here, you can see Windows XP running inside Windows Virtual PC on top of Windows 7.

That said, for the best results, anyone utilizing Virtual PC to run an older operating system such as Windows XP along with whatever set of Windows 7–incompatible applications is well served to pack the host PC with as much RAM as physically possible. For typical PCs today, that means loading up with 4GB. Remember: you're running two operating systems and any number of applications simultaneously. That old Pentium 3 with 256MB of RAM just isn't going to cut it.

Secret

Windows Virtual PC is available in separate 32-bit and 64-bit versions. Make sure you download the correct version for your PC.

Secret

Windows Virtual PC has specific hardware requirements, and thanks to the vagaries of microprocessor marketing, your PC may not be up to snuff. The only important consideration, indeed, is the microprocessor: in order to run Windows Virtual PC (and, thus, XP Mode as well), you need a microprocessor that supports hardware-assisted virtualization. And you must be able to enable this functionality in the PC's BIOS. If you don't have such support, you'll see the error message shown in Figure 3-13 when you try to install Windows Virtual PC.

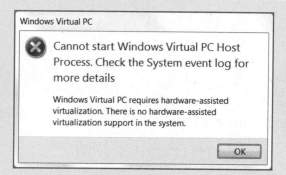

Figure 3-13: Windows Virtual PC has very specific hardware
requirements and won't work on all PCs.

This technology goes by different names depending on which microprocessor
vendor you're talking about. With Intel, it's called Virtualization Technology (Intel
VT). And with AMD it's simply called AMD Virtualization (AMD-V). The vast
majority of modern (for example, 64-bit and multicore) AMD processors include
AMD-V, so you're generally in good shape if you're running a PC with an AMD
processor. But in the Intel world, you have some work ahead of you.

Let's get the simple part out of the way first. If your PC utilizes an Intel i7 or
i7 Extreme processor, you're all set. All of these products include the necessary
hardware support. For the remainder of Intel's modern CPU lineup, however, you
can refer to Tables 3-1 and 3-2.

**Table 3-1: Intel Desktop Microprocessor Support for
Hardware-Assisted Virtualization**

Intel Microprocessor	Supports Hardware-Assisted Virtualization
Core 2 Duo E4300, 4400, 4500, 4600, and 4700	No
Core 2 Duo E6300, 6320, 6400, 6420, 6540, and 6550	Yes
Core 2 Duo E6600, 6700, 6750, and 6850	Yes
Core 2 Duo E7200, 7300, 7400, and 7500	No
Core 2 Duo E8190	No
Core 2 Quad Q6600 and 6700	Yes
Core 2 Quad Q8200, 8200S, 8300, 8400, and 8400S	No

continues

Table 3-1: Intel Desktop Microprocessor Support for Hardware-Assisted Virtualization *(continued)*

Intel Microprocessor	Supports Hardware-Assisted Virtualization
Core 2 Quad Q9300, 9400, and 9400S	Yes
Core 2 Quad Q9450, 9550, 9550S, and 9650	Yes
Pentium D Pentium EE 805, 820, 830, and 840	No
Pentium D Pentium EE 915, 925, 935, and 945	No
Pentium D Pentium EE 920, 930, 940, 950, and 960	Yes
Pentium D Pentium EE 955 and 965	Yes
Pentium for Desktop E2140, 2160, 2180, 2200, and 2220	No
Pentium for Desktop E5200, 5300, and 5400	No

Table 3-2: Intel Mobile Microprocessor Support for Hardware-Assisted Virtualization

Intel Microprocessor	Supports Hardware-Assisted Virtualization
Core 2 Duo Mobile L7200, 7300, 7400, and 7500	Yes
Core 2 Duo Mobile P7350, and 7450	No
Core 2 Duo Mobile P7370	Yes
Core 2 Duo Mobile P8400, 8600, 8700, 9500, and 9600	Yes
Core 2 Duo Mobile SL9300, 9400, and 9600	Yes
Core 2 Duo Mobile SP9300, 9400, and 9600	Yes
Core 2 Duo Mobile SU9300, 9400, and 9600	Yes
Core 2 Duo Mobile T5200, 5250, 5270, 5300, 5450, and 5470	No
Core 2 Duo Mobile T5500, and 5600	Yes
Core 2 Duo Mobile T5550, 5670, 5750, 5800, 5850, 5870, and 5900	No
Core 2 Duo Mobile T6400, and 6570	No

Intel Microprocessor	Supports Hardware-Assisted Virtualization
Core 2 Duo Mobile T7100, 7200, 7250, 7300, and 7400	Yes
Core 2 Duo Mobile T7500, 7600, 7700, and 7800	Yes
Core 2 Duo Mobile T8100, and 8300	Yes
Core 2 Duo Mobile T9300, 9400, 9500, 9550, 9600, and 9800	Yes
Core 2 Duo Mobile U7500 and U7600	Yes
Core 2 Extreme Mobile QX9300	Yes
Core 2 Extreme Mobile X7800 and 7900	Yes
Core 2 Extreme Mobile X9000 and 9100	Yes
Core 2 Quad Mobile Q9000	Yes
Core 2 Quad Mobile Q9100	No
Core 2 Solo SU3300 and 3500	Yes
Core 2 Solo U2100 and 2200	Yes
Core Duo L2300, 2400, and 2500	Yes
Core Duo T2050 and 2250	No
Core Duo T2300, 2400, 2500, 2600, and 2700	Yes
Core Duo T2300E, 2350, and 2450	No
Core Duo U2400 and 2500	Yes
Core Solo T1300 and 1400	Yes
Core Solo T1350	No
Core Solo U1300, 1400, and 1500	Yes

If the PC you're using does not include a microprocessor that supports hardware-assisted virtualization, you have two options: you can use a different PC, of course. Or you could use a competing virtualization solution that doesn't include such a limitation. (Note, however, that no competing virtualization products include a free copy of Windows XP.) We favor VMWare Workstation (www.vmware.com/products/ws) but if you would like a free solution, check out VirtualBox (www.virtualbox.org) instead.

Secret

The previous tables were current when this book was written, but of course AMD, Intel, and other microprocessor makers are always updating their product lines. So be sure to check this book's Web site, www.winsupersite.com/book, for the latest processor compatibility tables.

Secret

If your PC's processor has hardware-assisted virtualization support but you failed to enable it in the BIOS, you will see the dialog shown in Figure 3-14 when you attempt to install XP Mode or another OS in a virtual machine. That means you have to reboot, enable the feature in the BIOS, boot into Windows again, and then rerun Windows XP Mode Setup. So get this set up first.

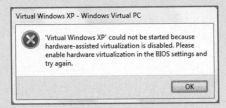

Figure 3-14: Enable hardware-assisted virtualization before running XP Mode Setup or configuring any other virtual machines.

You manage Windows Virtual PC from a very simple Virtual Machines explorer, rather than from the console application window that accompanied previous versions. Shown in Figure 3-15, this window provides a toolbar button from which you can create a new virtual machine.

The Create a virtual machine wizard (see Figure 3-16) can create new virtual environments using an existing virtual disk, or, more likely, by creating a new one from scratch. In the latter case, you install a new operating system just as you would normally, using the original setup CD or DVD, or an ISO image, which can be "mounted" so that it works like a physical disk from within the virtual environment.

After determining the name of the virtual machine, how much RAM it will use, and the location of the virtual hard disk, it's time to install an operating system. You're welcome to install virtually any modern, 32-bit version of Windows, but Windows Virtual PC natively supports Windows 7, Windows Vista with SP1 or higher and Windows XP with SP3 in a special way: in these environments, you can install integration components that take guest-to-host integration to the next level.

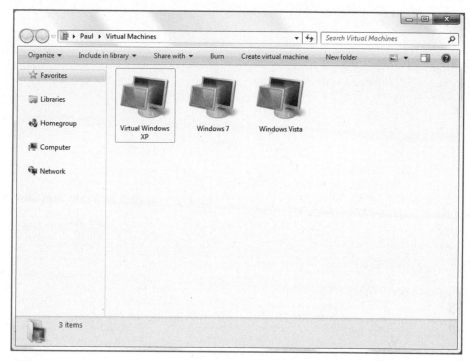

Figure 3-15: Console be gone: Windows Virtual PC is managed from a simple explorer.

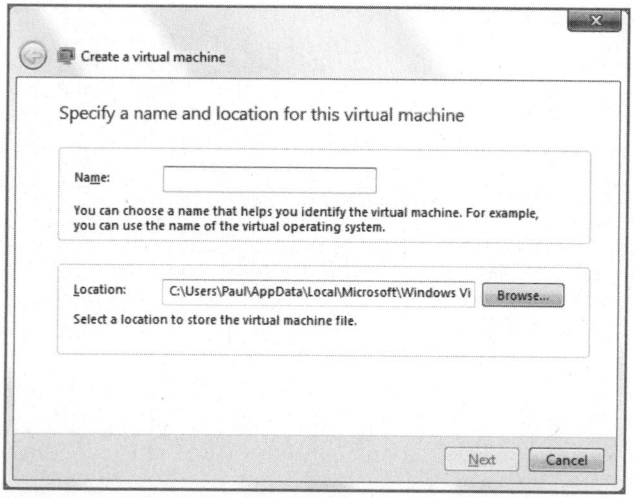

Figure 3-16: Virtual PC's Create a virtual machine wizard helps you determine the makeup of the virtualized environment.

Secret

Though Windows Virtual PC is available in a 64-bit version, the product supports only 32-bit guest operating systems.

Noticeably absent from this list, incidentally, is any form of Linux. You can, in fact, try to install various Linux distributions in Windows Virtual PC, but this install type has some limitations, chief among them a lack of integration with the host environment that supported guest operating systems receive. That said, many modern Linux distributions don't work correctly in Windows Virtual PC unless you are capable of some serious tinkering. In this case, Google is your friend.

Secret

While Windows Virtual PC supports both Windows Vista and Windows 7, the emulated graphics subsystem utilized by this environment is not powerful enough to render the operating systems' Windows Aero user interface. Therefore, if you choose to run Windows Vista or 7 in a virtual machine, you have to make do with the Windows Basic user experience.

To manage any virtual machine environment you've created, just select it in the Virtual Machines explorer and click the Settings button that appears. The resulting Settings window (see Figure 3-17) lets you configure individual VM settings, including the RAM, virtual hard disk(s), and other devices associated with the VM.

In use, virtual machines are like slower versions of "real" PC installs. You can continue running guest operating systems in a Windows Virtual PC window side by side with the host Windows 7 system, or you can run the guest OS full-screen, making it appear as if your modern Windows 7–based PC has gone back in time. Windows Virtual PC supports a variety of niceties for moving information back and forth between the host and guest operating systems, including cut-and-paste integration and the notion of a shared folder that exists in both systems so you can move files back and forth.

But what really makes Windows Virtual PC special is that those integration components allow compatible operating systems to publish their applications into the host PC environment. That way, you don't have to launch and manage a second PC desktop. Instead, you can simply use the application(s) that caused you to install Windows Virtual PC in the first place.

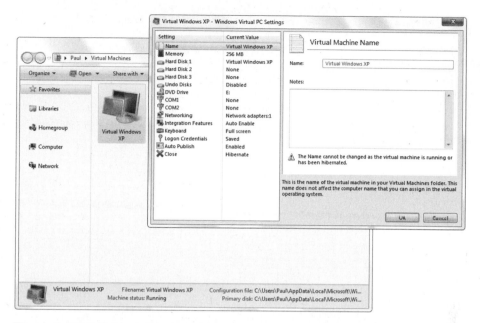

Figure 3-17: Individual virtual machines are managed with a single window too.

Taking It to the Next Level: Windows XP Mode

For users of Windows 7 Professional, Enterprise, and Ultimate, Microsoft provides a freely downloadable, prepackaged, and fully licensed copy of Windows XP with SP3 as a perk. Called Windows XP Mode, this feature allows you to run XP applications side by side with Windows 7 applications using Windows Virtual PC. Yeah, it really is that cool.

When you download and install Windows XP Mode and run it for the first time, you are prompted to provide a non-optional password for the default user account in Windows XP, which is imaginatively titled *User* (see Figure 3-18).

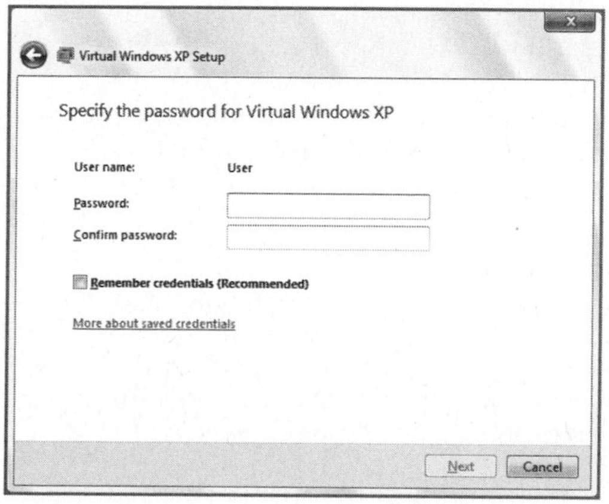

Figure 3-18: You must create a password, but the Remember credentials option is even more important.

The more important option is Remember credentials (recommended). We, too, recommend that you select this option, as the point of XP Mode is that you can seamlessly run XP applications side-by-side with Windows 7 apps. If you do not allow the system to remember your logon credentials (for example, your user name and password), you will be prompted to provide them every time you run an XP application.

You're also prompted to configure Automatic Updates, as shown in Figure 3-19. Again, you should do so, as you want the underlying XP system to take care of itself. After initial configuration, you should be able to forget it even exists for the most part.

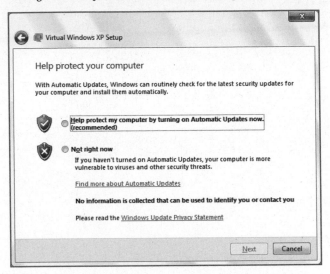

Figure 3-19: Make sure you enable Automatic Updates.

After this, you will have to wait quite a while as Windows Virtual PC steps through the process of starting the virtual machine, setting up Windows XP Mode for first use, starting the OS, and enabling integration features. What's happening behind the scenes is that Windows Virtual PC is actually moving through the post-Setup steps, creating the user and configuring the Automatic Updates setting you previously defined. When it's ready, the familiar Windows XP Desktop will appear in a window on top of your Windows 7 Desktop, as shown in Figure 3-20.

Of course, running a virtual environment inside of a host OS like Windows 7 isn't the end goal here. The reason you're running Windows XP virtually in the first place is that you want access to that system's larger (and older) software library. From here on out, any application you install under Windows XP will actually appear in the Windows 7 Start menu, as shown in Figure 3-21.

In this way, XP Mode is *publishing* installed applications to Windows 7. And when you run these apps from the Windows 7 Start menu, naturally, they run side-by-side with native Windows 7 applications, share the same clipboard and file system with the host environment, and so on. And really, that's the point: XP Mode isn't about running Windows XP. It's about getting incompatible applications to work properly again.

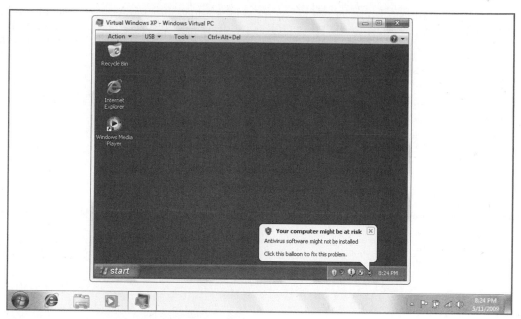

Figure 3-20: Ah, the good ol' days.

Figure 3-21: When you install applications in the virtual Windows XP environment, they also appear in the Windows 7 Start menu, so you can run them from there.

It's not obvious, but this ability to run virtual applications inside of Windows 7 is not limited to Windows XP Mode. Nor is it limited to virtualized instances of Windows XP. You can do the same thing with virtualized Windows Vista and Windows 7 applications, too.

Publishing applications is nice, but what about XP's built-in apps, like Internet Explorer 6? You can manually publish built-in Windows XP apps using the following workaround: launch Windows XP Mode, right-click the XP Start menu, and choose Open All Users. In the Explorer window that appears, navigate into the Programs folder. Now, drag a shortcut for the application you'd like to run into the Programs folder. Close it, close XP Mode, and check the Windows 7 Start menu: success!

Looking to the Future

As it stands today, Windows Virtual PC is an interesting and, in many cases, desirable solution, especially with Windows XP Mode. But the underlying technology is still based on the legacy Virtual PC code and not on newer, hypervisor-based virtualization solutions like Hyper-V, part of the Windows Server 2008 product line. This technology runs closer to the metal than Windows Virtual PC, so it offers much better performance and is more secure and easily maintainable. Despite utilizing a different architecture, however, Hyper-V is compatible with the same VHDs used by Windows Virtual PC, ensuring that customers who adopted Microsoft's virtualization products early in the game could move their virtualized environments forward.

Microsoft also offers more managed application virtualization products, which today are, of course, geared toward larger companies. Microsoft purchased a company called SoftGrid and relaunched its application virtualization solution as Microsoft Application Virtualization, or App-V. This software enables Microsoft customers to stream applications to the desktop in special virtualized packages. Instead of delivering an entire virtualized environment to end users, companies can deliver individual applications in a package, along with any required dependent files. These packages break the application/operating system lock and allow for some interesting scenarios, including the ability to run multiple versions of the same application on a single OS.

Then, in 2007, Microsoft purchased another innovative company in the virtualization space, Kidaro. This acquisition gave Microsoft the final piece of the puzzle: the ability to combine the power of Virtual PC with the application independence of SoftGrid. The resulting product, Microsoft Enterprise Desktop Virtualization (MED-V), is basically a server-based version of XP Mode.

Looking ahead, it seems like future versions of Windows will include a virtualization solution based on Hyper-V and some combination of the SoftGrid and Kidaro technologies. This would expand on the work done in Windows 7 but provide additional performance and manageability benefits. Then, in these future Windows versions, Microsoft will be able to move in completely new technical directions, secure in the knowledge that its virtualization platform will enable users to install virtually (sorry) any application that works on older versions of Windows. The key is packaging them into mini-virtualized environments that include only those parts of Windows XP, Windows 98, or whatever they need in order to run.

Windows Virtual PC and Windows XP Mode are just one step down this road. They are an important step, of course.

Summary

Windows 7 constitutes, in many ways, a break with the past, but that doesn't necessarily mean you have to make a break with your existing hardware or software just yet. Using Microsoft's Windows 7 Upgrade Advisor, you can determine whether your current PC is powerful enough to run Windows 7 and, if so, which of your existing hardware devices and software applications will work properly after the upgrade. After installing Windows 7, however, you're not on your own. Features such as the Program Compatibility Wizard and the Program Compatibility Assistant can force older Windows applications to run fine in Windows 7. If that doesn't work, there are always virtualization solutions, including Microsoft's free Windows Virtual PC and the seamless Windows XP Mode environment. Chances are good there's a way to make your existing devices and applications work with Windows 7. You just need to know where to turn.

Part II

The New and Improved Windows 7 User Experience

What's New in the Windows 7 User Experience

◆ ◆

In This Chapter

Exploring the various Windows 7 user experiences

Understanding what you need to run Windows Aero

Personalizing the Windows 7 desktop

Examining the Windows 7 shell with Explorer

Touching Your Computer with Windows Touch

◆ ◆

Gazing upon Windows 7 for the first time, either you will feel a sense of déjà vu or you will immediately be struck by how different everything looks, depending on whether you're coming from Windows XP or Vista. For XP users, the translucent and glasslike windows and the subtle animations and visual cues will all be new. For Vista users, the interface has been refined, enhanced, and sped up. Regardless of your background, this new interface leaves no doubt: Windows 7 is a major new Windows version, with much to learn and explore. In this chapter, we'll examine what's changed in the Windows 7 user interface since Windows XP and Vista, and explain what you need to know to adapt to this new system.

Understanding the Windows 7 User Experience

When the first PCs hit the streets over 20 years ago, users were saddled with an unfriendly, non-intuitive user interface based on the MS-DOS command line and its ubiquitous C:\ prompt. Since then, computer user interfaces have come a long way, first with the advent of the mouse-driven graphical user interface (GUI) on the Macintosh and later in Windows, and then with the proliferation of Internet connectivity in the late 1990s, which blurred the line between local and remote content and led to the currently emerging era of "cloud computing," where PC-like user interfaces are available on the Web.

Microsoft has done much to evolve the state of the art of computer GUIs for the masses over the years. Windows 95 formalized the notion of right-clicking on objects in the operating system to discover context-sensitive options. Windows 98 introduced a shell, Explorer, that was based on the same code found in the Internet Explorer Web browser; and Windows XP began a trend toward task-oriented user interfaces, with folder views that changed based on the content you were viewing or had selected.

In Windows Vista, the Windows user interface, or as Microsoft likes to call it, the Windows *user experience*, evolved yet again, presenting users with a translucent, glasslike interface called Aero that takes the Windows user interface metaphor to its logical conclusion. That's right: for the first time, in Windows Vista, windows actually appeared to be made of glass, just like real windows.

The Windows 7 user interface is based on that from Windows Vista. It features a further evolved version of the Windows Aero interface that debuted in Windows Vista, but this time around there's even more glass and even more special effects. There are new keyboard shortcuts to learn and new ways of managing running applications and other open windows.

For all the changes, it may be comforting to know that much in Windows 7 has not changed since XP. That is, you still press a Start button (though it's now officially called the Start Orb, a term we'll simply dispense with) to launch the Start menu. From the Start menu, you can perform tasks such as launching applications, accessing the Control Panel, networking features, and other related functionality, and turn off the system. A taskbar still runs along the bottom of the Windows Vista desktop; and while it's far more powerful than that found in previous versions, it still contains buttons for each open window and application. A system tray still sits in the lower-right corner of the screen, full of notification icons and the system clock. The desktop still contains icons and shortcuts. Windows still appear to float above this desktop, and all of your familiar applications and documents will still work, especially if you install the optional new XP Mode feature. The Windows Aero user experience is shown in Figure 4-1.

Figure 4-1: As with Windows Vista, most Windows 7 users will see the glasslike Windows Aero user interface.

Secret

While most people will see Windows Aero, some won't. What you do see in Windows 7 depends largely on the Windows 7 product edition you're using, the hardware in your system, and your own personal preferences. More confusing, perhaps, is that you likely won't see options for all of the user experiences.

You access the different Windows 7 user experiences via the Personalization control panel (see Figure 4-2). Windows Aero is the high-end user experience and the one you'll likely want (though it's not available in Windows 7 Starter or Home Basic). Windows 7 Basic is the simplest version of the new user interface, and it is available to all Windows 7 editions. Windows 7 Standard (not to be confused with the old Windows Standard color scheme) is available only in Windows 7 Home Basic, so many readers will not see this option. Windows Classic is available to one and all.

continues

continued

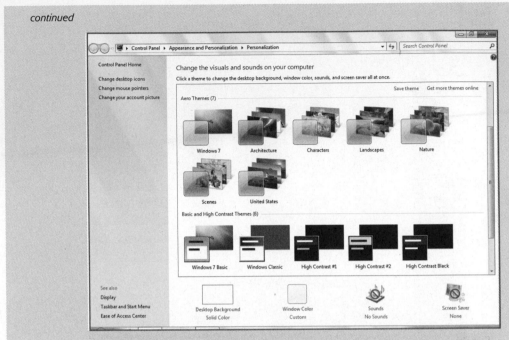

Figure 4-2: The Personalization control panel is pretty well hidden, but it's the secret to switching between various user experience types.

Table 4-1 summarizes the different user experiences and which product editions you need to access them.

Table 4-1: Which User Experiences Work in Which Windows 7 Product Editions

User Experience	Available in Which Windows 7 Product Editions
Windows 7 Classic	All
Windows 7 Basic	All
Windows 7 Standard	Home Basic only
Windows Aero	Home Premium, Professional, Enterprise, Ultimate

There are other requirements for some of these user experiences, however. In the sections that follow, we'll highlight the different user experiences that Microsoft has included in Windows 7, and explain how and when you might see them.

Windows Classic

Windows 7 includes a user experience called Windows Classic that resembles the user interfaces that Microsoft shipped with Windows 95, 98, Me, and 2000. (It most closely resembles Windows 2000.) This interface is available on all Windows 7 product editions, including Starter Edition. Classic is included in Windows 7 primarily for businesses that don't want to undergo the expense of retraining their employees to use the newer user experiences. It's also there for you masochists. The Windows Classic user interface is shown in Figure 4-3.

Secret

While Windows Classic does resemble the Windows 2000 look and feel, there are in fact numerous differences. So users will still require some training when moving to Windows 7 and Windows Classic mode. Some older interfaces are no longer possible. For example, the Windows 7 Start menu still retains the layout that debuted with Windows XP, and not the cascading menu style you might remember from Windows 2000. (In Windows XP and Vista, this older-style Start menu could still be used if desired. It's gone from Windows 7.)

Figure 4-3: Windows Classic lets Windows 7 users enjoy a Windows 2000-like user interface.

Windows 7 Basic

Windows 7 Basic is the entry-level desktop user experience in Windows 7 and the one you're going to see on Windows 7 Starter or Home Basic or in other editions if you don't meet certain hardware requirements, which we'll discuss in just a bit. From a technological perspective, Windows 7 Basic renders the Windows desktop in roughly the same way as Windows XP did, meaning it doesn't take advantage of the graphical prowess and enhanced stability offered by Aero. That said, Windows 7 Basic still provides you with many of the unique features that make Windows 7 special. The Windows 7 Basic user experience is shown in Figure 4-4.

Secret

Windows 7 Basic isn't as attractive as Windows Aero, but there are actually some advantages to using it. For starters, it offers better performance than Aero, so it's a good bet for lower-end computers. Notebook, Tablet PC, and netbook users will notice that Windows 7 Basic actually provides better battery life than Aero, too. So if you're on the road and not connected to a power source, Windows 7 Basic is a thriftier choice if you're trying to maximize runtime.

On the flip side, Windows 7 Basic has a few major if non-obvious disadvantages. Because it uses XP-era display rendering techniques, Windows 7 Basic is not as stable and reliable as Aero and could thus lead to system crashes and even Blue Screen crashes because of poorly written display drivers. Aero display drivers are typically far more reliable, and the Aero display itself is inherently superior to that offered by Basic. Nor does Windows 7 Basic offer some unique Windows 7 features, like Aero Peek, Flip 3D, and taskbar thumbnails.

Figure 4-4: Even Windows 7 Basic is capable of displaying Live Icons, which contain previews of the underlying documents and files.

Secret Even if you are running Windows Aero, you may still run into the occasional issue that causes the display to flash and suddenly revert back to Windows 7 Basic. For example, some older applications aren't compatible with Windows Aero; when you run such an application, the user experience will revert to Windows 7 Basic. When you close the offending application, Aero returns. In other cases, certain applications that use custom window rendering actually display in a Windows 7 Basic style, even though all of the other windows in the system are utilizing Aero. These are the issues you have to deal with when Microsoft makes such a dramatic change to the Windows rendering engine, apparently. The good news is that these glitches are significantly less common with Windows 7 than they were with Windows Vista. Most modern Windows applications work just fine with Aero.

Windows 7 Standard

This oddball user experience is an olive branch of sorts, extended to those who are stuck with Windows 7 Home Basic but have the hardware required to run Windows Aero but cannot do so because that user experience is not included in Home Basic.

Secret Windows 7 Standard has the same hardware requirements as Aero, which we'll examine in the next section.

Windows 7 Standard is essentially a visual compromise between Windows 7 Basic and Windows 7 Aero. That is, it features the look and feel of Windows Aero, minus the translucency effects. Under the hood, however, it utilizes the less sophisticated display technologies utilized by Windows 7 Basic.

In addition to losing Aero's transparency feature, Windows 7 Standard also dispenses with many other Aero features, such as Flip 3D and live taskbar thumbnails. Windows 7 Standard is shown in Figure 4-5.

tip If you are running Windows 7 Home Basic and would like to upgrade to Aero, you need to utilize Windows 7's unique Windows Anytime Upgrade service—available to Windows 7 Home Basic and Home Premium customers—to upgrade to Windows 7 Home Premium or Ultimate Edition. We discuss Windows Anytime Upgrade in Chapter 2.

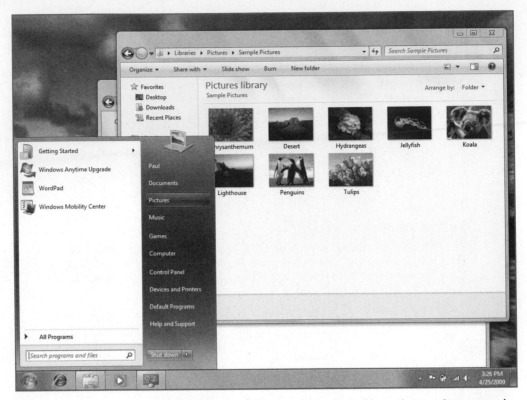

Figure 4-5: Windows 7 Standard looks like Windows Aero, but without the translucency and Aero effects.

Secret

If you're using Windows 7 Home Premium, Professional, Enterprise, or Ultimate, you can emulate Windows 7 Standard: just disable transparency. To do so, open the Personalization control panel, click Window Color, and then uncheck *Enable transparency.*

Windows Aero

Windows Aero is the premium user experience in Windows 7 and the one most users will want to access. Fortunately, it's also the one most users *will* access. It provides a number of unique features.

First, Windows 7 Aero enables the Aero Glass look and feel in which the Start menu, task-bar, and all onscreen windows and dialogs take on a glasslike translucent sheen. While this effect debuted in Windows Vista, it's been enhanced in Windows 7. In Figure 4-6, you can see how overlapping objects translucently reveal what's underneath.

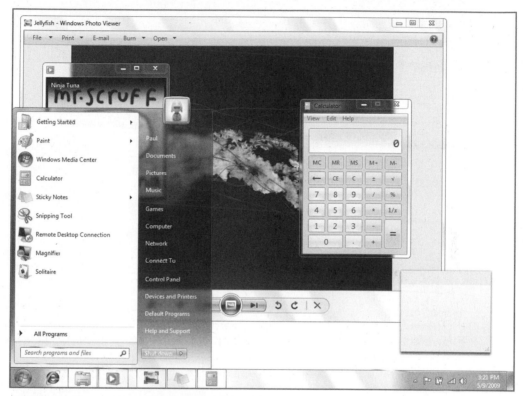

Figure 4-6: The Aero Glass effect provides a heightened sense of depth and a more professional-looking user experience.

Aero Glass is designed to move the visual focus away from the windows themselves and to the content they contain. Whether that effort is successful is open to debate, but it's certainly true that window borders lose the vast, dark-colored title bars of previous Windows versions and provide a softer-looking and more organic-looking container around window contents. Compare Windows XP's My Computer window to Windows 7's Computer window in Figure 4-7.

tip When you have a lot of Aero windows open onscreen, it's often hard to tell which one is on top, or has the focus. Typically, that window will have a bright red Close window button, while lower windows will not.

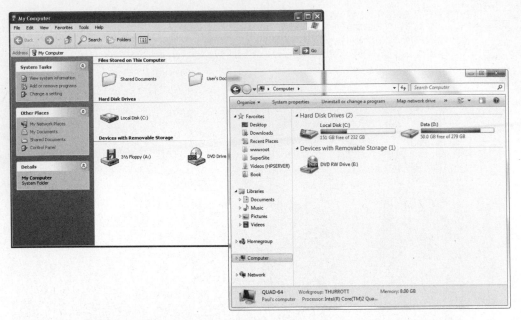

Figure 4-7: In Windows XP, too much of the visual focus is on the title bar, whereas the software window chrome in Windows 7 puts the focus on the contents of the window.

When you utilize the Windows Aero user experience, you receive other benefits. Certain Windows 7 features, for example, are available only when you're using Aero. Windows Flip and Flip 3D, two task-switching features, are available only in Aero. Windows Flip 3D is shown in Figure 4-8.

Aero also enables dynamic window animations, so that when you minimize a window to the taskbar, it subtly animates to show you exactly where it went. This kind of functionality was actually first introduced in Windows 95, but it has been made more subtle and fluid in Windows 7. Aero also enables *live taskbar thumbnails*: when you mouse over buttons in the taskbar, a small thumbnail preview will pop up, letting you see the window or windows represented by that button without having to actually activate it first, as shown in Figure 4-9.

In addition to its obvious visual charms, Windows Aero also offers lower-level improvements that will lead to a more reliable desktop experience than you might be used to with previous Windows versions. Thanks to a graphics architecture that's based on DirectX video-game libraries, Windows 7 can move windows across the screen without any of the visual tearing or glitches that were common in Windows XP. The effect is most prominent in windows with animated content, such as when you're playing a video in Windows Media Player (WMP). But it's not just about looks. Windows Aero is simply more reliable than the other user experiences. To understand why that's so, we need to examine Aero's hardware and software requirements.

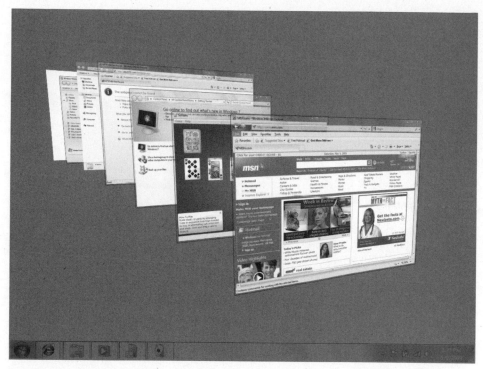

Figure 4-8: Flip 3D enables you to visually inspect all of the running tasks and pick the window you want.

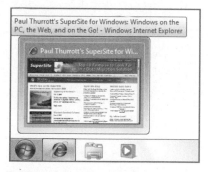

Figure 4-9: Live taskbar thumbnails make it possible to preview windows without maximizing or bringing them to the forefront.

Secret

Windows Flip and Flip 3D are typically accessed via keyboard shortcuts. The problem, of course, is that you have to know what those shortcuts are. To use Windows Flip, hold down the Alt key and tap the Tab key to cycle between all of the running applications and open windows. To use Flip 3D, hold down the Windows key and tap the Tab key to cycle between these windows.

Windows Aero Requirements

As noted earlier, you have to be running Windows 7 Home Premium, Professional, Enterprise, or Ultimate Edition in order to utilize Windows Aero. Windows Aero is not available in Windows 7 Starter or Home Basic.

Next, your display adapter must meet certain technical requirements. That is, it must support DirectX 9.0 with Pixel Shader 2 in hardware and be supported by a modern Windows Display Driver Model (WDDM) driver. The WDDM driver requirement is part of the reason why Aero is so much more reliable than other Windows 7 user experiences: to become WDDM certified, a driver must pass certain Microsoft tests aimed at making these drivers of higher quality.

Additionally, your graphics card must have enough dedicated memory (RAM) to drive your display. Table 4-2 explains how much video RAM you need to run Windows Aero at particular screen resolutions.

Table 4-2: Video RAM Needed to Drive Certain Resolutions

Video RAM	Display resolution
64MB	Lower than 1,280 × 1,024 (fewer than 1,310,720 pixels)
128MB	1,280 × 1,024 to 1,920 × 1,200 (1,310,720 to 2,304,000 pixels)
256MB	Higher than 1,920 × 1,200 (more than 2,304,000 pixels)

Secret

Microsoft critics made these requirements sound difficult and complicated when they first arrived with Windows Vista. But the truth is, virtually every 3D graphics card on the market, as well as all modern integrated graphics chipsets, are capable of running Windows Aero. And most of today's graphics cards come with at least 128MB of RAM. Note, however, that some older integrated graphics chipsets, such as those found on most notebooks and Tablet PCs sold before 2005, are not compatible with Windows Aero. Furthermore, in order to obtain Aero on a system with integrated graphics, at least 512MB of system RAM must be available after the integrated graphics reserves whatever it needs.

Personalizing the Windows Desktop

If you're not a big fan of the translucent glass effects provided by Windows Aero but would still like to take advantage of the other unique features and reliability offered by this user experience, take heart. Microsoft has nicely provided a number of ways in which you can fine-tune how it looks. As with Windows Vista, you're free to manually change various aspects of Aero's visual style individually. In Windows 7, Microsoft has introduced a new feature called Aero Themes that helps you access and create unique visual themes that affect multiple UI elements at once. The next section takes a look.

Using Aero Themes

Aero Themes is a formal combination of desktop background, Aero glass window color, sound scheme, and screen saver. Windows 7 comes with a number of built-in Aero Themes and users can create their own by building off of them. Aero Themes can be saved, of course, and they're also portable, meaning they can be packaged up and copied from machine to machine. Microsoft expects users and third-party partners to trade and perhaps even sell Aero Themes online when Windows 7 is finalized.

Also, Microsoft is building on a feature that was previously unique to Windows XP/Vista Starter Edition by providing built-in Windows 7 Aero Themes that are unique to different regions around the world. Pre-release versions of Windows 7, for example, include Aero Themes oriented towards Australia, Canada, Great Britain, the United States, and South Africa.

Secret

Most of these locale-specific Aero Themes are not available by default, but you can find several of them hidden in C:\Windows\Globalization\MCT.

Aero Themes can optionally take advantage of another new bit of functionality called *desktop slide shows*. This feature allows you to specify multiple pictures for the background image and then have the system rotate between them on a set schedule.

Working with Aero Themes and Theme Packs

Aero Themes are accessed via the new Personalization option on the context menu that appears when you right-click the Windows desktop. (You can also launch this control panel by typing **Personalization** in Start Menu Search.) The Personalization control panel is shown in Figure 4-10.

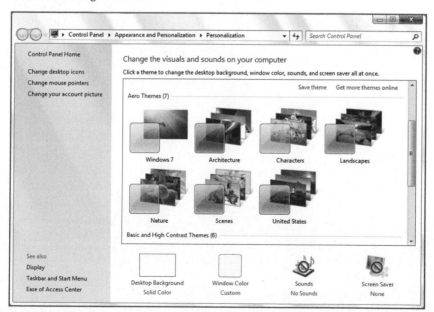

Figure 4-10: Aero Themes are configured via Windows 7's Personalization control panel.

As you can see, a stock Windows 7 install includes whatever Aero Themes you've created (or are currently using), several built-in Aero Themes, and several Basic and High Contrast Themes, the latter of which includes styles based around the Windows 7 Basic and Windows Classic themes and four high-contrast themes.

The following Aero Themes are available in Windows 7:

◆ **Windows 7:** The default Windows 7 Aero Theme utilizes the default Sky (clear, light bluish) glass color, the Windows Default sound scheme, and no screen saver. This is a great theme from which to create your own theme. Figure 4-11 shows the effects of configuring a typical theme.

◆ **Architecture:** This Aero Theme features a desktop slide show of six alternating architectural images, the Twilight (deep blue) glass color, the Cityscape sound scheme, and no screen saver.

◆ **Characters:** This Aero Theme features a desktop slide show of six alternating whimsical cartoon-type images, the Taupe (light pink) glass color, the Characters sound scheme, and no screen saver.

◆ **Landscapes:** This Aero Theme features a desktop slide show of six alternating landscape images, the Slate (dusty brown) glass color, the Landscape sound scheme, and no screen saver.

◆ **Nature:** This Aero Theme features a desktop slide show of six alternating plant- and leaf-based images, the Lavender (bright pink) glass color, the Garden sound scheme, and no screen saver.

◆ **Scenes:** This Aero Theme features a desktop slide show of six alternating artistic images, the Violet (soft purple) glass color, the Quirky sound scheme, and no screen saver.

◆ **Theme for [your region]:** This Aero Theme is customized for the region in which you live. So in my case, it is customized for the United States. It features a desktop slide show of six alternating country- or region-specific images, a custom glass color (medium tan for the U.S.), a custom sound scheme (Delta for the U.S.), and no screen saver.

Secret

Aero Theme files are, in fact, simple text files, similar to XML or INI files, so you can open them with a text editor, like Wordpad, to see what they're made of. A typical section in an Aero Theme file looks like so:

```
[VisualStyles]
Path=%SystemRoot%\resources\themes\Aero\Aero.msstyles
ColorStyle=NormalColor
Size=NormalSize
ColorizationColor=0X45409EFE
Transparency=1
VisualStyleVersion=10
```

The problem with Aero Theme files is that they're not portable: if the Aero Theme you're using includes background images, sounds schemes, or screen savers that aren't found in a default Windows 7 install, you won't be able to pass them around to others. Fortunately, there's a way around this issue: you can also save Aero Themes as a Theme Pack (*.themepack), which packages all of the needed files into a single archive that can then be distributed to others.

Note that Theme Pack files are really just ZIP files with a different extension. That means you can open them—and extract their contents—with any ZIP extractor, including Compressed Folders, WinRAR, WinZIP, and others.

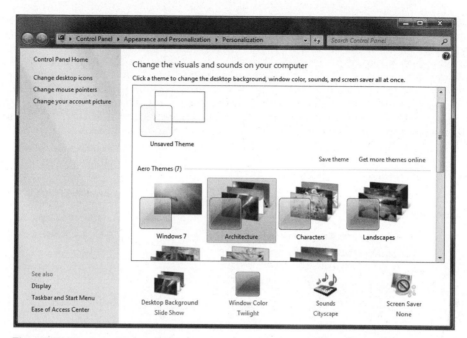

Figure 4-11: Aero Themes include desktop backgrounds, Aero glass colors, and other configuration options.

To save an Aero Theme, click the Save theme link, which is subtly located near the bottom right of the My Themes section. Aero Themes are saved as a single file with a *.theme extension. These files can then be copied to other PCs and used elsewhere.

Secret   Microsoft offers a number of wonderful pre-built Theme Packs on the Windows 7 Web site (windows.microsoft.com/en-US/Windows7/Personalize). To download and install these Theme Packs, click the link "Get more themes online" in the bottom-right corner of the My Themes section of the Personalization window. This site also offers downloadable desktop backgrounds, desktop gadgets, and Sideshow gadgets.

Creating a Desktop Slide Show

As noted previously, most of the built-in Aero Themes utilize a desktop background slide show feature, which is also new to Windows 7. This works similarly to the static background image feature which has been available in Windows for years. But now, you can configure the desktop to switch between two or more pictures on a set schedule. Here's how it works.

When you enter the Desktop Background control panel (via the Personalization window), you will see the interface shown in Figure 4-12. You can choose between different background types, such as Windows Desktop Backgrounds (the high-quality wallpaper provided by Microsoft), Pictures Library (pictures and other images you've stored in your My Pictures folder and other locations aggregated by the Pictures Library), Top Rated Photos (based on a metadata ranking system most users probably haven't used), Solid Colors, and, perhaps, other locations if you've ever manually browsed to a different location using this UI. For all of these options (except, oddly, Solid Colors), a new feature has been added in Windows 7: you can multi-select images.

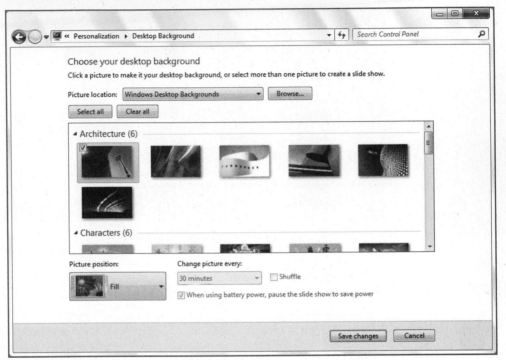

Figure 4-12: The Desktop Background control panel

Multi-select works here as it does elsewhere in Windows: you can Ctrl+click each item you wish to include. Or, you can single-click the new check box that appears in the upper-left corner of each picture thumbnail, as shown in Figure 4-13.

When you do select two or more items, some new options become available at the bottom of the Desktop Background window. You can determine how often the images change (30 minutes is the default), whether to shuffle them so that they display in a random order, and whether to disable the slide show when on battery power in order to save power.

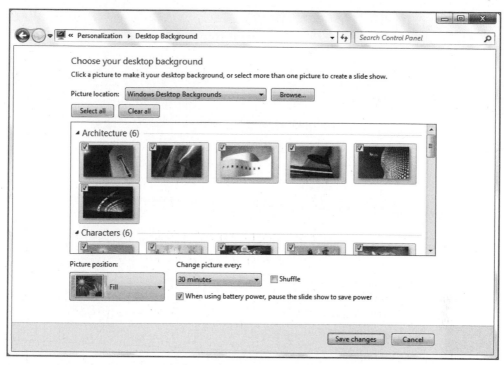

Figure 4-13: You can create a desktop slide show using multi-select.

Exploring with the Windows 7 Explorer Shell

Aside from the user experiences and different personalization options that are available in Windows 7, you're going to notice a number of other visual and functional changes as you begin navigating around this new system. In this section, we highlight the most important changes you should be aware of and help you resuscitate some old favorites that have been lost in the transition.

Start Menu

The Windows 7 Start menu, shown in Figure 4-14, has been enhanced since Windows XP and Vista and is now easier to use and better looking. Like its predecessor, you access the Start menu by pressing the Start button, which now resembles a rounded Windows flag. It no longer includes the word Start, as did XP: presumably, most users understand how this button works now. (That said, if you mouse over the Start button, the word *Start* will appear in a tip window. You know, just in case.)

Figure 4-14: The Windows 7 Start menu

As with the Windows XP and Vista Start menu, the Windows 7 Start menu is divided vertically into two halves. On the left half is a list of your most recently used (MRU) applications. But whereas Windows XP and Vista would automatically pin the default Web browser and e-mail to the top of this list, Windows 7 no longer does so. That's because Microsoft is moving to a system where the taskbar, instead of the Start menu, is used to access your most frequently needed applications. We'll look at the brand-new Windows 7 taskbar in just a bit, don't worry.

On the right of the Start menu, as before, is a list of commonly accessed shell folders and other system locations and tasks.

Secret

Though Windows 7 no longer includes any pinned Start menu shortcuts, you can still pin shortcuts to your favorite applications into the Start menu MRU. To do so, select the shortcut you want to pin from the Start menu and drag it up to the top of the most recently used application list. Or, right-click a shortcut in the Start menu and choose Pin to Start Menu. To remove a pinned shortcut from this area, right-click it and choose Unpin from Start Menu.

Secret

Windows Vista included an application called the Welcome Center that provided links to commonly needed post-setup tasks. This application has been replaced in Windows 7 by the new Getting Started application. Getting Started, by default, can be found at the top of the Start menu MRU, on the left side.

Accessing Start Menu Jump Lists

While the Windows 7 Start menu works largely like that of its predecessor, there has been one major change: now, items in the Start menu (and, as you will see, in the taskbar as well) can optionally have associated Jump Lists, which provide access to documents or tasks associated with those items. Jump Lists expose themselves a bit differently in the Start menu than they do in the taskbar, but the idea is the same: instead of launching an application and then finding the document, picture, song, or other bit of data you're really looking for, you can now access this information directly, without a lot of mousing around. Jump Lists also help reduce clutter.

Secret   You can think of Jump Lists as mini Start menus for each item. For example, whereas the Windows 7 Start menu is of course global to the entire PC, a Jump List for Microsoft Word would be specific to that application.

The Getting Started application, shown in Figure 4-15, is a good example of a Jump List. When you highlight this item in the Start menu (by mousing over it—you don't have to click on it), the right side of the Start menu fills up with the contents of its Jump List. As you can see from the figure, the Getting Started Jump List corresponds to the options available in the application itself.

Figure 4-15: A typical Jump List, as seen in the Start menu.

While not all Start menu items will have Jump Lists, those that do display a small black triangle graphic, indicating that that item expands to display its Jump List when highlighted.

Secret

Jump Lists represent a bit of a navigational challenge for keyboard mavens. If you're used to moving around the Start menu with the arrow keys, you'll discover that moving right from an item that contains a Jump List will cause that Jump List to open, instead of causing you to navigate to the right side of the Start menu, as you might expect. In order to move right through the Start menu with the keyboard, then, you need to be vigilant and ensure that you're on an item that does not provide a Jump List. Remember, these items do not display the little black arrow graphic.

Jump Lists vary from application to application. After you've used Paint for a while, for example, that application's Jump List will include recently saved graphics files. Microsoft Word provides a list of recent documents. These lists make a lot of sense, given the purpose of the applications. But some Windows 7 applications provide custom Jump Lists, and Microsoft has opened up the programming interfaces for this so that any application in the future can do so as well.

The Windows Media Player Jump List provides a list of recently accessed media files, of course, but it also has links for Media Player–specific tasks, as shown in Figure 4-16.

cross ref Windows Media Player is discussed further in Chapter 11.

Figure 4-16: Windows Media Player provides a custom Jump List.

Internet Explorer also provides a custom Jump List. Here, you'll see recently accessed Web pages, as expected. But the IE Jump List also includes access to IE-specific features, such as InPrivate and New Tab, as shown in Figure 4-17.

cross ref Check out Chapter 20 for more information about InPrivate, New Tab, and other IE8 features.

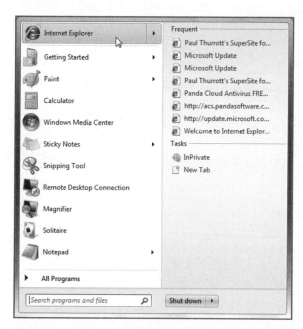

Figure 4-17: The IE Jump List surfaces frequently needed IE8 features as well as recently accessed Web pages.

These aren't the only examples of custom Jump Lists in Windows 7, of course. As you gain experience with the system, you'll discover that many applications provide access to unique functionality in this way as well.

Accessing All Programs

At the bottom of the most recently used applications list, you'll see the familiar All Programs link. However, in Windows 7, this link behaves quite differently than it does in Windows XP, which launches a cascading series of menus when clicked. The All Programs link in Windows 7, like that in Vista, expands the Start menu's All Programs submenu directly within the Start menu itself. And you don't have to click the link to make that happen. Instead, you can simply mouse over it. In Figure 4-18, you can see how the All Programs submenu opens up inside of the Start menu, temporarily replacing the most frequently used application list.

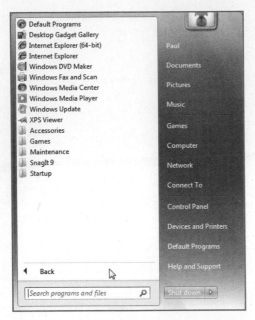

Figure 4-18: No more fumbling with cascading menus.

Secret

This change was made for a number of different reasons. First, expanding All Programs inside the Start menu eliminates the sometimes maddening pause that would occur in Windows XP when you clicked or moused-over the All Programs link. Second, many users found the cascading menu system used previously to be hard to navigate. How many times have you expanded submenu after submenu and then inadvertently moved the mouse cursor off the menu, only to cause the whole thing to disappear? It's happened to the best of us.

To navigate through the various submenus linked to from All Programs, you simply have to click various folders. When you do so, the menu expands, in place, and scroll bars appear so you can move around within the menu structure. As you can see in Figure 4-19, submenus that expand within the current view are easier to navigate than cascading menus.

Secret

Those more comfortable with the keyboard can easily navigate the new Start menu as well. To do so, tap the Windows key or the Ctrl+Esc keyboard shortcut to open the Start menu. Then, press the Up Arrow key once to highlight All Programs. To expand All Programs, press the Right Arrow key. Then, use the arrow keys to navigate around the list of shortcuts and folders. Anytime you want to expand a submenu (indicated by a folder icon), press the Right Arrow key. To close, or contract, a submenu, press the Left Arrow key. To run the selected shortcut, tap Enter.

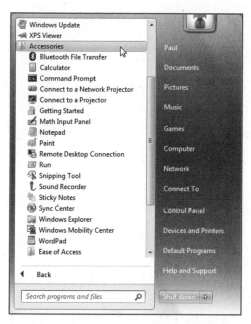

Figure 4-19: With the Windows 7 Start menu, you never have to worry about losing your place.

Searching for Applications

One of the best features in Windows 7 is its integrated search functionality. Although you might think that this feature is limited only to finding documents and music files, you can actually use it for a variety of things, and depending on where you are in the Windows 7 interface, those searches will be context sensitive. So when you search from the Start menu's useful new Search box, located on the left side of the menu underneath All Programs, you will typically be searching for applications. You can also use this feature, called Start Menu Search, to quickly launch applications, when you know their names. This is especially useful for applications that are infrequently used and thus buried deep in the Start menu. It's also a boon to touch typists, as you don't have to take your hands off the keyboard to use it.

Secret

The Search menu's search feature isn't limited to searching applications. You can also use it to search documents, pictures, and other files. To find out more about searching the file system and constructing your own saved searches, please refer to Chapter 5.

Here's how it works. When you open the Start menu and begin typing, whatever you type is automatically placed in the search box. So say you want to run Notepad. You could always click the Start button, expand All Programs, expand Accessories, and then click on the Notepad icon. Or, you could tap the Windows key and just type **notepad**. As you type, applications that match the text appear in a list, as shown in Figure 4-20. When you see the application you want, use the arrow keys (or mouse cursor) to select it, and then the application will start normally.

Figure 4-20: Start Menu Search makes short work of finding the application you want.

Start Menu Search is even better than this. You don't have to type the entire name of an application. Instead, you can just start typing the first few letters. On most systems, just typing **pa**, for example, should be enough to display Paint as the first choice in the found programs list. So you could just type **pa** and then tap Enter to run Paint. Try this shortcut with some favorite applications to see how little typing is actually required.

It's possible that some users will prefer to use the old Run command, which brings up a small dialog that maintains a history of previously accessed commands. (We're looking at you, Luddite.) Good news: even though the Run command is missing from the default Windows 7 Start menu, you can turn it on. To do so, right-click the Start button, choose Properties, and then click the Customize button. Scroll down the list until you see the Run command option (the list is alphabetical) and then select it. Click OK and then OK again, and you'll see that the Run command is back where it used to be (on the right side of the Start menu).

Accessing Shell and System Locations

On the right side of the Start menu, you'll see a list of commands that are vaguely similar to what appeared on the XP and Vista Start menu. However, if you're coming from XP, many of the names have changed. For example, the old My Documents link has been replaced by one named Documents, My Pictures is now Pictures, My Music is now Music, My Computer is now Computer, and My Network Places is now Network. There are some new items, too, as well as some missing items that were present in XP.

Secret

In Windows XP and Vista, some of these links pointed to *special shell folders,* special physical folder locations that were reserved for specific purposes. In Windows 7, these links no longer point to special shell folders; they point instead to Libraries, a new Windows 7 feature. From a usage standpoint, Windows 7 Libraries work similarly to special shell folders from previous Windows versions. We explore this new feature thoroughly in Chapter 5.

At the top of the right side of the Start menu, you will see a link that has the same name as your user account. For example, if you're logged on as Paul, the first link on the right side of the Start menu will also be named Paul. When you click this link, it opens a Windows Explorer window displaying the contents of your user folder, which is found in C:\Users*Your Username*, by default. This folder contains folders such as My Documents, My Pictures, My Music, and so on. It's unclear why you would ever need to access this folder, except in rare circumstances. For this reason, you may simply want to remove it from the Start menu and replace it with a more frequently needed command (like Videos). We cover Start menu customization.

The Games link debuted in Windows Vista and opens the Games Explorer, which provides access to both games that came with Windows and those you might purchase separately.

cross ref

We examine Vista's Games functionality in Chapter 16.

tip

One feature some people might miss with the new Start menu is the ability to quickly cause the system to shut down, restart, sleep, or hibernate using just the keyboard. In Windows XP, you could tap the Windows key, press U, and then U for shut down, R for restart, S for sleep, or H for hibernate (the latter of which was a hidden option). Because of the Start Menu Search feature in the Windows 7 Start menu, these shortcuts no longer work. However, you can still perform these actions with the keyboard in Windows 7. Now, however, you have to tap the Windows key and then press the Right Arrow key three times to display the submenu shown in Figure 4-21, which provides links to the aforementioned options as well as Switch User, Log Off, Lock, and, if you have a notebook computer with a docking station, Undock. The default option—on the button, not the menu—is shut down.

continues

continued

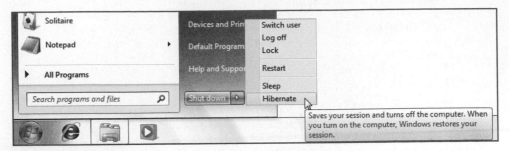

Figure 4-21: Options related to shutting down, sleeping, and locking the PC are available via this mini pop-up menu.

While we're on this topic, notice that this menu is, alas, a pop-up menu similar to the All Programs menu in Windows XP. Why Microsoft killed pop-up menus in one place but added them in another is a mystery.

Start Menu Customization

While the Windows 7 Start menu is a big improvement over its predecessors, you will likely want to customize it to match your needs. We've already discussed how you access this functionality: right-click the Start button, choose Properties, and then click the Customize button. Table 4-3 summarizes the available options.

Table 4-3: Start Menu Customization Options

Start Menu Option	What It Does	Default Value
Computer	Determines whether the Computer item appears as a link or a menu, or is not displayed. This was called My Computer in Windows XP.	Display as a link
Connect To	Determines whether the Connect To item appears. If you have a wireless network adapter, this item will trigger a submenu.	Enabled
Control Panel	Determines whether the Control Panel item appears as a link or a menu, or is not displayed.	Display as a link
Default Programs	Determines whether the Default Program item appears. This item was called Set Program Access and Defaults in Windows XP with Service Pack 2. In Windows 7, it launches the new Default Programs control panel.	Enabled

Start Menu Option	What It Does	Default Value
Devices and Printers	Determines whether the Devices and Printers entry appears. This new interface largely replaces Device Manager from previous Windows versions. This link also replaces the Printers link from previous Windows versions.	Disabled
Documents	Determines whether the Documents item appears as a link or a menu, or is not displayed. This was called My Documents in Windows XP.	Display as a link
Downloads	Determines whether the Downloads link appears as a link or a menu, or is not displayed. This corresponds to the Downloads folder in your user folder, which is the default location for Web downloads from IE and other browsers.	Disabled
Enable context menus and dragging and dropping	Determines whether context menus appear when you right-click items in the Start menu, and whether you can drag and drop icons around the Start menu in order to change the way they are displayed.	Enabled
Favorites menu	Determines whether the Favorites menu item appears	Disabled
Games	Determines whether the Games item appears as a link or a menu, or is not displayed	Enabled
Help	Determines whether the Help item appears. This item launches Help and Support.	Enabled
Highlight newly installed programs	Determines whether newly installed applications are highlighted so you can find them easier.	Enabled
HomeGroup	Determines whether the HomeGroup link appears in the Start menu. This corresponds to the HomeGroup control panel, which helps set up Windows 7's simple new sharing feature. We discuss HomeGroup in Chapter 9.	Disabled
Music	Determines whether the Music item appears as a link or a menu, or is not displayed. This was called My Music in Windows XP.	Enabled
Network	Determines whether the Network item appears as a link or a menu, or is not displayed. This was called My Network Places in Windows XP.	Enabled
Open submenus when I pause on them with the mouse pointer	Determines whether mousing over a submenu (like All Programs) will cause that submenu to open (or expand)	Enabled
Pictures	Determines whether the Pictures item appears as a link or a menu, or is not displayed. This was called My Pictures in Windows XP.	Enabled

continues

Table 4-3: Start Menu Customization Options *(continued)*

Start Menu Option	What It Does	Default Value
Recent Items	Determines whether the Recent Items entry appears. This item provides a pop-up menu that lists numerous documents and other data files you've recently accessed.	Disabled
Recorded TV	Determines whether the Recorded TV item appears as a link or a menu, or is not displayed	Disabled
Run command	Determines whether the Run command item appears	Disabled
Search other files and libraries	Determines whether searches from Start Menu Search include or exclude public folders	Public folders are included
Search programs and Control Panel	Determines whether searches from Start Menu Search include programs and Control Panel items in addition to data files	Programs and Control Panel items are included
Sort All Programs menu by name	Determines whether the All Programs submenu is organized alphabetically	Enabled
System administrative tools	Determines whether the Administrative tools submenu appears on the All Programs menu, on the All Programs menu and the Start menu, or is not displayed	The Administrative tools submenu is not displayed
Use large icons	Determines whether the left side of the Start menu renders large icons. Otherwise, small icons are used.	Enabled
Videos	Determines whether the Videos item appears as a link or a menu, or is not displayed. This was called My Videos in Windows XP. Note that this item could not be added to the Windows XP or Vista Start menu for some reason.	Disabled

Secret

While power users will likely disable the *Highlight newly installed programs* item pretty quickly, it's become more useful in Windows 7 than it was in Windows XP and Vista. Because of the enhanced shortcut pinning functionality in this release, and the new taskbar behaviors we'll discuss soon, Microsoft thought it would make sense to "surface" recently installed applications briefly so that you could choose to pin them to the Start menu or taskbar. So when you install a new application, you may see an entry for it appear in the bottom of the Start menu MRU (on the left), as shown in Figure 4-22. This is your opportunity to pin the shortcut, if it's something you think you'll access frequently. That way, you won't have to dive into the Start menu to find it later.

Figure 4-22: Recently installed applications will display a shortcut at the bottom of the Start menu MRU so that you can pin them to the Start menu or taskbar if needed.

Advanced Start Menu Customization

One feature of the Start menu that's not immediately obvious is that it is composed of items from the following two different locations, both of which are hidden by default:

- ◆ **Within your user profile:** By default, C:\Users*Your Username*\AppData\Roaming\ Microsoft\Windows\Start Menu
- ◆ **Inside the profile for the Public user account that is common (or public) to all users:** Typically, C:\ProgramData\Microsoft\Windows\Start Menu

If you navigate to these locations with Windows Explorer, you can drill down into the folder structures and shortcuts that make up your own Start menu (see Figure 4-23). What's odd is that these two locations are combined, or aggregated, to form the Start menu display you access every day.

You used to be able to access these folders by right-clicking on the Start button. That is no longer possible in Windows 7.

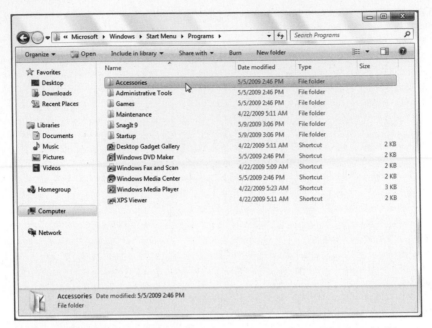

Figure 4-23: Fully customizing the Start menu requires a bit of spelunking in two different folder structures.

So why would you want to access these locations? Although it's possible to customize the Start menu by dragging and dropping shortcuts like you might have done back in Windows XP, doing so can get tedious. Instead, you could simply access these folders directly, move things around as you see fit, all while opening the Start menu occasionally to make sure you're getting the results you expect. For example, you might want to create handy subfolders such as Digital Media, Internet, and Utilities, rather than accept the default structure. Or, you could stop trying to micro-manage everything and use Windows 7 technologies like taskbar and Start menu pinning and Start Menu Search to find what you need.

Secret

Be careful when you customize the Start menu this way. Any changes you make to the Public Start menu structure will affect any other users that log on to your PC as well.

Desktop

At first glance, the Windows 7 desktop looks very similar to that of Windows XP. Well, looks can be deceiving. In fact, Microsoft has made some long-overdue and quite welcome changes to the Windows desktop, although of course with these changes comes a new set of skills to master.

For the most part, you access desktop options through the pop-up menu that appears when you right-click an empty part of the Windows desktop. In Windows XP and Vista, this menu had options such as Arrange Icons By, Refresh, Paste, Paste Shortcut, Undo, New, and Properties. In Windows 7, naturally, this has all changed.

At the top of the right-click menu is a submenu called View, which is shown in Figure 4-24. This submenu enables you to configure features Windows users have been requesting for years: you can now switch between Large Icons, Medium Icons, and Small Icons (the latter of which was called Classic Icons in Vista). You can also select auto-arrange and alignment options, and hide the desktop icons altogether, as you could in XP. Additionally, you can choose to hide desktop gadgets, discussed later in this chapter.

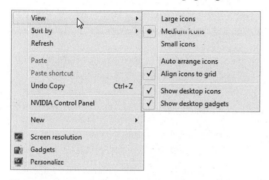

Figure 4-24: Something old, something new: Microsoft changes menus arbitrarily again, but this time at least we get some new functionality.

The Sort by submenu is similar to the top part of the Windows XP Arrange Icons By submenu (and the Sort submenu in Windows Vista). Here, we get sorting options for Name, Size, Item type (as in file extension), and Date modified. On the main pop-up menu, the Refresh, Paste, Paste shortcut, Undo, and New items all carry over from XP and Vista as well.

As with Windows XP and Vista, Windows 7 includes a New menu item in the Desktop properties menu that lets you create new objects on the desktop. These objects include folders, shortcuts, and a variety of document types; the exact document types you see here will vary from system to system, depending on which applications you've installed. Some of these document types are installed as part of Windows 7, like Bitmap image and Text document, while others will show up as part of a separate application install. The option Microsoft Office Word Document, for example, is installed with Microsoft Office or Word.

Secret

Most of these objects are pretty useless: when was the last time you needed to create an empty bitmap image on your desktop? As it turns out, these are relics from Windows 95, with which Microsoft was pushing a then-new document-centric computing model that, frankly, never took off. That said, you may find the New Folder option to be quite useful. Our vote for most useless new object, however, has to go to New Shortcut, which may never actually be used by a single Windows 7 user. We're astonished it's still available in this release.

At the bottom of the right-click menu is another new option, dubbed Personalize. This item debuted in Windows Vista and replaces the Properties option from XP. But it now displays the Personalization control panel section when selected. From here, you can access a wide range of personalization options, only some of which have anything to do with the desktop. (We discuss the personalization features elsewhere in the chapter.)

Secret

One of the big questions you likely have, of course, is what the heck happened to the familiar Display Properties dialog that has graced every version of Windows from Windows 95 to Windows XP? Sadly, that dialog is gone, but pieces of it can be found throughout the Personalization control panel if you know where to look. Table 4-4 shows you how to find the different sections, or tabs, of the old Display Properties dialog, which have been effectively scattered to the winds.

It's unclear whether Windows 7's approach is better, but if you're looking for XP Display Properties features, you really have to know where to look.

Table 4-4: Where to Find Old Display Properties Tabs in Windows 7

Display Properties Tab	Where It Is in Windows 7
Themes	Control Panel ⇨ Appearance and Personalization ⇨ Personalization ⇨ Themes
Desktop	Replaced by the new Desktop Background window, found at Control Panel ⇨ Appearance and Personalization ⇨ Personalization ⇨ Desktop Background
Screen Saver	Control Panel ⇨ Personalization ⇨ Screen Saver
Appearance	Control Panel ⇨ Personalization ⇨ Visual Appearance ⇨ Open classic appearance properties
Settings	Control Panel ⇨ Personalization ⇨ Display Settings and Control Panel ⇨ Appearance and Personalization ⇨ Display ⇨ Screen Resolution

You could see other options in the Desktop properties menu, but these are not typically installed by Microsoft. For example, some graphics chipset makers install links to their own utilities and figure that the Desktop properties menu is the logical place to access those tools. Intel adds two menu options, Graphics Properties and Graphics Options, on systems using some of its embedded graphics solutions. Since these options are not part of Windows 7 per se, and will vary from system to system, that's about all we have to say on the topic.

Secret

The Desktop tab of the Display Properties dialog in Windows XP had a Customize Desktop button that launched a Desktop Items dialog from which you could configure which icons appeared on the desktop, and other related options. But in Windows 7, the Desktop tab has been replaced with the new Desktop Background window, which does not provide a link to this functionality. To access the Desktop Icon Properties dialog, as it's now known, you must select Control Panel ⇨ Appearance and Personalization ⇨ Personalization, and then choose Change desktop icons from the Tasks list on the left. Some functionality, however, is missing. You can no longer run the Desktop Cleanup Wizard or place Web items on your desktop, as you could in XP. However, Start Menu Search comes to the rescue with Disk Cleanup: to run Disk Cleanup in Windows 7, just open the Start menu, type **Disk Cleanup** and then tap Enter.

Customizing How Windows Appear on the Desktop

Most Windows users are probably familiar with the fact that windows in, ahem, Windows can appear to float onscreen, be maximized to occupy the entire desktop, and be minimized so that they are hidden in a taskbar button. There's no need to belabor these obvious capabilities here: windows in Windows 7 work pretty much like they always have.

There are a few differences, however, and some cool capabilities you might not be aware of. First, if you're running the Windows Aero user experience, you will notice that the window Minimize, Restore/Maximize, and Close buttons adopt a pleasant glowing effect when you mouse over them, as they did in Windows Vista. The Minimize and Restore/ Maximize buttons glow blue, indicating that clicking these buttons is a non-destructive act. The Close button, meanwhile, glows a menacing red color. The intent is clear: click with caution.

Secret

Early versions of Windows featured something called the window control button, which was previously denoted by a small icon in the upper-left corner of most windows. In Windows 7, these icons are gone, replaced by the same translucent glass look that graces the rest of the tops of most Aero windows. Amazingly, the window control button still exists: it's just hidden, an archaic artifact from the Ghost of Windows Past. To see it, just click in the upper-left corner of most windows, including all Explorer windows. Ta-da! You'll see the old pop-up window with options like Restore, Move, Size, Minimize, Maximize/Restore, and Close, as shown in Figure 4-25.

Figure 4-25: It's a blast from the Windows 3.1 past: the window control button still works, though it's hidden in Windows 7.

Exploring the New Windows 7 Desktop Effects

While the Windows 7 desktop may artificially resemble that of previous Windows versions, Microsoft has actually imbued it with a number of unique desktop effects, sometimes called *Aero desktop enhancements*. These effects make Windows 7 a pleasure to use, are visually stimulating, and provide some important productivity advances.

Aero Snaps

Aero Snaps expands on previously available window management functionality in Windows and makes it easier to do so without the use of standard window controls, which are getting smaller and harder to use as we move to extremely high resolution displays. What Aero Snaps does is provide a way to maximize, minimize, and stack windows side-by-side. And it works using natural and easy-to-remember mouse movements that don't require precise mouse clicks. (There are also some simple keyboard shortcuts for each Aero Snaps effect, as you'll soon see.)

Aero Snaps provides a number of new ways to position and resize windows. And none of them actually require new onscreen controls, so they work fine with both the mouse and with Windows 7's new touch controls (described later in this chapter). These methods include the following:

◆ **Maximize:** To maximize the currently focused and floating window, click and hold the title bar area and drag the window up toward the top of the screen. When the cursor hits the top edge of the screen, the window will maximize as shown in Figure 4-26.

Figure 4-26: Aero Snaps provides a new way to maximize windows.

tip

The Aero Snaps Maximize keyboard shortcut is WinKey+Up Arrow.

♦ **Maximize vertically:** If you just want the current window to maximize vertically, both up and down (but not horizontally, or left and right), you can grab the top or bottom edge of the currently focused and floating window and drag it toward the closest (top or bottom) edge of the screen. When the cursor hits the edge of the screen, the window will maximize vertically, as shown in Figure 4-27.

Figure 4-27: New to Windows 7, you can now maximize windows only up and down, but not left and right.

tip

The Aero Snaps maximize vertically keyboard shortcut is WinKey+Shift+Up Arrow.

♦ **Snap left:** To snap the currently focused and floating window to the left side of the screen, drag it to the left. When the cursor hits the left side of the screen, the window will snap to that edge and occupy the leftmost 50 percent of the screen, as shown in Figure 4-28.

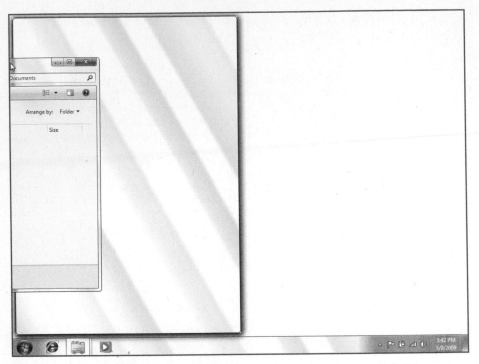

Figure 4-28: Now you can easily snap a floating window to the left side of the screen.

tip

The Aero Snaps left keyboard shortcut is WinKey+Left Arrow.

Secret

Snap left works uniquely on multiple monitors as well: as you repeatedly tap the keyboard shortcut, the window moves left across the displays, snapping to various screen edges as it goes. It will eventually make a complete round-trip between the various displays.

◆ **Snap right:** To snap the currently focused and floating window to the right side of the screen, drag it to the right. When the cursor hits the right side of the screen, the window will snap to that edge and occupy the rightmost 50 percent of the screen, as shown in Figure 4-29.

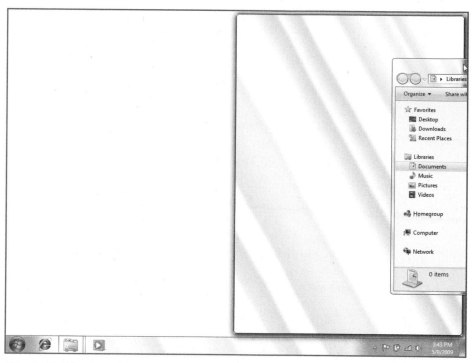

Figure 4-29: Likewise, you can also easily snap a floating window to the right side of the screen.

---

tip

The Aero Snaps right keyboard shortcut is WinKey+Right Arrow.

As with Snap left, Snap right works uniquely on multiple monitors too: as you repeatedly tap the keyboard shortcut, the window moves right across the displays, snapping to various screen edges as it goes. Again, it will eventually make a complete round-trip between the various displays.

---

tip

Aero Snap left and Aero Snap right are often used together. So you may snap one window to the left side of the screen, one to the right, and then drag and drop files between them or perform other similar tasks. This is shown in Figure 4-30. In previous windows, you could achieve a similar effect, but it was far more convoluted and less discoverable.

continues

continued

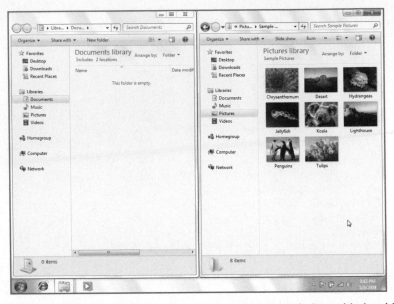

Figure 4-30: Aero Snaps makes it easy to place two windows side-by-side.

◆ **Restore:** To restore a maximized or snapped window, simply drag it down from the top or other edge of the screen by clicking and holding in the title bar area as shown in Figure 4-31. If you maximized or snapped the window using Aero Snaps, it will return to its previous size and position.

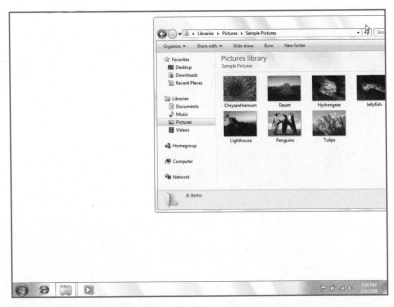

Figure 4-31: You can restore any snapped windows by dragging them off the screen edge to which they are attached.

tip The Aero Snaps restore keyboard shortcut is WinKey+Down Arrow.

Aero Peek

Aero Peek is one of many technologies that Microsoft has implemented over the years to combat the problems caused by excessive multitasking: if a user opens too many windows on the desktop, it's easy to lose track of those windows and the desktop, the latter of which can contain valuable shortcuts and other icons; and, in Windows 7, any number of desktop gadgets. (See the section titled "Using Desktop Gadgets.")

Aero Peek is used to literally "peek" behind all of the open windows on your system so you can get a look at the desktop. Previous to Windows 7, various Windows versions (including XP and Vista) included a feature called Show Desktop that was typically exposed by an icon in the Quick Launch toolbar in the taskbar. This Show Desktop functionality worked like a toggle: if you clicked it once, all of the open windows on your system would be minimized and you could access the desktop. Click it again, and all of the windows that were previously open would be returned to that state.

In Windows 7, Show Desktop has been effectively replaced by Peek at Desktop, though you can optionally cause this feature to work like the old Show Desktop if you're so inclined. Instead of a taskbar icon, Peek at Desktop is enabled by mousing over a new glass rectangular area found in the lower rightmost corner of the screen; it's to the right of the system clock in the taskbar. When you do mouse over this little panel, all of the open windows are hidden and replaced by window outlines, as shown in Figure 4-32.

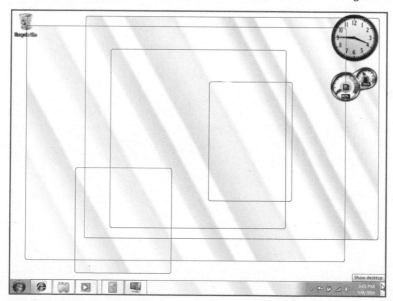

Figure 4-32: Aero Peek provides a way to peek behind onscreen windows and see what's on the desktop.

Aero Peek is of minimal usefulness for shortcuts and other icons, because once you move the mouse off of this panel, the windows return to the forefront, masking the desktop; but it's very useful if you take advantage of the new desktop-based gadgets in Windows 7, described in the section titled "Using Desktop Gadgets."

tip To trigger a true Show Desktop effect, you can click this panel instead of just mousing over it. Doing so causes all open windows to minimize, as they did for the Show Desktop icon for previous Windows versions.

tip The Aero Peek feature is used elsewhere in Windows 7, too. When you mouse over a taskbar button's Live Preview, you will see the underlying window displayed as a full-screen preview too. (We look at the new Windows 7 taskbar in just a bit.) Also, when you use the Windows Flip windows-switching keyboard shortcut—Alt+Tab—Aero Peek is used to preview each window as you move around the z-order.

 **Secret** Don't like Aero Peek? That's okay: you can turn it off. To do so, right-click a blank area of the taskbar and choose Properties. In the Taskbar tab of the Taskbar and Start Menu Properties window that appears, uncheck the option Use Aero Peek to preview the desktop.

Aero Shake

Aero Shake is as easy to describe as it is difficult to discover: simply click and hold on the grabbable area of any floating (nonmaximized) window and shake the mouse left and right vigorously. (This works much better with a true, external mouse than it does with a trackpad or other pointing device.)

When you do so the first time, all other open windows are minimized. Repeat the action, and those minimized windows will be restored to their prior state.

Aero Shake is designed as an adjunct to Aero Peek, though it works a bit differently. In this case, the focus is on the selected window, as you'd expect. And other windows are truly minimized: that is, they disappear from the screen entirely and you don't see a ghost window outline as you do with Aero Peek.

tip You can also trigger the Aero Shake effect—well, not the shaking bit—with the keyboard shortcut WinKey+Home.

Aero Shake is almost impossible to convey in a screenshot, so we've created a short video demonstrating this feature instead. You can see it at `tinyurl.com/aeroshake-video`.

Using Desktop Gadgets

With the proliferation of local and global digital information since the advent of the public Internet, Microsoft has been working on ways to integrate the data you need most often in a seamless way with the Windows desktop. In Windows Vista, the company created a feature called Windows Sidebar, which would typically sit on the edge of the PC display and provide an environment for Windows Gadgets, mini-applications that provide valuable information at your fingertips.

In Windows 7, Windows Gadgets are largely unchanged from Windows Vista. But the Vista Sidebar is gone. Instead, Gadgets now appear only on the desktop and cannot be hosted inside of a visible, side-mounted panel. Also unlike with Vista, no Windows Gadgets appear on the desktop by default; you need to enable them first.

Adding Gadgets to the Desktop

You access Windows Gadgets from the Windows Gadget Gallery, shown in Figure 4-33. You can launch this application from the Start menu (just type **gad** in Start Menu Search) or by right-clicking the desktop and choosing Gadgets from the pop-up menu that appears. (If you already have one or more gadgets displayed on the desktop, you can also right-click a gadget and choose Add gadget from the resulting pop-up menu.)

Figure 4-33: Manage Windows Gadgets using this simple application.

Secret

Windows Vista users will recognize Windows Gadget Gallery because it debuted in that OS (as did the Add Gadgets window for Windows Sidebar). More alarming, however, is this: of the 10 Gadgets that come with Windows 7, only one is new to this version (Windows Media Center). The other nine come over virtually unchanged since Windows Vista. Boring!

There are two ways to add a gadget to the desktop:

Double-click the gadget in Windows Gadget Gallery. When you do so, the gadget is placed in the top-right corner of the desktop. Subsequent gadgets are added down the right side of the screen. So if you were to add three gadgets using this method, the screen might resemble Figure 4-34.

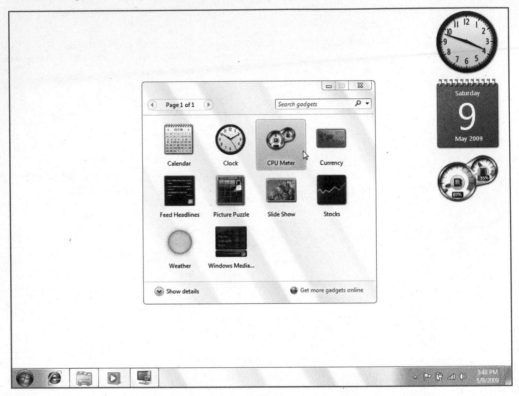

Figure 4-34: You can emulate the old Vista Sidebar by double-clicking gadgets.

This method of adding gadgets simulates how gadgets would appear in Windows Vista. Remember, in that OS, the gadgets would appear in the Windows Sidebar, which, by default, sat on the right edge of the screen.

Drag and drop a gadget onto the desktop, as shown in Figure 4-35. When you add gadgets to the desktop using this method, they will sit wherever you drop them.

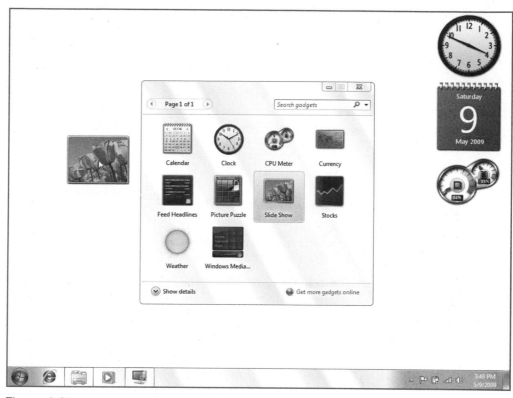

Figure 4-35: You can also drag gadgets directly onto the desktop.

However you add gadgets, you can move them around on the desktop as you'd like. Unlike with desktop icons, they can be moved indiscriminately around on the desktop, as they're not bound by the positioning rules that govern icons.

You can also add multiple copies of any gadget to the desktop if you'd like. This is handy for certain gadgets, such as the Clock (each instance of which can be set to a different time zone) and Weather (as each can be configured to display the weather for a different place).

Looking at the Built-In Gadgets
Table 4-5 summarizes the gadgets that ship with Windows 7.

Table 4-5: Built-In Windows Gadgets

Gadget	What It Does
Calendar	Provides a handy onscreen calendar with both day and month views. Note that there is no settings window for Calendar: it's designed to tell you the date and day of the week only.
Clock	A clock that can be configured to show the time in any time zone or city worldwide, or just use the current system time. Clocks can be named and you can choose between eight different clock styles. You can also choose whether to enable the second hand.
CPU Meter	A set of two gauges that tracks the load on your PC's microprocessor and RAM, using percentage only. There is no settings window for this gadget.
Currency	A simple currency converter. It's handy if you want to see how poorly the U.S. dollar is doing today against the euro. There is no settings window for this gadget.
Feed Headlines	An RSS client that integrates with the RSS feeds to which you've subscribed in Internet Explorer. You must click the View Feeds button before it will display the results of any feed. To view more information about a particular feed, click the feed and Feed Headlines will expand out with a larger text view. To view the actual feed or Web page in Internet Explorer, click the headline in the expanded window. (Please see Chapter 20 for more information about RSS feeds.) The Feed Headlines settings window enables you to configure which of IE's RSS feeds to display and how many headlines to show at a time.
Picture Puzzle	Remember those little handheld tile games in which you move tiles around until the picture displayed on the front of the tiles is complete? Well, here it is in gadget form. You can choose from 11 pictures, enable a timer, and click a small button to see what the finished picture is supposed to look like.
Slide Show	A photo slide-show gadget with a host of options. You can pick the folder from which to obtain the pictures (the default is the Public Pictures folder), the amount of time to display each image, which of 15 transitions to use, and whether the pictures should be shuffled. While the gadget is running, you can also mouse over its surface to access a small controller overlay with Previous, Play/Pause, and Next buttons, as well as a View button that displays the current picture in Windows Photo Gallery.
Stocks	An electronic stock ticker that integrates with Microsoft's MSN Money Central to provide constant stock price updates. By default, this gadget displays the Dow Jones Industrial Average, the NASDAQ composite, and the S&P 500 index, but you can add and remove stock symbols as you see fit.
Weather	A weather gadget that can be configured for any town and display the temperature in Fahrenheit or Celsius. Note that you can search by town/city name (as in *Paris, France*) or by zip code (like *02132*).
Windows Media Center	New to Windows 7, this gadget provides a handy front end to the recorded TV and Internet TV content in Windows Media Center. (See Chapter 15 for more information about Media Center.)

Some of these gadgets are obviously just for fun, but some are truly useful, especially for serious multitaskers.

Configuring Gadgets

When you have one or more gadgets displayed on the desktop, you'll probably want to configure them in some way. Some gadgets offer no customization per se, but many expose their customizable features via a Settings window. The way you access this information is identical for any gadget. If you move the mouse cursor over a gadget, you'll see one or two small user interface items appear in the top-right corner of all gadgets, as shown in Figure 4-36: a small Close button (resembling an x), which is always present, and possibly a small wrench. This second item appears only on gadgets that offer some form of customization.

Figure 4-36: When you mouse over a gadget, you'll see some new UI appear around the edges.

If you click the Close button, the gadget will close and disappear from the Sidebar without any warning dialog. But if you click the wrench, the gadget will display its Settings window. Each gadget will display a different set of Settings options. Figure 4-37 shows the Settings option for the Clock gadget.

Figure 4-37: From the Clock Settings window, you can select a clock name, the time zone, and optionally show the clock's second hand.

In Windows 7, most gadgets support two views: a standard size and a larger size. To trigger the larger size, mouse over a gadget and look for the Larger size button to appear; it will be directly below the Close button and resemble an arrow inside of a box. When you click this button, the gadget will expand. Most gadgets don't just get larger, however. Instead, they typically provide additional information or functionality. The Calendar gadget, for example, displays a second panel with a full month view in its larger size. And the Weather gadget provides a three-day outlook in its larger size, as shown in Figure 4-38.

Figure 4-38: Many gadgets also provide a larger size view that includes more information.

To access common gadget options, you can right-click any gadget. This displays a pop-up menu from which you can control the opacity, or translucency, of the gadget (20, 40, 60, 80, or 100 percent, where 100 percent is the default) and access other options.

New to Windows 7, you can globally hide gadgets by right-clicking the desktop, choosing View from the pop-up menu that appears, and then de-selecting Show desktop gadgets. (You can also separately hide desktop icons from the same submenu.)

Gadgets remember where you left them. If you hide the gadgets and then later enable them, all of the gadgets will reappear exactly where you left them. (This includes multiple monitor setups as well, which is nice.)

tip   Remember, you can always use the new Aero Peek feature to view gadgets that are hidden by floating windows. Or just tap WinKey+D to show the desktop (and thus the gadgets) without the Aero Peek effect.

tip   Gadgets can also be configured to permanently float above all other windows if needed. Simply right-click the gadget you'd like to see on top of other windows and select Always on Top from the menu that appears. Obviously, this wouldn't be a desirable effect for gadgets floating around in the middle of the screen, but it's not a bad idea for gadgets attached to the side of the screen or displayed on a second monitor.

Removing Gadgets

To remove a gadget from the desktop, simply right-click it and choose Close gadget. Or, mouse over the gadget and click the small Close button that appears. This will not delete a gadget from your system, of course. You will be able to re-add any removed gadgets later from the Add Gadgets window.

Finding New Gadgets

In order to make it easy for users to find new Windows Gadgets, Microsoft has created a Web community called Windows Live Gallery (`gallery.microsoft.com`). Actually, this community is designed for users of all kinds of gadgets, including those that run on the Windows Live Web sites, Windows Live Messenger, Windows Live Toolbar, Windows Sideshow, as well as Windows Sidebar (in Windows Vista) and the on the Windows 7 desktop.

Microsoft has basically created three different gadget environments to date:

- ◆ Sidebar and the Windows 7 desktop
- ◆ Live.com and various other Windows Live Web sites
- ◆ Windows Sideshow, an external display that is beginning to appear on new notebook computers, Tablet PCs, and other devices.

Secret Unfortunately, the three environments are not entirely compatible, so you can't just create one gadget that works in all three. If you wanted to get a gadget that would display your e-mail, for example, you would need different versions for Windows Gadgets, Windows Live, and Sideshow. That said, gadgets for all three environments could be built using the same HTML, DHTML, and JavaScript technologies and could share some code.

On the Windows Live Gadgets Web site, shown in Figure 4-39, you can find galleries of downloadable gadgets, information for developers who would like to make their own gadgets, forums for providing gadget feedback, and other information.

Figure 4-39: Windows Live Gadgets is a Web community for finding Windows Gadgets.

Windows Live Gallery includes a wealth of information and documentation about building gadgets that work in any or all of the supported environments. If you are a developer, all of your skills writing Web applications and Web sites are easily transferable to gadget design and development.

The New Windows 7 Taskbar

In Windows 7, the system taskbar works similarly to the way it did in Windows XP and Vista but it's been significantly enhanced as well, and is now more easily customized. More dramatically, the Windows 7 taskbar has picked up some functionality that was previously the purview of the Start menu: it can be used as an application, folder, or document launcher as well.

Secret

Chances are this functionality isn't as jarring as it sounds. Mac users will smugly point out that their version of the taskbar, called the Mac OS X Dock, has combined shortcuts with icons for running applications and open windows since 2001. But the Windows 7 taskbar isn't a Mac knock-off. Instead, it combines functionality that previously appeared in early versions of the Windows taskbar with that of the Quick Launch toolbar. In Windows Vista and earlier versions of Windows, you could click shortcuts from the Quick Launch toolbar and then manage open applications and other windows from the taskbar. In Windows 7, these functions have simply been combined. So instead of separate places for performing these tasks, you can do it all from a single, more customizable location.

Every time you open an application or Explorer window, you will see a new button appear in the taskbar. When you click one these buttons, the selected window comes to the forefront. If that window was already at the forefront, it will be minimized. If you simply mouse over the button, you'll see a live thumbnail preview, as shown in Figure 4-40.

Figure 4-40: A live taskbar thumbnail

When a taskbar button does represent multiple windows, the button image is slightly different. As you can see in Figure 4-41, a button with multiple underlying windows takes on a more 3D look, providing a hint that there's more underneath. And when you mouse over it, you'll see multiple thumbnails, each representing one of the open windows.

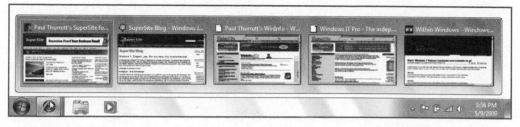

Figure 4-41: The Windows 7 taskbar hides multiple windows under a single button.

When you right-click a blank area of the taskbar, you get a pop-up menu with links to enable toolbars, arrange desktop windows in various ways, show the desktop, access the Task Manager, toggle taskbar locking, and access the Taskbar and Start Menu Properties window, from which you can configure various taskbar options. This window is shown in Figure 4-42.

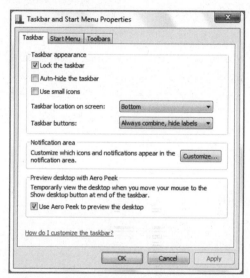

Figure 4-42: From here, you can customize certain taskbar features.

Secret

You don't have to accept Microsoft's default button view and, to be honest, we recommend that you not. If you're put off by the fact that a single button is representing multiple underlying windows and would rather know exactly what's open on your desktop without having to continually mouse over buttons, simply visit the Taskbar tab in the Taskbar and Start Menu Properties window and choose *Combine when taskbar is full* from the Taskbar buttons drop-down list. As shown in Figure 4-43, this choice results in a more readily useful taskbar display.

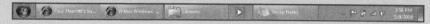

Figure 4-43: You can make the Windows 7 taskbar work more like that in Windows XP and Vista if you'd like. We recommend it.

Secret

There's another glaring gotcha in the new taskbar. Say you've got multiple windows open and you're trying to find just the right one. So you mouse over the individual buttons in the taskbar, triggering various live previews as you go. If you then mouse up to one of the previews, that window will appear on the desktop, and the system will hide all of the other open windows using the previously discussed Aero Peek feature (see Figure 4-44). *Voila!* You've found what you're looking for, right? So you mouse up from the preview to the window that's peeking through and…poof! It's gone. In order to actually select this window, you have to click the preview, not mouse off of it. This is a mistake that every single Windows 7 user will make at least once. It's kind of like touching a lit burner on a stove in that you'll never make the same mistake twice. At least you don't literally hurt yourself.

Figure 4-44: If you mouse over a taskbar thumbnail, Aero Peek will hide the other windows and display just the one window represented by the thumbnail.

Customizing the Taskbar

While most Windows users are probably familiar with the stock taskbar, this handy Windows feature can be configured in a number of ways, many of which dramatically change its appearance. This means you can make the taskbar work the way you want it to: you don't have to accept the taskbar as delivered by Microsoft.

There are two major new taskbar customization capabilities included in Windows 7: you can now pin items to the taskbar so that you can access them more quickly. And you can reorder taskbar buttons so that they appear in the order you want, and not in some arbitrary order determined by when windows were opened and closed.

Pinning Items to the Taskbar

Remember, the Windows 7 taskbar doesn't just contain buttons for running applications and other open windows. In this Windows version, the taskbar can also contain pinned shortcuts for applications, folders, documents, and other items. As shown in Figure 4-45, different types of taskbar buttons look different. The Explorer button represents a pinned taskbar shortcut, and because no Explorer windows are open, its button appears to float on the taskbar, without any border. The Windows Media Player button, however, has a single rectangular border around it. This means that the Media Player application is active and running. And the Internet Explorer button has a bigger, more 3D border, indicating that multiple IE windows and/or tabs are open.

Figure 4-45: Windows 7 shortcuts are said to be pinned to the taskbar.

By default, Windows 7 pins three buttons to the taskbar for you: IE, Explorer, and Windows Media Player. But you can pin your own items to the taskbar, and you can unpin the default buttons if you don't want them there.

There are a few ways to pin an item to the taskbar. The most obvious is to open the Start menu's MRU or All Programs list, navigate to the shortcut you want, right-click it, and choose Pin to Taskbar from the pop-up menu that appears, as shown in Figure 4-46.

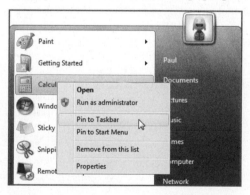

Figure 4-46: You can pin Start menu items to the taskbar.

If you pin an item from the Start menu MRU to the taskbar, it will no longer appear in the Start menu MRU. So if you'd like to also pin this item to the Start menu, you have dig deeper into the Start menu's All Programs list to find it.

You can also drag and drop items onto the taskbar to pin them. As shown in Figure 4-47, the system will alert you that dropping the item will cause it to be pinned.

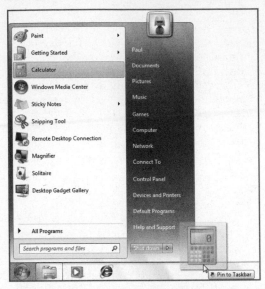

Figure 4-47: You can pin Start menu items to the taskbar using drag and drop, too.

The problem here is that some items can't apparently be pinned. Some exceptions we've discovered include the following:

◆ **You cannot have multiple Explorer buttons.** If you leave the default Windows Explorer button pinned to the taskbar, subsequent attempts to pin other Library or folder locations to the taskbar will not work as expected. (That is, they will not be given a separate pinned button, as you may prefer.) Instead, as you drag such an item over, you'll be alerted that the item will be pinned to Windows Explorer. This means that it will appear at the top of the already pinned Windows Explorer button's Jump List, as shown in Figure 4-48.

Figure 4-48: You cannot pin multiple items of the same type to the taskbar. They appear under a single button's Jump List instead.

◆ **Some items cannot be pinned.** Some system items simply cannot be pinned to the taskbar. As shown in Figure 4-49, any attempt at pinning a network connection to the taskbar is met with failure. This is also true of individual control panels.

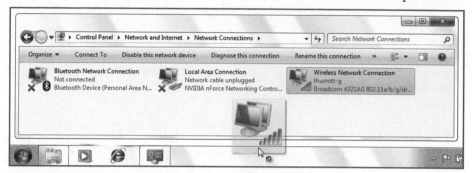

Figure 4-49: Some items cannot be pinned to the taskbar at all.

Because the default drag and drop behavior for the Start menu is Pin, you need to hold down the Shift key when you're dragging and dropping to the taskbar in order to open a document or other data file with a non-default application. For example, say you want to open a Microsoft Word document (*.docx) with WordPad, a built-in Windows 7 application. You could pin WordPad to the taskbar, and then drag and drop a Word document to that button while holding down the Shift key. As shown in Figure 4-50, you'll be notified that this will cause WordPad to open the document.

Figure 4-50: To open a document with a non-default pinned application, hold down the Shift key.

To unpin an item from the taskbar, right-click its taskbar button and choose *Unpin this program from taskbar*. You can do this whether any windows are open or not.

Reordering Taskbar Buttons

You can also reorder taskbar buttons so that they appear in the order you prefer. Doing so is simple: just grab one of the buttons and drag it left or right. This is shown in Figure 4-51.

Figure 4-51: You reorder taskbar buttons using drag and drop.

Secret

There's a secret way to launch applications and other pinned or open windows from the taskbar using just the keyboard. This trick works only with the first 10 taskbar items, however. To do this, just tap WinKey+*[a number from 1 to 0]*, where the number corresponds with the position of the button on the taskbar. To launch the application or window associated with the second taskbar button, for example, you'd tap WinKey+2.

Notification Area and System Clock

Way back in Windows 95, Microsoft introduced a number of user interface conventions that still exist in Windows 7. These include, among others, the Start button and Start menu, the taskbar, the Windows Explorer windows, and the notification area, which sits at the right end of the taskbar by default. You'll typically see three types of items here: various notification icons, the system clock (which is technically considered a notification icon for some reason), and the Desktop Preview button (Aero Peek). Some of the notification area icons are visible by default in Windows 7, such as Action Center, Network, Volume, and Power (on mobile computers only). The stock Windows 7 notification area is shown in Figure 4-52.

Figure 4-52: The Windows 7 notification area

Other icons appear when needed or are installed by third-party applications. For example, Windows Home Server and many security applications install notification icons.

 tip   Like a certain demonic creature, the notification area goes by many names. If you see references to such things as the "system tray" or the "tray notification area," these are referring to the same place in the Windows 7 UI: what's now simply called the *notification area*.

As the name suggests, the notification area is designed for notifications and shouldn't be used as a taskbar replacement, although some developers try to use it that way for some reason (some applications inexplicably minimize to the tray, rather than to the taskbar as they should). Applications like Microsoft Outlook, which need to alert the user to new instant messages, e-mails, or online contacts, also use the tray, and display small pop-up notification windows nearby. However, in Windows 7, these icons are all hidden by default, so the tray won't become cluttered. Of course, this hiding has two bad side effects: sometimes features you want aren't visible, and you aren't alerted to the fact that some applications are silently running in the background.

You can access hidden notification icons by clicking the Show hidden icons button, a small white arrow to the left of the notification area. When you do so, a small window pops up, showing you the hidden notification icons (see Figure 4-53).

Figure 4-53: Hidden notification icons can be accessed via a pop-up window.

Customizing the Notification Area

If you're not happy with the default notification area layout, you can do something about it. You can remove or enable default notification icons, and choose whether to hide other icons and their notifications.

To do so, right-click a blank area of the taskbar and choose Properties. In the Taskbar and Start Menu Properties window that appears, click the Customize button on the Taskbar tab to display the new Notification Area Icons control panel shown in Figure 4-54.

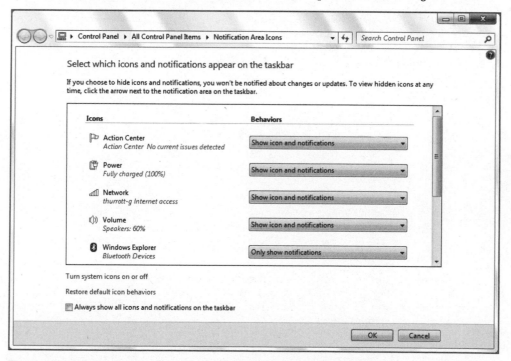

Figure 4-54: You can determine how notification icons display using this control panel.

For all system and non-system notification icons, you can choose from three options:

- ◆ **Show icon and notifications:** In this case, the icon appears directly in the notification area and will display any notifications the underlying application displays.
- ◆ **Hide icon and notifications:** In this case, the icon will not appear in the notification area and will not display any notifications. You can access these icons by clicking the Show hidden icons button.
- ◆ **Only show notifications:** In this case, the icon will not appear in the notification area but the underlying application will still be able to display notifications. Again, you can access these icons by clicking the Show hidden icons button.

In addition to this control, you can also access options that are unique to the built-in system icons by clicking the link titled *Turn system icons on or off*. When you do, the System Icons control panel appears, shown in Figure 4-55. This interface enables you to control the display of the Clock, Volume, Network, Power, and Action Center icons. (The Power icon option will be disabled on desktops PCs, however.)

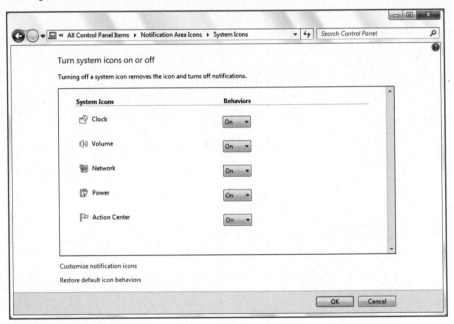

Figure 4-55: System icons can be independently enabled and disabled as well.

Like taskbar buttons, most notification area icons can be reordered using drag and drop. And this applies to the hidden icons, too: you can drag hidden icons down into the notification area to cause them to be displayed. There is one exception: you cannot change the location of the Clock.

Speaking of the Clock …

Exploring the System Clock

Microsoft changed the system clock pretty dramatically in Windows Vista, and these changes carry over to Windows 7. But because they will be new to so many readers, we cover this feature here as well.

At first glance, it's not obvious what has changed. The clock displays the time, as you'd expect, and a shortened version of the date in the default display. And if you mouse over the clock, a pleasant-looking balloon tip window appears, providing you with the day and date. So far, it's not so different from the clock in XP.

In Windows XP, you could access the system's Date and Time Properties dialog by double-clicking the clock. This doesn't work in Windows 7. Instead, you can single-click the clock to display a pop-up window, shown in Figure 4-56, which provides a professionally formatted calendar and analog clock. There's also an option to change the date and time settings.

Figure 4-56: Windows 7 includes a nice-looking calendar and clock display.

When you click that link, you'll see the Date and Time window, as shown in Figure 4-57. Here, you can configure options you'd expect, such as date, time, and time zone; but you can also configure additional clock displays, which is an excellent feature for travelers or those who frequently need to communicate with people in different time zones.

Figure 4-57: The Date and Time window has been completely overhauled.

From the Additional Clocks tab of this dialog, you can add up to two more clocks. Each clock gets its own time zone and optional display name. What's cool about this feature is the way it changes the clock displays. Now, when you mouse over the clock, you'll see a pop-up that lists data from all of your clocks, as shown in Figure 4-58.

Figure 4-58: You can configure up to three clocks in Windows 7.

And when you click the clock, you'll see the nice display shown in Figure 4-59.

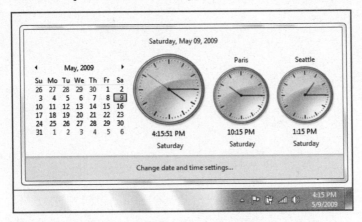

Figure 4-59: This handy and speedy time and date display can also handle up to three clocks.

Windows Explorers

No discussion of the Windows 7 user experience would be complete without a look at the ways in which Microsoft has evolved Windows Explorer in this release. Windows Explorer first appeared in Windows 95, replacing the many horrible "manager" programs (File Manager, Program Manager, and so on) that plagued previous Windows versions. It was a grand idea, but then Microsoft made the mistake of combining Internet Explorer with the Windows shell. Starting with an interim version of Windows 95, the Windows Explorer shell has been based on IE, and since then we've suffered through a decade of security vulnerabilities and the resulting patches.

In Windows 7, that integration is a thing of the past. Windows Explorer has been completely overhauled, and it's quite a bit better than the Explorer shell in Windows XP, and also quite a bit different. (It's also quite different from the Windows Vista shell, which can be disconcerting.) Microsoft has also introduced some new terminology into the mix, just to keep us on our toes. So My Documents is replaced by the Documents library in Windows 7, for example. (Likewise with all the other special folders: there are now Libraries for Pictures, Music, and Videos, and you can make your own libraries. We look at this functionality in Chapter 5.)

From a usability perspective, much has changed since XP. Consider a typical Explorer window, as shown in Figure 4-60. The menu bar is gone, replaced by a hidden menu bar (called Classic Menu in Windows Vista), which can be dynamically triggered by tapping the Alt key. The main toolbar is also gone, replaced by Back and Forward buttons, an enhanced address bar, and the Windows Search box.

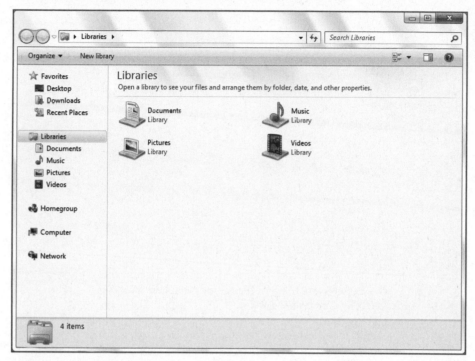

Figure 4-60: Like many user interface pieces in Windows 7, Explorer windows have changed fairly dramatically.

Below those controls is a new toolbar, which includes context-sensitive commands, that replaces the old task pane from Windows XP Explorer (and the command bar from Windows Vista). In other words, the options you will see in the toolbar will vary from window to window according to what's selected. On the bottom of each window is a Details pane, which also varies according to the current window and what's selected. Are you sensing a theme here?

In the center of the window, you'll see a Navigation pane with various system shortcuts, a large icon display area, and, optionally, a Preview pane. Now it's time to see what all of these features do.

Menu Bar

One of the guiding principles in Windows 7 is simplification. In previous Windows versions, virtually every system window and application included a top menu structure. In Windows 7, however, these menus are typically either nonexistent or are hidden by default. To display the menu bar in an Explorer window temporarily, simply tap the Alt key. (See Figure 4-61.)

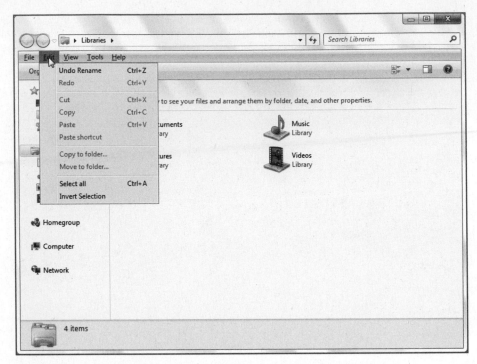

Figure 4-61: The Explorer menu bar is hidden by default in Windows 7 but can be displayed by tapping the Alt key.

Or, you can enable it permanently by choosing Organize in the toolbar, followed by Layout, and then Menu bar. There's precious little reason to do this, however. The menu just takes up valuable space.

> **tip** The Explorer menu bar is virtually identical to its XP counterpart. One major exception is that the Favorites menu does not appear in Windows 7, because IE is no longer integrated with the Windows shell.

Enhanced Address Bar

The Windows 7 address bar works almost identically to that in Windows Vista, but if you're coming from XP, prepare for a bit of a shock. Now, instead of the classic address bar view, the address bar is divided into drop-down menu nodes along the navigation path, making it easier than ever to move through the shell hierarchy. This interface is referred to as the *breadcrumb bar*, though we're pretty sure there isn't a gingerbread house at the end with a witch living in it.

To see how this works, open the Documents window—that is, the Documents *library*—by clicking the Documents item in the Start menu and observing the address bar. It is divided into three nodes: an icon, a node representing Libraries, and Documents. Each has a small arrow next to it, indicating that you can click there to trigger a drop-down menu.

To navigate to a folder that is at the same level in the shell hierarchy as the Documents library, click the small arrow to the left of Documents. As shown in Figure 4-62, a drop-down menu appears, showing you all the folders (in this case, Libraries) that are available. You can click any of these to navigate there immediately. Note that doing something similar in XP requires two steps. First, you have to click the Up toolbar button; then, you have to double-click the folder you want. That's progress, ladies and gentlemen.

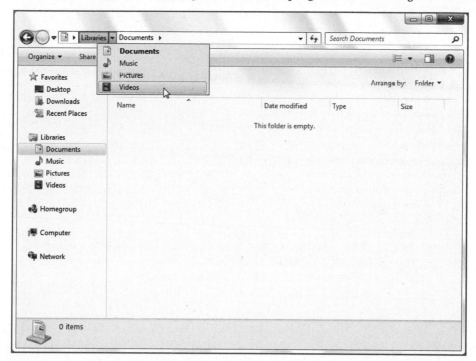

Figure 4-62: The new address bar makes it easier to move through the shell hierarchy.

Secret

To create a shortcut to the current shell location in the current view, click the icon that appears in the leftmost part of the address bar.

To simply move back up a level, click the node to the left of the current location. In this example, we would click the node that is denoted by Libraries. (Or, click Alt+Up Arrow.)

Secret   To see the classic address bar, simply click a blank area of the enhanced address bar. Now, the breadcrumb bar disappears and the arcane, text-based address appears in all its colon and forward slash goodness. To return to the safety of the breadcrumb bar, click elsewhere in the window.

Windows Search

Windows 7 has Start Menu Search, search in Internet Explorer, a new Search window (hidden, but you can tap F3 to see it), and even a Windows Search box in every Explorer window. The reason this is useful is that the Windows Search box is context sensitive. Sure, you could search your entire hard drive if you wanted, but what's the point? If you're in a folder, and you know that what you're looking for is in there somewhere, maybe in one of the subfolders, then the Windows Search box is the tool to use.

To search for a document or other file in the current folder or one of its subfolders, just click the search box and begin typing. (You can also tap Ctrl+F to select the Windows Search box with the keyboard.) Your results will begin appearing immediately. For more information about Windows 7's Instant Search functionality, please see Chapter 5.

Toolbar

The new Windows 7 toolbar combines the functionality of the toolbar and task panes from the Windows Explorer windows in Windows XP in a new, less real estate–intensive space. Like the task pane in XP, portions of the toolbar are context sensitive, and will change depending on what items you are viewing or have selected.

That said, the following portions of the toolbar will remain constant regardless of what you're viewing:

◆ **Organize button:** Appears in all Explorer windows and provides you with a drop-down menu from which you can perform common actions like create a new folder; cut, copy, paste, undo, and redo; select all; delete; rename; close; get properties; and change the window layout.

◆ **Views button:** Lets you change the icon view style for the current window. This option is uniquely configurable on a folder-by-folder basis.

◆ **Show the preview pane:** This toggles the Preview pane.

◆ **Help:** A button that launches Windows Help and Support. (You can also just tap F1.)

The other options you see in the toolbar depend on the view and selection. For example, Figure 4-63 shows how the toolbar changes in the Documents library window when you select a document file.

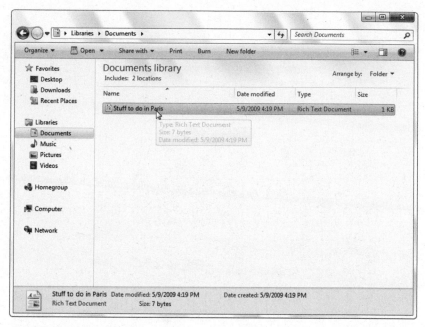

Figure 4-63: The Explorer toolbar provides options that are specific to what you're doing.

Navigation Pane

On the left of every Windows Explorer window is an area called the Navigation pane, shown in Figure 4-64. This pane features a list of favorite shell locations (like Desktop, Downloads, and Recent Places), a list of Libraries (Documents, Music, Pictures, and Videos), Homegroup locations, Computer locations, and Network locations.

You can add locations to the Favorites list by dragging them in from the display pane.

Figure 4-64: The Navigation pane includes links to commonly needed shell locations.

Live Icons and Preview Pane

In Windows 7, document icons are "live" and can provide you with a rich preview of their contents depending on which view style you're using, as shown in Figure 4-65.

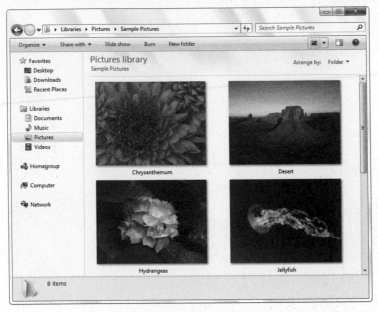

Figure 4-65: In Windows 7, document icons are "live," providing you with a preview of their contents.

But even when you're using one of the smaller view styles, you can get live previews: simply enable the Preview pane (also a global option), and as you select individual documents, you'll see a preview in that pane, which is located on the right side of the window. This is shown in Figure 4-66.

Details Pane

By default, every Windows Explorer window includes a Details pane at the bottom that provides a list of properties about the currently selected file or document. Previously, you had to open the file's Properties sheet to view this information. As you can see in Figure 4-67, the amount of detail shown in this pane increases dramatically as you resize it.

Secret

Note that this feature is global: once you resize the Details Pane, this setting will be preserved in all subsequent Explorer windows.

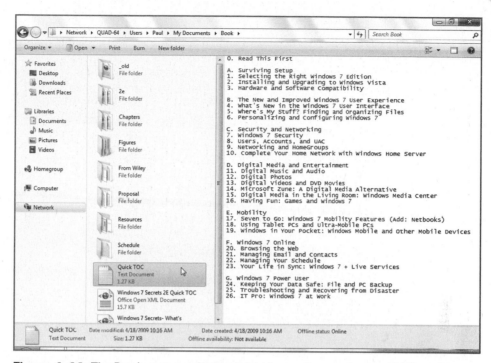

Figure 4-66: The Preview pane takes up a lot of space but can be used in lieu of actually opening a document in a separate application.

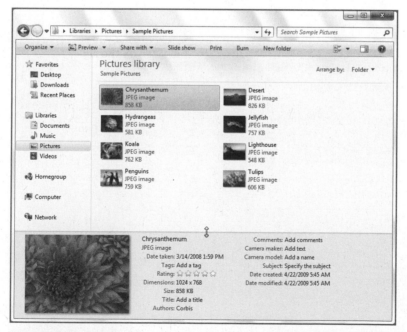

Figure 4-67: The Details pane will show more information if you make it bigger.

Bundled Windows 7 Applications

We'd like to spend a bit of time discussing some of the built-in applications that Microsoft bundles with Windows 7. These aren't major-league applications, like Internet Explorer and Windows Media Player (which demand full chapters of their own), but rather smaller applets that may be of interest. More important, each of application has either changed dramatically in this release or is new to Windows 7. As such, they impact the overall Windows 7 experience in generally positive ways.

Calculator

In Windows 7, Calculator gets a surprisingly major update and the first serious functional refresh since Windows 95. For the first time since that release, Calculator gets a new default layout, shown in Figure 4-68, and it has been significantly resized so that it will work better with Windows 7's multi-touch capabilities. (That's right: for the first time, a significant percentage of Windows users will actually be able to "press" the Calculator buttons with their own fingers, as we do with physical calculators.)

Figure 4-68: Windows Calculator gets a new layout and big, touch-compatible buttons.

But the biggest change in the Windows 7 version of Calculator is that it now supports different modes of operation. And within these modes, you can also configure Calculator to expand to display additional functionality, including some useful new templates.

Calculator modes include the following:

◆ **Standard:** This is the classic Windows Calculator and works largely like all of the Calculator versions included with Windows 95 through Windows 7. One change is that in addition to the Memory Clear (MC), Memory Recall (MR), Memory Store (MS), and Memory Add (M+) buttons, the Windows 7 version of Calculator adds a Memory Subtract (M-) button.

◆ **Scientific:** As with previous Windows versions, the Windows 7 Calculator includes a Scientific Calculator mode as well. This is shown in Figure 4-69.

Figure 4-69: Calculator's new Scientific mode

♦ **Programmer:** New to the Windows 7 Calculator is a Programmer mode that provides such things as number format conversion (hexadecimal, decimal, octal, binary), data type conversion (BYTE, WORD, DWORD, QWORD), and the like. Programmer mode is shown in Figure 4-70.

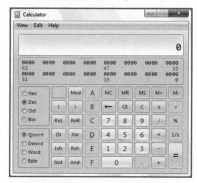

Figure 4-70: Calculator's new Programmer mode

♦ **Statistics:** Also new to the Windows 7 Calculator is a new Statistics mode, shown in Figure 4-71.

Figure 4-71: Calculator in Statistics mode

Each mode requires a certain bit of expertise, as Calculator provides little or no explanation for how these modes can be used or the purpose of various buttons.

Secret

You can also access the following additional Windows 7 Calculator functionality via the new Options menu:

• **Basic:** In this display, Calculator includes only those buttons required by the current mode.

• **Unit Conversion:** When enabled (see Figure 4-72), Calculator expands to the right and provides angle, area, energy, length, power, pressure, temperature, time, velocity, volume, and weight/mass conversion functionality. Each offers unit-specific options. For example, with temperature, you can convert to and from Celsius, Fahrenheit, and Kelvin. Area supports to and from conversion of acres, hectares, square centimeter, square feet, square inch, square kilometer, square meters, square mile, square millimeter, and square yard.

continues

continued

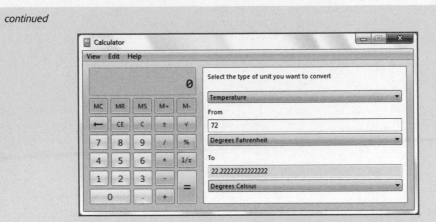

Figure 4-72: Here, we're converting from Fahrenheit to Celsius.

- **Date Calculation:** In this display (see Figure 4-73), Calculator provides various date/time calculations, including the difference between two dates and adding or subtracting days to a specific date.

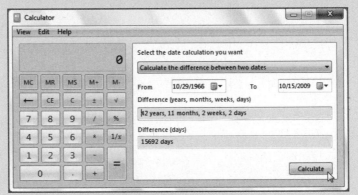

Figure 4-73: Calculating Paul's age with the Windows 7 Calculator

- **Templates:** In the Templates display, you will see a variety of other calculations, such as Gas Mileage, Lease Estimation, and Mortgage Estimation, each of which includes various template-specific options. Gas Mileage, for example, provides entry fields for distance, fuel consumption, and mileage; fill in two and the third will be calculated.

Scenic Ribbon Applications: Paint and WordPad

For Office 2007, Microsoft created the innovative ribbon user interface, which replaced old-school menus and toolbars with new bands called *ribbons* that include contextual tabs, mini-toolbars called *chunks*, and style galleries. While there will always be dissenters, the Office 2007 ribbon has proven wildly popular with users because it surfaces, or exposes, functionality that used to be buried deep within the applications' submenus and options dialogs. In fact, the Office 2007 ribbon UI was designed specifically to overcome the biggest single problem with Microsoft's productivity suite: Previous to Office 2007, most of the new feature requests the company received were for features that were already available in the product. Customers just didn't know how to find them.

Windows 7 includes dramatic updates to two legacy Windows applications, Paint and WordPad, which take advantage of the second-generation ribbon UI, called *Scenic Ribbon*. Both of these apps, shown in Figure 4-74, expose all of their various functions and options via graphic, easy-to-use ribbons that extend across the top of the application windows. The ribbon is divided into task-specific chunks, making it easier than ever to find out what features are available.

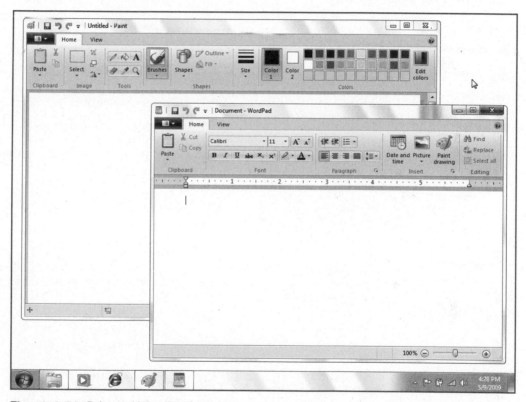

Figure 4-74: Paint and WordPad both feature Scenic Ribbon user interfaces.

Best of all, because the Scenic Ribbon interface is part of Windows 7, application developers will be able to create their own ribbon-based Windows applications in the future.

Sticky Notes

Windows Vista included a desktop gadget called Notes that let you jot short notes to yourself within the context of the Sidebar. In Windows 7, this functionality has been replaced by the new Sticky Notes application, shown in Figure 4-75.

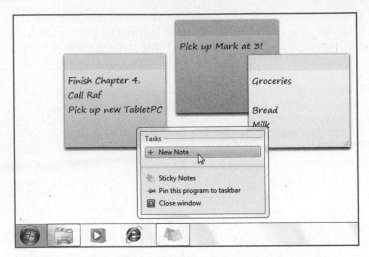

Figure 4-75: Windows 7's New Sticky Notes application

Sticky Notes is superior to the old Notes gadget in many ways. First, it runs as a normal application, and is thus available via Windows Flip (Alt+Tab) and on the taskbar like any other application. It integrates directly with the enhanced Windows 7 taskbar, too, providing some unique Jump List functionality. It also integrates with Windows Search: so if you remember jotting down a note but can't quite remember its full contents, you can just launch Windows Search and find it that way.

Secret Like the physical Post-It Notes they emulate, Sticky Notes come in different colors. To change the color of a note, right-click it and choose from the colors in the list that appears.

Windows Touch: Reach Out and Touch Some Screen

In many ways, we've saved the best for last. No Windows 7 feature is as exciting and profoundly futuristic, perhaps, as Windows Touch, which provides both touch support and *multi-touch* support to Windows 7. That means that, with the proper computing hardware, such as a touch-compatible desktop computer like HP's excellent TouchSmart line of products (see Figure 4-76), or touch-compatible Tablet PCs, you can actually interact with Windows 7 almost entirely using just your fingers. It's a liberating experience.

Touch support is pervasive throughout Windows 7. When we were first drafting an early Table of Contents for this book, we originally envisioned an entire chapter devoted to this technology. But then it became obvious that Windows Touch wasn't so much a separate bit of functionality as it was a fully integrated way of interacting with the system, much like the keyboard and mouse have been for the past few decades. So the truth is, once you get the hang of the basics, you can pretty much use Windows Touch as your only interface to the system if you'd like. So we'll cover what you need to get started here. And we think you'll come to agree that the Windows 7 touch interface is so natural and so obvious that you'll be up and running in no time at all.

Figure 4-76: The HP TouchSmart PC touched off a new generation of touch-compatible PCs.

Touch-compatible PCs operate much like the Tablet PC and Ultra-Mobile PCs (UMPCs) we discuss in Chapter 18. That is, the system can be navigated with a keyboard and mouse, as usual, but if you actually tap the screen with one or more fingers, you'll see a new mouse cursor, which looks a bit like a small star, appear as you tap the screen. This is shown in Figure 4-77.

Figure 4-77: Windows 7 lets you touch the desktop and other UI bits with your finger.

Windows 7 also makes some minor changes to the default UI when it is installed on touch-compatible hardware. For example, the size of onscreen elements is changed from the default Smaller (100 percent) setting to Medium (125 percent) so that window controls, buttons, and other UI objects are a bit larger and, thus, finger-friendly. (You can change this setting from the Display control panel.)

Tapping the screen to select items works just like clicking the mouse button. To right-click, hold down your finger on the screen for a few seconds. When a graphical circle appears around your fingertip, as shown in Figure 4-78, let go. Then, the expected right-click menu appears.

Figure 4-78: You can right-click a touch screen by holding down your finger on the screen.

Every Windows 7 application can be accessed via touch, and indeed some of them have been dramatically updated to take advantage of unique Windows Touch functionality. For example, in Paint, you can paint with your finger, which is of course fun. But you can also use multi-touch to paint with two fingers simultaneously, as shown in Figure 4-79.

Figure 4-79: Paint becomes Finger Paint with Windows Touch.

Other applications, like Internet Explorer and Windows Explorer, support finger flicks, which let you navigate back and forth from view to view by flicking your finger. In IE, for example, you can emulate the Back command by flicking your finger to the right within IE. To go Forward, flick to the left.

Media Center (covered in Chapter 15) is another application that is uniquely suitable for Windows Touch because of its overly large buttons and other UI controls. Media Player, too, is designed for touch access.

And it's no mistake that taskbar buttons are large and square in Windows 7: they're touch friendly. To trigger a taskbar button Jump List, just tap the button and, while holding down, swoop upwards. As you can see in Figure 4-80, the Jump List will spring to life. (You can emulate this with a mouse too, if you're looking for unique new ways to use a mouse in Windows 7.)

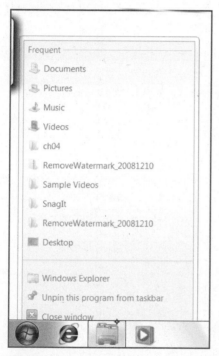

Figure 4-80: Jump Lists can be activated via a finger swoop too.

Aero Peek is designed for touch, too: on a touch-enabled screen, it's twice as wide as usual so it can accommodate your fingertip (see Figure 4-81).

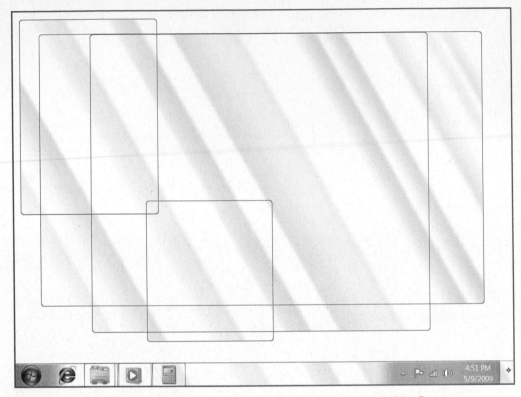

Figure 4-81: Aero Peek gets bigger so you can activate it with your chubby fingers.

Table 4-6 highlights some of the touch gestures that are now available in Windows 7.

Table 4-6: Windows Touch Keyboard Shortcuts

Command	Gesture	What It Does
Click	Tap	Selects an object
Double-click	Double tap	Opens selected object
Right-click	Press and hold (or press and tap with second finger)	Emulates a right-click
Drag	Touch object and slide finger across screen	Operates like selecting and dragging with a mouse
Scroll	Drag up or down inside of document area of the window	Works like using the scrollbars
Zoom in	Pinch two fingers together	Zooms in on the current view
Zoom out	Pinch two fingers apart	Zooms out in the current view
Return to default zoom	Two-finger tap	Returns the view to the default zoom

Command	Gesture	What It Does
Rotate	Touch two spots and spin fingers	Rotates current view (supported applications, like Paint, only)
Navigate back	Flick right	Emulates the Back command
Navigate forward	Flick left	Emulates the Forward command

Touch-screen users should be on the lookout for fun new games and other applications that take advantage of the unique properties of their PC hardware. One of our favorites is the air hockey game shown in Figure 4-82.

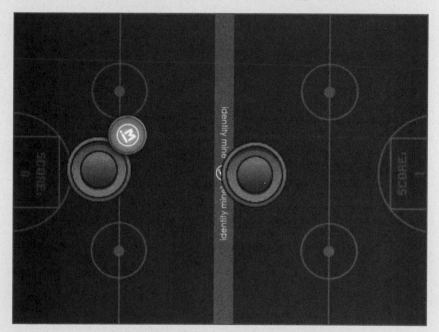

Figure 4-82: Windows Touch makes it possible for two people to play air hockey using just their fingers to control the on-screen paddles.

More to Come ...

There's so much more to know about the Windows 7 user experience, including the move to virtual folder-based Libraries, new icon view styles and arrangements, saved searches, and more. We will look at all of those features in upcoming chapters.

Summary

Anyone who uses Windows 7 will need to deal with its user interface, which is both brand-new in many ways but also extremely familiar to anyone who has used Windows XP or Vista. Like its predecessors, Windows 7 features a Start button and Start menu, a taskbar, a notification area, and a desktop. But Windows 7 improves on each of these features while adding user experiences such as Windows 7 Basic and Standard and Windows Aero, and other unique features. Thanks to these many enhancements, Windows 7 is the most efficient and attractive version of Windows yet.

Where's My Stuff? Finding and Organizing Files

Chapter

5

◆ ◆

In This Chapter

Understanding Libraries

Using the Windows shell

Understanding virtual folders

Working with Windows Explorer

Finding the documents and files you want

Creating and using custom Libraries and saved searches

◆ ◆

W indows 7 finally fulfills a longtime Microsoft plan: to incorporate a virtualized file system whereby physical drive letters, folder locations, and other file system arcana of the past disappear behind a much friendlier interface that works more like you do. From a technical perspective, while Windows 7 includes yet another updated version of the Explorer file system, it begins the transition away from the notion of *special shell folders*, replacing it with a new Libraries system in which much-needed data files such as documents, digital photos, digital music, and videos are aggregated and displayed for you automatically.

Libraries are a dramatic and important extension of the *virtual folders* technology that Microsoft first introduced in Windows Vista. In fact, they're really just search folders, and you can make your own as well, a confusing but powerful capability. In this chapter, you will explore the Windows shell and learn how to take advantage of the new file organization features Microsoft added to Windows 7. Get your Library card out, we're heading in.

Understanding Libraries

Most *Windows 7 Secrets* readers are probably familiar with basic computer file system concepts like files, folders, and drive letters; but you may not realize that certain locations in the Windows shell—that is, Windows Explorer, the application with which you literally explore the contents of your PC's hard drives—have been specially configured to work with particular data types and live in the shell hierarchy outside of their physical locations. In previous Windows versions, these locations were called *special shell folders*, and they included such things as My Documents, My Pictures, and My Music.

In Windows 7, these special shell folders still exist, sort of, but now they are just normal folders that can be found inside of your personal folder (typically at C:\Users*your username*). You can still manually copy documents to My Documents, as you did in Windows XP, and copy pictures to My Pictures. But in Windows 7, the old special shell folders aren't particularly accessible because they've been effectively replaced by something called Libraries.

---

tip | **To see the folders contained within your *home folder* in Windows 7, open the Start menu and click your user name on the top right. The Explorer window that opens displays the contents of your personal folder.**

Instead of the My Documents folder, you'll typically access the Documents library. The My Pictures folder has been replaced by the Pictures library. And so on. As Libraries, and, thus, virtual folders, are central to the entire shell and user experience, we want to step back for a second and explore virtual folders.

Virtual Folders 101

Early in the several-year development life cycle of Windows Vista, Microsoft began talking up a new file management system that would be based on a new user interface construct called a *virtual folder*. As the name suggests, virtual folders are a special kind of folder, one that does not actually represent a physical container in the file system like a "real" folder. You may recall that the constructs we call folders and special shell folders do, in fact, correspond to discrete locations in the shell namespace. That is, they are what we might call *real* or *physical* folders.

Virtual folders are not the same as real folders. They're not even really folders at all, though they do appear to contain files and folders. Actually, virtual folders are files that describe (or appear to contain) *symbolic links*, or shortcuts, to real files and folders. And the way that virtual folders are created might surprise you: they're really just the physical embodiment of a file search. That's right: virtual folders contain search query results, presented in a way that is virtually (ahem) indistinguishable from the display of a real folder.

We know. It sounds confusing. But in day-to-day usage, virtual folders work almost exactly like regular folders. We'll describe the differences—and the very real advantages of Libraries—in just a moment.

Secret

Virtual Folders—A Short History Lesson

In order to truly understand virtual folders, it's important to first understand the thinking that went into this feature. And since this is a feature that was originally scheduled for the ever-delayed Windows Vista, it might also be helpful to know about Microsoft's original plans for the Vista shell and virtual folders and compare the plans with what eventually happened.

Microsoft originally envisioned that it would not include in Vista a traditional file system with drive letters, physical file system paths, and real folders. Instead, the software giant wanted to virtualize the entire file system so that you wouldn't need to worry about such arcane things as "the root of C:" and the Program Files folder. Instead, you would just access your documents and applications, without ever thinking about where they resided on the disk. After all, that sort of electronic housekeeping is what a computer is good at, right?

This original vision required a healthy dose of technology. The core piece was a new storage engine called *WinFS* (short for Windows Future Storage), which would have combined the best features of the NTFS file system with the relational database functionality of Microsoft's SQL Server products. As of this writing, Microsoft has been working on WinFS, and now its successors, for about a decade.

There was just one problem: the WinFS technology wasn't even close to being ready in time for Windows Vista, so Microsoft pulled WinFS out of Vista and began developing it separately from the OS. Then, it completely cancelled plans to ship WinFS as a separate product. Instead, WinFS technologies would be integrated into other Windows versions—including Windows 7—and other Microsoft products.

Even though WinFS was out of the picture, Microsoft figured it could deliver much of that system's benefits using an updated version of the file system indexer it has shipped in Windows for years. And for about a year of Vista's development in 2004–05, that was the plan. Instead of special shell folders like Documents, users would access virtual folders such as All Documents, which would aggregate all of the documents on the hard drive and present them in a single location. Other special shell folders, like Pictures and Music, would also be replaced by virtual folders.

continues

continued

Problem solved, right? Wrong. Beta testers—who are presumably more technical than most PC users—found the transition from normal folders to virtual folders to be extremely confusing. In retrospect, this should have been obvious. After all, a virtual folder that displays all of your documents is kind of useful when you're looking for something, but where do you save a new file? Is a virtual folder even a real place for applications that want to save data? And do users need to understand the differences between normal folders and virtual folders? Why are there both kinds of folders?

With the delays mounting, Microsoft stepped back from the virtual folder scheme, just as it had when it stripped out WinFS previously. Therefore, the file system that appeared in Windows Vista was actually quite similar to that in Windows XP and previous Windows versions. That is, the file system still used drive letters, normal folders, and special shell folders like (My) Documents and (My) Pictures. If you were familiar with any prior Windows version, you would feel right at home in the Vista shell. (Likewise, if you found the Windows file system to be a bit, well, lackluster, all the same complaints still applied in Vista as well.)

There was, however, one major difference between Vista's file system and that of previous Windows versions, and this difference has been made central to the Windows 7 file system. Even though Microsoft had temporarily decided not to replace special shell folders with virtual folders in Windows Vista, the company still shipped virtual folder technology in the OS. The idea was that users could get used to virtual folders, and then perhaps a future Windows version would simply move to that system, and eventually we'd reach some "nerdvana" where all the silly file system constructs we use today were suddenly passé.

That nerdvana, arguably, has arrived in Windows 7. No, Microsoft hasn't relegated drive letters and physical folders to the dustbin of history, at least not yet. But they have implemented one of the early Vista file system plans in Windows 7: now, traditional special shell folders (but not the entire file system) have been replaced by virtual folders. This time around they're called Libraries.

On a side note, the capability to create your own virtual folders is also available in Windows 7, just as it was in Vista. And as in Vista, this feature is somewhat hidden. Okay, it's *really* well hidden, maybe even devilishly well hidden. That makes it a power-user feature and thus, for readers of this book, inherently interesting. Most people won't even realize that Libraries are virtual folders, let alone discover that you can create your own virtual folders with their contained shared searches. But if you do want to harness some of the most awesome and unique technology in Windows 7, this is the place to start.

Libraries and Windows 7

Okay, enough background. It's time to see what's changed with regard to user folders, Libraries, and special shell folders. The first thing to understand is that while your typical special shell folders—My Documents, My Music, My Pictures, and My Videos—still exist in Windows 7, inside of your user folder, you will rarely need or want to access them directly. Instead, you will work with the content types stored in these folders via Windows 7's new Libraries.

Think about how you might typically access My Documents in Windows XP: there's a very handy My Documents link right there in the Start menu. In Windows Vista, it was called Documents. Well, Windows 7 has a Documents link in the Start menu too. But when you click on that link, the window that opens displays the Documents library, not the (My) Documents folder, as was the case in previous versions. Ditto for Pictures, Music, and Videos.

Yes, you read that last sentence right: for the first time, you can link to your Videos library directly from the Start menu. It's not enabled by default, however. If you'd like to enable this access, right-click on the Start button, choose Properties, and then click the Customize Button in the Taskbar and Start Menu Properties window that appears. Scroll down the list in the Customize Start Menu window that appears until you find Videos (it's at the very bottom). Then choose Display as link or Display as a menu. *Voila.*

Each of the built-in Libraries in Windows 7 can be quickly accessed via the Windows Explorer shortcut that's pinned to the taskbar. When you click this shortcut, the Libraries view opens in Windows Explorer, as shown in Figure 5-1.

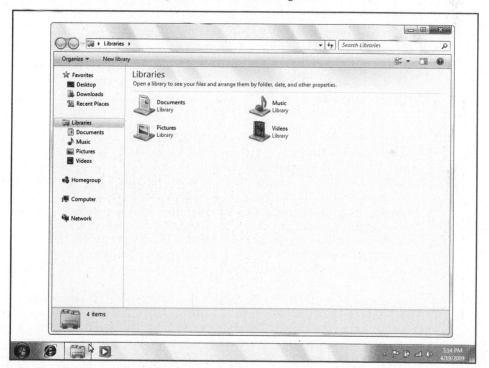

Figure 5-1: Windows 7 Libraries

Secret So what is this Libraries window? Where does that thing exist? As it turns out, the Libraries folder can be found at C:\Users*your username*\AppData\Roaming\ Microsoft\Windows\Libraries, which is hidden by default. Like special shell folders from Windows past, the Libraries folder is really just a special location in the shell namespace and is there for your convenience. In addition to the pinned tray shortcut, you can access this folder at any time, in any Windows Explorer window, by clicking the Libraries link in the navigation pane.

Because Libraries aren't really folders, there are a few additional concepts to understand about this change: yes, Libraries do effectively *replace* special shell folders in that you access them from the Windows Start menu. And yes, when you save and open files via virtually any application, you'll do so via the various Libraries that Windows 7 provides. There's just one thing: these Libraries aren't real *places*. In fact, they're simply files themselves, files that describe the contents of a thing that is presented to the user as a folder—or something like a folder. Something *better* than a folder.

Secret If you're familiar with Windows Media Center (Chapter 15) or Zune (Chapter 14), you may recall that these applications use a system called *monitored folders* to watch, or monitor, folders in the file system for new or changed files. The system used by Windows 7's Libraries is functionally identical. If anything changes in a physical folder that is being monitored by a Library, that change will be reflected in the Library.

Here's how Libraries are different, from a usage standpoint:

◆ **Libraries look different than folders:** If you compare a typical Library window and a typical folder window side-by-side, you'll see a few subtle but important differences. Libraries include a header area that lists the name of the library and links for Includes and Arrange by, as shown in Figure 5-2.

These links provide access to additional Library functionality that we'll discuss in just a moment. But as important as the UI difference is, it's equally important to understand that the header area you see in a Library is available continuously as you drill down into the folders it "contains." You won't see this header—or gain access to its functionality—if you access the same shell locations via normal folders.

◆ **Libraries are collections:** By default, each of the four Libraries that ship with Windows 7—Documents, Music, Pictures, and Videos—collects, or aggregates, content from two physical locations on your hard drive and displays them in a single location. For example, the Documents library collects content from your My Documents folder (C:\Users*your username*\My Documents) and the Public Documents folder (C:\Users\Public\Public Documents). You are free to add and remove the folders that a library monitors for content.

To view or modify the folders that are monitored by a Library, click the link next to Includes in the Library header, which, by default, will read as *two locations*. As shown in Figure 5-3, the resulting Locations window lists the shell locations monitored by the Library; has an Add button for adding new locations to monitor; has a Remove button for removing monitored locations; and references something called the default save location, which we will discuss next.

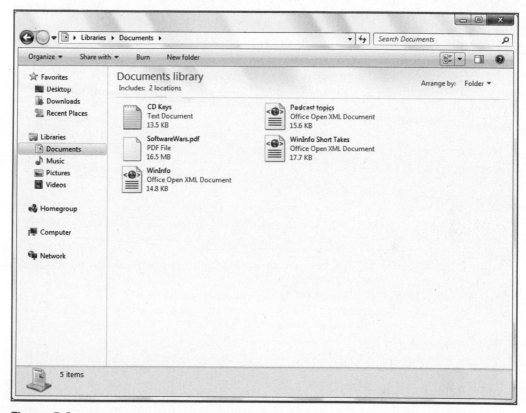

Figure 5-2: Libraries include a header area that's not seen in, and not available to, normal folders.

Secret

You may want to add a network share to the list of locations as well. While this is certainly possible, and recommended, there's a catch. The device or server housing this share must *index*, or catalog, the files within and provide results to Windows 7 clients on-demand. While this requirement can easily be met on a Windows platform by installing Windows Desktop Search, you may run into difficulties with other non-Windows devices.

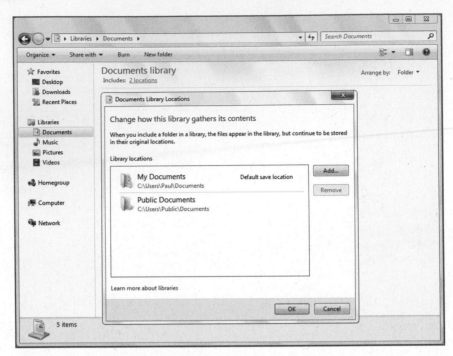

Figure 5-3: You can configure individual Library behaviors via the Locations window.

♦ **Libraries support a default save location:** Because Libraries are not really folder locations, and because they can monitor multiple folder locations, you need some way of knowing what happens when you save a file or folder to a Library. That is, where does it go? What happens to it?

Each default Library—Documents, Music, Pictures, and Videos—uses the appropriate special shell folder inside of your user folder as its default save location. For example, for the Document folder, the default save location is My Documents. For Pictures, it's My Pictures. And so on. This makes plenty of sense, and it's certain easy enough to handle when you're just using the two default monitored folder locations for each Library.

Things can get a little more complicated when you start monitoring folders on different drives or on remote network locations. Both of these are possible, but doing so introduces some a few twists. Consider simple file copy operations. When you drag a file from folder to folder on the same drive, Windows uses a move operation by default. But when you drag and drop from drive to drive, or across the network, the file is copied, not moved. These different file operations will occur within your Libraries too, if the monitored folders in question are located off of the main hard drive. It's something to think about.

♦ **Windows Media Player and other applications utilize Libraries:** In previous versions of Windows Media Player, you could set up the file locations the player would use to monitor for content. That's no longer the case in Windows Media Player 12. Now, the player simply utilizes the Music, Pictures, and Videos libraries for content. (We look at Windows Media Player 12 in Chapter 11.) While some other Windows 7 applications also utilize Libraries, some do not (at least not yet). Windows Live Photo Gallery, for example, still uses a pre-Library folder monitoring system of its own.

♦ **Libraries are the basis for Windows 7's network sharing capabilities:** In previous versions of Windows, you had to explicitly share folders so that they could be accessed by other PCs and compatible devices across your home network. Windows 7 makes this much easier with a new feature called HomeGroups. While we discuss HomeGroups in Chapter 9, it's worth at least mentioning here that four of the five objects that Windows 7 shares via HomeGroups—pictures, music, videos, and documents—are shared via Libraries. (The fifth shared object, printers, is of course separate.) Yes, you can still share things the old-fashioned way if you want, but Libraries, combined with HomeGroups, make sharing easier than ever.

♦ **You can arrange Library views in ways that aren't possible with folders:** While Libraries support the Sort by and Group by options utilized by folders, they also offer a unique visualization option called Arrange by that is not offered to traditional folders. We examine Sort by, Group by, and Arrange by later in this chapter.

Special Shell Folders…Now Just User Folders

We mentioned earlier that Windows 7 still sports a full collection of special shell folders, and that's true, though these folders really aren't that special anymore given the prominence of Libraries. These folders exist inside your user folder, which can be found at C:\ Users*your username* by default, as shown in Figure 5-4.

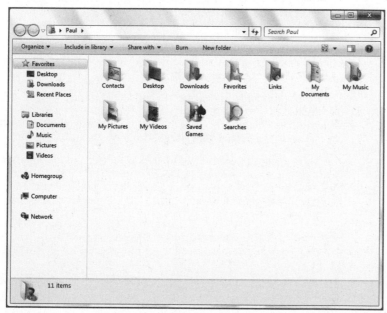

Figure 5-4: Windows 7 special shell folders are just folders inside your home folder.

These special shell folders are listed in Table 5-1.

Table 5-1: Special Shell Folders

Contacts	Contacts was introduced in Windows Vista as a central database for contacts management, and it was used by Windows Mail. Contacts, alas, is deemphasized in Windows 7; it's really just there for upgraders and backward compatibility. Microsoft latest e-mail client, Windows Live Mail, utilizes its own cloud-based contacts scheme, and Microsoft expects third-party e-mail application developers to follow suit.
Desktop	This folder represents your Windows desktop. Any folders, files, or shortcuts you place on the desktop will appear in this folder too (and vice versa). There's one exception: if you enable certain desktop icons—like Computer, User's Files, Network, Recycle Bin, or Control Panel via the Desktop Icon Settings dialog—these icons will not appear in the Desktop folder.
Downloads	This folder is the default location for files downloaded from the Web with Internet Explorer and other Web browsers, including Mozilla Firefox. New to Windows 7, you can add a Downloads link or menu to the Start menu and use it as a download manager of sorts.
Favorites	A central repository for your Internet Explorer Favorites (what other browsers typically call Bookmarks). The Favorites folder has been in Windows for several years. You can find out more about IE in Chapter 20.
Links	Links is a vestigial folder location from previous Windows versions and is there for upgraders and compatibility purposes only. Links has been replaced in Windows 7 by the Favorites locations in Windows Explorer and the Favorites bar in Internet Explorer 8.
My Documents	This folder is specially configured to handle various document types, such as Word documents, text files, and the like. My Documents is the default save location for the Documents library.
My Pictures	The My Pictures folder is designed to handle digital photographs and other picture files, and work in tandem with other photo-related tools such as Windows Live Photo Gallery and the Import Pictures and Videos wizard. My Pictures is the default save location for the Pictures library.
My Music	The My Music folder is designed to work with digital music and other audio files. If you rip music from an audio CD or purchase music from an online music service such as Apple iTunes, those files will typically be saved to your My Music folder by default. My Music is the default save location for the Music library.
My Videos	This folder is designed to store digital videos of any kind, including home movies. It is the default save location for the Videos library.
Saved Games	The Saved Games folder is designed as a place for Windows-compatible game titles to store saved game information. We discuss Windows 7 and video games in Chapter 16.
Searches	This folder contains built-in and user-created saved searches. We examine this functionality later in this chapter.

> **tip** In Windows XP, you had to run Windows Movie Maker once before the My Videos folder would appear. This is no longer the case in Windows 7, and the My Videos folder is always available under each user's Home folder.

In Windows Vista, Microsoft removed the word "My" from many of the special shell folders. But with the migration to the Library system in Windows 7, the company has returned the word "My" to special shell folders but left them off of the related Library names. Confused? Hey, that's what Microsoft does.

If you are coming from Windows XP, there are also some differences in the way that pre-existing special shell folders are organized in more recent Windows versions. For example, folders such as My Pictures, My Music, and My Videos were physically arranged below (and logically contained within) the My Documents folder in Windows XP and earlier. But in Windows Vista and 7, the new versions of these folders are found directly below each user's home folder, alongside My Documents. This won't affect typical users, who will likely access special shell folders virtually through Libraries. But more advanced users will want to be aware of the changes.

> **tip** The Windows 7 home folder layout is actually quite similar to that used by Unix and Linux systems, including Apple's Mac OS X.

Where Is It Now?

One of the challenges facing anyone moving to Windows 7 is that Microsoft chose to change the location of many user interface elements, which might make it hard for you to navigate around the shell in some instances. In Table 5-2, we summarize some of the changes you can expect to see, and how to work around them.

Table 5-2: Where to Find Common Shell Features from Previous Windows Versions in Windows 7

Windows XP	Windows Vista	Windows 7
My Documents folder	Documents folder	Documents library, My Documents folder
My Recent Documents (Start menu item)	Recent Items (Start menu item)	Recent Items (Start menu item, disabled by default)
My Pictures folder	Pictures folder	Pictures library, My Pictures folder
My Music folder	Music folder	Music library, My Music folder
My Video folder	Videos folder	Videos library, My Videos folder
My Computer	Computer	Computer
My Network Places	Network	Network

continues

Table 5-2: Where to Find Common Shell Features from Previous Windows Versions in Windows 7 *(continued)*

Windows XP	Windows Vista	Windows 7
Control Panel	Control Panel	Control Panel
Connect To	Connect To	Connect To (no longer displayed on the Start menu by default)
Set Program Access and Defaults	Default Programs	Default Programs
Printers and Faxes	Control Panel ⇨ Printers (was removed from the default Start menu)	Devices and Printers
Help and Support	Help and Support	Help and Support
n/a	Start Menu Search	Start Menu Search
Search	Removed from Start Menu in SP1; available via F3 or Explorer-based search boxes	Available via F3 or Explorer-based search boxes
Run	Start Menu Search (Run can still be optionally added to the Start menu if desired)	Start Menu Search (Run can still be optionally added to the Start menu if desired)
Windows Explorer and Folders View	Rather than use separate My Computer and Explorer view styles, all shell windows in Windows Vista incorporate an optional and expandable Folders pane in the bottom-left corner.	Via Folder Options, you can enable the Folders pane in the Explorer window Navigation pane.
Explorer Menu System	Renamed to Classic Menus and hidden by default, but you can view it by pressing the Alt key.	Same as Windows Vista
Folder Options	Available from the hidden Tools menu and via Folder Options applet in the Control Panel	Available from the hidden Tools menu, via Organize ⇨ Folder and search options, and via Folder Options applet in the Control Panel
Explorer Status Bar	Replaced by the Details Pane, which now sits at the bottom of all shell windows by default. Curiously, you can still enable the old status bar by tapping Alt and choosing Status Bar from the View menu.	Same as Windows Vista, but you can also optionally display the old Status bar if desired
Map/Disconnect Network Drive	Accessible via the hidden Tools menu	Toolbar button in Computer window

Visualization and Organization: How to Make the Windows Shell Work for You

In each Windows version, you can utilize a number of shell view styles, each of which presents the files and folders (and now, Libraries) you're looking at in a slightly different way. These view styles—and the ways in which you access and configure them—have changed again in Windows 7.

tip	For purposes of this discussion, we treat Libraries just like any other folders. It's just simpler that way, and the view styles work identically across folders and Libraries with one crucial exception, which we'll call out when appropriate.

Windows XP offered six Explorer view styles: Thumbnails, Tiles, Icons, List, Details, and, for folders containing digital pictures, Filmstrip; and you could arrange the files in folders in various ways, such as by name, type, or total size, or in groups, where icons representing similar objects would be visually grouped together. All of these options could be configured in a number of ways, including via buttons in the Explorer window toolbar, by right-clicking inside of an Explorer window, or from the View menu.

Windows Vista bumped the number of Explorer view styles to seven but, confusingly, it dropped some of the options that were previously available in Windows XP. In Vista, you could choose between Extra Large Icons, Large Icons, Medium Icons, Small Icons, List, Details, and Tiles views.

One thing that both Windows XP and Vista shared, sadly, was that they would often forget or override folder view styles, either on a per-window or system-wide basis. This is one of the weird areas in which Windows XP and Vista were inferior to previous Windows versions. Thankfully, this situation has been rectified in Windows 7: the system no longer forgets view styles.

Table 5-3 describes the eight view styles that are available in Windows 7. And in Figure 5-5, you can see the latest member of the view style family, Content view.

Table 5-3: Explorer View Styles

View Style	Description
Extra Large Icons	This absolutely gigantic view style takes full advantage of Windows 7's near photographic quality icons, which are rendered at 256 x 256 pixels.
Large Icons	Similar to the Windows XP Large Icons view, this view style provides 128 x 128 icons laid out in a conventional grid.
Medium Icons	A new style that was added to Windows Vista, Medium Icons are similar in style to Large Icons, but smaller, at 64 x 64 pixels.
Small Icons	Small icons appeared in Windows 95, Windows 98, Windows Me, and Windows 2000, but were exorcised from Windows XP for some reason, much to the chagrin of many users. They returned in Windows Vista and still remain today in Windows 7, sizing in at 32 x 32 pixels.

continues

Table 5-3: Explorer View Styles *(continued)*

View Style	Description
List	A columnar version of Small Icons view, with the same size icons but a more linear look
Details	A columnar view style that uses the same icon size as Small Icons but presents them in a more regulated fashion.
Tiles	A view that presents information about each folder and file to the right of the icon, as with Small Icons and Details, but utilizes a much larger icon (it's the same icon used by Medium Icons view). Because of the extra space available, Tiles view can present more than just the icon's name. What you see varies according to file type. Microsoft Word documents, for example, include both the name of the file and the notation "Microsoft Word Document." Digital photos include the name and the date the picture was taken.
Content	A view that combines the medium-icon behavior of the Tiles view (although these icons are strangely a tad smaller) with the behavior of the informative Details view. The columnar information you would normally see in Details view piles up to the right of each icon, space permitting.

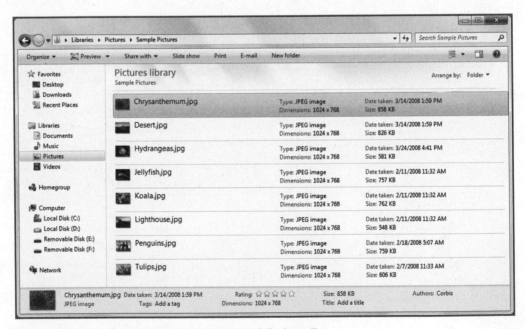

Figure 5-5: The Content view style is new to Windows 7.

You can access these styles in manners that are similar to those in Windows XP and Vista—via the Views button in an Explorer window toolbar, via the View submenu on the menu that appears when you right-click a blank area of the current Explorer window, or, if you have the Classic Menus option enabled, via the View menu.

tip   As with Windows Vista, Windows 7 enables you to choose different icon view styles for the desktop as well as for normal Explorer shell windows. To access these view modes, right-click a blank area of your desktop and choose View. You'll see three view styles here: Large Icons, Medium Icons, and Small Icons, which was called Classic Icons in Windows Vista. (Details, Extra Large Icons, Small Icons, Tiles, and Content are not available on the desktop.)

Secret

For some reason, clicking the Views button toggles between all but one of the available view styles. If you want to use Extra Large Icon view, you have to do a bit more work: click the More Options button to the right of the Views button to display the Views drop-down menu and then select Extra Large Icons.

What's interesting is that these shell view styles are not your only view style options. You can also access intermediary view styles between each of those stock settings using a new slider control that pops down when you click the More Option button next to the Views toolbar button (it resembles a small arrow), as shown in Figure 5-6. This control enables you to fine-tune the look and feel of individual Explorer windows, so you can arrive at a view style that matches your preferences and system capabilities. For example, on a large wide-screen display, you might prefer larger icons, whereas a smaller notebook display might look better to your eyes in Details view. It's up to you.

Secret

You can also move the slider with the scroll wheel on your mouse if it's so equipped. Simply open the slide control by clicking the arrow as noted previously and then use the scroll wheel to find the view style you like.

Alternately, skip the More Options button entirely: while viewing any Explorer window, simply hold down the Ctrl button on your keyboard and scroll with your mouse's scroll wheel. The icon sizes in the current window will change in real time.

Figure 5-6: You needn't be constrained by the stock view styles; Windows 7 enables you to select styles that fall somewhere between the presets.

Sorting and Grouping the Explorer View Styles

All Explorer windows, including Libraries in their default view styles, support various icon sorting and grouping options. In Details view, you can access the sorting options in an obvious fashion because they're available as column headings, as shown in Figure 5-7; but in other view styles, you'll need to employ right-click.

The sorting and grouping options in Windows 7 will be new to those coming from XP, but they're quite similar to what was available in Windows Vista. That is, you can sort a folder by Name, Date Modified, and other criteria, and this will affect the order in which items in that folder are displayed. (Folders are always displayed first, followed by files.)

You can also group files and folders by name, date modified, keywords, author, type, and other criteria, and your grouping options will vary according to the contents of the folder you're currently viewing.

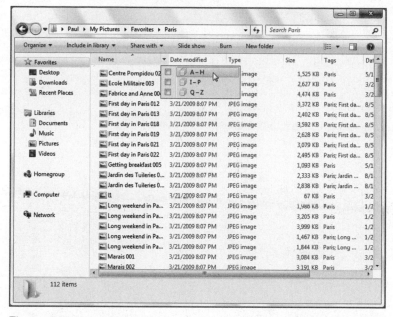

Figure 5-7: Only Details view lets you sort without resorting to right-click.

These options are available under the Group by submenu by right-clicking in any open Explorer window. As shown in Figure 5-8, numerous sorting and grouping options are available.

Figure 5-8: All Explorer windows and Libraries support the same range of Sort by and Group by options.

Arranging: The Organizational Advantage of Libraries

Sorting and grouping hasn't really changed much since Windows Vista, except that in Windows Vista you could access Details view–style column heads in almost any view style, a feature subsequently removed from Windows 7, presumably because of Microsoft's simplification mantra for this release. What has changed is that, with Libraries, you have an additional viewing option. Yes, you can sort and group, as with any Explorer window, but Libraries also enables you to *arrange*.

To understand how this functionality is exposed in the UI, check out Figure 5-9. Here, you can see two windows, side by side. On the left is a subfolder in the Pictures library; on the right is the same subfolder in the current user's My Pictures folder. See the difference?

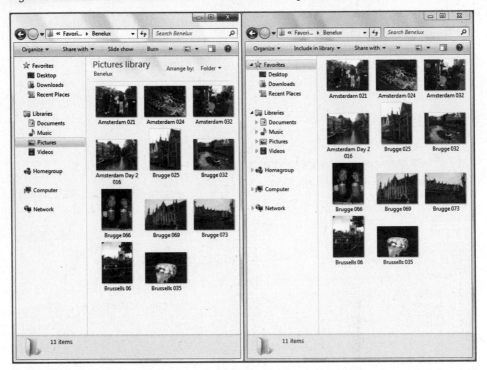

Figure 5-9: Library windows (like that on the left) offer a few advantages over standard folders.

Okay, enough guessing games. Libraries have an additional panel at the top of the window, below the toolbar, that provides access to two crucial Library features. The first, Library Locations, lets you determine which physical folders are monitored to create the current Library view. However, the second feature, Arrange by, is what interests us at the moment.

Arrange by provides a number of options, but what you'll see will differ according to which Library you're viewing. All of them use "Arrange by Folder" as the default choice, however, and in this arrangement, a Library will display just like any other folder.

If you choose one of the other arrangements, the Library will change into the Stack view that was first used in Windows Vista. Stacks represent files as visual stacks of paper, much like stacks of paper might be arranged on a real desk. (Yes, Microsoft is taking the PC's desktop metaphor a bit far these days.) To better understand what this means, take a look at Figure 5-10, which shows the Music library arranged by Artist.

If you arrange the Pictures library by Month, it should resemble Figure 5-11. Neat, eh?

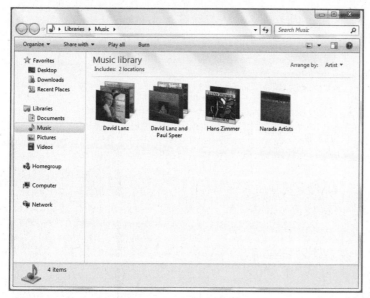

Figure 5-10: The Music library, arranged by Artist.

Figure 5-11: Library arrangements look best when the content is very visual, like pictures.

As with Sort by and Group by, you can also access Arrange by if you right-click an empty area of a Library window. Note, however, that this option is only available in Libraries. You won't see an Arrange by option in the pop-up menu that appears in regular folder windows.

Custom Libraries and Saved Searches

While Microsoft has finally taken virtual folders mainstream with the Libraries feature in Windows 7, the company has also provided a number of virtual folder features for power users. Some, like saved searches, were also available in Windows Vista, while others, like the ability to create your own custom Libraries, are new to Windows 7. Take a look.

Creating Custom Libraries

As noted earlier, Windows 7 includes four default Libraries, each of which handles a specific content type (documents, music, pictures, and videos). These Libraries will likely offer enough diversity for most users, but power users may be interested in creating custom Libraries of their own. It's unlikely that you'll need to create your own Library for a specific content type, but it's easy to understand why you might want to create custom Libraries for specific projects, or for special content groups that you'd like to keep separate from the default Libraries for some reason.

Imagine, for example, that Rafael and Paul are working on a book called, say, *Windows 7 Secrets*. Sure, we could organize the working files for this book in a folder found inside of My Documents, and accessed via the Documents library. But since we're going to need to access those files so frequently, it may make sense to create a Windows 7 Secrets library for this purpose. Then, it would always be one click away: we could access it via the Windows Explorer shortcut in the taskbar, or from the Library section in the Navigation pane of any Explorer window.

To create a new Library, open the Libraries window and click the New Library button in the toolbar. A New Library entry will appear with a generic Library icon, as shown in Figure 5-12. You can give this Library any reasonable name you'd like, as you could with a regular folder.

Note, too, that the new Library appears in the Libraries list in the Windows Explorer Navigation pane.

When you navigate into this virgin Library, you'll see that you need to monitor, or include, at least one folder before it will be useful. As shown in Figure 5-13, Windows will prompt you in this regard with an Include a folder button. Click the button and then navigate to the folder you'd like to include, and repeat as necessary. (Remember, you can include multiple folders in any Library.)

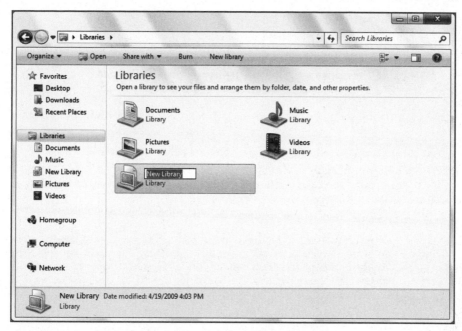

Figure 5-12: You can create your own Libraries in Windows 7.

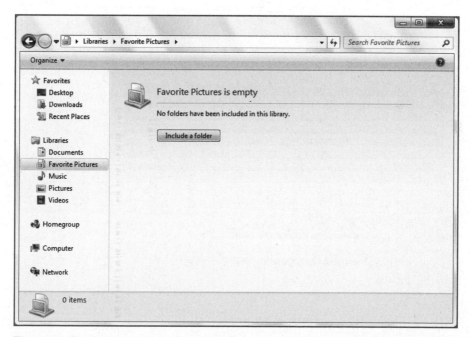

Figure 5-13: A new Library will need at least one monitored folder before it can be used.

Secret

Because Libraries are simply views of data, you can actually include folders that are within a Library in other Libraries. For example, you could include the My Documents folder in multiple Libraries if desired.

The first folder you include in a custom Library will, of course, be the default save location for that Library. You can, as always, change that later at any time using the Includes link in the Library window.

Secret

One question you may have about custom Libraries is, how does Windows determine which Arrange by options to provide? For example, the Documents library provides links for arranging by folder, author, date modified, tag, type, and name. Pictures, meanwhile, has folder, month, day, rating, and tag. But when you create a custom Library you get folder, date modified, tag, type, and name. What the . . .? Turns out that Libraries have customization options similar to folders, and that Windows 7 supports five different ways in which you can optimize a Library: General Items, Documents, Music, Pictures, and Videos. To change how your custom Library (or one of the default Libraries, for that matter) is optimized, right-click on the Library in the Windows Explorer Navigation pane, or in the Libraries window, and choose Properties. You'll see the window shown in Figure 5-14. Simply make the appropriate choice in the "Optimize this library for" drop-down list. Note that you can also use this dialog to remove a Library from the Explorer Navigational pane.

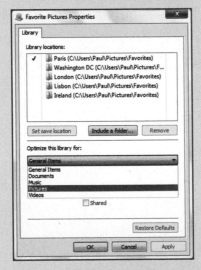

Figure 5-14: You can customize Libraries in a manner similar to the way you customize folders.

Secret   When you delete a Library, the underlying files are not deleted. In this way, Libraries work just like other shortcuts, which makes sense. Still, it's always frightening to test this kind of thing before you're sure.

Using Saved Searches

While Libraries are awesome for specific projects, sometimes you just want to search for certain kinds of files, regardless of where they're located, and then save this search for later use. This functionality is called *Search Folders*. These folders are built using Windows's indexing engine and stored in an XML file format that developers can easily access, modify, and extend. For users, they can be accessed at any time, like a regular folder.

There are two types of saved searches:

♦ Libraries
♦ Those that you build yourself

We've already spent a lot of time on Libraries, so now we want to take a look at custom saved searches.

Saved searches are dynamic, meaning that they can change every time you open them (and cause their underlying search query to run). For example, if you create a saved search that looks for all Microsoft Word (*.doc and *.docx) files (which, admittedly, wouldn't be hugely useful), you may produce a search result containing 125 matches; but if you add a new Word document to your My Documents folder and re-open the saved search, you'll see that you now have 126 matches. The point here is that saved searches aren't static, and they don't cease being relevant after they're created. Because they literally re-query the file system every time they're run—that is, when the folder is opened—saved searches will always return the most up-to-date possible results.

Searching for Files

To create a saved search, you must first search your hard drive for some kind of information. In a simple example, you might simply look for any files on your hard drive that contain your full name. To do so, open a Search window by tapping WinKey+F. If you don't have a Windows key on your keyboard, open the Start menu and tap the F3 key. This displays the Search tool, as shown in Figure 5-15.

Secret   Searching is context sensitive. If you bring up the Search tool as described here, Windows 7 will search the most common locations where documents might be stored in the file system. (These locations are called *Indexed Locations* in Windows: They are the locations in the file system that are indexed, or kept track of, by the Windows Search indexer.) However, if you use the search box in any Explorer window, Windows 7 will search only the current folder (and its subfolders).

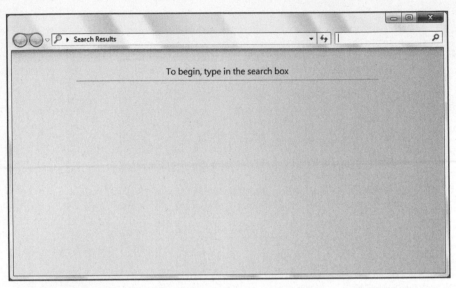

To begin, type in the search box

Figure 5-15: The Windows Search tool is a standard Explorer window. Simply type the word or phrase you are looking for into the search box.

In the Search window, select the search box in the upper-right corner of the window (it should be selected by default) and begin typing your search query. As you type, Windows Search queries the index of files contained on your hard drive and returns the results of your in-progress search in real time, as shown in Figure 5-16.

Secret

In the original shipping version of Windows Vista, Microsoft included a Search entry on the right side of the Start menu. This entry is missing in Windows 7 (it was first removed with the release of Service Pack 1) and it cannot be added back via the Taskbar and Start Menu Properties interface, as you may expect. That's because Microsoft has bowed to pressure from its competitors—specifically Internet search giant Google—which complained that the integrated search functionality in Windows made it too difficult to sell competing desktop search solutions like Google Desktop Search. To appease Google and avoid a lengthy and potentially costly antitrust investigation, Microsoft agreed to make some changes, essentially treating search like other so-called Windows "middleware" that can be replaced by users. There are several components to this change, but the obvious visual change is that the Start menu's Search entry is now missing in action. (This change does not affect Start Menu Search, however, which is denoted by the "Start Search" box in the lower-left corner of the Start menu.)

tip

If you want the absolute best performance, consider moving the index to your fastest hard drive. To do this, open Indexing and Search Options and click the Advanced button.

Secret

Not surprisingly, you can change the locations that Windows indexes by default. Equally unsurprisingly, finding the user interface for this requires a bit of spelunking. Fortunately, we've done the dirty work for you: just open the Start menu and type **indexing options** (you should see it appear after just ind) and tap Enter to display the Indexing Options control panel. A word of caution: you don't actually want to add too many file system locations to the Included locations list, and certainly not the whole hard drive, because doing so could adversely affect your PC's performance. The only reason to change this setting is if you regularly keep your document files in a nonstandard location (for example, not the Documents, Music, or Pictures Libraries, or other logical locations). To add a location to the Included locations, click the Modify button, and then the Show all locations button in the Indexed Locations dialog that appears. In the next window, you can expand the locations—like Local Disk (C:)—that appear in the Change selected locations list. As you expand the tree view, you can place a check next to those folders you'd like indexed.

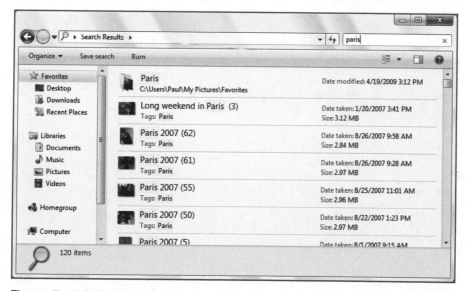

Figure 5-16: Windows Search truly is instant, assuming you're using the search box: here, search results are returned as you type.

This feature is called *as-you-type-search* or *word-wheeling*. Contrast this with most search tools, whereby you type a search query and then press Enter or a user interface button in order to instantiate the actual search. The reason Windows Search performs search queries as you type is that the information it's looking for is instantly available because it is indexed: on a typical PC, there's no performance penalty.

As Windows Search displays the search results, a green progress bar will throb through the Search window's address bar. When the query has completed, the progress bar will disappear.

Secret

Although you're probably familiar with file and folder searching using the Find function in previous Windows version or a third-party tool like Google Desktop or MSN Desktop Search, you may not be familiar with some commonly used wildcard characters, which can help fine-tune your searches. For example, the character * stands for one or more letters, whereas the ? character is used to represent any one letter.

Filtering the Search Results

A search query as general as your name can result in hundreds or thousands of hits, so it's more useful to filter the search results down a bit to make the search more specific. You do this by using the special search filter drop-down that's available from the search box. To make it appear, click anywhere in the search box, as shown in Figure 5-17.

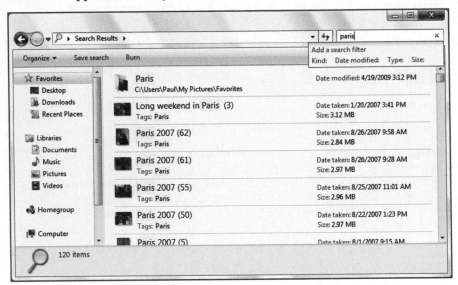

Figure 5-17: You can filter search results via a handy drop-down on the search box.

You can filter by kind, date modified, type, or size. To select one of these criteria, click the appropriate link. When you do so, Windows Search provides an appropriate drop-down list of options. The date modified option is particularly nice, providing a calendar control for picking the date, as shown in Figure 5-18.

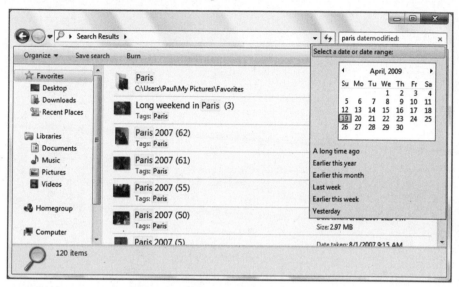

Figure 5-18: Some of the filter types are pretty creative.

You can, of course, mix and match filters too. That is, you can specify multiple filters until you have exactly the search query you're looking for.

Saving a Search

After you've created a search, especially a fairly complicated one that you may need to repeat later, it's a good idea to save it. The easiest way is to use the Save Search button on the toolbar. Alternately, tap Alt to bring up the Classic Menu, and then select Save Search from the File menu. This displays a standard Save As dialog box, where you can provide a name for your saved search. By default, saved searches are saved, naturally enough, to your Searches folder (found under your user's Home folder), but you can change the location if you'd rather save a search to your desktop, the My Documents folder, or another location. You can also drag any saved search over to the Favorite Links section of the Navigation pane in Windows Explorer so you can access it easily later.

Saved searches use the blue "stacks" icon that debuted in Windows Vista; and because they're treated like Libraries, you get the header area and resulting Arrange by options, so you can view your search results via organizational stacks, as shown in Figure 5-19.

Figure 5-19: Saved searches employ the little-used "stacks" icon from Windows Vista.

Secret

When you save a search it is automatically added to the Favorites list in the Explorer Navigation pane as well. Apparently, Microsoft feels that if you went to all that trouble, then you must really intend to keep using this saved search.

Configuring Search

In Windows 7, Windows Search options have been added to the classic Folder Options window. To access these options, open Folder Options—the fastest way is by typing **folder options** into Start Menu Search—and navigate to the new Search tab, shown in Figure 5-20.

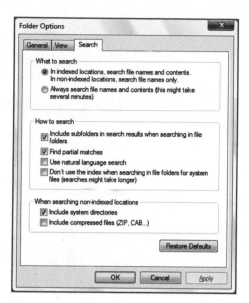

Figure 5-20: Windows Search is now configured via Folder Options.

Summary

Microsoft may have abandoned WinFS, but the heart and soul of that technology lives on in the Library and saved search functionality in Windows 7. Windows Search in Windows 7 is a huge improvement over the far more limited Find functionality in Windows XP, with numerous entry points in the OS, including every Explorer window, and intelligent results based on where the search was instigated. You can even search for applications, documents, and other objects directly from the Start menu. Windows Search functionality also includes a pretty well-hidden ability to save searches as dynamic virtual folders called *saved searches* that you can access again and again as if they were normal shell folders. It's no wonder that even innovative Apple copied this functionality from Microsoft: the deep OS integration in its Mac OS X Spotlight feature was directly inspired by the integrated search work Microsoft first announced it would include in Windows Vista. That integration is even deeper and more impressive in Windows 7.

Personalizing and Configuring Windows 7

Chapter

6

◆ ◆

In This Chapter

Customizing the Start menu

Configuring folders

Replacing Windows 7's compressed folders with something useful

Replacing the user interface

Branding Windows 7

"Decrapifying" your PC

Making Windows 7 boot faster

Improving Windows 7's performance

Monitoring Windows 7's reliability

Customizing Virtual Memory

Utilizing ReadyBoost

Adding more RAM to a Windows 7–based PC

◆ ◆

Windows 7 is the most capable version of Windows yet created, with an unprecedented collection of useful application software and a technically impressive and elegant user interface. Of course, Windows 7 is just software, so it's not perfect; and depending on your needs or wants, you may prefer to customize Windows 7 to make it your own and to have it provide a more comfortable environment for your day-to-day work. This chapter presents a collection of ways to personalize and customize Microsoft's latest operating system.

Virtually anytime you see words like *personalize* and *customize*—or, heaven forbid, *tweak*—used together with Windows, you can expect Microsoft's most controversial tool, the Registry Editor, to raise its ugly head. Well, we're not going down that road. Life is too short to waste an entire chapter of this book—not to mention hours of your life—teaching you how to spelunk around the archaic and arcane depths of Windows' bowels. Sure, you'll see a handful of references to the Registry Editor in this book—in this chapter even—but only when no simpler alternatives are available. And just as you don't need to know how an internal-combustion engine works in order to drive a car, there are ways to make Windows 7 your own without resorting to an ancient tool like the Registry Editor. You're going to customize Windows 7 the smart way!

The Windows 7 User Interface

Although Microsoft improved the Windows user interface in ways both subtle and profound in Windows 7, that doesn't mean it's perfect out of the box. Everyone's needs and wants are different, and fortunately Microsoft has engineered Windows 7 in such a way that you can configure the system to your preferences. This section describes some of the ways in which you can tame the Windows 7 UI and make it your own.

Customizing the Start Menu

As discussed in Chapter 4, the Windows 7 Start menu is an evolution of the Start menu that debuted in Windows XP, and it offers a much smarter interface for interacting with the applications, documents, and other content on your PC than did the Start menus from previous Windows versions.

As shown in Figure 6-1, the Windows 7 Start menu is divided into a number of logical areas, each of which covers specific functionality.

These areas include the following:

♦ **Pinned items:** Found at the top-left corner of the Start menu, this area contains shortcuts that are permanently displayed regardless of how often you use them. Unlike Windows Vista, there are no pinned shortcuts displayed by default in Windows 7.

♦ **Most Recently Used (MRU) list:** Here, taking up the majority of the left side of the Start menu window, is a list of the applications you use most frequently. The algorithm Microsoft uses to determine this list is decidedly hokey, because it gives precedence to an application you just used instead of one you use regularly, every single day. It also doesn't take into account applications that were not launched from the Start menu at all.

♦ **All Programs:** This link reveals the All Programs list, a combination of the shortcuts stored in your user profile's Start menu folder structure and the Public account's Start menu folder structure. Unlike Windows XP, the All Programs list appears inside of the Start menu window instead of popping up in a separate, hard-to-navigate cascading menu.

Figure 6-1: The Windows 7 Start menu

♦ **Start Menu Search:** Arguably the single greatest Windows feature in over a decade, and easily the best feature of the Start menu, Start Menu Search enables you to quickly and easily find any application, shortcut, document, e-mail, contact, or other searchable object. It's magic, and we love it.

Secret

How incredible is Start Menu Search? It can sometimes even sense what you're looking for. Say you want to work with Windows 7's disk partitioning tools, but you can't think of the name of the tool, let alone where to find it. Start typing *partition* in Start Menu Search and, sure enough, an option entitled *Create and format hard disk partitions* appears. The tool it launches? The Disk Management console, of course. Magic!

♦ **User picture:** Here you will see the user picture you configured when you created your user account. It changes to different system icons as you mouse over the links on the right side of the Start menu.

♦ **Links:** This is a list of important system locations that Microsoft thinks you will need regularly. These include such things as special shell folders (Documents, Music), common shell locations (Computer, Games), configuration settings (Control Panel, Default Programs), and Help and Support.

♦ **Sleep/Shutdown:** On the bottom right of the Start menu are two buttons, the right-most of which includes a cascading pop-up menu with various power-management and shutdown-related options. These two buttons are configured differently by default depending on your system's power-management capabilities. (They can be modified, as discussed in Chapter 17.)

Most Start menu customizations occur via the Taskbar and Start Menu Properties dialog, shown in Figure 6-2. You can display this dialog by right-clicking the Start button (sometimes called the *Start Orb*) and clicking Properties. A related dialog, Customize Start Menu, is displayed by clicking the Customize button.

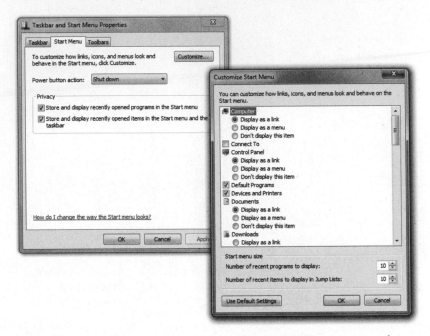

Figure 6-2: Start menu customization typically starts here.

The Windows 7 Start menu is full-featured, but you may decide to tailor it to fit your needs. Here are some of our favorite Start menu tweaks.

Changing Your Logon Picture

Microsoft supplies 36 user pictures from which you can choose, an improvement from Window Vista's 12. Instead of using Windows 7's built-in images, why not use a favorite photograph or other image? Here's how: open the Start menu and click on the user picture at the top-right corner of the Start menu. This causes the User Accounts window to open. Click the link titled Change Your Picture, and you'll see the interface shown in Figure 6-3.

Click the Browse for More Pictures link and then use the standard Open File window that appears to find a favorite photo.

Secret

Because your account picture always appears inside of a square area, you may want to edit a photo before performing these steps, cropping it accordingly into a square shape. That way, Windows 7 won't have to do its own (non-optimal) cropping.

Figure 6-3: You don't have to settle for Windows 7's built-in account pictures.

Adding, Configuring, and Removing Start Menu Links

Microsoft's options for Start menu links—those important system locations shown on the right side of the Start menu—are serviceable, but there's always room for improvement. To configure which items appear in the list—and remove the links you don't want while adding back those you do—open the Customize Start Menu window. There's a list at the top of this window that enables you to configure which links appear and, in many cases, *how* they appear; some links can appear as cascading submenus instead of standard buttons that launch separate windows. Here are the Start menu links you can configure from this UI:

- ◆ **Computer:** Can be displayed as a link, as a menu, or disabled. This item is displayed as a link by default.
- ◆ **Connect To:** Can be enabled or disabled. Unlike Windows Vista, this item is disabled by default.
- ◆ **Control Panel:** Can be displayed as a link, as a menu, or disabled. This item is displayed as a link by default.
- ◆ **Default Programs:** Can be enabled or disabled. This item is enabled by default.
- ◆ **Devices and Printers:** Can be enabled or disabled. This item is enabled by default.
- ◆ **Documents:** Can be displayed as a link, as a menu, or disabled. This item is displayed as a link by default.
- ◆ **Downloads:** Can be displayed as a link, as a menu, or disabled. This item is disabled by default.
- ◆ **Favorites menu:** Can be enabled or disabled. This item is disabled by default.

✦ **Games:** Can be displayed as a link, as a menu, or disabled. This item is displayed as a link by default on Windows 7 Home Basic, Home Premium, and Ultimate. It is disabled by default on Windows 7 Professional.

✦ **Help:** Can be enabled or disabled. This item is enabled by default.

✦ **HomeGroup:** Can be enabled or disabled. This item is disabled by default.

✦ **Music:** Can be displayed as a link, as a menu, or disabled. This item is displayed as a link by default.

✦ **Network:** Can be enabled or disabled. This item is disabled by default.

✦ **Personal folder:** Can be displayed as a link, as a menu, or disabled. This item is displayed as a link by default.

✦ **Pictures:** Can be displayed as a link, as a menu, or disabled. This item is displayed as a link by default.

✦ **Recent Items:** Can be enabled or disabled. This item is disabled by default.

✦ **Recorded TV:** Can be displayed as a link, as a menu, or disabled. This item is disabled by default.

✦ **Run command:** Can be enabled or disabled. This item is disabled by default.

✦ **System administrative tools:** Can be displayed as a link, as a menu, or disabled. This item is disabled by default.

✦ **Use large icons:** This item is enabled by default.

✦ **Videos:** Can be displayed as a link, as a menu, or disabled. This item is disabled by default.

For the most part, the defaults are acceptable. You can safely remove Default Programs, as you're unlikely to need it very often. One thing you might want to experiment with is changing some links into menus. As shown in Figure 6-4, the effect is quite interesting. Some love it, some don't.

Additionally, this section of the Customize Start Menu window provides a few options that aren't related to the Start Menu Links area, though they're no less important. Key among them is Highlight Newly Installed Programs, which can be enabled or disabled. This item is enabled by default, but we strongly recommend disabling it, as the effect when enabled is very annoying.

Figure 6-4: Certain Start menu links can be configured as menus.

Configuring Folder Options

Although the version of Windows Explorer found in Windows 7 is quite a bit different from that found in Windows XP and Windows Vista, some things haven't changed much at all. One of these things is Explorer's Folder Options functionality, which is typically accessed via the (hidden, in Windows 7) Tools menu. (You can also access Folder Options directly via Start Menu Search; just type **folder options**.) The Folder Options dialog, shown in Figure 6-5, presents three tabs that are chock-full of configurable goodness.

Figure 6-5: Folder Options hasn't changed much since Windows Vista, which is fine, as it's still very useful.

On the default General tab, you'll see options that broadly affect all Explorer windows. For example, you can switch between opening each folder in its own window or a single window and choose whether or not to automatically show all folders in the Navigation pane.

Things really get interesting on the View tab. As shown in Figure 6-6, this tab provides a massive number of settings, so it's easy to get lost.

Some of the key settings you can configure here include the following:

- **Always show menus:** By default, menus are hidden (made visible by pressing the Alt key).
- **Hidden files and folders:** By default, hidden files and folders are...hidden.
- **Hide extensions for known file types** and **Show drive letters:** In a long-standing bid for simplicity, Microsoft is working to at least hide things that confuse people, such as drive letters and file extensions. You can re-enable the display of file extensions, however, and you can hide the display of drive letters.
- **Hide protected operating system files (Recommended):** There are hidden files, and then there are *hidden* files. Protected operating systems are the latter, and they are replaced automatically by Windows 7 if you try to modify or delete them, so Microsoft just hides them to avoid any confusion.

◆ **Use check boxes to select items:** This feature is covered in Chapter 19 because it's enabled by default on Tablet PCs (and Ultra-Mobile PCs) but disabled by default on all other systems (including touch-based PCs, where this functionality would also be quite useful).

◆ **Use Sharing Wizard:** When you right-click a folder and click Share with, then click Specific people, Windows 7 utilizes an easy-to-use File Sharing Wizard, a feature covered in Chapter 9. If you disable this option, you will be left with the old XP-style Sharing dialogs and tab. While normally we would prefer the latter, Windows 7's File Sharing Wizard is refreshingly simple and easy to use. You should leave it enabled, really. (Remember, too, that Windows 7's HomeGroup feature makes it easier to share digital media content, documents, and printers without resorting to these legacy sharing technologies.)

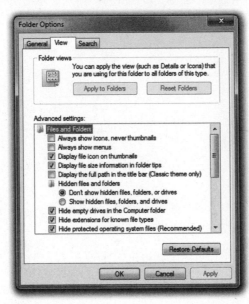

Figure 6-6: Virtually anything you'd like to configure about Explorer windows happens right here.

Replacing Windows 7's Compressed Folders with Something More Useful

Microsoft has included ZIP compression compatibility in Windows for a while now courtesy of an incurably lame feature called Compressed Folders. This feature is still present in Windows 7, but it's pretty basic, so we recommend replacing it with a worthier alternative—WinRAR (www.rarlabs.com), which works with the more efficient RAR compression format as well as older formats such as CAB, ARJ, and TAR. WinRAR is shown in Figure 6-7.

WinRAR isn't the only compression game in town. If you're looking for maximum squeeze capabilities, look into WinRK (www.msoftware.co.nz). Other more popular alternatives to consider include PKZIP for Windows (www.pkware.com), WinZIP (www.winzip.com/), SecureZIP (www.securezip.com), and 7-Zip (www.7-zip.org).

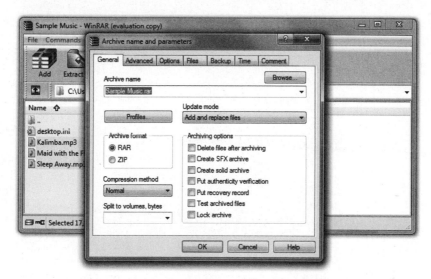

Figure 6-7: WinRAR is an awesome compression utility and far superior to Compressed Folders.

Replacing the User Interface

We happen to believe that Windows 7's user interface is a tremendous improvement over those of both its predecessors, Windows XP and Windows Vista, and various competing operating systems such as Mac OS X. You may not agree. If that's the case, you might consider one of the utilities out there that enable you to replace the standard Windows 7 UIs with new skins, some of which are quite attractive. The best of the lot is Stardock WindowBlinds, which offers custom UI skins with configurable color schemes (see Figure 6-8).

An alternate (and wildly popular) approach is to replace several system files with modi-fied ones to enable Windows to use homebrew Microsoft Styles (.msstyle) files. Rafael has been modifying the system files responsible for "theming" in Windows since they debuted in Windows (code-named as Whistler) and upkeeps a repository of files on his site (www.withinwindows.com/uxtheme-files).

Microsoft Styles files, unlike Theme (.theme) and Theme Pack (.themepack) files, enable you to control how all the various UI elements in Windows look, like the Start button, the Taskbar's height, and even the appearance of window shadows. If you're interested in creating your own Microsoft Style, and have a lot of time on your hands, check out Ave's Windows 7 Style Builder (www.win7stylebuilder.com).

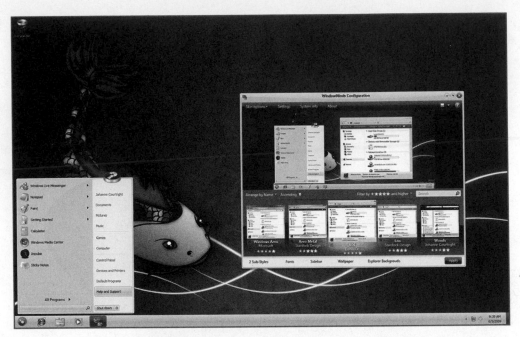

Figure 6-8: Tired of the stock Windows UI? WindowBlinds is the tool for you.

Secret   You may be wondering why Microsoft would lock down the use of custom styles. Branding and support are two reasons. Imagine the nightmare scenario of trying to explain where the Start Orb is located when it has been modified to appear as a sunflower instead.

Branding Windows 7 like a PC Maker

This one is just good old-fashioned fun: if you've ever purchased a new PC, you've probably noticed that the PC maker has customized the System Properties window with their logo and other information. Well, you can customize this information yourself. There are two ways to handle this. You can muck around in the Registry, which is time-consuming and difficult, or you can simply use the wonderful freeware utility called WinBubble (`http://unlockforus.blogspot.com`), shown in Figure 6-9.

Figure 6-9: WinBubble provides a number of tweaking features, including the capability to modify the OEM branding.

Once you apply the changes, check out the System Properties window to see the havoc you've wrought (see Figure 6-10). Neat, eh?

> **tip**
>
> In case it's not obvious, WinBubble can also be used to *remove* branding, so if you purchased a PC and want to get rid of that HP logo in the System Properties window, this is a great way to do so.

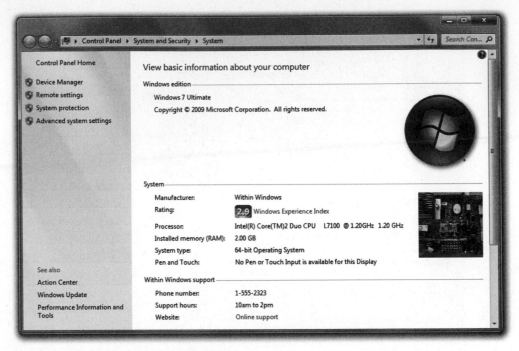

Figure 6-10: A customized System Properties window, courtesy of WinBubble

Secret

WinBubble does *a lot* more than just help you change the branding. In fact, this handy utility is, we believe, the tweaking tool that's closest in spirit and functionality to Microsoft's long-admired TweakUI. Microsoft never made a version of TweakUI for Windows Vista or Windows 7 for some reason, but it doesn't matter: WinBubble fills that gap quite nicely.

Unfortunately, WinBubble hasn't been updated to take advantage of the ability to brand the logon screen, new to Windows 7. This tweak isn't difficult to implement, however. Simply open the Registry Editor (Start Menu Search, type **regedit**) and navigate to HKEY_LOCAL_MACHINE\Software\Microsoft\Windows\CurrentVersion\Authentication\LogonUI\Background. Then, click Edit ➪ New ➪ DWORD, and name it "OEMBackground," as shown in Figure 6-11. Finally, double-click the newly created value name and assign it a data value of 1.

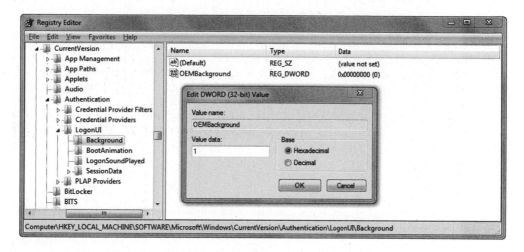

Figure 6-11: Adding the OEMBackground DWORD

After turning on this feature, navigate to the C:\Windows\System32\Oobe\Info\ Backgrounds folder (creating any missing folders in the process) and drop your background image inside. There are a few rules you must follow, however:

◆ The image must be *less than* 256 kilobytes in size.
◆ The image must be named as background<*height*>x<*width*>.jpg (e.g., background1920x1200.jpg).

Secret

Changing your theme will unfortunately trample over your logon background.

Secret

Due to the number of different resolutions out there, you may have issues changing the logon background image. The supported resolutions follow:

768×1280, 900×1440, 960×1280, 1024×768, 1024×1280, 1280×960, 1280×768, 1280×1024, 1360×768, 1440×900, 1600×1200, 1920×1200

If you don't see your resolution in the preceding list, rest assured there's a failsafe. Simply rename your image to "backgroundDefault.jpg," and you'll be good to go. Keep in mind, however, your image may be resized, stretched, or otherwise distorted to fit your weird resolution.

Making It Faster: Performance Tweaks

One of the biggest complaints about upgrading Windows, especially from those coming from Windows XP, is that the new system doesn't perform as speedily on the same hardware. Truth be told, Windows 7 works just fine if you operate the system with reasonable hardware specs, and of course it performs much better than Vista. Regardless of the performance attributes of your PC, faster is always better. In this section, we'll show you some ways you can make Windows 7 run more efficiently.

Taking Out the Trash

While we do recommend buying a new PC with Windows 7 preinstalled to get the best experience, the truth is that many PC makers seem to go out of their way to screw up what should be a happy experience. They do so by loading down their new PCs with extensive collections of largely useless utilities, a practice that's gotten so out of hand that the industry has adopted the term *crapware* to describe it. Fortunately, there are a few things you can do to avoid crapware. First, you can purchase PCs only from those PC makers that offer no crapware, such as Dell. Or you can simply not worry about it and download a wonderful free utility called the PC Decrapifier (`www.pcdecrapifier.com`), which automates the removal of trialware and other annoying crapware that PC makers tend to preinstall (you know, for your convenience).

The PC Decrapifier, shown in Figure 6-12, is free for personal use and highly recommended if you're looking for that new-PC smell. However, be sure to uncheck any items you do want to keep, as some of the so-called crapware that PC Decrapifier finds might actually be useful.

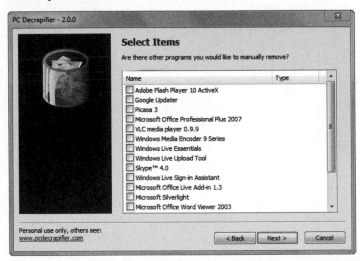

Figure 6-12: The PC Decrapifier will help you clean the junk off your PC.

---

tip   The PC Decrapifier works perfectly well on any PC, not just new PCs. In fact, it's a great tool for automating the cleanup of a PC you've been using (and abusing) for a long time.

Making It Boot Faster

Throughout the years, all Windows versions have shared a common problem: they degrade in performance over time and boot more slowly the longer the computer is used. Microsoft addressed this gradual sludgification somewhat in Windows Vista, and even more in Windows 7. Compared to Windows XP there are certainly some improvements. For example, unlike XP, it's actually possible to take an aging Windows 7 install, clean some things up, and get it back in tip-top shape. With XP, you'd eventually be forced to reinstall the entire OS in order to regain lost performance.

Boot-up speed, of course, is a primary concern. In order to speed up the time it takes for your PC to return to life each time you sit down in front of it, you can take a number of steps:

◆ **Remove unwanted startup items:** Over time, as you install more and more software on your computer, the number of small utilities, application launchers, and, most annoyingly, application *prelaunchers* (which essentially make it seem like those applications start more quickly later because large chunks of them are already preloaded) that are configured to run at startup multiply dramatically. There are several ways you can cull this list, but the best one is to use Autoruns, a Microsoft Sysinternals freebie (`technet.microsoft.com/en-us/sysinternals/bb963902.aspx`).

To cull the list of startup applications, download and open Autoruns (Start Menu Search, and enter `http://live.sysinternals.com/autoruns.exe`) and click Run. You'll be presented with the scary-looking window shown in Figure 6-13.

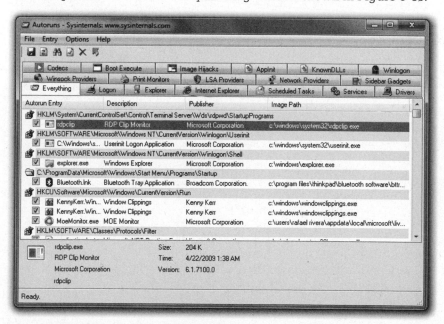

Figure 6-13: Autoruns at first glance looks daunting but it's actually very simple to use.

Before attempting to make any systemwide changes, click File ⇨ Run as Administrator. This will restart the application under administrative credentials to give you full access to startup entries on the system. After dealing with the User Account Control prompt that appears, click the Logon tab to view a list of programs that execute right after you log in. By clicking Hide Microsoft and Windows Entries in the Options menu, you can narrow the list down to just third-party gunk. Finally, if you'd rather disable than delete, simply uncheck the entries you wish to disable and you're set. Later, when you feel comfortable without the gunk, you can return to Autoruns and delete it once and for all.

Secret While Autoruns sports a dizzying array of other tabs, such as LSA and Winsock Providers, KnownDLLs, and Drivers, we suggest you limit clean-up activities to the safer Logon, Sidebar Gadgets, and Scheduled Tasks tabs. As Autoruns provides an unbiased view into the internal wiring of various Windows components, you could inadvertently and irreparably break Windows.

Secret Windows XP and Vista users can use the Software Explorer feature of Windows Defender to remove unwanted startup items as well. This feature, alas, was removed from Windows 7, because Microsoft believed that it detracted from the main function of Defender (the removal of malware). We disagree: the line between true malware and unwanted preloaders is pretty gray.

♦ **Do a little cleanup:** There are a number of things you can clean up on your PC that will have mild effects on performance. One of the more effective is Windows 7's hidden Disk Cleanup tool (Start Menu Search, and type **disk clean**), shown in Figure 6-14. This little wonder frees up hard drive space by removing unused temporary files. (Free hard drive space is important for keeping virtual memory and other applications (like Adobe Photoshop) running optimally. Virtual-memory optimization is covered in just a bit.)

♦ **Don't shut down the PC:** This one may seem obvious or even humorous, but think about it: why are you shutting down the PC anyway? Windows 7 supports advanced power management states, including Hybrid Sleep and Hibernation, and these states enable your PC to "shut down" and "power on" far more quickly than actual shutdowns and power-ups. We examine Windows 7's power-management functionality in Chapter 17, but don't be thrown by the chapter title: the power-management information there applies to both desktop PCs and mobile computers.

Secret

You can automate Disk Cleanup using another hidden Windows 7 utility—the Task Scheduler. This process is documented in Windows 7's Help and Support: Search for *Schedule Disk Cleanup* to learn more.

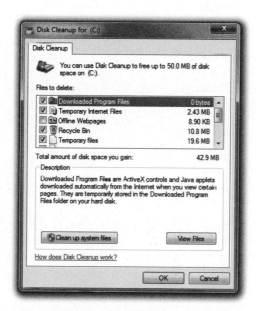

Figure 6-14: The Disk Cleanup utility can clear out unneeded files.

Using Windows 7's Performance Options

While all the performance tools are available individually throughout the system, Windows 7 introduces a nice list of available tools, if you can find it. To unearth the listing, first type **performance info** into Start Menu Search and press Enter. In the Performance Information and Tools view, click Advanced Tools in the left-hand pane. You will now see a listing, as shown in Figure 6-15, of all available performance-related tools within Windows, each of which is described in Table 6-1.

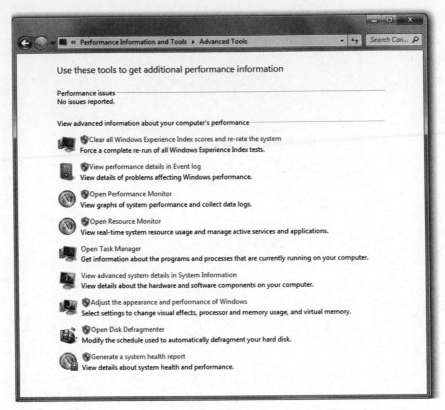

Figure 6-15: Windows 7's Advanced Performance Tools—all in one, neat list.

Table 6-1: Windows 7 Performance Tools

Performance Tool	What It Does
Clear all Windows Experience Index scores and re-rate the system	Re-assesses system performance and generates a new Windows Experience Index (WEI) score. You would typically run this after installing newer, faster hardware components (for example, a video card).
View performance details in Event Log	Provides insight into any performance-related warnings or errors. Unfortunately, clicking this link does not open the Event Viewer with Performance Information upfront. You need to navigate to Applications and Services Logs ⇨ Microsoft ⇨ Windows ⇨ Diagnostics-Performance, and then click Operational.
Open Performance Monitor	Enables you to view and gather performance data, either in real time or from a log file, and generate reports.

Performance Tool	What It Does
Open Resource Monitor	Enables you to view information about hardware (for example, CPU, memory, and so on) and software (for example, handles) resources in real time.
Open Task Manager	Infamous tool that enables you to display (and, more important, kill) running programs, processes, and services. It also provides network status and basic performance information.
View advanced system details in System Information	Enables you to view details about your computer's hardware configuration, computer components, and software, including drivers. Very handy and can even be run via the Command Prompt.
Adjust the appearance and performance of Windows	Enables you to tweak visual effects, processor and memory usage, and virtual memory settings. We'll be using this tool in the next section.
Open Disk Defragmenter	Rearranges bits of files and folders on your disk (defragments) for faster, more efficient hard disk access. With solid-state drives on the rise, the usefulness of this tool is declining.
Generate a system health report	Analyzes your system from top to bottom and provides a *very* thorough report on various performance warnings and problems detected. If you suspect performance issues, run this tool first.

Secret

When you are generating a system health report, the result is quite hard to read. You may find it easier to read the HTML report by exporting it (click File ⇨ Save As).

Appearance and Performance Tweaking

Windows 7 continues to use an advanced desktop composition engine and provides a number of subtle but pleasing UI animations by default. Some of this stuff, however, may be a bit much; and all of it takes its toll on the performance of your PC. Fortunately, the operating system includes a number of configurable performance options worth tweaking if you have an older PC and have noticed some slowdowns with Windows 7.

To open the *classic* Performance Options window (identical to the *Adjust the appearance and performance of Windows* tool in the previous section), type **adjust perf** into Start Menu Search. Here you can choose between three automated settings (Let Windows choose what's best for my computer, Adjust for best appearance, and Adjust for best performance).

Alternately, you can click the Custom option and then enable and disable any of the 15 user-interface-related options that appear in the custom settings list. Most of these options should be self-explanatory, and many appeared in previous versions of Windows, but a couple of options are worth highlighting:

◆ **Animations in the taskbar and Start menu (New to Windows 7):** With the debut of the new taskbar, a number of new animations have been added (for example, the fading in and out of Jump Lists). If you'd rather these menus just appear, shortening menu display time, disable this feature.

◆ **Use visual styles on windows and buttons:** Disabling this feature causes Windows 7 to revert to the ancient-looking Windows Classic user interface. It will dramatically increase the performance of your PC at the expense of attractiveness and graphical reliability.

Monitoring Performance and Reliability

Windows has had a Performance Monitor since the earliest days of NT, but with Windows Vista, Microsoft debuted an amazing new utility, the Reliability Monitor, which tracks the overall reliability of your PC over time, ever since the first day you booted. Both utilities used to be part of a combined Reliability and Performance Monitor tool, but now, in Windows 7, they exist as separate tools. You can access the Reliability Monitor, shown in Figure 6-16, by typing **relia** into Start Menu Search.

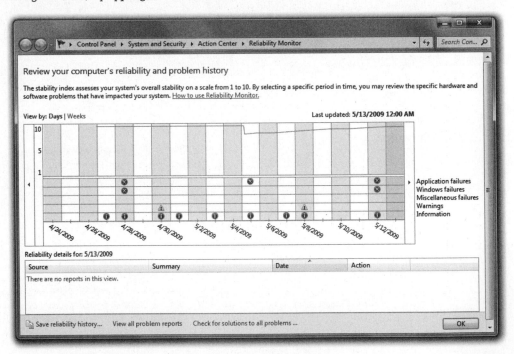

Figure 6-16: Another hidden wonder: the Reliability Monitor.

The Reliability Monitor assigns a reliability rating to your PC on a scale from 1 to 10, where 1 is horrible and 10 is perfect. Out of the box, Windows 7 gets a perfect 10 but from there on its all downhill: any glitch or failure in any application, hardware, or Windows will cause the reliability rating to plummet. Meanwhile, days with no problems are barely rewarded, with only a slight bump. If anything, we think Windows is being too hard on itself.

Consider Figure 6-17. Here you see a decidedly different reliability picture, a PC on which multiple applications have failed, repeatedly, over a period of time. While you can't see it in this window, the reliability rating of this machine is sad.

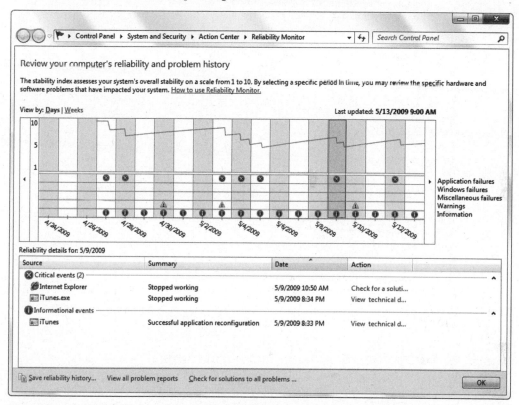

Figure 6-17: Ouch. Windows 7 is painfully honest about unreliable systems.

What went wrong with this disaster of a PC? We must be miserable using that machine, right? Not exactly. The Reliability Monitor shown in Figure 6-17 is from a daily-use desktop PC. This machine is used to test a wide range of software, and many of the application failures are related to beta versions of a single application that was known to have issues at the time. You can see individual problems by clicking on dates and viewing what went wrong, as shown in Figure 6-18.

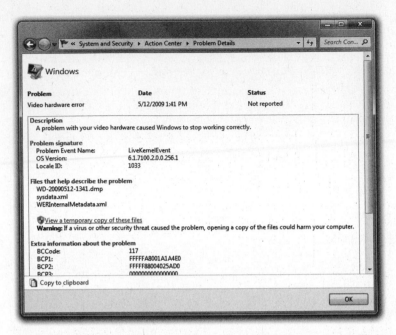

Figure 6-18: Dive in and you can see where Windows—or, more likely, a third-party application—let you down.

That's what's beautiful about the Reliability Monitor. It gives you a place to see exactly what is causing the problems. Then you can take steps to fix those problems. (In this case, that simply meant waiting for an updated version of the poorly performing application.)

This illustrates why we think the Reliability Monitor is a bit harsh. Over the period shown, this PC was actually quite reliable.

Improving Windows 7's Memory

A long time ago PCs of a bygone era had woefully inadequate amounts of RAM, and the versions of Windows used back then had to regularly swap large chunks of RAM back to slower, disk-based storage called *virtual memory*. Virtual memory was (and still is, really) an inexpensive way to overcome the limitations inherent in using a low-RAM PC; but as users ran more and more applications, the amount of swapping would reach a crescendo of sorts as an invisible line was crossed and performance suffered.

Today, PCs with 4 to 8GB of RAM are commonplace, so manually managing Windows 7's virtual memory settings is rarely needed. That said, you can still do so if you want. In older versions of Windows, you had to jump through quite a few hoops. With Windows 7's Start Menu Search enhancements, finding and opening this dialog is much easier.

1. Open the *classic* Performance Options dialog by performing a Start Menu Search for **adjust perf**.

2. In the Performance Options dialog that appears, navigate to the Advanced tab and click the Change button. The Virtual Memory window will appear, as shown in Figure 6-19.

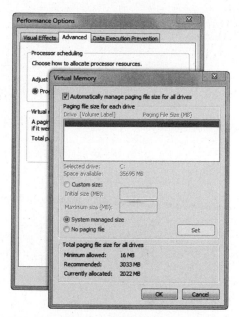

Figure 6-19: Virtual Memory options

By default, like previous versions of Windows, Windows 7 is configured to automatically maintain and manage the paging file, which is the single disk-based file that represents your PC's virtual memory. Windows 7 will grow and shrink this file based on its needs, and its behavior varies wildly depending on how much RAM is on your system: PCs with less RAM need virtual memory far more often than those with 4GB of RAM (or more with 64-bit versions of Windows 7).

While we don't generally recommend screwing around with the swap file, Windows 7's need to constantly resize the paging file on low-RAM systems is one exception. The problem with this behavior is that resizing the paging is a resource-intensive activity that slows performance. Therefore, if you have less than 2GB of RAM and can't upgrade for some reason, you might want to manually manage virtual memory and set the paging file to be a fixed size—one that won't grow and shrink over time.

To do this, uncheck the option titled *Automatically manage paging file sizes for all drives* and select Custom size. Then determine how much space to set aside by multiplying the system RAM (2GB or less) by 2 to 3 times. On a PC with 2GB of RAM, for example, you might specify a value of 5,120 (where 2GB of RAM is 2,048MB, times 2.5). This value should be added to both the Initial size and Maximum size text boxes to ensure that the page file does not grow and shrink over time.

Secret

Optionally, you can put the paging file on a faster, separate hard disk (a physical hard disk, not just a second partition) for better performance.

Using ReadyBoost

Another way to improve performance on systems with 2GB or less of RAM is to use a new Windows 7 feature called *ReadyBoost*. This technology uses spare storage space on USB-based memory devices such as memory sticks to increase your computer's performance. It does this by caching the most frequently accessed information to the USB device, which is typically much faster than reading directly from the hard drive. (Information cached to the device is encrypted so it can't be read on other systems.)

There are a number of caveats, of course. First, the USB device you choose to use must meet certain speed requirements or Windows will not allow it to be used in this fashion. Second, storage space that is set aside on a USB device for ReadyBoost cannot be used for other purposes until you reformat the device.

Secret In previous versions of Windows, you were limited to the use of only one USB device and a maximum ReadyBoost cache size of 4GB. Both of these limitations have been lifted in Windows 7.

In our testing, ReadyBoost seems to have the most impact on systems with less than 1GB of RAM, and it clearly benefits netbooks and notebooks more than desktop PCs, as it's often difficult or impossible to increase the RAM on older portable machines.

When you insert a compatible USB device into a Windows 7 machine, you will see a Speed Up My System option in the Auto Play dialog that appears. When you select this option, the ReadyBoost tab of the Properties dialog of the associated device will appear, as shown in Figure 6-20, enabling you to configure a portion of the device's storage space. It recommends the ideal amount based on the capacity of the device and your system's RAM (ensuring a RAM-to-cache minimum of 1:1 and a maximum of 2.5:1).

Obviously, ReadyBoost won't work unless the USB memory key is plugged into your PC. This can be a bit of a hassle because you need to remember to keep plugging it in every time you break out your portable computer. Still, ReadyBoost is a great enhancement and a welcome feature, especially when a PC would otherwise run poorly with Windows 7.

Secret If you're using a PC containing a solid-state drive (SSD)—a drive similar to a flash stick vice a spindle of spinning platters—ReadyBoost will be turned off, because the disk is fast enough that ReadyBoost will unlikely provide any additional gain in performance.

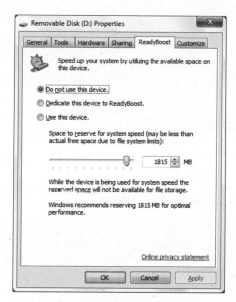

Figure 6-20: ReadyBoost provides an inexpensive and simple way to boost performance on low-RAM PCs.

Adding More RAM

This final tip may seem a bit obvious, but Windows 7 is a resource hog (albeit less so than Windows Vista), and it will steal whatever RAM you throw at it. Our advice here is simple: 2GB of RAM is the minimum for a happy Windows 7 PC; most PC users would be better off with more. If your PC can support 4GB or even 8GB of RAM, upgrade. Memory is inexpensive these days, so cost is rarely an issue.

Microsoft says that 32-bit versions of Windows support up to 4GB of RAM (while 64-bit versions support quite a bit more). While this is technically true, 32-bit versions of Windows are actually limited in their support of RAM because of its underlying architecture. Therefore, even on systems with a full 4GB of RAM, 32-bit versions of Windows can really access only about 3.12GB to 3.5GB of RAM, depending on your configuration. In the initially shipped version of Windows Vista, the System Information window would accurately portray how much RAM it could access, but this confused (and probably infuriated) those who paid for and installed 4GB of RAM, so with Windows Vista Service Pack 1 (SP1), Windows now reports that your PC has 4GB installed, even though it can't use all of it. Windows 7 carries over this behavior unaltered.

The obvious question is whether you should even bother upgrading to 4GB of RAM when your 32-bit version of Windows 7 can't actually address almost 1GB of that storage space anyway. The answer is an unqualified yes, for two reasons. First, you'd have to really go out of your way to upgrade a PC to 3GB of RAM instead of 4GB, and the cost differential would be minimal. Second, who says you're always going to be using a 32-bit version of Windows? You may later decide to go the 64-bit route. When that happens, you'll be happy you went for the full 4GB of RAM instead of saving a few pennies to no good end.

continues

continued

For the record, we max out the RAM on every single PC we purchase because the costs are so minimal and the effect is extremely positive. You just can't overstate how important more RAM is to Windows. 8GB of RAM may have been a fantasy a few years ago, but for a modern, Windows 7–based PC, that's just a starting point.

Summary

Windows 7 supports a wide range of configuration options and other tweaks, and only some of them are found in this chapter. Throughout the book, we provide advice and tips about configuring and personalizing various aspects of the OS as well; but with a system as vast and complicated as Windows 7, there's always more to be done, and entire books have been written solely about optimizing, customizing, and otherwise tweaking Windows. It is hoped that this chapter gives you some idea of the kinds of things you can do to make Windows 7 a truly personalized experience.

Part III

Security and Networking

Windows 7
Security Features

Chapter
7

◆ ◆

In This Chapter

Using Action Center to monitor the health of your PC

Using Windows Defender to defend your PC against spyware

Protecting your system with Windows Firewall

Keeping your PC secure with Windows Update

Browsing the Web securely with Internet Explorer 8

◆ ◆

Although visual, up-front features like Windows Aero get all the press with Windows 7, some of the more important, if less obvious, changes in this new operating system occur under the hood. For example, Microsoft further componentized its core OS in Windows 7, a change that enables more efficient updating and servicing. The more important under-the-hood work in Windows 7, of course, involves security changes. Whereas Windows XP had to be changed dramatically in Service Pack 2 (SP2) to be more secure, Windows 7 was designed from the outset to be as secure as possible, building off and expanding on the work the company first did in XP SP2 and Windows Vista. In this chapter, you examine the new security features in Windows 7 that will affect you in day-to-day use.

Security and Windows 7

It's been a tough decade for Windows users. As Microsoft's operating system entered the dominant phase of its existence, hackers began focusing almost solely on Windows, as that's where all the users are. As a result, various Windows versions have suffered through a seemingly never-ending series of electronic attacks, security vulnerabilities, and high-profile malware breakouts.

In 2003 Microsoft halted development of its major operating system and application products and began an internal review of its software-development practices. The company reexamined the source code to its then-current projects and developed a new software-engineering approach that is security-centric. Now the software giant will not release any software product that hasn't undergone a stringent series of security checks. Windows Vista was the first client operating system shipped that was developed from the get-go with these principles in mind. That is, it was architected to be secure from the beginning. Windows 7 continues this trend quite nicely and builds off the work begun in Windows Vista.

Is Windows 7 impenetrable? Of course not. No software is perfect; but Windows 7 is demonstrably more secure than its predecessors. And although Windows users will no doubt face awesome security threats in the future, Microsoft at least has the lessons it learned from the mistakes of the past to fall back on. Many people believe that the security enhancements in Windows 7 will prove to be a major reason many users will upgrade to this version. This is completely valid.

Secret

We want to expose one myth right now: while proponents of UNIX-based systems like Apple Mac OS X and Linux like to tout the supposed security benefits of their systems over Windows, the truth is that these competitors benefit primarily from *security by obscurity*. That is, so few people use these systems relative to Windows that hackers don't bother targeting the minority operating systems. Consider this: in 2007, the installed base of Windows-based PCs exceeded 1 billion, but the maker of the number-two OS, Apple, claims just 25 million users. That's right, only 2.5 percent of the Windows user base is using the number-two most frequently used OS on earth. Hackers may be evil but they're not dummies: they know where the numbers are.

This isn't a partisan attack on Mac OS X or Linux. Both are fine systems, with their own particular strengths; and as far as security by obscurity goes, it's certainly a valid enough reason to consider using OS X or Linux instead of Windows. It's one of the reasons we both use Mozilla Firefox instead of Internet Explorer: in addition to various features that Firefox offers, the browser is hacked a lot less often than IE simply because fewer people use it.

Windows 7's security features permeate the system, from top to bottom, from the high-profile applications, applets, and control panels you deal with every day to the low-level features most Windows users have never heard of. This chapter highlights most of the Windows 7 security features that affect the user experience, starting with those you will likely have to deal with as soon as you begin using Microsoft's latest operating system. First, however, take a look at the first thing Windows 7 users need to do to thoroughly secure their system.

Securing Windows 7 in Just Two Steps

Out of the box, Windows 7 includes antispyware functionality in the form of *Windows Defender*, a two-way firewall in Windows Firewall; a hardened Web browser (Internet Explorer 8); and automatic updating features that keep the system up-to-date, every day, with the latest security patches. Also included are changes to the User Account Control (UAC) feature, covered in the next chapter, making it less annoying and less likely to be turned off, thus reducing your exposure to malware. It would seem that Windows 7 comes with everything you need to be secure.

Sadly, that's not quite the case. First, Microsoft makes it too easy for users to opt out of one of the most important security features available in the system. In addition, one glaring security feature is missing from Windows 7. You'll want to make sure you correct both of these issues before using Windows 7 online. Fortunately, doing so takes just two steps:

1. **Enable automatic updating:** If you set up Windows 7 yourself, one of the final Setup steps is configuration of Automatic Updates, the Windows Update feature that helps to ensure your system is always up-to-date. However, Automatic Updates can't do its thing if you disable it, so make sure at the very least that you've configured this feature to install updates automatically. (Optionally, you can enable the installation of recommended updates as well, but these are rarely security oriented.) We can't stress this enough: this feature needs to be enabled. If you're not sure how it is configured, run Windows Update (Start Menu Search and then type **windows update**) and click Change Settings in the left side of the window. Make sure the option under Important updates *Install updates automatically (recommended)* is selected.

2. **Install an antivirus solution:** Many new PCs are preinstalled with security suites from companies such as McAfee and Symantec. While these suites are better than nothing, they're also a bit bloated and perform poorly in our own tests. We prefer standalone antivirus solutions for this reason. There are many excellent options, including ESET NOD32 Antivirus, which in our own tests has proven to do an excellent job with minimal system impact. You can find out more about ESET NOD32 Antivirus from ESET directly (www.eset.com).

Secret

While commercial antivirus solutions are generally more effective, you might be surprised to discover that you can get a perfectly good antivirus solution free, which is perfect for budget-minded students and other individuals. The best free antivirus solution we've used is AVG Anti-Virus Free Edition. It's not quite as lightweight as ESET NOD32 Antivirus, but it's close. And it's not as bloated as those unnecessary security suites. Best of all, did we mention that it is free? You can find out more about AVG Anti-Virus Free Edition on the Web (free.grisoft.com).

Security in Windows 7 starts with this simple rule: leave all the security settings on, at their defaults, and install an antivirus solution. That said, a full understanding of what's available in Windows 7 from a security standpoint is, of course, beneficial. That's what this chapter is all about.

Now it's time to take a closer look at Windows 7's security features.

Action Center

When Microsoft shipped Windows XP Service Pack 2 (SP2) in the wake of its 2003 security-code review, one of the major and obvious new features it added to the operating system was the Security Center, a dashboard or front end of sorts to many of the system's security features. In Windows XP SP2, the Security Center was designed to track the system's firewall, virus protection, and Automatic Updates features to ensure that each was enabled and as current as possible. If any of these features were disabled or out-of-date, the Security Center would warn the user via a shield icon in the notification area near the system clock, or via pop-up warning balloons.

Security Center continued in Windows Vista and picked up even more security monitoring duties. But in Windows 7, the Security Center has been rebranded and dramatically updated to support new security features, house common tasks, and provide notifications in a less intrusive way. Shown in Figure 7-1, Windows 7's Action Center is barely recognizable as the successor to the XP and Vista Security Center. There's actually a lot more going on there once you begin examining its new functionality.

The core behavior of this tool hasn't changed in Action Center. The Action Center still tracks certain security features and ensures that they're enabled and up-to-date. If they're not, the Action Center subtly notifies you by changing its notification area flag icon (using a small red "x" icon overlay), instead of irritating you with a pop-up balloon as before.

As noted previously, Action Center now tracks far more items. Here's the list:

- ◆ **Security Features**
  - **Network firewall:** The Action Center ensures that Windows Firewall (or a third-party firewall) is enabled and protecting your PC against malicious software that might travel to your PC via a network or the Internet.
  - **Windows Update:** Like Windows XP and Vista, Windows 7 includes an Automatic Updates feature that can automatically download and install critical security fixes from Microsoft the moment they are released. Action Center ensures that Automatic Updates is enabled.
  - **Virus protection:** Although Windows 7 doesn't ship with any antivirus protection, Action Center still checks to ensure that an antivirus service is installed and up-to-date. Modern antivirus solutions are designed to integrate with Windows Action Center so that the system can perform this monitoring function.
  - **Spyware and unwanted software (malware) protection:** Windows 7, like Vista, ships with Windows Defender, the malware protection suite. Action Center will monitor Windows Defender (or your anti-spyware solution of choice) and ensure it's running and using the latest definitions.
  - **Internet security settings:** The Action Center ensures that Internet Explorer 8 is configured in a secure manner. If you change any IE security settings Action Center will warn you about this issue.

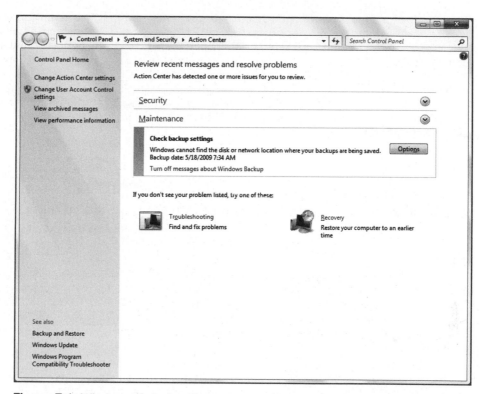

Figure 7-1: Windows 7's Action Center now tracks more than just security features.

- **User Account Control:** The Action Center also ensures that the User Account Control (UAC) technology is active. This tool is described in Chapter 8.
- **Network Access Protection:** Network Access Protection, first broadly provided with Windows Server 2008, enables IT administrators to protect the security of a network by ensuring that connected PCs (running Windows XP, Vista, or 7) pass software and settings checks, created by the administrator. These checks, for example, can reveal a required piece of corporate software or ensure that certain network authentication settings are configured properly. Any deviations from this configuration will be picked up and passed on to you by the Action Center.

✦ **Maintenance Features**

- **Windows Backup:** The Action Center takes note of whether or not you're performing backups of your crucial data.
- **Windows Troubleshooting:** The Windows Troubleshooting platform in Windows 7 ties directly into the new Action Center. Action Center will alert you to any problems that should be sent to Microsoft for further analysis and any solutions that were found to solve existing issues. (Windows 7's new troubleshooting tools are covered in Chapter 25.)
- **Problem reports:** If you run into a software issue, Windows 7 can automatically report the problem to Microsoft and check whether a resolution is provided. Action Center monitors this feature to see whether it is enabled.

If all of the features that the Action Center is monitoring are enabled and up-to-date, you won't ever see this feature unless you manually navigate to it. (You can find the Action Center in Control Panel ⇨ System and Security ⇨ Action Center, or by typing **action center** in Start Menu Search.) However, if one or more of these features are disabled, misconfigured, or out-of-date, the Action Center will provide the aforementioned alerts. It also displays its displeasure with red prefixed sections in the main Action Center window. In such a case, you can usually resolve the issue by simply using the button provided. For example, if you don't install antivirus software, in Action Center you'll see a Virus protection alert along with a "Find a program online" button. After installation of the antivirus software, this alert will disappear.

tip If you install Windows 7 yourself, you will see a red Action Center icon in the notification area of the taskbar. This is because Windows 7 doesn't ship with any antivirus solution: To make this warning disappear, install a third-party antivirus solution.

Secret In some cases, you might want to configure Action Center to not monitor a certain feature, such as Windows Backup after installing third-party backup software. Simply open Action Center and click the Change Action Center settings link in the task list on the left. This will display the Change Action Center settings control panel shown in Figure 7-2. From here, you can specify which features Action Center should and should not monitor, eliminating any unwanted alerts.

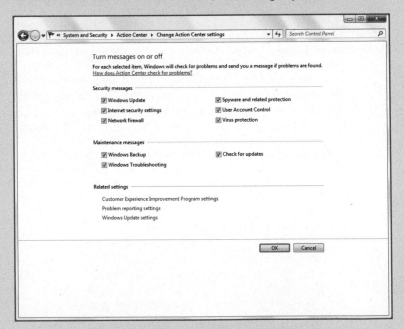

Figure 7-2: You can disable Action Center alerting of certain features, like Windows Backup.

At the bottom of this area, Action Center also provides handy links to configuring various related features such as the Customer Experience Improvement Program, problem reporting, and Windows Update.

Secret   Action Center provides a number of Application Programming Interfaces (APIs) for all the various antivirus vendors to tie into the Action Center. If you installed antivirus software that doesn't appear in Action Center, it is likely out-of-date or simply not worth using. All modern, capable AV solutions will natively support Action Center.

Windows Defender

Over the years, hackers have come up with new and inventive ways to attack PCs. Recently, spyware, one of the most pervasive and difficult forms of malware yet invented, has become a serious issue. For this reason, Windows 7 includes an integrated antispyware and anti-malware package called Windows Defender. Unlike some security products, you won't typically see Windows Defender, as it's designed to work in the background, keeping your system safe; but if you'd like to manually scan your system for malware or update your spyware definitions, you can do so by loading the Windows Defender application, available through the Start menu.

tip   Windows Defender does occasionally show up as an icon in the taskbar notification area. This generally happens when the tool has been unable to download new definitions, the files it uses to ensure that its antispyware database is up-to-date. In such a case, you can click the Windows Defender icon and trigger a manual download of the latest updates.

Shown in Figure 7-3, Windows Defender has a simple interface. You can trigger a malware scan, view the history of Defender's activities, or access various options.

Secret   Security researchers almost unanimously agree that no one antispyware product is enough to completely protect your PC from malware attacks. For this reason, you should consider running two antispyware products at the same time. And yes, that's entirely okay: unlike with AV products, multiple antispyware solutions can happily co-exist on the same PC, all running at the same time.

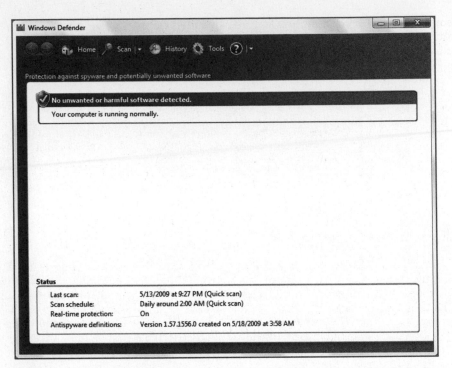

Figure 7-3: Windows Defender runs silently in the background and works well. What more could you ask?

Windows Firewall

When Microsoft first shipped Windows XP in 2001, it included a feature called Internet Connection Firewall (ICF) that could have potentially thwarted many of the electronic attacks that ultimately crippled that system over the ensuing several years. There was just one problem: ICF was disabled by default and enabling and configuring it correctly required a master's degree in rocket science (or at least in computer security). Microsoft wised up and shipped an improved ICF version, renamed as Windows Firewall, with Windows XP SP2. Best of all, it was enabled by default. Sure, it broke many applications at first, but now, years later, virtually all Windows applications know how to live in a firewall-based world.

In Windows Vista, we were given an even better version of Windows Firewall. Unlike the XP SP2 version, the version in Windows Vista enabled monitoring both outbound and inbound network traffic. While Windows 7 doesn't bring many Windows Firewall additions, it does feature a much more informative interface, as shown in Figure 7-4.

Windows Firewall is initially configured to block any unknown or untrusted connections to the PC that originate over the network. You can enable exceptions to this behavior via the Allowed Programs list, which you can access by clicking the link *Allow a program or feature through Windows Firewall.* Typically you just leave the settings as is, of course. Depending on the network type (Home, Work, or Public) chosen when Windows 7 connects to a network, some programs and features are automatically configured to communicate through the firewall, as shown in Table 7-1.

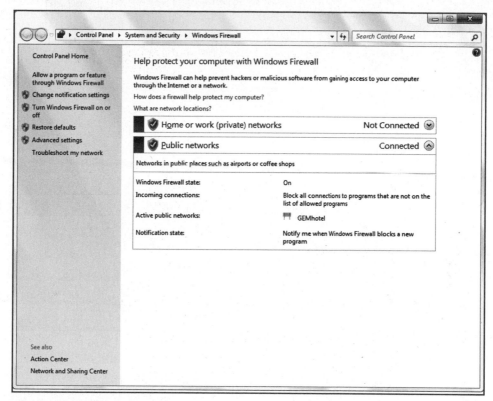

Figure 7-4: Windows Firewall

Table 7-1: Automatically Configured Programs and Features

Allowed Program/ Feature	What it does	Home/work (private) networks	Public networks
Core Networking	Performs basic (and required) network tasks, such as obtaining an IP address	Allowed	Allowed
Network Discovery	Allows other networked computers and devices to be detected *and* for them to detect your computer	Allowed	Blocked
Remote Assistance	Enables others, upon invite, to connect to your computer for remote assistance	Allowed	Blocked

Secret

Microsoft includes a more verbose interface to Windows Firewall called Windows Firewall with Advanced Security. You can access it by simply typing **advanced firewall** into Start Menu Search. (You can also access this tool from Windows Firewall. Just click the link *Advanced settings* in the task list on the left. As shown in Figure 7-5, the tool loads into a Microsoft Management Console (MMC).

Figure 7-5: Windows Firewall with Advanced Security

Here, you can inspect and configure advanced firewall features, such as inbound/outbound connection rules, and so on. This tool is almost identical to the one Microsoft ships with Windows Server 2008 and should be of most interest to advanced users and, of course, IT administrators who need to centrally manage hundreds or thousands of Windows 7 installations. The latter market, of course, is who Windows Firewall with Advanced Security is really aimed at.

Secret

As good as Windows 7's firewall is, you should absolutely use a third-party firewall instead if you're using a security software suite. In such cases, the security suite will typically disable Windows Firewall automatically and alert Windows Action Center that it is now handling firewalling duties. In contrast to antispyware applications, never run two firewalls at the same time, as they will interfere with each other. If you're not running a third-party security suite, Windows Firewall works just fine: it's all you're likely to need from a firewall.

Windows Update

With Windows 98 over a decade ago, Microsoft introduced a Web-based service called Windows Update that provided software updates to Windows users. That service has since been superseded by Microsoft Update, which also provides updates to many other Microsoft software products. In Windows Vista, Windows Update was moved into the operating system and made a client application, eliminating the number of Web browser hoops you had to jump through to keep your operating system up-to-date. Windows 7 continues to carry the Windows Update torch, making a few subtle changes for the good.

As shown in Figure 7-6, Windows Update remains a client application that you can access from the Start menu. From here, you can check for and install new updates, hide updates you don't want to be alerted about anymore, and view the history of updates you've already installed. You can also click a link to enable Microsoft Update functionality, enabling Windows Update to download and install updates for other Microsoft applications, such as Microsoft Office and various Windows Live products.

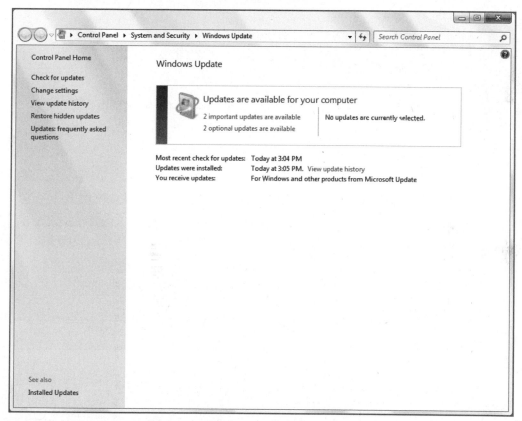

Figure 7-6: Windows Update in Windows 7

<table>
<tr><td>cross
ref</td><td>In addition to the features discussed in this chapter, Windows 7 includes two major technologies that help protect different types of user accounts from outside threats. Dubbed User Account Control and Parental Controls, these technologies are discussed in Chapter 8.</td></tr>
</table>

Internet Explorer 8 Security Features

Internet Explorer 8 comes with Windows 7 and includes a vast number of security improvements that make this the safest version of IE yet. This section examines the security features Microsoft added to Internet Explorer 8. These features were absolutely necessary: ever since Microsoft integrated Internet Explorer with the Windows shell beginning in the mid 1990s, Internet Explorer has been a major avenue of attack against Windows.

<table>
<tr><td>cross
ref</td><td>Chapter 20 covers the functional aspects of Internet Explorer 8.</td></tr>
</table>

<table>
<tr><td>tip</td><td>Yes, Internet Explorer 8 is available for Windows XP and Vista users too.</td></tr>
</table>

InPrivate Browsing

Internet Explorer 8 can optionally run in a new InPrivate Browsing mode, shown in Figure 7-7, effectively hiding your tracks as you travel around to the more nefarious parts of the Web or, what the heck, secretly shop for a spouse's birthday present online. More specifically, InPrivate Browsing turns off IE's ability to locally store or retain browser history, temporary Internet files, form data, cookies and user names, and passwords. It does allow you to download files and add sites to your Favorites. By default, IE add-ons like toolbars are disabled in InPrivate Browsing mode, but you can change that from Internet Settings if desired.

A related feature, InPrivate Filtering, is a first step in addressing the way in which many Web sites share data with each other. Consider a mainstream Web site like wsj.com, for *The Wall Street Journal*. This site is certainly reputable, but it utilizes advertising services that work across multiple non-WSJ Web sites. Once these services have collected information about you on wsj.com, they can track you across other sites that utilize the same services. This is usually innocuous, but it's possible that a malicious site could take advantage of this capability and deliver dangerous content via other sites.

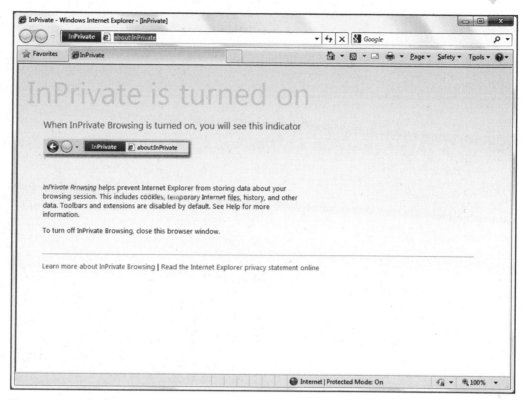

Figure 7-7: InPrivate is sometimes referred to as *porn mode.*

InPrivate Filtering provides basic protection against this potential kind of attack by preventing, by default, more than 10 cross-site calls. It's not enabled by default, however,
but once you enable it you have decent control over how it works. For example, you could
lower the threshold for cross-site content (down to a minimum of three), choose to allow
or block specific sites, and so on. It's interesting to look at just to see what the sites you
visit are up to. You might be surprised.

SmartScreen Filter

IE8's SmartScreen Filter is the new version of the anti-phishing filter that debuted in IE7.
It's been renamed to reflect the fact that it now performs both anti-phishing and anti-
malware functions, protecting you and your PC from electronic attacks. So if you attempt
to browse to a site that is known to deliver malware, or you attempt to download a known
bad file, IE8 will prompt you with a warning, as shown in Figure 7-8.

You can manually check the current Web site if you're unsure of something. When you
do so, the SmartScreen Filter tells you what it knows about the site. You can also report a
Web site that you think might be fraudulent. Microsoft says that almost 50 percent of the
data in its SmartScreen database comes from users.

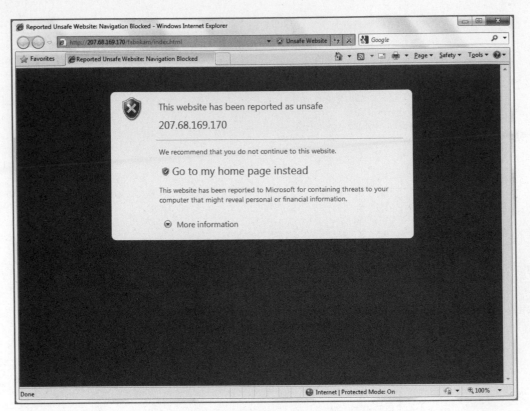

Figure 7-8: Redrum, redrum. Here, you see IE8's reaction to a malicious site.

Address Bar Domain Name Highlighting

It seems like a small thing, but IE8 also highlights (bolds) the **domain name** in the URL, helping to ensure you're visiting a legitimate Web site. Consider the following complex (but imaginary) URLs to see why this is important:

```
https://secure.winsupersite.com?key=10923
```

```
https://secure.winsupersite.com.h4x.com?key=10923
```

If you weren't paying attention—and who is, really?—you might miss the fact that the second address points to a malicious Web site. But when you highlight the domain name as follows, the difference is a bit more apparent. It's like the third brake light on automobiles:

```
https://secure.winsupersite.com?key=10923
```

```
https://secure.winsupersite.com.h4x.com?key=10923
```

Other Internet Explorer Security Features

The list of Internet Explorer security features is vast, although you won't likely run into most of them unless you're truly unlucky. IE8 integrates with Windows Defender to provide live scanning of Web downloads to ensure that you're not infecting your system with spyware, and it integrates with Windows 7's parental controls as well as Windows Live Family Safety (both described in Chapter 8) to ensure that your children are accessing only those parts of the Web you deem safe. In addition, various low-level changes prevent increasingly common cross-domain or cross-window scripting attacks and blocks malicious malware installation attempts.

Secret Should Internet Explorer 8 somehow be compromised, there's a way out. An Internet Explorer mode called Add-ons Disabled Mode loads IE with only a minimal set of add-ons so you can scrub the system of any malicious code. You can access this mode by navigating to All Programs ⇨ Accessories ⇨ System Tools ⇨ Internet Explorer (No Add-ons) in the Start menu. Alternately, you can use Start Menu Search to find Internet Explorer (No Add-ons).

Summary

Although much is made of Windows 7's new user interface and other highly visible features, its new security features are, beyond a doubt, a major reason to consider upgrading to this new operating system. Although it's possible to duplicate many of the end-user features in IE8 by using it on Windows XP or Vista, Windows 7's many security improvements are available only to those who upgrade to the latest Windows version. Security isn't something that's easy to sell per se, and various vulnerabilities will still crop up over time; but make no mistake: Windows 7's security improvements are important. Windows 7 is an evolution of Windows Vista and vastly more secure than Windows XP can ever be.

Users, Accounts, and UAC

Chapter

8

◆ ◆

In This Chapter

Understanding the types of user accounts you can create in Windows 7

Using User Account Control to protect your system

Configuring User Account Control

Turning off User Account Control

Applying and configuring Parental Controls for your children

How Parental Controls work and how you can override their settings

Using Windows Live Family Safety

◆ ◆

By now most Windows users are probably familiar with the notion of user accounts and how all users on a PC can have their own individual settings, documents, and other features. In Windows Vista, Microsoft simplified the user account types down to just two, and locked them down to make the system more secure. Windows 7 takes this approach a step further and makes it easier to configure how user accounts behave and are protected. And thanks to features such as User Account Control, Parental Controls, and Windows Live Family Safety, Windows 7 is not only more secure than previous Windows versions, but also easier to configure from a user account perspective. This chapter describes these features and explains how they can be put to the best possible use.

note   Windows 7 user accounts include a variety of obvious functionality that is not covered here explicitly because this book focuses on secrets, those features that are brand-new to Windows 7 and/or are so well hidden you'd never normally know about them. So, yes, you can add cute pictures to your user account; add, change, and remove passwords; and even change your account type, but you can do much more than that. This chapter looks at the new and improved functionality that makes user accounts so much better in Windows 7 than they were in Windows XP and Vista.

Understanding User Accounts

Starting with Windows XP, Microsoft began to push PC-based user accounts to consumers. That's because XP, unlike previous consumer-oriented Windows versions (such as Windows 95, 98, and Me), was based on the enterprise-class Windows NT code base. NT originally was developed in the early 1990s as a mission-critical competitor to business operating systems such as UNIX. Previously, consumer Windows products such as Windows 95 and Windows Me were based on legacy MS-DOS code and provided only the barest possible support for discrete and secure user accounts. That's because those systems were originally designed for single users only.

Eventually, however, Microsoft began moving the two products together. Windows XP, released in 2001, was the first mainstream NT-based Windows version, and this product marked the end of the DOS-based Windows line. Windows Vista, like Windows XP, was based on the NT code base, which means that Microsoft marketed separate versions of Vista to both individuals and businesses. Additionally, Vista retained—and even enhanced—the paradigm of all users having their own user account for accessing the PC.

As an updated version of Windows Vista, Windows 7 offers an evolution of the user account capabilities from its predecessor. That said, some of the changes dramatically alter the experience of using and protecting user accounts. Therefore, it's worth discussing how user accounts have changed in Windows 7 compared to both Windows XP and Vista.

First, however, a short review may be in order. When you installed or configured Windows XP for the first time, you were prompted to provide a password for the special administrator account and then create one or more user accounts. Administrator is what's called a *built-in account type*. The administrator account is traditionally reserved for system housekeeping tasks and it has full control of the system. Theoretically, individual user accounts—that is, accounts used by actual people—are supposed to have less control over the system for security reasons. In Windows XP, that theory was literally a theory. Every user account you created during XP's post-setup routine was an administrator-level account, and virtually every single Windows application ever written until fairly recently assumed that every user has administrative privileges. This resulted in an ugly chicken-or-egg situation that has caused several years of unrelenting security vulnerabilities because malicious code running on a Windows system runs using the privilege level of the logged-on user. If the user is an administrator, so is the malicious code.

In Windows Vista, everything changed. Yes, you can still create user accounts, and hopefully, you create accounts with strong and secure passwords. (Microsoft still doesn't require this is in Windows 7, for some reason.) And you would still log on to the system to access applications, the Internet, and other services, just as you did in Windows XP. But in Windows Vista, user accounts—even those that were graced with administrative privileges—no longer had complete control over the system, at least not by default. Microsoft, finally, was starting to batten down the virtual hatches and make Windows more secure. Although there were (and still are) ways to counteract these preventive measures, the result was a more secure operating system than previous Windows versions, one that hackers have found and will continue to find more difficult to penetrate.

Microsoft's approach to user account security in Windows Vista was hugely successful. According to the software giant, Vista users experienced 60 percent fewer malware infections than did XP users. Windows 7 continues using the infrastructure Microsoft created for Vista while adding a few changes at the requests of its customers. The following sections look at what has changed.

Creating the Initial User Account

When you install Windows 7 for the first time or turn on a new computer that has Windows 7 preinstalled from a PC maker, you will eventually run into the so-called out-of-box experience (OOBE), sometimes called the Day One Experience, whereby Windows 7 prompts you for a few pertinent bits of information before presenting you with the Windows desktop for the first time—information used to create your initial administrative account. While this account is technically granted administrative privileges, remember that this privilege isn't as all-powerful as it was in XP. You'll see why in just a moment.

Are you wondering why Microsoft doesn't give you the chance to make your initial user account a non-administrator account? The reason is simple: you still need at least one account on each PC that has administrative privileges. If you didn't have such an account, there would be no way for you to access those features and services that do require administrative privileges.

One feature that's missing from Windows 7, incidentally, is that it's no longer possible to create up to five user accounts during setup, as it was in XP setup. (In this case, Windows 7 behaves as Vista did.) You can create only a single user account while configuring Windows 7 for the first time, so if you want to create more accounts, you have to do that after you log on. Those accounts, by default, are *not* created with administrative privileges unless you change the settings (a process described fully in just a moment).

Understanding Account Types

Windows 7, like Windows Vista, but unlike XP, supports just two account types:

◆ **Administrator:** This is (almost) exactly what it sounds like, and is basically the same as the administrator account type in Windows XP. Administrators have complete control of the system and can make any configuration changes they want, though the method for doing so has changed somewhat since XP.

◆ **Standard user:** A standard user can use most application software and many Windows services. Standard users, however, are prevented from accessing features that could harm the system. For example, standard users cannot install most applications, change the system time, or access certain Control Panel applets. Naturally, there are ways around these limitations, discussed in a bit.

Secret

So, what's missing? Windows XP supported something (under the hood) called a *power user* account type, which was supposed to convince people who would normally want administrative privileges to accept a slightly less risky account type. It never really took off, and it's gone in Windows Vista and 7.

Microsoft would like most people to run under a standard user account; and although this would indeed be marginally safer than using an administrator account, we don't recommend it, assuming that you log on to your account with a password. That's because Microsoft has actually locked down the administrator account in Windows 7, making it safer to use than ever before. More important, perhaps, you'll ultimately find an administrator account to be less annoying than a standard user account, even given some of the changes Microsoft has made in this release. To find out why that's so, you need to examine an important security feature in Windows 7: User Account Control.

User Account Control

No Windows feature has proven as controversial and misunderstood as User Account Control, or UAC. When it debuted in Windows Vista, tech pundits screamed far and wide about this reviled feature, spreading mistruths and misunderstandings and generally raising a lot of ruckus about nothing. If these pundits had just calmed down long enough to actually use User Account Control for longer than a single afternoon, they'd have discovered something very simple: it's not really that annoying, and it does in fact increase the security of the system. Indeed, we would argue that User Account Control is one of the few features that really differentiate modern Windows versions from the increasingly crusty XP, because there's no way to add this kind of functionality to XP, even through third-party add-on software. User Account Control is effective, and as ongoing security assessments have proven, it really does work.

Great, but what is it exactly? In order to make the operating system more secure, Microsoft has architected Windows so that all of the tasks you can perform in the system are divided into two groups, those that require administrative privileges and those that don't. This required a lot of thought and a lot of engineering work, naturally, because the company had to weigh the ramifications of each potential action and then code the system accordingly.

The first iteration of UAC was implemented in Windows Vista with what Microsoft thought to be a decent technical compromise. In response to overwhelming user feedback surrounding the frequency of prompts, however, Microsoft modified UAC in Windows 7 to make it "less noisy" (that is, less annoying) by default. They did this by implementing a pair of "Notify me only when. . ." options, letting users perform common configuration tasks, prompting only when something out of the ordinary is done (for example, changing important configuration settings). The result is that UAC in Windows 7 is more configurable and less irritating than it was in Vista. But it's even more controversial, because it's not clear that it's as secure as it used to be.

How UAC Works

Every user, whether configured as a standard user or an administrator, can perform any of the tasks in Windows 7 that do not require administrator privileges, just as they did in Windows XP. (The problem with XP, from a security standpoint, of course, is that *all* tasks were denoted as not requiring administrative privileges.) You can launch applications, change time zone and power-management settings, add a printer, run Windows Update, and perform other similar tasks. However, when you attempt to run a task that does require administrative privileges, the system will force you to provide appropriate credentials in order to continue. The experiences vary a bit depending on the account type. Predictably, those who log on with administrator-class accounts experience a less annoying interruption.

Standard users receive a User Account Control credentials dialog, as shown in Figure 8-1. This dialog requires you to enter the password for an administrator account that is already configured on the system. Consider why this is useful. If you have configured your children with standard user accounts (as, frankly, you should if you're going to allow them to share your PC), then they can let you know when they run into this dialog, giving you the option to allow or deny the task they are attempting to complete.

Figure 8-1: Standard users attempting to perform admin-level tasks are confronted by the User Account Control credentials dialog.

Administrators receive a simpler dialog, called the User Account Control consent dialog, shown in Figure 8-2. Because these users are already configured as administrators, they do not have to provide administrator credentials. Instead they can simply click Yes to keep going.

By default, administrators using Windows 7 are running in an execution mode called Admin Approval Mode. This is why you see consent dialogs appear from time to time even though you're using an administrator-type account. You can actually disable this mode, making administrator accounts work more like they did in XP, without any annoying dialogs popping up (something that was not possible in Vista). However, understand that disabling Admin Approval Mode could open up your system to attack. If you're still interested in disabling this feature, or disabling User Account Control, you will learn how at the end of this section.

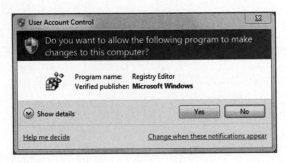

Figure 8-2: Administrators receive a less annoying dialog.

Conversely, those running with administrative privileges who would like Windows 7 to be even more secure—and really, why aren't there more people like you in the world?—can also configure the system to prompt with a User Account Control credentials dialog (which requires a complete password) every time they attempt an administrative task. This option is also discussed shortly.

The presentation of these User Account Control dialogs can be quite jarring if you're not familiar with the feature or if you've just recently switched to Windows 7 from XP. (Vista users are very well accustomed to this effect.) If you attempt to complete an administrative task, the screen will flash, the background will darken, and the credentials or consent dialog will appear somewhere onscreen. Most important, the dialogs are modal: you can't continue doing anything else until you have dealt with these dialogs one way or the other.

The screen darkening and modal nature of the UAC prompts indicate that Vista has moved into the so-called *secure desktop,* which is a special, more secure display mode that Microsoft also uses during logon and when you access the Ctrl+Alt+Delete screen. It's possible to configure UAC to work without the secure desktop, but this is not recommended because UAC dialogs could be spoofed by malicious hackers if you do so. You'll examine various UAC configuration options later in this chapter, including the removal of the secure desktop.

There's also a third type of User Account Control dialog that sometimes appears regardless of which type of user account you have configured. This dialog appears whenever you attempt to install an application that has not been digitally signed or validated by its creator. These types of applications are quite common, so you're likely to see the dialog shown in Figure 8-3 fairly frequently, especially when you're initially configuring a new PC. Over time, these prompts will occur less and less because you won't be regularly installing applications anymore.

By design, this dialog is more colorful and "in your face" than the other User Account Control dialogs. Microsoft wants to ensure that you really think about it before continuing. Rule of thumb: you're going to see this one a lot, but if you just downloaded an installer from a place you trust, it's probably okay to go ahead and install it.

Figure 8-3: This dialog (colorful onscreen) appears whenever you attempt to execute an application installer from an unknown source.

The behavior of User Account Control has led some to describe this feature as needlessly annoying and a contributing factor to the (perceived) demise of Windows Vista. In reality, however, Windows Vista wasn't the first operating system to use this type of security feature: Mac OS X and Linux, for example, have utilized a UAC-type user interface for years now. (You can see Mac OS X's version of UAC—which debuted way back in 2001—in Figure 8-4.)

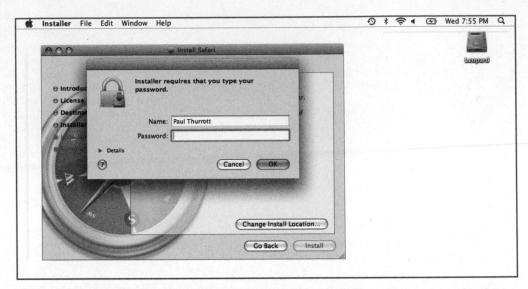

Figure 8-4: Mac OS X users have been putting up with a UAC-like security prompt for almost a decade, and we don't hear them complaining.

And unlike with other operating systems, User Account Control actually becomes less annoying over time. That's because most UAC dialogs pop up when you first get Windows 7. This is when you'll be futzing around with settings and installing applications the most; and these two actions, of course, are the very actions that most frequently trigger User Account Control. The moral here is simple: after your new PC is up and running, User Account Control will rear its ugly head less and less frequently. In fact, after a week or so, User Account Control will be mostly a thing of the past. You'll forget it was ever there.

How UAC Has Changed in Windows 7

User Account Control debuted in Windows Vista to a resounding thud, for both users and reviewers. And that's too bad, because as we've noted again and again, UAC is both effective and far less annoying than many realize. But Microsoft is a customer-centric company, and when people complain, they actually listen. And sometimes, when the stars align just right, they do something about it.

In the case of UAC, this action took a number of forms. At a general level, Microsoft has dramatically reduced the number of tasks that require UAC elevation prompts. So the overall experience should be less annoying, assuming you're used to how UAC works in Windows Vista. And Microsoft has even given users a graphical interface, logically called User Account Control settings, for adjusting how UAC behaves.

Secret

This graphical interface is only available to those users with administrative privileges. This wasn't always the case, however. During the Windows 7 beta, Rafael and another blogger discovered and reported that UAC did not require confirmation when changing its slider setting, leaving it vulnerable to malware attack. Stubbornly, Microsoft did not budge at first, claiming that UAC worked as designed. It was not until after the issue gained international attention that Microsoft reversed its decision and made several changes to UAC, requiring administrative privileges being one. You can read more about this event on Rafael's blog, Within Windows (see `http://tinyurl.com/win7uacissue`).

You access User Account Control settings from the Action Center; there's a link in the side pane titled User Account Control settings that will trigger the UI shown in Figure 8-5. Or, simply type **user account control** in Start Menu Search.

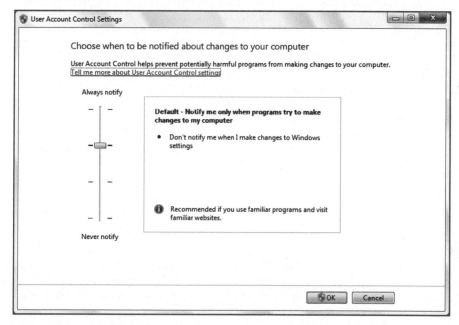

Figure 8-5: This slider control lets you literally tune UAC to be less—or more—annoying.

User Account Control settings couldn't be easier: there's a simple slider control with four settings, which one might think of as "really annoying," "annoying," "less annoying," and "Windows XP." (Homeland security might consider a similar scale.)

More formally, these settings are as follows:

- ♦ **Always notify:** At this most heightened level, UAC will prompt you anytime a software install or configuration change is detected, or whenever the user makes changes to Windows settings—just like Windows Vista.

- ♦ **Notify me only when programs try to make changes to my computer:** This is indeed the default setting. Here, UAC will prompt you anytime a software install or configuration change is detected. But it will not prompt when the user makes changes to Windows settings. Initial setup tasks like setting the clock, updating device drivers, and formatting partitions can now be performed speedily without having to confirm each time.

- ♦ **Notify me only when programs try to make changes to my computer:** This setting is almost identical to the previous setting, but with one important difference: UAC does not invoke the secure desktop during prompts. This has a few ramifications. First, UAC will be less annoying (though no less frequent) than with the default setting, because you won't see that jarring flash that occurs when the secure desktop is invoked. The screen will not go dark, and the UAC prompt will not be modal, meaning you can do other things instead of addressing the prompt immediately. (On the flip side, you can also easily lose track of the UAC prompt because it will just be one of many potential windows on screen and won't appear prominently or appear special in any way.) Finally, it will be slightly less secure: the secure desktop feature ensures that malicious software applications cannot spoof the UAC dialog.

- ♦ **Never notify:** In this least secure setting and least recommended setting, UAC will not warn you when software is installed or changed, or when the user makes changes to Windows settings.

So, with all these options, I know you're eagerly awaiting our expert opinion on what it is you should do. And that's maybe the easiest advice we've ever given: you should do nothing. In fact, you should never even visit this UI. Just leave UAC alone and let it do its thing. UAC is there for a reason and, as noted earlier, it gets less annoying over time anyway. There is absolutely no reason to change how UAC works.

Secret

When UAC is left at its default setting, Windows 7 automatically elevates a hand-picked list of applications, further reducing the UAC dialogs you see. These applications are referred to as being *white-listed* for auto-elevation. They include the following:

\Windows\ehome\Mcx2Prov.exe

\Windows\System32\AdapterTroubleshooter.exe

\Windows\System32\BitLockerWizardElev.exe

\Windows\System32\bthudtask.exe

\Windows\System32\chkntfs.exe

\Windows\System32\cleanmgr.exe

\Windows\System32\cliconfg.exe

```
\Windows\System32\CompMgmtLauncher.exe
\Windows\System32\ComputerDefaults.exe
\Windows\System32\dccw.exe
\Windows\System32\dcomcnfg.exe
\Windows\System32\DeviceEject.exe
\Windows\System32\DeviceProperties.exe
\Windows\System32\dfrgui.exe
\Windows\System32\djoin.exe
\Windows\System32\eudcedit.exe
\Windows\System32\eventvwr.exe
\Windows\System32\FXSUNATD.exe
\Windows\System32\hdwwiz.exe
\Windows\System32\ieUnatt.exe
\Windows\System32\iscsicli.exe
\Windows\System32\iscsicpl.exe
\Windows\System32\lpksetup.exe
\Windows\System32\MdSched.exe
\Windows\System32\msconfig.exe
\Windows\System32\msdt.exe
\Windows\System32\msra.exe
\Windows\System32\MultiDigiMon.exe
\Windows\System32\Netplwiz.exe
\Windows\System32\newdev.exe
\Windows\System32\ntprint.exe
\Windows\System32\ocsetup.exe
\Windows\System32\odbcad32.exe
\Windows\System32\OptionalFeatures.exe
\Windows\System32\perfmon.exe
\Windows\System32\printui.exe
\Windows\System32\rdpshell.exe
\Windows\System32\recdisc.exe
\Windows\System32\rrinstaller.exe
\Windows\System32\rstrui.exe
\Windows\System32\sdbinst.exe
\Windows\System32\sdclt.exe
```

continues

continued

\Windows\System32\shrpubw.exe

\Windows\System32\slui.exe

\Windows\System32\SndVol.exe

\Windows\System32\spinstall.exe

\Windows\System32\SystemPropertiesAdvanced.exe

\Windows\System32\SystemPropertiesComputerName.exe

\Windows\System32\SystemPropertiesDataExecutionPrevention.exe

\Windows\System32\SystemPropertiesHardware.exe

\Windows\System32\SystemPropertiesPerformance.exe

\Windows\System32\SystemPropertiesProtection.exe

\Windows\System32\SystemPropertiesRemote.exe

\Windows\System32\taskmgr.exe

\Windows\System32\tcmsetup.exe

\Windows\System32\TpmInit.exe

\Windows\System32\verifier.exe

\Windows\System32\wisptis.exe

\Windows\System32\wusa.exe

\Windows\System32\oobe\setupsqm.exe

\Windows\System32\sysprep\sysprep.exe

This list is representative of information available at time of publication. Be sure to check http://www.withinwindows.com **for the latest version.**

Changing How UAC Works (The Hard Way)

Okay, we recognize that giving advice is easier than taking it. With that in mind, there are a number of low-level changes you can make to this infamous Windows feature outside of the previously described new UI. If you really must futz around with UAC, look to User Account Control settings first. Or, if you're a real meddler, you can try the less obvious methods described in this section.

Disabling User Account Control

We don't recommend this; but as mentioned earlier, many people are going to be annoyed by User Account Control despite its good intentions, and they're going to want to simply disable it. As it turns out, Windows 7 makes disabling User Account Control very easy, much easier than it was in Vista. Simply open the Start menu and type **user account**

control into Start Menu Search and press Enter. Then, drag the slider to its lowest setting, as shown in Figure 8-6.

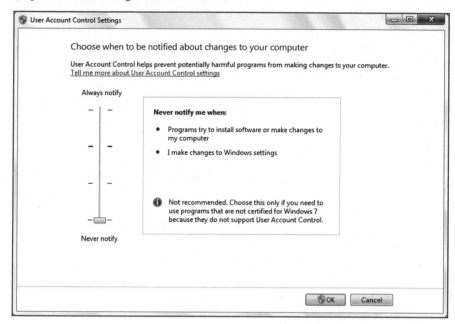

Figure 8-6: Wait a second. There's actually a UI for disabling User Account Control now?

After clicking OK, two things will happen immediately. First, UAC will prompt you to confirm the change with a UAC dialog! (Naturally.) Then, Action Center will throw out a balloon help window warning you that you must restart the system in order for the change to take place (see Figure 8-7). If you miss this prompt, you can simply click the Action Center tray icon, which has taken on a red "x" overlay.

Figure 8-7: It doesn't get much simpler than this, but actually there's a catch.

Or you can choose to open Action Center, as shown in Figure 8-8.

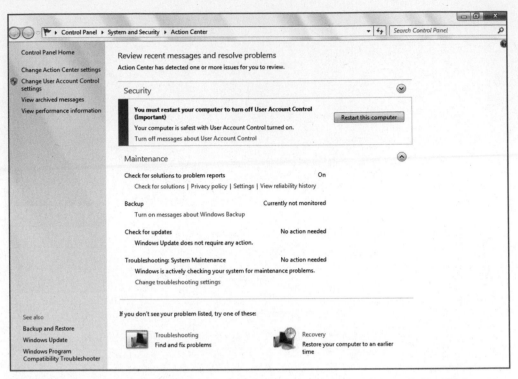

Figure 8-8: Action Center provides more information about what you're doing to UAC.

If you later change your mind, you can re-enable User Account Control by simply re-opening User Account Control settings and dragging the slider back up to the desired position. As is the case with disabling UAC, a reboot is required to fully re-enable it.

Configuring User Account Control

If you're the tweaker type and are running Windows 7 Professional, Enterprise, or Ultimate, Microsoft makes a number of User Account Control settings available through the hard-to-discover Local Security Settings management console. To launch this console, open the Start menu and type **secpol.msc** in Start Menu Search. This displays the administrative console shown in Figure 8-9.

To access the User Account Control options, expand the Security Settings and Local Policies nodes in the tree view in the left pane of the management console and then select Security Options. When you do so, the right pane will be populated with a list of security options. Scroll to the bottom, where you will see several options related to User Account Control. You can see this in Figure 8-10.

Table 8-1 highlights these settings and explains what each one does. To change a setting, double-click it. In the resulting dialog, just select the option you want (Enabled or Disabled for most of the UAC-related features) and then click OK.

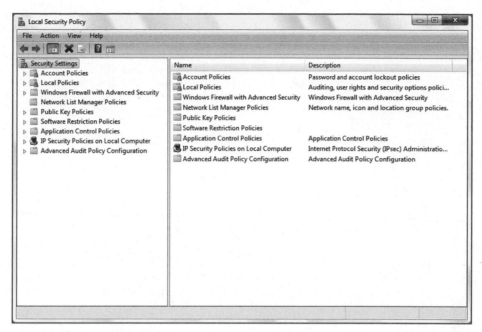

Figure 8-9: The Local Security Policy management console enables you to configure various security features, including User Account Control.

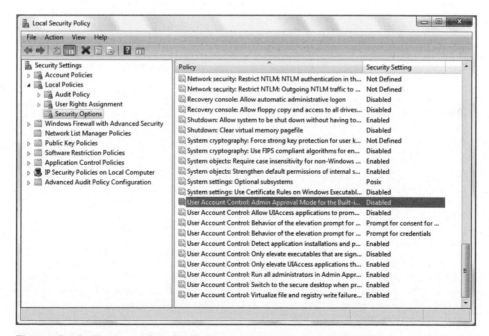

Figure 8-10: The Local Security Policy management console provides a number of configurable options related to UAC.

Secret   The Local Security Policy management console should be used only on PCs that are not centrally managed by a Windows Server–based Active Directory (AD)–based domain. Unless you work for a large company, it's unlikely that your PC is centrally managed in this way.

Table 8-1: Customizable User Account Control Features

Security Option	What It Does	Default Setting
Admin Approval Mode for the built-in administrator account	Toggles Admin Approval Mode for the built-in administrator account only. When Admin Approval Mode is off, UAC is said to be in "quiet" mode.	Disabled
Allow UIAccess applications to prompt for elevation without using the secure desktop	Determines whether properly installed applications that need to be run with administrative privileges can prompt for elevation without entering the secure desktop. "UIAccess" applications are applications that are installed in "trusted" shell locations such as the Windows directory or the Programs Files directory.	Disabled
Behavior of the elevation prompt for administrators in Admin Approval Mode	Determines what type of prompt admin-level users receive when attempting admin-level tasks. You can choose between a consent dialog, a credentials dialog, and no prompt.	Prompt for consent
Behavior of the elevation prompt for standard users	Determines what type of prompt standard users receive when attempting admin-levels tasks. You can choose between a consent dialog, a credentials dialog, and no prompt.	Prompt for credentials
Detect application installations and prompt for elevation	Determines whether application installs trigger a User Account Control elevation dialog	Enabled
Only elevate executables that are signed and validated	Determines whether only signed and validated application installs trigger a User Account Control elevation dialog	Disabled
Only elevate UIAccess applications that are installed in secure locations	Determines whether only properly installed applications can be elevated to administrative privileges	Enabled

Security Option	What It Does	Default Setting
Run all administrators in Admin Approval Mode	Determines whether all admin-level accounts run in Admin Approval Mode, which generates User Account Control consent dialogs for admin-level tasks. When Admin Approval Mode is off, UAC is said to be in "quiet" mode.	Enabled
Switch to the secure desktop when prompting for elevation	Determines whether the secure desktop environment appears whenever a User Account Control prompt is initiated by the system	Enabled
Virtualize file and registry write failures to per-user locations	Determines whether User Account Control virtualizes the Registry and file system for legacy applications that attempt to read from or write to private parts of the system. Do not disable this option.	Enabled

If you're running Windows 7 Starter, Home Basic, or Home Premium, you need to edit the Registry to manipulate these UAC policies:

1. Open the Start menu, type **regedit** into Start Menu Search, and press Enter.

2. Navigate to HKEY_LOCAL_MACHINE, Software, Microsoft, Windows, CurrentVersion, Policies, and finally System. The resulting display is shown in Figure 8-11.

3. In the right pane, double-click the value name associated with the setting you want to edit and set its value data appropriately, using Table 8-2 for reference.

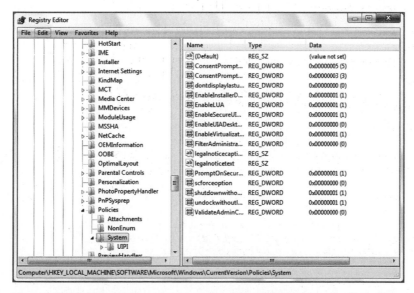

Figure 8-11: Users with nonmanaged versions of Windows 7 will need to use the Registry Editor to make low-level UAC changes.

Secret

If a value doesn't exist, fear not. Simply click Edit ⇨ New ⇨ DWORD (32-bit) Value from the Registry Editor menu and then type in the appropriate value name and value, according to Table 8-2.

Table 8-2: User Account Control Features and Their Corresponding Registry Value Names

Security Option	Registry Value Name	Possible Data Values
Admin Approval Mode for the built-in administrator account	FilterAdministratorToken	0 – Disabled 1 – Enabled
Allow UIAccess applications to prompt for elevation without using the secure desktop	EnableUIADesktopToggle	0 – Disabled 1 – Enabled
Behavior of the elevation prompt for administrators in Admin Approval Mode	ConsentPromptBehaviorAdmin	0 – Elevate without prompting 1 – Prompt for credentials 2 – Prompt for consent
Behavior of the elevation prompt for standard users	ConsentPromptBehaviorUser	0 – Automatically deny elevation requests 1 – Prompt for credentials
Detect application installations and prompt for elevation	EnableInstallerDetection	0 – Disabled 1 – Enabled
Only elevate executables that are signed and validated	ValidateAdminCodeSignatures	0 – Disabled 1 – Enabled
Only elevate UIAccess applications that are installed in secure locations	EnableSecureUIAPaths	0 – Disabled 1 – Enabled
Run all administrators in Admin Approval Mode	EnableLUA	0 – Disabled 1 – Enabled
Switch to the secure desktop when prompting for elevation	PromptOnSecureDesktop	0 – Disabled 1 – Enabled
Virtualize file and registry write failures to per-user locations	EnableVirtualization	0 – Disabled 1 – Enabled

Parental Controls

Although Windows XP was the first version of Windows to make user accounts truly usable, Windows Vista was the first to make them safe for children. In that OS, Microsoft first offered Parental Controls that can be applied to your children's accounts to keep them away from the bad stuff online and off, and give you peace of mind that was previously lacking when the kids got on a computer. Like Windows Vista, Windows 7's Parental Controls are available on a per-user basis.

Secret Parental Controls are available in Windows 7 Home Basic, Home Premium, and Ultimate, but not Professional or Enterprise.

Configuring Parental Controls

To set up Parental Controls, you first need to configure one or more user accounts as standard user accounts; these are the accounts that your children will use.

Secret Parental Controls cannot be applied to an administrator-class account. They can be applied only to standard users. In addition, there's another limitation. While it's technically possible to configure Parental Controls on a system in which one or more administrators do not have passwords, doing so would be folly. Parental Controls rely on the controlled accounts (your kids' accounts) not having access to administrator accounts. If one or more administrator-class accounts do not have passwords, your kids will be able to bypass any controls you set up. Thus, be sure that any administrator-class accounts on the PC have passwords.

Then, from an administrator account, you can configure Parental Controls. To do so, just type **parental** in Start Menu Search to locate and access the Parental Controls application (Figure 8-12). Then select the user to which you'd like to add Parental Controls. You will see the User Controls dialog.

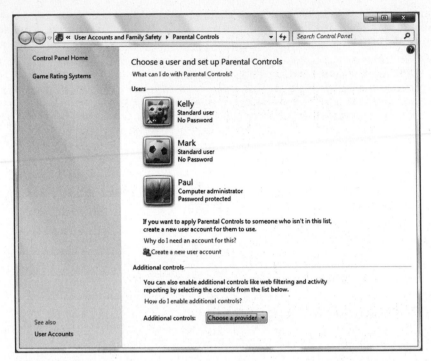

Figure 8-12: Parental Controls enable you to configure various restrictions for your children.

Secret

You will most likely see a message in the Parental Controls control panel stating that web filtering and activity reporting are not available on this computer, as shown in Figure 8-13. In Windows Vista, these features were part of the built-in Parental Controls functionality. But in Windows 7, these features are now part of Windows Live Family Safety, which you must install and configure separately. We look at Family Safety—and these features—later in this chapter.

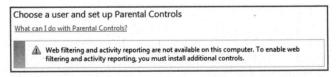

Figure 8-13: Don't worry about the warning. You can add this functionality later with Windows Live Family Safety.

tip

You can configure Parental Controls on only one account at a time. If you have three children to whom you'd like to apply identical Parental Controls, unfortunately you will have to repeat these steps for each of your children's accounts.

By default, Parental Controls are not enabled for any standard user accounts. When you do enable Parental Controls by checking the option titled On, enforce current settings, you can configure the features discussed in the following sections.

Time Limits

This is one of our favorite Parental Controls because it's so obvious and graphical. The Time Restrictions Parental Controls provides a graphical grid that enables you to configure exactly when your kids can use the computer. By default, Windows 7 users can use the PC on any day at any time, but by dragging your mouse around the grid shown in Figure 8-14 you can prevent your children from using the computer at specific hours, such as late at night or during school hours.

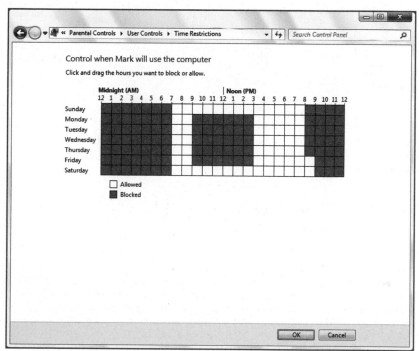

Figure 8-14: This simple and effective interface helps you configure when your kids can and cannot use the PC.

Games

The Game Restrictions Parental Controls specifies whether your children can play games on the PC and, if so, which games they can access. By default, standard account holders can play all games. Of course, you can fine-tune that setting using the screen shown in Figure 8-15, which appears when you click Set game ratings.

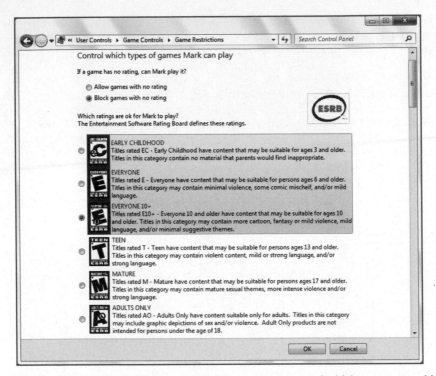

Figure 8-15: With the games restrictions, you can control which games your kids play.

Here you can set acceptable game ratings using the rating system enabled on your PC. The most common and default system (regardless of where you are in the world) is the Entertainment Software Ratings Board's (ESRB). Additionally, you can block games based on content, using a surprising range of content types, including unrated online games, alcohol and tobacco reference, alcohol reference, animated blood, blood, blood and gore, cartoon violence, comic mischief, crude humor, drug and alcohol reference, drug and tobacco reference, drug reference, edutainment, fantasy violence, and about 200 others. It's a long list.

Finally, you can also block or allow specific games, which is surprisingly helpful because many Windows games do not digitally identify their rating. The nice thing about this UI, shown in Figure 8-16, is that Parental Controls sees which games are already installed on the system and enables you to supply a Caesar-style yea or nay.

Allow and Block Specific Programs
This final setting lets you manually specify applications that you do or do not want your child to use. By default, standard users can access all of the applications installed on the system. However, using the interface shown in Figure 8-17, it's possible to fine-tune what's allowed. If you don't see an application in the list, click Browse to find it.

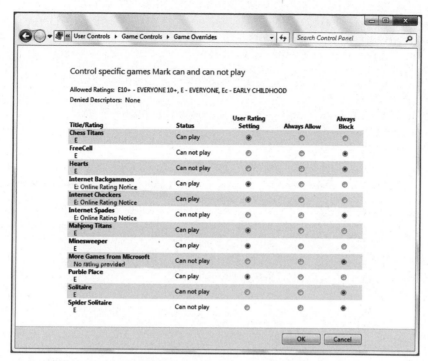

Figure 8-16: Use this dialog to block or allow specific game titles.

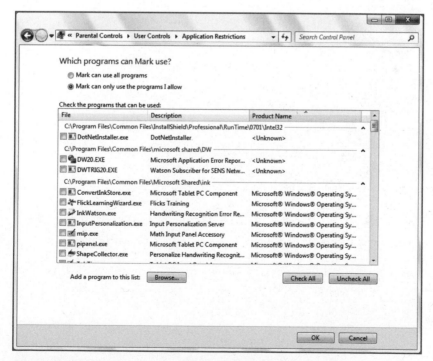

Figure 8-17: Use this dialog to block or allow specific programs.

Where Did the Activity Reporting and Web Filtering Features Go?

Users of Windows Vista's Parental Controls feature will probably notice two features missing after upgrading Windows 7. To streamline Windows 7, Microsoft removed the Activity Reporting and Web Filtering features, replacing it with a behind-the-scenes framework that allows trusted third-party providers to extend Windows' built-in Parental Control functionality.

These features aren't really gone, though. Microsoft simply moved these features into their free Windows Live Family Safety product, which comes bundled with code that hooks directly into Windows 7. We will go over Windows Live Family Safety in a moment.

Secret

One of the most unique features of Windows 7's Parental Controls is that they don't necessarily have to be limited to children. Indeed, many security-conscious users will find that it's worth setting up a standard user account for themselves, applying various Parental Controls to it, and then using that account for their normal PC operations. Why would you want to do such a thing? Well, for starters, you might want to protect yourself from some of the nastier things that happen online. It's something to think about.

Running as Standard User with Parental Controls

You may be wondering what the experience is like running a standard user account to which Parental Controls have been applied. For the most part, it's just like running a standard account normally, but certain actions will trigger Parental Controls blocks, depending on how you've configured Parental Control restrictions. For example, if the user attempts to log on to the system during a restricted time period, he or she will be prevented from doing so, as shown in Figure 8-18.

Figure 8-18: Sorry, Johnny: your parents say it's too late to be computing.

Similarly, if you try to run an application that is not explicitly allowed by Parental Controls, you will see the dialog shown in Figure 8-19.

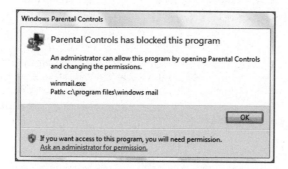

Figure 8-19: Sorry, but this application is being blocked by Windows 7's Parental Controls.

Note that you can ask for permission to run individual blocked applications. When you choose this option, the User Account Control credentials dialog appears (see Figure 8-20) giving parents a chance to review the action and decide whether or not to give their permission.

Figure 8-20: If parents are around, they can okay blocked activities.

Incidentally, some activities are simply blocked and can't be overridden. If you specifically block a game or application, for example, even a parent can't unblock it on the fly, as shown in Figure 8-21. Instead you have to make a configuration change in Parental Controls, back in your own account.

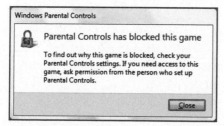

Figure 8-21: Programs that are specifically blocked can't be overridden on the fly.

Extending Parental Controls with Windows Live Family Safety

Windows Live Family Safety is a cloud-based service that offers parental controls to Windows XP and extends the parental controls that are native to Windows 7 with a variety of Web, e-mail, and instant messaging protections aimed at keeping your children safe online. As such, it's best used on PCs that are shared between parents and children. We'll take a look at each feature of Windows Live Family Safety in the following sections.

> **tip**   Windows Live Family Safety is installed as part of Windows Live Essentials, which we discuss throughout the book. If you do not yet have Windows Live Essentials, please install it now by visiting the suite's Web page at download.live.com.

If Family Safety is installed, you can access its functionality via the Parental Controls control panel or via the standalone Family Safety Filter application, which is shown in Figure 8-22. The easiest way to find this application is to type **family** in Start Menu Search.

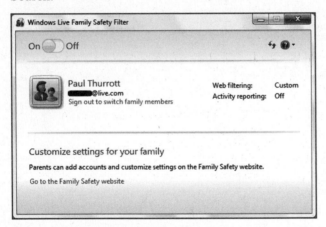

Figure 8-22: Windows Live Family Safety offers a simple interface, but then most options are configured from the Web.

As a Windows Live service, you actually do most Family Safety features configuration from the Web. The Windows application shown above simply determines whether Family Safety is enabled on that computer and provides a little refresh button for manually getting the latest family controls from the Web site.

To access the Family Safety Web site, click the link "Go to the Family Safety website." You should see something like the screen shown in Figure 8-23.

From this Web site, you need to create a Windows Live ID for each child you will be protecting and then associate those IDs with your own Windows Live ID. This is a bit onerous, but once you've got all that configured, you can get up and running with Family Safety's core functionality: Web filtering, activity reporting, and contact management.

cross ref   We discuss Windows Live IDs in more detail in Chapter 23.

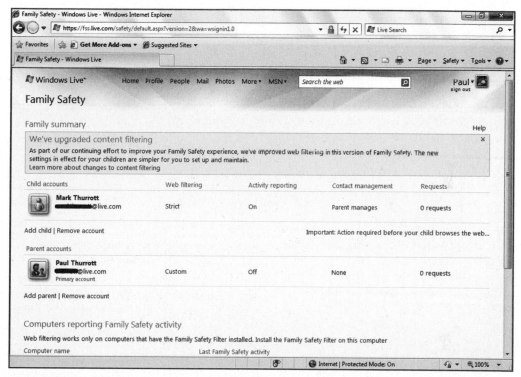

Figure 8-23: The Windows Live Family Safety Web site is where the magic really happens.

Web Filtering

Using the Windows Live Family Safety Web filtering option, shown in Figure 8-24, parents can configure which types of Web sites their children can visit using a number of content categories that are specified on a per-child basis.

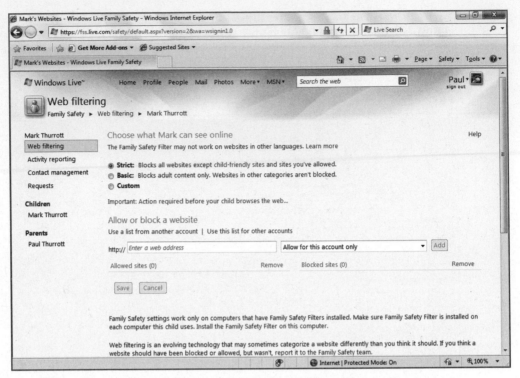

Figure 8-24: Family Safety's Web restrictions will keep your children safe online.

You can choose which sites your children see using simple settings such as the following:

◆ **Strict:** Family Safety blocks all Web sites except for a list of child-friendly Web sites that Microsoft has created as well as whichever sites you've manually configured.

◆ **Basic:** Family Safety blocks adult content only.

◆ **Custom:** If you choose the Custom restriction level, you can determine exactly what kind of Web content you'd like to block. In Windows Vista, you could actually choose to block vast swathes of objectionable subject matter such as adult content, Web mail, social networking sites, anonymizer sites, and other types of sites. But that's not how it works in Family Safety. Now, you can only allow or block specific sites. If you're really worried about the Web, you can block all Web sites except those you explicitly allow.

Activity Reporting

When this feature is enabled, your children's Web- and Internet-related activity is recorded and presented to you periodically in report form. The reports include such things as Web sites visited, instant-message conversations, and e-mails received and sent. Compared to Windows Vista's activity reporting, however, Windows Live Family Safety lacks the ability to monitor webcam and audio usage, game play, file exchanges, SMS messages, media (audio, video, and recorded television) access and logon times. You can see the Activity reporting configuration page in Figure 8-25.

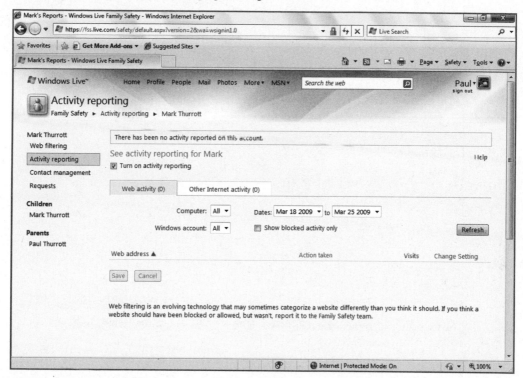

Figure 8-25: With Family Safety activity reporting, you can view your children's online activities.

Contact Management

Windows Live Family Safety's contact management feature enables you to explicitly control which contact-driven Windows Live services your children can use and which contacts they can communicate with. Specifically, you can control access to Windows Live Messenger (instant messaging), Windows Live Hotmail (Web-based e-mail), and Windows Live Spaces (blogging), and manage your children's contact list, removing and adding contacts as you see fit. This is shown in Figure 8-26. Finally, if you wish, you can give your children the freedom to manage their own contacts, but retain the ability to check in from time to time and intervene when necessary.

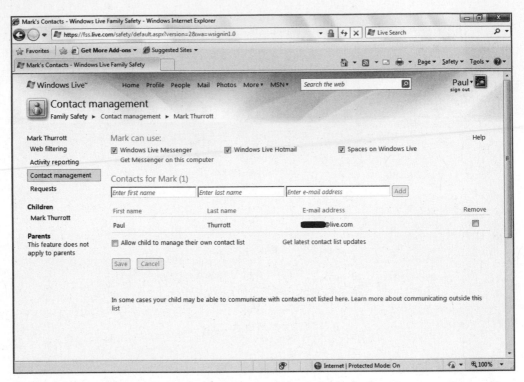

Figure 8-26: Contact management enables you to keep track of who can communicate with your children online.

> **caution**
> Note that while Live Family Safety's contact management feature works well, it does nothing to block people from services outside of Windows Live from contacting your children. You will have to rely on the service's Web filtering functionality to keep away predators that might be lurking on MySpace or other non-Microsoft Web services.

Requests

There may come a time when your child wants to add a particular Web site to his or her Allow list or perhaps add a friend to the contact list. At that time, a window will pop up, and they will be given two ways to ask for your permission—in person or via e-mail. This is shown in Figure 8-27.

Clicking "Ask in person" will simply ask the child to call you over to sign in and authorize the transaction by providing your administrative password. Clicking "E-mail your request," however, will do two things. First, an e-mail is generated and sent to your account. This e-mail simply states your child is trying to do something that requires your permission and that you should visit the Family Safety Web site (http://fss.live.com) to approve or deny this request. Second, a request is added to the Requests page on that site. This page will identify the Web page or contact your child wishes to add and when the action was requested. You can then OK—or deny—the request.

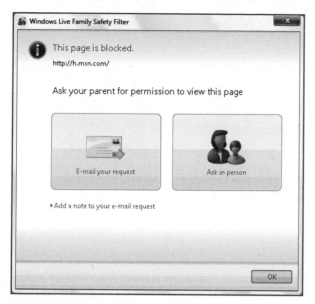

Figure 8-27: Family Safety provides a requests interface so your children can ask permission for certain activities.

Secret

Requests will sit in queue for 30 days. If a request expires, it is automatically denied and removed from the queue.

Summary

Windows 7 continues the tradition of making it possible for users to run the system in more secure ways, thanks largely to advances in the way that user accounts are handled. Although features such as User Account Control will often seem annoying, the alternative is worse, as evidenced by the past half-decade of Windows security vulnerabilities. Windows 7's parental controls, meanwhile, continue to extend a measure of safety to your children, whether they're using local applications or browsing the Web. Sadly, they're not as powerful as the parental control functionality built into Windows Vista, even when you add Family Safety to the mix. But since Microsoft has made parental controls extensible, it's likely that third-party developers, perhaps those that make the more popular security suites, will step in to fill that gap.

Networking and HomeGroup Sharing

Chapter
9

♦ ♦

In This Chapter

♦ ♦

Windows networking has come a long way since the days of Windows 95. Back then, the big news was the move to 32-bit computing, but Windows networking was still largely a heterogeneous affair, with Windows 95 supporting a confusing mix of networking technologies, including Banyan, LAN Manager, Novell NetWare, IPX/SPX, and a then-emerging dark horse called TCP/IP, which forms the underlying foundation for the Internet. Since then, the industry—and Windows along with it—has embraced TCP/IP-based networking as the de facto standard, and support for staples of the previous decade of networking—such as dial-up networking or Microsoft's workgroup-oriented NetBEUI protocol—have been either removed from Windows entirely or depreciated in anticipation of future removal.

Today, networking is all about TCP/IP, wireless, WAN, Ethernet connections, and pervasive connectivity; and Windows 7 is right there, as was its Windows 95 predecessor at the time, supporting all of the new and emerging networking technologies that are relevant now and in the future. If you made the transition from earlier versions of Windows XP to Windows XP with Service Pack 2 (SP2), you're already pretty far down the road to understanding how networking has improved since Windows Vista and again in Windows 7, as that update brought with it a number of modern networking-related improvements. But even Windows XP with SP2 can't hold a candle to Windows 7's networking prowess. In this chapter we'll show you why that's the case and how you can best take advantage of Windows 7's networking capabilities.

Windows XP with SP2: A First Look at Today's Networking Infrastructure

Windows XP is fondly remembered today, but in fact the initially shipped version of that operating system was probably the most insecure product Microsoft has ever shipped. That wasn't obvious at the time, of course, but during the first year of XP's release, hackers launched an unprecedented number of electronic attacks on the system, causing Microsoft to halt new OS development for about nine months so that it could devise its Trustworthy Computing initiative and apply the security principles it learned during this process to its products. The first product to ship after this period was Windows XP Service Pack 2 (SP2), which included a number of security technologies that Microsoft had originally intended to ship first in its next OS, now called Windows 7.

Before moving on to what's changed since then, we will look at the security technologies Microsoft introduced in XP SP2 to see how they compare to their Windows 7 counterparts. Why look at security in a chapter about networking? When you think about it, many OS security features are directly related to networking because the most common way for hackers to attack a PC is electronically, over the network; and with pervasive broadband Internet connections becoming increasingly common, understanding these technologies is critical for anyone using a Windows PC today:

♦ **Automatic Updating:** Beginning with Windows XP with SP2, Windows users received a full-screen advertisement for Automatic Updating, the Windows Update–based service that automatically keeps your Windows PC up-to-date with the latest critical security updates. Microsoft also began using subfile patch-management technologies, keeping the download sizes to a minimum and speeding updates.

♦ **Windows Firewall:** While the originally shipped version of Windows XP did in fact ship with firewall software, it was disabled by default and most Windows software was written with the assumption that no firewall existed. Because firewalls are designed to control the network traffic coming into and going out of your PC, this type of software is key to preventing unwanted software—such as viruses and other malware—from performing dangerous actions and potentially enabling a hacker to remotely control the PC.

cross ref   Chapter 7 covers Windows Firewall.

♦ **Windows Security Center:** In XP SP2, this dashboard monitors the state of the firewall, antivirus, and automatic updating functionality installed on the computer and ensures that they're running and up-to-date. (The Windows Vista version was improved to monitor other security features, including antispyware, User Account Control, and Internet Explorer 7's anti-phishing feature, among others.) In Windows 7, this functionality has been expanded yet again to include system maintenance and other monitoring. As a result, the feature has been renamed *Action Center*.

cross ref   Action Center is also covered in Chapter 7.

♦ **Internet Explorer:** IE6 was dramatically improved in SP2 with a new pop-up blocker, protection against so-called "drive-by" downloads, a new Manage Add-ons applet, and other security-oriented features. Manage Add-ons was significantly enhanced in IE7 and Windows Vista, and of course IE8 adds even more security controls.

cross ref   We look at Internet Explorer in detail in Chapter 20.

♦ **Attachment blocking:** Both Outlook Express (e-mail) and Windows Messenger (instant messaging) were upgraded with blocking functionality for unsafe attachments in XP SP2. Today, both products have been upgraded significantly and moved into the Windows Live initiative, with Windows Live Mail (Chapter 21) and Windows Live Messenger (Chapter 23), respectively.

♦ **Wireless networking:** In the originally shipped version of Windows XP, wireless networking configuration was almost nonexistent. If there was a wireless network nearby, the system would simply connect to it, security be damned. Microsoft changed this behavior slightly in Service Pack 1, adding a block that prevented automatic connections to insecure networks. In SP2, Microsoft applied several changes that were later included in Vista as well, including a new Wireless Connection application and a simple Wireless Network Setup Wizard. Things are even simpler in Windows 7, as you'll soon see.

Put simply, Windows XP Service Pack 2 was a tough upgrade because the security improvements broke a lot of existing applications, causing headaches for users, IT administrators, and application developers at the time. However, these security changes were necessary and have made the transition to Windows Vista and Windows 7 that much easier.

What's New in Windows 7 Networking

Starting with the solid base established in Windows Vista, the focus for Windows 7 networking is to make things as simple as possible while keeping the system as secure and reliable as possible as well. At a low level, Microsoft rewrote the Windows networking stack from scratch for Windows Vista in order to make it more scalable, improve performance, and provide a better foundation for future improvements and additions. (And it has been fine-tuned further for Windows 7.) Understanding the underpinnings of Windows 7's networking technologies is nearly as important (and interesting) as understanding how your car converts gasoline into energy. All you really need to know is that things have improved dramatically.

Secret

In addition to standard IP-based networking, the Windows 7 networking stack also supports the next-generation IPv6 (IP version 6) network layer. (The current version has been retroactively renamed to IPv4.) The big advantage of IPv6 is that it provides a much larger address space than IPv4. IPv6 provides 128-bit IP addresses, compared to 32-bit addresses in IPv4. The IPv6 address space isn't four times as large as that of IPv4, as you might assume, however; it is, in fact, quite a bit bigger. Whereas IPv4 supports 2^{32} IP addresses (approximately 4 billion IP numbers), IPv6 supports 2^{128} addresses, or about 340 quadrillion unique addresses.

That said, IPv6 is still a bit futuristic. There are no mainstream implementations of the technology anywhere yet; but when it happens—and invariably, the Internet itself will have to make the switch—Windows 7 will be ready.

Here are some of the major end-user networking interfaces available in Windows 7:

◆ **HomeGroup sharing:** This is big one. While Windows XP and Vista both supported traditional network-based resource sharing as well as a slightly simpler model, Windows 7 takes it to the next level with HomeGroup sharing. Rather than replace the sharing schemes in previous versions, HomeGroup sharing complements them; this also enables Windows 7 to easily share digital media content, documents, and printers with both Windows 7–based PCs and those based on previous Windows versions.

◆ **Network and Sharing Center:** This interface provides a single place to go to view, configure, and troubleshoot networking issues, and access new and improved tools that take the guesswork out of networking.

◆ **Seamless network connections:** In Windows XP, unconnected wired and wireless network connections would leave ugly red icons in your system tray, and creating new connections was confusing and painful. In Windows 7, secure networks connect automatically. Windows 7 will also automatically disable networking hardware that isn't in use, a boon for mobile computer users on the go who want to preserve battery life.

- **Network explorer:** The old My Network Places explorer from previous versions of Windows has been replaced and upgraded significantly with the new Network explorer. This handy interface supports access to all of the computers, devices, and printers found on your connected networks, instead of just showing network shares, as Windows XP did. You can even access network-connected media players, video game consoles, and other connected device types from this interface.

- **Network Map:** If you are in an environment with multiple networks and network types, it can be confusing to know how your PC is connected to the Internet and other devices, an issue that is particularly important to understand when troubleshooting. Windows 7's new Network Map details these connections in a friendly graphical way, eliminating guesswork.

The following sections cover these features and other new Windows 7 networking features. Note that we save HomeGroup sharing for the end of the chapter, as this is the most major change, and the one that seriously differentiates Windows 7 from both XP and Vista.

Network Locations

If you already have a wired or wireless home network (or, more typically, a home network that features both wired and wireless connection types) or you bring a Windows 7–based mobile computer to a new networking environment (such as an Internet cafe, coffee shop, airport, or similar location), you will run into one of Windows 7's best features: the Set Network Location wizard. Shown in Figure 9-1, this wizard will appear during Setup if it detects a network connection. Or you will see it later, whenever you connect to a new network for the first time. (This is true for both wired and wireless networks.)

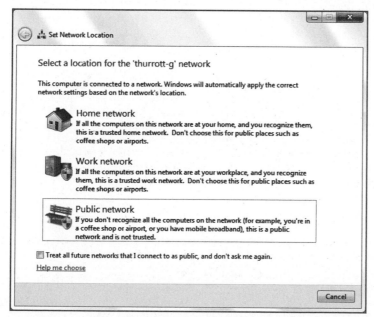

Figure 9-1: Plain English rules: the new Set Network Location wizard makes it easy to configure a network connection securely.

Secret

You can also manually view a similar window by clicking the Network icon in the notification area, choosing Open Network and Sharing Center, and then clicking the link titled either *Home network, Work network* or *Public network* under the View your active networks heading.

The Set Network Location wizard takes the guesswork out of connecting to a network by providing clear explanations of the different ways in which you can make the connection. It offers three options:

♦ **Home network:** Used for your home network or other trusted network type. When connected to such a network, your computer will be *discoverable*, meaning other computers and devices on the network will be able to "see" your PC and, with the appropriate credentials, access any shared resources your PC may provide. Additionally, you will be able to discover other PCs and devices connected to the network.

♦ **Work network:** Used for your workplace or other trusted network type. As with the Home location, a network configured for the Work location provides discoverability of network-based PCs and devices.

♦ **Public network:** This is used for any public network connection, especially Wi-Fi connections you might run into at the aforementioned cafes, coffee shops, airports, and similar locations. With a Public network type, you're assumed to need Internet access and little else: network discoverability is kept to a minimum and software on your system that might normally broadcast its availability—such as shared folders, printers, and media libraries—remains silent.

Secret

Given the apparent similarities between Home network and Work network, there must be some difference between the two, right? Microsoft wouldn't create two different network locations that were, in fact, exactly the same, would it? Actually it would (and did): from a functional standpoint, Home and Work are in fact identical. The only difference between the two is the name and the icon used to denote each network location type: the Home network location features a friendly-looking home icon, whereas the Work network location is denoted by a more industrial-looking office building.

Why have two different locations when a single "Home or Work" location would have achieved the same goal? Keep in mind that the point of the Set Network Location wizard is to make things easy. To the average consumer, Home and Work are obvious options, whereas a combined "Home or Work" might cause a bit of wasted time pondering what that was all about.

Behind the scenes, the Set Network Location wizard is, in fact, working with just two location types, one of which covers both Home and Work and one that represents the Public location. So Home network and Work network are, in fact, really of type Private and Public network is really of type Public.

Setting the network location is generally a "set it and forget it" affair. Windows 7 will remember the unique setting you configure for each network you connect to and then reapply those settings when you reconnect. This is especially handy for mobile computers. When you're at home or work, Windows 7 ensures that your network location type is Private (Home network, typically); but when you connect to the Internet at a coffee shop you may frequent, the location type will be set to Public.

Truth be told, Windows 7 actually does support three network location types, but the third is for networking domains based on Microsoft's enterprise-oriented Active Directory technologies. Because most people don't have Active Directory domains in their homes, we don't examine this network location type too closely in this book. Instead we focus on so-called "workgroup" computing, or what the rest of the industry calls *peer-to-peer networking*. In domain-based networking, all of the security and configuration settings are maintained on central servers, whereas in workgroup computing environments, PCs are islands of functionality and each maintains its own set of users and shared resources.

While Windows 7 does utilize workgroup-type networking by default, the notion of workgroups is now depreciated, especially with the onus of resource sharing largely resting on the shoulders of the HomeGroup technology we discuss later in the chapter. In Windows XP and previous versions of Windows, you could automatically connect to shared folders on other computers only when they were in the same workgroup—that is, on the same network (or IP subnet). But this is not true in Windows 7. In fact, you could configure every single PC in your home with a different workgroup name and you'd still have no issues sharing information between them (and this is true whether you use HomeGroup or not). The only time workgroups are relevant in Windows 7 is when your home network has both Windows 7–based PCs and PCs that are based on older Windows versions. In such a case, you should configure the workgroup name to be identical on all PCs. You do this in a similar manner to how it is done in Windows XP and Vista: from the Start menu, right-click Computer, choose Properties, and then click the *Change settings* link under the heading *Computer name, domain, and workgroup settings*.

What's the real difference between Private and Public network locations? (Or, if you like, Home/Work network locations and Public network locations?) In both location types Windows Firewall is on, but configured somewhat differently. Network discovery is on while connected to Private networks, but off for Public networks. Sharing of folders, printers, and media is on by default in Private networks, but off in Public networks.

When you're connected to a network, you'll see a Network icon appear in the taskbar notification area. (This icon was called a "connectoid" in previous Windows versions.)

This icon can have different states, and while the states are identical between wired and wireless network types, the icons are different. The following states are available:

◆ **Connected with Internet access:** In addition to being able to connect to resources on the local network, you are also connected to the Internet. This icon type is shown in Figure 9-2.

Figure 9-2: This is what you're looking for:
a healthy network connection.

◆ **Connected with local access only:** You are connected to the local network but do not have Internet access, as shown in Figure 9-3.

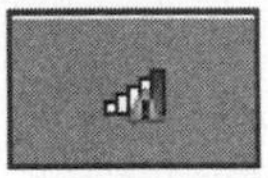

Figure 9-3: This icon means you won't
be connecting to the Internet.

◆ **Disconnected:** We noted previously that Windows 7, unlike XP, doesn't leave stranded disconnected network icons littered around your taskbar notification area. Here is the exception: if you're connected to a network and that connection is severed—perhaps because the gateway or switch sitting between your PC and the network has been disconnected—and there are no other networks to which you can connect, you will see the notification icon shown in Figure 9-4.

Figure 9-4: Houston, we have a problem.

Network and Sharing Center

Most people will simply boot up Windows 7 for the first time, configure the network location for a Home, Work, or Public network location, and go about their business. But Microsoft provides a handy front end to all of the networking-related tasks you'll ever have to complete in Windows 7. Called the Network and Sharing Center, and shown in Figure 9-5, it is indeed a one-stop shop for all your networking needs.

You can access the Network and Sharing Center from a variety of locations. The most obvious is via the taskbar notification area Network icon discussed in the previous section. Just click it once and then click the Network and Sharing Center link in the pop-up window that appears. We recommend the Start menu approach: open the Start menu and type **sharing** in Start Menu Search.

However you enable this utility, the Network and Sharing Center provides a wealth of configurable networking information, as outlined in the following sections.

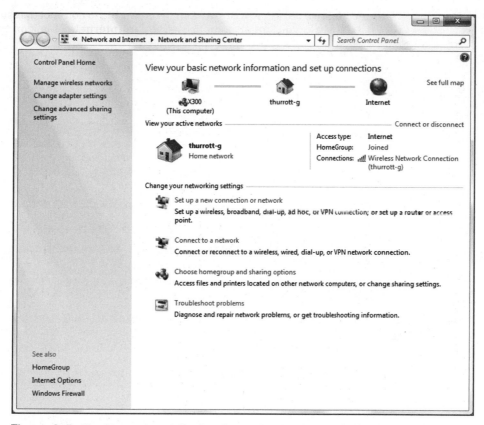

Figure 9-5: The Network and Sharing Center is a front end to virtually all of your networking needs.

Looking at the Network Map

At the top of the Network and Sharing Center window you will see a simple network map depicting the basic relationship between your computer, the local network to which you're connected, and the Internet (see Figure 9-6). For wired networks, on the top, the network name is simply called Network by default. With wireless networks, the network name represents the actual name that was given to the wireless network.

Figure 9-6: A basic Network Map

Secret

Oddly enough, the items in this basic network map are interactive. If you click the computer icon on the left, a Computer explorer window appears. If you click the Network icon, the Network explorer window appears. And if you click the Internet icon, Internet Explorer opens and navigates to your home page.

The Network and Sharing Center can also display a more detailed network map that shows you a topographical view encompassing other PCs and devices on your home network. You can see this map by clicking the link titled *See full map*. As shown in Figure 9-7, this map can be quite full indeed. (More often than not, however, the full map offers information that isn't any more useful than the information provided on the basic map.)

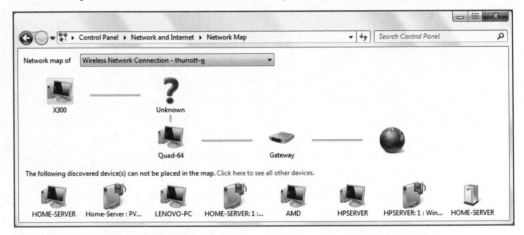

Figure 9-7: Network Map provides a visual representation of your home network.

Viewing Active Networks

Below the basic network map is a list of one or more active (or what you might think of as "connected") networks. Figure 9-8, for example, shows a computer with two active network connections, one wired and one wireless. It's not hard to imagine other multiple network connections. For example, some people may have wireless network access through a high-speed wireless card provided by their cellular company as well as either an Ethernet-based wired network connection or a traditional Wi-Fi-based wireless network connection.

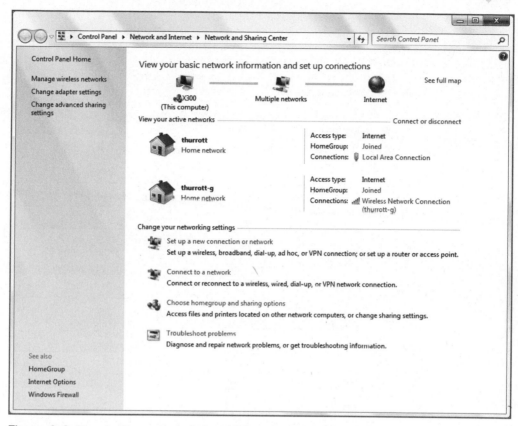

Figure 9-8: You can be connected to multiple networks simultaneously.

In Windows Vista, each active network offered various configuration options. For example, you could rename networks, reassign location types, and even change the icon used to represent the network in Network and Sharing Center. These options were all considered frivolous and useless (which they were) and they've been removed from Windows 7 as part of Microsoft's simplification initiatives in this release. Bravo, we say.

Changing Network Settings

In this section of the Network and Sharing Center, you can configure a number of properties related to network discovery and sharing. The following settings are available:

♦ **Set up a new connection or network:** This triggers the Set Up a Connection or Network wizard, which enables you to manually configure a new network connection.

♦ **Connect to a network:** This triggers the View Available Networks window, which is also seen when you single-click the Network notification icon.

♦ **Choose HomeGroup and sharing options:** This launches the HomeGroup control panel, from which you configure Windows 7's new HomeGroup sharing feature.

♦ **Troubleshoot problems:** This launches the Network and Internet troubleshooter, which is part of Windows 7's new troubleshooting platform.

We discuss most of these features later in the chapter.

Setting Up a New Connection or Network

The *Set up a new connection or network* link in Network and Sharing Center launches the Set Up a Connection or Network wizard, shown in Figure 9-9. This wizard is a handy front end to all of the network connection types you can create in Windows 7. (You will see more options in this window if you are using a wireless-equipped PC.)

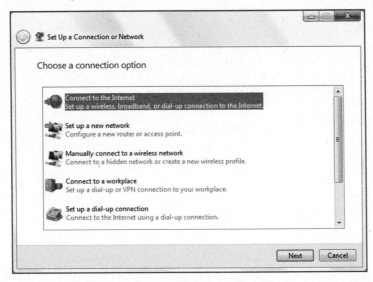

Figure 9-9: Need to set up a network connection? This is the place to be.

Your options here are many, but Microsoft breaks them down to obvious subsets:

♦ **Connect to the Internet:** Choose this if you need to set up a wireless, wired, or dial-up connection to the Internet. Generally speaking, you will almost never need to use this option, but there are two exceptions. One, you may have a DSL or similar broadband connection type called PPPOE (called Point-to-Point Protocol over Ethernet) that requires you to actually enter a user name and password before you can get online. Two, you're using a wireless network (though this option will simply launch the View Available Networks window).

♦ **Set up a new network:** If you just purchased a new Internet router or have just recently subscribed to a new Internet service, you may need to access this option, which looks for wireless routers, access points, and other network connection hardware devices on your network—a process that can take quite a bit of time—and then attempts to configure it for you. Frankly, this type of thing is best handled by either the service provider or directly from the device's own user interface, assuming you know what you're doing. But newer network devices based on the Universal Plug and Play (UPnP) standard can be configured directly from Windows 7. The wizard will detect your network hardware and settings and then forward you to the networking hardware's Web-based configuration. Of course, this varies from device to device, as will your success rate.

♦ **Manually connect to a wireless network:** This connection type is available only on wireless networks. It provides an alternative to the View Available Networks window and is only really needed when you want to connect to a network connection that does not broadcast its SSID (and is thus normally "invisible"). As shown in Figure 9-10, you'll need a bit more information than is normally the case, including the name (SSID) of the network, the security and encryption types, and the security key (passcode).

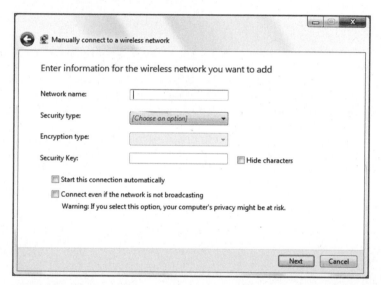

Figure 9-10: Windows 7 can help you connect to hidden wireless networks, too.

♦ **Connect to a workplace:** Choose this option if you need to create a VPN (virtual private network) or direct-dial connection to your workplace. Some businesses require a VPN connection so that any connections between your PC and the corporate network are electronically separated from the public Internet, and thus somewhat protected from snooping. You either need a VPN connection or you don't; and if your company doesn't explicitly configure your PC for this feature or provide their own custom VPN software solution, they will provide instructions on how to get it to work.

Secret

VPNs are notoriously finicky and difficult to configure, connect to, and use. For this reason, Windows 7 includes two technologies aimed at helping users who require this sort of connection. The first is VPN Reconnect, which automatically reestablishes lost VPN connections, without any user action. The second is DirectAccess, a simple and secure VPN-like connection technology that may one day render VPN obsolete. There's just one problem with DirectAccess: it requires your workplace to have implemented this feature on the server end as well, functionality that's available only in Windows Server 2008 R2 or newer.

◆ **Set up a dial-up connection:** The 1990s are calling: if you're stuck in dial-up hell (that is, you need to connect to a dial-up Internet connection via a telephone line and computer modem), this option will get you started. Note that traditional dial-up services such as AOL and NetZero often provide special software and don't require you to use this sort of interface.

◆ **Set up a wireless ad hoc (computer to computer) network:** This option provides a way to set up a temporary peer-to-peer (P2P) network between two closely located PCs with wireless adapters. Why might you want to do such a thing? It can be a handy way to share files or even a (wired) Internet connection. Note, however, that creating such a network disconnects you from any traditional wireless networks, which is why it's rarely needed or used.

◆ **Connect to a Bluetooth personal area network (PAN):** This connection type is available only on PCs with Bluetooth hardware. It provides access to Windows 7's Bluetooth Personal Area Network Devices explorer, shown in Figure 9-11. A Bluetooth PAN is a special kind of ad hoc or P2P network that is typically created to facilitate file sharing between a PC and a Bluetooth-capable device, or between a small collection of Bluetooth-capable devices (such as smartphones, Palm devices, and the like). Note that not all Bluetooth-capable devices support PAN functionality, however.

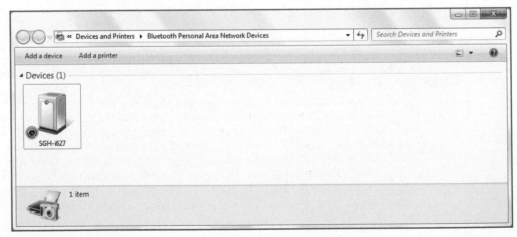

Figure 9-11: Windows 7's Bluetooth capabilities are best suited for device interoperability.

Secret

If you wanted to, you could actually create a PAN between two or more Bluetooth-equipped Windows 7–based PCs. This would enable you to share files using the Bluetooth File Transfer Wizard, shown in Figure 9-12. That said, Bluetooth connections are pretty slow and require the devices to be very close to each other. You're almost certainly better off sharing files over a traditional network, a temporary ad hoc (P2P) network, or via a USB storage device.

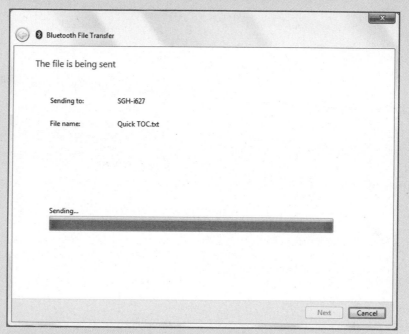

Figure 9-12: Bluetooth file transfers are okay for smaller files only.

Connecting to a Network

Windows 7 offers various ways in which you can connect to networks. The most common, of course, are wired and wireless connections, but wireless networks typically require the most work. With Ethernet-based wired connections, the configuration is simple: you plug one end of the network cable into your PC and connect the other end to your router or other networking interface. If all goes well, you'll be connected to the Internet rather quickly.

For those with a wireless network adapter (including users with both wired and wireless connections), the Set Up a Connection or Network wizard typically presents many more options, as shown in Figure 9-13.

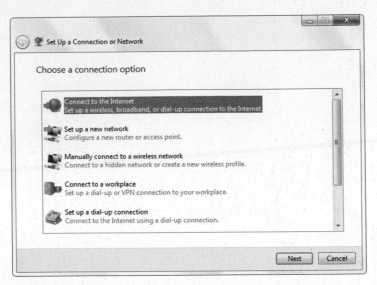

Figure 9-13: With a wireless adapter, you'll usually see more connection options.

The View Available Networks window offers more information than you'll see with a wired connection. From this simple interface, shown in Figure 9-14, you can see which wireless network you're connected to, which kind of access you have, and which other networks are within range.

Figure 9-14: You'll see more in View Available Networks if you're using a PC with a wireless adapter.

Secret

As noted previously, Windows 7's networking stack is dramatically improved over those in older Windows versions; but even Windows 7 can't overcome the limitations and problems caused by home networking equipment and service providers. We've found that many connection problems are caused by either the balkiness of the networking hardware we use or our service providers. In the former case, resetting the hardware gateway/switch often solves connection problems, while resetting the PC's network adapter can sometimes help as well: choose Reset the Network Adapter from the Windows Network Diagnostics wizard to attempt that fix. If the problem is the service provider, sometimes all you can do is call and complain.

Managing Network Connections

If you're coming from Windows XP, one of the biggest network-related changes you'll notice in Windows 7 is what happens when you right-click the Network link in the Start menu (called My Network Places in XP) and choose Properties. In XP, this launches Network Connections, a Windows Explorer view of the various networking devices in your PC. In Windows 7, of course, doing this launches the Network and Sharing Center, a much more comprehensive resource for all your networking needs. (In Windows 7, the Start menu does not display a Network link by default.)

What if you really do want to access your network connections for some reason? In Windows 7, you do this by first launching the Network and Sharing Center and then selecting the Tasks link titled *Change adapter settings*. As in XP, the Explorer location that opens is called Network Connections, and the functionality it provides is virtually identical (see Figure 9-15). It's just harder to get to.

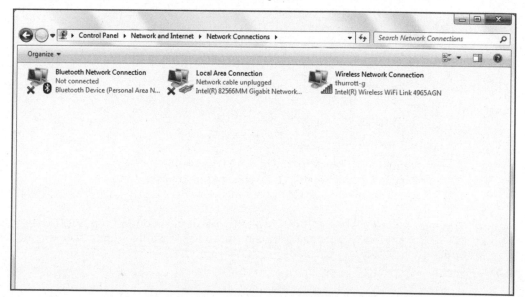

Figure 9-15: Windows 7's Network Connections works just like the XP version.

The big difference is that the visible network connection options—shown when you select a particular network connection—appear in the Explorer window's toolbar instead of in a Network Tasks pane, but the options are the same:

- ◆ **Disable this network device:** Clicking this will disable the device hardware and disconnect you from any connected networks.
- ◆ **Diagnose this connection:** This launches the Windows Network Diagnostics wizard.
- ◆ **Rename this connection:** This option enables you to rename the connection from the bland but descriptive defaults Microsoft chooses (e.g., Local Area Connection and Wireless Network Connection).
- ◆ **View status of this connection:** This launches the connection status window, described previously.
- ◆ **Change settings of this connection:** This option brings up another blast from the past, the old Network Connection Properties window, from which you can view and configure the various network types, protocols, and other networking technologies supported by the connection. As shown in Figure 9-16, this dialog hasn't changed much since Windows 95.

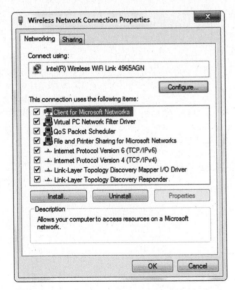

Figure 9-16: Proof that the good old days weren't really that good. Windows networking used to mean actually configuring these options manually.

You may also see a View Bluetooth network devices option if your PC has Bluetooth capabilities. Finally, note that you can right-click a connection to access many of these options.

Secret
Because previous versions of Windows didn't provide a handy front end to all of the system's networking features, accessing Network Connections used to be a common activity. However, thanks to the Network and Sharing Center, this is no longer the case. Therefore, while these options are all still available, chances are good you will almost never need to navigate this far into the UI for any reason. You know, unless you're one of those old-school types.

Other Network-Related Tasks

In the left side of the Network and Sharing Center, you will see a list of two or three tasks, depending on what types of network connections are available in your PC. (The first task, Manage wireless networks, will not appear unless you have a wireless network adapter.)

◆ **Manage wireless networks:** Clicking this link displays a unique Windows 7 interface called Manage Wireless Networks (see Figure 9-17). From this window, you can configure various options for each wireless connection in your PC, including a rather unique one: you can rename the connection by right-clicking it and choosing Rename. Why would you want to do this? We can't think of a single reason.

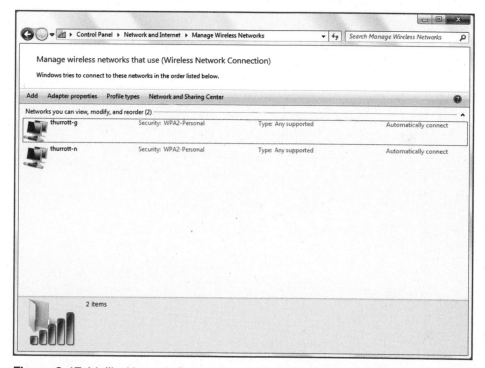

Figure 9-17: It's like Network Connections, but only for wireless connections, and with some unique extra options.

- ❖ **Change adapter settings:** As noted previously, this option navigates to the Network Connections explorer.
- ❖ **Change advanced sharing settings:** This link triggers the Advanced sharing settings window, which enables you to manage network discovery, file and printer sharing, public folder sharing, and other sharing features. We examine sharing later in this chapter.

Using Network Explorer

In previous versions of Windows, the Network link was prominently displayed right in the Start menu, providing you with a quick way to access resources on your home network. In Windows 7, Network does not appear on the Start menu by default. You can enable it via Taskbar and Start Menu Properties if you think you're going to use it a lot (as we do), or you can simply enter **network** in Start Menu Search and choose the Network entry from the search results list that appears.

Either way, when you do so you'll see the Network Explorer, shown in Figure 9-18. Compared to the My Network Places view in Windows XP, the Network Explorer is quite an improvement. (It's very similar to Network Explorer in Windows Vista, however.)

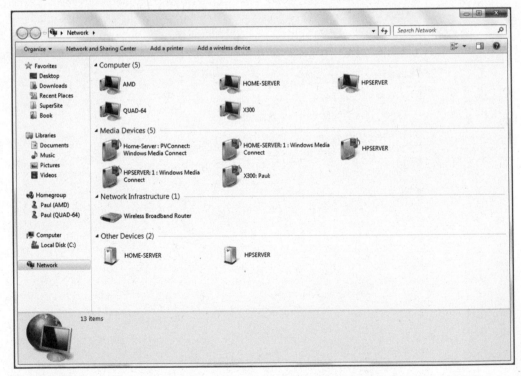

Figure 9-18: Windows 7's Network Explorer connects to far more than just folder shares.

From the Network Explorer, you gain access to the following:

♦ **Discovered computers:** These are computers on the local network that offer folder and printer shares. You should be able to connect to any PCs on a Home or Work network, but only the local PC on a Public network. If you double-click on a discovered computer, you'll see a list of the folder and printer shares available on that system, as shown in Figure 9-19, assuming you have the correct access privileges.

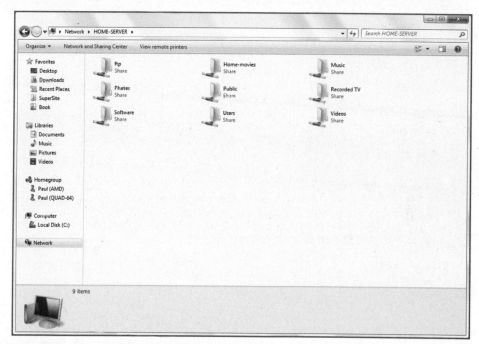

Figure 9-19: You can navigate into discovered PCs to see which shared resources are available.

♦ **Media devices:** This includes digital media–oriented hardware devices, such as Xbox 360 video game consoles, Media Center Extenders, and other digital media receivers, as well as any shared media libraries on Windows-based PCs. Each of these items behaves a bit differently. For example, if you click a shared media library, Windows Media Player 11 will load and display the shared library. Double-click a Media Center Extender and Windows Media Center will launch, enabling you to configure connectivity between the two. And if you double-click an Xbox 360 or other digital media receiver, Windows Media Player will launch and present its Media Sharing interface so you can configure sharing with that device.

♦ **Network infrastructure:** Your broadband router will show up here as long as it's compatible with modern networking technologies such as Universal Plug and Play (UPnP). Double-clicking this icon usually loads the device's Web-based management console, which varies from manufacturer to manufacturer.

♦ **Other devices:** When Network Explorer detects other network devices but can't correctly identify them, it places them in the Other Devices category and provides a generic icon. Windows Home Server (Chapter 10) causes such an icon to appear, for example. Double-clicking one of these icons triggers a UPnP event which, in the case of Windows Home Server, launches IE and displays the server's Web-based welcome page.

Sharing Between PCs

Generally speaking, networking is designed to facilitate two things: a connection between your PC and the outside world—including other PCs as well as the Internet—and sharing resources between your PC and the outside world. For the latter case, Microsoft has been building sharing features into Windows for years in the form of shared folders, shared printers, and shared media libraries, and this functionality is even easier to use in Windows 7 than it was in XP or Vista because of the advent of HomeGroup sharing.

HomeGroup Sharing

When you think of "sharing" with regard to PCs on home networks, you generally mean two types of resources: files and printers. For a long time, Microsoft has supported sharing these types of resources in various ways, but there was always a level of complexity involved. In Windows 7, there's a better way. And while it requires two or more PCs in your home to be using Windows 7, the result is worth it: HomeGroup sharing makes sharing documents, music, pictures, video, and other files, as well as printers, easier than ever.

Secret HomeGroup sharing does not replace the workgroup network scheme that was previously discussed. In fact, to use HomeGroup sharing, you must be on a workgroup. HomeGroup sharing does not work with domain networks like those found in corporations. It is very specifically a consumer-oriented feature aimed at home users.

tip It's very important to understand HomeGroup permissions. With the old-style workgroup sharing scheme we discuss later in the chapter, shared resources are global in that they work across all of the user accounts configured on a PC; but in order to seamlessly access shared folders on other PCs, you would need to make sure each PC has user accounts with the same names and passwords. With homegroups, shared resources are also global in the sense that they work across all user accounts, but the ability to access shared resources is also global: to connect a PC to a homegroup, you just need the homegroup password. And once you're in, you're in. And that's true for all user accounts.

Secret Microsoft's use of the word HomeGroup may seem inconsistent because the word appears variously as *HomeGroup*, *Homegroup*, and *homegroup* throughout the Windows 7 user interface. However, Microsoft tells us this is all by design. The word *HomeGroup* is a trademarked term and refers to the Windows 7 sharing feature. A *homegroup*, meanwhile, is the generic "thing" that is created by the feature, as you will see. And if you see it spelled as *Homegroup* (with a capital "H" but a small "g"), that's just because it's a title or other place in the UI where an initial capital letter is required. Seriously, they told us this.

HomeGroup sharing is so important to Windows 7 that Microsoft actually makes joining or creating a homegroup part of the Windows 7 Setup experience. As you can see from Figure 9-20, you're given this opportunity in one of the final phases of Setup.

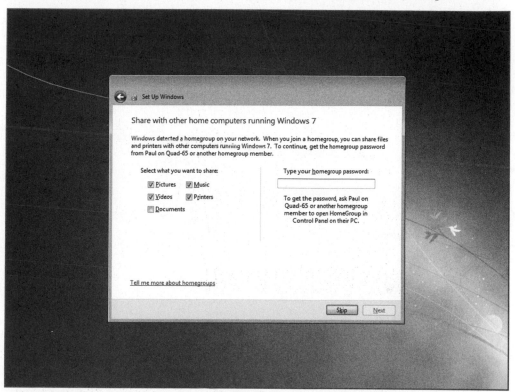

Figure 9-20: You can create or join a homegroup during Windows 7 Setup.

We recommend not configuring a homegroup until you already have Windows 7 up and running. If you run the HomeGroup control panel (either by typing **homegroup** in Start Menu Search or by clicking *Choose homegroup and sharing options* in the Network and Sharing Center) in Windows 7, you'll see a window like that shown in Figure 9-21.

---

tip Well, you'll *probably* see that window. Depending on the status of homegroup sharing and your network connection type, you may see that this computer already belongs to a homegroup, that there is already an existing homegroup configured on the current network that you can try to join, or, if you're joined to a Public network (or domain), that you cannot connect to a homegroup. Here, we will assume that you are setting up a homegroup for the first time.

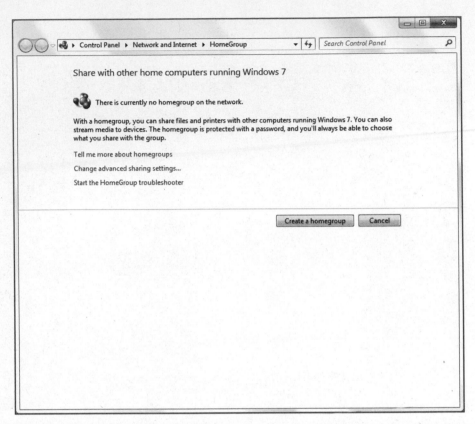

Figure 9-21: The HomeGroup control panel is ready to make network-based resource sharing easier than ever.

Creating a New Homegroup

To create your homegroup, click the Create a homegroup button. The Create a Homegroup wizard appears, shown in Figure 9-22. From this window, you can choose which resources you'd like to share. These include pictures, music, videos, documents, and printers.

Once you've chosen, click Next. HomeGroup will set up your homegroup and then you'll be presented with the password, as shown in Figure 9-23. The wizard recommends jotting this password down, as you will need it on other PCs that want to join the homegroup, but you can skip that step: we're going to change the homegroup's password next.

Click Finish to close the wizard.

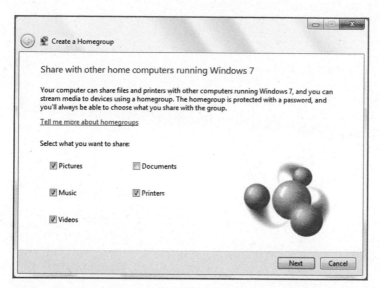

Figure 9-22: When setting up a new homegroup, the first step is to determine which resources you'd like to share.

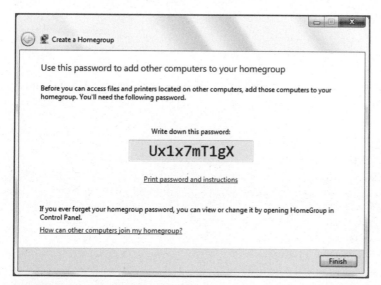

Figure 9-23: The Create a Homegroup wizard provides a homegroup password, but you can change it later.

Joining a Homegroup

Once a homegroup has been created on your network, you can connect to it from other PCs. To do so, you will again access the HomeGroup control panel. Only this time, because there is already a homegroup on the network, the window looks a bit different (see Figure 9-24).

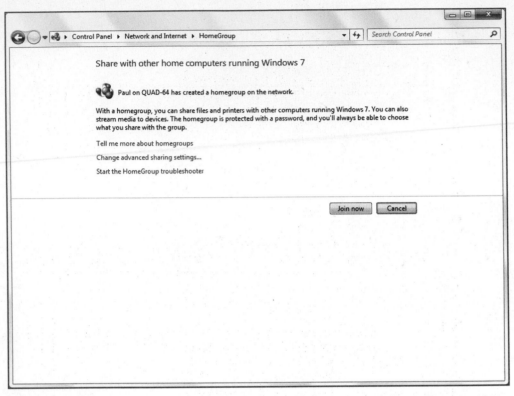

Figure 9-24: If there's already a homegroup on the network, the HomeGroup control panel will let you connect.

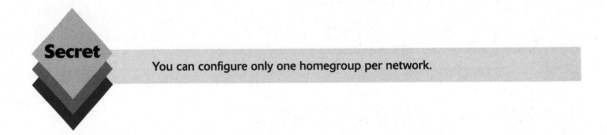

Secret

You can configure only one homegroup per network.

To join the existing homegroup, click the Join now button. You will be prompted to pick the resources you want to share and then enter the homegroup password before you are allowed to join.

Configuring a Homegroup

Once you've created or connected to a homegroup, you can use the HomeGroup control panel to configure it in various ways. As shown in Figure 9-25, once there is a homegroup on your network and you are joined to it, the HomeGroup control panel changes yet again. Now, it's designed to help you make changes to the homegroup configuration.

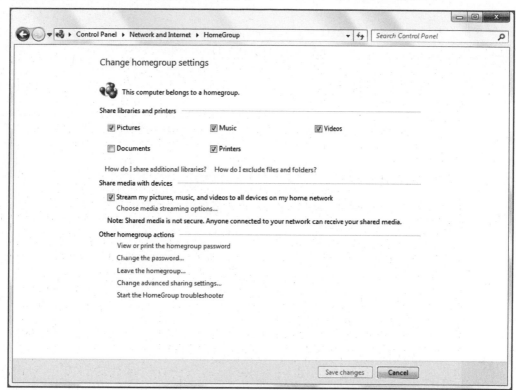

Figure 9-25: Once you're joined, you can start configuring your homegroup.

Secret

Homegroups are not tied to the PC from which they were created. Instead, any PC that is joined to the homegroup can be used to make configuration changes.

Here are the changes you can make to your homegroup from this interface:

◆ **Change which resources you're sharing from this PC.** At the top of the HomeGroup control panel is a section called Share libraries and printers. From here, you can check (enable) and uncheck (disable) the sharing of pictures, documents, music, videos, and printers. The first four items are shared on a per-Library basis.

Secret

You can, however, share other items via the homegroup. There are two instances in which this may be desirable. First, you may have created custom libraries. Second, you may simply have a folder of whatever files somewhere, outside of a library, that you'd like to share. To share nonstandard libraries or any other folders via your homegroup, simply navigate to that location with Windows Explorer. Then, click the Share toolbar button and choose Share with and then either *Homegroup (Read)* (for read-only access) or *Homegroup (Read/Write)* (for full access).

◆ **Share media with devices.** Since all media sharing now occurs via the HomeGroup mechanism, you can access the Media Sharing options window. We discuss this interface in Chapter 11.

◆ **View or print the homegroup password.** This one is pretty self-explanatory but note that you cannot change the homegroup password from this interface.

◆ **Change the password.** This allows you to change the homegroup password. We recommend doing so, and using a password that you will remember if you need to join the homegroup from another PC.

◆ **Change advanced sharing settings.** The enormous window (see Figure 9-26) that appears when you select this option lets you access a number of important network- and sharing-related features. These include network discovery (which determines whether your PC can find other computers and devices on the network and vice versa), file and printer sharing (which can be globally enabled or disabled), public folder sharing (which can be globally enabled or disabled), media streaming (which is accessed via a separate Media streaming options interface we discuss in Chapter 11), password-protected sharing (which affects the old-school sharing methods discussed at the end of this chapter), and HomeGroup connections (which determines whether to allow Windows to utilize simple homegroup-based sharing or to revert to the sharing technologies provided by previous Windows versions).

Secret

All of the settings in Advanced sharing settings can be configured separately for Home/Work networks and Public networks. As you might imagine, most of these options tend to be enabled for wide open sharing on Home or Work network types and are disabled by default on Public network types.

Finally, you can use this interface to trigger a HomeGroup troubleshooter.

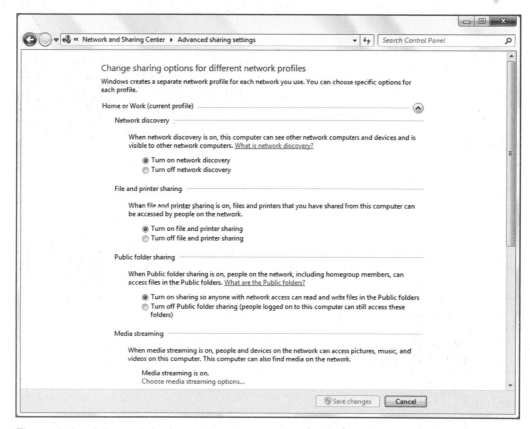

Figure 9-26: Advanced sharing settings is a dumping ground for networking and sharing options that have no other home.

Old-School Sharing

If homegroups are too simple (or too earthy-crunchy) for your tastes, or if you simply want to share files and folders on your Windows 7–based PCs with PCs that are running earlier versions of Windows, fear not: you can still access the old-school network-based sharing technologies that have been available in previous Windows versions for years. In fact, they work much like they did in both Windows XP and Vista: you can choose between a simple, wizard-based sharing mechanism or a slightly more complicated, but much more capable (and, let's face it, *really* old school) method.

Secret

By default, Windows 7 is configured so that folder sharing requires password protection. For example, if you configured a user named Paul with the password 123 on a computer named PC-A and have likewise configured a user named Paul with no password (or a different password) on a computer named PC-B, the user Paul on PC-B won't be able to access any folders shared by Paul on PC-A unless he provides the appropriate logon information when prompted. To bypass this issue, it's best to use passwords for all accounts on all PCs and use the same password when you configure identically named accounts on different PCs.

Sharing a Folder: The Wizard-Based Approach

Microsoft's wizard-based approach to folder sharing is simple enough. Navigating with Windows Explorer, locate and select the folder you'd like to share on your home network. Then click the Share with button in the toolbar, followed by Specific people. The File Sharing wizard, shown in Figure 9-27, will appear.

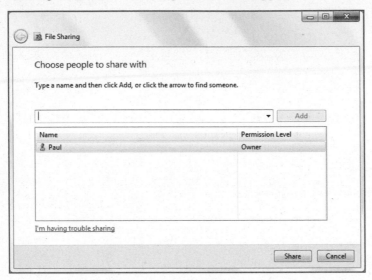

Figure 9-27: Windows 7's File Sharing wizard provides a more fine-grained approach to sharing than did XP's simple file sharing.

In the first stage of the wizard, you set the permission level for each user configured on the system, and remove those users to whom you do not wish to give access. By default, you are configured with Owner permissions, while all other users are configured with Read permissions.

Secret

What's missing, by the way, is the notion of "all users." To give blanket permission to anyone to access a share, you need to access the drop-down box to the left of the Add button and then select Everyone (All Users in This List).

The following permission types are available:

◆ **Owner:** This is essentially admin-level permissions, and you are free to view, add, edit, or delete any shared file, as well as configure or remove the folder share.

◆ **Read/Write:** Users with this permission level can view, add, edit, or delete any shared file. (This permission level was called Co-owner in Windows Vista.)

◆ **Read:** Users with this permission level can view shared files but not add, edit, or delete them.

Once you're done configuring permissions, click the Share button and you're good to go. To change sharing permissions or stop sharing the folder, select it again, choose Share with and then Specific people, and then choose the appropriate option from the File Sharing wizard, which will now resemble Figure 9-28.

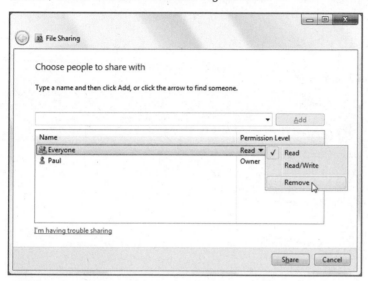

Figure 9-28: The File Sharing wizard can also be used to reconfigure or stop sharing.

Advanced Sharing

The File Sharing wizard works well enough, but if you've been sharing folders with Windows for a while now, as we have, you may actually be more comfortable with Windows 7's alternative sharing UI, which very closely resembles classic file sharing from Windows XP. To access this interface, locate the folder you'd like to share, right-click, and choose Properties. Next, click the Sharing tab, shown in Figure 9-29.

If you click the Share button, you'll see the now-familiar File Sharing wizard. Instead, click Advanced Sharing. This launches the Advanced Sharing dialog, which is very similar to the Sharing tab of a folder's Properties window in Windows XP (when classic file sharing is enabled, as it is by default in Windows XP Professional). The Advanced Sharing dialog, shown in Figure 9-30, assumes you know what you're doing, but it's very easy to use.

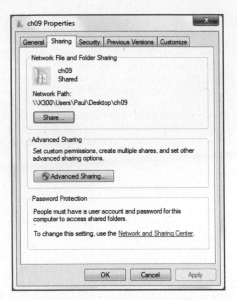

Figure 9-29: Like XP and Vista, Windows 7 offers two ways to share folders: Sharing for Dummies (the wizard) and Advanced Sharing.

Figure 9-30: If you don't mind getting your feet wet, Advanced Sharing is the way to go.

To share a folder this way, select the option titled Share this folder. Then, accept or edit the share name and click the Permissions button to display the Permissions window. From here you can set the permission level for users and groups. By default, only the Everyone group, which represents all user accounts on the system, is present, but you can click Add ➪ Advanced ➪ Find Now to choose other users and groups individually if needed. Click OK when you are done.

Advanced Sharing provides a number of features that aren't available via the File Sharing wizard, and that's why it's good to know about. One is a limit on how many people can be connected simultaneously to the share. Windows 7 limits the number of users who can simultaneously connect to the PC to 10. But you can reduce the number of connections to a given folder in the Advanced Sharing window. (You cannot, however, raise the limit beyond 10.)

Another unique feature of Advanced Sharing is the capability to configure folder caching, which determines whether connected users can cache the contents of shared folders locally for use offline. You access this functionality via the Caching button in Advanced Sharing.

While some people will no doubt have very specific sharing needs, most simply want to open up a portal from which they can share files with others or with other PCs. In this case, Advanced Sharing is actually quite a bit quicker than the wizard.

Sharing Printers

While network-attached printers are becoming more common these days, many people still use printers that are directly connected to an individual PC, typically by a USB cable. In such cases, it's nice to be able to print to that printer from other PCs on the home network. Although you could temporarily unplug these printers and plug them into a different machine, an easier way is available. You can share these printers so that other PCs on the network can access them.

For this to work, the PC to which the printer is connected must be turned on, and not asleep, in hibernation, or shut down. You don't need to leave it logged on with a particular user account, however.

In Windows 7, you share printers via HomeGroup sharing. HomeGroup sharing is simple and requires you to just check the Printers box in the HomeGroup control panel. Simple, no?

Summary

Windows 7 offers the simplest yet most powerful networking functionality of any Windows version to date, with everything you need to create and connect to home networks and the Internet. While all of the features available in Windows XP and Vista are still available in Windows 7, they've all been updated and enhanced. And if what you want to do is share media, documents, or printers on your home network, the new HomeGroup feature makes it easier than ever.

Complete Your Home Network with Windows Home Server

Chapter

10

♦ ♦

In This Chapter

Installing and configuring Windows Home Server

Understanding the Windows Home Server Console

Utilizing Windows Home Server's unique features

♦ ♦

Windows 7 is Microsoft's most impressive desktop operating system to date, but in today's world, few users actually access a single PC. In addition, you use online services, have portable devices such as smart phones and portable media players, and manage home networks with two or more PCs, some of which are laptops and other mobile computers. Throughout this book, we've tried to maintain this sense of perspective, because Windows 7 doesn't exist in a vacuum. Instead, it's part of a complex and growing electronic ecosystem of products and services. That's why we also cover Zune, Windows Mobile, and Microsoft's Live services in this book. They're all interrelated.

But if you're looking for one product that can really simplify the management of a multi-PC home, Windows Home Server has no peers. Don't let the name scare you: though this product is indeed based on Microsoft's enterprise-class servers, Windows Home Server is designed for home users, and it is surprisingly easy to use, given its vast capabilities. In this chapter, we'll examine Windows Home Server, Microsoft's solution for the multi-PC home.

Introducing the Home Server

In late 2007, Microsoft's PC maker and hardware partners began shipping specially designed home server products based around a new operating system called Windows Home Server. Code-named "Q" (and previously code-named "Quattro"), Windows Home Server is just what its name suggests, a home server product. It provides a central place to store and share documents, along with other useful services for the connected home.

Windows Home Server is designed to be almost diabolically simple, and after 2½ years of active development, Microsoft decided that it had achieved an interface that was both simple enough for the most inexperienced user and powerful enough for even the most demanding power user.

Okay, maybe that's a bit of a stretch; but given what it does—bring the power of Microsoft's server operating system software into the home—Windows Home Server is pretty darned impressive. And if you're in the Windows Home Server target market—that is, you have broadband Internet access and a home network with two or more PCs—this might just be the product for you. In many ways, it's the ultimate add-on for Windows 7.

From a mile-high view, Windows Home Server provides four basic services: centralized PC backup and restore, centralized PC and server health monitoring, document and media sharing, and remote access. We'll examine all of these features in just a bit.

Secret

Truth be told, Windows power users don't have to buy a prebuilt home server to get Windows Home Server, though we've both had excellent results doing so ourselves. Instead, if you'd like to purchase just the Windows Home Server software and install it on your own PC-based server, you can do so. Just visit an online electronics retailer such as Newegg.com and search for **Windows Home Server**. The software typically costs less than $100 in the United States.

Windows Home Server Evolution

The initial Windows Home Server generation, which is still current at the time of this writing, is based on Windows Server 2003, a previous generation version of Microsoft's enterprise-class server OS. In addition to the initial release, Windows Home Server has also seen two major updates, Power Pack 1 (PP1) and Power Pack 2 (PP2).

The first version of Windows Home Server provided all of the basics, which are still present in today's product: PC backup and restore functionality, PC and server health monitoring, document and media sharing, remote access, and, as crucially, an extensibility model that enables developers to create add-ins, small software updates that enhance Windows Home Server's capabilities in fun and interesting ways.

Windows Home Server PP1 was released in mid-2008. This update includes compatibility for 64-bit (x64) versions of Windows Vista (and Windows 7), server backup capabilities, improvements to remote access, and a number of other changes. Key among these is a fix for a data corruption bug that affected almost no users but was widely reported by the press.

Windows Home Server PP2 debuted in April 2009 and included features that made this product more interesting to the hardware makers that sell Home Servers. It adds support for the Italian language (in addition to the currently supported Chinese, English, French, German, Japanese, and Spanish languages), improves the SDK for developers, and vastly simplifies the "day one" experience (what used to be called OOBE, or out of box experience), reducing the number of steps a new user has to complete from 23 to 13. PP2 also includes a simplified and improved remote access experience, and enhanced media sharing, especially for Media Center (see Chapter 15) users.

Of course, Microsoft is also working on a next-generation Windows Home Server code-named Veil, which will ship after Windows 7. Windows Home Server v2 will be based on the Windows Server 2008 R2 generation of server products that appeared along-side Windows 7 and will no doubt interact seamlessly with Windows 7 features like HomeGroups. Sadly, that product wasn't ready for testing at the time of this writing.

Secret

In addition to Microsoft's work on Windows Home Server, some key hardware partners have been working over the years to steadily improve their Windows Home Server machines with innovative hardware designs and interesting software solutions that extend core functionality through high-quality add-ins. Key among these is HP, whose MediaSmart Server line has proven to be the customer favorite in the United States, and for good reason: these machines consistently provide an even better experience than the stock Windows Home Server experience documented here. And yes, both Paul and Rafael rely on HP MediaSmart Servers in their own homes. These are excellent servers.

HP currently markets two different MediaSmart families of servers. The high-end MediaSmart EX series is the mainstream Home Server and supports multiple internal hard drives. It's shown in Figure 10-1. The HP MediaSmart Server LX series, meanwhile, is a one-hard-drive option that is aimed at the low end of the market. Shown in Figure 10-2, these servers can be expanded externally.

continues

continued

Figure 10-1: HP MediaSmart EX series Home Server

Figure 10-2: HP MediaSmart LX series Home Server

Windows Home Server Installation and Configuration

Depending on how you acquire Windows Home Server, your one-time install and initial configuration experience will either be long and reasonably difficult or long and reasonably easy. Those who purchase new home server hardware will have the simpler—and likely superior—experience, but configuring the server is a time-consuming proposition in either case. That said, it's a one-time deal. For the most part, you'll install the server just once and then access it remotely occasionally after that.

Secret

Some PC makers, notably HP, have gone to great lengths to make the Windows Home Server initial setup experience much easier than the Microsoft default. See Paul's reviews of HP's MediaSmart Servers on the SuperSite for Windows (www.winsupersite.com/server) to see what we mean.

Once you've purchased a Windows Home Server machine, you simply plug it into your home network, turn it on, and then access it remotely from other PCs on your network. (Check the server documentation for the exact setup procedure, which varies from PC maker to PC maker.)

You won't normally sit down in front of your home server with a keyboard, mouse, and screen, and access it as you would a normal PC. Indeed, many commercial home server machines don't even come with a display port of any kind, so you couldn't plug in a monitor even if you wanted to. Instead, Microsoft expects you to interact with Windows Home Server solely through a special software console.

Secret

You may not be surprised to discover that you can bypass the Windows Home Server administrative console and access the bare-bones operating system if you know the trick. Here's how it works: on a Windows 7–based PC, launch the Remote Desktop Connection utility (type **remote** in Start Menu Search), type the computer name (hostname) of your home server into the Computer field (typically something like HOME-SERVER), and supply the name *administrator* as the user name and the password for the master account that you configured during home server setup. Ta-da! You can now access the Windows Home Server Desktop, shown in Figure 10-3, just as you would any other computer. Note, however, that Windows Home Server is designed to be used remotely via the console, and not interactively, so be careful about installing software or making other changes via this remote desktop interface.

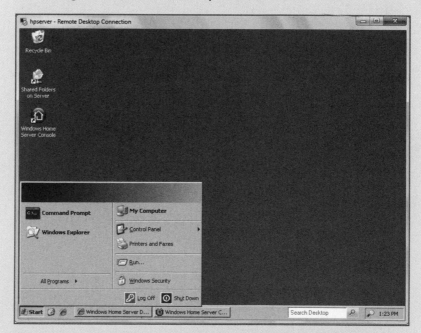

Figure 10-3: If you remotely access the server, you'll find a stripped-down version of Microsoft's enterprise-oriented Windows Server products.

The initial configuration of Windows Home Server involves first installing the Windows Home Server Connector software, which comes on its own CD, on a client PC running Windows XP with Service Pack 2 or 3 or any version of Windows Vista or 7. (You can also access the Connector software via your home network; it can be found at **\\(computer name)\Software\Home Server Connector Software** by default.) The installer will "join," or connect, your PC to the server (see Figure 10-4) for later backup purposes and then complete the setup process.

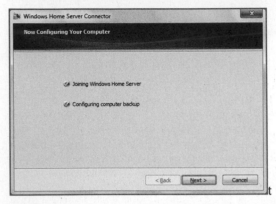

Figure 10-4: Windows Home Server connects to your PC, establishing a backup and management relationship.

Secret

As is the case with any other PC-like network resource, you must log on to the Windows Home Server in order to access it remotely, and that's true regardless of how you plan to access the server (via shared folders, the administrative console, or the Connector tray software). While it's possible to maintain different logons on your PC and the server, it's simpler to make them identical. That way, you will automatically and silently log on to the server every time you need to access it. In fact, Windows Home Server will prompt you to do this, as shown in Figure 10-5, if the passwords don't match. Note, too, that if you configure Windows Home Server for remote access (detailed later in this chapter), the passwords you use need to meet minimum length and complexity guidelines, for your security.

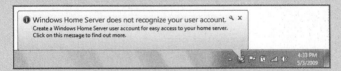

Figure 10-5: It's not required, but your life will be easier if you sync passwords between your PC and your Windows Home Server user account.

Admin Console Drive-By

You can launch the Windows Home Server Console from the Windows Home Server Connector icon in the taskbar notification area. (Remember that Windows 7 will hide this icon under "Show hidden icons" by default.) This icon is a colored square with a white home on it. The color of the icon relates to the overall health of your home network and home server: green is healthy, yellow indicates a warning, and red means something is very wrong.

The Windows Home Server Console, shown in Figure 10-6, is a unique application running remotely on the server. It's an odd little application.

You log on to the console with the Windows Home Server password you configured during initial setup. Once the (overly lengthy) logon process completes, you'll be presented with the UI shown in Figure 10-7. From here, you can manage and configure the various features of the Windows Home Server.

On a standard Windows Home Server install, you'll see a very simple interface with tabs at the top titled Computers & Backup, User Accounts, Shared Folders, and Server Storage. There's also a Network Healthy shield icon and links for settings and help.

Secret

Companies that sell prebuilt Windows Home Server solutions, like HP, often include other tabs in this interface. These tabs expose functionality that is unique to those products.

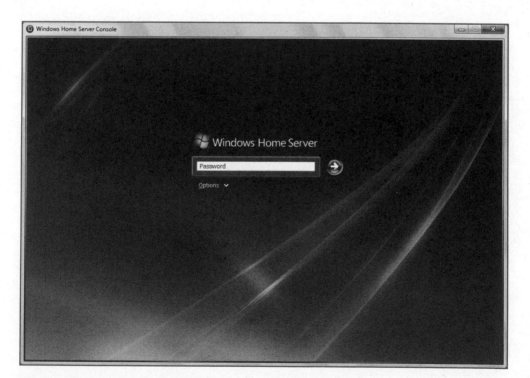

Figure 10-6: The Windows Home Server Console logon interface

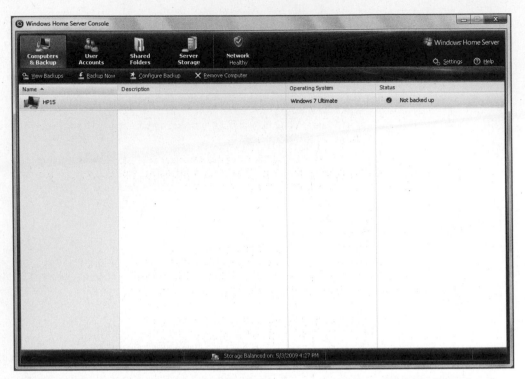

Figure 10-7: The Windows Home Server Console presents a simple, multi-tabbed user interface.

The following sections describe what's available in every Windows Home Server Console user interface, regardless of how you obtained the server.

Computers & Backup

From this tab, you manage the computers connected to Windows Home Server (that is, the systems on which you've installed the Windows Home Server Connector software). A connected PC is one that will be completely backed up to the server by default, but you can configure this at the drive level. For example, you might want to back up only one hard drive on the system regularly, but not the other. By default, Windows Home Server will back up individual PCs overnight.

To configure backups on a PC-by-PC basis, navigate to the Computers & Backup interface in the Windows Home Server Console, right-click the PC you'd like to manage, and choose Configure Backup. The Backup Configuration Wizard shown in Figure 10-8 will appear, enabling you to choose which disks to back up and other details related to the process.

You can manually trigger a backup from the Connector tray icon on the client PC (as shown in Figure 10-9) or from within this interface. (Using the tray is much faster than waiting for the admin console to load, of course.) You can even trigger backups from other PCs if you'd like. Remember: Windows Home Server is all about central management of your PCs, so you're free to trigger backups and other activities from any PC that has access to the Windows Home Server Console.

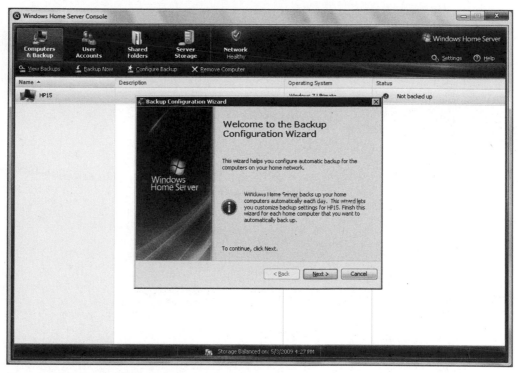

Figure 10-8: The Backup Configuration Wizard

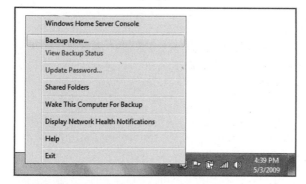

Figure 10-9: You can also trigger backups from the Windows Home Server Connector tray icon on your PC.

User Accounts

In the User Accounts tab, you can create user accounts that allow individuals to access various features of the server. By default, there is a guest account (disabled), but you will typically create accounts that map to accounts on the PCs you use, and thus to people in your home. For example, Paul created a *paul* account, assigned it a complex password (required in Windows Home Server by default), and gave it Full access to all shared folders (see Figure 10-10).

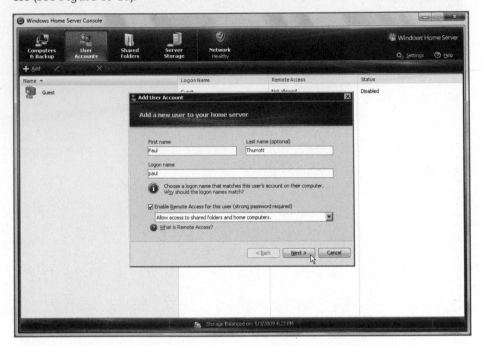

Figure 10-10: Individual user accounts are configured via a simple dialog.

If you want to provide remote access, you need an even more complex password; and you can, of course, specify which users can access which shared folders (described in the next section). That way, your children, for example, could have access to certain shared folders but not others that you want to keep private.

Shared Folders

Here you'll see all of the shared folders that are configured on the server, along with a simple Duplication option for each. This option specifies whether data in that folder is copied to two hard disks for reliability purposes. (Note that you must have at least two physical hard disk drives in the server to access this feature.) You can add and configure shares from here and determine access rights on a user-by-user basis. The Shared Folders tab is shown in Figure 10-11.

Server Storage

This section of the Windows Home Server user interface lists all of the hard drives currently attached to your server, whether or not they're configured for use by the server, and other related information, as shown in Figure 10-12. You can add new storage to the server here or repair a hard drive that's encountering errors. (When this happens, you'll see a health alert in the Windows Home Server Connector tray icon on each connected PC.) You can also remove a hard drive using this interface if necessary.

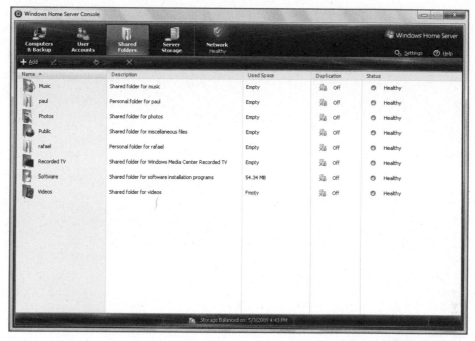

Figure 10-11: This interface is a front end to all of the shared folders on the server.

Figure 10-12: Server Storage shows which drives are configured for use with the server and how storage is allocated.

What you can't do in Windows Home Server is specify where files will be stored. This is handled automatically by Windows Home Server. All you do is create shares, determine whether they're duplicated across disks, and then copy files to that location. In the Server Storage tab, the only thing you can do with a healthy disk is choose to remove it. Simple, right?

Settings

The inconspicuous little Settings link in the upper-right corner of the Windows Home Server Console opens the most complex UI you'll see here, as shown in Figure 10-13—a Settings dialog with eight sections by default, though preinstalled versions of the server may have more.

Figure 10-13: The most complex UI in Windows Home Server is accessed via an almost hidden link.

Default sections in the Settings dialog include the following:

♦ **General:** Configure date and time, region, Windows Update, and other basic settings.

♦ **Backup:** Configure various default settings related to PC backups, including the backup time window (12:00 a.m. to 6:00 a.m. by default); how much time to retain monthly, weekly, and daily backups; and so on.

♦ **Passwords:** Windows Home Server requires very strong passwords by default, because malicious hackers accessing the server over the Web could gain control over the system, and thus over all of your valuable files and, potentially, other PCs on your network if they were able to brute-force attack their way past a weak password. That said, you can change the password policy here if desired. We don't recommend it.

◆ **Windows Media Center:** New to PP2, Windows Home Server can automatically configure Windows Media Center on your connected PCs to "see" the media shares on your home server. There's no interface to the Windows Media Center tab in Windows Home Server Settings per se, but rather some information about the update. But when you run Windows Media Center on a connected PC for the first time, you'll see the prompt shown in Figure 10-14. Click OK to install the Windows Media Center Connector.

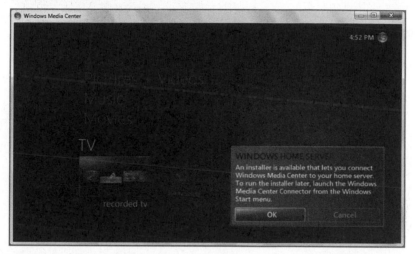

Figure 10-14: Windows Home Server includes Windows Media Center Connector software that provides a seamless interface between the content on your home server and Microsoft's premier digital media solution.

◆ **Media Sharing:** Windows Home Server can share digital media files via default Music, Photos, and Videos shared folders. This interface uses standard Windows Media Connect technology to do so, so if you enable this sharing, PCs and compatible devices on your network (e.g., an Xbox 360 or other Windows-compatible digital media receivers) will "see" the Home Server shares and be able to access that content over the network.

◆ **Remote Access:** In this important and sometimes confusing section, shown in Figure 10-15, you can turn on the Home Server's Web server, configure your home router for remote access and Web serving, and configure your custom domain name (*something*.homeserver.com).

◆ **Add-ins:** Here, you can install or uninstall any Windows Home Server add-ins.

Secret

Microsoft maintains a list of Windows Home Server add-ins on its Web site (www .microsoft.com/windows/products/winfamily/windowshomeserver/ add-ins.mspx) but there's a better list on the Home Server plus Web site (www .whsplus.com).

◆ **Resources:** This last section acts as an About box for Windows Home Server.

◆ **Other settings:** Depending on how you acquired your Windows Home Server, you may see other settings listed in this dialog. For example, the HP MediaSmart Servers we use have additional settings that are unique to HP's hardware; and some Windows Home Server add-ins place their own link here as well.

Figure 10-15: Remote Access is a bit of a black art, but Windows Home Server will try to automatically configure your router.

Deep Dive: Windows Home Server Features

Mousing around the Windows Home Server Console UI is a nice way to see what's available, but it's time to take a closer look at each of the core features of Windows Home Server, with an emphasis on the benefits that each feature offers.

PC Backup and Restore

With the advent of Windows Home Server, Microsoft now offers multiple levels of backup protection to Windows users. Windows 7 features the Backup and Restore control panel, for image-based backup of the entire PC as well as more typical file backup. Windows 7 also includes Previous Versions, a way to retrieve older versions of documents and other files directly from the file system, as well as tools such as System Restore. (These tools are all described in Chapters 24 and 25.)

Windows Home Server offers another level of backup protection via its PC Backup functionality. This Windows Home Server feature provides a centralized backup solution that applies to all of the PCs on your home network (up to 10 PCs). Sure, you could individually configure a Windows 7 Backup on each PC, but Windows Home Server is a better solution because the backups are stored in a more logical place—the headless "back room" Home Server—and because it reduces the required hard drive space by not creating duplicate copies of files that haven't changed.

Windows Home Server Backup provides two basic services: it backs up the entire PC and then performs incremental backups on a daily basis going forward, enabling you to restore your computer to a previous state using a Computer Restore CD that's included with the server. It also provides a way to access and restore individual files and folders, similar to the way Previous Versions works on the local system.

This interface is a bit hard to find. Open the Windows Home Server Console and navigate to the Computers & Backup tab. Then, right-click the computer whose backups you'd like to access and choose View Backups. The dialog shown in Figure 10-16 will appear.

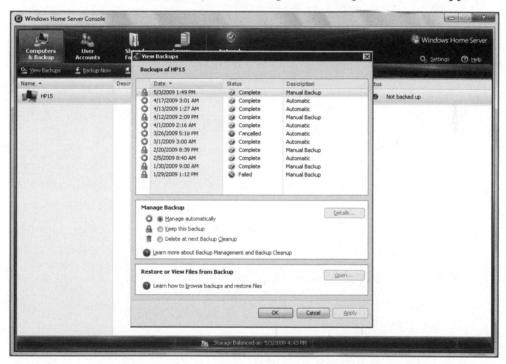

Figure 10-16: You can view all of the backups associated with a particular PC.

To access backed-up files from a specific date, choose the date from the list at the top and then click Open. If the backup contains files backed up from two or more drives or partitions, you'll be prompted to pick one. Then, Windows Home Server will open the backup—a process that can take a few minutes depending on the size of the backup—and provide a standard Explorer window, like that shown in Figure 10-17.

From here, you can navigate around the virtual file system of the backup, find the files you need, and drag and drop them onto your PC as you would any other files. When you close this special Explorer window, the connection with the backup is lost.

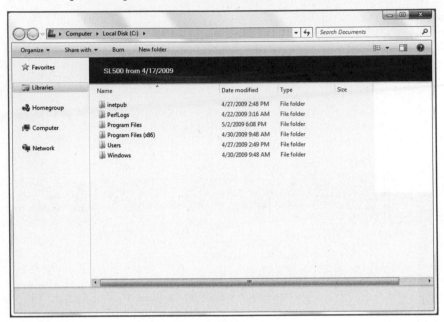

Figure 10-17: Backup sets can be navigated using a standard Windows Explorer window.

PC and Server Health Monitoring

Windows Home Server includes health monitoring, both for the server itself and all of the connected PCs. The overall health of the entire network—the home server and all of the connected clients—is optionally communicated via the Windows Home Server Connector icon that appears in the notification area of any connected PCs. If it's green, all is well; yellow indicates a risk; red is a critical problem; and blue means that the PC is being backed up.

Windows Home Server monitors several things to determine overall health. On the server, it monitors the integrity and free space of the attached hard drives (both internal and external). On the PC clients, it monitors backups to ensure they're proceeding without problems, and, on Vista systems in particular, it integrates with Windows Security Center to ensure that each PC is up-to-date with anti-virus and other security controls. That way, you know when a PC elsewhere in the house is behind on updating its security features and can take proactive steps to correct the situation.

Notifications, which appear when there are issues, can be annoying, as anyone who has used Windows OneCare or similar notification-based security software will know, but individual users can elect to just turn off tray-based health notifications, which isn't a bad idea for all the non-administrators in the house (that is, everyone else in your family).

Document and Media Sharing

While it's relatively simple to share content with HomeGroups or even create a shared folder manually on a Windows 7 PC, Windows Home Server builds on this basic functionality in a number of ways. From a general standpoint, a server is an ideal place to store file archives of any kind, though this may be a foreign concept to many consumers currently. Though we had both been using Windows Server–based servers for years at home, we switched over entirely to Windows Home Server when the product first shipped in late 2007. It's a product we both use and recommend, for its simplicity, functionality, and extensibility.

From a file-sharing perspective, Windows Home Server works like any Windows-based machine. It includes a number of prebuilt shares, such as Music, Photos, Public, Software, and Videos, and it creates a default share for each user you create (at \\home-server\users\ *username* by default). These shares have standard rights associated with them, so whereas even a guest has read access to the Public folder, only a user who was explicitly given the correct credentials can access any share with Full rights. The UI for configuring this is far simpler than what's available in Windows 7, and you can, of course, add other shared folders if you wish. To do so, just navigate to the Shared Folders tab in the Windows Home Server Console and click the Add toolbar button.

Windows Home Server isn't just about simplicity. In addition to making it very easy to access and control access to whatever is available on the server, Windows Home Server also includes a unique and innovative approach to disk storage. Instead of using the arcane drive letter layout that still hobbles Windows 7 today, any hard drive you connect to Windows Home Server is added to the pool of available storage, and you don't need to deal with any disk management arcana. Just plug in the drive, external or internal, navigate to Server Storage, right-click it, and choose Add.

In a nice nod to future expansion, Windows Home Server will work with as much storage as you can throw at it, and it's basically limited only by the USB 2.0, FireWire, ATA, and S-ATA connections on your server. Our Home Server setups both utilize about 4TB of storage, although much of that is used for file duplication.

Indeed, this file duplication functionality is another innovative Windows Home Server feature. Rather than burden users with complicated existing technologies like RAID, Windows Home Server instead supplies a very simple interface that ensures that important files are duplicated across at least two physical drives, so if one drive fails, you won't lose anything critical. Paul has configured Windows Home Server so that all of his digital photos and documents are duplicated in this fashion, for example, while videos are not. File duplication is configured on a per-share basis and is automatic if you have two or more drives connected. You can, however, configure this feature as you will.

Finally, Windows Home Server also makes it easy to remove storage. This way, if you want to disable older, less voluminous storage devices and plug in newer, bigger drives, you can do so without interruption. Windows Home Server first copies whatever data is on the older drives to other drives, and then it removes that drive from the storage pool so you can disconnect it. (Obviously, this requires enough free space on other drives.) It's a brilliant scheme and works as advertised.

More important, perhaps, you can also use the Windows 7 Library feature to monitor Windows Home Server–based folder locations alongside those that are available on your local PC. As you may recall from Chapter 5, the Windows 7 Documents, Pictures, Music, and Videos libraries automatically aggregate content from two locations each on your PC. There's no reason you couldn't also include locations on your Home Server. After all, that's where your content will typically reside anyway.

Here's how: using the Pictures Library as an example, say that you would like this library to monitor a Windows Home Server–based Photos share as well as whatever local folders are already being monitored. To do so, open the Pictures Library and click the locations link under the Pictures Library name in the folder header. This opens the Pictures Library Locations window. Click Add to add a new location. Then, browse to your Home Server's Photos share on the network and click Include folder. Then, click the OK button to close the Pictures Library locations window.

Now, as shown in Figure 10-18, you can see that the Pictures Library is monitoring three locations: the My Pictures and Public Pictures folders on your local PC, and the Photos share on your Home Server.

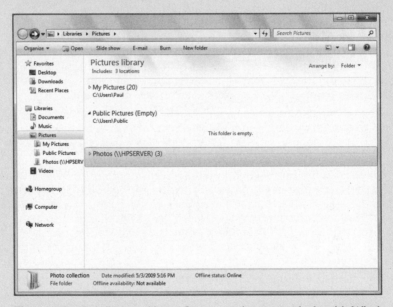

Figure 10-18: Windows Home Server can integrate nicely with Windows 7.

Remote Access

Paul used to subscribe to Logmein.com's Log Me In Pro service at a cost of about $100 a year. This service enabled him to connect to his home-based Windows Server machine, which until late 2007 was his main data archive. From anywhere in the world, he could find an Internet connection. For someone who travels as much as Paul does, this kind of service is crucial: he can't tell you how often he's been out on the road and realized he forgot to copy an important file to his laptop. With Log Me In, he was able to download those files and even remotely access the server UI over the Internet to perform other tasks. It was incredibly valuable.

Windows Home Server includes a superset of this functionality, and it does so at no additional or annual cost. Thanks to the Windows Home Server remote access features, you can access the home server as well as most connected PCs in your home network using a simple and effective Web interface, shown in Figure 10-19.

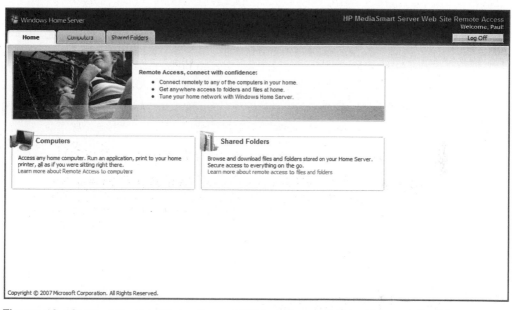

Figure 10-19: The Windows Home Server Web interface enables you to use all of the server's remote access features.

Note the word *most* there: due to limitations of Microsoft's home-oriented Windows versions, you can only remotely control PCs on your home network running Windows XP Pro or XP Tablet PC with Service Pack 2 or higher, Windows Vista Business, Enterprise, or Ultimate, or Windows 7 Professional, Enterprise, or Ultimate.

Secret

Fortunately, you can bypass this built-in remote desktop limitation with Microsoft's Live Mesh software, a free solution described in Chapter 23.

Remote access consists of three related features:

◆ **Windows Home Server shared folders:** The contents of any folders that are shared from Windows Home Server, such as Music, Photos, Public, Software, and Videos, as well as any other folders you've shared, are accessible via the Web interface, shown in Figure 10-20. There's even a Windows Live Search box to help you find exactly what you need.

◆ **Connected PCs:** PCs that are connected to Windows Home Server can be remotely controlled, similar to the way you can control a Windows client or server using Remote Desktop. Obviously, the experience can be fair to middling depending on your connection speed, but it's still great to be able to do this with desktop machines when you're on the road.

◆ **Windows Home Server Console:** You can also access the Windows Home Server Console when you're online but off the home network. The management experience is identical to when you're connected locally, aside from potential speed issues and the fact that the console appears within the browser and not via the traditional console window.

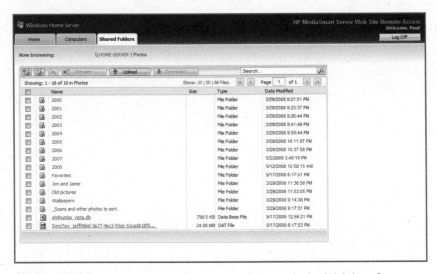

Figure 10-20: Access server-based shared folders via the Web interface.

In addition to all this great functionality, Microsoft has made it really easy to configure and use. By default, remote access is disabled, so you need to utilize the Remote Access link in the Settings dialog to first turn it on and then configure it. Enabling remote access can be either dead simple or utterly painful, depending on what kind of router you're using on your home network. The trick is to use a modern, Universal Plug and Play (UPnP) router: Windows Home Server will automatically configure it for remote access, and all will be well. If you don't have such a device, you need to manually configure your router using fairly technical instructions in the Windows Home Server help files.

Secret

To enable remote access to specific PCs, you need to do a little work on each PC, as there's no way to make it work using just the Windows Home Server Console. On a Windows 7–based PC, open the Start menu, right-click Computer, and then select Properties. Then, click Remote Settings located in the left pane of the System Properties dialog that appears. Under Remote Desktop, select *Allow connections from computers running any version of Remote Desktop (less secure)*, as shown in Figure 10-21. If you choose the *more secure* option, it won't work.

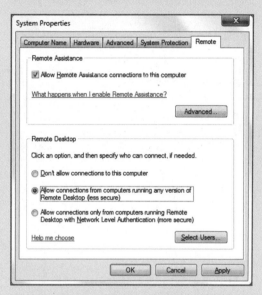

Figure 10-21: Configure Windows 7 for remote access.

Once remote access is up and running, Microsoft (or the PC maker from whom you purchased the server) will give you a free custom URL like *something*.homeserver.com where *something* is replaced by whatever name you prefer. Then you can access your home server resources from the Web using a standard Web address.

Summary

While Windows 7 is an excellent solution for standalone PCs, you must look to additional tools if you want to manage multiple PCs on your home network from a central location. Microsoft offers such a solution in Windows Home Server, which is typically obtained with new home server hardware but can also be purchased separately. Windows Home Server provides four basic services: centralized PC backup and restore, centralized PC and server health monitoring, document and media sharing, and remote access. The combination of Windows 7 and Windows Home Server provides a comprehensive management suite suitable for any home network.

Part IV

Digital Media and Entertainment

Digital Music and Audio

Chapter
11

◆ ◆

In This Chapter

Using Windows Media Player to play and manage music

Understanding the new Windows Media Player user interface

Working with digital music, photos, videos, and recorded TV

Ripping and burning CDs

Accessing your media from Explorer

Synchronizing with portable media devices, including the iPod

Sharing your media library with other PCs, devices, and the Xbox 360

Buying music online

◆ ◆

W indows has always included playback capabilities for digital audio, though those capabilities were admittedly basic until early the 1990s. By the time it was getting ready to retire its legacy DOS-based versions of Windows, however, Microsoft had turned its flagship OS into a multimedia maven. And with the launch of its first all-in-one digital media player—Windows Media Player 7, with Windows Millennium Edition (Me) in 2000—the company made it clear that music and audio were only the beginning.

Today, Windows 7 includes a number of audio technologies that are dramatic improvements over previous Windows versions. Key among them is Windows Media Player 12, which supports all kinds of digital media content, including digital audio and music, videos, photos, recorded TV shows, streaming Internet media, and more.

In Windows 7, Microsoft has augmented Windows Media Player in several important and exciting ways. The player thoroughly integrates with new Windows 7 shell features, providing a custom Jump List and taskbar thumbnail window for a truly unique experience. It is far more compatible with important new audio and video formats like Advanced Audio Coding (AAC), the successor to MP3, and H.264, the video format used by the iPod and Zune. It offers a nice new Now Playing mode that lets you place the player to the side while you get other work done. And it offers a neat new Play To feature that lets you wirelessly push your media library around your home to other PCs and compatible devices, including the Xbox 360. You can even share your media library across the Internet. It's the full meal deal.

As the front end for your digital media content, Windows Media Player really is the only digital media software you'll ever need (well, with one major exception: Windows Media Player still doesn't natively support Apple's dominant iPod, the best-selling portable MP3 player on the planet). In this chapter, you'll learn how to get the most out of Windows 7's digital audio and music prowess, which is exposed largely through Windows Media Player.

Secret   Microsoft is so taken with Apple's iPod that it has emulated that product with its own Zune platform, which includes portable media player devices, Zune PC software, and online services. In fact, Zune directly competes in many ways with Windows Media Player, offering an alternative to the program that Microsoft ships with Windows 7. For this reason, we look at Zune separately in Chapter 14.

Media Player Basics

As is the case throughout this book, we assume you're familiar with basic operations in Windows and its many bundled applications. And because Microsoft has included a full-featured, all-in-one player since Windows Me, it's likely you're at least passingly familiar with this solution.

That said, Windows Media Player 12 can be fairly complicated if you don't understand what it's doing and how it has changed over the past few versions. So we'll get started by examining this new Media Player version and its core functionality before moving on to more complex topics and the neat new functionality Microsoft added this time around.

Setting Up Windows Media Player 12

The very first time you launch Windows Media Player 12, you're forced to step through a quick wizard that enables you to configure various options, as shown in Figure 11-1. Don't just select Recommended settings here, as doing so will configure Windows Media Player using some presets that might have undesired consequences. Instead, you will want to very carefully read through the options. It's possible to configure these options after the fact, of course, but it's better to do so now, as you'll see in a moment.

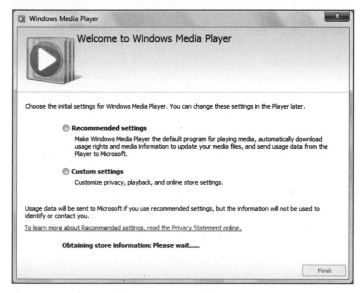

Figure 11-1: Don't ever accept Microsoft's default values.

Secret

On the first page of the wizard, you're asked to choose between Recommended settings and Custom settings set-up choices. You should always choose Custom settings. Recommended settings may be quicker, but it doesn't give you access to the most important Windows Media Player 12 configuration options and instead chooses defaults that benefit Microsoft, not you.

This weird little wizard is a holdover from the Windows XP and Vista days, when Microsoft offered the ability to configure Windows Media Player to work with a default online music store. For example, in the initial shipping version of Windows Vista, Microsoft offered access to an online music service called MTV URGE. Since that time, however, Microsoft and MTV have gone their separate ways: URGE is still available, but it's now part of RealNetworks' Rhapsody online service. Microsoft, it seems, would rather have you purchase music from its Zune Marketplace, which we cover in Chapter 14.

After you choose Custom settings and click Next, you'll be presented with the dialog shown in Figure 11-2, which is very similar to the initial dialog that first appeared in the versions of Windows Media Player that came with Windows XP and Vista. Here, you pick various privacy options.

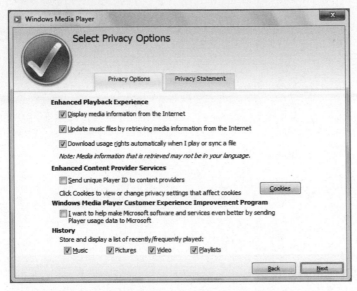

Figure 11-2: Thanks to near-constant lawsuits, Microsoft cares very much about your privacy.

Here are the options you need to think about.

In the Enhanced Playback Experience section, you will want to weigh the second option very carefully. If you already have a finely crafted media library, in which you've lovingly downloaded and applied album art for all of your ripped music files, you will definitely want to uncheck the check box titled *Update my music files by retrieving media information from the Internet*. If you don't do so, you will find that your media library will, over time, become a jumbled mess as Media Player changes your nicely formatted music files to match what a third-party library on the Internet says are the correct song, album, and artist names, often with disastrous results. On the other hand, if you're just starting out and intend to use Windows Media Player to rip your CDs to the PC, you can safely leave this option checked: those who are less precise with their music files—most people, we'd imagine—will actually benefit from this functionality.

In Windows 7, Microsoft has changed the settings for History. In previous versions of the player, Media Player would, by default, save file and URL history. Now, however, you can choose to store and display a list of recently played and frequently played music, pictures, video, radio, and playlists. Each option is selected by default, but each can be individually deselected as well. Our advice is to simply be aware that this is happening but to leave these options selected: it's often handy to be able to find the content you frequently enjoy in this manner.

The other options should be pretty self-explanatory and can be left selected as is.

A second tab on this section of the setup process provides links to two online privacy statements. These statements explain Microsoft's stance on user privacy with regard to the data it collects via Windows Media Player and other applications. It's not as scary as it sounds, and it hasn't changed notably since Windows Vista.

Speaking of Windows Vista, a step in the previous version of this wizard is now missing in Windows 7. Previously, when you clicked Next here, you were presented with a window that allowed you to place Media Player shortcuts on the desktop and Quick Launch toolbar, respectively. These options are no longer available. The Quick Launch toolbar was removed in Windows 7, and a Windows Media Player shortcut now appears by default in the Windows 7 taskbar. In Windows 7 parlance, it is *pinned* to the taskbar.

The next window in the wizard lets you choose to make Windows Media Player the default music player for all of the media types it supports, or you can choose the exact file types that it will play (see Figure 11-3).

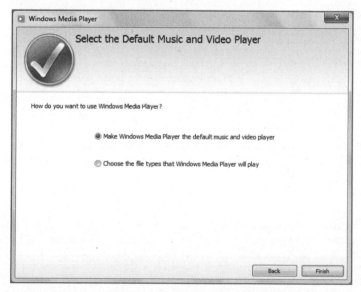

Figure 11-3: Be careful here: the choices are really between utter simplicity and mind-numbingly confusing.

It may not be obvious, but this phase of setup is aimed at experts, and for the most part you should simply choose the first option, Make Windows Media Player the default music and video player. However, if you have strong feelings about using a different media player for specific file types, you can choose the second option. If you do, understand that you'll need to deal with Windows 7's horrible and unfriendly Set Program Associations utility, which is shown in Figure 11-4. Here, you can configure which media file types will be associated—that is, played—with Windows Media Player.

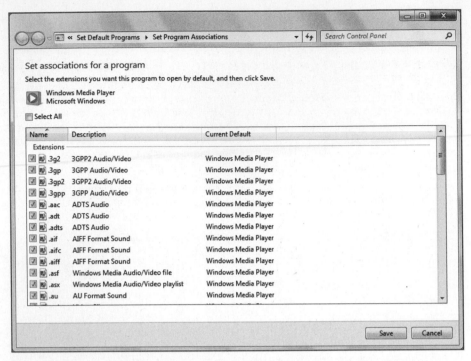

Figure 11-4: In previous Windows versions, this information was buried in the system and configured directly through Windows Media Player. Now it's right up front and personal, but confusing to use.

Secret

What you see here will vary depending on which media player software is already installed on your PC. If you or your PC maker has installed other media player solutions, such as Apple QuickTime Player, Apple iTunes, Microsoft Zune, and the like, you may see that certain file types are configured to work with different applications. Again, this is a power user feature, so unless you really know what you're doing, your best bet is to select the option titled Select All and then click Save.

Note too that these settings are all configured on a per-user basis. If you have multiple users configured on the PC, they can each select different media player applications and associate digital media file types with whatever applications they happen to prefer. Put in more simple terms, you may choose to use Windows Media Player while your children might like iTunes instead. Everyone can make different choices without affecting the other users on the machine.

If you don't choose to alter the file types that are associated with Windows Media Player here, fear not: you can do it later, and at any time. To make this change later, open the Start menu and click Default Programs. Then, click Set your default programs. In the Set Default Programs window that appears, select Windows Media Player from the list on the left. Then, select either *Set this program as the default*, which will assign all possible defaults to Windows Media Player, or *Choose defaults for this program*, which will bring you to the view shown in the previous screenshot.

And that's it, you're done. Once you click the Finish button, you're presented with the actual Windows Media Player user interface.

Understanding the Windows Media Player User Interface

Shown in Figure 11-5, Windows Media Player 12 is an evolution of previous Windows Media Player versions, with a simpler, less cluttered user interface and a visual media library view that relies heavily on album art and photo and video thumbnails. (This latter feature explains the player's desire to connect to the Internet to retrieve media information, by the way.) Also, Windows Media Player 12 adopts the Windows 7 look and feel, with glasslike window borders and the new bland blue color scheme that Windows 7 uses throughout the new shell.

Figure 11-5: It's not your father's media player: Windows Media Player 12 is more graphical, with rich views of your music, photos, and videos.

Secret

Few people realized it, but in Windows Vista, Microsoft used different toolbar color schemes for different types of applications. For example, productivity applications like Windows Calendar and Windows Contacts—neither of which are available anymore in Windows 7—had deep blue toolbars. Media applications, like Windows Media Player 11, had black toolbars. In Windows 7, these distinctions are gone and all applications utilize the same bland blue color scheme instead.

tip Windows Media Player 12 ships with a small selection of sample music and video content, which you can see in the previous screenshot. This lets you get started with the player even if you don't have any content of your own. However, we've loaded up the player with our own content, which makes for some more interesting examples.

Compared to its predecessors, Windows Media Player 12 offers a number of improvements and changes. First, the player no longer uses a hokey, pseudo-rounded window that doesn't quite work correctly (maximize Windows Media Player 10 in Windows XP to see what we mean by this). Instead, Windows Media Player 12 looks and acts like other Windows 7 applications. There's no menu bar by default (though you can access one if you wish), for example.

Windows Media Player sports two bands, or toolbars. In the top band, you'll find Back and Forward buttons, similar to those in Internet Explorer and Windows Explorer, which let you to easily move between the available Media Player experiences. Next to that is a modified version of the breadcrumb bar that first appeared in Windows Media Player 11; this one has been designed to mimic the Windows 7 HomeGroup sharing scheme. On the right side of this top band, you'll find tabs for Play, Burn, and Sync. These tabs toggle various types of playlists that you may want to access as you use the player.

In the second, more traditional-looking toolbar, you'll see items that were inspired by and meant to resemble items found in Windows 7's Windows Explorer. There are Organize, Stream, and Create playlist toolbar items, all of which trigger pop-down menus, on the left. On the right are familiar View Options, Search, and Help items.

Below these you'll see a Navigation pane, for selecting content, the View pane, for browsing and managing content, and, if enabled, a Play, Burn, or Sync pane. Below this large area, near the bottom of the player window, are playback controls.

Okay, it's time to dig a bit deeper.

Using the Back and Forward Buttons

Here's an example of how Back and Forward work in Windows Media Player. If you're browsing your Music library—that is, the Music item is selected in the Library tab—and then click the Video item, you'll find yourself transported to the Video library. You can press Back to get back to the previous experience you visited (for example, the Music library). If you do navigate back to the Music library, you can subsequently click Forward to return to the Video library again. In other words, the Forward and Back buttons work just like their equivalents in Internet Explorer and the Windows shell. Figure 11-6 demonstrates how it works.

Secret

At one time, Microsoft hoped to establish a standardized user interface convention whereby every single Windows application utilized this style of navigation, with Back and Forward buttons in the top toolbar. Over time, however, it became clear that UI navigation wasn't always required and that in certain application types, like wizards, prominent Forward buttons were non-intuitive. Long story short, you'll see these UI elements only in certain places in Windows 7, and typically only where they really make sense.

Figure 11-6: Follow the progression as the user navigates to the Video library, then uses Back to return to the Music library, and then uses Forward to return again to Video.

Using the Library Link, Breadcrumb Bar, and Navigation Pane to Find Your Way

To the right of Back and Forward, you'll see a breadcrumb bar that helps you navigate through the various media libraries you'll access in Windows Media Player 12, including Music (the default), Video, Pictures, and Recorded TV. This UI element first appeared in Windows Media Player 11 (the previous version) and works similarly this time around. Much of it is also repeated in the player's Navigation pane, so you can choose between the two navigational elements when switching between player experiences.

Previous to Windows Vista, Microsoft divided up your media library by media type using an expanding tree view in Windows Media Player that many users found difficult to use, especially those with large media libraries. Regardless of your experience, however, the tree view was a lousy user interface because it was too easy to get lost. Now, Windows Media Player does away with this interface, replacing the tree view with a simpler breadcrumb bar (similar to what is used in the Windows Explorer address bar) that is triggered by the Library link. If you click the arrow to the right of this link, as shown in Figure 11-7, you can choose between the various media types Media Player supports and see only that part of the media library you need. These media types map to the media-oriented Libraries that are present in Windows 7—for music, videos, and pictures—as well as other content types.

Figure 11-7: Media Player isn't just about music.

Secret

The Library link doesn't actually represent the "top" of the Windows Media Player namespace. To the left of the Library link you will see a caret (or sideways arrow) graphic. If you click this, you may see other media libraries on your home network, or that are associated with connected portable devices. That's because Windows Media Player is now aware of libraries beyond your PC. You can select these other libraries and browse them—and play back content—in the same way you would with your own media library (only slower, in most cases).

By default, Windows Media Player displays the Music library, since most people use Windows Media Player to play music. You'll notice that the breadcrumb bar to the right of the Library button lets you dive into your media library in various ways. For example, by default, an All Music view of your media library displays your music content organized by artists, albums, and songs, but you can change this view by clicking on the various nodes in the breadcrumb bar. Say you wanted to view just the albums, and not the individual songs. To do so, click the arrow to the right of Music in the breadcrumb bar and select Album, as shown in Figure 11-8.

Figure 11-8: Media Player's media library view can be changed in a multitude of ways to match your preferences.

What you see in the breadcrumb bar varies according to which section of the media library you are viewing. For example, Music has options for Artist, Album, All Music, Genre, Year, Rating, Contributing Artist, Composer, Parental Rating, Online Stores, and Folder, whereas Video has options for All Video, Actors, Genre, Rating, Parental Rating, Online Stores, and Folder.

As previously noted, many of the locations in the breadcrumb bar are replicated in the more visible Navigation pane, which takes up the left side of much of the player. In fact, as you navigate around with the breadcrumb bar, the Navigation pane view will change to match. The reverse is also true: as you select different media libraries and other views in the Navigation pane, the breadcrumb bar will also change to match.

Which you use is a matter of personal preference. The advantage of the Navigation pane is that it makes it much easier to move arbitrarily around your media libraries. For example, if you're viewing your albums as shown above and suddenly want to look at your digital videos, you can just click the Video link in the Libraries pane and you're there, in a single click. Doing that with the breadcrumb bar would take two or more clicks.

Using the Windows Media Player Toolbar Options

The second, more traditional toolbar in Windows Media Player houses a number of useful options. On the left are three toolbar menu items: Organize, Stream, and Create playlist. These items work like the toolbar menu items in Windows Explorer, so they expose various options via drop-down menus. While not all of these are power user features, some are, and some are simply new to Windows 7. We will examine those here.

Organize

In the Organize menu, you will find a menu item called Manage Libraries, with four submenu items for Music, Video, Pictures, and Recorded TV. As you might expect, these items each launch the Locations dialog associated with the appropriate Library type, as described in Chapter 4. As such, they provide a way for you to determine which physical folders are aggregated to form each Library view. As you can see in Figure 11-9, the Music Library is made up of content from your own Music folder and the Public Music folder, by default.

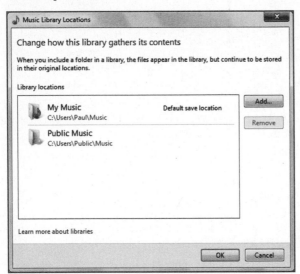

Figure 11-9: The Music Library consists of content culled from two physical locations on your hard drive by default.

You can, of course, determine which folders are represented in your Music Library (and in other Libraries) by adding new locations and, potentially, removing some that were previously configured.

As its name suggests, the Customize Navigation Pane option provides a handy UI for determining which items appear in the Navigation pane. Shown in Figure 11-10, this window provides a simple way to hide items you'll never access, and add those you will.

Finally, the Options item opens Windows Media Player's now well-hidden Options dialog. We will examine that feature more closely later in the chapter.

Figure 11-10: Don't like the Navigation pane layout? No problem: just customize it.

Stream

In the Stream toolbar menu, you'll see only three items, but they're all very important. They're also new to Windows 7 and Windows Media Player 12, owing to the new sharing options that have been exposed by the HomeGroup sharing scheme. We examine these options very closely later in the chapter, so stay tuned.

Create Playlist

The Create Playlist toolbar menu provides options for creating new playlists and auto-playlists, the latter of which are automatically updated as you add new content to your library that matches the playlist's criteria.

Secret

In Windows Vista, Windows Media Player included a separate Layout Options button to the left of the View Options button and Search box in the player tool-bar. This button, alas, is missing in Windows 7, a victim of Microsoft's aggressive anti-clutter campaign with this release. You may be wondering whether the functionality exposed by this button is simply missing in action or is located elsewhere in the Windows Media Player 12 user interface.

Some options literally are missing. For example, you can no longer toggle the display of the player's Navigation pane in this release; it's on for good. And the List pane view has been replaced in this version with separate Play, Burn, and Sync panes, each of which can be toggled via a dedicated tab in the top-right corner of the Media Player window. Other options can be found elsewhere as well: Show Classic Menus (now renamed simply Menu bar) and Choose Columns are both now found in the Organize toolbar menu.

Secret

To access the Windows Media Player 12 menu system without enabling the menu bar, simply tap the Alt key at any time. Alternatively, right-click any empty spot in Windows Media Player's black toolbar button. Either way, you'll see a fly-out version of the Media Player menu appear, as shown in Figure 11-11.

Figure 11-11: No need to enable Classic Menus: the Windows Media Player menu is always available if you just know where to look.

View Options

The View Options button, found to the left of the player's Search box, triggers a pop-out menu, but this one includes just a few options, all of which are related to the way the current media library view is displayed. There are three options here: Icon, Tile/Expanded Tile (depending on the content being viewed), and Details.

In Icon view, the media library displays each item as an icon. Albums appear as they do in a real music store, with colorful and easily recognizable album art. Artists and other groups appear as *stacks*, as shown in Figure 11-12, when there is more than one contained item. For example, if you have two or more albums by Collective Soul ripped to your hard drive, the Collective Soul icon will display as a stack, not a standard square icon, which denotes a single album.

Stacks are cool because they are immediately obvious. They look just like a stack of paper on your desk or, in this case, like a stack of CD cases. You'll see a lot of stacks in both the Genre and Year views in the Music portion of the media library. When you drill into a stack—by double-clicking it—you'll typically see a standard icon view. For example, navigating into the Collective Soul stack mentioned previously shows a display of albums by that band, as shown in Figure 11-13.

Figure 11-12: Stacks denote that the icon contains other items that can be represented by their own icons.

Figure 11-13: Inside a stack, you'll see the contained items.

In Details view, the media library behaves like it did in older Windows Media Player versions: as a textual list of information. This interface, which seems to be modeled after 20-year-old MS-DOS database applications like dBASE III+, is utilitarian, but it also performs a lot faster than the more visual Icon and Tile/Expanded Tile views. If you have a slower computer, a massive music collection, or a low-resolution display, this might actually be your best bet. It will certainly provide the best performance.

tip Depending on what you're viewing, some view styles will not be available. For example, in the All Music view, you can choose the Expanded Tile or Details view but not Icon. But, why would you ever want to view songs in Icon mode?

Instant Search

In keeping with one of the biggest selling points of Windows 7, Windows Media Player includes an Instant Search box so that you can quickly find the content you want. Predictably, the search box in Windows Media Player is indeed instant: as you type in the name of an artist, album, song, or other media information, the media library view is filtered in real time. In other words, it doesn't wait for you to press Enter; it searches as you type.

Secret Instant Search is context sensitive. If the media library is in the All Songs view, it will search for songs that match your search query. If you're viewing artists, it will search artist names instead. If you aren't interested in Media Player trying to outthink you, however, you can apply your search to other criteria—like the entire library—by clicking the drop-down arrow to the right of the Instant Search box and picking the option you want. You'll see options such as Library, Artists, and Albums, as shown in Figure 11-14. These options will vary, of course, according to which media library view you're currently using.

Figure 11-14: Instant Search works well in Windows Media Player and can be used to quickly find particular items in even the biggest media libraries.

Help

New to Windows Media Player in Windows 7 is a blue Help button, which triggers the player's online help. There's not much to say about it, other than that it's new.

> **tip** Oh, what the heck. You can also tap F1 to bring up Windows Media Player help.

Keyboard Shortcuts for Media Player Navigation

If you're a keyboard jockey, you'll appreciate the fact that Windows Media Player includes a wealth of keyboard shortcuts related to navigating around the Media Player user interface. These shortcuts are summarized in Table 11-1.

Table 11-1: Keyboard Shortcuts for Navigating Windows Media Player

Navigation Operation	Keyboard Shortcut
Navigate backward to the previous Media Player experience (identical to pushing the Back button)	Alt+Left Arrow
Navigate forward to the previously accessed Media Player experience (identical to pushing the Forward button)	Alt+Right Arrow
Switch to full-screen mode	Alt+Enter
Switch to skin mode	Ctrl+2
Select the Instant Search box (in Library view only)	Ctrl+E
Display Windows Media Player Help	F1

Playing Music and Other Media

As with previous Windows Media Player versions, you can easily select and play music in the media library; but the range of options you have for doing so has increased over the years, and in Windows 7, Microsoft has put some frequently needed playback options, like Shuffle and Repeat, right up front where they belong. The company has also added a cool, new Now Player mode in this release.

Normal Playback

To play a single song in Media Player, simply double-click the item in any music-based media library view. The song will begin playing immediately. To play a complete album, double-click the album's album art. Simple, right? Most items work this way in the media library.

Secret   There are, of course, exceptions. You can't play a stack of items by double-clicking it, for example. Instead, doing so simply opens the stack and displays the items it contains. If you want to play a stack, right-click it and choose Play. If you want to play it after the currently playing selection, choose Play Next.

In the bottom of the Media Player interface you'll see the universal media playback control, which is centered in the application window and provides simple access to the most frequently needed playback features (see Figure 11-15).

Figure 11-15: The universal media playback control puts the most frequently needed playback buttons up front and center.

These are, from left to right, Shuffle, Repeat, Stop, Previous, Play/Pause, Next, Mute, and a volume slider. The use of these controls should be obvious, but what might not be obvious is how you trigger these features, plus other playback controls, using the keyboard. These keyboard shortcuts are explained in Table 11-2.

> **tip**   The first two buttons, Shuffle and Repeat, are actually toggles, so they can be selected or deselected. When selected, the functionality is enabled.

Table 11-2: Keyboard Shortcuts for Controlling Media Playback in Windows Media Player

Playback Operation	Keyboard Shortcut
Start or pause playback	Ctrl+P
Stop playback	Ctrl+S
Stop playing a file and close it	Ctrl+W
Toggle Repeat (audio files only)	Ctrl+T
Navigate to the previous item or chapter	Ctrl+B
Navigate to the next item or chapter	Ctrl+F
Toggle Shuffle	Ctrl+H
Eject optical disk (CD or DVD)	Ctrl+J
Toggle the Classic Menus in Full mode	Ctrl+M
Fast forward	Ctrl+Shift+F
Change playback to fast play speed	Ctrl+Shift+G
Change playback to normal speed	Ctrl+Shift+N
Change playback to slow play speed	Ctrl+Shift+S
Toggle Mute	F7
Decrease the volume	F8
Increase the volume	F9

Using the New Now Playing Mode

Also not obvious, perhaps, is the new Switch to Now Playing button, which can be found in the bottom right of the Windows Media Player window. In previous versions of the player, Now Playing was a view style, like Library, Rip, Burn, or Sync, that would literally take over the entire player window. This time around, Microsoft has come up with a more elegant solution.

You toggle the new Now Playing view by clicking the Switch to Now Playing button. When you do so, the player switches into the small and clean display shown in Figure 11-16. In this view, only the necessary UI bits are available, and then only when you mouse over the window. Leave it alone, and the player window will display only the song name, artist, album title, and album art of the currently playing selection.

Figure 11-16: The new Now Playing view is small, uncluttered, and graphical.

When you do mouse over the player in this view, you'll see a miniature version of the universal media playback control, with Stop, Previous, Play/Pause, Next, and Volume controls. This is shown in Figure 11-17.

Figure 11-17: When you mouse over the Now Playing view, playback controls appear.

There are also other buttons. The Switch to Library button, in the upper right of the window, switches Windows Media Player back to the default application window view style. And the View Full Screen button, as its name implies, switches the player into full screen mode. This mode makes a lot more sense for video, of course, than it does for music. In fact, unlike with music, video content played in Windows Media Player actually causes the application to enter Now Playing mode automatically, and resize to the dimensions of the video.

Finding and Managing Your Music

If you already have a bunch of CDs that you've ripped to the PC, music you've purchased from an online store, or other digital media content, and you want to make sure you can access it easily from Windows Media Player, take a moment to tell Media Player where that content is.

By default, Windows Media Player monitors your Music Library for music and other audio content, your Videos library for video content, and your Pictures Library for photos and other images. (These libraries aggregate content from the current user's Music folder, the Public Music folder, the current user's Pictures folder, the Public Pictures folder, the current user's Videos folder, and the Public Videos folder.) The player also monitors the Recorded TV folder, which is in the Public folder structure. You can add other folders to this watch list as well.

Secret Recorded TV functionality is available in Windows 7 Home Premium, Professional, Enterprise, and Ultimate editions. We discuss this feature in Chapter 15.

Finding Your Music

In previous versions of Media Player, you could speed media detection by telling it to manually search for media. This was especially helpful when you stored media in a nonstandard location.

This no longer works in Windows Media Player 12. In fact, it's simply unnecessary. That's because the underlying OS has become more sophisticated. In Windows 7, the new Libraries infrastructure formalizes what was previously an application-specific feature and makes it part of the base OS. Now, you use your Music, Pictures, and Videos libraries to determine which physical folders are monitored for content. And Windows Media Player 12 uses these libraries to determine which music, photo, video, and recorded TV files are presented in the player. (We previously discussed how to determine which folders are monitored for the Music library, but as a reminder, it's Organize, Manage Libraries, and then the name of the Library you'd like to manage—Music, in this case.)

If you want to manually add songs to the media library, you can also select them in Windows Explorer and simply drag them into Windows Media Player's media library. Behind the scenes, Windows Media Player will not add those folder locations to its monitored folders list, but will only add the dragged media to the media library.

Power users forego the muse as much as possible. Table 11-3 highlights the keyboard shortcuts used for managing the media library.

Table 11-3: Keyboard Shortcuts for Finding and Organizing Media in Windows Media Player

Media Management Operation	Keyboard Shortcut
Create a new playlist	Ctrl+N
Open a file	Ctrl+O
Edit media information on a selected item in the library (typically rename)	F2
Refresh information in the panes	F5
Specify a URL to open	Ctrl+U

Managing Your Music

As you add music to your collection, you may discover that Windows Media Player's reliance on album art as a visual means for quickly finding your music is a liability, as some music won't have the correct album art. Instead, you'll just see a black square. If this happens, fear not: it's easy to add album art to your blanked-out music. There are two ways: manual and automatic.

To manually add album art to your blanked-out albums, search the Web or browse to a Web site like Amazon.com using your Web browser and then search for each album, one at a time. The Amazon Web site is an excellent repository of album art: Simply click the See Larger Image link that accompanies each album and then drag the image from the Web browser onto the blanked-out image in Windows Media Player, as shown in Figure 11-18. *Voilà!* Instant album art. (You can also use Copy and Paste to apply album art: just use the Windows Copy functionality from Explorer; then right-click the album cover in Windows Media Player and choose Paste Album Art from the pop-up menu that appears.)

Figure 11-18: Album art is only a drag and drop away.

continues

continued

The manual approach works well if you are missing only a few bits of album art, but if you are missing multiple pieces of album art, then you'll want to use a more automated method. There are many ways to do this, but Windows Media Player includes a Find Album Info feature that, among other things, helps you add missing album art. To trigger this feature, navigate to an album that's missing album art in the Media Player media library, right-click the offending album, and choose Find album info. This displays the Find Album Info window. Find Album Info is pretty simple: choose the correct album from the available selections and you're off and running. However, this tool has a huge problem: it works on a track-by-track basis, even when you select an entire album—and that's not automated enough.

Instead of Find Album Info, try another right-click option, Update Album Info (unless, of course, you don't want Microsoft messing with your carefully massaged media files, in which case you've probably skipped over this section anyway). Update Album Info is totally automated: if the online database that Microsoft licenses for Media Player has your album correctly listed, you should see the album art appear pretty quickly.

Playing with Photos, Videos, and Recorded TV Shows

In keeping with its name, Windows Media Player is about more than just music. You can also manage and access other digital media content, including photos and other pictures, videos, and recorded TV shows. For the purposes of Windows Media Player, "recorded TV shows" refers to files that are stored in Windows Recorded TV Show (.wtv) format. This is the format used to record TV shows with Windows Media Center, which you can examine in Chapter 15. (In previous versions of Windows, Media Center used an earlier version of the format called Microsoft Digital Video Recording instead.) But you don't need to use Windows Media Center to access these recorded TV shows; they work fine in Windows Media Player as well.

Accessing Photos with Media Player

To access your photo collection in Windows Media Player, click the Pictures node in the Navigation pane. This will put the media library in Pictures view, shown in Figure 11-19. By default, you will see all photos.

Secret

When you double-click a photo in Pictures view, Media Player switches to its new Now Playing mode and displays the image in a slide show with the other pictures around it, as shown in Figure 11-20. You can use the standard Media Player navigational controls to move through the playlist, shuffle the order, and so on. You can also click the Switch to Library button to get back to the media library.

Figure 11-19: Windows Media Player in Pictures view

Figure 11-20: It's not the optimal way to do this, but Windows Media Player can be used to view photos in a pinch.

Media Player's support of photos isn't fantastic, and you should probably use Windows Live Photo Gallery—described in Chapter 12—to manage your photos instead, because that application includes decent editing tools and is optimized for this task. But there's a reason why Media Player supports photos: so you can synchronize them with a portable device and enjoy them on the go. We look at Windows Media Player 12's support for portable media devices later in this chapter.

Secret   There are many other reasons to use Windows Live Photo Gallery instead of Windows Media Player, at least for photos. Case in point: while you can set the speed of photo slide shows in Photo Gallery, Windows Media Player–based slide shows are always stuck at the same speed (5 seconds per picture). And unlike with Photo Gallery, there's no way to change the theme or the type of the slide show. That said, Windows Media Player is decidedly better than Photo Gallery when it comes to videos, even though Photo Gallery does technically support videos as well as photos.

Playing Videos and DVD Movies

Because of its history as an all-in-one media player, Windows Media Player is an excellent solution for managing and playing videos that have been saved to your PC's hard drive. These movies can be home movies you've edited with Windows Movie Maker (see Chapter 13) or videos you've downloaded from the Internet. Windows Media Player also makes for an excellent DVD player.

You access digital videos in Media Player by choosing Video in the Navigation pane. Videos display as large thumbnails in the media library by default, and double-clicking them, of course, plays them. But it doesn't just play them. New to Windows 7 is a svelte new Now Playing mode that Windows Media Player switches to when playing a video. As you can see in Figure 11-21, this mode is streamlined and sized to the dimensions of the video that's playing.

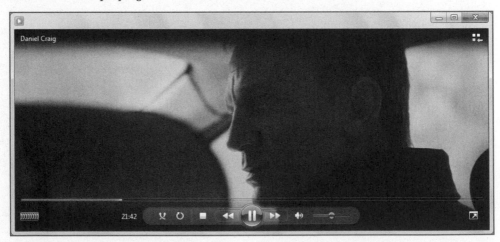

Figure 11-21: Windows Media Player 12 is a particularly excellent way to enjoy video content.

tip You can make video playlists, which is actually pretty useful. Just open the List pane and drag over the videos that you want in a new playlist.

Like previous versions of the player, Windows Media Player 12 supports a wide range of legacy video formats, including MPEG-2, Windows Media Video (WMV) and WMV-HD, and AVI. But Media Player 12 finally makes good on its promise to be the only video player you'll ever need: it also supports modern and popular formats like DivX and XViD, Apple QuickTime, and, most important, MPEG-4/H.264. In the past, you had to download and install balky codec packages to get these formats working, if poorly, in Windows Media Player. Now they're just part of the package.

Windows Media Player also includes DVD playback capabilities.

In pre-Vista versions of the player, you needed to download a $10 DVD decoder in order to add this functionality. DVD playback is shown in Figure 11-22.

Figure 11-22: Now you can play DVD movies in Windows Media Player without purchasing additional software.

Note that Windows Media Player changes a bit when you are watching a DVD movie. The universal media playback control drops the Shuffle and Repeat buttons, which don't make sense in the context of DVD movie playback, and picks up a new DVD button. When you click this button, you'll see the menu shown in Figure 11-23. This provides you with quick access to the root and title menus of the DVD and lets you access other DVD features, like languages, captions, and angles.

Figure 11-23: The DVD menu lets you access features that are specific to DVD movies.

tip

Note that the time display to the left of the DVD button can be toggled between three views: time elapsed (the default), time elapsed and total play time, and total play time. To toggle between these view, just click the time display. Each time you click, the time display changes.

Secret

Instead of spending money on a third-party DVD playback application, you might want to invest in something that's even more useful: software that makes the DVD playback experience demonstrably better. It's called SlySoft AnyDVD and this little wonder provides a wealth of features, including the following:

- Removes region code limitations so you can play back DVDs from outside your country or region
- Prevents DVDs from launching annoying PC-based software automatically
- Allows you to skip directly to the main DVD menu or the start of the actual movie, bypassing those annoying previews and other junk that movie makers always put at the beginning of DVDs
- Bypasses DVD encryption so you can "rip" a DVD to your hard drive and watch the movie without the disc

AnyDVD isn't free, but I think it's worth it. You can find out more from the SlySoft Web site: www.slysoft.com/. I discuss this application a bit in Chapter 13 as well, where I describe DVD ripping techniques.

Regarding DVD navigation—that is, the process of selecting items from menus in the DVD movie you're watching—you will typically want to use the mouse, as keyboard control seems to be unreliable. To navigate DVD menus with the mouse, just move the mouse pointer over items in the menu and watch for selection graphics to appear (these vary from DVD to DVD). Then, you can trigger a selected item by tapping the primary mouse button.

Secret

Windows Media Player 12 is missing only one major compatibility piece that we can think of: it can't play Blu-Ray disc-based movies out of the box. But this isn't actually a huge issue: if your PC came with a Blu-Ray drive, you will have been provided with a third party Blu-Ray player as well, or perhaps an add-on that provides this ability to Windows Media Player. You will get similar software if you purchase a Blu-Ray drive separately.

Playing Recorded TV Shows

If you're using a Media Center PC, or a PC running Windows 7 Home Premium or Ultimate edition and a TV tuner card that's connected to a TV signal, you have the capability to record TV shows (discussed in Chapter 15). TV shows recorded with Windows Media Center are visible in and playable by Windows Media Player as well, and appear in the media library when you select Recorded TV from the Navigation pane. Recorded TV works just like any other videos, as shown in Figure 11-24, but occupy a lot of disk space, thanks to Microsoft's use of an inefficient video codec.

Figure 11-24: Recorded TV shows are like videos, except that they're humongous files.

As with videos, recorded TV shows are shown in a nice thumbnail icon view by default; but if you already have Media Center on your PC, why would you want to access these shows in this fashion? Actually, there are a few reasons.

First, you might want to synchronize your recorded TV content with a portable device so you can access these shows during the morning commute, on a plane, or in other mobile situations. And as you might expect, that's indeed the primary reason this content type shows up in Media Player. But what about users with laptops? You might have Media Center on your desktop PC or Media Center PC, but if you're running a different version of Windows 7 (or a previous version of Windows) on your notebook computer, you can still use Windows Media Player to access that content: just copy the unprotected shows—those that are not protected with digital rights management, or DRM, technology—you want to watch to your notebook, take them on the road, watch them, and then delete them when you're done. (Most TV shows recorded with Media Center are not protected in any way, but individual networks can choose to protect their content. Some, like HBO, do so.)

Secret Seriously, delete them. Media Center content takes up massive amounts of hard drive space. Thirty minutes of recorded TV takes up almost 2GB in Media Center. Yikes.

As you might expect, Windows Media Player supports a wide range of keyboard shortcuts that are related to videos, DVDs, and recorded TV shows. Table 11-4 shows them.

Table 11-4: Keyboard Shortcuts for Video in Windows Media Player

Video Operation	Keyboard Shortcut
Zoom the video to 50 percent of its original size	Alt+1
Display the video at its original size	Alt+2
Zoom the video to 200 percent of its original size	Alt+3
Toggle display for full-screen video	Alt+Enter
Return to full mode from full screen	Esc
Rewind	Ctrl+Shift+B
Toggle captions and subtitles on or off	Ctrl+Shift+C
Fast forward	Ctrl+Shift+F
Change playback to fast play speed	Ctrl+Shift+G
Change playback to normal speed	Ctrl+Shift+N
Change playback to slow play speed	Ctrl+Shift+S

Ripping CDs to the PC

If you haven't yet copied your audio CD collection to the PC, Windows Media Player makes doing so as painless as possible. Know, however, that *ripping* a CD collection—as those in the know call the copying process—can be quite time-consuming, especially if you have a large CD collection. But before you can get started, you need to make a few configuration changes. (What else is new?)

Secret

Configuring Media Player to Use the Right Audio Format

To configure Windows Media Player for CD ripping, right-click a blank area at the top or bottom of the Windows Media Player application window and choose Tools and then Options from the pop-up menu that appears. Then, navigate to the Rip Music tab of the Options window, which is shown in Figure 11-25.

Figure 11-25: Make sure you've set up Media Player to rip music correctly before starting.

There are a number of options here, but we are primarily concerned with Rip settings, which determine the file format Media Player will use for the music you copy. By default, Media Player will rip music to Microsoft's proprietary Windows Media Audio (WMA) format. We cannot stress this point enough: do not—ever—use this format.

continues

continued

Here's the deal. WMA is a high-quality audio format, and much more desirable from a technical standpoint than competing options such as MP3 or Advanced Audio Coding (AAC), the format Apple uses for its own music. But because WMA is not supported on some of the most popular music devices on the planet (including the iPod), we advise against storing your entire collection in a format that could be a dead end in a few years (and potentially incompatible with the device you're using right now).

Instead, we recommend the MP3 format, which is a de facto audio standard that is supported by every single audio application, device, and PC on the planet. Yes, MP3 is technically not as advanced as WMA, or even AAC for that matter. But that's okay. Thanks to today's massive hard drive sizes, you can simply encode music at a high bit rate. The higher the bit rate, the better the quality. (And, not coincidentally, the bigger the resulting file sizes. But again, who cares? Storage is cheap.)

Here's how you should configure Windows Media Player for ripping CDs. First, choose MP3 from the Format drop-down list box. Then, using the Audio quality slider, change the quality setting so that it is three-quarters of the way up the scale (256 Kbps) or higher. The highest setting, 320 Kbps, is even better, but you might not notice a difference between the two.

Prior to Windows Media Player 10, Microsoft did not even include integrated MP3 creation capabilities in its media players. But this functionality is now included at no extra cost, as are DVD viewing capabilities.

Ripping Music

To rip, or copy, an audio CD to your PC, simply insert the CD into one of your PC's optical (CD, DVD) drives. An AutoPlay dialog box is displayed, asking you what you'd like to do. Dismiss this dialog box immediately: instead of choosing Rip music from CD—which is one of the choices you'll see in the AutoPlay dialog—you will want to first ensure that Media Player has correctly identified the disk.

You can completely disable AutoPlay, or just disable it for audio CDs, if you think you're smart enough to remember that you just inserted a disc and don't need to be reminded by Windows. If this is the case, open the Start menu and type *AutoPlay* to locate the AutoPlay control panel. In the window that appears, navigate to the option titled Audio CD (it's the first one) and choose *Take no action*, or whatever choice you prefer. To turn off AutoPlay universally, uncheck the box titled *Use AutoPlay for all media and devices*.

The CD you've inserted should show up in Media Player, as shown in Figure 11-26.

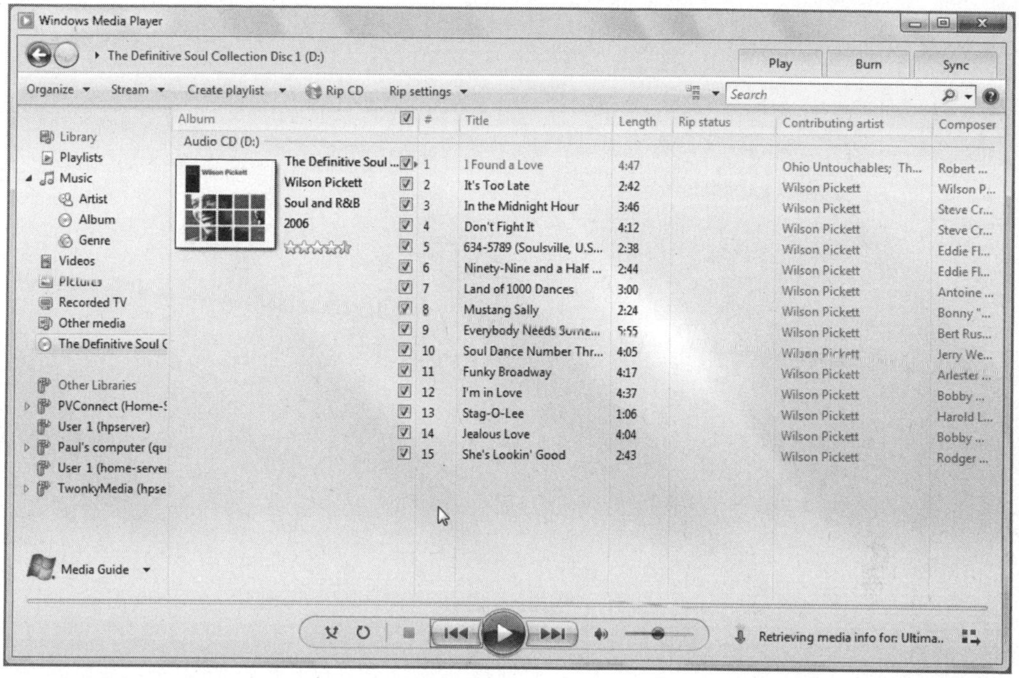

Figure 11-26: Windows Media automatically gets ready to rip any audio CD you insert into your PC's optical drive.

Examine the disk name, artist name, genre, date, and each track name to ensure that they are correct. If anything is wrong—and chances are something will be wrong given the quality of the online service Microsoft uses for this information—you can edit it now before the music is copied to your computer. To edit an individual item, right-click it and choose Edit.

To edit the entire album at once, right-click any item and choose Find Album Info. This displays the Find album information window, shown in Figure 11-27, which compares a unique identifier on the CD with a Web-based database.

If you find a match for the CD you've inserted, select it, click Next, and then confirm that you chosen the correct album.

When everything is correct, click the Rip CD button (hidden in the toolbar) to begin the copy process. Under the Rip Status column, you'll see progress bars for each song that mark the progress of the CD copy. This is shown in Figure 11-28.

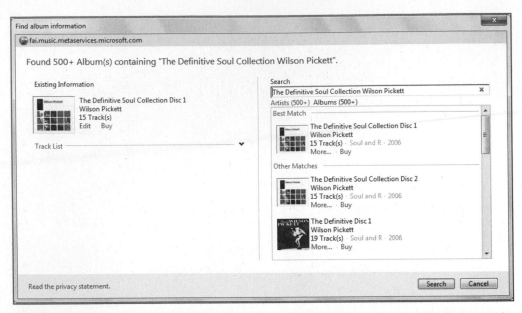

Figure 11-27: Windows Media Player can look up your CD online and, hopefully, find a match.

Figure 11-28: Windows Media Player provides you with an ongoing status update as you rip a CD to the hard drive.

Secret

By default, Windows Media Player copies music to your my Music folder. First, it creates a folder named for the group, and underneath that it will create a folder named for the album. Inside of the album folder, you'll find the individual files that make up each of the tracks in the copied album. You can change the place to which Media Player stores your songs, and the template used to name each file, in the Rip Music pane of the Windows Media Player Options windows.

Burning Your Own Music CDs

When you have a lot of your music on your PC, you're going to want to listen to it in various ways. You can create custom playlists of songs you really like in Windows Media Player, and if you have a Media Center PC, you can even interact with these playlists using a remote control, your TV, and (if you're really on the cutting edge) a decent stereo system. But if you want to take your music collection on the road with you, there are other options. You can synchronize music with a portable device, as described in the next section. Or you can create your own custom mix CDs, using only the songs you like. These CDs can be played in car stereos, portable CD players, or any other CD players.

As with CD ripping, you're going to want to configure Media Player a bit before you burn, or create, your own CD. To do this, open the Burn experience by clicking the Burn tab. As you can see in Figure 11-29, a Burn pane opens on the right side of the player.

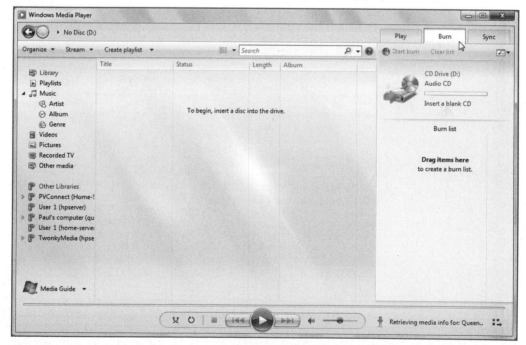

Figure 11-29: The Burn pane lets you burn items to disk and configure disc burning.

To access the various available disc burn options, click the Burn options button in the Burn tab. As you can see in Figure 11-30, a number of options are available right there in the menu, and you can choose More burn options to see more advanced options on the Burn tab of the Windows Media Player Options window.

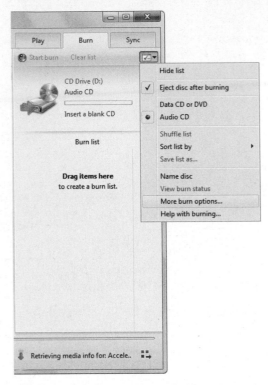

Figure 11-30: It's pretty well hidden, but this menu lets you control disc burning.

Secret You won't normally need to access this interface, with one possible exception: if you notice that your created discs aren't playing properly in your CD player, you can turn down the burn speed of your CD/DVD burner, which might result in more reliable discs.

Secret If you have a CD or DVD player that can play back data CDs or data DVDs, that option will enable you to create disks with far more music. For example, a typical audio CD can contain about 80 minutes of music maximum, but a data CD—with 700 MB of storage—can store 10 times that amount. And DVDs are even larger. Check with your CD player or DVD player's instructions to see if it is compatible with data disks.

When you're sure that you're set up for audio CD creation, insert a blank CD. Windows will display an AutoPlay dialog boxes with two choices by default: burn an audio CD (using Windows Media Player) or Burn files to disc (using Windows). You can choose the first option or dismiss the dialog box and navigate to the Burn experience in Windows Media Player by clicking the Burn tab if it's not already open. When you do so, Media Player displays the Burn pane and creates an empty Burn list.

To add music to this list, navigate through your music collection. Then, drag the songs you want on the disk over to the List pane, as shown in Figure 11-31. (Or use an existing playlist.)

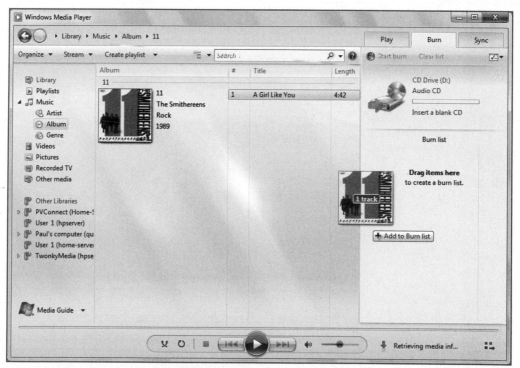

Figure 11-31: Setting up disc burning is as easy as drag and drop.

At the top of the Burn pane, Media Player provides a handy progress bar and time limit gauge so you can be sure that your Burn List isn't too long to fit on the CD. Fill up the Burn list with as much music as you'd like, making sure that you don't go over the time limit. When you're ready to create the disk, click the Start burn button at the top of the Burn pane. When you do so, Media Player begins burning the disk.

You'll see progress bars appear next to each song as they're burned to disk. CD burning moves along pretty quickly, especially on a modern optical drive.

Accessing Media from the Windows Shell

While most users will prefer to manage their digital audio and music (and video) content directly from within Windows Media Player, Microsoft has added unprecedented digital media integration into the Windows 7 shell, and some of this functionality will make accessing digital media directly from the Explorer shell a viable option as well. Key among these integration pieces, of course, is the new Library functionality, which provides rich new Arrange By views and other niceties. (We examine Libraries in Chapter 5.)

But Windows Media Player integrates with the Windows shell in other ways too. For example, it heavily utilizes the new Windows 7 Jump List feature, which exposes itself when you right-click the Media Player's taskbar button when the application is running. As you can see in Figure 11-32, the Windows Media Player Jump List provides access to recently played content as well as Media Player–related tasks and other shortcuts.

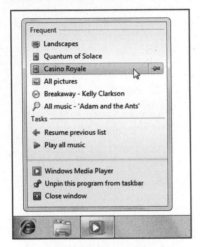

Figure 11-32: You can quickly find recently accessed media from Windows Media Player's custom Jump List.

Additionally, Windows Media Player provides a unique taskbar thumbnail. This thumbnail replaces an option in previous versions of the player that enabled you to minimize the application as a taskbar toolbar. As shown in Figure 11-33, this thumbnail is indeed live, so you'll see album art, a playing video, visualizations, or whatever else is happening in the player at the time. It even includes minimal playback controls.

Figure 11-33: The Windows Media Player live taskbar thumbnail is indeed live.

Synchronizing with Portable Devices

Although the iPod gets all the press these days, a popular family of Windows Media Player–compatible portable players offers better features and functionality than Apple's devices, and often at a better price. Although it's not possible here to enumerate through every single non-Apple device on the market, mostly because new devices enter the market almost every month, what you're looking for, generally, is a portable device that's made for Windows.

Secret

Devices that are compatible with Windows Media Player used to be labeled as *PlaysForSure*-compatible. PlaysForSure was a Microsoft marketing campaign aimed at educating consumers about which devices work seamlessly with Windows Media Player. Unfortunately, Microsoft killed this program, replacing it with the semi-related and pre-existing "Made for Windows" logo program. For the most part, most Windows-compatible devices work just fine with Windows Media Player, including those made by companies such as Creative, iriver, Samsung, and SanDisk. Even Sony is starting to come around: though its devices were previously compatible only with its own proprietary software, newer Sony devices work just fine with Windows Media Player as well. If in doubt, check the box. Or, do some research first: Microsoft lists compatible devices on its Web site: www.microsoft.com/windows/windowsmedia/devices.

Secret

Technically, Windows Mobile-based smart phones fall into the "Made for Windows" category, and they can certainly sync media content with Windows Media Player. We examine Windows Mobile in Chapter 19.

Using Windows Media–Compatible Devices

If you do go the Windows Media route, you'll find that setup and configuration are simple: just plug the device into a USB port on your Windows–based PC and wait a few seconds while Windows 7 automatically downloads and installs the correct drivers. Once that's complete, you'll see something new to Windows 7: Device Stage. As shown in Figure 11-34, this new interface provides a front end for all of the things you can do with compatible devices, including such things as portable music and video players.

Device Stage presents a list of options that are unique to each device. Windows Media Player–compatible devices will typically include an option titled Manage media on your device (or similar). Double-click this option to launch Windows Media Player.

tip   If the player isn't Device Stage–compatible, you'll just see a standard AutoPlay dialog appear. Choose the option that opens Windows Media Player.

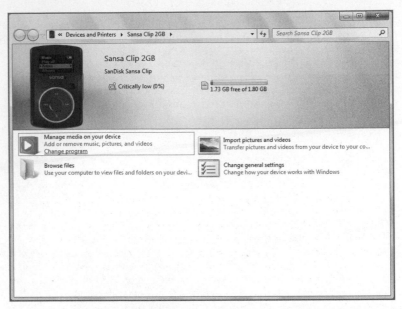

Figure 11-34: When you connect a compatible device, Windows 7 will display this attractive front end, called Device Stage.

Windows Media Player starts up in Sync mode, with the Sync pane displayed and the device loaded up, as shown in Figure 11-35. From here, you can synchronize music and, if the device is compatible, photos, movies, and recorded TV shows as well. What you'll be able to do is determined by the capabilities and capacity of the player you select.

Figure 11-35: Windows Media Player is ready to sync content with your device.

tip

For those with light needs—a few hundred songs but no photos or videos—a low capacity 1GB to 2GB flash-based device should work just fine. But even some of these small players are stepping up with video and photo support, so look for crisp color screens, even at the low end.

For the ultimate in portable entertainment, you'll want a device with a large color screen and a massive hard drive. With enough storage space, you'll have no problems storing all the photos, home movies, and recorded TV shows you want to watch. Whichever device you choose, configuration is largely hands-free and occurs behind the scenes.

In addition to the prominent Sync pane, you should see the player listed in the Navigation pane. This Navigation pane entry enables you to navigate through the media in your player in the same way you would the media on your PC. So you can click into the device and see what content is already on there, as shown in Figure 11-36.

Figure 11-36: You can navigate into compatible devices via the device entry in the Windows Media Player Navigation pane.

That's pretty interesting, in some ways and it enables you to manually manage the content you're carrying around with you. But where Media Player really shines when it comes to devices is in its ability to automatically synchronize content between the player and the device. Synchronizing is about more than just copying media to the device. It's about ensuring that the media on your device is always what you want and always up-to-date.

tip

You can toggle the Sync pane by clicking the Sync tab.

Synchronizing with a Portable Device

You'll handle all of your device synchronization through the Sync experience in Media Player which, logically enough, is accessed through the prominently displayed Sync button in the application's toolbar. Technically, there are two kinds of synchronization: *automatic sync* and *Shuffle*. You will typically use automatic sync when you have a large-format portable device (that is, one with multi-gigabytes of storage). Shuffle is aimed a smaller players, where you can't possibly fit all of your music collection on the device, but you'd like to get a sampling of your collection on there.

To set up a device for automatic sync, ensure that the Sync pane is open and that the device you wish to configure is displayed. Then, click the small Sync Options button directly below the Sync tab and choose Set up sync. This launches the Device Setup dialog, shown in Figure 11-37, from where you will configure which media files you want automatically synchronized with the device.

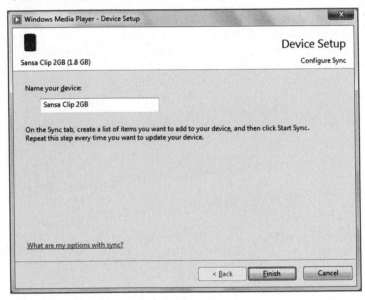

Figure 11-37: Think you know what you're doing? Then choose automatic sync and let your media fly free.

From this interface, you can do a few things. You can set up automatic synchronization, and, depending on the capabilities of your device, sync all of your music, photos, and videos accordingly. If the device is too small to hold all of that content, Media Player will pick which content to sync, based on criteria such as ratings and so on. (This is essentially what shuffle does.)

Secret   Don't worry about multigigabyte video files clogging up your portable device. Windows Media Player uses a technology called *transcoding* to copy large video files (and even, optionally, high-quality music files) into smaller versions that are tailored to your device. We examine this capability in the next section.

If you're the type of person who makes a lot of hand-crafted playlists, you can use the Device Setup window to ensure that only the music you care about is synchronized with the player. Just select the playlists you want copied to the device and those playlists, as well as the music contained in each, will be copied over. It's all up to you.

If you choose a playlist or playlists that are too large to fit on the device, Windows Media Player will simply copy over as much as it can. Click the Shuffle option to randomly select the content that will be synced to the device.

Secret

One final point about Sync: we mentioned earlier that synchronization was about more than just copying. Here's why that's true: if you configure a portable device to synchronize with certain playlists, or even, say, your entire music library, the content on the device will be updated every time you make a change to those playlists or libraries. So, if you rip a new CD to your PC and then connect the device to the PC, and that device is synchronized with your entire music library, that new content will silently and automatically be copied to the device. Likewise, if you add (or remove) a song from a playlist that is synchronized with a device, the next time you connect the device, its music library will be updated to reflect the changes you made on the PC. Maybe Bill Gates was on to something when he started talking about the "magic of software" after all.

Using Shuffle

If you're using a small-capacity device, typically one that is based on Flash RAM and contains only a few gigabytes or less of storage space, you might want to configure the device to Shuffle rather than Sync. In Shuffle mode, the entire contents of the device are replaced with a random selection of songs from your music library, so you always have a fresh set of tracks each time you connect the device and reshuffle it.

To set up Shuffle, click the Sync Options button in the Sync pane, and choose the name of the device and then Shuffle. You could also manually just drag songs into the Sync pane and then click the Sync Options button in the Sync pane and choose Shuffle list to shuffle that manually created list of content.

tip
Shuffle isn't the answer for many people, however. If you have a wide selection of music types in your media library, you might find it a bit jarring as your player moves from, say, classical Mozart to hard rock Van Halen to new age David Lanz. Indeed, many people use smaller Flash-based players while working out, and it's likely that such people will want a particular kind of music on their players. (David Lanz is a hugely talented pianist, but he just doesn't make good workout music.) So be sure you know what you're doing before picking Shuffle.

Whichever sync type you choose, Windows Media Player uses a Sync status view to show the progress of file copying, as shown in Figure 11-38. To get to it, click the device in the Navigation pane and then choose Sync status. Once all of the files you've chosen have been synced to the device, you can unplug it, pop in the headphones, and rock out.

Figure 11-38: During sync, Windows Media Player shows the status of each file it's copying.

Managing Portable Devices in Windows_Media_Player

Primarily, most of your PC-to-portable device interactions will involve synchronizing content between the two (and charging the portable device, which occurs while it's connected to the PC via a USB cable). However, there are a number of ways you can configure portable devices in Windows Media Player, and some of these options are important if you want to get the most out of your devices.

To change the name of your device as it appears in Windows Media Player, right-click the device in the Navigation pane and select Properties from the pop-up menu that appears. In the Sync tab of the Properties window that appears (see Figure 11-39), you can rename the device. If you're not using the Shuffle option, you can also use this interface to determine various synchronization options, such as how much space on the device you'd like to reserve for file storage. (Many portable devices have enough capacity that they serve as excellent general-purpose file storage devices as well as media players.)

In the Quality tab of the same window, you can control how Media Player transcodes music, videos, and recorded TV that is synchronized with the device. The issue here is simple: A 19GB video file might look great on your PC, but few portable devices are capable of HDTV-quality video and surround sound. So rather than waste valuable storage space on your device, Windows Media Player can make copies of these content types that are smaller and more in line with your player's capabilities.

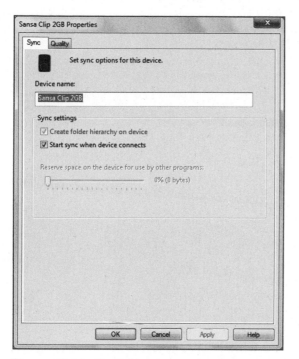

Figure 11-39: The Properties window helps you configure your portable media device.

tip

Transcoding can be quite time consuming, so Windows Media Player does it in the background. If you often take your device along for the morning commute, it might be a good idea to leave Media Player on overnight so it can transcode and synchronize any new content.

You can separately configure how Media Player transcodes music and videos/recorded TV. By default, Media Player will automatically transcode content as required. Or, if you feel really strongly about file sizes and quality, you can manually choose how the player handles these media types.

Secret

Audiophiles can actually use this feature to ensure that Media Player does not transcode music to lower-quality files, ensuring that what they hear on their music player is at the same quality level as the original recordings.

You can also access some portable device options from the Devices tab of the Windows Media Player Options dialog. The quickest way to access this dialog is to tap the Alt key and then select Tools and Options from the pop-up menu that appears. Then, navigate to the Devices tab. From here, you can select the device you'd like to configure and then click the Properties button to display the Properties dialog described previously.

Alternately, you can click the Advanced button to display the File Conversion Options dialog, shown in Figure 11-40. This dialog enables you to choose advanced transcoding options, such as whether video and audio files are converted in the background (which is recommended) and where Media Player stores temporary files.

Figure 11-40: You can really micromanage the transcoding functionality of Media Player if you'd like.

Sharing Your Music Library

One of the nicest features of Windows Media Player is its *media sharing* functionality. This feature enables you to share your Media Player–based music library with other PCs that are running Windows Media Player, various Windows Media–compatible devices, and Microsoft's multimedia game machine, the Xbox 360. This was true of previous versions of Windows Media Player, too, within the confines of your home network. But Windows 7 adds an exciting new twist on this functionality: Now, for the first time, you can also share your music library—and of course your other media—over the Internet. We'll examine all of these capabilities now.

tip
Unlike with previous versions of Windows Media Player, Microsoft will not be making Windows Media Player 12 available to previous Windows versions. But the media-sharing features still work with Windows Media Player 11, so you can share content with XP- and Vista-based PCs too, if you'd like.

Why would you want to share music and other media? Well, with many homes having two or more PCs these days, it makes sense to save some disk space and utilize your Wi-Fi (or wired) home network to access music, photos, and videos that are stored on other PCs. In one typical scenario, you may have a desktop PC with a large hard drive on which you store all of your media content. Using a wirelessly equipped notebook, you can easily access that content from elsewhere in the house. Or you can access that content using a network-attached device such as a media receiver or Xbox 360, neither of which offers a lot of local storage. Or—and this is a fun one—maybe you're on a business trip or vacation and would like to access your home PC-based media collection from the road, using a Windows 7–equipped notebook computer. Now, you can.

Share and Share Alike: Setting Up Your PC for Sharing

Before you can share your media library content, however, you'll have to do some configuration work. First, the PC must be connected to your home network, and you must have already configured the PC's network connection to access your network as a private network (for example, with a Home or Work network profile). If you haven't done this, here's the quickest way.

Right-click the network connection icon in the system tray and choose Open Network and Sharing Center. Then, in the Network and Sharing Center window that appears, view the type of network that's listed next to the icon and under the bolded text "Network." If it doesn't say "Home network" or "Work network," click the network type. In the Set Network Location dialog that appears, choose Home network or Work network for location type and then click Close. (Make sure you do this for your home network only, and not for any public networks you might visit.)

> **tip** Please note that you'll need to repeat this process on any other Windows 7–based PCs with which you'd like to share media libraries.

Accessing Other Shared Media Libraries

At this point, you can already access other shared media libraries on your home network, so if you have other PCs (or a home server, as described in Chapter 10) that are sharing their own media libraries, you will see these libraries appear in the Windows Media Player Navigation pane. And you can navigate through them just as you would your own media library, playing content remotely over the network via the player. This is shown in Figure 11-41.

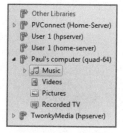

Figure 11-41: Shared media libraries show up in the Windows Media Player Navigation pane.

Enabling Media Streaming Features

Accessing shared libraries is one thing. You may also want to share your own media library. To do so, you must first configure Windows Media Player for sharing, or what Microsoft calls *media streaming*. Open Windows Media Player and then take a look at the Stream button that appears in the top-left corner of the application window. When you click it, you'll see a pop-up menu appear with three options: allow Internet access to home media, Allow remote control of my Player, and Turn on media streaming. Choose the latter option. When you do, the Media streaming options control panel appears, as shown in Figure 11-42.

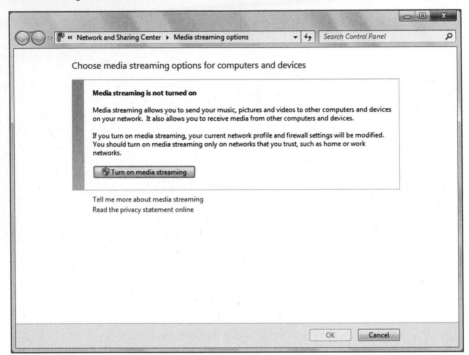

Figure 11-42: It's just one big switch, and when you enable it, your media can go out over the network.

To share your media, click the button titled "Turn on media streaming." The control panel will change to give you more fine-grained control over the devices in your network, as shown in Figure 11-43. By default, all of your media is shared with all devices, but you can use this interface to change those settings, and you can do so on a device-by-device basis if you're a control freak.

You could just accept the defaults, though we recommend at least providing your PC's shared media library with a unique name. (For some reason your user name is the default.) When you're done, click OK to close the control panel and return to Windows Media Player.

Figure 11-43: Once media streaming is enabled, you can control how media is shared with devices on your home network.

Okay, now go back to that Stream button. Now, when you click it, you'll see three options—only one of which is enabled, as shown in Figure 11-44—and a link for more streaming options in the pop-up menu. These items are the key to sharing media with Windows Media Player.

Figure 11-44: From this innocuous button, a host of sharing options.

It's time to see what each option does. Because they're sorted in a rather odd order, however, we're going to cover them in the order that makes the most sense.

Allowing Remote Control of My Player

If you choose the second Stream menu option, Allow remote control of my Player, you'll be confronted with the Allow Remote Control window shown in Figure 11-45. Again, this is an either-or question: you are either going to allow other computers and devices (including Windows Mobile-based smart phones) to *push* media content like music, pictures, and videos to this PC's install of Windows Media Player, or you're not.

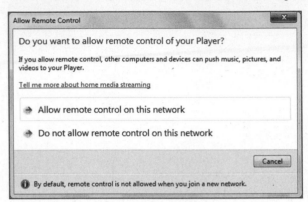

Figure 11-45: If you choose to allow remote control of your media, users on other PCs in your homegroup can use the Play To function to cause media playback to begin on your PC.

This is an exciting new Windows 7 capability and it turns the media sharing equation on its head. In traditional media sharing scenarios, you access, or *pull*, media content from other media libraries. But Windows 7 also allows you to push media content to other end points, including Windows 7–based PCs. This functionality is enabled here and then accessed via a new Windows Media Player 12 feature called Play To.

Play To requires at least one Windows 7–based PC (the "sending PC") and then either of the following:

◆ Another Windows 7–based PC (the "receiving PC")

◆ A compatible media device, including the Popcorn Hour or a Windows Media Center Extender (including the Xbox 360; we cover Media Center Extenders in Chapter 15)

Since the simplest example is PC-to-PC Play To, take a look at that first. To push content to another Windows 7 PC via Play To, you must first enable media streaming on both PCs as described above. Then, you must configure the receiving PC to allow remote control via the instructions earlier in this section. Once you've done that, you will see a new Play To submenu appear in the menu you get when you right-click any content in Windows Media Player on the sending PC (see Figure 11-46).

To push media to the receiving PC, simply select that PC from the Play To submenu. When you do, the new Play To window appears on the sending PC as shown in Figure 11-47.

Figure 11-46: The Play To menu enables you to push content to any compatible devices on the home network, including other instances of Windows Media Player 12.

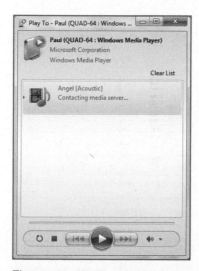

Figure 11-47: The Play To window helps you control the pushing of media content to other PCs and devices on your home network.

Meanwhile, on the receiving PC, the media will simply begin playing in Windows Media Player, as shown in Figure 11-48.

Figure 11-48: On the receiving PC, media simply begins playing.

The Play To window on the sending PC provides a few simple management features (Figure 11-49). You can add and remove items from the Play To list that appears in this window, for example, and control features like volume and repeat. You can even drag items in from the main Media Player interface if you'd like and create a kind of on-the-fly playlist.

Figure 11-49: The PlayTo window provides simple playlist management features, including the ability to drag and drop content in from Windows Media Player.

> **tip** Some devices—like Media Center Extenders—don't allow you to adjust the volume from the sending PC.

While Play To is applicable to a variety of uses, we think it makes the most sense in a home entertainment situation. For example, you may have an Xbox 360 or a Media Center PC in your living room, attached to a good stereo and HDTV. But your media collection may be otherwise trapped on a PC in your home office. While you could always *pull* the media from the device based in the living room, you could also sit down at your home office PC, construct a playlist for a party or other event, and then simply *push* it to the living room device using Play To. Neat!

> **tip** In case it's not obvious, the receiving PC isn't a slave to the sending PC. From that PC, you can always stop the playback, change the song, and so on. You can view the currently playing Play To playlist on the receiving PC by clicking the Play tab.

Allowing Internet Access to Home Media

Yes, it's the final frontier: with this option, you can bypass the limitations of this mortal coil and…well, it's not *that* good. But if you do enable Internet access to home media, as Microsoft calls it, you'll be able to share your digital media content far beyond your home network. In fact, you should be able to access it from anywhere in the world. The trick is that you have to enable Internet sharing on two Windows 7 PCs: one that will remain at home (or wherever) and one that you'll bring with you on your travels.

> **tip** Some corporate networks block the firewall ports required for this feature to work, so don't be surprised if you cannot, in fact, access your home media from a work-based PC.

Here's how you make it work.

As before, click the Stream toolbar button. This time, choose All Internet access to home media from the pop-up menu that appears. You'll be confronted with the Internet Home Media Access window shown in Figure 11-50.

Click the link titled Link an online ID. This will display the Link Online IDs control panel. Because this is the first time you've encountered this window, you need to add an online ID provider. As of this writing, the only online provider is Windows Live, so you'll need a Windows Live ID first (see Chapter 23 if you're not familiar with this). Potentially, other online ID providers will come on board over time, so if you maintain an online persona at another service that's supported here, you could use that instead.

Click the link titled Add an online ID provider. This launches an Internet Explorer window that navigates to Microsoft's online list of Windows 7 online ID providers. Click Windows Live. You will be prompted to download the Windows Live ID Sign-In Assistant. Do so and install it; the Windows Live ID Sign-In Assistant setup is straightforward.

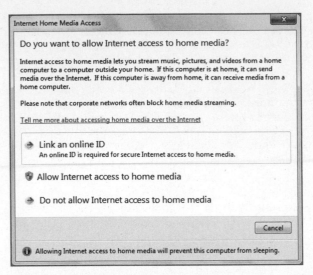

Figure 11-50: Here is the launching point for your Internet-based media sharing.

When the Sign-In Assistant is installed, return to the Link Online IDs control panel. As shown in Figure 11-51, you will now have an option to Link your Windows Live online ID to the user account you configured on the PC.

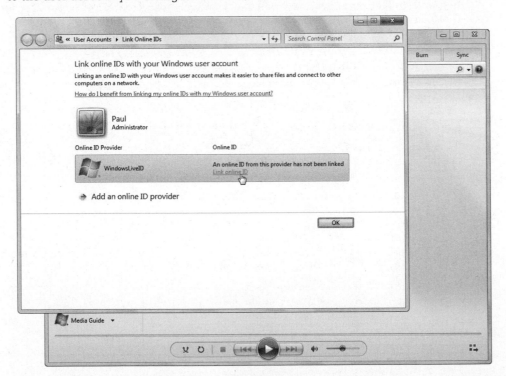

Figure 11-51: Once the Windows Live Sign-In Assistant is installed, you'll see an option for linking your Windows Live ID to your user account.

Click the link titled Link online ID. You'll be prompted to sign in to your Windows Live account. Once that's completed, you can close the Link Online IDs control panel and return to the Internet Home Media Access window. Click the link titled Allow Internet access to home media. As shown in Figure 11-52, you will be told that Internet home media access is now correctly configured.

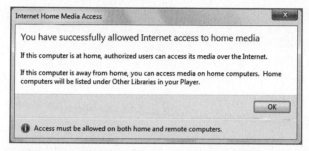

Figure 11-52: Success! You can now share your media library over the Internet.

You will need to repeat these steps on a second PC, of course.

In use, Internet media sharing works just like sharing over your home network, with the following caveats:

♦ It's slower. As you might expect from such a transfer, changing content is accompanied by a bit of a lag, and you will experience much better results with music than with video.

♦ You will see only the shared libraries from PCs for which you have configured Internet sharing. That means that you will typically only see a single library in the Other Libraries section of the Windows Media Player Navigation pane, as shown in Figure 11-53.

Figure 11-53: Shared libraries appear at the bottom of the Navigation pane.

tip   Internet sharing of digital media content is not available in Windows 7 Home Basic or Starter editions.

Connecting to a Shared Music Library with Xbox 360

With Xbox 360 game consoles now found in tens of millions of homes worldwide, Microsoft has found a perfect way to remotely access PC-based music libraries with a device that is probably connected to the best TV display and stereo system in the home. Thankfully, the process is incredibly simple.

Secret   The Xbox 360 can actually share PC-based media in two ways: what we're documenting here, and also as a Media Center Extender. We look at Extender functionality in Chapter 15.

1. After you've configured Windows Media Player to share its media library, ensure that your Xbox 360 is connected to the home network, and then turn it on. Navigate to My Xbox ➪ Music Library in the Xbox 360's New Xbox Experience.

2. In the Select Source dialog that appears, pick your Windows 7–based shared library from the list. It will take the form machine-name: [share name]. You may see a number of options, depending on how many PCs and devices are sharing media.

3. In the next screen, you can choose from the Albums, Artists, Saved Playlists, Songs, and Genres that make up your shared media library. The Xbox 360 includes a simple but decent media player for playing back this content.

As you might expect, photos and videos are accessed in a very similar manner.

Secret   The Xbox 360 isn't the only electronics device that can access digital media content on your Windows 7-based PC over the home network. A variety of hardware makers, such as D-Link, Linksys, and others, sell so-called digital media receivers, which are simple set-top boxes that bridge the gap between your home stereo and TV and your PC. Sony's PlayStation 3 (PS3) also offers Xbox 360-like media connectivity functionality, also using Microsoft Windows Media Connect technology. Increasingly, it's getting easier and easier to access your content regardless of where you are.

Accessing Online Music Stores

In previous versions of Windows Media Player, Microsoft pushed a collection of online music services that could be accessed from directly in the player. In the past few years, however, a few market forces have collided to make these types of services superfluous. First, the music industry has finally embraced the concept of copy-protection-free (also called DRM-free) music. Second, the industry has very clearly rallied around non-Microsoft formats, primarily the MP3 format. (The most popular service, Apple iTunes, sells songs in unprotected AAC format instead.)

There are numerous services selling DRM-free MP3 tracks these days. Unprotected MP3 is important because this format is the most compatible across all the devices, PCs, and software you use—both today and tomorrow. And it works just great with Windows Media Player 12.

Because it's no longer necessary to access only those services that are provided through the player, we'll simply ignore them. The best services, it turns out, can be found outside of Windows Media Player. The next sections take a look.

Amazon MP3

At a very basic level, all online music services perform the same functions. They provide music for sale (so-called a la carte downloads, whereby you can purchase individual songs or albums) or, in some cases, provide subscription music services, which enable you to access all of the service's music, on a number of PCs and even portable devices, for a monthly or yearly fee. Music services also typically offer editorial content, ways to discover new music, or find out additional information about your favorite artists and albums. They often supply custom playlists and other content.

Amazon MP3, which, as the name suggests, is part of the Amazon.com online retailing site, is actually fairly bare-bones, in line with Amazon's policy of keeping things simple. That is, the service is offered only via the Web, and there's no downloadable media management application (though Amazon does offer a very simple PC-based song downloader, as you'll soon see). What you get is access to millions of unprotected MP3 tracks, either individually or within prepackaged digital albums, using Amazon's familiar interface.

To see Amazon MP3 in action, open Internet Explorer or your favorite Web browser and navigate to www.amazonmp3.com. Shown in Figure 11-54, this part of Amazon's site should be immediately familiar if you're a frequent visitor.

You can browse Amazon MP3 in any number of ways. The service calls out new and notable albums, top songs and albums, and editor's pick selections. And you can browse via genre, album price range (there's a surprisingly good selection of low-cost MP3 albums available), and via a variety of promotions. This being Amazon, of course, one of the best ways to find content is to use the site's integrated search functionality. If a particular song or album isn't available digitally, Amazon will offer you a chance to purchase it in a more traditional (albeit less instantly gratifying) CD-based format.

Figure 11-54: Amazon MP3 combines the convenience of Amazon's e-commerce site with a millions-strong collection of unprotected MP3 songs.

Purchasing Music from Amazon MP3

When you've found an album you might be interested in, you'll see some surprising niceties. As with more traditional online music stores, Amazon MP3 offers 30-second previews of each song, accessed from directly within the Web browser. Just click the little play button next to any song name, as shown in Figure 11-55, to get a preview.

Amazon also offers a wealth of customer reviews, its patented one-click ordering capability, and links to related music, including music that was purchased by people who also purchased the album you're currently viewing.

To purchase an album, click the button labeled *Buy MP3 album* (or *Buy MP3 Album with 1-Click*). Or, you can purchase individual tracks by clicking the *Buy MP3* button found next to each track name. Amazon provides a handy Amazon MP3 Downloader application that you can install on your PC, and you'll be prompted to do so the first time you purchase a song or album. This application manages music downloads from the service. More important, it integrates with Windows Media Player (or, if you prefer, Apple iTunes), automatically adding any music you purchase from Amazon MP3 to your Windows Media Player–based media library.

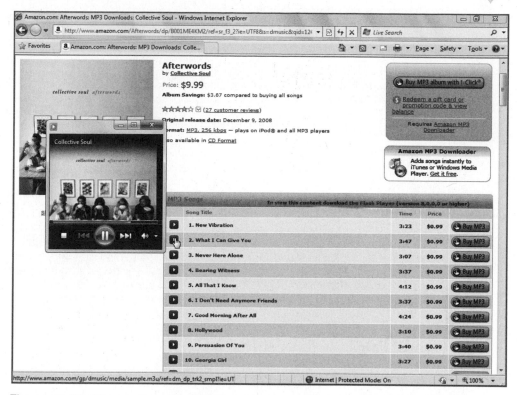

Figure 11-55: You won't need to launch a separate application to get song previews.

Because of some configuration options, you may want to manually download the Amazon MP3 Downloader before purchasing any music:

1. Navigate to the Amazon MP3 store and click Getting Started.

2. Locate the link for downloading the Amazon MP3 Downloader and then download and install the application.

3. Open the Start menu and type **Amazon MP3 Downloader** to manually launch the application. (It will later launch automatically whenever you download music from Amazon.) From this application, select File ➪ Preferences. You'll see the dialog shown in Figure 11-56.

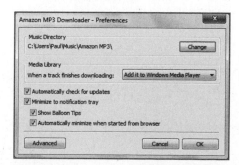

Figure 11-56: Amazon MP3 integrates with either Apple iTunes or Windows Media Player.

4. In the Media Library section, choose "Add it to Windows Media Player" from the drop-down list box so that songs downloaded from the service are automatically added to Windows Media Player. Click OK and you're good to go.

Now, when you purchase songs or albums from Amazon MP3, you don't have to worry about any management issues: They'll be downloaded directly to your Music folder (under an Amazon MP3) subfolder and added to your Windows Media Player media library. *Voila!*

Other Music and Audio Stores

Although Amazon MP3 is pretty exciting, it isn't the only online music service game in town. It isn't possible to cover them all here, but a few do stand out, so we examine these next.

Apple iTunes

The most popular online media store, Apple's iTunes Store, is accessed via that company's PC software, offering music, movies, TV shows, music videos, audiobooks, podcasts, and other content, including iPod games. Apple's service has proven hugely popular with consumers largely because of its tie-in with the iPod and the iPhone. In truth, it's a decent application in its own right, but the Windows version suffers from performance and stability issues.

In the good news department, Apple has jumped onboard the DRM-free music bandwagon, and though the AAC format they use for music isn't as compatible as MP3, it does work fine with Windows Media Player and Windows Media Center in Windows 7. (You may have issues with synced portable devices and network-connected devices, however.)

www.apple.com/itunes

Audible.com

Audible.com, now owned by Amazon, offers over 60,000 audiobooks and other content, including newspapers. If you're interested in listening to Audible audiobooks on a portable player, you should ensure that the device is compatible: Audible maintains a useful database of devices that work and can help you download correctly formatted audiobooks.

www.audible.com/

RealNetworks Rhapsody

If you're more the subscription music kind of fan, the Rhapsody service might be of interest. This service provides access to millions of tracks for a monthly fee, and it's also compatible with a wide range of portable devices. However, Rhapsody must be accessed via a proprietary RealNetworks application, which we find a bit bizarre and hard to use.

www.rhapsody.com/

Microsoft Zune

Finally, Microsoft has followed in the footsteps of Apple and created a separate digital music platform called *Zune* that closely mimics the iPod/iTunes ecosystem. Microsoft's contribution to this market isn't just a copycat, however; the Zune portable players, PC software, and online services all offer features and functionality that's nowhere to be found on the iPod or iTunes. And because it's from Microsoft and likely the future of the company's digital media efforts, 'we cover the Zune extensively with its own chapter in this book, so you can find out all about the Zune in Chapter 14.

http://www.zune.net

Summary

Windows Media Player 12 is the most full-featured version of Media Player yet, with a simpler and more visual user interface, awesome media sharing capabilities, and much better compatibility with music and video formats people are really using. You can even make Windows Media Player 12 work with Apple's stunning iPod, if you really want to. There are plenty of free competitors out there, but many Windows users will find almost everything they need right there in Windows Media Player. If not, you might want to check out Microsoft's Zune, which promises to be Microsoft's next step in this space. You can take a look at that digital player in Chapter 14.

Organizing, Fixing, and Sharing Digital Photos

Chapter
12

To say that Microsoft's approach to digital photos has been somewhat schizophrenic across the past several versions of Windows is an understatement. In Windows XP, Microsoft took a task-based approach to digital images, whereby you would manage them directly in the Explorer shell. In Windows Vista, that all changed: although some digital image tasks were still possible from the shell, Microsoft for the first time provided a discrete application, Windows Photo Gallery, for managing, editing, and sharing these files.

In Windows 7, it's all changed yet again. This time, Microsoft has changed the Windows shell dramatically to support virtual folder technology called Libraries. The Windows Photo Gallery was removed from Windows 7 and is included instead in the Windows Live Essentials application suite as Windows Live Photo Gallery. (As we noted very early in this book, Windows Live Essentials is indeed a very essential part of the Windows 7 experience, and thus we assume you will have downloaded and installed it if it did not already come preinstalled on your PC.)

In this chapter, you'll examine the many ways in which the Windows shell has changed in Windows 7 with regard to digital photos, and then take an extensive look at the new Windows Live Photo Gallery, which helps you organize, fix, and share your photos. Finally, you'll also look at Microsoft's Windows Live online services for photos and some third-party solutions that truly complete the digital photo experience in Windows 7.

---

tip   As noted throughout this book, no Windows 7 install is complete without Windows Live Essentials. You can download Windows Live Essentials—which includes Windows Live Photo Gallery—from the Microsoft website `http://download.live.com`.

A Look Back: Photo Management in Windows XP and Vista

If you're used to either Windows XP or Vista for photo management, Windows 7 requires you to change your ways yet again. To understand why, you need to first look back to how this worked in previous versions of Windows.

When Windows XP first shipped several years ago, Microsoft imbued the system with a number of task-centric user interface elements that made it fairly easy to work with digital media files directly in the Explorer shell. For example, the My Pictures special shell folder provided a number of picture-specific tasks, such as *Get pictures from camera or scanner*, *View as a slide show*, and *Order prints online*, among others. Windows XP also included a number of picture-specific folder views, such as Filmstrip, which made viewing pictures from Explorer reasonably pleasing. The Windows XP My Pictures folder is shown in Figure 12-1.

Other operating systems, such as Mac OS X, offer fewer shell-based digital photo management features than does Windows, but Mac users have come to love the iPhoto digital photo management application; and on Windows, applications such as Google's Picasa have proven hugely popular with users. For this reason, Microsoft stepped away from the task-centric user interfaces it developed for Windows XP and instead created the iPhoto-like Windows Photo Gallery application for Windows Vista.

Figure 12-1: With Windows XP, digital photo management occurred directly in the Explorer shell, not within a separate application.

Windows Photo Gallery provided some decent if basic capabilities. It provided a friendlier place to manage photos than the Windows Vista shell, certainly. It had basic editing capabilities, with auto adjustment, exposure and color adjustment, cropping, and red eye reduction functionality. You could share photos from the application via e-mail, videos (via Windows Movie Maker), and DVDs (via Windows DVD Maker), and you could print, both to your own printers and to various online photo services. Windows Photo Gallery is shown in Figure 12-2.

While hardly exceptional, Windows Photo Gallery hit all the high points. The problem is that the application was bundled with Windows, a practice certain regulatory agencies—especially in Europe—complained about. But from a functional standpoint, it also meant that Microsoft could not update it very frequently and that doing so would require the company to pass such updates through the rigorous testing cycle that accompanies any Windows update.

To combat these issues, Microsoft began developing Windows Photo Gallery outside of Windows. Renamed to Windows Live Photo Gallery, this new version of Windows Photo Gallery has been updated significantly since Vista first shipped and is available as a free download. It is now included as part of the Windows Live Essentials suite, which, again, we do consider an essential part of the Windows 7 experience.

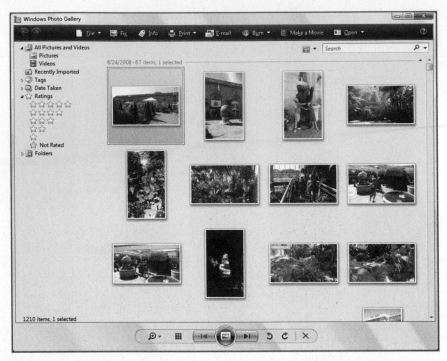

Figure 12-2: In Windows Vista, a bundled application called Windows Photo Gallery provided basic digital photo management, editing, and sharing functionality.

Secret

Windows Live Essentials—and, thus, Windows Live Photo Gallery—is available to users of Windows XP and Vista as well.

A bare install of Windows 7 does not include Windows Photo Gallery or Windows Live Photo Gallery, though it does include a stripped-down viewer application called Windows Photo Viewer, also discussed in this chapter. However, we will treat Windows Live Photo Gallery as a core part of Windows 7 regardless. This is an application that Microsoft would include in the OS if it weren't for antitrust-based bundling concerns.

Oddly enough, Microsoft also significantly enhanced the ways in which you can manage photos and other pictures via the Windows 7 shell, so we will begin our examination of Windows 7's image management capabilities there.

Using the Pictures Library

In Windows 7, Microsoft has finally come through with the virtual folder technologies it only tepidly started with Windows Vista. In this version of Windows, special shell folders like Pictures (My Pictures in XP) and Music (My Music in XP) have been replaced in the Start menu with new virtual folders called Libraries that each aggregate content from a variety of physical folders. The Library for photos is called, logically enough, *Pictures*.

---

cross ref   Remember, we examine the new Libraries system in more detail in Chapter 5.

The old physical folders still exist, of course. Here, confusingly, Microsoft has gone back to the old "My" naming scheme for physical folders. In the context of digital photos and other picture-related folders, this means that each user account gets its own pictures folder, which is named "My Pictures" when that user is logged on, or "[*Username*]'s Pictures" when accessed from a different account. (For example, if you logged on to my PC with a different user account, or accessed it from the network, my pictures folder would be named "Paul's Pictures.")

Additionally, there is always a universally available public folder structure, and the pictures-oriented folder there is called "Public Pictures."

---

tip   The availability of a Public Pictures folder is interesting for a couple of reasons, but one of the top reasons is that Microsoft provides a number of sample pictures in Windows 7, which are accessible through the Public Pictures folder. To find them, access the Sample Pictures shortcut in your Pictures folder, which points to C:\Users\Public\Public Picture\ Sample Pictures. As shown in Figure 12-3, this folder contains a number of beautiful background images that are suitable for your desktop or enjoying in other ways.

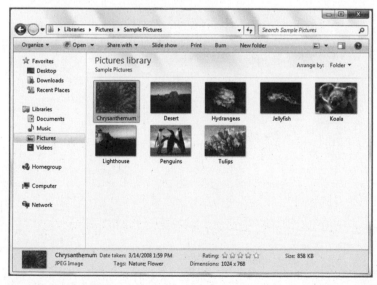

Figure 12-3: Windows 7 comes with a number of high-quality sample pictures.

Secret

Oddly enough, these aren't the only sample pictures found in Windows 7. Microsoft also provides a wide range of other high-quality, high-resolution images, which it intends for you to use as desktop backgrounds. But if you know where to find them, you can make copies in the Public Pictures folder (or any other folder) and access them more directly. There are two places to look.

The first is the Wallpapers folder. To find it, navigate to C:\Windows\Web\. You'll notice that there is a folder called Wallpaper here, with various subfolders inside. Each contains stunning high-res Windows wallpapers.

The second is the regional wallpapers folder. This is found in a hidden location: C:\Windows\Globalization\MCT. To find it, select Search from the Start menu, type in that address, and tap Enter. A new shell folder will open with that location displayed. Inside, you will see a variety of folders with names like MCT-xx where xx represents a region of the world. Each contains a folder with more stunning wallpaper, and there are other items related to Windows 7 Themes, which we examine in Chapter 4.

To copy pictures from these locations to Public Folders, right-click the folder and choose Copy. Then, navigate to Public Folders, right-click a blank area of the window, and choose Paste. *Voila!* Lots of gorgeous pictures to play with.

The big change in Windows 7, of course, is a new Libraries infrastructure. When you click on Documents, Pictures, or Music in the Start menu, you do not open My Documents, My Pictures, or My Music (respectively). Instead, what you're opening is a virtual folder, called a Library, that displays content from a number of different physical folders. In the case of the Pictures link in the Start menu, what you're opening when you click on that is the Pictures library, which is shown in Figure 12-4.

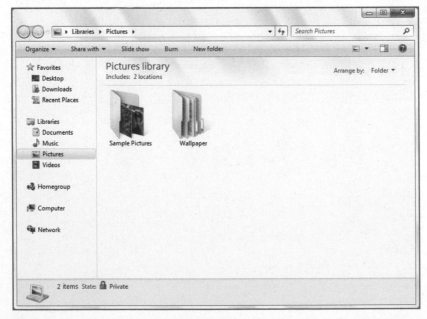

Figure 12-4: The Windows 7 Pictures library displays picture content from two physical folder locations in a single place.

By default, the Pictures library aggregates, or "includes," content from both My Pictures (that is, your own physical pictures folder) as well as the globally available Public Pictures folder. For the first-time Windows 7 user, the change isn't really all that profound, however. Most people simply copy photos and other pictures into their My Pictures folder anyway, so for a good number of users, the Pictures library and the My Pictures folder can be used interchangeably.

Secret

Indeed, this brings up an interesting point. What happens when you "copy" or "move" content into the Pictures library? After all, it's not a real location on the hard drive, but a view of two other locations (by default), mixed together. As it turns out, each Library has a default save location. For Pictures, that location is your My Pictures folder, so any content that you copy or move to Pictures actually ends up in My Pictures. See below for information about changing the default save location.

Of course, you may be wondering at this point whether there are any picture management capabilities left in the Windows 7 shell. It's a valid question with a complicated answer. Yes, you can still manage digital photos in Windows 7's Explorer shell, but many things have changed, depending on whether you're coming from Windows XP or Vista. We'll take a closer look at these changes.

Where Is It Now?

Table 12-1 summarizes some of the picture-related changes you can expect to see in the Windows shell, and how to find similar features in Windows 7.

Table 12-1: Where Common Picture-Related Features Are in the Windows 7 Shell

Windows XP feature	Windows Vista feature	Where it is in Windows 7
Web Publishing Wizard (accessed via *Publish this folder/picture to the Web* option in the folder task area)	Removed. Users were expected to utilize Microsoft's blogging service, Windows Live Spaces, to publish photos online.	Now, Microsoft has created a new picture-centric Windows Live Photos service, which we examine later in this chapter.
Share this folder	Share toolbar button	New "Share with" toolbar button that integrates with Windows 7 homegroups
Get pictures from camera or scanner	Missing. Users were expected to utilize the AutoPlay dialog and acquire pictures with Windows Photo Gallery.	Still missing, but the responsibility for photo acquisition has moved to Windows Live Photo Gallery

continues

Table 12-1: Where Common Picture-Related Features Are in the Windows 7 Shell (continued)

Windows XP feature	Windows Vista feature	Where it is in Windows 7
View as a slide show	Replaced by the Slide Show toolbar button. Windows Vista offers dramatically better Explorer-based photo slide shows than does either Windows XP or—gasp!—Windows 7.	Also includes a Slide Show toolbar button, but Windows 7's slide shows are far more basic than those in Windows Vista, and do not include such things as slide show themes or onscreen controls
Order prints online	You must launch Windows Photo Gallery to access this functionality.	You must now launch Windows Photo Live Gallery to access this functionality.
Print this picture/print the selected pictures	Replaced by a new Print toolbar button	Works as it does in Windows Vista
Set as desktop background	You could launch Windows Photo Gallery to access this functionality. Alternatively, you could still right-click a picture and choose Set As Desktop Background from the menu that appears.	Works as it does in Windows Vista
E-mail this file/e-mail the selected items	Replaced by a new E-mail toolbar button	Works as it does in Windows Vista
Preview picture	Replaced by a new Open toolbar button, which offers enhanced functionality thanks to an attached drop-down menu that enables you to choose which application to use to preview the selected image	Works as it does in Windows Vista
Edit picture	Missing, but if you select an application from the new menu attached to the Open button, which includes editing functionality (for example, Paint or Windows Photo Gallery), you can edit the picture that way.	Works as it does in Windows Vista
Shell-based photo and photo folder views	Mostly missing. You can use Windows Photo Gallery and its organizational view styles to view your photo collection in a variety of different ways.	Works as it does in Windows Vista. Windows 7 does add one new folder view style (Content) but it's not particularly applicable to photos.

Managing Content in the Pictures Library

The Pictures library works like other libraries and most other shell locations in Windows Explorer and provides the standard Address bar, Search box, toolbar, Navigation bar, and Details pane. It also includes a number of features that are specific to pictures. For example, while all libraries include Organize, Share with, Burn, and New folder toolbar buttons, Pictures also includes a Slide Show button that enables you to trigger a full-screen picture slideshow. (We discuss this feature later in the chapter.)

You can organize photos and other pictures in various ways in the Pictures library. The Change your view toolbar button enables you to cycle through various shell view styles, including some, such as Extra Large Icons and Large Icons, which are particularly nice for viewing a folder full of pictures, as shown in Figure 12-5.

Secret

You can access Extra Large Icons only by clicking the More options arrow next to the Change your views button and selecting Extra Large Icons from the list. If you simply toggle through the various views with the button, Extra Large Icons will never come up.

Figure 12-5: Some of the Windows 7 view styles are particularly nice when used with pictures.

tip

In Windows 7, like Windows Vista, you can view picture thumbnails on the desktop. (This wasn't possible in Windows XP.) Previously, this functionality was available only in traditional folder windows. That said, the Windows desktop is still limited to three view styles only: Large, Medium, and Small Icons. In Windows Vista, Small Icons is called Classic Icons.

Additionally, you can use the organizational capabilities of Windows 7 to view picture thumbnails in a wide variety of interesting ways. As with Windows Vista, Windows 7 includes file organizational features such as Stacks and Groups, which can be quite handy when used in conjunction with Picture files.

tip

We examine Stacks and Groups in more detail in Chapter 5.

To sort the Pictures library or any folder full of pictures, right-click a blank area of an open folder and choose Sort by. This triggers the submenu shown in Figure 12-6, enabling you to choose from a variety of sorting options, including Name, Date (modified), Type, Size, and others. For the most part, these options are straightforward, although the Tags option and other picture sorting criteria are described during our examination of Windows Live Photo Gallery later in the chapter.

Figure 12-6: Windows 7's file sorting options let you sort your pictures in various ways.

The Group By and Arrange By options are somewhat more impressive. In the same pop-up menu described above, you can choose Group By and then Name, Date (modified), Type, Size, Tags, or Date, and choose whether to group in ascending or descending order. For example, you might choose to group by name, which would alphabetize the list of pictures and segregate them into groups such as A–H, I–P, and Q–Z by default, as shown in Figure 12-7. If you check the Descending option, the list will sort in reverse order.

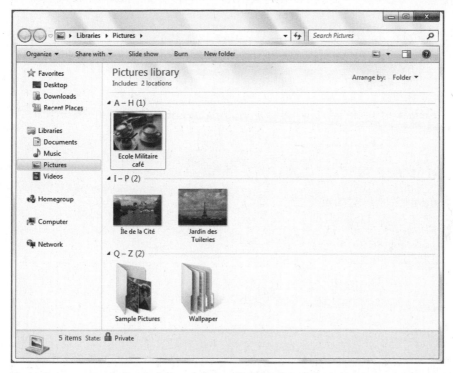

Figure 12-7: Group By enables you to segregate the current view into logical groups.

| tip | You may have noticed there's also a More option in the Sort By and Group By sub-menus. If you click this option, you'll be treated to a Choose Details dialog that actually enables you to choose which items will appear in that submenu. That means you can remove some of the default options and choose from dozens of other related options. The lists are quite extensive, but of course many of the options apply only to non-picture files. Furthermore, this list can be customized on a folder-by-folder basis. |

Secret To remove an applied Group By view, right-click as you did above and simply choose the new (None) option that appears in the context menu. This option isn't available to Sort By, however. It's unclear why there isn't a simple (None) option in the Group By submenu. However, the default is Name.

Windows Vista included a little-known and thus little-used user interface element called Stacks. This enabled you to organize files by category as if they were virtual stacks of paper, and it was heavily promoted in that version. It's no longer included in Windows 7, but its successor, Arrange By, carries on in the same tradition. There's just one caveat: arrange By is not available in any folder. It is only available in a library view like Pictures.

To access Arrange By, open the Pictures library. You'll see an Arrange By link near the top right corner of the window. By default, the Arrange By view is Folder, which displays the contents of the library in a normal, Explorer-style view. But there are four other options here: Month, Day, Rating, and Tag. Clicking one causes the library to change into a dramatic new view, whereby the contents of the library are sorted into stacks of pictures organized by the criteria you chose. This is shown in Figure 12-8.

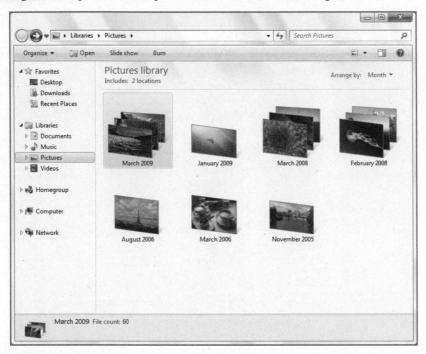

Figure 12-8: Stacks live on in Windows 7's new Arrange By view styles.

If you're familiar with the virtual folder capabilities in Windows 7, you'll recognize the Arrange By displays as in-place searches that can be optionally saved for later use. (Otherwise, please refer to Chapter 5 for more information.) That is, you can save these views as *saved searches* and access them later whenever you want. Saving an Arrange By view isn't obvious at all: to do so, tap Alt to display the hidden menu, choose File, and then Save Search. You'll see a standard Save As dialog appear, and you can save the search to the Searches folder associated with your user account or any other location in the file system. You might use this feature to create a virtual folder called "Favorite Pictures" that is populated only with photos that have been rated with four or five stars, for example.

Secret

Windows 7 saved searches use the blue Stacks icon from Windows Vista.

Viewing Information about Pictures

To view information about a picture, hover over a picture file with your mouse and wait until a pop-up window appears. What you see in this pop-up depends on the type of picture it is. For photos you've taken yourself with a digital camera, you typically see its type, date taken, rating, dimensions, and size information. Scanned images display type, rating, dimensions, and size information only. Meanwhile, other images simply display their type, dimensions, and size. This latter display is pretty much the least information a picture can supply to Windows Vista because type, dimension, and size are common to all images. The other information is presented if provided by the underlying photo. This information, called *metadata*, varies from file to file.

The Details pane at the bottom of the Explorer window also populates with a variety of unique information in addition to the information you see in the pop-up. Note that the Details pane almost always shows more information than the fly-over pop-up and that you can resize the Details pane to show even more info, as seen in Figure 12-9.

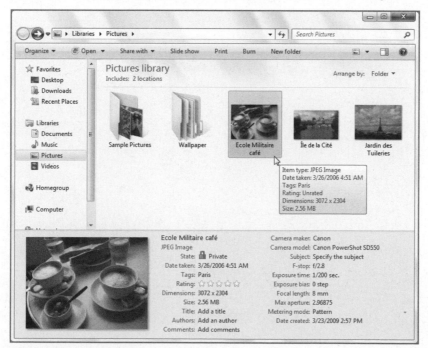

Figure 12-9: Selected images cough up their deepest secrets in the Details pane.

Secret   To find out even more information, or metadata, about a picture file, including such esoteric data as the make and model of the camera used to take the image, the F-number, and ISO speed, and other information, right-click an image, choose Properties, and navigate to the Details pane.

Viewing Photos

To view an image at a size larger than its thumbnail, double-click it or select it and then click the Open button in the window's toolbar. Depending on how your system is configured, this will cause the Windows Photo Viewer, Windows Live Photo Gallery, or a third-party application to open, displaying the selected image. Windows Photo Viewer is the default application until you've run Windows Live Photo Gallery, so we'll focus on that first.

Viewing Photos with Windows Photo Viewer

The Windows Photo Viewer application is very similar to the Photo Gallery Viewer from Windows Vista, and is much more powerful than the old Windows Picture and Fax Viewer from Windows XP. Shown in Figure 12-10, Windows Photo Viewer contains many of the picture-specific features found in Windows Live Photo Gallery, but none of the organizational or editing features.

Figure 12-10: Windows Photo Viewer is like Windows Live Photo Gallery Lite.

Put another way, Windows Photo Viewer is designed for working with single images only, whereas Windows Live Photo Gallery is aimed at managing your entire collection, or library, of digital images. While we will examine Windows Live Photo Gallery in much more detail later in the chapter, Figure 12-11 shows what the application looks like when viewing an individual photo.

Figure 12-11: Windows Live Photo Gallery is the full meal deal, with editing capabilities and other more advanced functionality.

Curious about the differences among the Windows XP Picture and Fax Viewer, the Windows Vista Photo Gallery Viewer, and Windows 7 Photo Viewer and Windows Live Photo Gallery? Table 12-2 shows you where to find features from older applications in Windows 7.

Table 12-2: Where Picture and Fax Viewer and Photo Gallery Viewer Features Can Be Found in Windows 7

Windows XP: Picture and Fax Viewer	Windows Vista: Photo Gallery Viewer	Windows 7: Windows Photo Viewer	Windows 7: Windows Live Photo Gallery
Previous Image	Previous button in navigational toolbar	Previous button in navigational toolbar	Previous button
Next Image	Next button in navigational toolbar	Next button in navigational toolbar	Next button

continues

Table 12-2: Where Picture and Fax Viewer and Photo Gallery Viewer Features Can Be Found in Windows 7 *(continued)*

Windows XP: Picture and Fax Viewer	Windows Vista: Photo Gallery Viewer	Windows 7: Windows Photo Viewer	Windows 7: Windows Live Photo Gallery
Best Fit	Not available, use the Change the Display Size slider instead	Not available, use the Change the Display Size slider instead	Not available, use the Actual size/Fit to window button or the Zoom in or out slider
Actual Size	Not available, use the Change the Display Size slider instead	Actual size/Fit to button in navigational toolbar	Not available, use the Actual size/Fit to window button or the Zoom in or out slider
Start Slide Show	Play Slide Show button in navigational toolbar	Play Slide Show button in the navigational toolbar (or press F11)	Slide Show (or press F12 or Alt+S)
Zoom In	Change the Display Size slider in the navigational toolbar	Change the Display Size slider and Actual size/Fit to window button	Zoom in or out slider
Zoom Out	Change the Display Size slider in the navigational toolbar	Replaced by the Change the Display Size slider and Actual size/Fit to window button	Zoom in or out slider
Rotate Clockwise	Rotate Clockwise button in the navigational toolbar	Rotate Clockwise button in navigational toolbar	Rotate Clockwise button
Rotate Counterclockwise	Rotate Counterclockwise button in navigational toolbar	Rotate Counterclockwise button in navigational toolbar	Rotate Counterclockwise button
Delete	Delete button in toolbar	Delete button in navigational toolbar (or Delete key)	Delete button (or Delete key)
Print	Print button in toolbar	Print button in toolbar	Print button in toolbar
(not available)	Print, Order prints...	Print, Order prints...	Print, Order prints...

Windows XP: Picture and Fax Viewer	Windows Vista: Photo Gallery Viewer	Windows 7: Windows Photo Viewer	Windows 7: Windows Live Photo Gallery
Copy To	File, Copy	File ⇨ Copy	File ⇨ Make a copy or File ⇨ Copy (Ctrl+C)
Edit	Open button in toolbar (also lets you choose which application to use)	Open toolbar button	Fix toolbar button or Extras ⇨ Open with
(not available)	E-mail	E-mail toolbar button	E-mail toolbar button
(not available)	Burn ⇨ Data Disc	Burn ⇨ Data Disc	Make ⇨ Burn a data DVD...
(not available)	Burn ⇨ Video DVD	Burn ⇨ Video DVD	Make ⇨ Burn a DVD...
Help	Help button in toolbar	Help button in toolbar	Help button in toolbar

Optimizing Folders for Pictures (But Not Libraries)

By default, any folder in Windows 7 that contains only image files will be optimized for this purpose. However, you can make sure that this is the case, or manually customize a folder with mixed content to work best with pictures if you'd like. This functionality dates backs to Windows XP, but it's changed a bit over the years.

In Windows XP, you could customize folders for pictures in a variety of ways. You could customize a folder for pictures in two ways in XP: Pictures (best for many files), which would present the folder in Thumbnail view, and Photo Album (best for fewer files), which would present the folder in Filmstrip view.

This functionality was detuned somewhat in Windows Vista because Microsoft moved the picture organizational features into Windows Photo Gallery. The popular Filmstrip view was removed, and there was only one picture-related folder customization option, called Pictures and Videos.

In Windows 7, it has changed yet again. First, you can't even use the Customize this folder option on a Library, so it's a nonstarter for many uses; but if you do navigate to a physical folder—such as My Pictures—accessing this option is the same as it was in Windows XP and Vista: right-click a blank area of an open folder (or right-click a folder icon) and choose Customize this folder. This causes the folder's Properties dialog to appear with the Customize pane displayed, as shown in Figure 12-12.

Now, instead of a single Pictures and Videos option, as you had in Vista, you will see a separate folder optimization for Pictures.

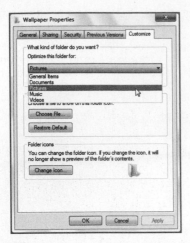

Figure 12-12: In Windows 7, folder customization options have been scaled back yet again.

Secret

If you really miss Filmstrip view, as I do, you can check out a similar if more unwieldy folder view in Windows 7 to see if it will meet your needs. It's called the Preview pane and you enable it by clicking the new Show the Preview pane toolbar button in the current window, as shown in Figure 12-13. The Preview pane occupies the right side of the window and shows an automatic preview of the currently selected file, much like the old Filmstrip view.

The problem with the Preview pane is that it's global. That is, once you enable this view, it will be applied to all subsequently opened Explorer windows.

Figure 12-13: Enabling the Preview pane in folders that contain images gives you an effect similar to that of the old Filmstrip view.

Playing Photo Slide Shows from the Shell

One last thing you can do from the shell is display very simple photo slide shows via the Slide Show toolbar button that you'll see in the Pictures Library and other photo-containing folders. These slide shows are pretty basic and cannot be configured in any meaningful way. There's no navigational UI, so to access the few configurable options—Play/Pause, Next, Back, Shuffle, Loop, and slide show speed (see Figure 12-14)—you have to right-click. You can also use the arrow keys as Back and Forward buttons, or tap Esc to exit at any time.

Figure 12-14: Windows 7 offers very basic picture slide show functionality right from Windows Explorer.

Secret

If your mouse has Back and Forward buttons, you can also use them to navigate through the slide show.

The Slide Show button appears in any folder that contains pictures. This includes the Pictures library, of course, as well as any subfolders that are displayed within this library.

Secret

If you just tap Slide Show without selecting any pictures, the slide show will include all of the pictures in the current windows as well as those in any subfolders. To restrict the slide show to a subset of pictures, simply multi-select individual pictures and/or folders and then tap the Slide Show button.

Managing Pictures with Windows Live Photo Gallery

If you were a fan of the shell-based photo management features in Windows XP, you might be somewhat disappointed that Microsoft removed a lot of that functionality from Windows Vista and Windows 7. But fear not: those features—and many more—are now available in the new Windows Live Photo Gallery. This easy-to-use application provides a single location from which you can organize, edit, and share your digital memories. And in an interesting twist, Windows Live Photo Gallery can even manage digital videos as well, despite its name. (It doesn't, however, provide video editing features. For that, you must use Windows Live Movie Maker, which is described in Chapter 13.)

First Things First

The first time you run Windows Live Photo Gallery, a couple of things will happen that are worth discussing before we get into actual application usage.

First, you will be asked to sign into your Windows Live ID account, as shown in Figure 12-15. Doing so plugs you into the wider family of Windows Live online services and provides for some nice integration between this application and other Windows Live applications and services.

You can use Windows Live Photo Gallery without making this connection, but if think you may want to publish your photos to Windows Live Photos or Microsoft's Windows Live Spaces blogging service, it's worth doing.

Next, Windows Live Photo Gallery will ask you if you would like to use this application to open common image file formats—instead of Windows 7's built-in Windows Photo Viewer (see Figure 12-16). We recommend using Windows Live Photo Gallery, and not Windows Photo Viewer, because the former application has so many more useful features.

Okay, now it's time take a lap around the Photo Gallery interface.

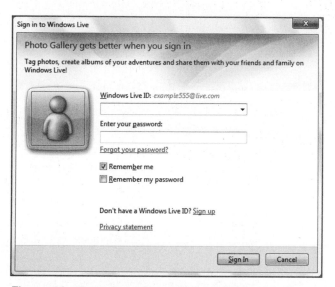

Figure 12-15: Windows Live Photo Gallery works better if you're connected to Windows Live.

Figure 12-16: Pick your poison. Or, in this case, a superior photo viewer.

Examining the Windows Live Photo Gallery User Interface

Windows Live Photo Gallery utilizes the now familiar Windows 7 application style, with a simple, light-blue colored user interface and no visible menus, as shown in Figure 12-17.

> **tip**
> If you're familiar with Microsoft's now-discontinued Digital Image Suite product line, you might find that Windows Live Photo Gallery looks and works similarly to Digital Image Suite Library. That's by design: Windows Live Photo Gallery offers a compelling subset of the features from Digital Image Suite, now available free.

Figure 12-17: Windows Live Photo Gallery looks basic but it's full-featured.

The Windows Live Photo Gallery user interface is divided into just a few main sections. Between the toolbar and bottom-mounted navigational controls, you'll see two areas, or panes, by default: a Navigation pane on the left that determines which photos (or videos) you will view, and the thumbnail pane, which displays the pictures (or videos) in the current view.

---

tip Windows Live Photo Gallery displays other panes under certain conditions. If you view a single image with the application or click the Info button in the toolbar, a right-mounted Info pane appears, providing information about the current picture. When you choose to edit an image—called Fix—a Fix pane appears with various editing options. We'll examine these functions in just a bit.

Secret

Picture Files: Where and Which Ones?

You may be wondering how Windows Live Photo Gallery aggregates the picture files found on your PC. Does it integrate with the Windows 7 HomeGroup feature? Access the same locations as your Pictures and Videos libraries? Or does it search your entire PC for content? Actually, it does none of those, betraying its pre-Windows 7 roots.

Instead, it simply looks in four locations by default. These locations happen to be the same ones that are aggregated by your Pictures and Videos libraries—your My Pictures and My Videos folders, and the Public Pictures and Public Videos folders—but that's more coincidence than anything. It's just that Windows Live Photo Gallery—which is also designed to work with Windows XP and Vista—is designed that way.

That said, you don't have to accept the application's defaults. You can add photos manually to the Windows Live Photo Gallery library by dragging them from the shell into the application. Or, you could simply add other folders to the Windows Live Photo Gallery list of watched folders. We show you how in the next section, but if you're familiar with the notion of Windows Media Player monitored folders, the concept here is similar.

What about picture file type support? Obviously, Windows Live Photo Gallery supports common image file types such as JPEG, (non-animated) GIF, PNG, TIFF, and Bitmap. Newer digital cameras support various RAW file types, which are uncompressed, and unfortunately Windows Live Photo Gallery cannot edit RAW images out of the box. But if you install a compatible Windows Imaging Components (WIC) driver from a camera maker, Windows Live Photo Gallery will allow you to edit RAW images and export them to JPEG. It cannot save edits directly to any RAW image.

Viewing Individual Photos

While Photo Gallery displays all of your photos in a grid of thumbnails, you will frequently want to view a single photo, either to simple admire it or to edit—or *fix*—it in some way. Doing so in Photo Gallery works identically to opening an image file in the Windows Explorer shell: you double-click the photo in question. When you do so, the Photo Gallery interface changes as shown in Figure 12-18.

A number of new features are exposed when you view a photo in this fashion. First, the application switches into a single-image view. To return to the thumbnail-based photo gallery view, click the Back to Gallery button, or the prominent blue Back button at the top of the window.

A new Info pane appears on the right side of the application window. From here, you can add tags, a caption, and a rating, and view detailed information about the photo. You can toggle this Info pane by clicking the Info toolbar button or, if it's visible, the close button in the upper-right corner of the Info pane. (It resembles a small "x.")

Using the bottom-mounted toolbar, you can move back to the previous image in the gallery, move forward to the next image, rotate the image counterclockwise or clockwise, delete the image, trigger a slide show, or zoom in and out. If you do zoom into the image, you can use the mouse cursor to scroll around within the display area, as shown in Figure 12-19.

Finally, you can also replace the Info pane with a Fix pane for editing the photo in various ways. We examine Fix later in this chapter.

Figure 12-18: When you view a single photo, the application display changes and exposes new functionality.

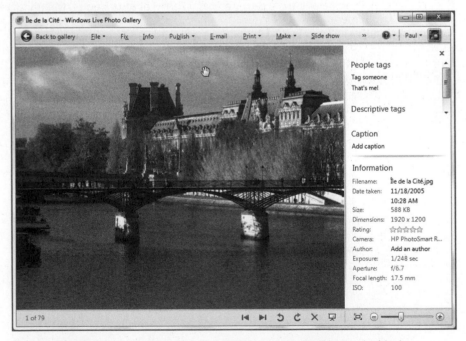

Figure 12-19: When zoomed into an image, you can scroll around with the dimensions of that image.

Changing How Your Digital Memories Are Displayed

Photo Gallery is a fairly versatile application. In the Navigation pane, you can choose to filter the view of photos and videos by various criteria. The top option, or node, is called All Photos and Videos. This entry lets you view all of the photos and videos you have in the My Pictures, Public Pictures, My Videos, and Public Videos folders (by default).

If you want to filter the view down a bit, you can expand and contract the various nodes found in the Navigation pane. For example, if you expand All Photos and Videos, you'll see subnodes in the tree for My Pictures, My Videos, Public Pictures, and Public Videos. Choosing one of those will filter the Thumbnail pane to show only the content in the selected folder. Other nodes in the Navigation pane include Date Taken, People Tags, and Descriptive Tags.

> **tip** The Folders nodes provide you with a close approximation to the old XP-style shell management. When you expand these nodes, you'll see a cascading set of folders representing the folders that Photo Gallery watches for new content.

Secret Although it's not obvious at all, you can actually add or remove folders from the list of folders that Windows Live Photo Gallery watches. To add a folder, simply navigate to that folder in an Explorer window and then drag it over to the Folders node. To remove a folder, including one of the default folders, right-click it inside of the Photo Gallery View By pane and choose delete. Be *very* careful here: when you delete a folder in this fashion, you are also deleting the original, so you will also delete the actual pictures as well. This is poor design on Microsoft's part, in our opinion.

As is often the case with any tree control–type user interface, the Navigation pane can grow beyond the bounds of the application window quite easily, especially if you've got a large image library with a lot of folders or tags. In such a case, the pane adopts a scrollbar so you can still access all of your pictures by navigating up and down through the list.

Grouping and Arranging in Photo Gallery

The thumbnail pane supports a number of organizational features that will be familiar to you if you've spent time playing around with similar features in the Windows shell (which are described earlier in this chapter). In fact, these features were clearly inspired by the Windows 7 shell.

The various organizational features are located below the toolbar and above the thumbnail pane. From left to right, these include the following:

♦ **Arrange By:** As with the Windows shell, Photo Gallery sports a handy way to arrange the items you're viewing. The default view is auto, which displays standard thumbnails in ascending order, with the oldest pictures at the top. However, you can click the Arrange By control to show different arrangements, including by Name, Date, Rating, Type, Tag, or Person. But here's where Photo Gallery wildly differs from the Windows 7 shell: instead of arranging the pictures into stacks,

Photo Gallery instead segregates the pictures vertically into groups, as shown in Figure 12-20.

These groups can be expanded and collapsed to save space. In Figure 12-21, you can see a few collapsed groups.

Figure 12-20: When you use Photo Gallery's Arrange By options, pictures are vertically segregated into groups.

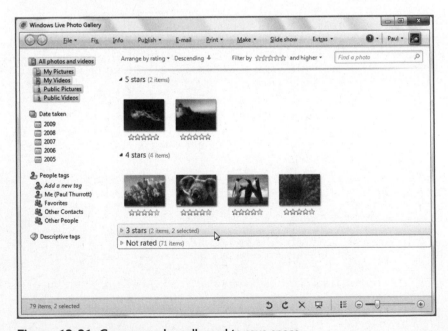

Figure 12-21: Groups can be collapsed to save space.

◆ **Arrange Order:** As you can in the shell, you can also order arranged items in either ascending or descending order. For example, if you choose Arrange By and then Date, and then use a descending arrange order, images will be displayed with the most recent images at the top. In ascending order, the oldest images will be shown at the top.

◆ **Filter By:** To the right of Arrange By and Arrange Order, you will see a Filter By control followed by a list of five grayed-out stars. This control enables you to filter the current view by rating. To view only those photos that are rated four stars, for example, click the fourth star from the left. This will highlight the first four stars and, naturally, display only the four-star-rated items, as shown in Figure 12-22.

Figure 12-22: Curiously, you can only filter by rating using the Filter By control.

You can fine-tune the filter a bit. To the right of the stars is a link titled "only." Tap this and you can choose "and higher" or "and lower." For example, to filter images in the current view down to those that are rated three stars and below, you would click the third star and then choose "and lower."

Note that the Filter By link now reads "Clear filter." To remove the filter, click this link.

◆ **Search:** Photo Gallery's search functionality is surprisingly complete. You can search by all kinds of things—file name, descriptive tags, people, date, and so on—further filtering the view. In Figure 12-23, you can see the results of searching for a specific tag, but we'll look at search a bit more later in the chapter.

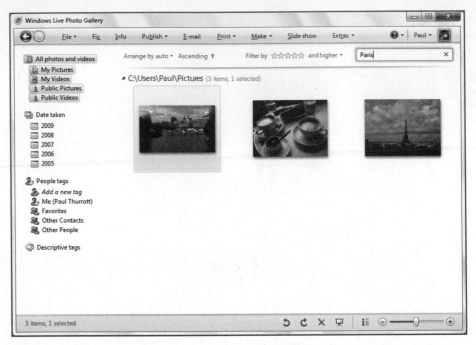

Figure 12-23: The search box enables you to find specific photos and filter the current view.

In addition to these UI controls, Photo Gallery also exposes shell-like grouping and sorting options, as well as a number of thumbnail view styles, most of which are unique to this application.

Grouping and sorting works largely as it does in the shell. To group thumbnails, right-click a blank area of the thumbnail pane and then choose Group by. Photo Gallery offers a much wider range of grouping options than does the Windows 7 shell. You can see the list of possibilities in Figure 12-24.

Photo Gallery's Sort By also offers more options than its Explorer counterpart. Here, you get Date taken, Date Modified, File Size, Image Size, Rating, Caption, and File Name.

Finally, Photo Gallery offers a wide range of view styles, all of which are specially tailored to photos. You access these options by right-clicking a blank area in the thumbnail pane and then choosing View and one of the following options:

◆ **Thumbnails:** The default view, this displays just thumbnail images with no surrounding text.

◆ **Thumbnails with date taken:** Here, a caption is added to the bottom of each thumbnail, describing the date and time that each photo was taken. This is shown in Figure 12-25.

Figure 12-24: Photo Gallery offers more grouping options than Windows Explorer.

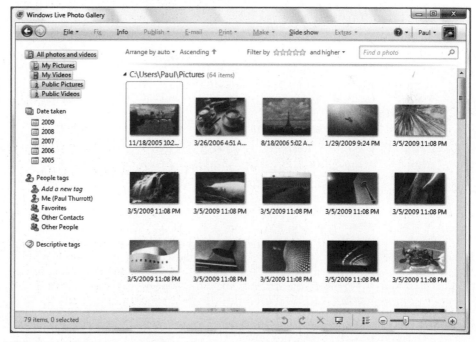

Figure 12-25: Want more than plain thumbnails? Photo Gallery offers various options, including this one, Date taken.

◆ **Thumbnails with date modified:** Here, the caption reflects the date and time the underlying file was last modified.

◆ **Thumbnails with file size:** In this case, the thumbnail caption will display the size of the underlying file, in kilobytes (KB) or megabytes (MB).

◆ **Thumbnails with image size:** This refers to the dimensions of the image, in pixels. For example, you may see captions such as 3328 × 1872 or 3072 × 2304.

◆ **Thumbnails with rating:** This is an excellent view style for those who want to rate their photos. It displays five grayed-out stars as the caption for unrated photos, or the correct rating in cases where one has been previously supplied. Note that this caption isn't read-only: you can also click within the stars to rate photos on-the-fly. This is shown in Figure 12-26.

Figure 12-26: With this view style enabled, you can rate individual photos.

◆ **Thumbnails with caption:** This view style provides a way to view and add captions to individual photos.

◆ **Thumbnails with file name:** This view style displays the photo's underlying filename as the caption. Interestingly, you can edit it, and when you do, the underlying filename is changed as well.

◆ **Details:** The unfortunately named Details view is, in fact, the very best view option of all. Don't be fooled by the name, as it has nothing to do with the Details view found in the Windows shell. This is no text view. Instead, each thumbnail is accompanied by a block of text to the right of the thumbnail, instead of the bottom. This text includes the image's filename, date and time taken, file size, image size (resolution), rating, and caption, as shown in Figure 12-27. The date taken, time taken, rating, and caption can all be edited in this view, which makes it very handy indeed.

Figure 12-27: Details view is the most complete and usable thumbnail view style.

Regardless of which view style you prefer, you can utilize the thumbnail resizing tool, found in the bottom right of the application window, to adjust the size of each thumbnail. As you can see in Figure 12-28, you're free to make the thumbnails as large—or small—as you want.

Figure 12-28: The thumbnail resizing tool lets you zoom in and out on the thumbnail images.

You can also resize the thumbnails in Windows Live Photo Gallery with the scroll wheel on your mouse, if you have one: just hold down the Ctrl key and scroll. No scroll wheel–equipped mouse? No problem: you can use the keyboard instead. Again, hold down the Ctrl key, but this time repeatedly tap the minus (-) key to zoom out or the plus key (+, really =) to zoom in.

Additionally, you can use the toggle to the left of the thumbnail resizing tool to toggle between the current view and the default thumbnails view.

To reset the thumbnails to their default size, tap Ctrl+0.

You can also enable a little-known Table of Contents pane from the Photo Gallery right-click menu. This adds a pane between the Navigation pane and thumbnail pane that corresponds to the current Group by setting. So, for example, if you're grouping by Date taken, the Table of Contents pane will list dates. If you're grouping by Rating, it will list ratings. The Table of Contents pane is shown in Figure 12-29.

Figure 12-29: The Table of Contents pane works better with some grouping styles than others.

Table of Contents acts like the Table of Contents in a book, enabling you to jump from group to group quickly. Say you have grouped by Year taken. The Table of Contents pane lists the name of each year for which you have one or more photos. Additionally, small blue meters below each year name visually hint at the number of pictures for each year. As you click year names in the Table of Contents, the Thumbnail pane scrolls down to display the corresponding group. Also, as it scrolls, a hazy blue box appears in the Table of Contents, visually showing you which portion of your pictures you're currently viewing.

Adding Captions, Ratings, and People Tags to Your Pictures

Although the Table of Contents feature is nice, you're probably going to want a more elegant way of filtering the view of your photo collection. For example, what if you'd like to see just your vacation pictures? Or pictures that contain only family members? Or any other criteria that might be important to you?

Photo Gallery offers a number of ways to help you filter your photo display so that you can see just the photos you want. The problem is that you have to do a bit of work to make these features useful. If you're really into digital photography, however, you may find it is worth the effort.

These features—tags, ratings, captions, and so on—are collectively called *metadata*. Technically speaking, metadata is "data about data," but in the context of a digital image, metadata is what describes and identifies that image. It is data *about* the image.

Secret

In older and non-Microsoft image editing programs, the metadata for each image wasn't always saved along with the image. This means that you could have spent hours fine-tuning your photo collection only to lose all the associated data later. Just to be clear, this is *not* an issue with Windows Live Photo Gallery: Anytime you add or edit any kind of metadata with this application, that information is stored inside of the image file. This means that an image's metadata will always be available going forward, both with other applications and with Web services such as Windows Live Photos.

For example, if you use Windows Live Photo Gallery to rate a picture with five stars, that rating will show up in Windows Media Player or other applications that are compatible with this kind of metadata. Likewise, if you change the rating, tag, or caption for a picture inside of Windows Media Player, that change is reflected in Windows Live Photo Gallery. It's the circle of life, people.

Using Descriptive Tags

The first of these features is called *descriptive tags* or, simply, *tags*. Tags are unique labels that you can apply to pictures to help you identify which ones are related. By default, your own photos will not include descriptive tags, though photos taken with digital cameras always include other metadata related to the technical details associated with the picture, such as its resolution, camera information, and the date and time the photo was taken.

Regardless of how you came to own a particular image, you can always create (and edit) tags, and you can of course apply them across multiple pictures as well. You can also apply multiple tags to each picture. Tags can be as detailed or generic as you want, but you might consider tags such as Family, Vacation, Personal, Work, Home, and so on.

To create a tag without applying it to a particular image, expand the Descriptive Tags node in the Navigation pane. Then, click the Add a New tag link, which is the top node in the list of descriptive tags. When you do so, an edit box appears with the text "Enter a new tag here," letting you create your own tag. Give it a name and then press Enter. You might want to do this repeatedly until you've created all the relevant tags you can think of.

To add these tags to your pictures, select the picture or pictures you'd like to tag and then drag them over to the tag name in the View By pane. As you do so, a small "Apply [*tagname*]" badge appears next to the dragged images, letting you know which tags you are adding. This is shown in Figure 12-30.

Figure 12-30: Tagging doesn't get any easier than this: use your existing drag and drop skills to get metadata to your digital photos and other images.

You can also drag pictures to multiple tags if you'd like, so, for example, some pictures might end up being tagged as Family, Vacation, and Personal.

If you want to remove all tags from a picture (or group of pictures), drag it to the Not Tagged node.

---

tip   You can also add tags in other ways. To add tags via the Info pane, select a picture or set of pictures and click the Add Descriptive Tags link in the Info pane. The new tag will be added to both the pictures and the list of available tags.

To remove a tag from the Info pane, select the photo or photos you'd like to adjust and then find the tag name in the list under Descriptive Tags in the Info pane. Click the "x" (Remove) button to the right of the tag name, as shown in Figure 12-31.

Figure 12-31: Tags can be viewed and removed from the Info pane.

> To display a view that includes more than one tag, Ctrl+click each tag name you want in the Navigation pane. *Voilà*, a custom view style.

After you've applied tags to your pictures, you can start filtering the view by this information. In the Navigation pane, simply select the tag you want and the Thumbnails view will change to display only those pictures that are tagged with that particular tag. In Figure 12-32, you can see the effect of viewing photos by tag.

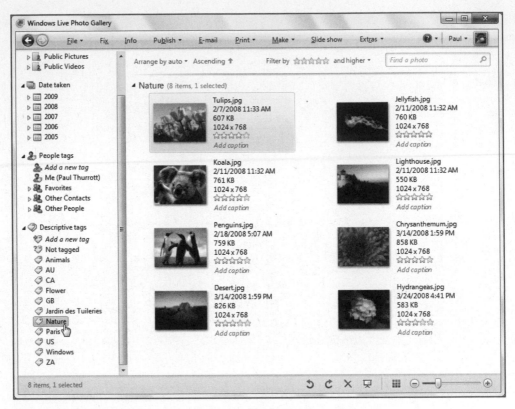

Figure 12-32: Tagging is ideal for filtering the view in Photo Gallery.

Using Captions

You can also optionally create a unique *caption* for each of your pictures if you'd like. These captions are simply descriptive text labels, so you can be creative and even verbose. (Descriptive tags, by comparison, are typically short words or phrases.) You might add text such as "Doesn't Kelly look surprised here?" or "Bob finally made it to the top of the mountain!" It's up to you.

Secret

Captions are limited to 255 characters, so you technically can't add *any* text you like.

To add a caption to a picture or group of pictures, select one or more pictures and then click the Add caption link in the Info pane under the Caption heading. Add any text you like.

You can also add captions to individual photos if you've set Photo Gallery to display in Details view. In this case, you can simply click the Add caption link you will see next to the photo, as shown in Figure 12-33.

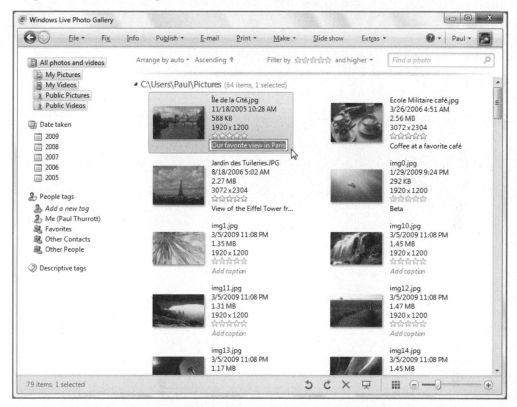

Figure 12-33: Captions can be added in Details view or via the Info pane.

Using Ratings

Another way to filter your images is to apply *ratings* to your pictures, on a scale from one to five stars. Pictures you really like could receive a five-star rating, whereas the duds might get one star. You can provide ratings via the Info pane or using two different thumbnail view styles.

To rate a picture via the Info pane, select the image you'd like to rate. Then, look for the Rating link and stars in the Information section of the Info pane. To give a picture a four-star rating, for example, click the fourth star, as shown in Figure 12-34.

Figure 12-34: Ratings provide a way for you to grade your pictures.

You can also apply ratings directly to thumbnails if you configure Photo Gallery to display in Thumbnails with rating or Details view. In these cases, the ratings stars will appear below, or right next to, each image thumbnail.

As you should expect by now, you can select multiple images and apply ratings to all of them simultaneously. To remove ratings, right-click one or more rated images and choose Clear rating from the pop-up menu that appears.

Secret

Thanks to improvements to Windows Explorer in Windows 7, you can also add or edit metadata to photos and other files directly from the shell. To do so, select one or more image files in Explorer and then note the Tags, Rating, and Title entries in the Details pane. (The Title entry is the same as Caption in Photo Gallery. Ah, the consistency of Microsoft software products.) You can edit these items directly from this location if you'd like.

Using People Tags

We've saved the best metadata functionality in Windows Live Photo Gallery for last, and think you'll agree that this is both the most interesting and potentially the most productive way to tag your photos. It's called *people tags*. People tags help you identify the people in your photos and then create tags for each. So you might create a separate people tag for each member of your family, each friend, and any other individuals you care about. Once you do this, it's a breeze to find the pictures you really care about.

This section explains how it works.

Creating People Tags

First, you need some people tags. Here's one example of when signing into your Windows Live ID account can save some time: if you did so, you will see a number of people tags ready to roll in the Navigation pane. There will be one called "Me (your name)" and then one or more groups, depending on how you may have configured contacts via Windows Live People, Windows Live Contacts, or Windows Live Messenger. (Remember: We examine these services in Chapter 23.) If you have logged on via Windows Live ID, you may already have a number of people tags, pre-made and ready to go.

If not, or if you'd like to manually create people tags that exist separately from any contacts (say, for children or others who are not part of your Windows Live "network"), you can create one or more people tags right here in Photo Gallery. These people will be added to a new group under People Tags called Other People.

To create the first people tag, click the Add a New Tag link below People Tags in the Navigation pane and start typing as shown in Figure 12-35. Then, repeat this for each people tag you'd like to make.

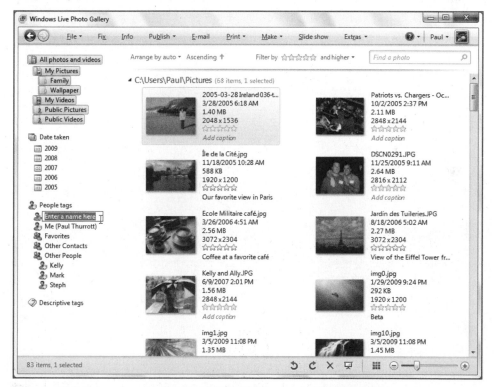

Figure 12-35: You can easily add a list of people tags in Photo Gallery.

Secret

The People Tags section in the Info pane also integrates with your Windows Live contacts, so you might use this instead if you're a Windows Live guy or gal: click the Add People Tags link and start typing; as you do, contacts from Windows Live contacts auto-fill so you can easily find who you're looking for.

Adding People Tags to Photos

Next, you can add a people tag to a photo. It's best to do this while viewing the photo, not in thumbnail view. Double-click on the photo you'd like to tag. Then, click the Tag Someone link in the Info pane, below People Tags. When you do so, an Add People Tag balloon help window appears, asking you to click on a face in the photo. You can either click in the center of someone's face, or you can draw a selection rectangle around a face using the mouse cursor. When you do, the Tag Someone palette pops up, letting you choose which person it is from the list of people tags you've created. This is shown in Figure 12-36.

Figure 12-36: Select the face, and then select the People Tag that matches.

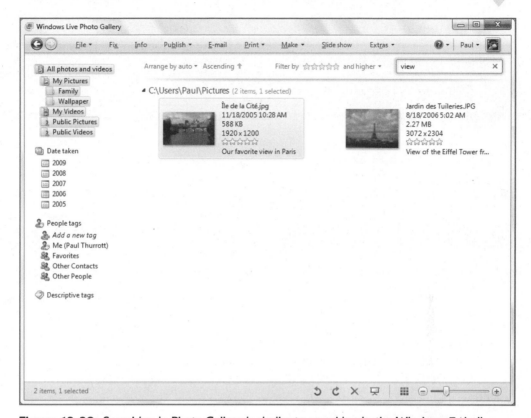

Figure 12-39: Searching in Photo Gallery is similar to searching in the Windows 7 shell.

Secret

As with shell-based searches, searching via Live Photo Gallery is nearly instanta-neous, so you will see search results appear as you type. By default, it searches in the current view, so if you've customized or filtered the view in any way, that will affect the search results. To search your entire photo library, click the See Other Options drop-down arrow to the right of the search box and choose Search All Items in Photo Gallery from the drop-down menu that appears.

Secret

Notice anything missing? Unlike with the Windows shell, there is no way to save searches inside of Windows Live Photo Gallery. There's no elegant solution to this, but you could apply a descriptive tag to a search result set (or any combination of filters and searches) to retrieve it later. Say you have 200 photos with the tag "Paris" but would like to segregate your very favorite Paris photos so that you can enjoy them in a slide show, a DVD movie, a movie, or wherever else. What you can do is Ctrl+click the ones you like best and then apply a new descriptive tag, perhaps *Favorites* or *Paris Favorites* just to those. That way, you can always get back to your favorite Paris photos simply by selecting the appropriate tag from the Descriptive Tags section in the Navigation pane.

Importing Pictures into Photo Gallery

If you already have pictures on your PC, you can add them to Photo Gallery by copying them into one of the folders Photo Gallery monitors, by adding their containing folders to Photo Gallery's watch folder list, or by dragging them directly into the application window. But what if you need to import new pictures via a digital camera, memory card, picture CD or DVD, or scanner? Like Windows XP and Vista, Windows 7 supports image acquisition via all of these sources. And it all happens via Windows Live Photo Gallery.

Secret If you do not have Windows Live Photo Gallery installed on your PC, there is no obvious way to import photos. You will basically need to install Windows Live Photo Gallery or a competing photo application to perform this function on Windows 7, short of a few cases—such as with a memory card, whereby you can simply drag raw image files over to the PC via Windows Explorer.

That said, what you see depends on whether you're importing from analog (scanner) or digital (camera or memory card) sources. We'll examine both here.

Importing Images with a Scanner

While the world has pretty much transitioned to digital photography, many people still have older photos and other paper-based content that they want to digitize and add to their digital photo collections. Devices called *scanners* have been designed for just this purpose, and you won't be surprised to discover that Windows Live Photo Gallery offers first-class support for scanners.

You can initiate a scan of a photo or other paper-based object in various ways. You can launch Photo Gallery, click File, and then select Import from a camera or scanner; Photo Gallery will present the Import Photos and Videos window from which you can choose the scanner. This is shown in Figure 12-40.

Figure 12-40: Scanners show up alongside cameras and other digital image sources in Photo Gallery.

Once you click Import, the New Scan wizard appears, as shown in Figure 12-41. From here, you can configure a bewildering series of scanning options.

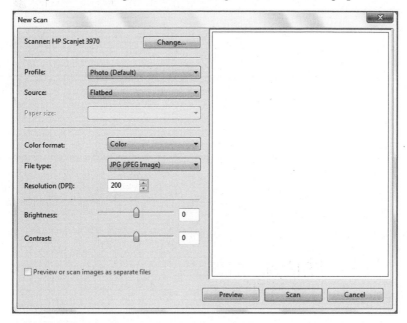

Figure 12-41: Here, you configure your scanner and prepare for scanning.

A few of these options are quite important:

 ◆ **Profile:** Make sure this is set accordingly. That is, use Photo (Default) for photos. (A second profile, Documents, is also included, but that is obviously optimized for documents.)

 ◆ **Source:** Typically, you'll be using a flatbed scanner for photos, but some scanners support other scanning methods, including slide and negative scanners.

 ◆ **Color format:** Here, you can choose between Color, Grayscale, and Black and White. You'll almost always want to use Color, but for black-and-white photos, choose Grayscale, not Black and White. You will typically use Black and White only for documents, though even in that case Grayscale often makes better sense.

 ◆ **File type:** Most of the time, you'll want to go with the default (JPG, for JPEG) if you're scanning photos; but other options are available, all of which are of higher quality than JPG. You may want to consider PNG for archival purposes, as it does not suffer from the same lossy compression issues that JPG does. Choose TIF for documents.

 ◆ **Resolution:** The default resolution here, 200 DPI (dots per inch), is pretty low. Depending on the capabilities of your scanner, you should select a higher value (I typically use 600 DPI, for example), which results in a higher-resolution image. But you can edit this image and resize it as needed. It's better to start off with a bigger source image and then downsize as needed.

There are also Brightness and Contrast sliders. Ignore these and use the photo editing features of Photo Gallery to edit the scan later.

Because most scans do not occupy the entire flatbed area, you should arrange the photos or other documents you wish to scan on the scanner and then click the Preview button. As shown in Figure 12-42, Windows Live Photo Gallery will do a preliminary scan so you can crop accordingly, using the onscreen markers.

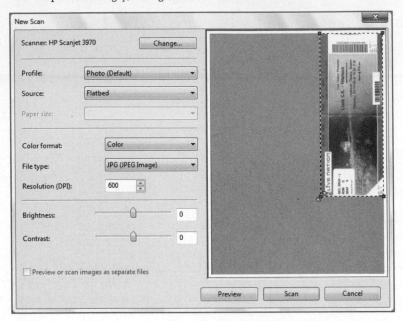

Figure 12-42: Once you've previewed a scan, you can use the onscreen guides to crop for the final scan.

After cropping as needed, click the Scan button to perform the actual scan. Photo Gallery will scan the image and prompt you to provide a tag for this picture, as shown in Figure 12-43.

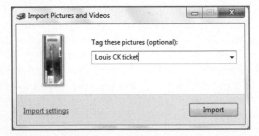

Figure 12-43: This tag will be used to name the underlying file.

This is optional, but the tag will also be used to name the photo file that's created, as well as the folder that contains it. So, for example, if you scan an image and then supply the tag "Celtics ticket," Photo Gallery will, by default, create a file called Celtics ticket.jpg inside a folder named "[*Date*] Celtics ticket" that exists under your Pictures folder.

Because scanning is more art form than science, chances are good you're going to want to make some edits before the rough scan can be considered a final image. You can use Photo Gallery or your favorite photo editing application to make these edits. You get a look at Photo Gallery's photo editing features later in this section.

Importing Images from a Digital Camera or Memory Card

When you plug in a compatible camera (via USB) or memory card (via a memory card reader), the Windows 7 Auto Play function will kick in by default, asking you what you'd like to do. Confusingly, there are two relevant options here: Import photos and videos using Windows and Import photos and videos using Windows Live Photo Gallery. The question of course is which one should you use?

You should use the Windows Live Photo Gallery version. That's because this importer includes one very important feature that is missing from the Windows 7 import option: it enables you to organize and group imported pictures and videos according to when they were taken. With Windows 7, everything you import is dumped into a single folder at the time of import, regardless of when the pictures were taken.

Beyond that, they both work similarly, but with two other minor differences:

♦ First, the Windows 7 import option will actually copy videos to a subfolder in your My Videos folder by default, instead of putting them with your photos in My Photos; The Windows Live Photo Gallery import option, meanwhile, puts camera-based photos and videos in the same folders under the My Photos folder.

♦ Second, the Windows 7 import option can be configured to open Windows Explorer to the folder containing the images you just imported when the import is complete. The Windows Live Photo Gallery option, meanwhile, can be configured to open Windows Live Photo Gallery when importing is complete.

Because Windows Live Photo Gallery is a complete end-to-end solution and offers vastly superior importing capabilities, we focus on that method here. So, without further ado, click Import photos and videos using Windows Live Photo Gallery from the Auto Play window. This runs the Import Photos and Videos wizard, which steps you through the process of acquiring your pictures. This is shown in Figure 12-44.

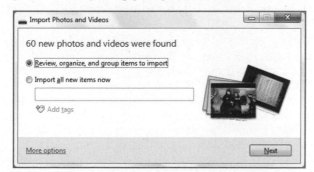

Figure 12-44: The Import Photos and Videos wizard does—well, you can guess what it does.

The first time you run this wizard, be sure to click the More options link to configure how Photo Gallery imports your photos. This is very important, as the default importing configuration is sub-optimal. Figure 12-45 shows the additional options that appear.

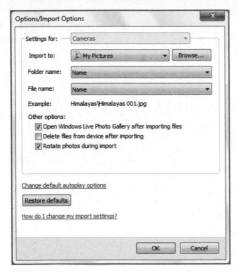

Figure 12-45: Do not pass Go, do not collect $200, before configuring Photo Gallery's import settings.

There are a number of important options in this dialog. Here, we list those options along with our advice for customizing them:

♦ **Import to:** By default, Photo Gallery will import your photos to the Pictures folder. Typically, this is exactly what you want, but if you're really living the multi-user dream, you could consider importing them to Public Pictures (or another shared location). We leave it alone.

♦ **Folder name:** By default, Photo Gallery will import photos into one or more folders, each of which is given the name you choose for the underlying photos. Say your digital camera has pictures from two separate events, a Disney trip and a birthday party. You might use the name Disney for the trip and the name Birthday Party for the party. But you can choose from a number of different options. We particularly like "Date Taken + Name," which would create folder names like "2009-08-01 Disney" and "2009-08-23 Birthday Party."

♦ **File name:** By default, Photo Gallery will import photos using their original file-name. This is completely unacceptable, and if you change nothing else, be sure to change this. Otherwise, your photos will all have names like "DSC_1234.jpg" instead of "Day at the beach 001.jpg." Which makes more sense to you? We recommend changing this to "Name" or perhaps "Name + Date Taken."

tip As you make changes to the preceding three options, an example filename will change in the dialog to match the selections you've made. This will help you pick options that make sense for you.

- ◆ **Open Windows Live Photo Gallery after importing files:** By default, Windows Live Photo Gallery will open after file importing is complete. This makes sense, as you will almost certainly need to edit, or "fix," many of the pictures you've taken. But if you don't wish that to happen, you can uncheck this option.

- ◆ **Delete files from device after importing:** This option is unchecked by default, which makes sense given its destructive nature. However, you may want to delete files from the camera as they're imported.

- ◆ **Rotate photos during import:** This option is checked by default, so Windows Live Photo Gallery will try to correctly rotate photos as they're imported. In our experience this works better with some camera models than it does with others, so your mileage may vary.

Once Windows Live Photo Gallery is correctly configured, click OK and you can begin importing photos. Note that you should always choose the first option in Import Photos and Videos, titled "Review, organize, and group items to import." That's because when you do so, the application will group your photos intelligently by event and create folders accordingly. Even so, you can still edit the groups to your preferences. It's really well done.

Once you select this option and click Next, the window will expand and you'll see the second section of this wizard, with photos grouped according to date and time. This is shown in Figure 12-46.

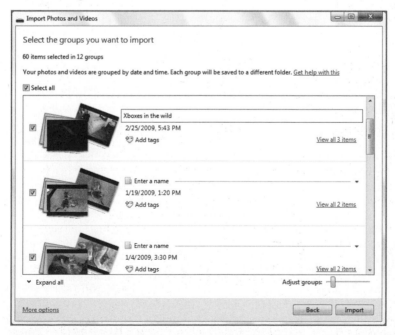

Figure 12-46: Here, you can determine exactly which photos to import and how they'll be grouped in folders on disk (and, logically, within Windows Live Photo Gallery).

Choose which groups of photos to import, using the check boxes on the left and the handy Select all button, and adjust the grouping using a simple slider (in which sliding to the left decreases the amount of time between groups, and sliding to the right increases the time). Even more important, you can provide a name and one or more tags for each group as you see fit. You can also click a View items link next to each group to ensure they're grouped exactly the way you want, as shown in Figure 12-47. (Finally, you can also contract each group again by clicking anywhere in the area above the photo previews.)

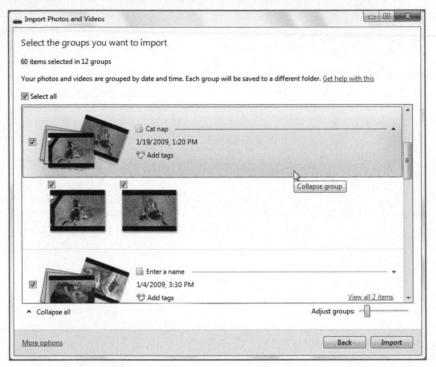

Figure 12-47: You can expand each group to see which photos will be included.

> **tip** If you don't have enough room in the Import Photos and Videos window, you can resize the window accordingly. Just grab the lower right corner of the window with the mouse cursor and go to town, or click the maximize window button if needed.

Once you've named, tagged, and grouped everything to your heart's content, click the Import button and Windows Live Photo Gallery will import the photos you've selected to the hard drive and into your Windows Live Photo Gallery photo library. If the target folder structure falls within a folder in your Pictures library, they will be added to that library as well.

> **tip** Even if you chose to not delete files as they're imported in the Import Options dialog previously, you can choose to do so on-the-fly every time you import photos: the import window includes an Erase After Importing check box for this very purpose.

Secret

You can also access the options for the photo import functionality by accessing the File menu in Photo Gallery and choosing Options. Then, navigate to the Import tab.

Editing Pictures

When you double-click an image in Photo Gallery, the application switches into a viewer mode, which is what you see when you open image files directly from the Windows shell. In this view, you'll often want to click the Fix button to display the application's image editing functions. This is a big change from Windows XP, which didn't typically offer much in the way of editing functionality beyond the very basic facilities of Windows Paint. Windows Live Photo Gallery is also a big improvement over the Windows Photo Gallery application with which Vista users are familiar.

When you preview an image and then click the Fix button in Photo Gallery, the display changes by replacing the Info pane with the Edit pane, providing a list of image editing features, as shown in Figure 12-48.

Figure 12-48: The editing features in Windows Live Photo Gallery enable you to perform several popular photo editing tasks.

The Photo Gallery image editing features are as follows:

◆ **Auto adjust:** This tool evaluates the picture and performs a variety of changes based on the needs of the image. Basically, it's a best-guess estimate of what needs to be fixed, and although it's often a decent try, you'll want to carefully evaluate the changes before committing them to the file. In fact, be very careful, because it seems that Photo Gallery wants to auto-straighten every single photo it comes across for some reason. This includes photos that really don't need such an adjustment.

Secret

Fortunately, Photo Gallery applies any changes you make to a copy of the original photo and archives the original photo on disk, at least by default. You can actually change this functionality so that the original versions of altered files are automatically moved to the Recycle Bin—via the application's Options dialog, which you can access via File ⇨ Options while Photo Gallery is in thumbnail view), but we recommend not doing so. Because of the compressed nature of JPEG images in particular, resaving digital photos can result in dramatic quality reduction. Be careful not to resave JPEG images too often; if you're going to edit a JPEG file, edit and save it once.

tip

If you don't like what Auto adjust does to your picture, click the Undo button at the bottom of the Info pane. If you've performed multiple operations, this button will invoke a pop-up menu that enables you to choose which operations to undo, or you can Undo All changes you've made.

Secret

The Undo button provides multiple levels of undo, so if you commit a number of changes, you can access its pop-up menu, as shown in Figure 12-49, to undo specific changes or multiple changes all at once.

Figure 12-49: Everyone makes mistakes.

◆ **Adjust exposure:** Unlike Auto adjust, this doesn't provide a single-click solution. Instead, when you click this option, the Info pane expands to display slider controls for Brightness, Contrast, Shadows, and Highlights, as well as a Histogram, as shown in Figure 12-50. Move these individual sliders to the left and right to adjust these properties until you're happy with the results.

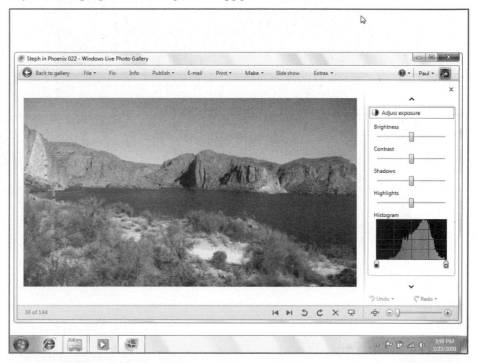

Figure 12-50: The Adjust exposure option provides access to a number of sliders that enable you to fine-tune the picture's exposure.

◆ **Adjust color:** This is also a little more involved. When you select this option, another new area expands in the Info pane, letting you use sliders to adjust the color temperature, tint, and saturation of the photo.

◆ **Straighten photo:** This tool superimposes a grid over the photo, as shown in Figure 12-51, enabling you to rotate the photo using a slide until the photo is level.

◆ **Crop photo:** This tool enables you to crop the current picture, to change its aspect ratio if needed or simply to edit out parts of the picture that are uninteresting. A Proportion drop-down box, shown in Figure 12-52, enables you to determine how you'd like the picture cropped. You can also use the Rotate frame tool to turn a horizontally aligned 16 × 9 photo into a vertically aligned 16 × 9 photo.

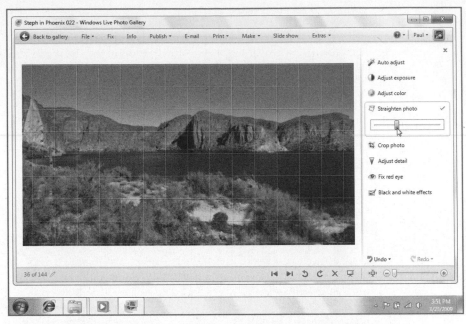

Figure 12-51: Here, you can straighten your photo with a grid and slider.

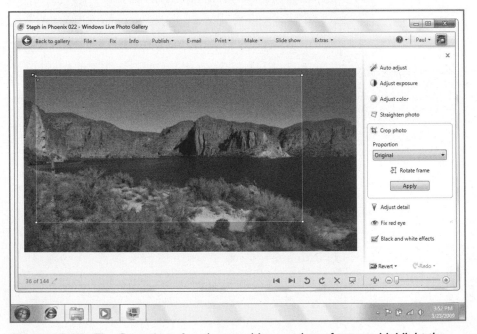

Figure 12-52: The Crop photo function provides a variety of ways to highlight the important parts of a picture.

After you have picked a proportion, you can use the onscreen guide lines to select the portion of the image you'd like cropped. It will retain the aspect ratio as you increase or decrease the size of the selection box.

♦ **Adjust detail:** When you click on Adjust detail in the Fix pane, you'll see a Sharpen slider appear, as shown in Figure 12-53. Sliding this bar to the right will increase the sharpness of the picture. This effect can be quite appealing, depending on the photo. Just be careful not to go too far with it, as oversharpened pictures tend to be a bit stark-looking.

Figure 12-53: New to Windows Live Photo Gallery is an Adjust detail tool, which enables you to increase the sharpness of a photo.

You can also use Adjust detail's Reduce noise tool to mitigate the effects of visual artifacts. Just click the Analyze button and Photo Gallery will check your photo and make the necessary adjustment. If it's not quite right, you can use the slider under the Analyze button to fine-tune things.

♦ **Fix red eye:** Red-eye correction is one of the most often-needed features in any photo-editing package. Fortunately, the one in Photo Gallery works pretty well. Simply click this option and then draw a rectangle around each eye you want to correct in the current picture, as shown in Figure 12-54. When you release the mouse button, Photo Gallery attempts to remove the red eye. It's usually pretty successful, but you may need to try a few times to get it just right.

Figure 12-54: Everyone appreciates a little red-eye removal.

◆ **Black and white effects:** Photo Gallery also includes five black and white filters that enable you to filter the image with an orange, sepia tone, yellow, red, or cyan filter.

There are some handy keyboard shortcuts you can use while editing pictures with Photo Gallery. For example, you can zoom in on a picture by pressing Ctrl (or Alt) and the + key at the same time, and zoom out with Ctrl (or Alt) and the – key. Normally, when you're zoomed in, you can move around the picture using the small hand cursor. But in certain edit tasks, such as Crop Picture and Fix Red Eye, the cursor changes for other purposes, preventing you from navigating around a zoomed picture. To return temporarily to the hand icon in these edits, hold down the Alt key and move around with the mouse. Then, release the Alt key and the cursor will return to the way it was before. By the way, Ctrl+0 zooms the picture back to its default zoom level (that is, the picture fills the entire viewing area).

Resizing Photos

While the crop functionality described previously works well for what it is, you often will want to resize a photo for specific needs. Perhaps you want to create something that correctly fits the resolution of your screen so it will make a good desktop wallpaper. Or maybe you want a version that is more appropriate for the small screen on your smart phone or other portable device. Whatever the reason, you can easily resize photos in Photo Gallery...if you know the trick.

The thing is, Resize isn't an option that appears overtly anywhere in the Windows Live Photo Gallery user interface. Instead, you need to right-click on an individual photo thumbnail to find the Resize option. When you select this, you'll see the Resize dialog shown in Figure 12-55.

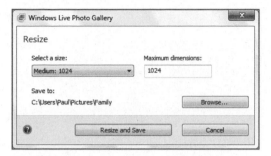

Figure 12-55: It's really well hidden, but once you find it, Resize works as well as can be expected.

To use Resize, select a size from the size drop-down, which includes various presets such as small, medium, and large. Or, input a pixel value into the Maximum Dimensions edit box. The value you enter here will be applied to the largest of the image's horizontal and vertical dimensions. For example, suppose you have a 3328 × 1872 image, which is a widescreen six-megapixel photo. If you set the Maximum Dimensions value to 1920 and click Resize and Save, the resulting photo will be resized to 1920 × 1080.

Creating Panoramic Photos

If you've ever vacationed in a scenic spot, you've probably engaged in an age-old ritual that's common to so many with a camera: you take a series of panoramic shots, moving from one side to the other, as you pan around to take in the entire view. The problem is, when you get home and copy those pictures to the computer, they're all disjointed, and it's not clear that they fit together at all. High-end photography tools like Photoshop have offered a way to stitch these photos back together again into a single very widescreen shot. And now Windows Live Photo Gallery offers this functionality as well.

The trick, of course, is to find two or more shots that can be visually connected in this fashion. Once you've done this, select them in Windows Live Photo Gallery, click the Make toolbar button, and choose Create Panoramic Photo from the drop-down menu that appears. Windows Live Photo Gallery will composite the photos and then prompt you to save the resulting combined image, using a standard Windows Save As dialog that's been renamed to Save panoramic stitch. Select a name and location for the resulting file and click the Save button to save the results.

At this point, Windows Live Photo Gallery will commit the newly stitched photo to disk, leaving the originals as-is, and display the new photo, as shown in Figure 12-56. As you can see, the stitching effect is usually seamless.

The one issue you'll have with stitched panoramic photos is that you will have to trim some excess black space in order to arrive at a normal, rectangular image. Just click the Fix toolbar button and then use the Crop photo tool in the Edit pane to do so.

Secret

Panoramic photos are usually too wide to make for good desktop wallpapers… unless you have multiple monitors. Later in this chapter, we'll explore how you can make a single panoramic photo display across multiple monitors as a seamless desktop background.

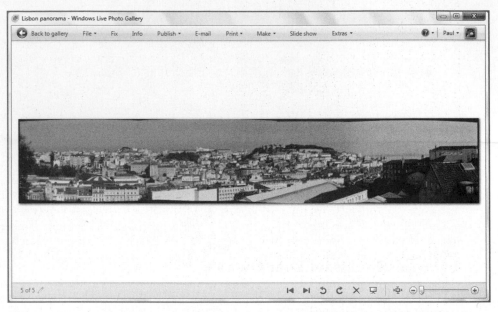

Figure 12-56: This panormaic cityscape was made by stitching four separate photos together.

Editing with Other Applications

Although the basic editing features in Photo Gallery should satisfy many people's needs, there are many other photo editing solutions out there, and you may want to use them to edit photos instead. A number of alternatives are available, including desktop applications like Adobe Photoshop Elements and Google Picasa, and you can access them directly from within Photo Gallery, which is pretty handy.

The key to doing so is the Open button on the Photo Gallery toolbar. If you don't have any third-party photo-editing applications installed, you will see Paint, Windows Live Photo Gallery, and Windows Photo Viewer listed in the resulting drop-down menu when you click this button. But if you installed a third-party application, it should appear in the list as well, as shown in Figure 12-57. This way, you can edit a photo in the application you like the most, while still using Photo Gallery's excellent management capabilities to perform other photo-related tasks.

Figure 12-57: You're not stuck with the useful but limited photo-editing features in Photo Gallery.

tip   What if your application doesn't appear in the Open with drop-down menu? You can
add it easily enough: simply select Choose program from the Open with drop-down
menu and then click the Browse button to find it on your hard drive. When you've
accessed a program in this fashion, it will be added to the drop-down list.

Sharing Photos with Others

Although you may find the process of managing, organizing, and editing photos to be
somewhat tedious, there is of course a wonderful payoff: once you've created an extensive
photo library containing your most precious memories, you can then share those photos
with your family, friends, and others in a stunning variety of ways. In other words, you
can consider Windows Live Photo Gallery to be only the means to an end: for the most
part, you'll use this application for the nitty-gritty management work, and then use its
sharing features to spread the wealth.

Enjoying Photos on Your Own PC

Before we get into the various ways in which you can share your digital memories with others, we want to examine a few ways in which you can enjoy your photos on your own PC.

Using Photos for Desktop Backgrounds

First, you can use any picture as a desktop background. This is easily done from within
Windows Live Photo Gallery or the Windows shell itself. Simply right-click the picture
file you want to use and choose Set as desktop background. In Photo Gallery, this works
from either the thumbnail view or when the application is displaying a single picture.

One of the cool new features in Windows 7 is that you can tile background images across
multiple monitors. First, you will need to add a second monitor to your PC and then use the
Screen Resolution control panel (right-click the desktop and choose Screen resolution) to
correctly position the monitors as they appear on your desk, as shown in Figure 12-58.

Figure 12-58: Windows 7 natively supports multiple monitors, which
has been shown to increase productivity. Plus, it's cool.

Then, access the Personalization control panel (right-click the desktop and choose Personalize) and click the Desktop Background link. In the next window, Choose your desktop background, navigate to a widescreen image, such as a panoramic photo you may have created as described earlier in the chapter. Then, choose Tile in the Picture Position drop-down. A typical two-monitor setup should resemble Figure 12-59.

Figure 12-59: In a multi-monitor setup, you can use a sweeping vista as your desktop background—one that extends across each display.

Using Photos as Screensavers

You can also use your favorite photos as a screensaver. To do so, choose Screensaver settings from Windows Live Photo Gallery's File menu. As shown in Figure 12-60, the Screen Saver Settings dialog will appear. (You can also access this UI from the Control Panel. The simplest way is to open the Control Panel and type **screen saver** into the Search box.)

Figure 12-60: One of the coolest ways to personalize your system is to use your own photos as a screensaver.

Now, click Settings. As shown in Figure 12-61, this dialog enables you to choose which pictures to use in your screensaver, along with various other related options. You can click Preview in the Screen Saver Settings dialog to see how your new screensaver looks.

Figure 12-61: Preview changes as you make them until the screensaver works exactly as you want.

Using Photos as Slide Shows

Finally, one of the neatest, if underappreciated, features in Windows Live Photo Gallery is its ability to create attractive photo slide shows. While Windows 7 offers a simple slide show capability via the shell, the slide show functionality in Photo Gallery is far more impressive.

To see it in action, just navigate to a favorite collection of pictures in Photo Gallery then click the Slide Show toolbar button. Photo Gallery prepares a full-screen photo slide show, as shown in Figure 12-62.

Because this slide show feature utilizes the underlying hardware-accelerated Aero features in Windows Vista, there are a few caveats. First, performance can be somewhat abysmal, particularly startup performance, if you're trying to trigger a slide show with too many photos on a low-end PC.

Second, the Photo Gallery slide show support offers a variety of themes, some of which are quite attractive, but not all of these themes are available on all systems. Those with low-end graphics hardware may only see a handful of themes, while those with a decent PC with 3D graphics hardware will have a choice of several themes. All of these themes are available from the Themes button on the floating navigational control that appears onscreen during slide show playback if you move the mouse around.

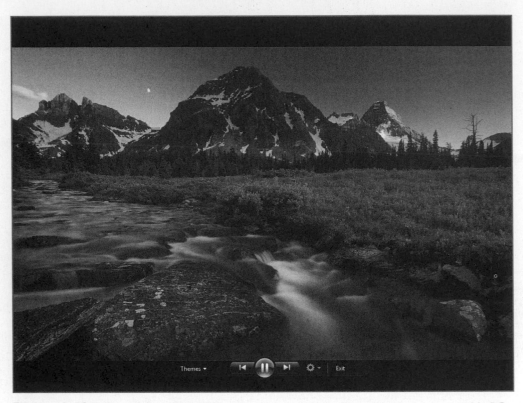

Figure 12-62: Photo Gallery Slide Show offers impressive-looking slide shows on capable PCs.

Here are the two basic slide show themes you will see on virtually any PC:

- ◆ **Classic**: An old-fashioned slide show with no panning or zooming effects. Transitions are non-existent, and new images simply pop onscreen.
- ◆ **Fade**: Similar to Classic except that new images fade in as the previous image fades out.

Most PC users should see the following additional themes as well:

- ◆ **Pan and zoom**: Inspired by the default slide show in Windows Media Center, this slide show animates images across the screen, panning and zooming each image.
- ◆ **Black and white:** Similar to Classic except that the images are shown in grayscale and utilize a fade effect.
- ◆ **Sepia:** Similar to Classic except that the images are shown in a sepia color scheme and utilize a fade effect.

If you're running Windows 7 Home Premium or higher and your PC utilizes 3D graphics hardware, you have several additional themes, including Album, Collage, Frame, Glass, Spin, Stack, and Travel. Each is attractive and worth investigating. The Travel theme is shown in Figure 12-63.

Figure 12-63: The Photo Gallery Slide Show provides various themes.

If you click the gear icon in the floating navigation bar in Photo Gallery, you see a variety of configuration options, including three speed-related options (Slow, Medium, Fast), Shuffle, Loop (repeat), and Mute.

Secret

That last bit is interesting because it suggests that there's some sort of integrated music playback option, a typical feature of most photo slide show options. This is misleading and then some. Unfortunately, there's no way to automatically kick-start a soundtrack for your slide shows with Photo Gallery Slide Show. Instead, you're expected to manually start playing the music of your choice and then start the slide show. If you select the Mute option in Photo Gallery Slide Show, it will globally mute any audio playback on your PC.

Click the Exit option in the floating navigational toolbar to end a slide show. Alternately, you can tap the Esc key to end a slide show.

Printing Pictures and Ordering Prints

If you want to share pictures with others, one of the most obvious ways is to create traditional paper-based prints. These can be wonderful gifts, and while the digital revolution is in full swing, not everyone has a PC or wants to enjoy pictures only with their computer. There are two ways to create picture prints in Windows 7. You can print pictures on your own photo printer, if you have one, or you can order prints online.

To print pictures from Photo Gallery, select the picture (or pictures) you'd like to print, click the Print button in the toolbar, and then choose Print from the drop-down menu. This action launches the excellent Print Pictures wizard, which is depicted in Figure 12-64.

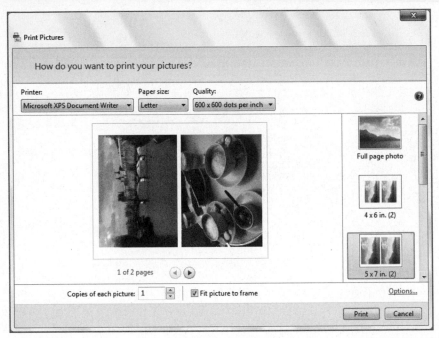

Figure 12-64: You may be surprised by how many options you have for printing photos in Windows 7.

From this deceptively simple wizard, you can customize the print job in a variety of ways, choosing what size prints to create, which printer to use, and a number of other options.

To order prints from an online photo service, select a group of photos and then choose Order Prints from the Print button's drop-down menu. This launches the Order Prints wizard, which provides a handy front end to various online printing services that have arrangements with Microsoft. Give it a second: the list of approved services sometimes takes several seconds to load (of course, it requires an Internet connection).

tip   You don't have to settle for the options Microsoft provides. Bypassing the Order Prints function in Photo Gallery, you can use Internet Explorer or another Web browser to discover, sign up for, and order prints from any number of web-based photo printing services. You can also bring a digital camera memory card into many pharmacies and photo printing retail kiosks and print photos from there.

Secret

One obvious feature that's missing from Windows Live Photo Gallery is the capability to create photo books, which can make great gifts or excellent keepsakes of family vacations and other events. There are a number of online services dedicated to helping you make your own books, but our two favorites, still, are **My Publisher** (www.mypublisher.com) and **Blurb** (www.blurb.com).

Adding Photos to Movies, DVDs, and Data Discs

Photo Gallery also offers basic integration features with Windows Live Movie Maker, Windows DVD Maker, and Windows' integrated CD and DVD burning capabilities to help you create movies of your photo slide shows or data discs full of your favorite pictures.

To create a digital movie of your favorite photos, select the photos you want in Photo Gallery, click the Make toolbar button, and then select Make a movie from the drop-down menu that appears. Windows Live Movie Maker will launch and import all of the selected photos into a new project, as shown in Figure 12-65, which you can then edit into a finished movie. We discuss Windows Live Movie Maker's movie-editing capabilities—including how you can use this tool to make movies of photos—in Chapter 13.

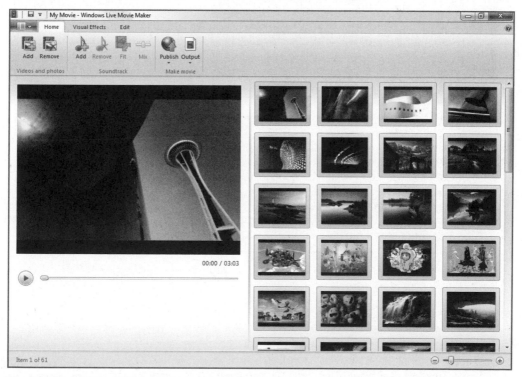

Figure 12-65: With Windows Live Movie Maker, you can turn a string of photos into a compelling animated home movie.

To add a similar slide show to a DVD movie, select the photos as before and then click the Make button followed by Burn a DVD. This will import the pictures into Windows DVD Maker, which enables you to create DVD movies, as shown in Figure 12-66. We discuss Windows DVD Maker in Chapter 13 as well.

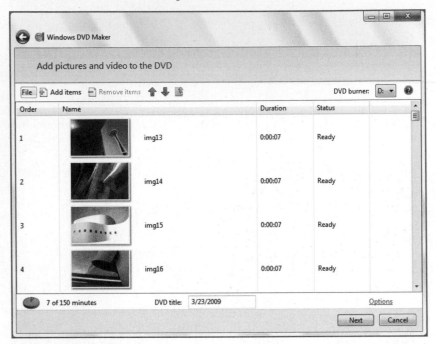

Figure 12-66: Windows DVD Maker lets you distribute your favorite photos via DVD movie.

If you want to create backups of your photo gallery, or share pictures with others via disc, Photo Gallery also enables you to create data disks, in either CD or DVD format, as well. Again, click the Make button on the Photo Gallery toolbar, but this time choose Burn a data DVD from the resulting drop-down menu. You'll be prompted to insert a blank CD or DVD disc into your recordable optical drive (see Figure 12-67), and then Windows 7 will use its integrated disc-burning capabilities to copy the photos onto the disc.

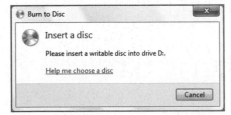

Figure 12-67: Okay, it's not that pretty, but if you're looking for a way to back up your photos to DVD or CD, Windows Live Photo Gallery has you covered.

Network-Based Library Sharing and Portable Device Syncing

You can also share your photos with other Windows–based PCs on your home network, and with compatible devices like the Xbox 360. You can also synchronize photos with a compatible portable device. However, these features are actually exposed through Windows Media Player, not Windows Live Photo Gallery. For this reason, we discuss this functionality in Chapter 11.

Sharing with E-mail

If you'd like to send a picture or group of pictures to friends or others, you can use the built-in e-mail sharing capabilities of Photo Gallery. As always, select the pictures you'd like to send first, and then click the E-mail button in the toolbar. The Attach Files dialog, shown in Figure 12-68, will appear. Here, you can choose how or whether to resize your images for transit, which is likely a good idea, as many of today's digital photos are quite large. Several picture size options are available, including Smaller (640 × 480), Small (800 × 600), Medium (1024 × 768, which is the default), Large (1280 × 1024), and Original Size. As you select a size, the total estimated size will change so you can gauge whether you're sending too many pictures at once.

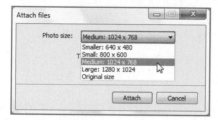

Figure 12-68: The Photo size drop-down enables you to choose from various preset sizes.

After your selection, click Attach and a new e-mail message will appear in Windows Live Mail (see Chapter 21) or whatever e-mail application you've specified as the default.

Sharing on the Web: Services Integration

As you might expect of a Windows Live application, Windows Live Photo Gallery offers unique integration points with other Windows Live online services, especially Windows Live Photos, Microsoft's photo-sharing service. Perhaps more impressive, it also offers some integration with non-Microsoft online services. It's time to examine this integration.

We previously discussed that Windows Live Photo Gallery allows you to log on to your Windows Live ID account using a handy Sign in link in the upper-right corner of the application. This is entirely optional (as are the other Windows Live integration features), but if you do use a Windows Live ID, you might find it convenient to automatically log on each time you use Windows Live Photo Gallery. Doing so will give you access to the other services with which this application integrates, meaning you won't have to manually log on later.

Most of the integration points are accessible via the Publish toolbar button. From here, you can publish photos online in the following ways:

♦ **Online album:** Any selected photo(s) will be published to Microsoft's Windows Live Photos service and added to an existing album or a new album. As shown in Figure 12-69, you can choose the upload size of the pictures (Original, Large, and Medium) in addition to the album in which they will be placed.

Figure 12-69: Want to share your photos with the world? This is the way.

◆ **Group album:** Any selected photo(s) will be published to Windows Live Groups, a Microsoft online service for groups of individuals who share similar hobbies or interests.

◆ **Event album:** Any selected photo(s) will be published to Windows Live Events, Microsoft's events service.

◆ **Soapbox on MSN video:** Any selected video(s) will be published to MSN Soapbox, Microsoft's answer to YouTube (`http://soapbox.msn.com`). The Publish wizard that appears lets you provide a title, a description, and up to five tags, and then select category and permission levels.

◆ **More Services:** If you haven't bought into the Microsoft ecosystem, this will be the most interesting option because it's the gateway to non-Microsoft services. Only one service, the Flickr photo-sharing site, is available off the bat, but you can download add-ons that make Windows Live Photo Gallery compatible with a variety of non-Microsoft online services, including such popular sites as Facebook (photos), YouTube (videos), SmugMug (photos), Google Picasa Web Albums (photos) and others. To see what's available, click Publish ➪ More Services ➪ Add a plug-in.

---

tip　Microsoft's complimentary online services are a big deal—big enough, in fact, to warrant their own chapter. We will examine Windows Live Photos, Events, Groups, and other services more thoroughly in Chapter 23.

Using Photo Gallery to Manage Digital Videos

Although the name Windows Live Photo Gallery suggests that this application is suitable only for pictures, it can also be used to manage digital videos as well. This actually makes sense: today, most digital cameras and many cell phones include video recording capabilities as well, and short videos created on these devices are already far more common than video shot with traditional video cameras.

Videos can be viewed in Photo Gallery by selecting All photos and videos, My Videos, or Public Videos in the Navigation pane, or any other video-related node you may have configured. This is shown in Figure 12-70.

Figure 12-70: Videos, too, can be organized in Photo Gallery.

By default, videos appear as thumbnails that provide a glimpse into the contained movie. If you double-click a video in Photo Gallery, the application switches into a special video preview mode so you can watch the movie, as shown in Figure 12-71. (Conversely, when you open a movie file from the Windows shell, it typically opens in Windows Media Player.) In this mode, the application's navigational control changes to add Play and Stop buttons, like a video player.

Figure 12-71: Videos that happen in Photo Gallery stay in Photo Gallery.

Even though the Photo Gallery toolbar doesn't change when you view videos or video previews, some options simply aren't available with videos. For example, the Fix menu returns a simple message, "Video files can't be fixed using Photo Gallery," if you try to access it.

Videos are fully compatible with the tag, rating, and caption metadata types that are utilized by pictures. This means that you can easily add this information to your videos, filter the view, and search for specific video content just as you do with pictures. Again, this makes sense given that most of the videos you have on your PC have likely come from a digital camera.

Summary

Windows 7 offers a nice "best of both worlds" approach when it comes to photo management, offering many of the familiar shell-based photo management functionality that was provided in Windows XP and expanding on the capabilities of Vista's Windows Photo Gallery with a new solution called Windows Live Photo Gallery. Now, Windows users have two excellent options for managing, editing, sharing, and otherwise enjoying digital photos (and videos) in Windows 7. And Windows Live Photo Gallery even offers a wealth of online services integration, giving you a connection to the future of computing.

Digital Videos and DVD Movies

Chapter 13

♦ ♦

In This Chapter

Learning how to manage your digital movies

Using Windows Live Movie Maker to import content, edit video, and publish completed movies

Editing TV shows and removing commercials with Windows Live Movie Maker

Sharing your videos on the Web

Using Windows DVD Maker to make DVD movies

Copying and ripping DVD movies to your PC

♦ ♦

Just a few short years ago, the notion of consumers using PCs to edit their home movies into professional-looking productions was science fiction. But then Apple came along with iMovie, proving not only that it was possible, but that high-quality video-editing tools could be both elegant and user-friendly. At that time, Microsoft had just released its first Windows Movie Maker tool, a crippled Windows Me application that was aimed only at the low end of the market. In Windows Vista, Microsoft introduced a variety of tools for managing, viewing, editing, and publishing digital video of all kinds. Now, in Windows 7, video editing has come full circle: thanks to the new Windows Live Movie Maker application, which is included as part of the free Windows Live Essentials suite, and Windows DVD Maker, you can even edit TV shows, remove commercials, publish videos to the Web, and make your own movie DVDs. And because this is a PC, with a rich ecosystem of third-party applications, it's possible to perform other related tasks in Windows 7 as well, including duplicating DVDs and "ripping" DVD movies to the hard drive. You can even duplicate and rip copy-protected DVDs if you know the right tricks. It's time to jump right in.

Managing Digital Movies

Like Windows Vista and Windows XP before it, Windows 7 includes a number of ways in which you can manage, view, and otherwise enjoy digital movies. You may recall that Windows XP included a special shell folder called My Videos. Actually, you will be forgiven for not remembering that—in Windows XP, the My Videos folder was curiously deprecated, unlike its My Documents, My Music, and My Pictures siblings. It didn't appear on the Start menu by default and couldn't be added later. In fact, My Videos didn't even appear in the Windows XP shell until you started up Windows Movie Maker for the first time.

In Windows Vista, the situation was only marginally different. In that release, the My Videos folder was replaced by the Videos folder, in keeping with Microsoft's Vista shell folder naming scheme. It was no longer a special shell folder, and it was not located in the file system inside of Documents as before. Instead, Videos sat under your Home folder (C:\Users*Your username* by default) alongside Documents, Music, Pictures, and other commonly needed folders. But it still didn't appear on the right side of the Start menu for some reason, and once again there was no way to make it appear there.

My Videos: Managing Digital Movies with the Windows 7 Shell

In Windows 7, finally, the Videos shell location has become a first-class citizen alongside your other commonly accessed user folders, though Microsoft continues to confuse with its folder names. What this means is that you now have physical video folders (including your personal My Videos folder at C:\Users*Your username*\My Videos, and Public Videos at C:\Users\Public\Videos), as well as a new Videos library—shown in Figure 13-1—which is a virtual folder that aggregates the content from other locations (My Videos and Public Videos, by default) into a single view. Of course, your Videos library can also be shared with others via Windows 7's new HomeGroup sharing scheme. While this evolution of the Videos folder may seem convoluted, it's actually quite a bit nicer in use than it used to be.

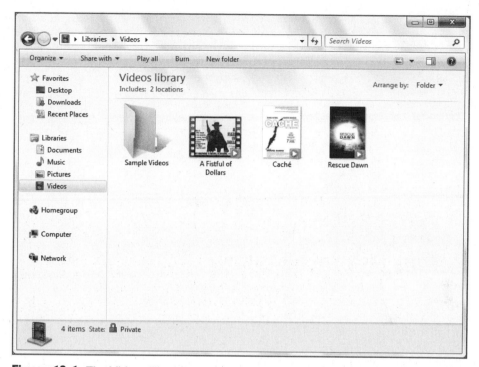

Figure 13-1: The Videos library aggregates content from My Videos, Public Videos, and, potentially, other locations, providing you with a single view into all of your video content.

cross ref We discuss the new Windows 7 Libraries feature in Chapter 5, and the HomeGroup sharing functionality in Chapter 9.

You can access Videos in various ways. The quickest is to click on the Windows Explorer taskbar button; this opens a view of the Libraries location, which by default displays icons for four libraries: Documents, Music, Pictures, and Videos, as shown in Figure 13-2.

You could also simply open the Start menu, select Search and type **Videos**, and then tap Enter.

Secret If you're familiar with the way that Windows 7 libraries work, you won't be surprised to discover that the Videos library aggregates content from two sources by default: your personal Videos folder (*C:\Users\Your username\My Videos*) and Public Videos (C:\Users\Public\Public Videos). Public Videos was called Shared Videos in Windows XP and was in a different location, but the Public Videos folder in Windows 7 works identically to that in Windows Vista.

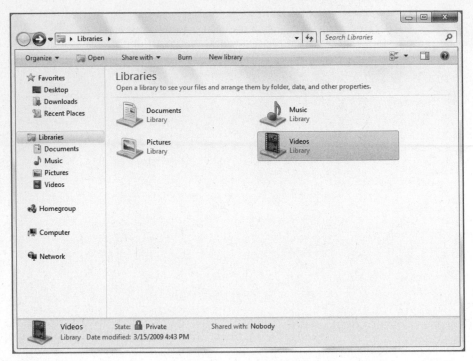

Figure 13-2: The Libraries shell location provides a way to access all of your libraries, including Videos.

Secret

The My Videos folder is the *default save location* for the Videos library, so when you copy content into Videos (the library), it is actually copied to My Videos (the folder).

tip

There's also a Sample Videos subfolder in Public Videos that includes a short sample video provided by Microsoft. There is a shortcut to this folder in your Videos folder, but the actual folder is located in C:\Users\Public\Public Videos\Sample Videos by default.

Because of the proliferation of digital cameras with video-taking capabilities, you could very likely also find videos scattered around inside of your My Pictures folder. When you copy pictures from a digital camera to Windows 7 (or to previous versions of Windows), any videos on the camera will be copied to the same location, which is typically a subfolder under My Pictures. You could easily use Windows 7's Library functionality to find and display these videos alongside the videos in My Videos and Public Videos. To do so, open the Videos library and click the link next to Includes (it will read *2 Library locations* by default). In the Videos Library Locations window that appears, click Add, and then navigate to My Pictures. Click Include folder, and then OK. Unfortunately, when you do so, the Videos library shows you all of the subfolders under My Pictures, not just the ones with videos, as shown in Figure 13-3.

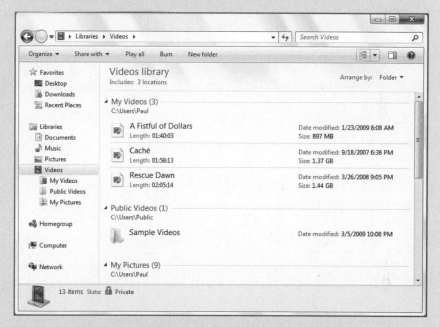

Figure 13-3: Look, ma! There are videos in the My Pictures folder.

With all these different locations for finding digital videos, you might wonder what Microsoft was thinking. Although we could never claim to offer any insight along those lines, we can tell you that video management, like that of music and photos, has changed dramatically between Windows XP, Vista, and 7. And though it's still possible to navigate around the Windows shell and double-click movies to play them in Windows Media Player or another software tool, Microsoft expects that most of its users will instead use

dedicated applications to manage and view digital movies. That said, the new Videos
library functionality is there for those who do wish to utilize the shell more heavily. In this
way, we think Microsoft struck a nice balance and has provided solutions that virtually
anyone will appreciate.

Secret

There's an even quicker way to access Videos than those we've mentioned so far. If
you're one of the many video enthusiasts who have been clamoring for Microsoft
to make it possible to add a link to Videos from the Start menu, rejoice: You can
now do so. To add this link to the Start menu, right-click the Start button and
click Properties. Then, click the Customize button in the Start Menu tab. In the
Customize Start Menu window that appears, scroll down to Videos and choose
from "Display as a link," "Display as a menu," and "Don't display this item." (The
latter is the default.) As shown in Figure 13-4, this link corresponds with the
Videos library, not the My Videos folder.

Figure 13-4: You can now add the Videos folder—really the
Videos library—to the Windows 7 Start menu!

Watching and Managing Movies with Windows Live Photo Gallery

While the new Videos library is the primary movie management tool in Windows 7, there are other ways in which you can manage videos. Believe it or not, one is Windows Live Photo Gallery. Why Microsoft didn't choose to name this Windows Photo and Movie Gallery is unclear, but the fact remains that you can organize and manage (and even play) virtually all of the digital video on your system with this tool. Although we describe this application in detail in Chapter 12, it may be worth a short side trip here to discuss how it works with digital movies specifically.

> **tip** Windows Live Photo Gallery is not actually included with Windows 7 for legal reasons, but is instead made available for free on the Web as part of the Windows Live Essentials suite (download.live.com). Because we consider Windows Live Essentials a key part of the Windows 7 experience, this chapter, like the rest of this book, assumes that you or your PC maker has installed the suite. Remember, no Windows 7 PC is complete without Windows Live Essentials.

By default, Windows Live Photo Gallery enables you to manage photos and videos together, and it's designed to search the My Pictures, My Videos, Public Pictures, and Public Videos folders for video (and photo) content by default. (You can manually configure Windows Live Photo Gallery to search other locations as well; see Chapter 12 for more information.)

> **Secret** Notice anything odd there? That's right: Windows Live Photo Gallery doesn't (currently) use the same Libraries management system that's exposed by Windows 7. Instead, it manually monitors specific folder locations on its own. So, if you do manually include other folder locations in the Videos library, these locations will not be monitored by Windows Live Photo Gallery unless you manually add them to the Gallery. We assume that a future version of Windows Live Photo Gallery will be updated for a more seamless experience in Windows 7.

When it comes to video, all the metadata application information works equally well with movies as it does with photos. That is, you can add tags, ratings, and captions to movies, just as you can with photos. That said, we don't expect many people will actually take advantage of that functionality because it's time consuming and, ultimately, of little value.

If you want to work just with movies in Windows Live Photo Gallery, you must multi-select the video-oriented entries under All photos and videos in the application's View By pane. (Use Ctrl+click to make that happen.) Now, you will see just videos in the Thumbnails pane, as shown in Figure 13-5.

Figure 13-5: Even video files are displayed with nice thumbnail images in Windows Live Photo Gallery.

As you mouse over individual videos, a pop-up window displays, showing a larger thumbnail, along with other information about the file, including its name, size, rating, and the date and time it was created. You can see this effect in Figure 13-6.

Secret

If you want to discover where an individual video is located in the file system, right-click it in Windows Live Photo Gallery and choose Open file location.

To play a video, simply double-click it. Curiously, videos opened in Windows Live Photo Gallery play in Windows Live Photo Gallery—and not in Windows Media Player, as you might expect. This is undesirable for a few reasons, but the most obvious is that the video playback pane in Windows Live Photo Gallery is only as large as the application window, which is often larger than the original video, causing blurry resizing effects. As shown in Figure 13-7, Windows Live Photo Gallery isn't the optimal place to play video files.

Figure 13-6: Nice flyover effects give you more information about individual videos.

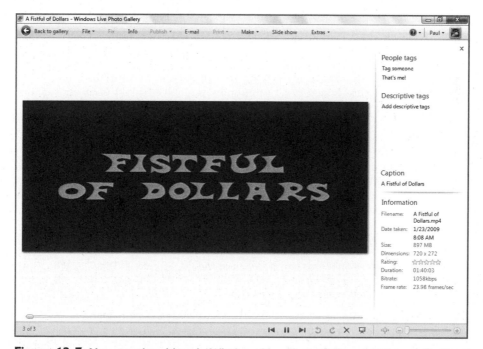

Figure 13-7: You can play videos in Windows Live Photo Gallery, but the application is better suited for just managing the files.

But you don't have to view videos this way. Instead, you can right-click a video file from within Windows Live Photo Gallery and then choose "Open with" from the pop-up menu. You'll see a list of applicable applications, including those that come with Windows 7 and any compatible third-party applications you may have installed yourself.

Secret There's no way to configure Windows Live Photo Gallery to *always* open video files in another application. Instead, you must choose a different application, manually, each time.

The Windows Live Photo Gallery video playback view does have some redeeming features. From this view, you can add descriptive tags and a caption, for example, and even edit the file's creation date and time data. What you can't do is edit the movie—clicking the Fix toolbar button just displays an unhelpful message. Our advice is to use Windows Live Photo Gallery to manage home movies only, use the shell for other video management, and use Windows Media Player, described in the next section, for playback. We discuss editing digital movies later in this chapter as well.

Watching and Managing Movies with Windows Media Player

Most people think of Windows Media Player as a music player, and sure enough, we do cover this application primarily in Chapter 11, which focuses on digital music and audio. But the truth is, Windows Media Player can also work with video and photo content as well, primarily so that you can synchronize the content with portable media players and share it with other PCs and compatible network devices.) This capability isn't new to Windows Media Player 12, the version that Microsoft ships with Windows 7. However, because videos do play natively in Windows Media Player 12, it's possible that you might want to manage videos, to some degree, in the player as well. Like Windows Live Photo Gallery, Windows Media Player 12 is configured to automatically monitor certain folders for digital media files, and those locations include, by default, your Videos folder and the Public Videos folder. No surprise there.

Secret Well, maybe there *is* a surprise there. Windows Media Player, like Windows Live Photo Gallery, doesn't automatically monitor your Videos library but instead manually monitors the My Videos and Public Videos folders instead. And there's no way to configure it to monitor other folders, as you could with previous versions of the player.

To configure Windows Media Player to display just videos, select Videos from the Navigation pane, as shown in Figure 13-8.

Figure 13-8: Windows Media Player can be the front end to your video files, assuming you store them in an obvious place.

From here, you can play, rate and rename individual videos, but that's about it. You can't add tags from within Windows Media Player, for example. (That is, if you right-click a video and choose Properties, the resulting dialog provides no way to edit tags, as you can with , say, Windows Live Photo Gallery, or from Explorer.) Typically, you're using this application to simply play videos. That's Windows Media Player's strong suit, and you can use the player's various controls to change the size of the video, display it using a nice full-screen mode, or even minimize the player to the system taskbar and watch it there while you get work done.

When you do play a video file, either from the shell or from within Windows Media Player itself, the player switches to a new Now Playing mode that automatically resizes the application window to match the size of the video (by default). As you can see in Figure 13-9, this new mode is attractive and space saving.

As the video begins playing, the playback controls fade away, giving you an even cleaner look. To return to the player's Library view, click the Switch to Library button in the upper-right corner of the window. (The controls will reappear when you mouse over the window.) Note that when you return to Library view, the currently playing video continues to play, even though you can't see it anymore. A Switch to Now Playing button in the bottom right of the Library view enables you to return to the show.

Figure 13-9: Windows Media Player has a new Now Playing mode in Windows 7 that is ideally suited for video content.

One nice side effect of Windows Media Player's capabilities is that you can actually create temporary or saved playlists of videos. That way, you can trigger a collection of videos to play in order, or randomly. It's not possible to do that from the shell or within Windows Live Photo Gallery. And if you save the playlist, you can access it from Windows Media Center, described in the next section.

Watching and Managing Movies with Windows Media Center

Windows Media Center is, of course, the premium environment in Windows for enjoying digital media content such as photos, music, movies, and, yes, even live and recorded TV shows. But Media Center—which we discuss in detail in Chapter 15—isn't just for people with expensive home theater setups. There's no reason you can't use Media Center with a mouse and keyboard on your desktop PC or notebook. In fact, you may find it quite enjoyable to do just that.

Because it is a premium feature, Windows Media Center is not available in all Windows 7 product versions. You have to be using Windows 7 Home Premium or better (Professional, Enterprise, or Ultimate) to get Windows Media Center.

As shown in Figure 13-10, Windows Media Center is a seamless, home theater–like application that works best full screen but can absolutely be enjoyed in a floating, resizable window alongside your other applications if you feel like doing a bit of multitasking.

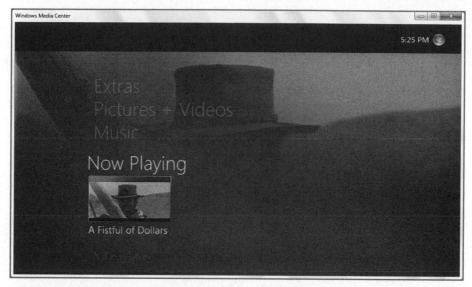

Figure 13-10: Windows Media Center is a nice graphical front end to a variety of digital media experiences.

To use Media Center to manage your digital movies, navigate to the Pictures + Videos experience in the Start page and then choose Video Library. The first time you enter this area, Media Center will ask if you'd like to choose other folders for locating videos. If you've already configured the Videos library to watch the folders you use for videos, or you intend to only use the default folders for video content, you can select No.

Unlike Windows Media Player and Windows Live Photo Gallery, Windows Media Center actually *does* integrate with the folders you monitor via the Videos library. So if you've configured Videos to aggregate content from other locations, those videos will automatically appear in this application as God intended. Hey, one out of three ain't bad when you're Microsoft.

Confusingly, the Windows 7 version of Windows Media Center also includes a top-level Movies option, so you're forgiven for thinking that this might be the place to go to see your digital movies. It is not. Instead, Movies is designed as a front end for online movies, like movie trailers, as well as DVD movies you might play via Media Center. Videos stored on your PC will be found in Pictures + Videos, Video Library.

If you choose Yes, Media Center will walk you through its Library Setup wizard. From here, you can easily add other folders to monitor for video content.

Secret If you do add monitored folders via Windows Media Center, those locations will be added to the appropriate libraries as well. So if you add a folder with video content here, that folder will be added to the Videos library too.

The Video Library experience, shown in Figure 13-11, provides a horizontally-oriented grid of videos through which you can navigate by either name or date. To watch a video, simply select it.

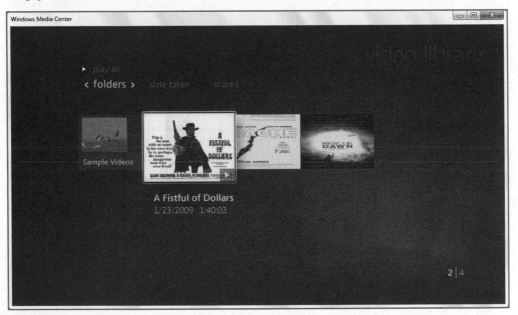

Figure 13-11: In Media Center, videos include graphical thumbnails, providing a highly visual navigation experience.

Secret Although Windows Media Center offers tag-based navigation for music and photos, it does not do so for videos. To navigate your video collection by tag, you'll need to use Windows Live Photo Gallery.

In a related vein, you can't tag, rate, or add captions to videos in Media Center. Essentially, Windows Media Center simply offers a high-end place for video consumption. If you want to interact with videos, you'll need to look elsewhere.

> **tip** As noted previously, Windows Media Center also works with live and recorded TV content. Although this content is technically digital video, we discuss this in more detail in Chapter 15, and later in this chapter where we discuss editing and republishing recorded TV content. Please refer to Chapter 15 for more information about Windows Media Player, especially those features that have been added or changed since Windows Vista.

Editing Digital Video with Windows Live Movie Maker

Microsoft first created an application called Windows Movie Maker as part of Windows Millennium Edition (Windows Me), which shipped back in 2000. Since then, both Windows XP and Vista also included updated versions of Windows Movie Maker. With Windows 7, Microsoft has stripped Movie Maker out of the operating system and made it part of the freely downloadable Windows Live Essentials suite instead. That way, the company can update the product more frequently and meet the product bundling requirements of various governments around the world. As always, we assume that you or your PC maker has downloaded and installed Windows Live Essentials. If not, you can find the suite at http://download.live.com.

Windows Live Movie Maker is Microsoft's tool for creating and editing digital videos and publishing them to the Web. You can import a variety of digital media types into the application, including home movies, photos, music and other audio files, and even recorded TV shows. Then, using simple editing techniques along with professional transitions and effects, you can create completed videos that can be shared with others on the Web.

Secret Windows Live Movie Maker can also output video files to your hard drive, but only in a limited range of formats. This is by design: whereas previous versions of Windows Movie Maker were aimed mostly at home users with camcorders who wanted to share videos in a variety of ways, including via DVD, times have changed, and Windows Live Movie Maker addresses those changes. Now, instead of supporting a bunch of special use cases, the application does what most people want: it publishes to the Web.

Windows Live Movie Maker is a simple and straightforward application, assuming you're comfortable with video editing. (And heck, who isn't?) But even for the uniniti-ated, Windows Live Movie Maker is pretty easy to use. You just need to know your way around.

Starting Windows Live Movie Maker

Typically, you start Windows Live Movie Maker by launching its shortcut from the Start menu. (Type **movie** in the Search box to find it quickly.) You can also find it buried in the Start menu All Programs list under Windows Live. The Windows Live Movie Maker application window is shown in Figure 13-12.

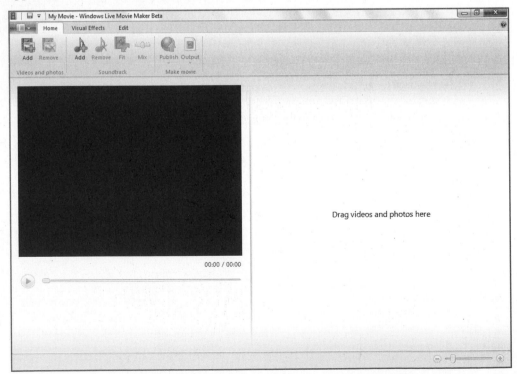

Figure 13-12: Windows Live Movie Maker is decidedly simpler than its predecessors.

Secret

In increasingly rare cases, you may get an error message when you try to launch Windows Live Movie Maker. If you see an error dialog like that shown in Figure 13-13, then your PC is not powerful enough to run Windows Live Movie Maker.

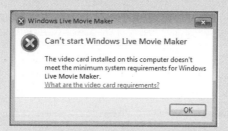

Figure 13-13: Uh-oh: it's time to upgrade.

You will only see this dialog if your PC does not meet the performance requirements for the application. These requirements include 1GB of RAM, a single-core 2.4 GHz or faster processor, and a video card that supports DirectX 9.0c (or later) and Pixel Shader 2.0 (or later). But we don't want to get bogged down in technical jargon here. If you have a reasonably modern computer, you'll have no issues with Movie Maker. We've successfully run Windows Live Movie Maker on a low-end netbook featuring a dual-core Atom processor running at just 1.6 GHz and utilizing integrated graphics, for example. So if you do see this dialog, you probably shouldn't even be running Windows 7.

Understanding the Movie Maker User Interface

Windows Live Movie Maker is divided into three basic areas from top to bottom: the new ribbon interface at the top, which replaces the old menu and toolbar; the Preview pane on the left, and the Contents pane on the right. As shown in Figure 13-14, these areas are clearly delineated.

This is the first version of Windows Live Movie Maker to utilize a ribbon interface, but you're probably familiar with it from newer versions of Microsoft Office and, of course, the new Paint and WordPad versions that are included in Windows 7. Basically, it combines the functions that used to appear in separate menus and toolbars, and presents them in a more graphical and discoverable way. The Movie Maker ribbon is quite simple, especially compared to the complex ribbons you sometimes see in Office. It features just three tabs: Home, Visual Effects, and Edit. We'll examine these as appropriate going forward.

Another change related to the ribbon is the new truncated File menu that appears if you click the Application menu button—the dark-blue box in the upper-left corner of the application window. This displays Windows Live Movie Maker's only true menu, as shown in Figure 13-15, though to be fair there's nothing in there that can't be accessed otherwise. (Even the Options dialog is empty at this point, though presumably Microsoft has big plans for future versions.)

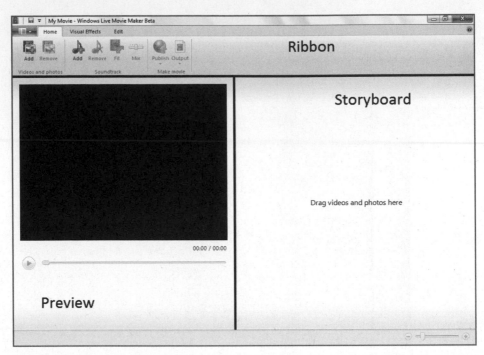

Figure 13-14: Windows Live Movie Maker takes digital media content in and spits out finished video after a bit of fine-tuning.

Figure 13-15: As with other ribbon-based applications, Windows Live Movie Maker does include a vestigial application menu.

Previous versions of Movie Maker offered a Tasks pane for stepping through the tasks needed to bring a custom video production to life. However, with the single-minded nature of Windows Live Movie Maker comes a much simpler way to work. You simply import content, position that content in the order in which you want it to appear, optionally apply a limited range of visual effects and titles, and then output your creation to disk and, usually, a Web-based video sharing site like MSN Soapbox or YouTube.

> **tip** Note that the Preview pane is resizable, so you can alternatively increase the size of the video output and decrease the size of the Contents pane, and vice versa, as needed. This is shown in Figure 13-16.

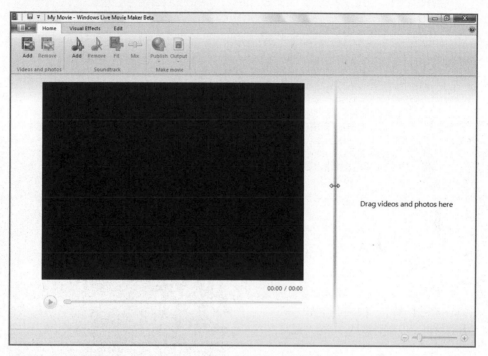

Figure 13-16: Give yourself space where you need it most

Working with Projects

Each time you work in Windows Live Movie Maker, you are creating a *project*. A Windows Live Movie Maker project is basically just a file that points to the various digital media files you're accessing, along with whatever transitions, effects, and titles you've made in the timeline or storyboard. This project does not *contain* any of the videos, photos, music files, or other content, so if you move these files around in the file system or delete them, Windows Live Movie Maker will not be able to use them in a saved project later. Instead, the project is simply a way to save your work so you can return to it later. You don't have to create your finished video in one sitting.

Importing Content

To start a new project in Windows Live Movie Maker, you first need a collection of shortcuts to digital media files that will be used in your final video. Windows Live Movie Maker can import a variety of video, audio, and picture files, and most of these files—with one glaring exception—can be assembled however you like in your project's storyboard or timeline. Table 13-1 highlights the formats you can use with Windows Live Movie Maker.

Table 13-1: Media Formats Supported by Windows Live Movie Maker

Movie formats	.ASF, .AVI, .DVR-MS, .M1V, .MP2, .MP2V, .MPE, .MPEG, .MPG, .MPV2, .WM, .WMV, .WTV
Audio formats	.AIF, .AIFC, .AIFF, .ASF, .AU, .MP2, .MP3, .MPA, .SND, .WAV, .WMA
Picture formats	.BMP, .DIB, .EMF, .GIF, .JFIF, .JPE, .JPEG, .JPG, .PNG, .TIF, .TIFF, .WMF

Secret

Windows Live Movie Maker cannot import some key digital media formats, including H.264/MPEG-4 video content and AAC audio content, which is odd because Windows 7 supports playing back these formats natively. Why is this? It turns out that while H.264 and AAC format support is a feature of Windows 7, Windows Live Movie Maker can also be downloaded, installed, and used on Windows Vista, an OS for which Microsoft has not paid the applicable format licensing fees. It is hoped that this issue will be resolved in the future.

Secret

There are other file types that Windows Live Movie Maker does not support, including copy-protected movies and TV show episodes you've purchased from an online service such as Apple iTunes, Amazon On Demand, and the like. These files are usually protected to prevent intellectual property theft and are thus specifically designed to prevent you from editing them in Windows Live Movie Maker or similar applications. When you import such a file, you will see a small red "x" on it in the Storyboard pane. Double-click it and you will see the error message shown in Figure 13-17. (This same error occurs when you try to use AAC or H.264 files.)

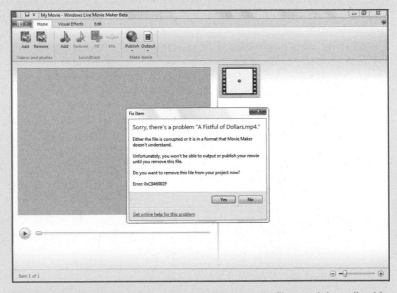

Figure 13-17: Protected and incompatible movie files can't be edited in Windows Movie Maker.

Another obvious source for video content is DVD movies. After all, wouldn't it be cool to include portions of your favorite movies in your own video creations? Maybe so, but Windows 7 doesn't include any way to acquire content from DVD movies, whether they're protected (as are Hollywood-created DVD movies) or not (as are most homemade DVD movies). Before you can use content from a DVD movie in Windows Movie Maker, you need to copy that content to your hard drive in a format that Windows Live Movie Maker understands. We explain how to do this later in the chapter.

Secret

The WTV (Windows TV) format is new to this version of Windows Movie Maker and replaces the DVR-MS format from previous Windows versions. This is the format Microsoft uses for its Media Center recorded TV shows. That's right: with a lot of work, you can use Movie Maker to edit TV shows. So if you'd like to save a movie or show you've recorded, or edit out the commercials or dead time at the beginning and end of the recording, you can now do so, though the process is somewhat mind-numbing, as explained in the next section.

There is one copy-protection caveat to this capability as well. Shows recorded on certain channels, such as HBO and Cinemax, cannot be edited (or, for that matter, copied to a PC other than the one on which it was recorded). That's because these shows are protected by so-called Broadcast Flag technology, which television stations can use to restrict copying. Currently, this technology is used mostly on pay cable channels in the U.S. market, but it will become more and more common going forward as the television industry looks to digital services like the iTunes Store, Amazon On Demand, and traditional cable On Demand to distribute their wares to paying customers only. (Free Web services like Hulu.com also fall into the "paid" category, of course, because they are ad-supported.)

You can import digital media content into Windows Live Movie Maker in a variety of ways. The easiest, however, is drag and drop: simply locate the photos, music, and/or video files you want to include in your project and drag them into the Storyboard pane as shown in Figure 13-18.

Or, you can use two different Add buttons in the application's ribbon. (For some reason, you can add videos and photos with one button, but must import music with a separate button.) Looking at the Home tab, you'll see two different Add buttons, one in the Videos and photos group, and one in the Soundtrack group. To add video or photo content to your project, click Add in Videos and photos. To add a music file, click the Add button found in Soundtrack. In both cases, you'll be presented with a standard Open File dialog (that's been appropriately renamed), allowing you to navigate around the file system and find the file(s) you want.

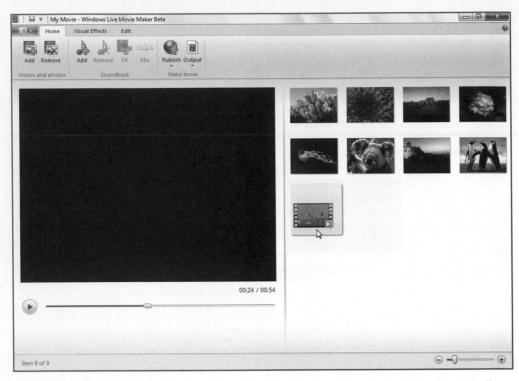

Figure 13-18: The simplest way to get content into Windows Live Movie Maker is good ol' drag and drop.

Secret

While you can add as many video and photo files as you'd like, you can only have one music file per project. This music, literally, will be used as the soundtrack of the entire video, and cannot be selectively applied to portions of the video. Therefore, if your project consists of both photos (in a slide show) and video content, the soundtrack will play during the entire presentation, and that's true even if the video content has its own audio (as video typically does). In this case, the audio from the soundtrack and the audio built into the video will play simultaneously. You can mute the video's audio on a per-clip basis (see below), but you cannot mute the soundtrack on a per-clip basis. Instead, the soundtrack is either there or it isn't.

Audio content that is added as the project's soundtrack appears as a textual note below the video preview display in the Preview pane, as shown in Figure 13-19.

Figure 13-19: It's subtle, but you can only add one song to a project, and that song is used as the video's soundtrack.

Photo and video content is added to the Storyboard pane. Each photo and each video is considered a *clip*, and you can drag and drop these clips to achieve the desired running order. That is, the resulting video you will create from this project will consist of the content shown in the Storyboard pane, and that content will play in order, from left to right, and from top to bottom. You can mix and match photos and videos as you see fit, using standard drag and drop.

In Figure 13-20, you can see a variety of media types located in the Movie Maker Imported Media pane, including JPEG photos, a WMV movie file, and a WTV recorded TV show.

Secret

Remember, when you import content into Windows Movie Maker, you're only telling Windows Live Movie Maker where to find that content. In other words, Movie Maker doesn't make a copy of the content; it only displays a shortcut to the original content. If you were to delete or move a file that Windows Live Movie Maker needs for a video project, it won't work properly anymore.

Figure 13-20: After you've assembled the pieces that will make up your video, it's time to start editing.

Editing Your Video

The simplest way to make a movie is just to grab some pictures and/or a video, and possibly an audio file for a soundtrack, and drag them into Windows Live Movie Maker. (A soundtrack obviously makes more sense for photo slide shows as sound in a video file would compete with the sound from an audio file.) Then, you can press Play in the Preview pane and watch your simple, unedited creation play through to completion. For the very simplest of videos, this is straightforward; but what if you want to take it to the next level, adding transitions, video effects, and titles? This section examines the editing capabilities, such as they are, of Windows Live Movie Maker.

Two things to remember before we get started: you can have only one soundtrack per project (and that's optional), and you can drag and drop the clips in the Storyboard pane to determine the running order of the video. Okay, it's time to get started.

Adding Transitions

Windows Live Movie Maker supports a small set of transitions that can be applied to both photos and video clips. These transitions are inspired by the transitions you see every day in TV shows and movies, and include such favorites as Crossfade, Slide, and Roll.

In keeping with the theme of Windows Live Movie Maker, we're oversimplifying. This application doesn't include "such favorites" as the three transitions mentioned above *among others*. It includes, literally, only those three transition types. To understand why this is an issue, note that the previous version of this application, Windows Movie Maker 6, supported *dozens* of transitions. So while Windows Live Movie Maker is simpler than its predecessor, it's also less powerful and useful as a result.

We're told, by the way, that Microsoft will be steadily improving Windows Live Movie Maker over time. So it's possible that by the time you read this, the application will have been updated with new transitions and other features. As always, stayed tuned to the book's Web site at www.winsupersite.com/book for the latest changes.

To access these transitions, click the Visual Effects tab in the ribbon. As shown in Figure 13-21, the available transitions can be found, logically enough, in the Transitions group.

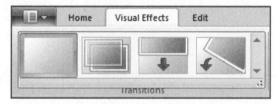

Figure 13-21: Windows Live Movie Maker includes just a limited set of video transitions.

You apply transitions on a clip-by-clip basis, and can apply only one transition to any photo or video clip. Also, transitions apply to the beginning of the selected clip and do not repeat. To add a transition, select the appropriate clip in the Storyboard and then click the transition you want to apply. To test the transition, click Play in the Preview pane. The video will begin playing at the selected clip with the transition in place, as shown in Figure 13-22. Repeat with other clips as needed.

You can also preview a transition by double-clicking the appropriate clip in the Storyboard.

Figure 13-22: Each transition can be tested in the Preview pane.

You can also choose the "No transition" option in order to remove a previously applied transition.

Adding Video Effects

In addition to transitions, you can also apply a limited selection of special effects to your videos. This time around, there are six effects, all of which are color tone changes like Black and white or Sepia tone. By contrast, previous versions of Movie Maker included a wide range of effects, such as blurring, brightness changes, various color fades, hue changes, and zooms. Video effects work much like transitions. They're available from the Effects group of the Visual Effects tab in the ribbon, and you can apply one effect per clip. Note, however, that transitions and video effects are configured separately, so you can have one transition and one effect per clip, which certainly spices things up just a little bit. In Figure 13-23, you can see a photo that has been given a Roll transition and a Sepia tone color cast, animating into the preview display. Look out, George Lucas.

Figure 13-23: As with transitions, you're given only a handful of effects to play with.

Using Titles

If the paltry selection of transitions and video effects hasn't gotten you down yet, wait until you see Windows Live Movie Maker's titling capabilities. Once again, whereas before we had a wide range of options, now we have a much more limited set of functionality that is entirely in keeping with the application's transition to Web-based videos. So instead of separate titles and credits, we can now add one single-line text box per clip.

For example, say you're editing a movie of your vacation to Hawaii. You might add a title at the beginning of the video, and then perhaps at various points throughout to describe where each scene occurred. And you might want to wrap up the video with a short farewell message. As with transitions and effects, you want to balance your use of titles so that they don't overpower the movie, but provide useful context. The simple titling capabilities in Windows Live Movie Maker help ensure that you're not making an animated version of a ransom note.

To add a title to a clip, navigate to the Edit pane in the Windows Live Movie Maker ribbon. There, you'll see two groups, Text and Font, that apply to titles. The first, Text, includes a single command, Text box, for adding a title to the currently selected clip. The second, Font, includes the standard set of font tools so you can control how the title looks. These groups are shown in Figure 13-24.

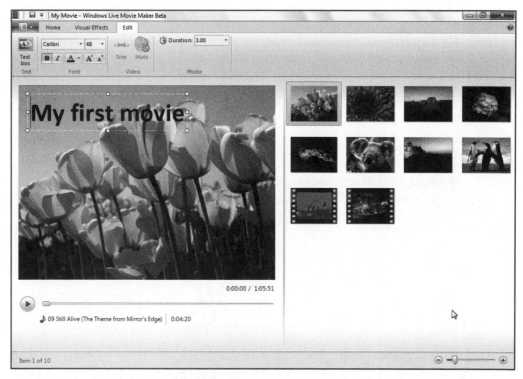

Figure 13-24: The titling capabilities in Windows Live Movie Maker can be found on the Edit tab.

The standard rules apply here: you can add only one title—excuse us, text box—per clip. You can't use Shift+Enter to create multiple-line titles, but if you do type more than one line can accommodate, the text will overflow and the box will grow to include it. Also, titles are attached to the body of the clip, so if you apply a transition that animates the introduction of the clip (like Roll), then the title will animate in with the clip. This speaks to another difference between earlier version of Movie Maker and this version: you can't separately animate a title as you could before. They're just static text boxes.

Trimming Video and Audio

In addition to transitions, effects, and titles, you can also perform a variety of other simple edits on your projects. In this section, we'll examine these trimming functions.

First, it's possible to trim video clips, though as usual only in very simplistic ways. This is an advantage for a number of reasons, but consider a typical example: you have a video clip you took with your digital camera. As is often the case with such clips, the beginning and end of the clip are pretty rough, so what you'd like to do is trim off the beginning and end of the clip so that it begins and ends in more meaningful places.

In previous Movie Maker versions, you could do these types of trims, but also edit out any portions of the video clips you wanted. Now, you can only trim the beginning and end of a clip; you're on your own with the middle. Here's how you make that happen.

Load the video clip you'd like to edit into the Preview pane by selecting it in the Storyboard view. Then, navigate to the Edit tab in the ribbon and click the Trim button in the Video group. As shown in Figure 13-25, the timeline under the preview display (and to the right of the Play button) picks up some scrubber tools. And a new Trim tab appears while you work.

Figure 13-25: Windows Live Movie Maker supplies simplistic video editing tools.

As you do so, the part in the middle—with the thick line, as shown in Figure 13-26—is the part that will appear in the final project. The rest is trimmed off.

Figure 13-26: As you move the scrubber bars, only the portion between them is used in the final video.

tip	Windows Live Movie Maker does not provide a way to really fine-tune the trim. You can't, for example, move the scrubber one frame at a time. What you can do while trimming, however, is maximize the size of the Preview pane by using the resizer control and dragging it all the way to the right. When you do this, the scrubber bar expands as well, making it easier to make finer edits.

Secret	Note that Movie Maker doesn't actually edit the underlying video file. Instead, it is simply creating pointers so that when your final video is created, only the parts of the video you want are included. No changes are made to the underlying digital media files that make up the project.

Click Save and close in the Trim tab to save your changes, or click Cancel to exit without saving.

In addition to this bit of video editing, you can also edit the audio mix that is applied to your project. This option—exposed by the Mix button in the Soundtrack group on the Home tab—only becomes active if you've added a sound file to use as a soundtrack. When you click this button, the small control shown in Figure 13-27 appears.

Figure 13-27: Control how the different audio sources interact.

By default, the audio mix is perfectly balanced between your soundtrack and whatever audio is present in the underlying video clips. However, if you'd prefer the soundtrack to take aural precedence (that is, be louder), you can slide this control to the right. Likewise, if you'd prefer for the underlying audio in the video clips to be louder than the soundtrack, you can slide this control to left.

Secret

If you slide the control all of the way in either direction, the opposite audio source will be completely muted. To utilize only your soundtrack and mute the video clips' underlying audio, slide the control all the way to the right.

Secret

This Mix control works for all clips in your project. That is, you cannot create a different audio mix for each clip.

Getting a Bit More Sophisticated

While simple home movies and photo slide shows are fun, you may occasionally want to make something a bit more sophisticated. For example, maybe you have a recorded TV show you'd like to edit. You will want to remove the dead space at the beginning and end of the show, at the very least. This was documented in the previous section and is an easy fix. But what if you also want to take the time to edit out any commercials, or edit out other bits of video that exist in the middle of a clip? You actually can do this with Windows Live Movie Maker, though the process is far more complicated in this version of the application and is not documented. It's time to see how it works.

tip	If you don't have a recorded TV show, perhaps because your PC isn't connected to a TV signal through a TV tuner card, fear not. You can use one of the sample recorded TV shows that comes with Media Center, or a sample video file that ships with Windows Vista. Or, grab some of your own home video footage. It's up to you.

note	Recorded TV shows are stored in C:\Users\Public\Recorded TV by default. There's no Recorded TV folder under a normal user account's Home folder. That's because recorded TV shows are shared by all of the users on the PC.

You may recall that each video clip you import into Windows Live Movie Maker is just a shortcut to an underlying file. As you make changes to that clip in your Movie Maker project—by adding things like transitions, effects, titles, and trims—the underlying file is not changed in any way. This is all fairly straightforward. But what you may not realize is that you can import the same video file into your project multiple times. This enables you to trim it down multiple times, into discrete and different video clips, each of which can contain a unique part of the video.

Consider Figure 13-28, a conceptual diagram representing a 30-minute TV show. In this fictional TV show, there is some introductory material (commercials, content from the previous show), some actual TV show content, a single commercial in the middle (hey, it's conceptual not realistic), more TV show content, and then some junk at the end (commercials, and perhaps the start of the next show).

Figure 13-28: Sometimes it helps to think of a TV show or other digital video file in terms of the content you want to keep and the content you'd like to edit out.

What you want from this video is the two bits of actual content, but none of the commercials and other non-TV show content. We know that Windows Live Movie Maker offers a way to trim the beginning and end of a single video clip, so that part of it is easy enough. What it doesn't offer is a way to trim out part of the middle of a clip. This seems insurmountable until you realize that you can simply import the same video file twice. (In this example, anyway. If you were really going to use this tool to edit out all of the commercials from a typical TV show, you'd have to import the same file several times.)

Here's how it works:

1. Start a new Movie Maker project by choosing New from the Application menu.
2. Using drag and drop or the Add button, import the recorded TV show or other video file you'd like to edit. This imported file will be used to create the first clip, sequentially.

3. Using the Trim functionality described in the previous section, trim off the beginning portions of the video that you'd like to leave out. Then, trim the end portion of the video clip so that the edited video ends right before the first commercial.

4. Click Save and close to save the changes.

5. Now, import the same file a second time and ensure that this second version appears to the right of the first, as shown in Figure 13-29.

Figure 13-29: There's no reason you can't import two or more copies of the same video clip.

6. With the second clip selected, go into Edit and then Trim again. This time, the open trim should start at the conclusion of the first set of commercials; and the end trim should be made at the conclusion of the TV show content. (If you're editing a real TV show, you will need to repeat this process for as many commercial breaks as there really are.)

When you're done, you can play back your completed project, ensuring that no commercials escaped your attention and that the edits were as clean as possible. Remember that you can always go back and re-edit any trims, and you can add transitions to smooth out jarring clip changes.

When you're done—*voilà!*—you've got a nicely edited TV show, sans commercials. Or perhaps a home video, without the boring parts.

Sharing Your Videos

The whole point of editing a home movie, TV show, or other video is to watch it and, preferably, share it with others. Unfortunately (but as we've come to expect), Windows Live Movie Maker offers only limited ways to share your completed videos. You can save them to your hard drive in reasonably high-quality, or you can publish them to the Web. That's it. In previous versions of Windows Movie Maker, you could publish to the PC, to DVD or CD, to e-mail, or back to a digital video camera. On the other hand, those products were clueless about popular video Web sites like YouTube. So this is progress, depending on your point of view.

The publishing capabilities of Windows Live Movie Maker are segregated into two separate options in the ribbon, Publish and Output. Publish enables you to upload your video to a video-sharing site, while Output is for creating local videos—that is, saving them to the PC's hard drive. (Presumably, you're free to then copy those files to DVD, CD, e-mail, or whatever, on your own.) We'll examine both options.

Publishing to the Web

Ultimately, Windows Live Movie Maker has been designed with one goal in mind: getting your videos online. And this is where that happens. The thing is, out of the proverbial box, the application only supports Microsoft's MSN Soapbox site. Don't feel bad if you've never heard of this site, as few people have. That said, it's not too shabby, and since this functionality is included with the product, we'll cover it here.

To publish to MSN Soapbox, click the Publish button in the ribbon's Home tab. (It's in the Make movie group.) You'll be prompted to log on to your Windows Live ID, and will then be presented with the Publish Your Video on MSN Soapbox window shown in Figure 13-30.

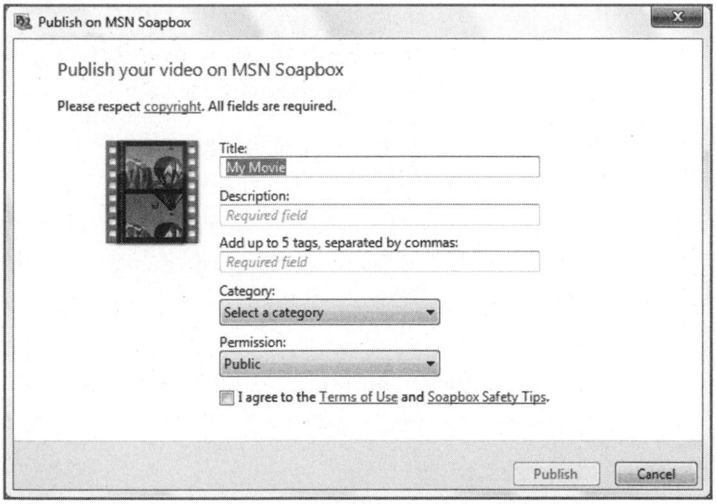

Figure 13-30: From this simple interface, you can publish your video creation to the MSN Soapbox video-sharing Web site.

Here, you should type in a name for your video, a description, and up to five descriptive tags (to help people searching for videos on the site). You'll also need to pick a category and a permission level (Public or Hidden). When you click OK, Windows Live Movie Maker will create your video, transcode it to the format required by MSN Soapbox, and then publish the finished product to the site. When that's done—the amount of time it takes varies according to how much content you've added to your project—you'll be prompted again, this time to view it online or open the Soapbox-compatible file it created (saved to My Videos, by the way). The resulting Web version of the video should look something like Figure 13-31.

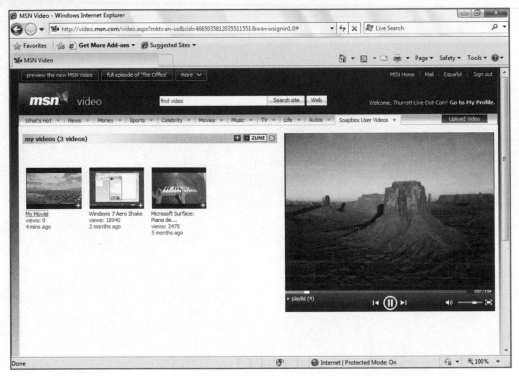

Figure 13-31: MSN Soapbox isn't particularly well known, but it's a decent place to share videos.

> **note**   Video upload—to MSN Soapbox, YouTube, or any other site—isn't instantaneous. Oftentimes, if you publish a video to the Web and then accept Windows Live Movie Maker's offer to view the video online, it won't actually be available immediately. Just give it a few moments: the site will do whatever preparatory work is required and get your video posted as quickly as possible.

Secret

Okay, so MSN Soapbox support is all well and good, but for the other 99 percent of the population, integrating with Google's super-popular YouTube service would be a lot more interesting. Sure, you could simply use the Output option, described below, to save a copy of your video to the hard drive and then manually upload it to YouTube using that site's Web-based controls. But wouldn't it be nice if you could simply upload to YouTube directly from Windows Live Movie Maker? Yeah, that would be nice, and we've got good news: It's completely doable.

To make this work, you need to install a Windows Live Movie Maker plug-in that adds YouTube compatibility to the application. So, instead of clicking the Publish button, click the down arrow underneath this button. You'll see two options in the pop-down menu that appears, Soapbox on MSN video and Add a plug-in. Click the second option to visit the Microsoft Web site and locate the LiveUpload to YouTube plug-in for Windows Live Movie Maker. (Alternately, simply navigate to the plug-in's Web site: `www.codeplex.com/liveuploadyoutube`). **Download the plug-in, close Movie Maker (saving your project if needed), and install it.**

Once the plug-in is installed, open Windows Live Movie Maker and reload your project. Then, click the down arrow under Publish. As shown in Figure 13-32, there is a new option in the pop-down menu, LiveUpload to YouTube.

Figure 13-32: With a little add-on love, you can now publish videos to a sharing site people actually know about and use.

Choose this option. You'll be prompted to sign into YouTube with your user name and password. Then you'll be presented with a view similar to that provided by MSN Soapbox, where you must provide a title, a description, keywords, a category, and a permission level (Public or Private, in this case). This is shown in Figure 13-33.

continues

continued

Figure 13-33: YouTube's metadata requirements for uploaded videos are quite similar to those for MSN Soapbox.

Windows Live Movie Maker will go through the same three steps as it does for MSN Soapbox—create, transcode, and publish—and create an identical movie to the version created for Microsoft's service. When you're done, you're given the same options for viewing the video locally or on YouTube's Web site. Figure 13-34 shows what a published video looks like on YouTube.

Figure 13-34: And there it is, in all its YouTube glory: your shared video.

Outputting to the PC

Publish is handy when you want to go directly to the Web, but the resulting files are pretty low quality and they're certainly not good enough for archival purposes. A better option is to output the video to the PC, and this is true even if you eventually intend to publish it to the Web: the resulting video file can be of much higher quality than what's available via Publish.

Windows Live Movie Maker can output video in just two formats:

♦ **Windows Media DVD quality:** This is a Windows Media Video (.WMV) file encoded at 2.8 Mbps with a resolution of 640 × 480 at 30 frames per second (fps). Technically speaking, this is actually sub-DVD quality (as DVDs are encoded at 720 × 480 in the U.S.) but it's close enough for horseshoes. You should generally choose this option when outputting to disk.

♦ **Windows Media portable device:** This is a Windows Media Video (.WMV) file encoded at 1.5 Mbps with a resolution of 320 × 240 at 30 frames per second (fps). This file will play well on a limited range of Windows Media–compatible devices and Windows Mobile-based smart phones.

To output your video to the PC, you can click the down arrow below the Output button in the Home tab to choose between the two aforementioned formats, as shown in Figure 13-35. Or, you can just click the Output button. When you do so, the higher-quality Windows Media DVD quality format is chosen for you.

Figure 13-35: Only two formats to choose from? What is this, Windows Me?

Not to beat this to death, but Windows Live Movie Maker's output options are woefully limited compared to what was possible in the Windows Vista version of this application. Back then, you could output in AVI as well as WMV, at standard definition resolutions up to and including 720 × 480, and in Hi-Def (HD) at 1280 × 720 (720p) and 1440 × 1080 (1080p). Our understanding is that Microsoft will update this product regularly, however, so it should become more powerful—and more interesting—in the future.

Creating DVD Movies with Windows DVD Maker

Windows 7, like Windows Vista before it, includes an application for *burning*, or creating, DVD movies. In fact, it's almost completely identical: Microsoft has barely updated Windows DVD Maker since it first debuted in Windows Vista. As you might expect from such an effort, Windows DVD Maker isn't a terribly sophisticated application, so the quality and variety of DVD movies you can make are fairly limited. On the plus side, DVD Maker does deliver the most commonly wanted DVD-making features, and, as a simple application, it's especially well suited for beginners. If you've never made a DVD movie, take heart. This is a great place to begin.

DVD Maker is available to users of Windows 7 Home Premium, Professional, Enterprise, and Ultimate. If you have a lower-end Windows 7 version—Windows 7 Starter or Home Basic—you will need to upgrade to one of these versions in order to use Windows DVD Maker. Or, you could purchase one of the many third-party DVD maker applications on the market. Note that any third-party package will be more sophisticated, but also more complex, than Windows DVD Maker.

There are actually several ways to start DVD Maker:

- From within Windows Live Photo Gallery, select a group of photos or videos. Select Make and then Burn a DVD from the toolbar.
- If you saved a DVD Maker project previously, you can double-click that project's icon in the shell and pick up where you left off.
- Simply find Windows DVD Maker in the Windows 7 Start menu and launch the application manually, and then add content to an empty project as you go.

Because the latter approach will gain you the skills necessary to explore the other options, we'll examine Windows DVD Maker as a standalone application here.

What you can't do anymore is access Windows DVD Maker from within Windows Live Movie Maker. The application is now designed solely to publish videos to the Web. If you are using Windows Live Movie Maker to edit videos, you will need to save them to your hard drive and then manually import them into Windows DVD Maker. We will, of course, examine this process in this chapter.

To start Windows DVD Maker, open the Start menu and locate the Windows DVD Maker shortcut in the All Programs group. Alternately, from the Start menu, type **dvd** in the Search box to find Windows DVD Maker more quickly.

Windows DVD Maker, shown in Figure 13-36, is a simple wizard-based application that steps you through the process of adding content and menus to your eventual DVD movie.

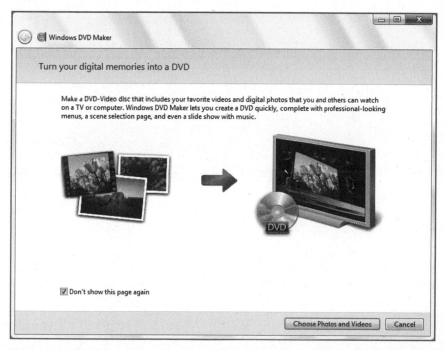

Figure 13-36: No frightening user interfaces here. DVD Maker is the definition of simplicity.

Secret

Like Windows Live Movie Maker, Windows DVD Maker works with something called a project, a file you can save and reload later that describes the DVD you're making. Unlike with Windows Live Movie Maker, there is no obvious way to save a project while you're compiling your DVD. However, if you look closely, you'll see a single menu item, File, in most of the Windows DVD Maker screens. When you click this menu, you'll see options for saving, loading, and making new projects. You can also save your project by clicking the more prominent Cancel button. This will close Windows DVD Maker, but the application will prompt you to save the current project first. (Hey, remember that you use a Start button to shut down the system. In Microsoft's world, this is all perfectly logical.)

note   DVD Maker projects are saved in your Videos folder by default.

Secret

Only one instance of DVD Maker can be running at a time.

Secret

While the Windows DVD Maker application looks and works like a typical Windows wizard, the application window can actually be maximized and resized as needed. So you can use the Maximize window button to maximize the application, as you would most other applications. You can also drag at the edge of any of the application's sides to resize the window manually in each of the four directions. Put simply: you don't have to put up with the curiously tiny default size of Windows DVD Maker: you can make it whatever size you'd like.

Adding Photos and Videos to Your DVD Project

As noted previously, Windows DVD Maker is a wizard-based application in which you move through a limited set of steps and end up, it is hoped, with a nice-looking DVD movie that will play on virtually any DVD player. In the first step of the wizard, shown in Figure 13-37, you add the content you'd like on the DVD.

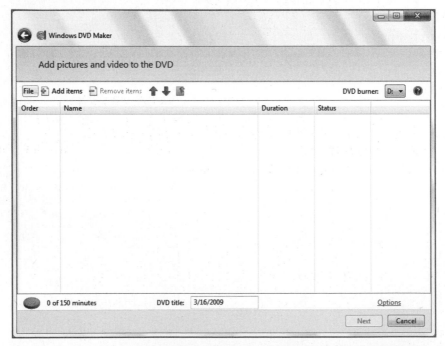

Figure 13-37: Every Windows DVD Maker project starts with this blank slate.

This content consists of pictures and video. You can drag items to the DVD Maker application using your standard drag and drop skills, or you can click the Add Items button, next to the File menu, to display a standard File Open dialog. Use this dialog to navigate to the content you'd like on your DVD movie.

note Windows DVD Maker, while certainly adequate for the job at hand, is a mess from a user interface perspective. There's no true menu structure, per se, just a single File menu jammed into the upper-left corner of the application window. You can add items to the current project in two different ways, one obvious and one hidden. The application's options are configured via an HTML-like Options link that sits in the lower-right corner of the window—that is, except for the DVD burner to use, which for some reason is always available in the upper-right corner of the first phase of the wizard. (Meanwhile, DVD burning speed is configured in the Options dialog.)

And while it features a prominent Internet Explorer-like "Back" button in the upper-left corner, Next is a more typical Windows-type button that sits, you guessed it, in the lower-right corner. This application deserves a special place in the User Interface Hall of Shame. It looks and works nothing like any other Windows 7 application. When you add videos to a Windows DVD Maker project, they appear in the wizard as you might expect. Pictures are a little different. If you drag one or more image files into Windows DVD Maker, the application will create a folder called Slide show, as shown in Figure 13-38. From this point on, any photos you add to the project are added to this one folder; and they are displayed as an animated slide show in the finished DVD.

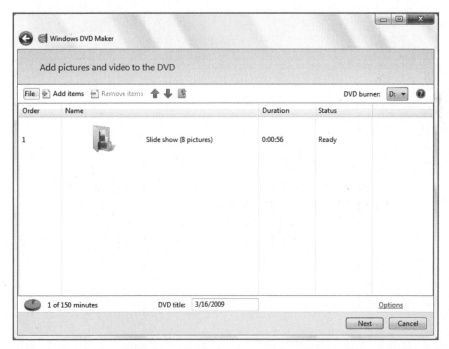

Figure 13-38: The Slide show folder will contain any pictures you add to your DVD project.

Secret

You can't have two or more photo slide shows on a single DVD. Only one is allowed.

Secret

You also can't add videos to the Slide show folder. If you try to add a video, it will be added to the root of the project instead.

Secret

You can navigate inside of the Slide show folder in Windows DVD Maker if you'd like. Just double-click it. To navigate back out to the root of the DVD, click the small Back to videos toolbar icon, shown in Figure 13-39.

Figure 13-39: Yet another nearly hidden user interface feature lets you escape from the Slide show folder.

To remove a video or picture, or the Slide show folder, select it in Windows DVD Maker and click the Remove Items button. Alternatively, click Delete or right-click the item and choose Remove.

DVD Storage Issues and Formats

One issue you should be concerned about is how much content will fit on the DVD. Windows DVD Maker works with standard recordable DVDs, so the storage capacities are based on the media you use. With a standard *single-layer* recordable DVD, you can have up to 60 minutes of high data rate (that is, DVD movie quality) video. With a standard *dual-layer* recordable DVD, you can store up to 120 minutes of high data rate video. With lower quality video, you can often fit more.

Secret

Another issue, of course, is that there are several recordable DVD types out there. To create a DVD movie that will work in virtually any DVD player in the world, use write-once DVD-R or DVD+R media. Both work well, though DVD+R seems to have won the format wars and is more common, while DVD-R offers better compatibility with older DVD players if that's an issue.

Avoid rewriteable DVD formats, such as DVD+RW or DVD-RW, because they won't work with most standalone DVD players (though they're fine for testing and PC-based use). If you see the acronym DL used, that describes dual-layer, a technology that doubles the capacity of a recordable DVD's storage space. Note that you might also be confined by the capabilities of your DVD writer. If your hardware is only compatible with, say, DVD+R, then obviously you will need to use DVD+R recordable disks; but if you have a multiformat DVD writer, it's your choice; you can use four different recordable DVD formats: DVD+R, DVD+RW, DVD-R, and DVD-RW. Confused? Welcome to the club.

Arranging Content

When you've added two or more items to your Windows DVD Maker project, you can start thinking about the order in which they will appear on the final DVD movie. While DVD Maker doesn't offer a huge selection of DVD menu layout options, it does let you reorder items. You'll notice that the list of videos and photo slide shows in the wizard has an explicit order, as noted by the Order column heading, which assigns each item a number, starting from 1.

You can easily reorder items in the following ways:

 ♦ **Drag and drop:** Using the skills you've no doubt honed over the years in Windows, simply grab an item in the list and drag it to the position in the order you'd like it to appear.

 ♦ **Move up and Move down buttons:** In the Windows DVD Maker toolbar, there are two arrow-shaped buttons, Move up and Move down, that enable you to reorder the selected item as indicated. This is shown in Figure 13-40.

 ♦ **Right-click method:** You can also right-click any item and choose Move Up or Move Down from the resulting pop-up menu.

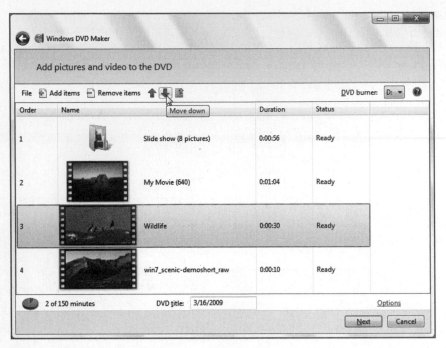

Figure 13-40: While customization is limited, you can at least change the order of items.

Secret

You can also move multiple items up or down in the order. To do so, first multi-select items by clicking them, in turn, with the Ctrl key held down. Then, right-click and choose either Move Items Up or Move Items Down.

Previewing Content

If you'd like to play a video or preview a photo that's in your DVD Maker project, simply double-click that item. Videos play back in Windows Media Player by default, while photos are previewed in either Windows Photo Viewer or Windows Live Photo Gallery, depending on which you've configured as the default picture viewer. (See Chapter 12 for a comparison of these two applications.)

Secret

Note that you cannot "play" the Slide show folder as an animated slide show. You can only open the folder and view the files inside, one at a time.

Naming Your DVD Movie

Under the content list of this initial window, you'll see a small and easily missed text box called DVD title. (This was called Disc title in Windows Vista.) By default, it's set to the current date in M/D/YEAR format, where M is a one- or two-number representation of the month (1), D is a one- or two-number representation of the day (30), and YEAR is a four-number representation of the year (2007).

You will want to change this title to something descriptive, because it will be used on the DVD's menu as the title of the DVD movie. A home movie DVD, for example, might be called *Our 2009 Summer Vacation* or similar.

Secret

You can pick whatever title you want, but only 32 characters are allowed.

Understanding DVD Movie Options

In keeping with the Salvador Dali–like user interface minimalism of Windows DVD Maker, you access the application's DVD Options dialog via a small Options link in the lower-right corner of its window (and not via a Tools ⇨ Options menu as you might expect). When you click this HTML-like link, the DVD Options dialog opens, as shown in Figure 13-41. Note that these options are related to the DVD you're creating and not to the Windows DVD Maker application per se.

The following options are available:

- ◆ **DVD playback settings:** You can configure your DVD movie to play its content in one of three ways:
  - • **Start with DVD menu:** Indicates that your DVD will behave like a typical Hollywood DVD and display a DVD menu on first start.
  - • **Play video and end with DVD menu:** Causes the DVD movie to play through the DVD content first and then display the menu only after the content is complete.
  - • **Play video in a continuous loop:** Simply plays the DVD content repeatedly, in a loop. Users will still be able to access the DVD menu, however, by pressing the Menu button on their DVD remote control or player.
- ◆ **DVD aspect ratio:** Enables you to configure whether the DVD's video playback and menu display in a 4:3 aspect ratio (which is not really square per se but certainly close) or in widescreen 16:9 aspect ratio. The choice you make here should be based on the aspect ratio of the screen on which the DVD will likely be accessed, and on the aspect ratio of the content you're using. Today, most home video content is still created in a 4:3 aspect ratio despite the widespread use of widescreen displays. That said, most television sets sold today are now widescreen. The choice is yours, and you can certainly make a version of the DVD in both formats just to see the differences, though that will be time consuming.

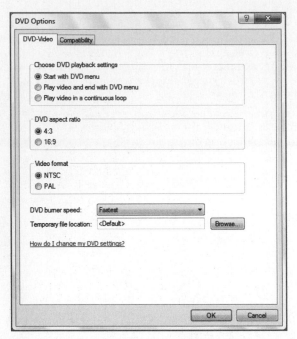

Figure 13-41: DVD Options lets you configure a small
number of settings related to the DVD you're creating,
not to the application itself.

◆ **Video format:** Enables you to choose whether the DVD will be created in the
NTSC or PAL video format. You should choose the format used in your locale.
For example, the NTSC format is correct for the United States, but PAL is used in
countries like France and Ireland.

◆ **Other DVD settings:** In the bottom of the DVD Options dialog, you can set options
for the DVD burner speed and the location where the application will store its
temporary files during the DVD creation process. Typically, you will want to leave
the DVD burner speed at the fastest setting, but if you run into problems burning
DVDs, you can change it to a slower speed (such as medium or slow). This will
increase the amount of time it takes to create your DVD movie but will result in a
more reliable burn experience. Similarly, most users will want to leave the temporary file location setting untouched, but if one of your hard drives is faster or has
much more space available, you can use this setting to change the location where
temporary files are stored and, possibly, speed up the DVD creation process.

Secret   You will need a hard drive or partition with at least 5GB of free space in order
to create a single-sided DVD movie. Dual-layer (DL) DVDs require at least 10GB
of hard drive space.

Secret   Do not attempt to create a DVD movie on a hard disk that is slower than 5,400 RPM. Faster drives—7,800 RPM and 10,000 RPM, for example—running on modern hard drive interfaces (e.g., SATA, or Serial-ATA, instead of IDE/ATA) will get better results.

Working with DVD Menus

After you've selected the content that will be included on the DVD movie and have set the DVD options, you can move on to the next step in the Windows DVD Maker wizard and select a menu style. As shown in Figure 13-42, this second and final step in the wizard can be skipped altogether if you like the default menu style: simply click the Burn button and off you go.

Figure 13-42: In the curiously named Ready to Burn DVD stage of the DVD Maker wizard, you can pick menu styles.

Secret

When you click the Next button to move to the second phase of the DVD Maker wizard, you will notice there is no corresponding Back button. That's because Windows DVD Maker adheres to a silly application style that debuted in Windows Vista: a round graphical Back button is illogically located in the upper-left corner of the application window. It resembles the Back button in Internet Explorer (that is, it's a white arrow in a blue circle). Why it's not next to a similar Next button is quite unclear.

It makes sense to spend a bit of time here and experiment with the built-in menu styles, as you might not be too excited by the default choice. Besides, you can do a number of other things here, including previewing the DVD, changing the menu text, customizing the menu, and adding music to and changing options for the photo slide show. We will look at those options in the next section.

Along the right side of the application window is a list of menu styles, each presented with a visual thumbnail to give you a rough idea of how it will appear in your DVD. Windows DVD Maker comes with roughly 20 DVD menu styles, and some are actually pretty decent. None, alas, are new to Windows 7: these themes all appeared in the Windows Vista version of this application as well.

To select and preview a different menu style, simply select it in the list. After churning for a few moments, the DVD menu preview display will change to reflect your selection, as shown in Figure 13-43.

Figure 13-43: Windows DVD Maker includes a decent selection of menu options.

Each menu style is quite different. Some offer an animated video preview running behind the menu text, while others offer multiple video previews, running simultaneously, or even animated menu text that flies in from the sides of the screen. Be sure to experiment here.

Changing Other DVD Options

To fully configure your DVD movie, and appreciate what effect the various DVD menu options will have on the finished product, you'll need to preview the movie and access the other options that are available in this step of the wizard.

Previewing the Movie

Even if you don't think you'll need to make any changes, you should always preview your DVD before committing it to disc. You do so by clicking the Preview toolbar button, which brings up a Preview Your DVD view with a virtual DVD player, complete with DVD controls such as Menu, Play, Pause, and so on, as shown in Figure 13-44.

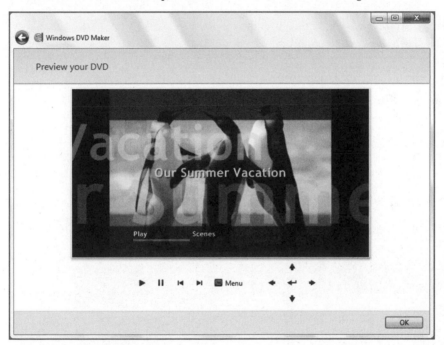

Figure 13-44: While previewing your DVD movie, you can see how it will behave and look in a real DVD player.

Here, you might discover that the font used for the menu text is ugly, that you made a bad decision about how the menu comes up, or that you might want to change to a different menu style all together. To make any changes, click OK (or the Back button) and get back to work.

Secret

And yes, you can also go back from the Ready to burn Disc phase to the first step of the DVD Maker wizard. The application will remember the settings you configured regardless of which direction you go in the user interface. That, at least, makes sense.

note Each "scene" in the DVD menu correlates to a video or photo slide show you imported into the Windows DVD Movie Maker project.

Changing the Menu Text

To change a variety of options related to the DVD menu text, click the Menu text button. Here, as shown in Figure 13-45, you can change the font (including color and bold and italic attributes, but not, curiously, the size), the disc title, and the text used for the Play, Scenes, and Notes links. You can also write a block of descriptive Notes text that will appear on a subpage of the main DVD menu.

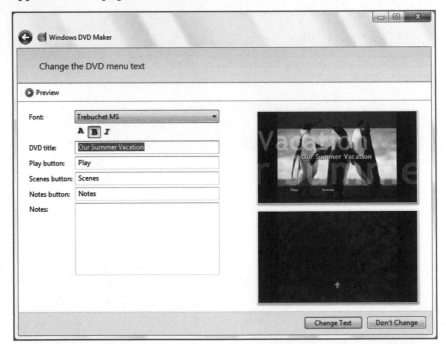

Figure 13-45: Here, you can change a variety of menu text options and add an optional block of Notes text.

Customizing the Menu

To customize the appearance of the DVD menu, click the Customize menu toolbar button. Curiously, you can change some font properties here again, duplicating the functionality of the menu text options described in the previous section. However, the rest of the disc menu options shown here are unique, as shown in Figure 13-46. You can change the videos that display in the foreground and background (the layout and appearance of which vary according to menu style), the audio that plays over the menu (you can't make it silent, however; it will default to the audio in the selected video clip if no audio file is chosen), and the style of the menu links, or buttons.

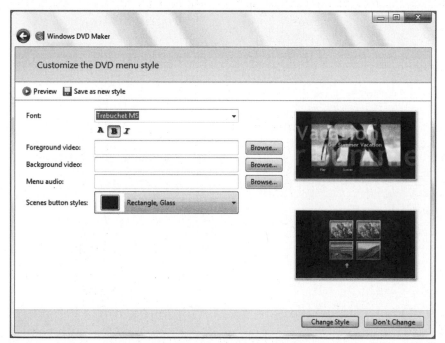

Figure 13-46: In addition to picking general menu styles, you can also configure various aspects of the DVD menu layout and presentation.

Secret   The video and audio used in the DVD menu don't even have to be related to the media files you chose for inclusion in the DVD movie itself. For example, you could select two movies and a photo slide show for the DVD itself, and separate third and fourth movies for the title if you want.

If you make enough changes, or want to reuse the customizations you made, you can actually save them as a brand-new style. When you do this, a new entry called Custom Styles is added to the drop-down menu above the list of menu styles in the right of the application window. Then you can choose between Menu Styles and Custom Styles.

Configuring the Photo Slide Show

If you've included a photo slide show in your DVD movie, you can customize it by clicking the Slide show button in the DVD Maker toolbar while in the Ready to burn DVD phase of the wizard. In the Change your slide show settings window, shown in Figure 13-47, you can add one or more songs (music files) to the slide show, alter the length of time each photo displays, choose a transition type (cross fade is the default), and decide whether to use pan and zoom effects, which provide a welcome bit of animation to the slide show.

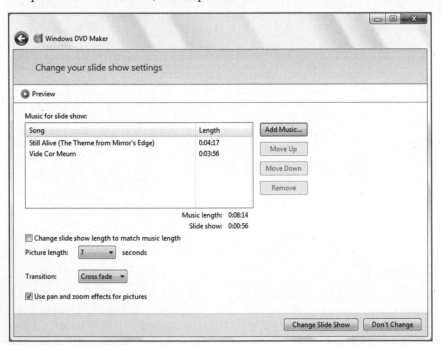

Figure 13-47: Here, you can configure a nice range of options for your photo slide show.

> **tip** Adding music and animation effects to a photo slide show dramatically improves its effectiveness, so spend some time playing around with these options.

Writing the Movie to Disc

When you're satisfied with the DVD movie, it's time to burn it to disc. Click the Burn button to proceed.

If there is no writeable DVD in the drive, Windows DVD Maker will prompt you to insert one. You should use the lowest capacity disc possible (4.7GB for one hour or less of video), as single-layer discs tend to be less expensive than the dual-layer versions. That said, a dual-layer (DL) disc will work just fine if that's all you have.

If your PC does not have a DVD burner, Windows DVD Maker will tell you that a DVD burner is required and recommend that you connect one before continuing. Optionally, you could save the project instead and install a DVD burner later.

Secret What you can't do easily is copy the DVD Maker project to a different PC with a DVD burner and then create the DVD there. That's because the project looks for the content needed to create the DVD in file paths relative to where they were on the original PC. In order to make this work, you would have to copy the content for the project to the same locations on the second PC as they were on the first. That's probably a nonstarter for most people.

After you've inserted a blank recordable DVD in the drive, DVD Maker will begin the creation process. This can be an extremely lengthy process, depending on the amount of content you've included. While DVD Maker is creating the DVD, the application window closes and a small Burning dialog appears in the lower-right corner of your screen, charting its progress.

When the DVD is completed, Windows DVD Maker ejects the DVD so you can go try it in a DVD player. You're also prompted to create another copy of the disc if you'd like. Click Close to cancel that option and return to the main DVD Maker application.

The Final Frontier: Duplicating and Copying DVDs

While it's likely that you have at least some video content of your own, the reality is that most home video tends to be short or at least short-lived. Many have had this same basic experience: excited at the beginning of a family or relationship, you purchase an expensive video camera, eager to document your lives, as though anyone, let alone you, will ever be particularly interested in watching most of the video you eventually shoot. Video cameras tend to gather dust in a closet somewhere, so you move on to digital cameras and even cell phones and smart phones, many of which now offer low-quality to decent-quality video capabilities in addition to their more common still picture functionality. But even that tends to be a low-impact hobby: most of the video I've taken with my digital camera, for example, has been created by mistake. I meant to take a still shot, but the camera dial had turned to the video setting while in my pocket. As I result, I've got dozens of five-second-long videos in which you can hear me in the background muttering about what went wrong. Its compelling footage, let me tell you.

While I have no doubt that some of you out there will become dedicated videographers, the truth is that most people enjoy an entirely different kind of video far more often than your own home movies, whether they were taken accidentally or on purpose. You rent and purchase DVD movies, for example, and, increasingly, even high-definition (HD) Blu-ray movies. You watch movies and TV shows on TV, and enjoy On Demand rental content. You watch short video clips on YouTube and other video-driven Web sites. And for a small minority of users, you even purchase and rent TV shows and movies electronically, using services such as Apple iTunes, Amazon On Demand, CinemaNow, Blockbuster Movielink, and others.

Wouldn't it be nice to get some of that content on your PC or portable media devices so you could enjoy it on the road, while commuting, at the gym, or in other situations in which it's not convenient or possible to be sitting on your couch watching TV, or sitting in front of your Internet-connected PC? Sure it would. In many cases, you can make it happen.

Some of the scenarios just listed are more problematic than others, but we'll focus on DVD movies here because these shiny, silver discs are, by far, the most common way to enjoy video entertainment. That said, it's worth at least a short side trip first to explain what's going on with these entertainment types:

◆ **Blu-ray:** As of this writing, the ability to create a DVD version or PC-playable file from a Blu-ray movie is somewhat of a pipe dream, though hackers are working on it. A bigger issue, from a PC perspective, involves Blu-ray playback. If you have a Blu-ray optical disc drive on your PC, you also need a variety of hardware that is *HDCP (High-bandwidth Digital Content Protection)* compatible. That is, Windows 7, like Windows Vista before it, has been engineered in such a way that your video card, sound card, monitor, and other hardware must all be HDCP compatible before you can play back that Blu-ray movie you legally purchased. That's because Blu-ray movies are essentially perfect digital copies of the original film, and Hollywood is understandably anxious to prevent consumers from illegally copying these perfect digital copies and giving them to friends. To be fair, any new PC, especially those that come with Blu-ray optical drives, should be fully HDCP compatible; but that doesn't help those who purchased lower-end PCs or built their own PCs. In the end, the consumer has a lot of work to do to ensure they can view Blu-ray content on a PC.

Secret

You could simply purchase a wonderful software product called AnyDVD HD. Available from SlySoft (www.slysoft.com/), AnyDVD HD enables you to watch Blu-ray movies on a non-HDCP-compliant PC. It also performs a number of other useful Blu-ray related jobs, including removing BD+ copy protection and region codes from Blu-ray discs, meaning you can watch international Blu-ray movies, a huge plus for movie buffs. AnyDVD HD also includes all of the other excellent features from the standard AnyDVD utility, which we examine more closely in just a bit. AnyDVD is a bit expensive, yes, but its cost pales in comparison to the potential cost of making your PC HDCP compliant.

That said, Windows 7 does include the capability to write Blu-ray data discs. And Microsoft has created the low-level underpinnings needed for third parties to add Blu-ray movie playback via their own applications.

◆ **Recordable TV content:** Windows 7 includes all the software tools you need to record TV shows from a variety of sources, including cable TV and HD sources such as HD cable and over-the-air (OTA) HD. We examine this functionality, which is part of the Windows Media Center software, in Chapter 15.

◆ **YouTube videos:** While online video entertainment sites like YouTube are enormously popular and make it easy to enjoy videos online, what they don't offer is a way to download your favorite videos so you can enjoy them offline.

Secret

To download unprotected copies of YouTube and other online videos to your hard drive, check out the free RealNetworks RealPlayer media player (www .realplayer.com/).

◆ **Content from online services:** Apple iTunes, Amazon On Demand, and other similar services rent movies and sell movies and TV shows in various formats. Fortunately, these movies arrive as PC-friendly video files, so you should have no problem accessing them offline on a portable computer or compatible device. Different services are compatible with different portable devices and digital media receivers, however. Apple's files are compatible only with its own hardware, including iPods, iPhones, and Apple TVs. Meanwhile, most other services have standardized on Microsoft's Windows Media Video (WMV) format and Windows Media DRM copy protection scheme, so these files should be compatible with any Windows-compatible devices that aren't made by Apple. Note, however, that all of this content is copy-protected, and as of this writing there's no way to remove that copy protection and use this content in your own projects. Some services do, however, allow you to burn purchased movies to DVD.

Okay, now it's time to take a look at the two biggest missing features in Windows 7 when it comes to digital video: duplicating DVD movies and ripping, or copying, DVD movies to video files that will play fine on PCs, Xbox 360s, Zunes, and many other devices, including Apple's iPod, iPhone, and Apple TV.

Duplicating DVD Movies

From a "fair use" perspective, it should be possible to make a backup copy of your legally purchased DVD movies, assuming you're doing so for archival purposes and will not be distributing those copies, or the originals, to others outside of your immediate family. This is a bit spurious from a legal standpoint, we think, but there is a compelling reason to back up a few DVD movies, and it has nothing to do with archiving.

If you travel a lot for work, as we do, you may sometimes like to bring along DVD movies for those otherwise wasted hours on planes and in hotel rooms. However, we don't want to subject expensive DVD purchases to the rigors of travel. Paul had a particularly maddening experience on a cross-country flight in which a few of his DVDs were actually cracked thanks to an overzealous fellow passenger jamming his too-large bag into a too-small storage compartment directly on top of his bag.

You'd think that Windows 7 would come up with some sort of basic DVD backup utility, even if it were designed to only function on that tiny percentage of unprotected (that is, homemade) DVDs that are out there. But it's not there: Windows 7 does include ways to burn data DVDs and Blu-ray discs and create DVD movies, but it's surprisingly light when it comes to DVD movie backup. For this reason, you're going to have to look elsewhere.

We've come across several excellent DVD backup utilities. Chances are good that your PC came with one of them. The Nero suite (www.nero.com/) and Roxio Creator (www.roxio.com/) are popular PC bundles, and of course, you can purchase these huge and sometimes confusing digital media suites on your own if you're looking for that kind of thing.

That said, we prefer simpler, more elegant solutions. For example, SlySoft's CloneDVD (www.slysoft.com/en/clonedvd.html) is an excellent and inexpensive way to back up entire DVDs or just the parts of a DVD you want. That's literally all it does, and it does it well. CloneDVD is shown in Figure 13-48.

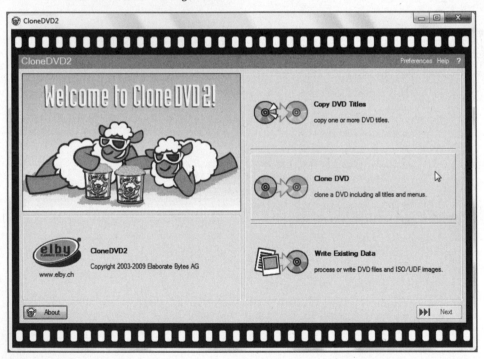

Figure 13-48: Looking to duplicate a commercial DVD movie? CloneDVD is the solution.

Secret

What all of these solutions lack, if it's not obvious, is a way to back up commercial, Hollywood-type DVDs. That's because these DVDs come with a form of copy protection that prevents such copying. In order to bypass this protection, you'll need something like SlySoft AnyDVD (or AnyDVD HD), www.slysoft .com/en/anydvd.html, which we both use and strongly recommend. AnyDVD removes the encryption from DVD movies, allowing you to back up Hollywood movies and other copy-protected DVDs. It removes the DVD region coding from DVD movies, so you movie buffs can enjoy DVD movies that are purchased outside of your locale. But AnyDVD isn't just about bypassing copy protection. In fact, other features make this a tool of interest to anyone who enjoys DVD movies regularly on a PC. It prevents the automatic launching of not-so-friendly "PC-friendly" software on video DVDs. It enables you to skip annoying trailers and other baloney that movie companies force on us, letting you jump directly to either the main movie or the DVD's title menu. And it does this automatically: pop in a disc and AnyDVD will do its thing under the covers. This is one of the best utilities we've ever purchased.

Ripping DVDs to the PC

While duplicating a DVD may be of limited interest, ripping (or copying) a DVD movie to your hard drive, much in the same way that you rip songs from an audio CD to your hard drive in MP3 format, is probably more interesting to a wider audience. This, too, would enable you to leave the master DVD copies of your movies safe at home while you travel or commute. It also means you don't have to travel with a bunch of discs, discs that incidentally aren't exactly the most battery-efficient thing to watch when traveling on a plane or in other locations where a power plug isn't available.

There are two major problems with ripping DVDs:

◆ First, you need a tool like the aforementioned SlySoft AnyDVD because Hollywood DVD movies are copy-protected and designed so that they cannot be copied to your PC.

Secret

You may not need to rip all of your DVDs. There is a growing generation of dual-use DVD discs out there that include both the standard DVD movie (which will, of course, work on all DVD players, including those in PCs) and so-called Digital Copy versions, which come in both iTunes- and Windows Media-compatible versions. The Windows Media Digital Copy version of these movies is a protected WMV file you can copy to your PC's hard drive and then to a compatible portable device. The first Digital Copy-compatible DVD movie, "Family Guy Blue Harvest," debuted in 2008. As of this writing, there aren't many Digital Copy DVDs, but if this format takes off, it could answer a lot of the complaints about fair use and DVD movies. There are even Digital Copy-compatible Blu-ray movies appearing now. Hey, you never know.

You can find out more about Digital Copy-compatible DVD and Blu-ray discs on Amazon.com: www.amazon.com/Digital-Copy-DVD/ b?ie=UTF8&node=721726011.

♦ Second, you need to figure out which tool you want to use to rip DVD movies, as Windows 7 doesn't come with such a thing. And on a related note, you have to settle on a video format for those ripped files. (In the music field, this is simple: MP3 is the universal standard for audio files and is the most compatible with software and devices. Video, alas, is a bit trickier.)

That latter issue used to be more of a concern. Windows Vista and earlier Windows versions were, of course, compatible with Microsoft video formats like Windows Media Video (WMV) and AVI—that is, if you wanted to play back a ripped movie in Windows Media Player, Zune, or Windows Media Center, you pretty much needed to rip it in WMV format. However, if you wanted to use the more popular and superior H.264 format—used by Apple's software and devices, and compatible with the Zune and Xbox 360—you couldn't use Windows Media Player or Media Center: earlier versions of those applications were not compatible with H.264.

In Windows 7, this has all changed. Now, Windows Media Player and Windows Media Center are completely compatible with H.264. This solves a compatibility issue, but only if you've completely migrated to Windows 7. If you have a mix of Windows 7–based PCs and PCs based on earlier Windows versions, you will want to carefully consider which format to use. Of course, you could always use Zune, QuickTime, iTunes, or other applications in Windows Vista or older Windows versions if needed.

Ripping DVDs in Windows Media Video Format

If you'd prefer to stick with the Windows Media Video format, you have an excellent (but not free) option for DVD ripping: SlySoft's CloneDVD mobile (www.slysoft.com/en/clonedvd-mobile.html). This software can rip DVD movies into a variety of formats, including WMV. It also offers a surprising array of quality options, so be sure to check the technical specifications of the portable device you'll be watching these movies on before ripping. (The exact resolution of the finished movie will vary based on the aspect ratio of the source movie, but you can choose between such resolutions as 320 × XXX, 480 × XXX, 640 × XXX, 720 × XXX, 852 × XXX, and 720 × 480 (NTSC TV), where XXX can vary.)

Here's how you can rip a commercial DVD movie to your hard drive in WMV format:

1. Insert a DVD movie into your optical drive.

2. Launch CloneDVD mobile. As shown in Figure 13-49, this wizard-based application supports a number of video formats (DivX, WMV, and so on) and comes with presets for numerous devices, such as the Xbox 360, PlayStation 3, Apple iPod and iPhone, Microsoft Zune, and many, many others.

3. Choose Generic WMV/WMA from the list of possible options in the first part of the wizard and then click the Next button.

4. In the next phase of the wizard, you have to choose the VIDEO_TS folder on the DVD. To do so, click the small Browse button on the right side and then navigate to the DVD movie in the dialog that appears, expanding the tree view if necessary to select the VIDEO_TS folder, as shown in Figure 13-50. Then, click OK.

5. Once you've selected the VIDEO_TS folder, CloneDVD mobile presents a list of the video tracks available on the DVD and will preview the selected track in the Preview tab. Generally speaking, the main DVD movie you want will be the longest video on the disk. Select it, ensure that it is correct using the Preview tab, and then click Next.

Figure 13-49: CloneDVD mobile enables you to rip DVDs into digital video files on your PC.

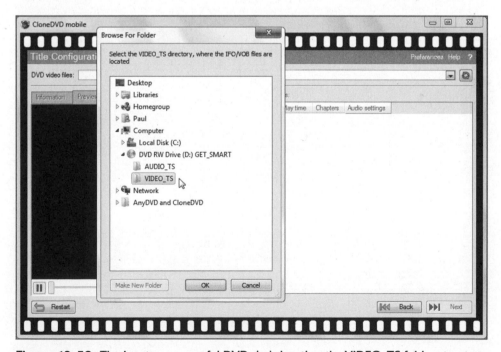

Figure 13-50: The key to a successful DVD rip is locating the VIDEO_TS folder structure on the DVD movie disc.

6. In the Audio and Subtitle Settings phase of the wizard, you can choose which audio stream to use (English by default in the U.S.) and whether you want subtitles hard-coded onto the movie (and if so, which language to use). Click Next when you've made the appropriate choices.

7. Finally, in the Output Method phase, shown in Figure 13-51, choose options such as resolution, video quality, and, perhaps, zoom settings. These options are very important, so you'll need to choose wisely.

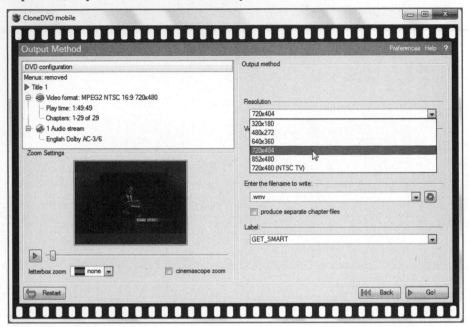

Figure 13-51: Here is where you'll determine the quality (and thus the size) of the resulting video.

In the Resolution drop-down, you'll see a variety of options (which, again, vary according to the actual aspect ratio of the original movie). Roughly speaking, the higher the resolution, the better the video will look, up to a certain point, and the larger the resulting file will be. Also, remember that it doesn't make sense to create digital videos that are larger than the source material: DVDs are always 720 × 480 or less, so you should ignore the 852 × XXX option for the most part. Finally, you'll want to ensure that the video you create will work on your portable device. If it's too big, Windows Media Player has to transcode it before copying it to the device, a process that can be time consuming. In my experience, videos that are 640 × 480 and below offer a good compromise between quality, size, and compatibility.

8. Select a resolution (typically 640 × 480 or less) and then click the "Default" button next to the Quality slider. (You can slide this to the right for better quality video, though these files will also be larger.) Then, provide a label for the video (Something like *Name of the Movie* instead of VIDEO_DVD or whatever).

Typically, you will want to leave the Zoom settings alone, but you can experiment with the Letterbox Zoom and Cinemascope Zoom settings to see how they change the resulting video.

9. Click Go when you're ready to encode, or create, the video. A Save As–type dialog will appear, enabling you to name the video file and pick a location for it on the hard drive. Videos are typically stored in the Videos folder, as you know, but you're free to create it virtually anywhere.

The amount of time this encoding process takes varies according to the performance characteristics of your PC. Generally speaking, it should take 50 to 100 percent of the length of time it would take to actually watch the movie if performed on a modern PC with decent 3D video hardware.

Once you've created a movie in this fashion, you can copy it to another PC, a portable device, or a digital media receiver (including the Xbox 360), or use it in Windows Live Movie Maker or Windows DVD Maker projects.

Ripping DVDs in H.264 Format

While Windows Media Video is a fine format, the future of digital video is clearly H.264. In fact, with Windows 7 natively supporting H.264, any previous rationale for holding off is quickly vanishing. H.264 is a modern, high-quality version of the MPEG-4 standard, and H.264 videos are compatible with iPods, iPhones, the Apple TV, the Xbox 360, Microsoft's Zunes, and a range of other devices. On the PC, H.264 also works fine with Apple QuickTime and iTunes, and with free media player software like GOM Player (www.gomlab.com/) and VLC Media Player (www.videolan.org/vlc/). And of course, H.264 video is now compatible with the Windows 7 versions of Windows Media Player and Windows Media Center. (Curiously, it's still not compatible with Windows Live Movie Maker and Windows DVD Maker, however.)

To rip to H.264 format in Windows 7, you have a variety of options. You can use the aforementioned CloneDVD or the very similar Nero Recode, which is part of the Nero suite (www.nero.com/). Both of these tools work similarly, but for H.264 we prefer and recommend the open-source HandBrake tool (http://handbrake.fr/), which has wonderful presets that work fine for the PC, Xbox 360, iPods and other Apple devices, the Zune, and just about anything else that's H.264 compatible.

Here's how you can rip a commercial DVD movie to your hard drive in H.264 format:

1. Insert a DVD movie into your optical drive.
2. Launch HandBrake. (Note that this application should be run with administrative privileges.) This application is shown in Figure 13-52.
3. Choose the VIDEO_TS folder on the DVD. To do so, click the Source button in the HandBrake toolbar and then the final entry in the pop-down menu. (It's the one below DVD/VIDEO_TS.) HandBrake presents a Reading Source dialog while it gets information about the DVD movie.
4. Once this process is complete, HandBrake tries to guess which title is the correct one to rip, but you can manually choose the correct title on the DVD via the Title drop-down menu, as shown in Figure 13-53. Generally speaking, the main DVD movie you want will be the longest video on the disk. Select it if it isn't already auto-selected for you.

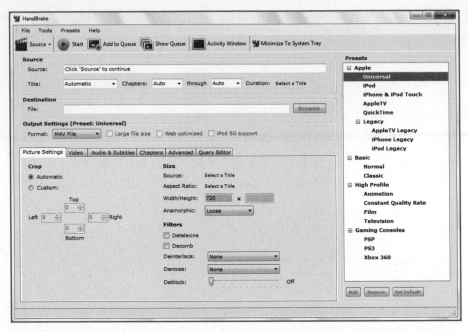

Figure 13-52: HandBrake is an open-source application that excels in ripping DVD movies to H.264 video files.

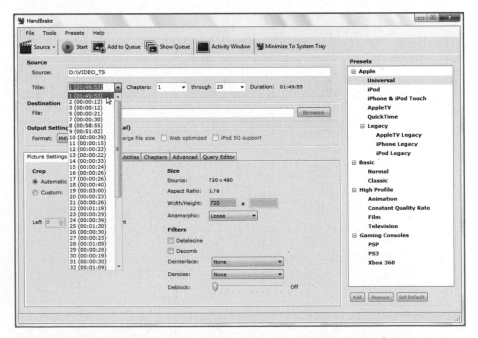

Figure 13-53: Sometimes you'll have a number of movies to choose from.

5. Click the Browse button next to the File text box in the Destination section. In the Save As dialog that appears, navigate to the location on the disk where you'd like to save the resulting file. Then, give it a plain English name and click Save.

Secret

Typically, H.264 video files utilize the .mp4 file extension. However, if you choose any of the Apple-oriented presets described below, HandBrake will use a more iPod-friendly .m4v file extension instead. This is fine: the underlying file isn't any different and .m4v files work just fine with Windows 7's Windows Media Player and Media Center, and with the Zune and Xbox 360 as well. (Of course, these files—and normal .mp4 files—work fine with all Apple hardware and software too.)

6. Select a preset from the list of Presets on the right of the application window. While you could choose a device-specific preset such as iPod, iPhone, or Xbox 360, it's best to simply choose the Universal preset, which encodes videos at a very high resolution (typically 720 × XXX or higher). These files are excellent for archival purposes, but they also offer excellent compatibility between iPods, iPhones, the Apple TV, Zunes, the Xbox, and, with Windows 7, the PC. You can choose optional video settings by clicking the Video tab. For example, you can enable two-pass encoding to obtain a somewhat higher-quality video file, though such files also take longer to rip (twice as long, in fact).

7. In the Picture Settings tab, make sure "Automatic" is selected under the Crop section. This ensures that the movie is cropped to the correct aspect ratio.

8. Finally, make any other changes you might need. For example, you can visit the Audio & Subtitles tab to change the audio track or add subtitles. Note that subtitles are hard-coded into the movie file, so only add them if you really need them.

9. Click the Start button to begin encoding.

H.264 video encoding, like that of WMV, is very much dependent on the performance characteristics of your PC. A decent PC with a dual-core CPU should be able to rip a DVD in roughly half the time it takes to watch the movie. (That is, a two-hour movie can be ripped in about 60 minutes.) Newer quad-core CPU-based PCs can rip DVDs in as little as 30 minutes, however. The more processor cores you have at your disposal, the faster it will go.

Once you've created a movie in this fashion, you can copy it to another PC, an Apple or Zune portable device, or a digital media receiver (including the Xbox 360 and Apple TV). You can also use it in Windows Live Movie Maker or Windows DVD Maker projects.

Summary

The digital video capabilities in Windows 7 are vastly superior to those offered in Windows XP, and thanks to H.264 compatibility, they are superior even to those of Windows Vista. You can manage your digital movie collection in a variety of ways, including the Windows shell, Windows Live Photo Gallery, Windows Media Player, and Windows Media Center. You can use Windows Live Movie Maker to edit and distribute your home movies, recorded TV shows, and other video-related content, including HD content, and can output the results in HD-compatible glory if you're so inclined. Using Windows DVD Maker, you can even publish movies and photo slide shows to standard DVD movies that will work in virtually any DVD player in the world. And if you don't mind spending a bit of money and taking the effort, you can even back up commercial DVDs and rip them to disc as unprotected digital video files.

Microsoft Zune: A Digital Media Alternative

Chapter
14

♦ ♦

In This Chapter

Discovering the Zune platform: Zune PC software, services, and devices

Understanding how the Zune PC software works and how it differs from Windows Media Player

Configuring Zune for your own needs

Enjoying music, podcast, video, and photo content in Zune

Sharing Zune content with the Xbox 360

Browsing Zune Marketplace for music, music videos, and podcasts

Subscribing to the Zune Pass service

Sharing your music and tastes with others via Zune Social

Picking a Zune device

Installing and configuring your device

Syncing content between your PC and the device

Using wireless sync

Keeping Zune up-to-date

♦ ♦

Microsoft surprised everyone in late 2006 by introducing its Zune digital media platform, an integrated set of software, services, and hardware that competes both with market leader Apple and with its own older digital media initiative, the Windows Media Player–based PlaysForSure. The first Zune didn't really take the world by storm, but a second-generation platform released a year later is much more impressive and provides a look at the future of Microsoft's digital media platform. This chapter examines the Zune platform, including the Zune PC software, the Zune Marketplace online store, the Zune Social Web-based community, and the growing family of Zune portable media devices.

> **tip**
>
> Okay, Microsoft's Zune platform isn't designed specifically for Windows 7—it runs on Windows XP and Vista as well—and it's not included in the box with Windows 7 like many of the features and products discussed elsewhere in this book. So why include an entire chapter about a software, hardware, and services player that essentially competes with what is included in Windows 7? As we'll explain in a bit, whereas Windows Media Player is a nod to the past, Zune is Microsoft's digital media mulligan, an attempt at a do-over. If the company could bundle Zune in Windows, it would; but because of heightened antitrust regulations around the world, Microsoft is instead keeping Zune separate, much in the same way that it has pulled various Windows Live services out of Windows. We're covering Zune here because it's important to Microsoft's strategy going forward: the software is being ported to the Xbox 360 and will be included in future versions of Windows Mobile. Zune, like Windows 7, *is* the future.

Why Zune?

Over the past decade, Microsoft has found that translating its success in operating systems into other markets isn't always a sure thing. Yes, its Microsoft Office productivity suite is a blockbuster success, and its enterprise-oriented Windows Server products aren't too shabby either, but these products are all obviously related. And Microsoft's Windows, Office, and Windows Server products are, in fact, still responsible for almost all of the company's revenues.

That's the problem. True financial success has eluded most of Microsoft's other products to date, including its digital media products, its Xbox video game business, and its Live and MSN online services. In each case, Microsoft's dominance in operating systems and office productivity software hasn't helped it expand successfully into other markets.

What's surprising about Microsoft's failure in the digital media market is that it actually does bundle its excellent Windows Media Player software with Windows, and it's done so for several years now. Despite this, Apple has taken a dominant position in the market with its iPod and iPhone portable devices, its iTunes PC software and iTunes Store online service, and related products such as the Apple TV set-top box. Apple's success is well-deserved—its products are routinely highly rated and are, in fact, almost universally excellent—but it has caused Microsoft's competing solution, based around Windows Media Player, to first falter and then fail in the market.

That solution, which was once called PlaysForSure, sought to duplicate Microsoft's experiences in the PC market. Microsoft created the software based on its Windows Media platform, consisting of Windows Media Player, Windows Media and Audio formats, Windows Media DRM (Digital Rights Management) for content protection, and much more. However, the company relied on a variety of hardware partners to design, ship, and market a set of competing portable devices and hardware, much like different PC makers make PCs. It also relied on a second set of partners to create online services for music, movies, and other content, all built on Windows Media.

It sounded like a great idea, but it wasn't really a great idea because Microsoft couldn't control the entire process. Even though it might introduce new platform features, it had to wait for the hardware makers and services to implement support, and when Apple came along with a centralized solution, controlled and designed by a single company, consumers took note. Today, PlaysForSure is essentially dead in the sense that you won't see PlaysForSure logos on any products at your local electronics retailer. Sure, numerous portable devices (made by companies such as Creative, Samsung, Sandisk, and others) still work just fine with Windows Media Player and online services such as Amazon Unbox, CinemaNow, and Napster, but the PlaysForSure ship has sailed, people, and the biggest indication that that's true is the fact that Microsoft, the originator of PlaysForSure and its underlying Windows Media platform, has moved on to something else, something called Zune.

Secret To be fair to Windows Media, the platform has a lot of life left in it; and as you discovered in Chapter 11, Windows Media Player, in particular, is an excellent bit of software. According to Microsoft, it intends to co-develop both Windows Media and Zune going forward, though the PlaysForSure logo program has been discontinued and rolled into the more nebulous Designed for Windows logo program (which, to my knowledge, few device makers and services have embraced with any particular gusto). Microsoft is throwing considerable resources at Zune as well and will improve this platform dramatically in the years ahead. If you're a gambler, this is the obvious pick, at least on the Microsoft side of the fence.

Zune 1.0

To the cynical, Microsoft's Zune platform is a fairly transparent copy of the Apple playbook. As with Apple's iTunes platform, Zune is centrally controlled by a single team, in this case from Microsoft. Like Apple's platform, Zune includes PC software for organizing and playing music and other content, accessing an online store, and managing compatible portable devices. Put another way, Zune is a closed platform, as is Apple's. The Zune devices work only with the Zune PC software, and the Zune PC software can't be used to manage any non-Zune devices. The advantages of this kind of solution are tighter integration between hardware and software and, in the case of Zune, a growing set of online services.

It's nice when it works out that way, but whereas Apple has gotten almost everything right with its iPod, iTunes, and related solutions, Microsoft has stumbled a bit as it tries to find its way. Today's Zune is a dramatic improvement over the first iteration, and no doubt future versions will be even better, and the Zune is an evolving platform, so it's improving steadily over time. As such, it has certain advantages over the Apple platform, but also some areas where it falls short.

Microsoft shipped the first Zune version in late 2006. There was a single Zune hardware device, the since-renamed Zune 30, which came in a classic iPod form factor and included a 30GB hard disk for storage. The original Zune hardware was decent if unexceptional, but the first Zune software—shown in Figure 14-1—was almost comically bad. It was essentially a rebranded version of Windows Media Player 11 with a weird gray skin. Zune's online store, Zune Marketplace, was accessed via this software interface.

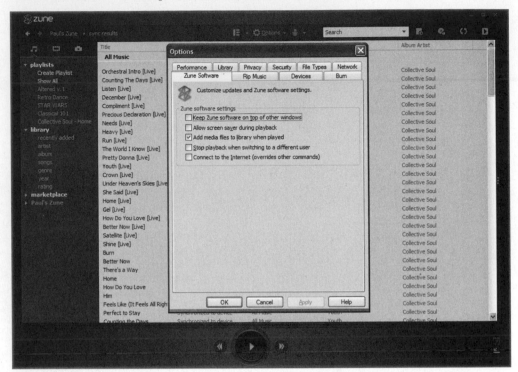

Figure 14-1: The first Zune software was just an ugly skin on top of Windows Media Player.

Was it successful? I guess that depends on how you define successful. Microsoft sold about 1.5 million Zune 1.0 devices in its first year on the market, just a tiny fraction of the number of iPods that Apple sold during the same time period; but Microsoft can and did accurately claim that this level of sales was enough to catapult the Zune to the number two position in the market for hard-drive-equipped MP3 players (behind, yes, the iPod—way behind). Just by entering this market, even with a decidedly lackluster product, Microsoft was able to immediately outsell all of the PlaysForSure and non-Apple competition. That's actually not too shabby.

Zune 2

The less that's said about Microsoft's first version of Zune the better. For the second itera-tion of the Zune platform, Microsoft set its sights considerably higher and the results were much more favorable. With the Zune 2 platform, released in late 2007, there were more devices, new device capabilities (all of which, amazingly, were ported back to the original Zune device), new PC software, a completely redesigned Zune Marketplace, a completely new Zune Social online community service, and even new hardware accessories. The Zune 2 PC software is shown in Figure 14-2.

Figure 14-2: Zune 2 included brand-new and innovative PC software.

Zune 2 was a revelation, and Microsoft really turned the Zune around by starting over from scratch. Whereas the first-generation Zune was all about the hardware, the second-generation platform expanded dramatically in all areas. The software was built from scratch and was dramatically better than the first, Windows Media Player–based, version. The hardware was expanded to include thin and light flash-based players, the Zune 4 and 8, and a new 80GB hard drive model, the Zune 80. It was all pretty well conceived.

However, as a new product essentially, Zune 2 had some issues. The initial release lacked the ability to create smart playlists, though Microsoft fixed that with a Zune 2.5 release in mid-2008. Microsoft's online store, Zune Marketplace, had over 1 million DRM-free tracks—that is, music not bound by copy protection schemes—but most of the songs sold there were still stuck in DRM hell. And the Zune Social, new to Zune 2 and discussed later in this chapter, was still sort of bare bones and couldn't be accessed from the devices or PC software; in this release it was purely Web-based.

Yes, as a new, built-from-scratch platform, Zune 2 had some holes, but Microsoft filled them over time. Zune 2.5 also added a number of new features, started a move toward a DRM-free Zune Marketplace, and offered better Zune Social integration.

Zune 3

In late 2008, Microsoft offered up its third-generation Zune platform, which was really just an evolution of Zune 2. The devices didn't change from a hardware perspective at all, though the capacities were upped to 8, 16, and 120GB, respectively. The PC software and device firmware was further refined with some nifty new features; and Microsoft expanded on Zune's social networking prowess with updates to the Zune.net Web portal and Zune Social. Zune 3 was all about finishing the work started with Zune 2, and it developed into an amazing platform for digital music and video. The Zune 3 PC software is shown in Figure 14-3.

Figure 14-3: With Zune 3, Microsoft finally closed the gap with Apple for good and offered some incredible new functionality.

At the time of this writing, Zune 3 is still the current version of the Zune software, but you can expect Microsoft to keep releasing new hardware, devices, and services and to generally improve the Zune platform. This chapter closely examines all of the functionality available in the Zune 3 platform—but first, allow us to present the best Zune secret of all.

Secret   You don't need to buy a Zune device to use the Zune software, Zune Marketplace, or Zune Social. The Zune software is freely available to anyone running Windows XP, Windows Vista, or Windows 7, as are the online services. That means you can very easily check out Microsoft's alternative digital media platform without first plunking down hundreds of dollars on a portable device.

tip   We'll continue covering future versions of Zune on the Web. For the very latest in Zune coverage, please stay tuned to Paul Thurrott's SuperSite for Windows, which has a dedicated Zune section: www.winsupersite.com/zune.

By itself, the Zune PC software is an excellent alternative to Windows Media Player, so we'll look at that first.

The Zune PC Software

Anyone with Windows 7, Vista, or XP can download and install the Zune PC software. It's free and is in many ways a better media player than Windows Media Player 12, which ships as part of Windows 7. Is Zune good enough to make you forego other media players? It's getting there, yes. Zune is still missing a few features that many readers will need—such as DVD playback—but its cool design and tight integration with online services and Zune devices is sure to win many people over. The following sections take a closer look.

Finding and Installing Zune

Like Apple, Microsoft no longer bundles its digital media software with its devices. Instead, it directs users to the Zune Web site (www.zune.net) where you can download the latest version of the Zune PC software. This is a smart move because Microsoft, again like Apple, updates its software fairly regularly. (Not providing an install disk also enables Microsoft to create smaller and more eco-friendly Zune packaging. You know, just like Apple.)

In addition, as with iTunes, you don't need a device to take advantage of most of this player's features. It works just fine as a standalone media player. You may find it taking the place of Windows Media Player for many of your day-to-day digital media playing needs.

From the Zune Web site, shown in Figure 14-4, you can do a number of things, including download the Zune software, which is what we're going to focus on here.

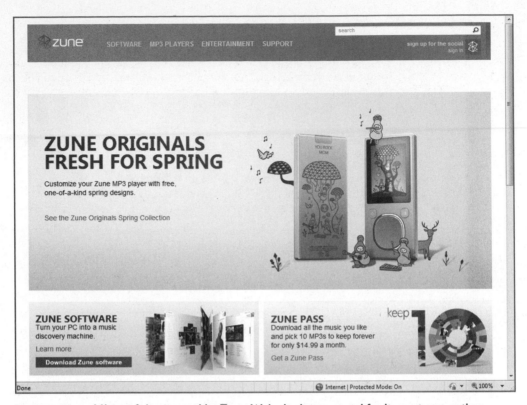

Figure 14-4: Microsoft has turned its Zune Web site into a portal for its next-generation digital media platform.

When you navigate to the Zune software download page, you have two options: Sign Up and Download or just Download. The former option steps you through a wizard that creates what's called a *Zune tag* for you. This Zune tag, which is tied to a Windows Live ID, can be valuable, especially if you want to take advantage of Zune's so-called social features. It is also a necessity if you ever plan to purchase music or other content from Zune's online store, Zune Marketplace. However, you don't need to configure a Zune tag just to use the Zune PC software, so you can skip that for now if you prefer. You'll look at Zune tags and related issues later in the chapter.

Make sure you download the correct version of the Zune software. Microsoft makes separate 32-bit (x86) and 64-bit (x64) versions available. If you're unsure, you can find out which version of Windows you have in the System Properties window (from the Start menu, right-click Computer, and then choose Properties). Next to System type, it will say "32-bit operating system" or "64-bit operating system."

Installing Zune is fairly straightforward. The setup application presents a simple wizard that installs the software and gets you up and running quickly without reboots. When setup is complete, you can run the Zune PC software for the first time. You'll be confronted with the screen shown in Figure 14-5. You can customize settings at this point or jump right into the player. We strongly recommend taking the time to customize settings. As with Windows Media Player, it's not wise to accept Microsoft's default settings. In fact, in one particular case, it can be downright dangerous.

Help — □ ✕

WELCOME TO ZUNE

go right to my collection ↗
Start me off with the default settings. I'll change them later if I want to.

- Add all media in my default Windows folders for music, video, and pictures.
- Make the Zune software my primary music and video player.
- Download song and album information from the Internet.
- Retrieve missing song information automatically.
- Send Microsoft anonymous usage data to help improve its products.

customize settings first ↗
I want to customize Zune software settings before I go to my collection. Settings include:

- Media locations (including external hard drives)
- Media types
- Privacy options

Customer Experience Improvement Program | Read the privacy statement online

Figure 14-5: Never accept the defaults from Microsoft. Customizing is key to making Zune work the way you want it to.

Secret

If you do skip the customization step here—and seriously, don't do that if you care about your music collection—you can always customize the Zune PC software settings later by clicking the Settings link in the upper-right corner of the Zune application window. In fact, even if you do customize settings right away, you should visit the link later, as Settings offers more options than what are exposed in the original wizard.

Configuring the Zune Software

If you opted to customize settings first, the setup wizard moves into a three-step phase whereby you can configure media locations, media (file) types, and privacy options. The first section refers to the media collection that you organize and enjoy in the Zune PC software, and which folders the Zune software will monitor.

As shown in Figure 14-6, you can configure monitored folders, just like in Windows Media Player, as well as related options, such as whether Zune should automatically update missing album artwork. And it is here that you should really pay attention. If you're a digital media newbie and don't have a large media collection yet, leave the default setting, whereby Zune will automatically update album art and metadata. Otherwise, uncheck that option: although Zune is pretty good at finding mainstream album art, we've been unhappy with how it has mauled our collections over time, and we now uncheck this option when installing the Zune software.

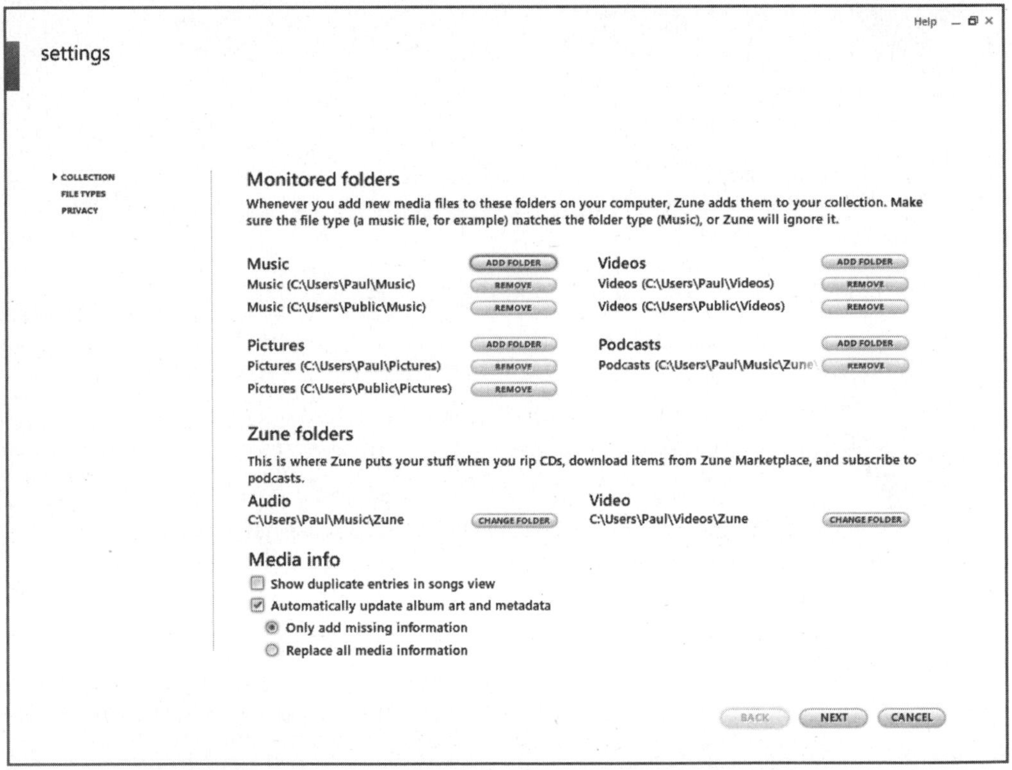

Figure 14-6: Use the Monitored folders setting to specify where Zune looks for content.

Unlike Windows Media Player, Zune enables you to remove default locations such as your Music, Pictures, and Videos folders from the Monitored folders list. I've never understood why this wasn't possible in Windows Media Player; after all, many users prefer to locate media in other locations and forego Microsoft's default folder structure. That said, it is technically possible in Windows 7 to remove, say, My Music from the list of folder locations that are used by the Music library. But that's sort of a balky workaround. It's nice to be able to do this on a per-application basis instead.

In the next step of the wizard, you determine the file types for which Zune will be the default player. Zune's format compatibility is an interesting combination of Windows Media Player and Apple iTunes. It supports Microsoft formats such as WMA and WMV, open formats such as MP3 and JPEG, but also Apple-friendly formats such as MPEG-4, H.264, and AAC.

Secret What Zune can't do, unfortunately, is play any protected content purchased from the iTunes Store, so TV shows, movies, and audiobooks purchased from iTunes are still incompatible with Zune. However, newer music files purchased from iTunes are A-OK: Apple switched to DRM-free music in 2008, and all the new stuff works just fine with Zune.

Until you're ready to commit to Zune full-time, you may want to unselect all the formats presented by the wizard, retaining the current default players. Later, when you've grown comfortable with Zune, you can decide whether to switch, just use it for certain file types, or dump it altogether.

Secret To change these settings later, you can always access Zune's Settings dialog, of course, but Windows 7 includes a handy Default Programs applet that works even better. From the Start menu, select Default Programs. Then, in the window that appears, choose Set Your Default Programs. Next, from the list that appears, select Zune (and/or other media player applications) and configure accordingly. For example, if you'd like Zune to be the default player for every file type with which it is compatible, you can select Zune from the list and then click the link titled "Set This Program as the Default." To use Zune for only certain file types, click "Choose Defaults for This Program" instead.

In the wizard's next step you can choose whether you want to automatically and silently participate in Microsoft's Customer Experience Improvement Program. We recommend doing so. Microsoft uses the anonymous data it collects to improve its software, and the results of this program have had an enormously positive impact on software as diverse as Windows, Office, and Zune.

Once that's done, the setup wizard ends and you're dumped into the Zune player's main user interface. (If you already have content on your PC, it's copied into Zune's media library. You'll look at that in the next section.) First, click the Settings link in the upper-right corner of the application window. This provides the three settings areas configured earlier, but it also includes a great number of others, as shown in Figure 14-7.

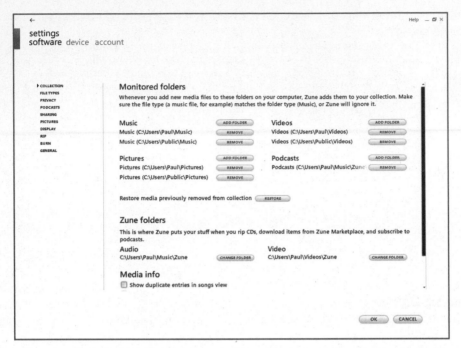

Figure 14-7: Here, you can configure many options that aren't available during Zune setup.

These additional settings include the following:

◆ **Podcasts:** Podcasts are the Internet's answer to radio, although they are pre-recorded audio files, not live streams. More important, podcast support is one of many advantages that Zune has over Windows Media Player. Unlike the bundled media player that comes in Windows 7, Zune actually understands and works natively with podcasts, enabling you to subscribe and listen to these unique content types in logical ways. In the Podcasts settings, you determine how many episodes of each podcast to keep and how they will be ordered for playback.

◆ **Sharing:** The Sharing settings pane includes a single option for sharing content between the Zune PC software and any Xbox 360 video game consoles that may be on your home network. You will look more closely at this functionality later in the chapter.

◆ **Pictures:** This simplistic settings pane provides just a single option: the length of time each photo will display during a photo slide show.

◆ **Display:** Display settings enable you to customize the Zune application window with any of several possible background designs, and configure onscreen animations and video enhancements.

◆ **Rip:** Rip settings offer a simple front end for various options related to CD ripping. Key among these, of course, is the format used. Zune defaults to WMA for some reason, but you should change this to 256 Kbps MP3 or higher for maximum compatibility and reasonable quality.

Secret

We mentioned earlier that Zune is missing a few key features. One that will be of importance to audiophiles is the capability to record MP3 using a so-called *variable bit rate (VBR)*, which generally provides better results, and smaller file sizes, than the *constant bit rate (CBR)* utilized by Zune. Apple's iTunes does offer this functionality for MP3 files.

◆ **Burn:** Burn settings are, of course, dedicated to Zune's CD and DVD burning capabilities. The application can burn audio CDs and data CDs or DVDs. You can also configure whether the disk is ejected on burn completion, and the burning speed.

◆ **General:** The General settings pane includes a few fairly innocuous options. None are particularly important.

When you're done configuring these various options, click the OK button. You'll be returned to the main application view.

Using Zune

The Zune user interface, shown in Figure 14-8, is a breath of fresh air compared to more staid digital media applications like Windows Media Player and, especially, Apple iTunes. This is by design. After basing the first version of its Zune PC software on Windows Media Player, Microsoft went back to the drawing board and built its Zune 2 software from the ground up as a brand-new application, and Zune 3 is an evolution of that design. The result is visually stimulating and, frankly, kind of pretty.

Figure 14-8: Zune is attractive and easy to use.

You may be interested to know that the Zune user interface was created by the same visual designers at Microsoft who were responsible for the UI of Windows Media Center.

Zune utilizes a single application window and typically uses a columnar display to present content in different, visual ways. There are four main UI views, or parts, in Zune:

◆ **Collection:** This default view shows the collection of media you have on your PC and are managing with Zune. It is in turn divided into subzones such as Music, Videos, Pictures, Podcasts, and Channels. Each represents content that is stored locally on your PC. We will examine the Zune's Collection view throughout this part of the chapter.

◆ **Marketplace:** This view connects to Microsoft's online store, Zune Marketplace. There are a number of subviews here—Picks, Music, Videos, Podcasts, and Channels. We describe Zune's online services later in this chapter.

◆ **Social:** Here you can access your Zune tag/Windows Live ID/Xbox 360 Gamertag friends list, personal information, and Inbox, the latter of which is much like e-mail but not nearly as useful. Don't worry; we'll explain this later in the chapter as well.

◆ **Device:** This view pertains to any Zune device (or devices) you own and have linked to this particular PC's collection. It is divided into subviews such as Status, Music, Videos, Pictures, Podcasts, Friends, and Channels. Later in this chapter, we will look at this view and how Zune devices work.

First, however, it's time to take a look at the main reason so many people are interested in Zune: digital music.

The Zune User Experience

Regardless of where you are in the Collection view, a few common elements are available. The Collection, Marketplace, Social, and Device links are common to all parts of the Zune UI, as are the Sign In, Settings, and Help links in the upper right corner of the application window. On the bottom is a series of three icons on the left (see Figure 14-9).

Figure 14-9: Inscrutable? Maybe. Useful? You bet.

These icons, from left to right, represent the following:

◆ **Device:** If you have a Zune portable device, you can access its sync status and other information from this first icon. (It also supports multiple Zunes for you Zune-crazy fans.)

♦ **Disk:** From here you can access Zune's disk play, rip, or burn functionality. You can also drag songs here to create a burn (play)list, which is used to create a custom audio CD.

♦ **Playlist:** This icon enables you to create new playlists and autoplaylists, access existing playlists, and add songs to the Now Playing playlist.

What you see in the bottom center of the application window depends on what's going on. If you're not playing any content, adding media, or performing other tasks, it is empty. When you're playing back some kind of content, you'll find a playback timeline with album art, the name of the media, the elapsed time, and the remaining time, as shown in Figure 14-10.

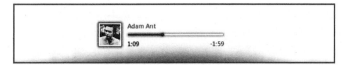

Figure 14-10: This timeline appears only when you actually play content.

Finally, on the bottom right of the application window, you'll see the playback controls shown in Figure 14-11. These controls include what you would expect: Play/Stop, Previous, and Next, as well as Repeat and Shuffle toggles. A final curious-looking pink icon launches Zune's amazing Now Playing view, which we'll examine shortly.

Figure 14-11: Zune's playback controls include the usual suspects plus one that's not so familiar.

If you mouse over the Volume text below the playback controls, you'll get a volume slider that you can use to adjust the playback volume.

Enjoying Music

In the Music view you get a three-pane look at your music collection by default (see Figure 14-12). On the left is a textual list of artists, which can be sorted alphabetically or in reverse alphabetical order. In the center, widest pane, are your albums, in graphical album art splendor; these can be sorted alphabetically, by release year, by artist, or by date added. On the right is a list of songs. These can be sorted alphabetically or by rating.

Secret

Sorting these columns is not obvious, but here's how it works: if you mouse over any of the three column headings, the heading name will be highlighted in gray. To change the sort type, just click this heading. It will toggle through each available option as you click.

Figure 14-12: The Music experience provides an attractive three-pane view.

Suppose you want to drill into your music collection. If you select an artist from the left-most Artists pane, the middle and right panes change to reflect this choice, as shown in Figure 14-13. For example, selecting Collective Soul from the collection will display what-ever Collective Soul albums are contained in the collection in the middle Albums pane; on the right, in the Songs pane, is a list of all of the Collective Soul songs in the collection.

Figure 14-13: Filtering the view to a single artist

You can drill down further, of course. If you select an individual album in the Albums pane, that album becomes selected and the Songs list is constrained to only those songs in the selected album, as shown in Figure 14-14.

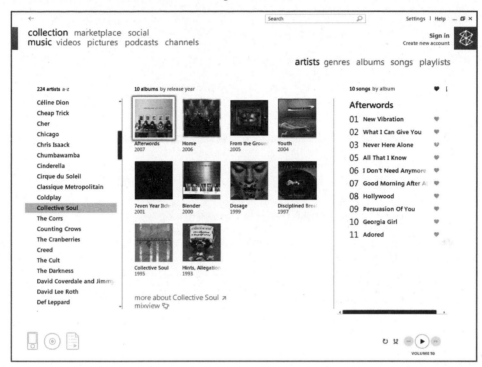

Figure 14-14: Filtering the view to a single album

To play an album or song, just double-click the item. The first song in the album (or the individual song you selected) will begin playing immediately. Meanwhile, a few things change in the Zune UI. The playback timeline appears, a small Now Playing icon appears next to the currently playing song in the Songs pane, and the Play button changes to Pause.

This is probably a good time to point out Zune's amazing Now Playing screen. You enable it by clicking the pink Now Playing button to the right of the Next button in the playback controls area. Alternately, you can click the Now Playing icon to the left of the currently playing song in the Songs pane. Either way, the Zune player UI switches to Now Playing mode, shown in Figure 14-15.

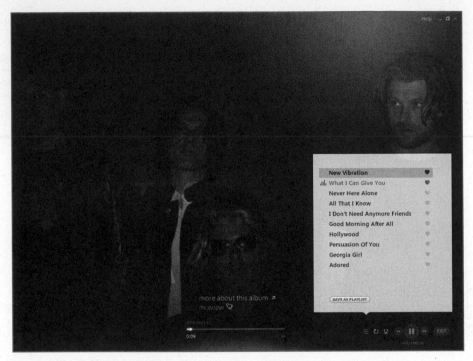

Figure 14-15: Zune's Now Playing mode is particularly impressive looking.

There's some information about the currently playing song over a cool backdrop composed of your collection's album art. In addition, temporarily, you'll also see the current playlist (what's displayed in the Songs pane), the playback timeline, and the playback controls. When you move the mouse off these elements they fade away, as shown in Figure 14-16.

If Zune doesn't have imagery and other information about the currently playing artist, the Now Playing view will instead show a grid-like collage of album art, as shown in Figure 14-17.

Secret

Look familiar? Microsoft liked this screen so much it also used it for the Now Playing view in its Windows Media Center software in Windows 7. We examine this software in Chapter 15.

To close Now Playing, click the Exit button in the bottom-right corner of the player window.

Figure 14-16: Stop moving the mouse and most of the onscreen fluff disappears.

Figure 14-17: Even when there's no artist info, the Now Playing screen is pretty cool.

Other Music Views

In addition to the default Artists view, Zune supports other Music views. These are accessible via a set of links that appear in the upper right side of the Zune application window. They include the following:

♦ **Genres:** In this view, the Zune player's three-column view changes to columns for Genres, Albums, and Songs, so the top-level sorting here is by genre: Alternative, Classical, Comedy, Pop, Rock, and so on. It will vary based on the types of content you have in your collection.

♦ **Albums:** In this attractive view style, Zune switches to a unique (for Music) two-pane view. Here, you will see large album art in the larger, leftmost pane, and a list of songs in the right pane. As shown in Figure 14-18, this view is quite visual and an excellent way to enjoy your music collection, especially if you're old-school and still think about music in terms of albums.

Figure 14-18: Albums view provides a very visual way to browse your music collection.

♦ **Songs:** In a nod to the textual, columnar media library style used by Apple iTunes, the Songs view provides a list-based look at your music collection. As shown in Figure 14-19, this view includes the columns Song, Song artist, Album, Genre, Rating (see the next section), and Device (that is, whether the song in question is synched to the attached Zune device).

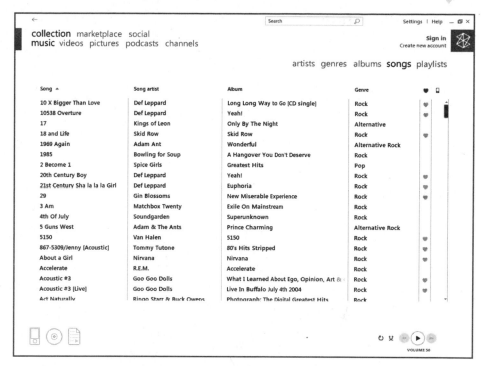

Figure 14-19: Look, it's iTunes! Okay, not really—but Zune can do text lists too.

♦ **Playlists:** From here, you can manage your playlists and autoplaylists. We examine this important functionality in just a bit.

Rating Content

While media players such as Windows Media Player and Apple iTunes support a ratings system whereby each song (or other content) can be rated on a scale from 1 to 5 (or from 0 to 5 if you consider no rating a 0), Microsoft has simplified this to the bare minimum in Zune. Instead of five stars, you can assign three different ratings:

♦ **Unrated:** In this case, the item has not been rated.

♦ **I Don't Like It:** This rating is reserved for songs and other items you specifically do not like.

♦ **I Like It:** This rating, of course, applies to songs and other content you enjoy.

Secret

What's interesting about the Zune rating system is that if you've already rated songs in either Windows Media Player or iTunes and then later install Zune, the Zune PC software will import your existing ratings and convert them to Zune-friendly values. Songs you've rated as 3 to 5 stars will be given the "I Like It" rating. Songs you've rated as 1 or 2 will receive "I Don't Like It." Unrated songs, of course, remain unrated.

Zune uses cute little heart icons to represent each rating. The I Like It rating is a solid heart, while the I Don't Like It rating, humorously, is represented by a broken heart. Unrated songs get no icon. Each icon option is shown in Figure 14-20.

Figure 14-20: Zune offers simple ratings with cute icons.

To set or change ratings, just click the heart icon next to each song in the Songs pane. Each time you click, the rating will toggle to the next available value. (You can also right-click songs and choose an appropriate rating from the context menu that appears. This method works for rating multiple songs simultaneously, though of course each will be assigned the same rating.) You cannot rate an entire album by right-clicking it in the Albums pane.

Secret

As with Windows itself, it's useful to remember that right-clicking throughout the Zune user interface can reveal some interesting features and options. The old adage is as relevant here as ever: when in doubt, right-click.

Working with Playlists

Like most media players, including Windows Media Player and iTunes, Zune supports both manually created playlists, which are simply called playlists, and automatically generated playlists, called autoplaylists. (Other media players call them smart playlists.)

Manual playlists aren't as smart as autoplaylists, but they're still a powerful tool, and they can and should be used to create lists of songs you're going to burn to CD or copy to a Zune portable device. Autoplaylists, meanwhile, are created using various filters, so they can change automatically over time. For example, if you create an autoplaylist of songs rated I Like It, that playlist will change over time as you rate more songs.

Here's how they work. The songs listed in the Songs pane are basically a temporary playlist. This temporary playlist changes as you select different items in the Artists and Albums panes; and when you actually start playing a selection of songs, it becomes the Now Playing playlist. This, too, is temporary in that it's not saved to disk or synchronized with any portable players. It's ephemeral, existing in the Zen-like now.

Zune provides a number of ways to formally construct a (manual) playlist that has a name and is saved to disk, including the following:

◆ **The Playlists icon:** In the lower-left corner of the Zune application window is a Playlists icon. (The icon resembles a dog-eared sheet of paper with a Play symbol on it.) If you mouse over this icon, a pop-up menu appears. It has three options by default: New playlist, New autoplaylist, and Now playing. If you create other playlists, they'll appear in the list as well, so everything in this list other than the first two items is there so that you can make it the current playlist. If you click the Playlists icon, the Zune UI will send you to the Playlists subview in Music.

◆ **Collection** ⇨ Music ⇨ **Playlists:** From this subview you can create new playlists or view or edit any playlists you may have already created. If you don't have any playlists, this view resembles Figure 14-21.

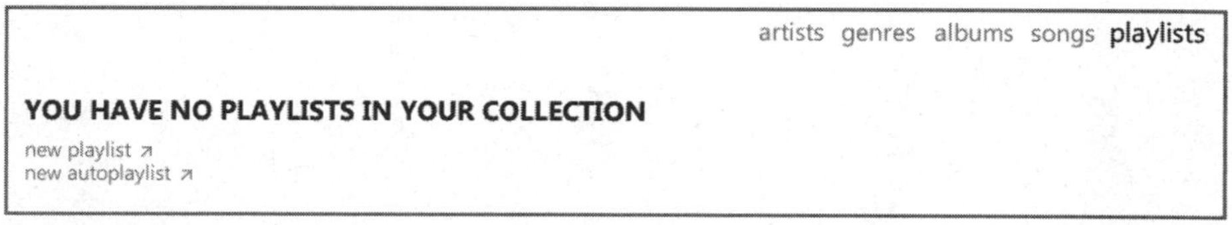

artists genres albums songs **playlists**

YOU HAVE NO PLAYLISTS IN YOUR COLLECTION

new playlist ↗
new autoplaylist ↗

Figure 14-21: It's empty by default, but savvy Zune users will soon fill up Playlists with their own manual playlists and autoplaylists.

◆ **Right-click:** A better way to interact with playlists is through the Zune software's right-click context menus. If you find an album or some songs you'd like to add to a new or existing playlist, just select them, right-click, and choose Add to playlist. When you do so, the Choose a Playlist dialog appears, shown in Figure 14-22. (If you have not yet created a playlist, however, you'll see a simpler Playlist dialog, from which you can create a new playlist.) From here, you can select an existing playlist or click the New Playlist button to create a new playlist.

Figure 14-22: From here, you can assign selected songs to particular playlists.

◆ **Drag and drop:** One of the more unexpected ways in which you can interact with playlists is similar to the right-click method except that you have to do a bit of work first. That is, you must mouse over the Playlists icon and either create a new playlist or select an existing playlist from the pop-up menu that appears; in either case, that will become the active playlist. Then, you can find content in the Artists, Albums, or Songs pane that you'd like to make part of that playlist, select it, and drag it over to the Playlists icon (see Figure 14-23).

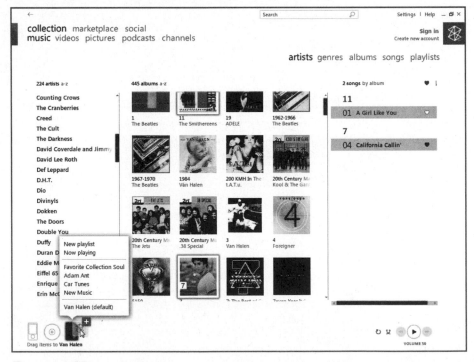

Figure 14-23: Content dragged onto the Playlists icon is added to the active playlist.

From the Playlists subzone, you can add items to the Burn list to burn them to a CD or DVD, in much the same manner as described above; drag and drop works just fine using the Disk icon you'll see there, as does the right-click menu. You can also use these methods to sync playlists to a device.

To create an autoplaylist, mouse over the Playlists icon in the lower left corner of the Zune application window and choose New autoplaylist from the pop-up menu that appears. Or, navigate to the Playlists subview and click the New Autoplaylist button. Either way, the Autoplaylist dialog appears, shown in Figure 14-24, enabling you to configure the filters that will determine which songs appear in the autoplaylist.

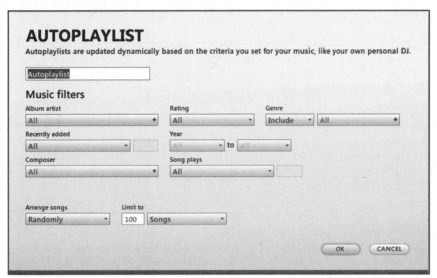

Figure 14-24: The Autoplaylist dialog works like the smart playlist generators in other media players.

Creating an autoplaylist might seem difficult at first, but it's actually pretty straightforward. Suppose you want to create a list of songs that were made in a certain decade (for example, the 1980s). To do this, you would simply change the years in the Year date fields to 1980 and 1989. Then click OK. It's that simple.

Working with Videos

Like Windows Media Player, Zune supports playing back various types of movies. There are some key differences between the two, however, including the following:

- ◆ **Windows Media Player has a more flexible UI:** WMP supports different video playback modes, including a true full-screen mode. Zune is far less configurable. It has a nice-looking full-screen mode (Now Playing), but it's not truly full screen in that it doesn't even hide the Windows taskbar, as shown in Figure 14-25.

Figure 14-25: It looks nice, but Zune's full-screen playback mode isn't really full screen.

♦ **They support different video formats:** Although there's some overlap—both Windows Media Player and Zune play nonprotected WMV and H.264 files, for example—video format support differs in important ways between each player. For example, Windows Media Player can play DRM-protected WMV videos from services such as CinemaNow and MovieLink, which Zune cannot.

The takeaway from all of this is that Zune cannot replace Windows Media Player when it comes to PC-based video playback, which again slightly lessens the ubiquity of this player. Instead, video support in the player seems to be there largely to facilitate synchronization with Zune devices. Presumably, Microsoft expects you to just watch your videos that way.

tip Syncing video with Zune devices works just like syncing music.

From an organizational standpoint, Zune offers some decent capabilities for your video collection. As with music, Zune supports a number of subviews for Videos:

♦ **All:** This view displays all of the videos stored in the folders that Zune monitors, regardless of type. To change the type of a video, right-click it and choose Edit. This will display the dialog shown in Figure 14-26. Click the Category button and choose the appropriate type—TV Series, TV Specials, TV News, Music, Movies, or Other—from the drop-down list that appears.

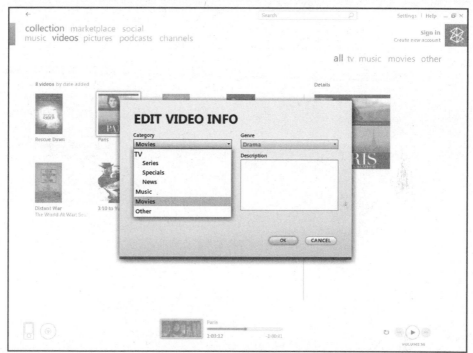

Figure 14-26: Zune lets you categorize your videos.

♦ **TV:** In this view, only the TV shows in your video collection are displayed. (Microsoft sells TV shows in Zune Marketplace.)

♦ **Music:** In this view, only the music videos in your video collection are displays. (Yes, Microsoft also sells music videos from Zune Marketplace.)

♦ **Movies:** In this view, only the movies (that is, full-length Hollywood-type movies) in your video collection are displayed.

♦ **Other:** Here, videos that are categorized as Other are displayed.

---

tip   Why categorize? Well, content sold via the Zune Marketplace is categorized, of course. But the real reason is that Microsoft's Zune devices also utilize these category types for navigational purposes. So you could view the TV shows and movies stored on your device in separate lists if you wanted.

Secret

Zune uses a thumbnail image to represent each video, and it doesn't offer a way to add DVD cover art, similar to music album art, to videos. But that doesn't mean you can't add DVD cover art to ripped DVDs and other video content: you could use another application, like Apple's iTunes, to add DVD cover art to a video file. When you do so, Zune recognizes it and uses it in the thumbnail display. As you can see in Figure 14-27, the effect is quite attractive

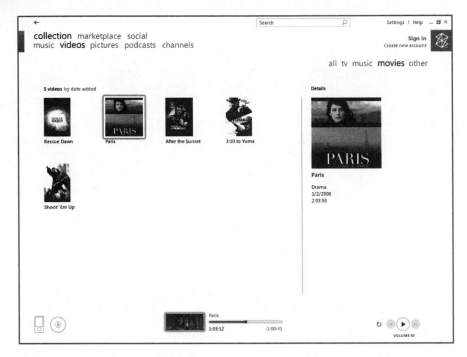

Figure 14-27: Zune doesn't let you add DVD cover art to videos, but it will utilize them if you add them with another application.

Organizing Pictures

Zune's support of pictures is pretty lackluster and seems to be oriented more toward device synchronization than actual PC playback. In this sense, the Zune software is much like Windows Media Player. It offers only basic picture viewing functionality, with simple slide shows. That said, the Zune does present folders of photos in a very visual way. As shown in Figure 14-28, folders of photos utilize a thumbnail and a large photo count within the Zune player.

Zune's slide show also works within the pseudo full-screen mode that's provided for videos, as shown in Figure 14-29.

tip   Syncing photos with Zune devices works just like syncing music.

Figure 14-28: Zune doesn't offer much in the way of photo functionality, but its presentation of photo folders is highly visual.

Figure 14-29: Photo slide shows utilize whatever playlist is currently playing for a full multimedia experience.

Radio in the 21st Century: Enjoying Podcasts with Zune

As the Internet's answer to radio broadcasts, podcasts are an awesome diversion, with topics ranging from the expected tech nonsense to travel, food, celebrity gossip, and more. In other words, it's just like radio from a content perspective. The problem with podcasts is that in order to enjoy them effectively, you need a software client that can work with the underlying technologies that distribute and manage these recordings.

Windows Media Player is not such a client. While you can of course play podcast files with Windows Media Player—they are typically delivered as standard MP3 files, after all—and even manage them manually if you're so inclined, this software has no understanding of the infrastructure that is used to post new podcast episodes.

Zune has no such problem. In fact, one of the major features of the Zune platform is that it's completely compatible with podcasts, so you can subscribe to podcasts with Zune and sync them with your Zune device if you have one.

Secret   In fact, you could use Zune to subscribe to podcasts even if you plan on usually using Windows Media Player. That's because Zune will save podcasts, by default, inside of your My Music folder, which is monitored by the Music library in Windows 7, and thus by Windows Media Player. Put another way, podcast content subscribed to by Zune automatically appears in Windows Media Player as well.

First, you might want to configure how the Zune PC software handles podcasts. This is done via the Podcasts section in Zune Settings, as shown in Figure 14-30. Here, you can determine how many episodes you want to keep of each podcast (three is the default, but you can keep as few as one at a time or as many as all of them) and how the podcast episodes are ordered (newest episodes first or oldest episodes first). Unfortunately, these settings are universal. You can't configure them differently for individual podcasts.

To subscribe to a podcast, you have two options. First, you can search podcasts via Zune Marketplace, discussed later in this chapter. As far as podcasts go, Zune Marketplace has a great selection, and its integrated search tool and genre-browsing capabilities make finding the right podcasts short work. A typical podcast entry in Zune Marketplace is shown in Figure 14-31. As you can see, you can easily download an individual episode to try it out, or click the Subscribe button to begin receiving new episodes automatically.

A less well-known method of subscribing to podcasts is via a standard RSS feed. To subscribe to a podcast this way, you need to visit the podcast's Web site in a Web browser and copy the URL for its RSS feed to your clipboard. Then, open the Zune PC software and navigate to Collection ⇨ Podcasts. In the lower-left corner of the player is an Add a Podcast button. Click this button and then paste the RSS feed URL into the dialog that appears, as shown in Figure 14-32.

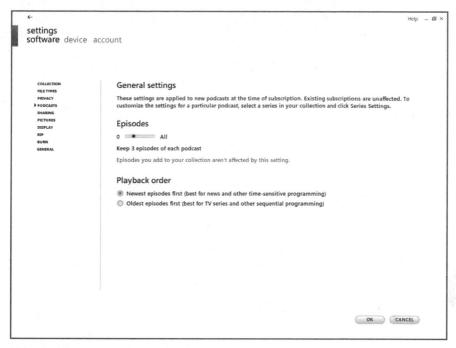

Figure 14-30: Before subscribing to any podcasts, you should configure how Zune handles podcast subscriptions and playback.

Figure 14-31: Now there's a handsome devil.

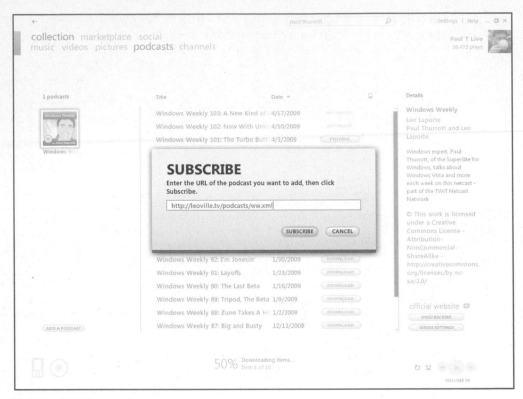

Figure 14-32: It's low-tech, but this works too.

To test this, use a random podcast RSS feed URL such as, oh, say, `http://leoville.tv/podcasts/ww.xml`. Paul would really appreciate it.

Secret Before you can subscribe to a podcast from the Zune Marketplace, you need to create and sign in to your Windows Live ID first.

Sharing Zune

If you're *really* living the digital media lifestyle, you might want to share the content in your Zune collection with other devices around your home, including PCs, digital media receivers, and the Xbox 360. Not surprisingly, this is all very possible.

Sharing with PCs and Other Windows Media Devices

Windows 7 already includes integrated digital media-sharing features, and those features (described in the previous chapter) continue to work just fine if you choose to use the Zune PC software to manage your music. That's because Zune integrates with this underlying technology and shares, by default, the same monitored folders and media folders as Windows Media Player and Windows Media Center. As long as you have correctly configured media sharing through Windows 7's HomeGroup feature as outlined in Chapter 11, it will work fine if you choose to use Zune instead of Windows Media Player.

Here's a shocker: this sharing capability extends even to Digital Rights Management– (DRM-) protected music that you've purchased from Zune Marketplace.

One interesting side note: while Windows Media Player works nicely with shared media libraries on other PCs thanks to its integration with Windows 7's HomeGroup functionality, Zune doesn't really offer any way to directly share content with other instances of the Zune software. For example, say you have Zune installed on two different PCs, both of which are connected to your home network, and you've decided to manage your music collection with this software. Even though Windows might be sharing your content on both PCs, the Zune software on either PC will never see the collection on the other. To do that, you have to use Windows Media Player. This, too, is another one of those areas in which the evolving nature of the Zune software makes it a little less viable as your sole solution for managing digital media content.

You can get around this limitation with a brute force approach if you really want to. To do so, visit Settings ⇨ Software ⇨ Collection in the Zune software and configure it to monitor one or more shared folders on your network that contain digital media content you'd like to enjoy. (You'll have to first set up sharing on the other PC, functionality we discuss in Chapter 9.)

Sharing with the Xbox 360

Zune also supports an optional media-sharing feature that's aimed at the Xbox 360, Microsoft's video game console. If you have one of these devices and think you may want to stream music, movies, and other content from your Zune media library over your home network, you'll need to enable this functionality first. To do so, navigate to Settings ⇨ Sharing.

Click the button labeled Enable Media Sharing with Xbox 360. Once you have done this, you can configure a few other sharing options, such as the name that will identify your media collection to the Xbox 360, which media types to share (music, video, and pictures are available, but only music is selected by default), and whether you want to share your media library with any nearby Xbox 360 or would prefer to specify a particular console. (The Zune-based PC and Xbox 360 must, of course, be on the same home network for the sharing feature to work.)

On the Xbox 360, media sharing is handled via the My Xbox section of the New Xbox Experience (NXE) user interface, just as it is for any other shared PC-based media libraries. To find your Zune, navigate to Music Library and then select the proper PC from the list in Select Source. (It will have a colorful purple and orange Zune logo next to it, so you can tell which one represents your Zune-based library.)

When you select the Zune-based library, you can choose between lists of Albums, Artists, Saved Playlists (which include both manual playlists and autoplaylists), Songs, and Genres.

Secret

Navigating through your Zune-based library from the Xbox 360 is pretty straight-forward, if not as graphical as doing so from the Zune PC software. However, the first time you try to play AAC (audio) or H.264 (video) content in this fashion, the Xbox 360 will alert you that you need to download a media update. This free update downloads and installs quickly.

Finding Zune-based photos and videos is handled similarly, using the Picture Library and Video Library options in My Xbox.

World Wide Zune: A Look at the Zune Online Services

With the first version of the Zune platform, Microsoft created its Zune Marketplace, an online store that sold only music that was protected by Microsoft's Windows Media DRM (Digital Rights Management) technologies. This limited the appeal of Zune Marketplace to the 17 or so people who bought the first-generation Zune devices. Clearly, some tweaking was in order.

Since then, Microsoft has significantly enhanced Zune Marketplace and added a second Zune-oriented online service, modeled on Xbox Live, called Zune Social. While Zune Marketplace is still accessed solely through the Zune PC software (much as the iTunes Store is typically accessed via the PC-based iTunes software), Zune Social is accessible via both the PC-based Zune software and the Web. Additionally, Zune Marketplace has been updated in some significant ways that make the service more appealing to people who are interested in using the Zune software but don't want to buy a Zune device. For example, Zune Marketplace sells only DRM-free music now, so any audio content you buy from this service will work just fine on any PC-based media player, including Apple's players and with the Xbox 306. This section examines both Zune Marketplace and Zune Social.

Zune Marketplace

As one of just four top-level menu items in the Zune PC software, Zune Marketplace offers an extremely rich and visual user interface. Shown in Figure 14-33, Zune Marketplace is designed to be more friendly and appealing than Apple's iTunes Store (shown in Figure 14-34). It certainly is that, which isn't hard to achieve given the ugly, busy UI that Apple employs.

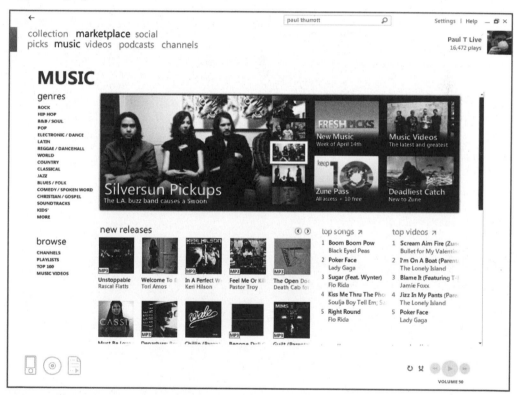

Figure 14-33: Zune Marketplace is open, airy, and visually appealing.

Figure 14-34: Contrast Zune Marketplace with the iTunes Store, a service so busy it's like the MySpace of online retailers.

Secret To be fair to Apple, it's easy to be beautiful and simple when you only sell movies and the occasional hard-to-find music video. That's the problem with Zune Marketplace: there are no Hollywood movies to download, for example, and the selection isn't as rich and deep as Apple's iTunes Store.

The layout of Zune Marketplace mirrors that of the PC software interface. You typically start in the Music section of the service—currently, there are only a few other sections, including Picks, Videos, Podcasts, and Channels—presented in a columnar view. If you're familiar with the Zune PC software you'll feel right at home in Zune Marketplace.

Browsing the Zune Online Store

When it comes to finding music online, of course, discoverability is key. One of the biggest failings of the iTunes Store is that it's not a friendly place to browse around and discover new music. Microsoft is seeking to avoid this problem by providing a more visual experience—one in which discovering new music is appealing and obvious.

Music, as you might expect, is at the center of the Zune experience. This is for practical reasons: the vast majority of portable media device buyers are interested in music above all else; hence, that is almost only what Zune Marketplace sells. (For now. Microsoft will no doubt begin selling and renting movies via Zune Marketplace soon, possibly by the time you read this.) In this area, Zune Marketplace does a reasonable job. There are several top-level genres, curiously ordered not alphabetically but rather in what is presumably some editorialized list according to user preference: Rock, Hip-hop, R&B/Soul, Pop, Electronic/Dance, Latin, Reggae/Dancehall, World, Country, Classical, Jazz, Blues/Folk, Comedy/Spoken Word, Christian/Gospel, Soundtracks, and Kids. Via a "More" option, you can access an additional five subgenres: Avant-Garde, Easy Listening, Miscellaneous, New Age, and Seasonal. There is also a separate Browse list below Genres that includes links for channels, Microsoft-created playlists, top-seller charts, and music videos.

Secret

For much of Zune Marketplace's existence, Microsoft sold two kinds of music, which was confusing. Most tracks were available as DRM-encoded WMA files, which we could not recommend purchasing: these tracks cannot play in iPods and are difficult to effectively archive and move forward to new PCs and devices. A minority of the tracks sold on Zune Marketplace, at first, were in DRM-free MP3 format, however. These types of tracks are highly desirable because they are compatible with virtually all PCs, devices, and software. As of 2009, however, Microsoft has transitioned to fully DRM-free MP3 files. Success!

Where Zune Marketplace really shines is with its artists pages. (A typical page is shown in Figure 14-35.) These pages are far better-looking than anything in iTunes, and they offer more useful information.

Figure 14-35: One of the nicest things about Zune Marketplace is the individual pages for artists.

For example, in addition to cool edge-to-edge graphical designs, you can get (often very detailed) biographical information, along with numerous photographs for top bands, and huge lists of related bands. You can switch between a graphical view of all available music from that band, and a subset of only that content you can actually purchase there. Many of the artist bios are like short novels, extending far below the lower edge of the application window and including numerous photographs.

Secret   In case you're wondering, this biographical information is not created by Microsoft. In fact, Apple licenses exactly the same artist bios in its iTunes Store. Missing from Apple's site is the other information, including the photos.

Zune Marketplace also offers excellent ways to find music that is similar to the artists you already know and love. Each artist page includes a list called Influenced By, which includes the bands that influenced the artist you're currently exploring. A Related Artists list is typically even longer, with numerous entries. A third list, Related Genres, provides yet another jumping-off point. It's an impressive store for music lovers.

Zune also provides a Picks section that is automatically updated with content the service thinks you'll enjoy, based on your listening habits. And Microsoft offers a Channel service to subscribers of the Zune Pass (see the next few sections) that provides continually updated auto-playlists of songs, helping you to find new music.

Podcasts

Microsoft was roundly criticized for its utter lack of support for podcasts in the first version of its Zune platform. They've clearly taken this criticism to heart since then, as podcasting is now a first-class citizen. Via the prominent Podcasts menu, you can access a basic collection of podcasts, one that increasingly approaches the selection available at iTunes.

Secret   Almost all podcasts are distributed in DRM-free MP3 format, regardless of where you find them. This means you can use the best tool for the job. For example, even if you're a Zune device owner who uses the Zune PC software and accesses Zune Marketplace regularly, you can still download podcasts with iTunes. They'll sync right up with the Zune device and work just fine.

The podcast section on Zune Marketplace has grown over time as users and podcasters have made suggestions; and, of course, you can manually subscribe to any podcast using an RSS-type URL via the Zune PC software as well. Finally, give Microsoft credit for actually calling them podcasts and not something lame like Zunecasts. You know they thought about it.

Spending Points: Purchasing Music Online

Zune Marketplace isn't ideal for a number of reasons. For example, it lacks a ton of commercial content such as movies, and there are no audiobooks (though you can separately use audiobooks with the Zune devices).

However, the single biggest problem, in our opinion, is that Microsoft makes it very difficult to purchase content online. They don't accept payment in the currency of the country in which you live. Instead, they use a bizarre electronic currency called Microsoft Points that seems designed to make Microsoft rich in the same way that Richard Pryor purloined leftover subpenny transactions in *Superman III*.

No, that's not a joke.

Instead of U.S. dollars or euros or whatever currency is legal tender where you live, Microsoft uses this Microsoft Points system because it can avoid the huge number of credit card transaction fees it would be forced to pay if it let you buy songs one at a time using a credit card. (Ignore for a moment that Apple and every other online store allows just that.) Here's how it works: instead of buying content online, you buy blocks of Microsoft Points. The cost of these points varies from region to region, but in the United States they break down as shown in Table 14-1.

Table 14-1: Microsoft Points vs. Reality

Points	Cost (US$)
100	$1.25
500	$6.25
1000	$12.50
2000	$25.00
5000	$62.50

When you purchase a block of Microsoft Points, they're applied to your Windows Live ID, so you can use them on Zune Marketplace (to buy music) or on Xbox Live, via an Xbox 360, to purchase Xbox Live Arcade titles, video rentals, and other items. Sticking with the Zune Marketplace discussion for now, as you purchase songs online, your pool of available points is depleted. Therein lies the problem with Microsoft Points: there's no actual way you'll ever evenly spend the points you've purchased. You're essentially giving Microsoft an interest-free loan.

Here's why: individual songs on Zune Marketplace are typically 79 Microsoft Points (which is equivalent to 99 cents, the same price that Apple typically charges for a single song), but 79 doesn't divide equally into 100, 500, 1,000, 2,000, or 5,000. Therefore, no matter what you buy, there will always be points left over. Points that you paid Microsoft for. Money that is now in Microsoft's bank account and not yours, accruing interest. That's right: you've given Microsoft a loan.

Our advice here is very simple. Don't buy content from Zune Marketplace, even if you are a huge believer in the Zune vision and think that the Zune devices are next to godliness. You're wasting your money.

Zune Pass: An All-You-Can-Eat Subscription Service

Okay, there is one exception to the preceding rule, which applies only to song purchasing. In addition to the dubious song purchasing plan that Microsoft invented to slowly siphon every last cent out of your wallets, the company has also created a Zune subscription service called Zune Pass. This service could actually make a lot of sense for you if two things are true: One, you're still young or interested enough to want to discover new music on an ongoing basis. Two, you own or are going to purchase a Zune device in addition to using the Zune PC software.

Here's the deal: Zune Pass costs $14.99 a month in the United States. Okay, this sounds a little steep at first, and Microsoft isn't offering special deals if you sign up for several months or one year at a time, but this $14.99 buys you ongoing access to all of the several million songs that Microsoft sells via Zune Marketplace. As long as your subscription is active, you can download and listen to any protected song they offer, both in the PC-based Zune software and on your Zune portable media player.

But wait, there's more. This $14.99 a month is actually a good value because each month, Microsoft allows you to download and keep up to 10 songs. That's a $10 value, so the real cost of this subscription part of the Zune Pass is only $4.99 a month, and that's a steal, especially if you are in the market for new music and are buying digital albums anyway.

As with anything that sounds too good to be true, there are some caveats. You can't burn any of the subscription-based songs to CD. The subscription covers music only, not music videos. And as soon as your subscription lapses—poof!—any songs you've downloaded are gone. (Except for the 10 free songs you get each month; those are yours to keep.)

If you're old and crusty, this may not seem like a good deal, but if you're young and have constantly evolving musical taste, Zune Pass may be just what the doctor ordered. Over time, you will discover more and more new music and find out what you really like. By the time your tastes settle down, you may be ready to start buying certain music.

Zune Social

The second Zune-oriented online service is called Zune Social. It's basically a duplication of much of the Xbox Live service but for Zune users. That is, it's essentially an online identity that is tied to a Windows Live ID account—giving others access, in this case, to your musical preferences. (By comparison, the Xbox Live service provides online access to your game playing.) It also provides other related services, such as an inbox for receiving, well, Zune messages.

Zune Social can be accessed in two ways. In the Zune PC software you can click the prominent Social link to access your friends list (arranged by Zune Card), your profile page (called Me in the menu), and Zune Inbox (which is identical to your Xbox 360 Inbox if you linked that to the same Windows Live ID as well). A Zune profile page is shown in Figure 14-36.

Figure 14-36: Zune is pretty social, letting you share information about yourself and your music preferences.

While the friends list and profile page are nicely done, the Inbox is particularly weak. Yes, you can read messages, reply to a message, or write a new message, but it's not a general e-mail client. It only works between users of the Zune software.

Secret

If you're an Xbox 360 gamer, chances are good you already have an Xbox 360 Gamertag. The Zune Card is the same thing, literally, so if you already have a Gamertag, and thus an associated Windows Live ID, then you already have a Zune Card as well, using the same online screen name. These online identities are all connected.

The Web-based version of Zune Social, found at `social.zune.net`, offers a more complete look at what Microsoft is trying to accomplish: making the act of listening to digital music, which is today very much a solitary experience, into a more social experience. Here, you will find the same social features available in the Zune software, but also gain a better idea of what's going on with those in your friends list or social circle. The site is shown in Figure 14-37.

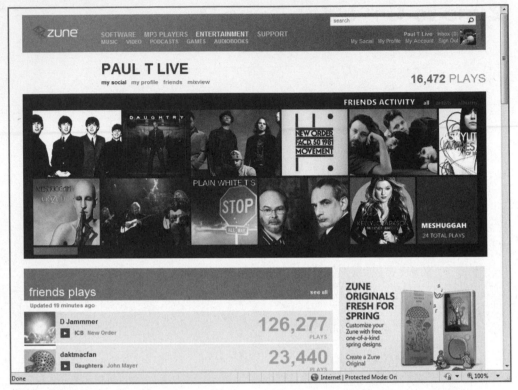

Figure 14-37: On the Zune Social Web site, others can view your Zune Card and check out your musical tastes—and vice versa.

Regardless of how you access Zune Social, the Zune Card is at heart of this system. This card is analogous to the Xbox Gamertag and tracks what you're listening to in the Zune software and devices, displaying that information for others to see.

Zune Cards are pretty graphical, with album art displays and three basic views. The default view, Home, displays the album art for the songs you've most recently played.

Clearly, Zune Social has the makings of a Facebook-style community, and we can envision some people rallying around similar music just as they do with video games now on Xbox Live. The idea is a good one. What it needs is a bigger market of users, sharing information about music with each other.

Secret

If you're freaking out about the privacy implications of this service, worry no more: Everything we have described here is opt-in. You can decide who sends you messages, who can see your friends list, and who can discover what music you've been listening to. (Each option can be configured as everyone, friends only, or blocked.)

Zune to Go: Using Zune Devices

The Zune PC software is free: You can download it, check it out, and dump Windows Media Player entirely if you'd like. Ditto for Zune Marketplace and Zune Social: While you do have to link your Zune tag to a Windows Live ID, both services can at least be accessed free. Of course, you'll need to spend some money if you want to buy music at Zune Marketplace.

The biggest investment you're going to make on the Zune platform occurs when and if you decide to go all in and snag a Zune portable media player. These devices, which compete with various Apple iPod models, are not inexpensive. They're high-quality, competitive devices, and if you like what you've seen with the Zune software and services, you're probably going to enjoy the Zune hardware too.

The current generation of Zune hardware is the second that Microsoft has offered in the market. Whereas the first-generation Zune platform included just a single hardware device—the 30GB Zune 30 player (see Figure 14-38), the second generation expands into a more complete product lineup. Interestingly, Microsoft didn't actually replace its Zune 30 player with a new model. Instead, it augmented that player with other new models and added new capabilities that are available on all players, old and new. (Microsoft no longer sells the Zune 30, however.)

Figure 14-38: Microsoft no longer sells the Zune 30 but it has augmented it with new Zune capabilities over time.

As of 2009, the second-generation players had been updated with two ultra-portable devices that utilize 8GB and 16GB of flash storage instead of heavier, bigger, and slower hard disks. Dubbed the Zune 8 and Zune 16, respectively, these devices come in a variety of colors, but color and storage capacity aside, they're all otherwise identical (see Figure 14-39).

On the high end, Microsoft has added a 120GB hard drive–based mode, the Zune 120, shown in Figure 14-40. This player is available only in black and red and is roughly the same size as the Zune 30, but is thinner and features a larger, nicer-looking screen.

Figure 14-39: The Zune 8 and Zune 16 utilize flash storage and offer a small form factor.

Figure 14-40: The Zune 120 is Microsoft's premium digital media player.

More Zunes are on the way (like the Zune HD), according to Microsoft, as are Zune software capabilities for Windows Mobile–based phones. By the time you read this, the Zune ecosystem will likely have grown somewhat.

Choosing a Zune

Pricing for the Zune lineup is similar to that of Apple's iPod lineup. At the time of this writing, the Zune 8 is about $140, while the Zune 16 comes in around $175. The Zune 30 has pretty much disappeared from the market, which makes sense given its age. Meanwhile, the Zune 120 retails for about $230. Zune HD pricing is dependent on capacity as well; check with your favorite retailer for the latest prices.

Even if you can find one, skip the Zune 30: It doesn't include some of the newer Zune hardware features discussed in this chapter, and it's slightly bulkier and heavier than the other models. It's also the model most likely to become obsolete first.

Secret If you purchase a Zune online through Microsoft's Zune Originals service (`http://zuneoriginals.net/`), you can choose from numerous custom, laser-engraved artwork designs and add your own text. These designs are applied to the back of the device. Zune Originals is not available for the Zune 30, yet another reason to forego this model.

Because the software-based functionality on all three Zune models is identical, any decision about models should come down to the following:

♦ **Form factor:** The Zune 8 and Zune 16 will appeal to those who have less content, and who value small size over capacity. If you're going to use a Zune while exercising, for example, a Zune 8 or 16 is ideal from a form factor perspective.

♦ **Capacity:** While a Zune 120 might seem like overkill from a capacity perspective, this is the device to have if you intend to load up with videos and large photo collections in addition to more typical audio content. Few people have tens of gigabytes of music, but video adds up very quickly.

♦ **Price:** Like other high-quality electronic devices, Zunes are fairly expensive. If you can't afford a Zune 120—or just don't want to drop $230 on what is essentially a digital bauble—the lower-end Zunes are also quite nice. Sometimes, simply meeting your budget is the most obvious and important factor of all.

Linking Your Zune: Installing and Configuring the Player

Whichever Zune you purchase, the process for connecting it to your PC and synchronizing the device with the Zune PC software is nearly identical. First, ensure that you have the latest version of the Zune PC software installed, using the instructions from earlier in this chapter to get it up and running and, preferably, connected to a Windows Live ID. After removing the Zune from its packaging, connect it to the PC with the included USB cable (which, sadly, is specially made for the Zune, so you can't just use any old USB cable) and then follow these steps:

1. Wait while Windows finds and then installs the drivers needed to interact with your Zune. This process, shown in Figure 14-41, is automatic and should conclude quickly. Once the drivers are loaded, the Zune PC software will appear.

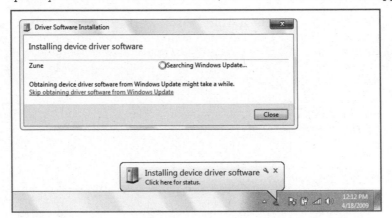

Figure 14-41: Zune drivers will be found and installed automatically the first time you plug in the device.

2. Launch the Zune software if you haven't already. The device setup process will begin. First, supply a friendly name for the device (see Figure 14-42) and determine whether you want to link the Zune to your Zune tag/Windows Live ID. If you've already begun using the Zune PC software and have established a Zune tag, there's no reason not to link it with the device now. That said, you can link the device to your Zune tag anytime.

3. In the next phase of device setup, you can optionally agree to send Microsoft information about any issues your Zune device may have. This improves the Zune experience for everyone and we recommend that you agree to do this.

4. At the final and most crucial phase of the setup wizard, shown in Figure 14-43, you determine how the Zune syncs with your media library. There are two general options, Smart Sync and Manual Sync. If you choose Smart Sync, you will get separate entries for music, video, pictures, podcasts, and friends, and in each case you can choose between Sync All and [*Content*] I Choose. With Manual Sync, you are selecting to individually sync content item-by-item in the Zune software. How you sync depends on a number of factors, including the size of your media collection and the capacity of your device. For example, if you have 30GB of music, you can't just use Smart Sync to sync all of your content with a Zune 8 because that device has only 8GB of storage. Because this is a big decision, we examine it further in the next section. For now, just select the [*Content*] I Choose options for each media type under Smart Sync and then click Finish to complete the wizard.

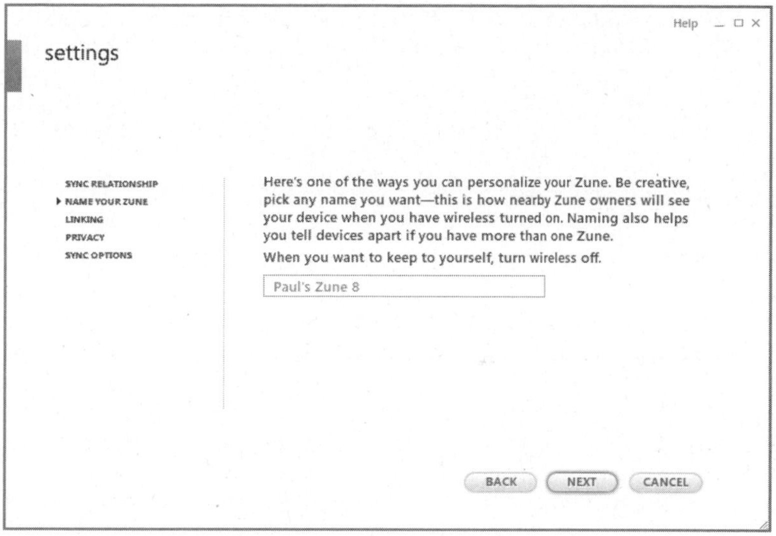

Figure 14-42: This time it's personal.

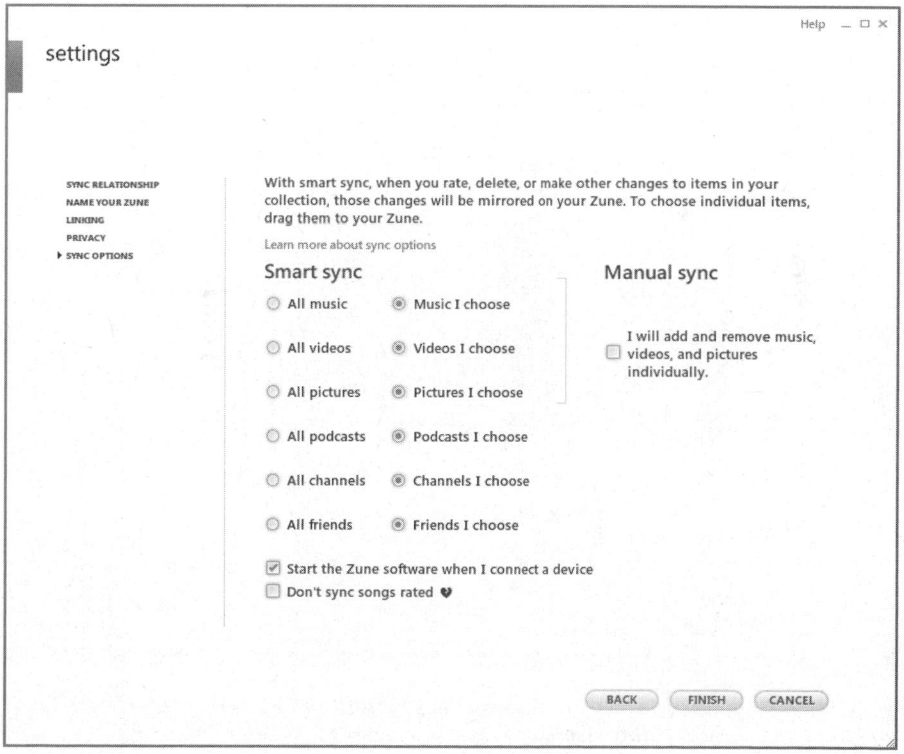

Figure 14-43: Zune's synchronization options are well thought out.

5. At this point, the Zune PC software displays the main screen (Collection ⇨ Music), which is a bit surprising, but if you look in the lower-left corner of the application window, you'll see a colored Zune icon—that matches the color and Zune device you purchased, by the way—that's lit up and synchronizing, as shown in Figure 14-44. You can watch the synchronization progress via the percentage text under the device icon.

Figure 14-44: It's subtle, but the Zune PC software
will trigger whatever sync options you set up in the wizard.

6. Click the Zune device icon to display the Device Status screen (Device ⇨ Status) shown in Figure 14-45. From here you can see an almost life-size device icon (again, in the correct color and style) with Just Added, Now Syncing, and Syncing sections that, together, give you an idea of how well the synchronization process is going. There's also a Total Space Used graph on the bottom that indicates how much of the device's storage space is used.

Figure 14-45: In Device Status, you can see how sync is going and find out how much of the device's capacity is utilized.

The Total Space Used graph is interactive: as you mouse over the various segments of the graph, it will tell you how much space each type of content—music, pictures, podcasts, and videos, as well as reserved space—uses individually.

You can sit and watch the device fill up with content (if you configured it to sync) or simply begin using any other part of the Zune PC software UI. You can also do other things while the device syncs, including shop in Zune Marketplace.

This one is kind of fun: Microsoft includes content on the Zune. This means you can actually view photos, watch movies, and listen to music on your new Zune before you even get it home and sync it with your computer. That's not to say you're going to enjoy any of this stuff, but it's an unusually generous preload.

Speaking of the content included with the Zune, one additional thing you should be aware of is that the Zune will not sync it back to your PC by default, so if you'd like to back it up, you should do so. Here's how: in the Zune PC software, navigate to Device and then Music, Videos, Pictures, and Podcasts in turn. In each of these sections, select the preloaded content, right-click, and choose Copy to my collection. This content will then automatically sync back to the PC. Music and podcasts are copied to your Music folder, while pictures are copied to your Pictures folder and videos are copied to your Videos folder.

To Sync or Not to Sync, That Is the Question

Okay, you've just purchased a new Zune device and you obviously want to get some content on there, and fast. The question is, how are you going to make that happen? The Zune PC software offers two basic options for synchronizing your media library with your Zune device. That is, you can automatically sync all content or you can manually sync only certain content.

Choosing a Sync Strategy

We want to be very clear about this choice: if you can do it—that is, if the capacity of your device is large enough to handle the size of your media library—the Smart Sync option is much simpler to use and manage than Manual Sync. That said, you may not want all of certain content types to sync with your device. For example, while a Zune 4 or Zune 8 is perfect for enjoying music and podcasts, its tiny screen makes it more difficult to enjoy pictures. And as for videos, forget about it.

Here are some basic rules for choosing how to sync:

◆ **If the device has enough storage, use Smart Sync:** If you can get every last song, picture, video, and podcast from your media library onto the device, do so. A Zune 120 should be enough storage for all but the most demanding users. Smart Sync is easier.

◆ **Unless you have specific needs, choose music first:** Choose music at the expense of other nonaudio content. Put simply, today's Zune is optimized for audio. In this case, you might choose All Music under Smart Sync and then [*Content*] I choose for the other content types.

◆ **Understand what you're getting into with Manual Sync:** The Zune's manual sync functionality is a bit harder to manage. There is a single place in the Zune UI to see what you're syncing to a particular device, but it's not clear.

Manual Sync

Suppose, for whatever reason, you've decided (or been forced) to manually sync content from your Zune media library to your device.

Here's how it works, using music as an example. As you navigate around your music library in the Zune PC software, you'll notice that you can manually sync artists, albums, and even individual songs with your device. To manually sync an artist, album, or individual song (or songs) you need to right-click one or more of those items and choose Sync with *device name* (where *device name* is the name of your Zune device) from the pop-up menu that appears (see Figure 14-46).

Figure 14-46: Manually syncing artists and albums isn't exactly intuitive.

When you choose this kind of synchronization, whatever content you've selected is copied to the device immediately, and the Zune creates something called a *Sync Group*, which is a collection of items that are synced together as a whole to a device. In the Songs column, you'll see a tiny On Device icon (in the shape of a Zune device) appear next to each song that is synced with the device.

Secret When you right-click individual songs in the Songs column, you'll see an additional option that's not available when you click artists or albums: never Sync with *device*. This provides you with some fine-tuning, so even if you choose to automatically sync everything by a particular artist, for example, you can manually exclude certain songs.

The problem with manual sync, of course, is that it's obvious where you go to see and manage what you're syncing. As you navigate around your music collection, tagging individual artists, albums, and songs for sync, the list of synced items is growing ever larger. You'll see those little On Device icons sprouting up here and there. How do you manage this mess?

As it turns out, this information is managed from within the Device section of the Zune PC software. This makes sense when you think about it, because it's certainly possible to own two or more Zune devices and configure sync differently for each. Therefore, to see which songs you're syncing, navigate to Device ⇨ Status. Then click the View Sync Groups button. You'll see a screen similar to the one shown in Figure 14-47.

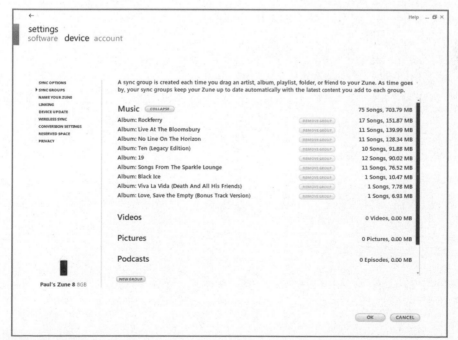

Figure 14-47: You can manage manual sync from within the **Device** area of the Zune PC software.

To stop syncing particular artists, albums, or songs, just right-click as appropriate. What you will see varies according to which items you've chosen to sync, and then which items you're choosing here in the UI. For example, say you've chosen to sync all music from the band Collective Soul. The way you did that was to right-click Collective Soul in the Artist list in Collection ⇨ Music and choose Sync to *device*. Okay, so now you navigate to Device ⇨ Music and you want to remove some items. Here are the options:

- ◆ **Right-click on the artist's name:** If you right-click on the artist's name in the left-most column, called Sync Groups, you see an option titled Remove group. If you select this, Zune will stop syncing music from this artist and will immediately remove all of the music that was previously synced to the device. (Obviously, the music will remain on your PC and in your Zune media library.)

- ◆ **Right-click on an individual album within a sync group:** You can delete individual albums from the device by choosing Remove group. When you do this, the album is deleted from the device only. More important, it is removed from the Sync Group as well (in this case, all music by Collective Soul), so when you sync the device in the future, music from that album will no longer be synced.

- ◆ **Right-click on an individual song within a sync group:** You can also delete individual songs from the device by choosing Remove group. As with albums, the song is deleted from the device and removed from the Sync Group.

If you navigate back to Collection ⇨ Music, you'll see that songs you have removed from Sync Groups have a small "Excluded" icon next to them instead of an On Device icon.

It's also worth pointing out that Sync Groups aren't always as clear-cut as an individual group. As you sync more and more content to your devices, a number of Sync Groups will appear, some of which are more arbitrary collections of music. And, of course, you'll have Sync Groups that comprise other content types such as podcasts, pictures, and video.

In any case, as you can see, manual sync is a lot of work. It's not so bad if you want to sync only a couple of items of a particular content type, but it can quickly get out of hand if you start adding more and more items. Smart Sync is the way to go if possible.

Wireless Sync

The type of synchronization we've been discussing thus far is very similar to the way that you would sync iPods, iPhones, and other portable digital media devices, but the Zune offers a fairly unique feature, called *wireless sync*, that enables you to synchronize content over your wireless home network.

Wireless sync works with all Zune models, including the older Zune 30, and requires an 802.11b/g Wi-Fi wireless network. (The PC can be connected via wired Ethernet.) Obviously, this kind of sync is slower than a USB tether, especially if you're stuck using the older, slower, and generally less desirable 802.11b variant. It's not particularly battery-friendly either. For this reason, Zune devices will not automatically sync wirelessly with your PC-based Zune library unless the device is powered somehow (either by a dock or a USB sync cable that's plugged into electric power with an optional Zune power adapter).

You can, however, trigger a manual wireless sync via the device. To do so, however, you must first configure the device for wireless sync using the Zune PC software. After ensuring that the device is connected to the PC via USB—you can't configure this feature otherwise—navigate to Settings ⇨ Device and then choose Wireless from the list of options. You'll see a screen like that shown in Figure 14-48. Click Set Up Wireless Sync to continue.

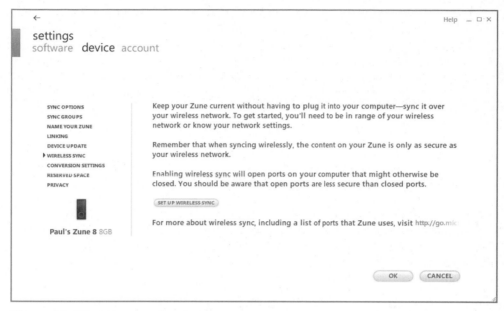

← Help ─ □ ·×

settings
software **device** account

SYNC OPTIONS
SYNC GROUPS
NAME YOUR ZUNE
LINKING
DEVICE UPDATE
▸ WIRELESS SYNC
CONVERSION SETTINGS
RESERVED SPACE
PRIVACY

Keep your Zune current without having to plug it into your computer—sync it over your wireless network. To get started, you'll need to be in range of your wireless network or know your network settings.

Remember that when syncing wirelessly, the content on your Zune is only as secure as your wireless network.

Enabling wireless sync will open ports on your computer that might otherwise be closed. You should be aware that open ports are less secure than closed ports.

(SET UP WIRELESS SYNC)

For more about wireless sync, including a list of ports that Zune uses, visit http://go.mi

Paul's Zune 8 8GB

(OK)   (CANCEL)

Figure 14-48: Before you can wirelessly sync with your Zune device, you must configure this feature in the Zune PC software.

At this point, the Zune software will search for available wireless networks. If you're connected to a wireless network already, Zune will ask if you'd like to use that network for wireless sync. If not, you can choose the appropriate wireless network from a list. Click Finish and Zune will connect to the wireless network and configure the device accordingly.

Secret

Can't connect? Zune has certain requirements for wireless networks, including compatibility with a limited range of wireless security technologies. These include open networks with no encryption (which, obviously, you would never do), WEP (64-bit or 128-bit key), WPA-PSK (TKIP), WPA-PSK (AES), WPA2-PSK (AES, not supported on Zune 30), and WPA2-PSK (TKIP, not supported on Zune 30). For more information and wireless sync troubleshooting tips, please visit the Microsoft Web site: `go.microsoft.com/fwlink/?linkid=103432`.

Once that's completed, perform a normal, wired sync with the device. Then unplug it from the PC to test wireless sync. On the device, navigate to Settings ⇨ Wireless ⇨ Sync and then select Sync with PC. The device will connect to your wireless network, connect to your PC, and perform a sync, albeit a bit slowly.

Aside from rampant abuse of battery power, why might you find wireless sync desirable? First, many people are now in the habit of charging their digital devices in a central location, perhaps using one of those charging stations you may have seen. This way, when they head off to work in the morning, everything is charged, ready, and accessible. By enabling wireless sync, you can charge your Zune along with your smart phone and other devices, and not worry about carting it over to the PC every few days to sync manually.

Second, and an arguably more interesting use for this technology, is home entertainment. Many people keep a digital media device dock next to their home theater so they can use this device with the best stereo in the house. (Note that because the flash-based Zunes don't support video out, this scenario would only include audio content such as music and podcasts with these particular devices.) If you keep your Zune by the home theater with an AV dock, you can ensure that it's always up-to-date, as it will be silently syncing back to the PC in the other room while it's docked.

Finally, many users simply forget to sync. Enabling wireless sync means that all you have to do is charge the device within range of your wireless network (typically almost anywhere in your home) and it will sync automatically.

Updating Zune

As with any electronic device, make sure your Zune is always up-to-date. That's because Microsoft often ships updates, both for the Zune's PC-based software and for the firmware that runs on the device itself. (For whatever its worth, Microsoft also updates Zune Marketplace and Zune Social regularly, but because those updates occur in the cloud, you don't have to do any work to stay up-to-date.)

The Zune PC software should alert you periodically when new updates are available. However, you can manually check for software updates by navigating to Settings ➪ Software ➪ General. Then click the Check for Updates button in the Software Updates section.

Likewise, the Zune PC software should periodically alert you when updates are made available for whatever Zune device(s) you own. To manually check for a firmware update, plug in the device and then navigate to Settings ➪ Device ➪ Device Update in the Zune PC software.

tip The Zune 8/16, Zune 30, and Zune 120 all use slightly different versions of the Zune firmware, so Microsoft makes different updates available for each of these devices.

Secret One feature that's not obvious is that you can restore your Zune device in various ways. If you just want to erase the content on the device and start over, you can do so from within the Zune PC software, but if you want to literally restore the Zune to factory condition—that is, with the firmware version that originally came on the device—you need to do that directly from the Zune itself. The process is somewhat complicated, but is described in Microsoft Knowledge Base Article 927001 (support.microsoft.com/kb/927001). Note that restoring your Zune in this fashion will not restore the music, photo, and video content that originally came on the device, so be sure to back that up before restoring the device. You can back up Zune-based content—that is, copy it back to the PC—by navigating to Device ➪ Music (or Device ➪ Videos or Device ➪ Pictures) in the Zune PC software, right-clicking the content, and choosing Copy to Collection.

Summary

Microsoft's Zune platform may not ship as part of Windows 7, but as with the company's Windows Live products and services, it extends Windows in fun and interesting ways and is an important step toward Microsoft's future platforms. The Zune PC software and services are free and available to all Windows users, even those who choose not to purchase a Zune portable media device. Those who do opt to buy into the Zune platform fully—by purchasing a Zune device and, perhaps, subscribing to Zune Pass—will discover a highly integrated digital media platform that, yes, takes a page from the Apple playbook but does so in a decidedly Microsoft way. Put simply, Zune is an excellent opportunity to see the future of Microsoft's digital media platform … today.

Digital Media in the Living Room

Chapter

15

◆ ◆

In This Chapter

Understanding how Media Center has evolved over the years

Seeing how Media Center has changed in Windows 7

Configuring Windows Media Center

Touring the Media Center user interface

Accessing the Media Center digital media experiences

Extending Media Center into other rooms with Xbox 360 and other Extenders

Synchronizing Media Center with portable devices and laptops

Using Media Center to burn your own CDs and DVDs

◆ ◆

Windows Media Center is one of the most innovative and entertaining technologies Microsoft has ever added to Windows. Essentially a wonderful, remote control–accessible front end to all of your digital media content, Windows Media Center helps you enjoy live and recorded TV shows, and digital videos, photos, and music. Media Center is equally at home in your living room or bedroom as it is in the home office or on a laptop during a cross-country flight. And in Windows 7, the Media Center environment has further evolved with added functionality and an improved user interface. It has also been made available in more versions of the operating system instead of just one or two as it was with Windows XP and Vista. Thus, it will reach a far wider audience than it did previously. In this chapter, we examine Microsoft's digital media solution for the living room, Media Center, as well as related products such as Media Center Extenders.

A Short History of Media Center

In January 2002, shortly after the release of Windows XP, Microsoft announced that it was working on software, then code-named Freestyle, that would extend the reach of Windows into the living room. Freestyle, which was eventually renamed to Windows XP Media Center Edition, was really just Windows XP Professional with the Media Center application and various Media Center–related services added on top. Media Center, the application, was and is a user interface designed for use with a remote control (although it works fine with a mouse and keyboard too, and, in Windows 7, with touch screens). This is what Microsoft calls the *ten-foot user interface* (compared to the mouse and keyboard interface, which the company refers to as the *two-foot user interface*.)

The original Media Center version included all of the basic features you've come to associate with Media Center in the intervening years. It supported a simple menu-based user interface with options for recording TV, watching live TV, controlling cable set-top boxes via a so-called *IR blaster*, and enjoying digital media experiences like music, pictures, videos, and DVD movies (see Figure 15-1). Windows XP Media Center shipped as a special new version of Windows in October 2002 and was available only with select Media Center PCs, a new generation of media-capable computers that, it was hoped, consumers would purchase and use in their home theater setups. Not surprisingly, the software was well received by reviewers, but it didn't sell very well because Media Center PCs were relatively expensive, and setting up TV tuner cards to work with cable signals was (and, sadly, still can be) difficult.

The second version of Windows XP Media Center Edition, code-named Harmony, shipped a year later as Windows XP Media Center Edition 2004. This version was also available only with new PCs and added support for FM radio tuner cards, online services, and functionality that Microsoft had previously left to the two-foot experience, like CD ripping. As you might expect, the product also included various UI and performance improvements as well.

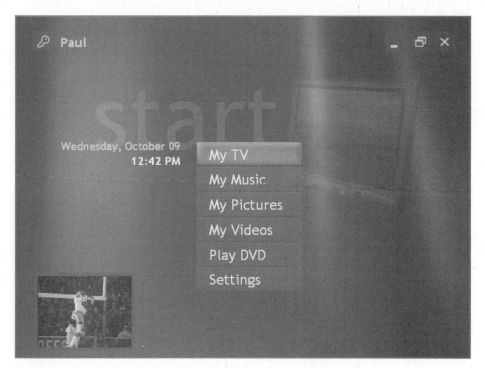

Figure 15-1: The original Windows XP Media Center Edition

In late 2004, Microsoft shipped the most extensive Media Center update yet, Windows XP Media Center Edition 2005, code-named Symphony. This version sported dramatic user interface improvements with a scrolling main menu, a much simpler setup experience, vastly improved TV picture quality with fewer MPEG-2 compression artifacts, and support for up to three TV tuners, one of which can be an over-the-air (OTA) HDTV tuner. Microsoft also added support for Media Center Extenders, hardware devices that resemble set-top boxes and enable you to access the Media Center experience remotely via your home network to other TVs in the house: that way, you can be watching a live TV show on one TV, with an Extender, and watching a recorded TV show on a different TV, using the Media Center PC. Media Center 2005 supported up to five Extenders, depending on the capabilities of the hardware on which the system resided. Microsoft also shipped Media Center Extender software for its Xbox video game console, enabling that device to be used like a dedicated Media Center Extender.

Although late 2005 didn't see a major Windows Media Center release, Microsoft did ship a Media Center update that year, ignominiously named Windows XP Media Center Edition 2005 Update Rollup 2 (UR2). This free update to Media Center 2005 added support for the Xbox 360 and its built-in Media Center Extender functionality, a feature called Away Mode that let newer Media Center PC models with modern power management features move quickly between on and off states that more closely resemble TV sets than PCs; DVD changer support; a new DVD burning utility; and support for up to DTV tuners). UR2 also added a wonderful new video Zoom feature that helps make 4:3 TV pictures look better on wide-screen displays, support for digital radio, and various bug fixes and performance improvements. Windows XP Media Center Edition 2005 UR2 is shown in Figure 15-2.

Figure 15-2: Windows XP Media Center Edition 2005 with UR2 was fast, stable, and lean looking.

Aside from the actual products that were rolled out over these years, Microsoft made some of its biggest improvements to Media Center from a marketing standpoint. Although the Media Center software was never released as a standalone add-on for all Windows users, Microsoft dropped the price of this XP version and stopped requiring PC makers to ship it only with new PCs that included TV tuners. Thus, over the years, Media Center quickly became one of the best-selling versions of Windows XP, and it's now installed on millions of PCs worldwide. Many Media Center users don't use the TV functionality at all, in fact, but use the software just to enjoy digital media. Today, Windows Media Center is a mature product that's benefited greatly from years of user feedback and constant improvements.

With Windows Vista, Microsoft stopped offering Media Center via only special Windows product editions and instead offered the software via two versions, Windows Vista Home Premium and Ultimate. The software's user interface was dramatically overhauled to better support 16´7 wide-screen HDTV displays and the underpinnings were enhanced in various ways, including support for the CableCARD cable TV standard. Sadly, Windows Vista also marked the end of a long line of Media Center yearly updates; despite promising to ship an interim update that would finish the UI changes that were only partially made across Media Center in Windows Vista, Microsoft never really delivered (Figure 15-3). Instead, it shipped a series of much smaller updates over the intervening years, including a so-called TV Pack in 2008 that added support for international television standards and a few other low-level changes. Unlike most previous Media Center updates, the TV Pack was made available only to users who purchased new Vista-based Media Center PCs from major PC makers. In other words, it never shipped to the public as a free download.

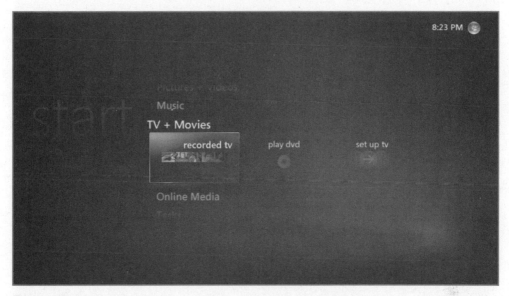

Figure 15-3: The Windows Vista version of Media Center was the most comprehensive yet, but the new UI was only partially implemented across the system.

Media Center in Windows 7

With Windows 7, Microsoft has made some big changes to Media Center. First, the software is no longer available only in two of the product editions. However, you still can't purchase Windows Media Center separately from Windows. Instead, you get Windows Media Center with three different Windows 7 product editions: Windows 7 Home Premium, Windows 7 Professional, and Windows 7 Ultimate.

Secret Okay, you can technically get Media Center in *four* Windows 7 product editions, as it's also available in Windows 7 Enterprise. However, this version of Windows 7 is made available only to volume license business customers and cannot be purchased by individuals, either at retail stores or with a new PC.

Secret Sadly, the version of Media Center that ships with Windows 7 is *still* only a half-realized version of where Microsoft hopes to take Media Center in the future. That is, while much of the Media Center interface changed dramatically back in Windows Vista, many of the subpages you'll navigate through while using this system in Windows 7 have not really changed since Windows XP Media Center Edition 2005, aside from a few theme changes to make these pages look more like the Windows 7 version.

In any event, from a high-level standpoint, Media Center has been upgraded in Windows Vista to be more intuitive and obvious. If you're used to XP Media Center versions, the changes will be a little jarring; but if you're familiar with the Vista version, you'll be right at home because the user interface differences between Media Center in Vista and in Windows 7 are very subtle. Microsoft hopes that the new user interface will help users find the content they want more quickly, with less navigating (and remote control button pushing). At a low-level, Media Center has been architected to be more scalable, so that Microsoft's partners can more easily extend Media Center to do more. It is hoped that this will result in more and better online experiences, applications, and other software that works both with and within Media Center.

Media Center also now supports a technology called CableCARD, which allows specially manufactured Media Center PCs to directly control cable systems without a jury-rigged IR blaster and cable set-top box. What CableCARD does is replace a cable box with a card that is plugged directly into the computer. It's a great idea, especially for anyone who has had to suffer through the performance issues incurred by IR blasting.

Secret

Stupidly, Windows Media Center's support for CableCARD cannot be added after the fact, nor can it be added to a PC that you have built yourself. Instead, CableCARD support can only be provided by a major PC maker at the time you purchase your PC. That's because Hollywood is freaked by the notion that users now have access to pristine, perfect digital copies of their HD movies and television shows, so it has created a copy protection scheme that ensures that digital content is protected from theft. This scheme is present in Windows 7, as it was in Vista. If it weren't, CableCARD and other HD technologies (such as support for HD Blu-Ray discs) simply wouldn't work. But the Draconian nature of Hollywood's control over this content makes it a lot harder on consumers. Go figure.

Finally, there's a fourth major difference. The version of Media Center in Windows 7 will not work with first-generation Media Center Extender devices, including the software-based version that shipped for the original Xbox. Instead, you will need to use a Vista-era Extender with the version of Media Center in Windows 7. This includes the Xbox 360 or a growing lineup of second-generation Extender-enabled devices, including set-top boxes, televisions, and DVD players. We will examine Media Center's Extender capabilities later in this chapter.

Configuring Media Center

Before you do anything in Media Center, you should configure it to work with your PC's display and sound system, Internet connection, and, if present, your TV signal. Unlike any other Windows feature, Media Center configuration is a bit time consuming and requires you to be prepared in advance. Unless you've done this before, plan on spending about an hour configuring Media Center for the first time.

When you launch Media Center for the first time, you will see a Media Center animation and then the screen shown in Figure 15-4, which enables you to navigate to the right and left and discover Media Center features and functionality. This is new to Windows 7.

When you click the Continue button, you can choose between Express or Custom initial configuration methods, or you can learn more via a third option, as shown in Figure 15-5. You can also optionally choose to run setup later by clicking Exit.

Figure 15-4: In Windows 7, Media Center first presents some promotional information about the product.

Figure 15-5: Media Center's notification dialogs aren't really separate windows, but are instead part of the underlying display. However, you still need to deal with these alerts before moving on and doing anything else in Media Center.

If you click Learn More, Media Center will navigate to another new Windows 7 feature: the Learn How section of MSN Video, as shown in Figure 15-6. Here, you can watch short instructional videos which explain how Media Center's various features work.

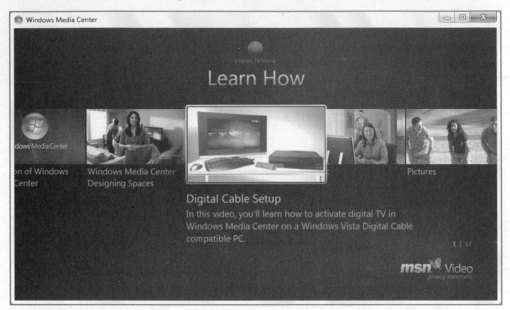

Figure 15-6: In Windows 7, Media Center includes some fun built-in help in the form of video how-to's.

> **tip** You must be connected to the Internet to watch these videos, as they are hosted on Microsoft's MSN service.

If you choose Express setup, Media Center will utilize the default settings. Generally speaking, we do not recommend allowing Microsoft to configure any of its software with the company's default settings, so our advice is to not choose the Express setup option. If you do choose Express setup, Media Center will be configured to download media information from the Internet and perform other Internet-based tasks you may not approve of.

If you choose the third option, Custom setup—which roughly corresponds to the setup experience used by previous Media Center versions—you will need to step through the Media Center Setup Wizard manually. Though it is a bit time consuming, we recommend you choose this option: even if you ultimately choose the options Microsoft would have configured for you automatically in Express options, at least this way you know exactly what you are getting—and you only have to do it once.

> **tip** Media Center actually enables you to skip the configuration stage and configure Media Center settings later. To do so, click the Exit button.

Running the Media Center Setup Wizard

To configure Media Center manually, choose Custom in the Welcome to Windows Media Center screen described previously. This launches the Media Center Setup wizard, as shown in Figure 15-7.

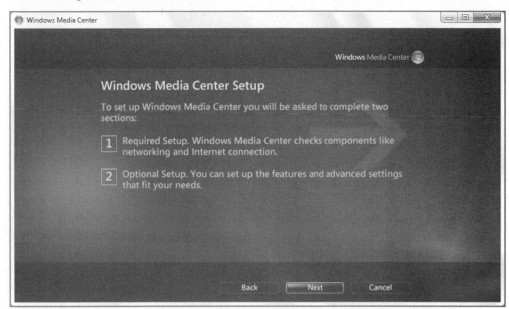

Figure 15-7: Media Center Setup will guide you through many of the configuration tasks you'll want to complete before using this interface.

The wizard steps you through the various options Media Center needs to run correctly, including your Internet connection (which includes a Join Wireless Network Wizard if you utilize a wireless connection), whether you'd like to join Microsoft's Customer Experience Program to help the company improve Media Center, and so on. We'll explain all of these steps as you continue through this section.

There are two sections to Windows Media Center Setup, Required Setup and Optional Setup. In Required Setup, the Setup wizard walks you through the process of configuring those features that are required for Windows Media Center to function properly.

You will experience the following configuration tasks in the Required section:

◆ **Help Improve Windows Media Center:** Here you will be asked if you'd like to join Microsoft's Customer Experience Improvement Program (CEIP). What Microsoft is really asking you is whether you'd like to have your computer automatically send anonymous reports about Media Center performance and reliability to the company over the Internet. In general, this is a wise option to enable because your Media Center experience will be aggregated with that of other Media Center users around the world to help find and fix issues with the software. But if you're a privacy aficionado and not particularly trusting of Microsoft, you can opt out of this program.

In this first Required Setup screen, you'll also have the option to read Microsoft's privacy statement. Microsoft is serious about your privacy. I know this because I have read their privacy statement. You should as well.

♦ **Get the Most from Windows Media Center:** In the second screen, you will be asked whether you'd like to let Media Center connect automatically to the Internet to automatically download music information, album art, and other data. Be very careful about allowing Microsoft to do this: if you have carefully crafted your ripped CD metadata, you might want to select No here. If, however, your digital media files are in need of some help—that is, you don't have album art associated with each of your ripped CD albums—you should choose Yes. Media Center's interface is very visual, and it looks and works better when it can display graphical representations of your digital media.

After this, you'll be told that the required components have been set up. You're probably thinking that wasn't so bad, but despite the naming conventions used, it is the Optional Setup section, shown in Figure 15-8, that is the more difficult. Therefore, we'll look at these customizations far more closely. In this section of Setup, you configure your TV tuners, TV signal and program guide (if your PC has one or more TV tuners installed), and your display, speakers, and media libraries. The advice here is simple: if you are going to be using Media Center at all, especially for watching and recording TV, you really need to take the time to go through each of these steps.

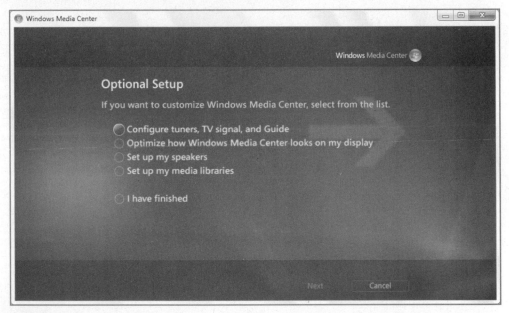

Figure 15-8: You've only just begun: the Optional Setup steps are far more time-consuming than the Required Setup section.

You will only see the first Optional Setup item, Configure the TV signal, if Windows Media Center detects that you have TV tuner hardware installed on your PC.

Configuring TV Tuners, Signal, and Guide

If your PC includes at least one TV tuner card that is connected to a TV signal of some sort, refer to your Media Center PC's or TV tuner card's documentation for information on setting up the required hardware. Then, you can configure Media Center to access and record televisions shows, as follows:

1. In Optional Setup, choose Configure tuners, TV signal, and Guide.
2. The wizard will ask you to confirm the region in which you live (United States in our case).

Secret

In case it's not obvious, you must have a live Internet connection in order to configure TV support within Media Center. In fact, Media Center relies on an Internet connection to keep its program guide, through which it displays the available TV shows at any given time, up to date. Although it's possible but not advisable to turn off the PC's Internet connection once you've configured its TV features, you will absolutely have to be connected to the Internet to complete this part of Setup.

3. Enter your ZIP code so that Media Center can provide the appropriate program guide data. Once you enter this, you'll be asked to agree to the Program Guide Terms of Service. (Unlike with services such as TiVo, the Media Center program guide is absolutely free.)
4. You'll also be asked to agree to the PlayReady PC Runtime EULA (End User License Agreement). PlayReady is Microsoft's Digital Rights Management (DRM) solution and it is used by licensees like Netflix to provide consumers with access to digitally streamed protected content. Media Center actually downloads and installs the PlayReady components once you agree to this EULA, which is an annoying extra process that wasn't present in Windows Vista or previous Media Center versions.
5. Media Center will examine your TV signal(s), another time-consuming process. When that is done, Media Center presents you with a list of the TV signals it has found. Here, you can choose to configure the system's TV features with the signals that were found, or you can force a redetection or try to configure the signals manually. In our experience, automatic configuration works best when you're connected to a TV signal via a cable set-top box and are using IR blasting in order to control the box's channel-changing functionality. Manual configuration works better for a direct TV connection, where a coaxial cable comes out of the wall and connects directly to your TV tuner card (that is, there is no set-top box), or with an over-the-air (OTA) HD antenna. Because the manual method always works and requires more thought, we'll cover that here. Choose the option titled "No, let me configure my TV signal manually" and then click Next.
6. In the next screen, you choose what type of TV signal you receive: Cable, Satellite, or Antenna. If you choose Cable or Satellite, you're asked whether you have a set-top box. If you do, Setup will walk you through a series of steps in which you configure the system to control your set-top box so that you can change channels, raise and lower the volume, and perform other actions from within Media Center while using the Media Center remote control. If you don't have a set-top box, or you are using an antenna-based configuration, you can simply skip that part. (If

you are using an antenna, you will be asked to choose between analog and digital (ATSC) types. Most likely, you are using a digital antenna.)

7. Next, you are asked if you need to configure another TV signal. This is because Media Center supports multiple TV signals. You might have a cable connection with two tuners, enabling you to watch one channel while you record another; or you might have two different kinds of signals, such as a cable signal and an OTA antenna-based signal. If you do have multiple signals, choosing Yes here will enable you to walk through the previous several steps for the next signal. Otherwise, click No and continue.

8. Next, Media Center will download the program guide. This, too, might take a few minutes depending on which type of TV signal you configured. Click Finish.

Secret Media Center downloads about two weeks' worth of program guide data at a time. The first time you do this, it will take a few minutes. But in the future, the guide download will occur in the background, and you won't even be aware it's happening. In this way, the program guide will always be up to date.

Optimizing the Display for Media Center

Media Center works with multi-monitor setups, which makes a lot of sense because many users will utilize the PC display for work and a separate HDTV display for Media Center. Therefore, in the first phase of this wizard, you'll be asked to verify that Media Center is appearing on the correct display. If it is, click Yes. Otherwise, click No and you will be able to move Media Center output to the correct display.

In the next step, you optimize Media Center for your display. Media Center natively supports these display types:

- ◆ **PC monitor:** For a CRT monitor connected via a VGA cable.
- ◆ **Built-in display:** For a notebook computer.
- ◆ **Flat panel:** For a flat-panel monitor connected via a VGA or a DVI cable.
- ◆ **Television:** For any type of TV connected via composite, S-video, DVI, VGA, HDMI, or component cable.
- ◆ **Projector:** For a dedicated projector connected via composite, S-video, DVI, VGA, HDMI, or component cable.

Choose the correct display type, as shown in Figure 15-9.

After you've chosen the display type, the wizard will prompt you to choose the Display Width (really, the aspect ratio) of your display. You have two options: standard (4:3) and Widescreen (16:9). Again, if you're not sure what to choose here, consult your display's documentation. (Or just look at the display: standard-width screens are basically square, whereas wide-screen displays are wide.) The wizard then checks the system and prompts you about the resolution of the display, as shown in Figure 15-10.

You can accept the value it provides (which you should do if it is correct) or select No. If you choose the latter option, you will be presented with a list of possible display resolutions, based on the capabilities of your display and whether you're using a wide-screen aspect ratio.

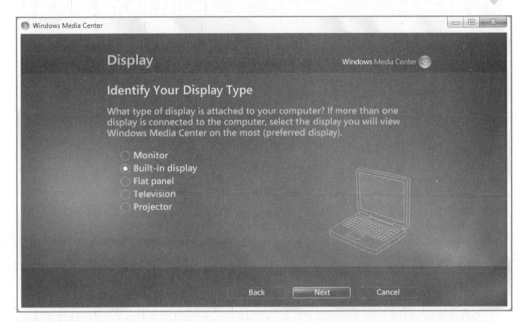

Figure 15-9: Media Center natively supports several display types and optimizes its display based on what you choose here.

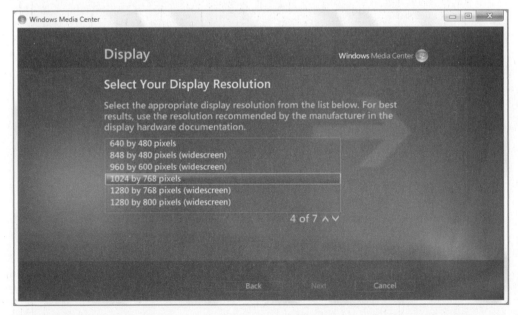

Figure 15-10: In general, you should ensure that Media Center is using the highest resolution supported by your display.

Next, you can optionally configure your display's controls, including calibrating the display's onscreen centering and sizing, aspect ratio, brightness, contrast, and RGB color balance. These controls are less important on VGA, DVI, and HDMI connections, but analog connections like composite and S-Video often benefit from some fine-tuning. If you're using Media Center on a PC display, simply click Finish This Wizard. Otherwise, you might want to take the time to fine-tune the display.

Configuring the Speakers

In the next part of Optional Setup for Media Center Setup, you will configure a number of options related to the speakers that are attached to your Media Center PC.

First, you'll be asked to configure the speaker connection type, as shown in Figure 15-11. This is a fairly technical question, and one that will differ wildly from system to system, so you may unfortunately need to consult your PC's documentation to make the right choice. (Or, you may be a stereo geek. No one is judging you either way.)

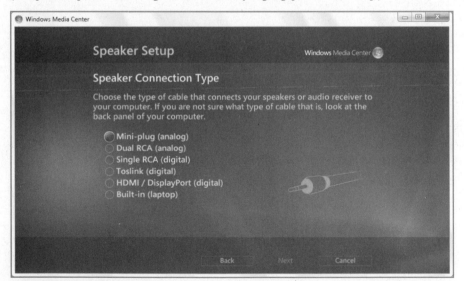

Figure 15-11: Time to reach for the documentation.

Next, you'll configure the number of speakers. Media Center supports three speaker configurations: two speakers (stereo), 5.1 surround sound (two front speakers, two rear speakers, and a center speaker), or 7.1 surround sound (two front speakers, two rear speakers, two side speakers, and a center speaker). Choose the configuration that most closely matches your hardware, and click Next.

In the Test Your Speakers window, click Test to ensure that everything works as expected, as shown in Figure 15-12. If you don't hear the test sounds in some or all of the speakers, the wizard will help you troubleshoot.

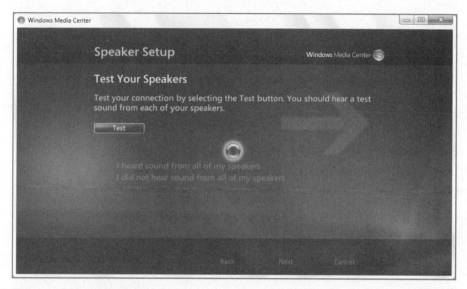

Figure 15-12: You'll hear a number of tones, hopefully in each of your connected speakers.

Secret

Media Center's speaker setup is quite a bit more limited than the speaker configuration options you get in Control Panel. There, you can configure stereo, quadraphonic, 5.1 surround, and 7.1 surround speaker setups. You can reach this control panel in various ways, but the most obvious is to right-click the volume icon in the tray notification area, select Playback devices from the menu that appears, and then select your speakers in the resulting dialog and click Configure. As shown in Figure 15-13, this control panel also enables you to test individual speakers separately.

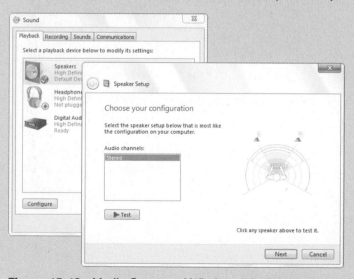

Figure 15-13: Media Center and Windows 7 both have their own ways of configuring sound.

Setting Up Your Digital Media Libraries

In the next phase, you can configure which folders Media Center monitors to fill your Music, Pictures, and Videos libraries with content. This is an interesting legacy feature from previous Windows versions and isn't strictly necessary. Here's why: by default, Media Center actually utilizes your Music, Pictures, and Videos libraries to determine which content it can use. That is, it monitors exactly the same physical folders that you configure in the Music, Pictures, and Video libraries. If you've already configured these Libraries to work the way you want, there may be no reason to change things here as well.

Secret   Folders you configure as Monitored Folders in Windows Media Center will actually be added to the appropriate library, so if you configure Media Center to watch, say, the D: drive for some reason, the contents of this drive will be aggregated by your Music, Pictures, and Videos libraries as well.

Secret   Intriguingly, Media Center offers an option that's lacking in Windows Media Player. That is, you can configure Media Center to stop monitoring default Library folders like C:\Users*Your User Name*\My Music, C:\Users*Your User Name*\ My Pictures, and C:\Users*Your User Name*\My Videos. Why you'd want to do this is unclear; and why it's possible in Media Center but not Windows Media Player is also unclear.

When you're done stepping through the Optional Setup section, select I am finished and then click Next. Media Center tells you you're done and provides yet another button (this time marked Finish) to click.

Exciting, right? Not quite. As it turns out, you're not really done.

Configuring Media Center Features after Setup

After you have configured Windows Media Center with the Setup Wizard, you'll be presented with the Media Center Start page. This is shown in Figure 15-14.

You can examine the finer points of this user interface in the next section, but for now, we need to discuss how you can configure Media Center further after completing the Setup Wizard. Some of the configuration information you'll see directly corresponds to features you configured in the wizard (or even runs part of the wizard in some cases). But you can access many more Media Center features from outside the wizard. For this reason, it's important to step through the Media Center Settings functionality to ensure that the system is configured exactly the way you want it.

You can actually access Settings from virtually anywhere in Media Center, but the simplest method is to navigate to the Start page (press the green Start button on the screen or on the Media Center remote) and then scroll down the main menu to Tasks. Then, click the Settings link, which is the default option. Shown in Figure 15-15, Settings includes links to several major areas.

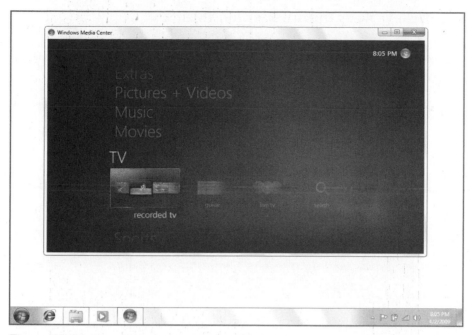

Figure 15-14: The Media Center Start page is your home base for all of Media Center's experiences.

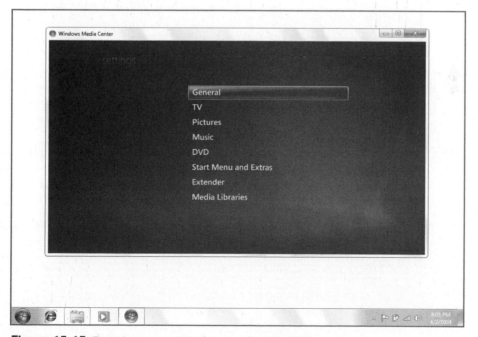

Figure 15-15: From here, a world of customization awaits you.

tip Old-school Media Center users will recognize that the Setup interface still looks like older, XP-era versions of the software. Microsoft has done precious little to update some parts of Media Center, and this is one obvious example. A different text style is used here as well. For example, all menu items are capitalized in Settings (like "Startup and Window Behavior") whereas they are not everywhere else in Windows 7 and in Media Center (as in "Startup and window behavior"). Not to beat it to death, but no one ever accused Microsoft of consistency.

There's little need to walk you through each and every feature here. Instead, in the Secret box that follows, we will highlight options that are new to Windows 7, those options that contain unlikely benefits, and the options you should absolutely consider changing.

Secret

General

The General Settings screen is shown in Figure 15-16. If you are using Media Center as the main interface to your TV in the living room, do the following:

1. Navigate into General ⇨ Startup and Window Behavior.
2. Select the top option, Always keep Media Center on top.
3. Select the option titled Start Windows Media Center when Windows starts.
4. Disable Show taskbar notifications, because you'll likely never see the Windows taskbar anyway.

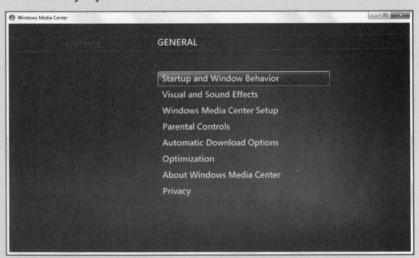

Figure 15-16: Here, you configure Media Center options that apply throughout the Media Center interface.

Got kids? Use the Parental Controls feature to access a suite of excellent ratings-based limitations that will prevent your children from viewing TV shows, DVD movies, or other media you find objectionable. You input a four-digit code to unlock these shows for yourself. Parental controls can be found in General ⇨ Parental Controls.

If you need to rerun Setup, or just part of Setup, you can do so from within the General Settings section. Click Windows Media Center Setup and then choose from Set Up Internet Connection, Set Up TV Signal, Set Up Your Speakers, Configure Your TV or Monitor, Join Wireless Network (if you have a wireless card), or Run Setup Again. That last option enables you to run through the entire Media Center Setup process again.

Media Center includes an unintentionally hilarious but useful optimization kludge: In General ⇨ Optimization, you can configure Media Center to reboot every morning at 4:00 a.m. (or any other time). This clears out any problems and is especially useful for people who use a Media Center as their TV interface. No, it's not elegant, but it does work wonders for stability.

TV

If you're hearing impaired, you can enable Closed Captioning, which is significantly improved in this version, by selecting TV ⇨ Closed Captioning. Closed Captioning can be on, off, or on when muted. Naturally, the quality of the actual captioning is dependent on the content creators who, unfortunately, have no federal requirements related to accuracy.

Pictures

Be sure to change at least two options in the Picture settings. First, navigate into Slide Shows and enable the option titled Show pictures in random order for better slide shows. Then, consider changing the transition time from 12 seconds to something smaller, like 5 seconds. You can also optionally enable captions (Show picture information), which is useful only if you've named your photographs logically (for example, "Day at the beach 06") instead of accepting the camera defaults (for example, P0000537).

There's also a Slide Show Screen Saver feature that's new to Windows 7. It's enabled by default and causes Media Center to slip into a full-screen photo slide show when the system has been idle for a set number of minutes. You can see the configuration screen for this feature in Figure 15-17.

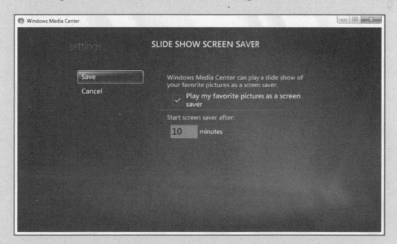

Figure 15-17: Configure the new slide show screen saver from here.

continues

continued

Also new to Windows 7 is a Favorite Pictures slide show, which automatically grabs pictures you've rated as four or five stars (typically in Windows Live Photo Gallery, as explained in Chapter 12). However, you can optionally configure the Favorite Pictures slide show to use all pictures or pictures in a particular folder.

Finally, Windows 7 has added yet another excellent (and related) feature to Media Center: the capability to rate pictures with the numeric keyboard on your PC or, better yet, the number keys on your Media Center remote. To enable this, navigate into Pictures ⇨ Ratings and then check the option titled "Let me use shortcut keys to set ratings." When you do so, you can then rate pictures as they appear on your TV or other screen, such as when you're viewing a slide show, as shown in Figure 15-18.

Figure 15-18: Now you can rate pictures as you watch a slide show.

Music

As with Pictures, Media Center now sports a Favorite Music playlist and a way to rate music as it's playing. You can access these options from Settings ⇨ Music.

Start Menu and Extras

This entire Settings section is new to Windows 7. From here, you can determine which items appear on the Media Center Start page, how various Media Center Extras behave, and which applications appear in the Extras library in Windows Media Center. This latter option is shown in Figure 15-19.

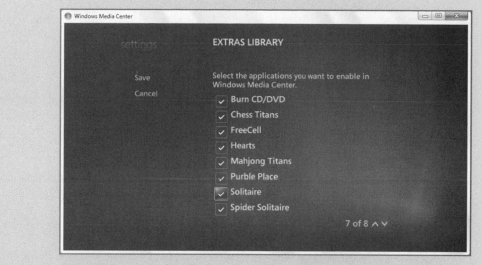

Figure 15-19: Media Center comes with a number of built-in Extras, and you can determine which show up in the UI here.

Media Libraries

If you skipped the Library Setup portion of Optional Setup described earlier, or simply want to add or remove monitored media folders, you can do so here.

A Continually Evolving User Interface

Okay, enough with the configuration already. Now it's time to take a look at the Windows Media Center user interface.

Prior to Windows Vista, Media Center presented most of its menus using lists of text that were formatted to be readable on TV displays. Now, as with Windows Vista, Media Center is more graphical and takes better advantage of the onscreen real estate offered by wide-screen displays such as HDTV sets. This interface may be a bit jarring if you're used to using older, XP-based Media Center versions, but others should find themselves able to adopt the new user interface fairly easily.

The main Media Center menu, or Start page, was shown in Figure 15-14. From here, you can scroll up or down to access top-level Media Center experiences like Extras, Pictures + Video, Music, Movies, TV, Sports, and Tasks, but you can also scroll left and right to access sub-options within each top-level experience. For example, if Pictures + Videos is selected, you can move left and right to access options such as Viral Videos, Picture Library, Play Favorites, and Video Library. This is shown in Figure 15-20.

Figure 15-20: It takes a bit of getting used to, but Windows Media Center's menu system scrolls both up and down and left and right.

Throughout the Media Center interface, you will run into these types of horizontally scrolling menu options, so it's a good idea to get used to them by experimenting with the Start page. How you navigate through the interface depends on whether you're using the keyboard, mouse, or Media Center remote control (which may have been included with your PC). Each can be used to navigate through the Media Center interface. Table 15-1 summarizes how you access the most common Media Center navigational options with each controller type.

Table 15-1: How to Get It Done in Windows Media Center

Media Center Action	Keyboard	Mouse	Remote Control
Open Windows Media Center or return to the Windows Media Center Start page.	Press the Windows key+Alt+Enter.	Select Media Center from the Start menu or click the Media Center logo while in Media Center.	Click the Start button.
Close Windows Media Center.	Press Alt+F4.	Select Shutdown and then Close from the Start page.	Select Shutdown and then Close from the Start page.
Select the highlighted option.	Press Enter.	Click the highlighted option.	Click OK.
Go back to the previous screen.	Press Backspace.	Click the Back button.	Click Back.

Media Center Action	Keyboard	Mouse	Remote Control
Go to the first item in a list.	Press Home.	Scroll to the top of the list with the mouse's scroll wheel.	Press the Page Up button until you reach the top of the list.
Go to the last item in a list.	Press End.	Scroll to the bottom of the list with the mouse's scroll wheel.	Press the Page Down button until you reach the bottom of the list.
Move left.	Press the left arrow.	Move to the left side of the menu and click the left arrow that appears; or, press left on a tilting scroll wheel–equipped mouse.	Click the Left button.
Move right.	Press the right arrow.	Move to the right side of the menu and click the right arrow that appears; or, press right on a tilting scroll wheel–equipped mouse.	Click the Right button.
Move up.	Press the up arrow.	Move to the top of the menu and click the up arrow that appears; or, scroll up on a scroll wheel–equipped mouse.	Click the Up button.
Move down.	Press the down arrow.	Move to the bottom of the menu and click the down arrow that appears; or, scroll down on a scroll wheel–equipped mouse.	Click the Down button.
Toggle full-screen mode.	Press Alt+Enter.	Click the Maximize button.	n/a

Secret

The four-way menu navigation isn't unique to Windows Media Center. Microsoft first used this navigational paradigm in its software for Portable Media Centers, but more recently you can see it used in the software that powers Microsoft's Zune portable media players (examined in Chapter 14) and in Windows Mobile, Microsoft's smartphone system (described in Chapter 19).

One feature you can access only with the mouse is the new controls overlay that appears when you move the mouse around while Media Center is enabled. Shown in Figure 15-21, these controls provide you with access to the Back and Start buttons in the top-left corner of the display and a rich set of playback controls perfect for music, TV, videos, or other multimedia content in the bottom-right corner.

Figure 15-21: Media Center's overlay controls are elegant looking and easy to use.

Previously, we noted that some of the screens in Media Center date back to much earlier versions of the software, while others are relatively new. In general, the Windows 7 version of Media Center uses a nearly identical graphical style to that of Vista, though many of the menu options have changed, even dramatically. The current Start page, for example, debuted in the Windows Vista version of Media Center. When TV, video, or a DVD movie is playing (but not, oddly, a photo slide show), and you return to the Start page, the Start page is overlaid over the video, as shown in Figure 15-22. Previously, the video was seen playing back in a small picture-in-picture (PIP)-type window in the lower-left corner of the screen.

There are a few new features in Windows 7. If you access the Program Info for a playing video, TV show, or other movie content (by right-clicking the screen or clicking the More Info button on the Media Center remote), you'll see that an overlay pops up over the video, as shown in Figure 15-23.

But then you navigate to Settings and it looks like Windows XP. This software is like an archaeological dig, with some bits dating to XP, some from Vista, and some new to Windows 7. You'll find inconsistencies like that throughout Media Center. Maybe someday they'll actually get a consistent UI. Maybe not. But Media Center is still pretty cool, regardless of how different bits of the UI look.

Figure 15-22: Movies and TV shows can be overlaid by the Start page.

Figure 15-23: New to Windows 7 is program information that appears over a playing video.

Exploring the Media Center Experiences

Media Center offers a rich and exciting way to access live and recorded television shows and movies, digital photos, home videos, digital music, and other digital media content, and it works equally well on a notebook, your desktop PC, or via an HDTV display in your living room. In this section, we examine the various digital media experiences offered by Media Center.

TV

The television experience sits up front and center in Windows Media Center, although it's unlikely that most Windows Vista users will have a TV tuner card installed in their system, let alone one that is connected to and controlling their TV source (cable, satellite, or whatever). And while that's too bad—Media Center's TV capabilities are most impressive and quite superior to competing digital video recording (DVR) solutions like TiVo—Microsoft does at least address the no-TV situation in Windows 7 with new Internet-based TV functionality. It's time to take a look.

Live TV

Assuming you went through the Set Up TV Signal wizard described earlier in this chapter, you should be able to click the Live TV button on your remote (or select Live TV from the TV entry on the Media Center Start page) and begin watching live TV immediately. Using your remote, you can change channels, view the program guide (see the section "TV Guide" later in this chapter), pause, rewind, and restart live TV, and perform all the other options you'd expect from a normal television.

---

tip   One caveat: if you're using an IR blaster to control your cable box or satellite dish, you may notice that some operations, such as changing channels, are much slower than they were when you accessed these devices directly. That's because Media Center (like other DVR solutions) employs a technique called *IR blasting*. That is, it has to translate the commands you press on the remote, send the control codes for the device via IR, and then wait while the device performs whatever action you requested. Because of this delay, you won't be able to quickly move through the channels to see what's on. No big loss, however: the integrated Program Guide and recording functionality largely eliminates this need.

One very cool feature of the TV, movie, and video experiences in Media Center is that playing content will continue to play in the background of the screen if you navigate back to the Start page or the program guide. The effect is somewhat stunning. To return to Live TV, press Back or the Live TV button.

Recorded TV

Live TV is neat...for the twentieth century. As you begin using Media Center, you'll quickly discover that it's so much better to record television and then watch it at your own convenience. Doing so has three big benefits when compared to live TV:

◆ You can skip over commercials and watch just the show itself.

◆ You can pause live TV if interrupted by the phone or some other annoyance.

◆ You can watch the show on your schedule, not that of the TV networks. Forget must-see TV. You can watch what you want, when you want.

And like live TV in Media Center, you can, of course, pause, rewind, and fast forward recorded TV.

There are many, many ways to record TV shows in Media Center, but the best way is to use Media Center's search capabilities to locate the shows you want. Then, you can configure it to record individual shows (such as when you want to record a movie or see what a particular TV show is like) or a series (for popular shows like *Lost* or *The Office* for which you don't want to miss a single show).

1. To search for a show to record, navigate to the Start page, TV, and then Search. (It's *waaaaay* over on the right.) As shown in Figure 15-24, you'll see a variety of ways to search, including by title, keyword, categories, actor, or director.

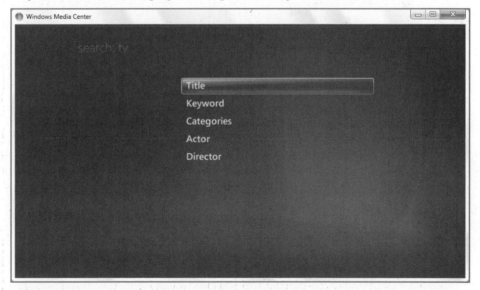

Figure 15-24: Media Center's searching functionality has improved dramatically in Windows 7.

2. For TV shows, the title is often the way to go. Choose Title and then type in the beginning of the show title until you see the show you want, as shown in Figure 15-25.

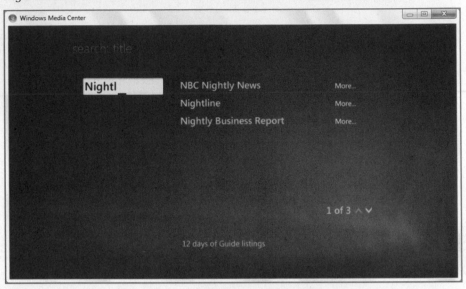

Figure 15-25: Keep typing until you've whittled the search results down to a manageable list.

3. Select the show's name from the list and you'll get a screen providing all of the times when that show is on.

> **tip** Some popular syndicated shows, like "The Simpsons," are on multiple times a day on multiple channels. Newer shows, those that are running for the first time, will usually be on less frequently and only on one station. One exception to this rule: many TV providers now supply two versions of local TV stations, one in standard definition and one in high definition (HD). Typically, it's advisable to record HD shows on the HD version of the station on which it appears—and vice versa.

- To record an individual show, select it from the list and click the Record button on your remote. (Alternatively, right-click the show title and choose Record.) You'll see a red circle appear next to the show, indicating that the show will record.
- To record a series, press the Record button twice (or right-click and choose Record Series). As shown in Figure 15-26, multiple red circles will appear next to the show, and possibly next to other episodes shown in the list.

Figure 15-26: When you record a series, you'll see this unique recording graphic.

For series recordings, make sure that you're recording exactly what you want. To do this, right-click one of the episodes that is marked with multiple red circles, and then choose Series Info (or select and click More Info on the remote). On the Series Info screen, you'll see the list of episodes that is currently scheduled to record. Click Series Settings to configure how the series will record.

On the Series Settings screen, you can choose when the recording will stop (on time, or some number of minutes after it's scheduled to end); which recording quality level to use (always choose Best); how long to keep each episode (until space is needed, until I watch, until I delete, and so on); how many recordings to keep at a time; which channels to record from; when to record; and which types of shows to record (first run only, or first run and rerun). You will want to spend some time configuring these options, both in general (via TV in Settings) or for individual shows. For example, if you know that a particular show always runs three minutes late, be sure to configure it to record late in Series Settings.

> **tip** You can view and configure various recorded TV shows and features from the Recorded TV screen. Just choose View Scheduled to see a list of shows that will be recorded in the future, to view all of the series you're recording, and to see a list of the shows you recorded in the past.

TV Guide

Media Center has always provided a free program guide that shows you a listing of the shows available on your TV provider. You can use this guide to view what's on right now, and what's coming up. It's also a handy way to find shows to record: if you happen to get a high-quality HDTV station, for example, you can scroll through the timeline on just that station and see what's coming up, marking shows and movies to be recorded as you go.

tip   To discover more about an individual show, select it in the guide and choose More Info. To watch a show that is on right now, simply select it. You can also filter the guide to show only the types of shows you want to see: to do so, click the Guide button while in the guide (or click the Categories bar at the left of the guide) and then select Most Viewed, Movies, HDTV, Sports, Kids, or any of the other categories. As shown in Figure 15-27, this can be a huge boon for anyone who wants to filter the programming chaff to only those shows of interest. This includes fans of HDTV programming, sports nuts, kids, and virtually anyone else.

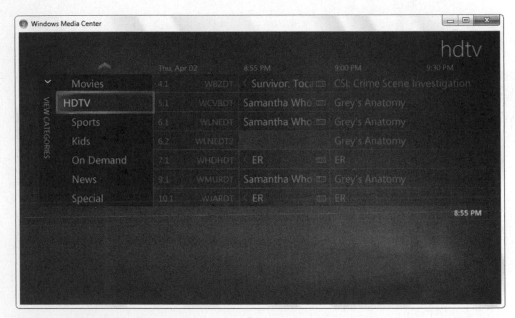

Figure 15-27: You can filter the guide to show only the types of shows you're interested in.

Internet TV

It's not available in the TV submenu for some reason, but if you access the Internet TV link in the Extras menu, you will find another excellent source of TV-type content, courtesy of MSN TV. It's certainly worth checking out, regardless of whether you've configured a traditional TV tuner card or not. There are even some entire TV seasons available free—with minimal advertising—including the highly recommended "Arrested Development."

Secret   If you don't have a TV tuner, the Guide will still show some Internet TV content.

Movies

In previous versions of Windows Media Center, movies were lumped in with TV, but they've been freed to their own devices in Windows 7 and now rate their own top-level Movies entry on the Media Center Start page. The Movies submenu, shown in Figure 15-28, provides a range of movie-related goodness, including access to Internet-based movie trailers, an online movie guide, and your own DVD collection.

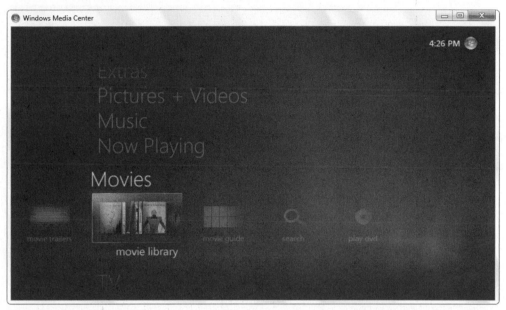

Figure 15-28: Movies is new to the Windows 7 version of Media Center.

Secret

You may have noticed that Media Center has a top-level Pictures + Videos entry as well as one for Movies. So what's the difference between Videos and Movies? In Media Center, there are videos and then there are…movies. Movies are videos that represent full-length feature films. Presumably, you will have acquired these movies from legitimate e-tailers like Amazon On Demand. Or perhaps you've ripped your own DVDs to disk using the techniques revealed in Chapter 13. Either way, you can collect these videos—sorry, movies—together under the Movies umbrella in Windows 7.

So what about videos? If you think for a moment about non-movie videos, you'll realize that lumping them in with photos in Pictures + Videos actually makes some sense. That's because most of the non-movie videos in your collection will be short home movies, perhaps those that were taken with your digital camera.

To ensure that movies and videos appear in the right place in Media Center, store them in separate locations and then use the system's Manage Library functionality to add libraries appropriately. In the Movies section of Media Center, for example, you can right-click (or tap the Info button on your remote) and choose Manage Library from the pop-up menu that appears.

The Movies submenu offers access to the following features:

◆ **Movie trailers:** Inspired, no doubt, by the success of Apple's QuickTime-based movie trailers service, Microsoft has added a similar feature to Media Center, enabling you to stream movie trailers over the Internet to your TV. Shown in Figure 15-29, the movies trailers submenu is a decent way to waste a bit of time.

Figure 15-29: Media Center now offers access to streamable online movie trailers.

◆ **Movie library:** Here, you will see all of your digital movies collected together. Movies you've purchased from online services will have nice DVD box art, while those you've ripped from DVD may not, though we describe how to make that work in Chapter 13. The Media Center movie library is shown in Figure 15-30.

◆ **Movie guide:** Although Media Center's program guide is nothing new, a new movie guide in this version provides a handy front end to all the movies that are available now and in the near future on your cable system or other TV source. Shown in Figure 15-31, this feature uses DVD box art to help you visually navigate through the list of available movie options that are on now and in the future via your TV provider. Because this feature requires a configured TV tuner card, it will not appear otherwise.

◆ **Search:** The search tool found in Movies works just like its cousin in TV and is, in fact, oriented around the movies that may be found via your TV provider. (That is, you cannot use it to search for movies on your hard drive.) In fact, if you don't configure a TV tuner card, this option won't even appear in the Movies submenu.

◆ **Play DVD:** As you might expect, Media Center is an excellent DVD player too, offering virtually all of the functionality of a standalone DVD player. When you insert a DVD movie into the PC while Media Center is running, it will start immediately. From there, you can use the DVD button on your remote to return to the DVD's main menu, or the remote-based or onscreen playback controls to, well, control playback.

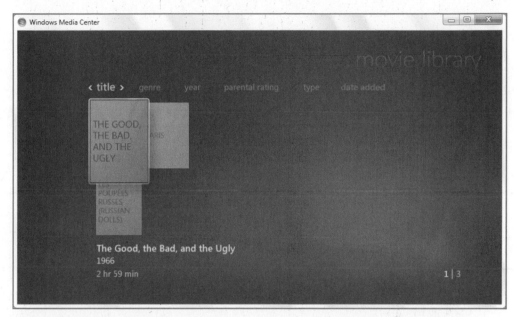

Figure 15-30: Media Center now provides a separate movie library for any full-length digital videos you may have acquired.

Figure 15-31: Movie guide is a great way to find movies to watch or record.

Whether you're watching TV, a movie, a video, or a DVD, be sure to experiment with Media Center's excellent Zoom feature, which cycles between four different zoom modes: Normal (1), Zoom (2), Stretch (3), and Smart (4). Users with wide-screen displays will want to check out smart zoom, because it intelligently zooms standard definition 4:3 content in such a way that it fills the entire screen without making people onscreen look stretched.

Media Center will also benefit from the SlySoft AnyDVD software (www.slysoft .com/) recommended in Chapter 13. Using this software, you can cause playing DVD movies in Media Center to jump directly to the title menu or even the start of the movie, bypassing all the junk that Hollywood studios put on the beginning of discs these days.

Pictures + Videos

You can access your digital photos (and other pictures), as well as any short home movies you may have created with your digital camera, in the Pictures + Videos section of Media Center. Here, you'll see four main items, described in the following sections.

Viral Videos

New to Windows 7, the viral videos link provides access to a YouTube-like collection of funny and interesting home movies. It's the sort of thing you might see on "America's Funniest Home Videos." You know, if you're lame enough to watch a show like that.

Picture Library

The Pictures experience in Windows Media Center is accessed via the Picture library item. As shown in Figure 15-32, it's a graphical grid, sorted by name by default, featuring nice-looking thumbnails of the subfolders and pictures contained in your Pictures folder and other monitored folders. You can choose to sort the library by various other criteria or run a slide show of all of your pictures from this screen.

When you navigate into a folder that contains individual photos, you'll see that the options remain the same: you can navigate horizontally through the collection of pictures, sort by name or date, or start a slide show.

tip   You should probably change some of those slide show settings. For example, you might want the pictures to display randomly, and you might find the default display time of 12 seconds to be quite a bit too long. We discuss this earlier in the chapter.

Figure 15-32: The Pictures experience is very graphical, with horizontally scrolling content.

Secret

To access the hidden Pictures options, right-click (or press the More Info remote button) on any selected photo or folder. You'll see a number of options, including Burn a CD/DVD (covered later in this chapter), View Small, Manage Library, and Settings.

- View Small will change the thumbnail images to smaller icons, which may make it easier to find content when many files are being displayed.

- Manage Library brings you to the Media Library wizard discussed previously in "Configuring Your Digital Media Libraries" earlier in this chapter.

- The Settings option navigates you to Media Center Settings. Here, you can choose Pictures and modify how slide shows work

Play Favorites

New to Windows 7, Play favorites plays a unique scrolling and zooming slide show of the photos you have marked as favorites. This is shown in Figure 15-33. You can determine which photos will be played by this slide show via the Settings interface. Navigate to Settings ➪ Pictures ➪ Favorite Pictures.

Figure 15-33: This cool new slide show feature zooms and scrolls around your favorite pictures.

Video Library

The Videos experience in Windows Media Center is accessed via the Video library item in the Pictures + Videos section of the Start page. Video library is sorted by folders by default (or date taken, optionally) and includes nice-looking thumbnails of the subfolders and videos contained in your monitored folders. When you click on a video, it begins playing immediately, as shown in Figure 15-34. You can use the onscreen controls (in two-foot mode) or the playback controls on your remote control to pause, fast forward, and perform other playback-related functions.

Secret

Unfortunately, the Video library will often show both home movies ("videos") and movies side by side. There's no easy way to prevent this. One thing you can do is not store home movies and movies in the same folder structure. Then, you could use Media Center's Manage Library functionality to add (or remove) the appropriate folders from being monitored by the Video and Movie libraries, respectively.

Figure 15-34: Videos behave much like TV shows, and offer the same controls.

Music

Media Center's Music experience is accessed via the Music item in the Start page. From here, you can access the Music library (that is, the songs and albums you've purchased online or ripped from CD to your hard drive); Radio, which enables you to access FM radio stations; and other features. Here's what's available from this interface.

Live Concerts

New to Windows 7, Live Concerts is a front end to the live music concerts that are offered through Microsoft's MSN Video service. There's a decent collection of shows available, and while each does come with limited commercial interruptions, the quality is pretty good, as shown in Figure 15-35.

Music Library

The Media Center's Music library organizes the digital music you're storing on your PC in an attractive, horizontally organized way, using album art information to identify each album. By default, Music library is organized by album, as shown in Figure 15-36.

Figure 15-35: Watch live concerts free with Windows Media Center.

Figure 15-36: The Music Library album view is graphical and fun to navigate, especially if you have a lot of music and good album art.

Unlike other Media Center experiences, you can choose to view your music in a wide variety of ways: artists, genres, songs, playlists, composers, years, or album artists. What's interesting here is that some of these views—like Artists, shown in Figure 15-37—are displayed in a textual, not graphical, format.

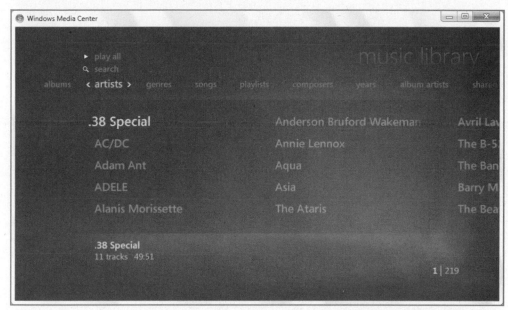

Figure 15-37: So much for the presentation: switch to Artists view and the list is presented in textual form.

As with other parts of the Media Center interface, you can navigate around, dive right in, and play any music at any time. And because of the concept of the Media Center Now Playing list, you can also add music, on the fly, to a temporary playlist called Now Playing. To do so, right-click an item and choose Add to Song List, as shown in Figure 15-38. (This was called Add to Queue in previous versions.) In this way, you can construct a playlist for an event, like a party, or to later synchronize with a portable device.

The first time you add music to the Now Playing list, it begins playing immediately and you'll see a thumbnail of the current song's album art appear in the lower left of the screen, as shown in Figure 15-39.

To access the new Now Playing view (shown in Figure 15-40), click this thumbnail. As you can see, it's now highly visual, with a scrolling background of album art.

Note that from this interface you can also play a picture slide show or visualization, and access other related options. Also, while the default view shows just the current song, you can also click the View Song List button to see a list of all the songs in the Now Playing list.

After you've collected a selection of music you like, you might want to save it as a permanent playlist. To do so, click View Song List and then click Save As Playlist. You can also change various playback options from this screen, including shuffle and repeat.

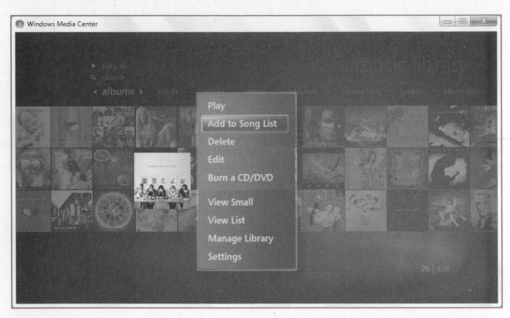

Figure 15-38: Queue up your music and party on.

Figure 15-39: The currently playing song appears at the bottom left of the Media Center display.

Figure 15-40: The full-screen Now Playing view is quite attractive as well.

Secret   New to Windows 7, you can now rate music on the fly. Just click the Info button on your remote, or right-click the Media Player window while a song is playing and you'll see a Rating bar of five stars in the top of the pop-up menu that appears. Click the appropriate rating to rate the song.

Play Favorites

New to Windows 7, the Play Favorites option will trigger a shuffled playlist of just your favorite songs. You determine which songs make up this playlist by visiting Settings ➪ Music ➪ Favorite Music. By default, the Favorite Music list is made up of songs that are rated 4 or 5 stars, are the most played, and/or have been added in the past 30 days, but you can choose from other criteria, such as a specific playlist or auto playlist you previously created.

Radio

If you have an FM radio tuner in your PC—they're common in Media Center PCs and are sometimes bundled into TV tuner cards—you can use this interface to enjoy FM radio broadcasts from Media Center.

Search

New to Windows 7, the Search option enables you to quickly find music in large collections. It searches all of the appropriate criteria (song, artist, album name, and so on).

Extras

New to Windows 7, the Extras menu is really just an improved version of the Online Media interface from Windows Vista. It provides an interface for accessing a library of online content that is tied into experiences such as TV + Movies, Music + Radio, and News + Sports. Here, you can access such utilities and services as the CinemaNow online movie service, XM radio, NPR, and Reuters news. The Extras library shown in Figure 15-41 provides a way to find new extras.

Figure 15-41: Most Media Center extras are online content services.

Microsoft also provides an online version of the MSNBC news channel via the Extras interface, as well as access to an Internet TV option.

Sports

Because Media Center has proven such a hit with sports fans—its ability to filter the TV program guide to show only sporting events is particularly nice—Microsoft had made a new Sports item available on the Media Center Start page. From here, sports fans can access several major interfaces that should be of interest.

If you have a TV tuner card configured, you will see On Now and On Later options that provide a list of the sports events found in your program guide. This works exactly like the On Now and On Later options that Media Center provides for Movies.

All Media Center users can access the three remaining options (Scores, Players, and Leagues) because these items utilize back-end Internet services for content. (You will need an active Internet connection, however.)

Scores, shown in Figure 15-42, provides a handy listing of all of the most recent sports scores and the current day's scheduled games, organized by league. The information is updated in real time and if you select an event, you can see period-by-period results.

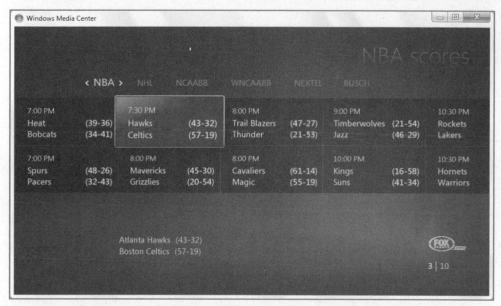

Figure 15-42: Check out the latest sports scores with Media Center.

Players enable you to track your favorite players in various sports. Once you've selected the players you want to track, it provides news items, player details (see Figure 15-43), and a schedule.

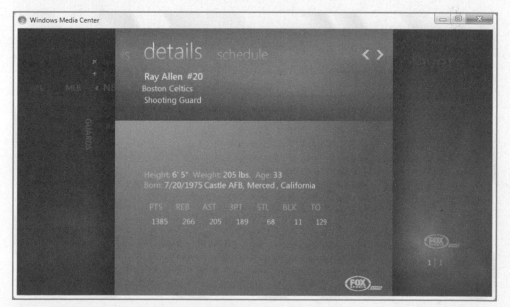

Figure 15-43: Follow your favorite players.

Finally, the Leagues entry enables you to configure which sports leagues you'd like to track. For example, if you'd like to leave out, say, the NHL, this is the place to do so.

Accessing Windows Media Center Away from the PC

Beginning in late 2004 with Windows XP Media Center Edition 2005, Microsoft and a handful of its hardware partners began shipping devices (or, in the case of Microsoft's solution, a software add-on for the original Xbox) called Media Center Extender. These Extenders (again, aside from the Xbox software) were set-top boxes, much like DVD players or cable boxes, which you would place on or near a TV somewhere in your house. They could then connect wirelessly if you had a wireless network, or via Ethernet cabling to your home network and thus to your Media Center PC. The idea is that Extenders can literally extend the reach of your Media Center, its stored multimedia content, and even live TV to other TVs around your home.

It was a good idea in theory. The problem is that first-generation Media Center Extenders weren't very good in practice. They were expensive, for starters, and lacked key features like built-in DVD players. (This was important because DVD content can't be extended from the PC to an Extender for copyright reasons.) And because they were based on low-end, Windows CE–based chipsets, Extender hardware wasn't capable of some of Media Center's nicer graphical effects. While many Extender users were unlikely to have missed some of the user interface–based animations, Extenders were also incapable of animating photos and transitions during photo slide shows. It was all rather inelegant.

Starting with the version of Windows Media Center in Windows Vista, Microsoft eliminated the first-generation Media Center Extenders for good. So if you have a hardware Extender or an Xbox with Microsoft's Media Center Extender software, they won't work with Windows Vista or 7. Instead, you will need to get an Xbox 360—which includes second-generation Extender software—or a second-generation Extender device. The Xbox 360 is powerful enough to render the graphical effects that first-generation Extenders could not, so you get the full Media Center experience. And while second-generation Extender hardware is still pretty low-rent compared to an Xbox 360, and thus lacks some of the animation features of Media Center, these devices are still decent all-around solutions. Instead of empty boxes with Extender chipsets built in, it's now possible to get Extender functionality in certain DVD players, TV sets, and other devices.

Secret   If an Extender is advertised as being Windows Vista compatible, it will work fine with Windows 7 as well.

Because the Xbox 360 video game console is so much more prevalent than dedicated Extender devices and probably always will be, we will focus on the Xbox 360 here; but using a device-based Extender is almost identical, although, of course, only the Xbox 360 can play blockbuster video games as well.

But using an Extender isn't the only way to get content from your Media Center out into the world. This section also describes how you can use Media Center to interact with portable devices and how to burn your own audio CDs and movie DVDs.

Using an Xbox 360 or Media Center Extender

The Xbox 360 is an interesting synthesis of video gaming, online services and communities, person-to-person interaction, and multimedia. It is, in other words, everything the first Xbox was plus a whole lot more. While it doesn't make sense to cover the Xbox 360 in depth here, suffice it to say that Microsoft's latest video game console is actually a multifunction device with impressive non-gaming capabilities in addition to its core features. This is especially true since Microsoft created the visual "New Xbox Experience" UI for the console, which makes it easier than ever to navigate around the console's non-gaming features.

If you do have an Xbox 360 (or have just purchased a Media Center Extender–capable device of any kind), connecting it to your Media Center PC is relatively straightforward. You'll want a 100 Mbps or 1 Gbps wired or 802.11n wireless home network for best performance, especially if you intend to stream live or recorded TV; but a 54 Mbps wireless network (802.11g or 802.11a) should suffice as well, assuming you're not doing a lot of other high-bandwidth networking activity while using the Extender.

> **tip** An 11 Mbps 802.11b network is completely inadequate for this functionality. However, note that most Media Center Extenders also work with 802.11n wireless networks. This type of wireless network is vastly superior to even 802.11g and performs pretty well even with HD video content. The Xbox 360 does not support 802.11n.

Your Xbox 360 includes instructions on connecting the device to your home network. Assuming you're up and running—you should be able to log on to the free Xbox Live service, for example—you're ready to link the Xbox 360 to your Media Center. To do so, ensure that Windows Media Center is running on your Windows 7 PC. Then, turn on the Xbox 360, being sure to eject whatever game DVD happens to be in the tray. On the Xbox 360, navigate to My Xbox ➪ Windows Media Center. The Xbox 360 provides some basic information about Media Center functionality via a Learn more button, or you can simply click Continue.

If the two machines are connected to the same network, you will see a Windows Media Center Extender dialog appear in Media Center. If you don't see this dialog, you can manually run the Extender Setup wizard, shown in Figure 15-44, by visiting Tasks ➪ Add Extender.

The wizard will walk you through the process of configuring the Xbox 360 (or other Extender) to work with your Media Center PC. Note that the Xbox 360 and other Media Center Extenders can be configured to work with only one Media Center PC at a time. (However, each Media Center PC can connect to up to five different Extenders.)

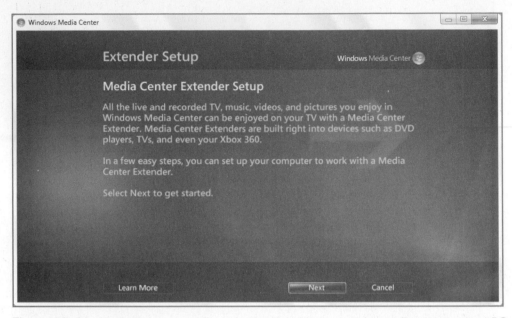

Figure 15-44: Media Center provides a simple wizard for connecting an Extender to your PC.

The only tricky part of this Extender Setup process is that you need to enter an eight-digit Setup Key in the Media Center Setup Wizard to link the two machines. When Media Center prompts you for this key, walk over to the Xbox 360 and write down the number displayed on the Xbox 360/Extender. Then, return to the PC and enter the Setup Key to continue, as shown in Figure 15-45. Click Next to continue.

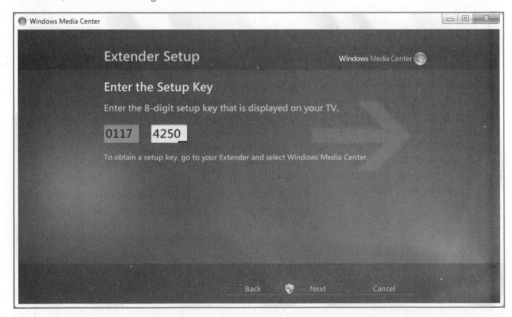

Figure 15-45: The Setup Key links an Extender to a single Media Center PC.

At this point, the Extender Setup wizard configures the PC to interact with the Extender. This process can take a few minutes, as part of the configuration is locating and identifying all of your media.

Meanwhile, the Xbox 360 will load the Media Center Extender software and connect to your PC over the network, and you will see the familiar Media Center experience appear on the Xbox 360 (or Extender).

From that point, using Media Center Extender via the Xbox 360 should be virtually indistinguishable from using it on the PC, albeit with possible lag time due to network slowness.

There is one minor difference. To exit the Media Center experience on the Xbox 360, choose Close from the Tasks menu. This will return you to the New Xbox Experience.

You can use the Xbox 360's hand controller as a remote control, or you can purchase an Xbox 360 media remote; several are available.

You can even use a Media Center PC remote with the Xbox 360, and this may in fact be the best solution, as these remotes tend to be more full-featured than the ones offered specifically for the Xbox 360. To use a Media Center PC remote with Xbox 360, you need to configure the machine first: navigate to My Xbox ➪ System Settings ➪ Console Settings, and then select Remote Control. From this user interface, choose Both Remotes (which enables you to use both Media Center PC remotes and Xbox media remotes).

A few quick if obvious points about Extenders. If you are using an Xbox 360 as an Extender, the visual experience should be identical to that on your Windows Vista PC, with a few exceptions. You can only run the Media Center experience full screen, for example, and you'll never see the control overlays that appear when you move the mouse around on the PC version. On dedicated Extender hardware, the visual experience is largely similar to that on the Xbox 360, except that some of the more subtle animation effects are missing. For example, the Start page background doesn't subtly animate as it does on the Xbox 360 and PC. Instead, it's a static bitmap.

Also, some Extenders include a DVD drive or are themselves embedded in other hardware, such as an HDTV display. In these cases, the hardware may have other non-Extender capabilities that may be of interest. These experiences occur outside of the Media Center environment, however. Consult your documentation for details.

After you've made the connection between your PC and Extender, Media Center will ask you if you'd like to tune your network. This is an optional performance test that you may want to run just to make sure you're using a network with acceptable bandwidth. For example, with an 802.11g-type network, Media Center will warn you that the Extender will not be able to stream HD content reliably. It also provides charts for the textually challenged.

After configuring an Xbox 360 or other Extender for use with Media Center, you can visit Settings ⇨ Extender in order to add other Extenders, configure a single Extender-related option (whether notifications are displayed when an Extender is connected), and view information about the Extenders that are already connected, as shown in Figure 15-46. From here, you can also run the network performance test again if you'd like.

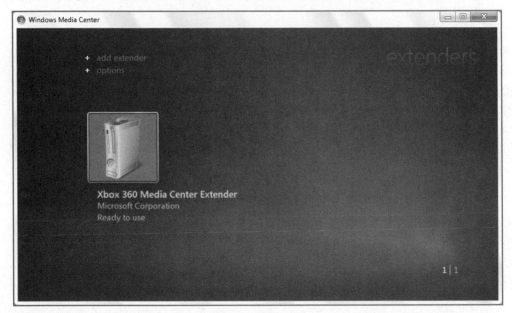

Figure 15-46: Media Center Extenders are configured through Settings ⇨ Extender.

---

tip

The Xbox 360 and other Media Center Extenders will appear in the Network location in the Windows 7 shell after you've configured them to work with Windows Media Center, as shown in Figure 15-47. If you double-click the Xbox 360 Media Center Extender or Extender device icon, Media Center will load and attempt to reconfigure the Extender. You can cancel this if you did so by mistake.

Figure 15-47: Configured Media Center Extenders also show up in the Windows 7 Network explorer.

Secret

When you configure any Media Center Extender device, Windows will silently create a new user account, with a name like Mcx1-*machine-name*, which is used by the Extender to access your PC's media resources. Mcx1-*machine-name* won't appear in the User Account control panel, as it did in Windows Vista, but you will see it if you navigate to C:\Users with Windows Explorer. That said, you shouldn't try to muck around in there in any way, because doing so might break the connection between the Extender and Media Center. Put simply, these accounts are configured automatically and should be ignored.

Synchronizing with Portable Devices

If you're using a portable MP3 player or other portable multimedia device, you may want to synchronize it with your digital media content using Windows Media Player, as discussed in Chapter 11. This is the recommended approach if the system you're using is a typical PC, where you interact with the machine using the mouse and keyboard while sitting at a desk.

If, however, you utilize Windows Media Center via a remote control in your living room, bedroom, or other non-home office location, you might want to use Media Center to synchronize with a portable device instead. As you might expect, Microsoft supports this scenario fully.

To synchronize content between Media Center and a portable device, plug in the device and ensure that it's fully supported by Windows 7. That is, if Windows 7 doesn't automatically recognize the device and install drivers, you might have to visit the device maker's Web site and download and install the drivers manually before proceeding. This is rare, however. Most portable media devices work fine with Windows 7, and automatically.

Secret

Note that while the process described in this section applies to virtually all portable media devices, it does not apply to Apple's iPod, iPhone, and other devices. These devices are not natively Media Center compatible. Chapter 11 describes how you can make an Apple device work better with Windows Media Player, and thus with Media Center as well.

Secret

The process described in this section also does not apply to Microsoft's own Zune. At this time, there's no way to directly link a Zune device with Windows Media Center, unfortunately. Instead, you'll need to use the Zune PC software as described in Chapter 14

When that's done, launch Media Center and navigate to Tasks ➪ Sync from the Start page. Media Center will pop-up an alert asking if you'd like to synchronize media content with the device (see Figure 15-48).

When you click the Yes button, the Manage List screen will appear, as shown in Figure 15-49. From this screen, you can determine which content from your Media Center PC will be synchronized with the device. By default, the Manage List screen displays a list of playlists you've created, which is to say there won't be any (most likely).

Secret

As with much of its other functionality, Media Center shares playlists with Windows Media Player, so any playlists you create in Windows Media Player will appear here in Media Center. The reverse is also true: playlists you create in Media Player appear in Windows Media Player, too.

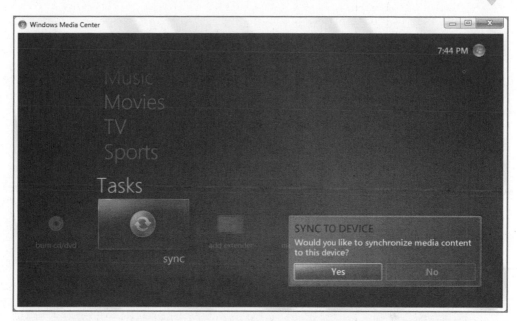

Figure 15-48: Yes, it's possible to bypass Windows Media Player and sync with devices directly from Media Center.

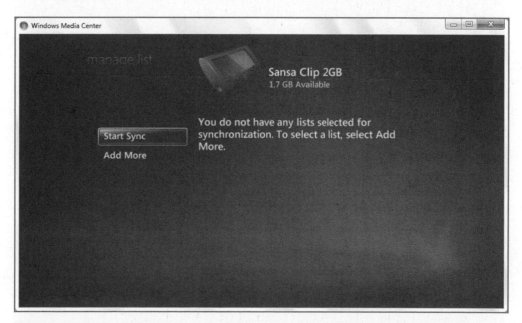

Figure 15-49: The Manage List screen determines which content is synchronized with a device.

While you could create playlists to handle the syncing of content between the PC and the device, Media Center provides built-in ways to sync content. To see them, click Add more and then choose the type of content you'd like to synchronize. (This could be any mix of Music, Pictures, Videos, and Recorded TV, depending on the capabilities of the device.) Each has similar built-in sync possibilities, but as you can see in Figure 15-50, the Music sync options are typical: you can choose All Music, Music added in the last month, Music auto rated at 5 stars, and more.

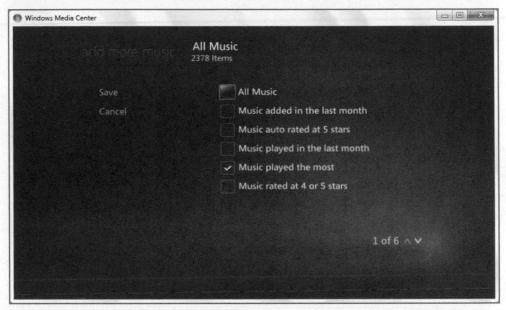

Figure 15-50: Sync it, sync it good: Media Center has nice built-in sync presets for different content types.

When you've determined which content to synchronize, press the Start Sync option. A Sync Progress dialog will appear while the content is synchronized between the PC and device. You can do other things in Media Center while this happens: just click the OK button to move along. When the sync process is completed, a Sync to Device notification will appear, alerting you.

Secret

What if you have more than one portable device? When you select Sync from the Settings menu, you'll be presented with a screen that enables you to choose which device to access.

Burning a DVD Movie or Music CD

Windows Media Center also includes native CD and DVD burning capabilities. This means that you can create your own audio CDs, data CDs (containing pictures, photos, TV shows, or whatever), DVD movies (typically of TV shows), or DVD data disks.

Creating an Audio CD

To create an audio CD:

1. Select an artist, album, playlist, genre, or whatever song list from within Media Center's Music library, right-click it (or press the More Info button on the remote) and choose Burn a CD/DVD. As shown in Figure 15-51, you will be prompted to insert media if you haven't already done so.

Figure 15-51: Various collections of music can be written to disc from Media Center, enabling you to enjoy your favorite tunes on the go.

2. Choose Audio CD in the next screen and then click Next. Provide a name for the CD (Media Center will default to the name of the media you previously selected).

Secret

Although it's possible you're going to want to recreate a CD you already ripped to the hard drive, it's more likely that you will you want to create what's called a mix CD, a CD of various content that you've hand-picked. For this reason, it's much easier to create a playlist first, add the songs you want to that playlist, and then start the audio CD creation process when you're done. Be mindful of the limits of a typical CD, which can store about 80 minutes worth of music.

3. In the next screen, Review & Edit List, click Add More and repeat the preceding steps until you've filled the CD or added everything you want.

4. Click Burn CD when you're ready. Media Center will make sure you want to proceed and then burn the CD.

Assuming you used write-once media (that is, not a rewriteable CD), the resulting CD should work fine in any CD player, including in-car, home, and portable CD players.

Creating a Data CD or DVD

To create a data CD or DVD—that is, a disc that contains the underlying media files, one that will not play back in a normal CD or DVD player:

1. Select an item in the appropriate Media Center experience, right-click (or press the More Info button on the remote), and choose Burn a CD/DVD.

2. If you haven't already inserted compatible writeable optical media, Media Center will prompt you to do so. In this example, assume you insert a blank CD-R.

3. In the next screen, choose Data CD (and not Audio CD) and then click Next.

4. Pick a name for the disc; Media Center will auto-select the name of the media you initially selected as the default.

5. In the next screen, Review & Edit List, click Add More and repeat the preceding steps until you've filled the CD or added everything you want.

6. Click Burn CD. Media Center will make sure you want to proceed and then burn the CD. Since CDs are relatively small, from a storage perspective, burning a CD does not take a lot of time.

The resulting CD will work only in a computer, for the most part.

Secret

That said, many car and home CD players are now compatible with MP3 and WMA formats. If this is the case, you can use this functionality to create a data disc of music files, and it should play just fine in such a player.

Creating a DVD Movie

To copy a recorded TV show to a DVD movie:

1. Open Recorded TV (by navigating to TV ⇨ Recorded TV) and select the movie or TV show you'd like to copy to DVD.

2. Right-click (or press the More Info button on the remote) and choose Burn a CD/DVD, as shown in Figure 15-52.

3. If you haven't already inserted compatible writeable optical media, Media Center will prompt you to do so.

4. In the next screen, Media Center will ask if you prefer a Data DVD or a Video DVD. Select Video DVD and click Next.

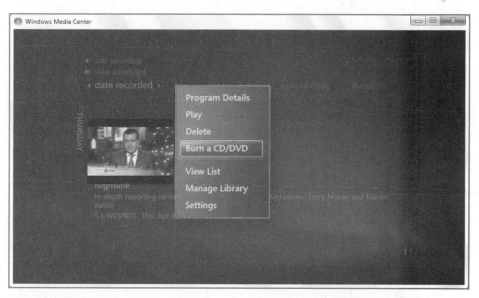

Figure 15-52: Media Center enables you to copy recorded TV shows and movies to DVD.

5. Pick a name for the DVD movie; Media Center will auto-select the name of the TV show as the default.

6. In the next screen, Review & Edit List, you can perform a number of actions. If the TV show you selected is the only one you want on the DVD, simply click Burn DVD to commit the movie to disc. Otherwise, click Add More and repeat the preceding steps.

Note that you can only add videos and recorded TV to DVD movies from Media Center in this fashion. If you want to add a photo slide show, you need to use Windows DVD Maker, which is covered in Chapter 13. Photos can be added only to data DVDs from within Media Center.

Some recorded TV shows cannot be burned to DVD. For example, shows on pay stations like HBO and Cinemax are referred to as *protected content* in Media Center. That means Microsoft is respecting the so-called broadcast flag technologies these channels are using to protect the content. The result is that HBO (which owns Cinemax too) and other channels have made the decision that they don't want users copying their content. This means that you can't copy a Media Center–recorded version of an HBO show to a portable device, or another PC as well, incidentally. It just won't work.

> **tip** If you select too much content, Media Center will warn you that the TV shows (or videos) must be burned at a lower-quality level in order to fit everything on the disc. You can choose to remove a TV show or video or accept the lower quality.

7. When you do finally set about actually burning the DVD, be prepared for a wait. DVD burning takes a long time, especially for video content. A. Really. Long. Time.

> **tip** You can do other things in Media Center when a DVD is burning, but the burning process will take even longer in such a case. You've been warned.

When the DVD is completed, it should work just fine in any DVD player, including the set-top box you probably use on your TV, portable DVD players, in-car DVD players, and laptops.

Summary

Windows Media Center is a wonderful environment for enjoying digital photos, music, videos, TV shows, and other digital media content. If you're lucky enough to be using this system via a Media Center PC or any Xbox 360 Media Center Extender functionality, that's even better—the best features of Media Center come to life when accessed via an HDTV set and remote control. But Media Center isn't just for TVs. Even on a more pedestrian portable computer, Media Center provides a highly visual way of enjoying digital media content. For many users, this program will be reason enough to upgrade to Windows 7.

Having Fun: Games and Windows 7

Chapter

16

♦ ♦

In This Chapter

Discovering the games that Microsoft supplies with Windows 7

Utilizing the Games Explorer

Installing and configuring other games

Utilizing game controllers and other game-related hardware

Accessing the Games for Windows - LIVE service

♦ ♦

Although the experts may extol the many productivity and usability enhancements in Windows 7, the truth is, we all need to relax sometimes. And sure enough, since the earliest versions of Windows, Microsoft has included a number of games with its operating system, from classics such as Minesweeper and Solitaire to lamented lost titles such as Pinball 3D. In Windows Vista, Microsoft provided users with a totally refreshed and modernized set of game titles, as well as a centralized Games Explorer that aggregates all of your game titles and related hardware devices, such as game controllers. These features have been enhanced in Windows 7 with new games, new capabilities, and, thanks to new online functionality, a whole new world of gaming possibilities. In this chapter, we're going to have a bit of fun, Windows 7 style.

Games That Come with Windows 7

If you were a fan of Minesweeper, FreeCell, or any of the other classic games from Windows' past, get ready for a fun surprise: With Windows Vista, many of these games were completely overhauled with new graphical treatments that take advantage of the underlying 3D graphics capabilities Microsoft introduced in that release. Windows 7 includes these new games plus a few popular Internet-based titles as well. Here are the games that ship with Windows 7.

Secret

Thanks to Microsoft's ongoing strategy of shipping numerous Windows product editions, not all of the games listed in this chapter are available in all versions of Windows 7. Microsoft separates these "inbox" games into two categories, basic games and premium games. Basic games are those games that come with every Windows 7 product edition, whereas premium games are those that ship only with so-called "premium" versions of Windows 7, including Windows 7 Home Premium, Professional, Enterprise, and Ultimate. This may seem like a problem, but remember that the vast majority of Windows 7 users—including, we imagine, virtually everyone who buys this book—will be running Windows 7 Home Premium or Professional. That means that most people won't have to worry about missing out on some of the nicer game titles mentioned here.

Chess Titans

What it is: A 3D chess title (see Figure 16-1).

Game type: Premium (Windows 7 Home Premium and up).

FreeCell

What it is: A variation of the Solitaire card game, sometimes called Klondike (see Figure 16-2).

Game type: Basic (All Windows 7 product editions).

Figure 16-1: Chess Titans

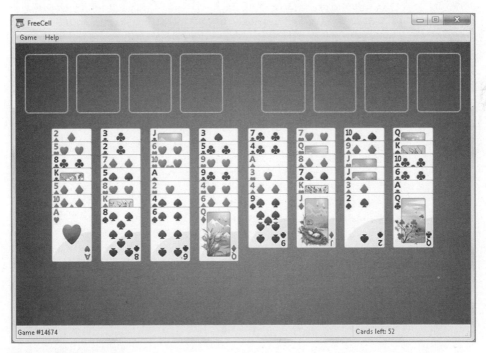

Figure 16-2: FreeCell

Hearts

What it is: A classic card game; a variation of whist (see Figure 16-3).

Game type: Basic (All Windows 7 product editions).

Internet Backgammon

What it is: New in Windows 7. An online version of the popular Backgammon board game. You must be online to play this game (see Figure 16-4).

Game type: Basic (All Windows 7 product editions).

Internet Checkers

What it is: New in Windows 7. An online version of the classic Checkers board game. As with the other Internet titles here, you must be online to play this game (see Figure 16-5).

Game type: Basic (All Windows 7 product editions).

Figure 16-3: Hearts

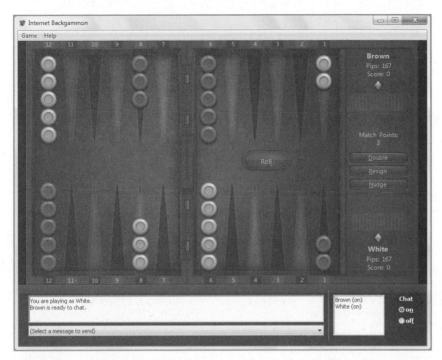

Figure 16-4: New to Windows 7, Internet Backgammon enables you to play this popular board game against others online.

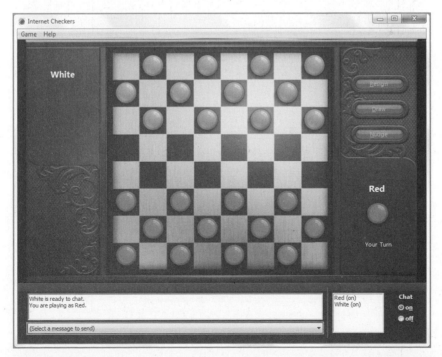

Figure 16-5: Windows 7 also includes an online version of the classic game Checkers.

Internet Spades

What it is: New in Windows 7. An online version of Spades, a fast-paced, team-based card game. This title requires Internet connectivity to play (see Figure 16-6).

Game type: Basic (All Windows 7 product editions).

Figure 16-6: With Internet Spades, you can compete in teams online with others in this fast-paced card game.

Mahjong Titans

What it is: A curiously addictive Chinese tile game (see Figure 16-7).

Game type: Premium (Windows 7 Home Premium and up).

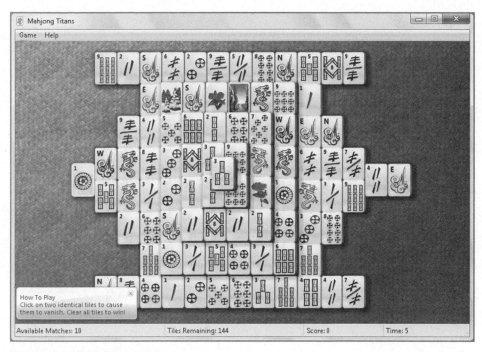

Figure 16-7: Mahjong Titans

Minesweeper

What it is: The timeless classic, updated for modern PCs, in which you must uncover all of the spots on a grid that do not include a hidden bomb (see Figure 16-8).

Game type: Basic (All Windows 7 product editions).

Figure 16-8: Minesweeper

Purble Palace

What it is: A set of children's games, including Comfy Cakes, Purble Shop, and Purble Pairs, that help teach memory, pattern recognition, and reasoning skills (see Figure 16-9).

Game type: Premium (Windows 7 Home Premium and up).

Solitaire

What it is: The classic single-player card game in which you try to rearrange a shuffled deck of card (see Figure 16-10).

Game type: Basic (All Windows 7 product editions).

Spider Solitaire

What it is: A two-deck variant of Solitaire (see Figure 16-11).

Game type: Premium (Windows 7 Home Premium and up).

Figure 16-9: Purble Palace

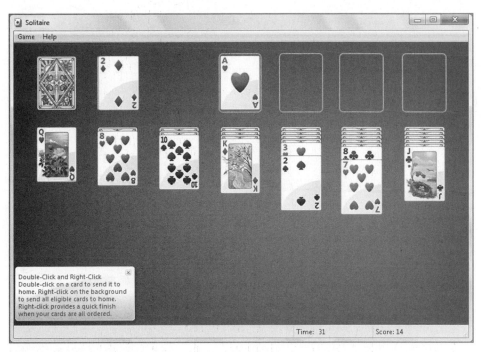

Figure 16-10: Solitaire

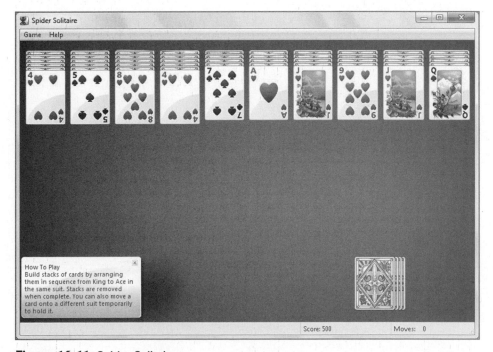

Figure 16-11: Spider Solitaire

Using the Games Explorer

Windows 7, like Windows Vista before it, includes a new Games Explorer that is prominently linked to from the right-most side of the main Start menu display, as shown in Figure 16-12.

Figure 16-12: Apparently, games are as important in Windows 7 as the computer and the network. Yeah, you bet they are.

Secret

Don't see it? If the Games link does not appear in your Start menu, you can easily add it back: right-click the Start button and choose Properties. Then, in the Start Menu tab, click Customize to display the Customize Start Menu window. In this window, scroll down to the Games link (the items are alphabetical) and choose from Display as a link (the default), Display as a menu, or Don't display this item.

tip

The first time you run Games Explorer, you'll be presented with a dialog, Set up Games, that asks whether you'd like to use recommended settings or customized update and folder settings. If you choose Recommended settings, Windows 7 will automatically check online for game updates, and the Games Explorer will automatically download game art and information, and collect information about the games you most recently played. We suggest simply using the recommended settings in this case.

When you select this option, you're shown the Games Explorer, as referenced in Figure 16-13 and oftentimes referred to simply as Games. Games is a handy front end to the games that are included with Windows Vista, as well as a number of other game-related features, including third-party games you install yourself, game hardware, parental controls, and other tools.

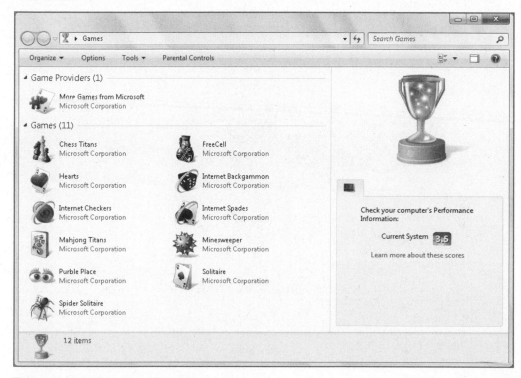

Figure 16-13: The Games Explorer

Actually, if this is the first time you've opened the Games Explorer, you'll see a slightly different display: Microsoft provides a window with which you can configure various options related to the Games Explorer and the built-in Windows 7 games, as shown in Figure 16-14.

The first choice you need to make is whether to let Games Explorer automatically update itself with game updates and—new to Windows 7—news about game-related products and services. You can also decide whether you want the Games Explorer to automatically download art and information about installed games—similar to the way Windows Media Player downloads album art—and collect information about the games you play. This latter feature isn't as Big Brother as it sounds. Instead, Windows 7 is simply creating a Most Recently Used (MRU) list so that it can display those games you've played recently and most frequently at the front of your list of games, if you so choose.

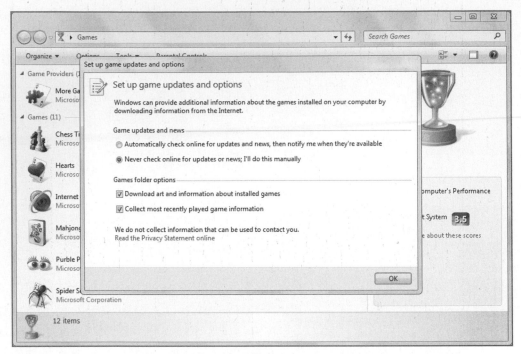

Figure 16-14: The first time you run Games Explorer, you can configure a few options.

> **tip**
>
> If you clicked through this window without paying attention, or think you may want to pick different options, fear not. You can make these configuration changes later. Just click the Options toolbar menu item in Games Explorer to redisplay the window.

Once you dispense with this window, you're free to, ahem, explore the Games Explorer. It works largely like the version from Windows Vista: as you select any of the built-in game titles, a large version of the game's icon and its Entertainment Software Rating Board (ESRB) rating is displayed in the Preview Pane, which is found on the right side of the Games window. (We take a look at performance ratings later in this chapter.)

This display has changed a little bit since Vista, however: thanks to a new tab-based user interface, you can toggle between the ESRB rating and a new Performance tab, shown in Figure 16-15, that provides the recommended and required Windows Experience Index (WEI) score for playing the game, as well as the WEI score for your PC so you can compare and contrast.

> **tip**
>
> Depending on how you've installed or acquired Windows 7, you may see additional games in the Games Explorer. For example, PC makers often include their own selection of game titles.

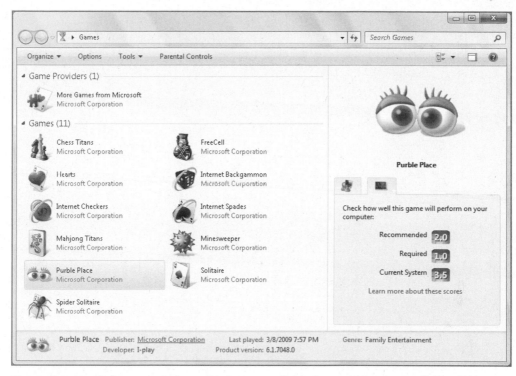

Figure 16-15: Performance information is now available from within a new tab-based user interface in Games Explorer.

To launch a game, simply double-click its icon. As shown in the figures earlier in this chapter, the games included with Windows 7 are significantly more attractive than the games in older Windows versions.

As a program explorer and shell location, the Games Explorer is customizable in certain ways. Via a standard Organize toolbar menu button, you can perform common shell tasks and change the layout of the window. The toolbar also includes links to Games Explorer options, game-related tools, and Windows 7's parental controls, the latter of which provide a way for parents to restrict which games their kids can play (among other related functionality; see Chapter 8 for more information about parental controls).

You can also right-click a game icon and choose the Play option if you think double-clicking is too simple and obvious. Glibness aside, there is a great new reason to right-click games in the Games Explorer: with Windows 7, two new Pin To options enable you to attach shortcuts to the Start menu or, more usefully, to the taskbar. So if you find yourself playing a certain game quite frequently, you can skip the rigmarole of navigating through the Start menu or using the Games Explorer and simply make that game a permanent inhabitant of your taskbar, as shown in Figure 16-16.

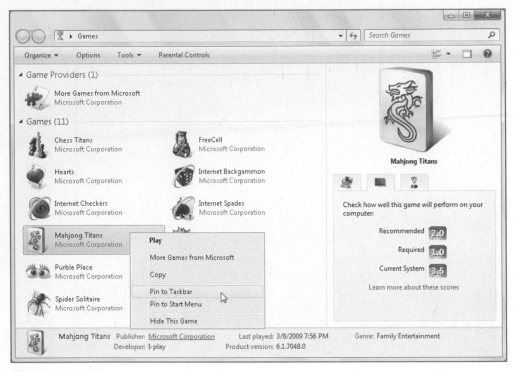

Figure 16-16: If you're a big fan of a particular game, you can pin it to your taskbar for even quicker access.

cross ref We look at the new Windows 7 Pin To functionality in Chapter 4.

Secret Here's a useless but fun fact: Microsoft did not create any of the games in Windows 7. Instead, they were created by third parties for the software giant. For example, Oberon Games was responsible for updating games such as Minesweeper and Solitaire.

Secret Some of the game-related options mentioned in this chapter appear only for built-in Windows 7 games. It's up to game publishers to specifically support this new functionality.

Customizing Games Explorer

In addition to the Set up game updates and options window, which is accessible from the Games toolbar menu item, there are a number of ways in which you can configure the Games Explorer in Windows 7.

New to Windows 7 is the More Games from Microsoft link in Games Explorer. When you double-click this icon, Internet Explorer (or your browser of choice) opens and navigates to the Microsoft Web site, as shown in Figure 16-17. From this page, you can explore Microsoft's nonbundled game options, which include a wide variety of online and downloadable games, some of which are free.

Figure 16-17: Microsoft offers far more for both casual and extreme gamers than the handful of titles that are bundled with Windows 7.

At the time of this writing, Microsoft's online PC game options were spread between three services: MSN Games, Windows Live Messenger, and Games for Windows - LIVE Messenger. The first two options include mostly casual games—card games such as Uno, board games like Checkers, and the like. Games for Windows, however, is far more involved and includes expensive retail offerings. We will look more at Games for Windows later in this chapter.

---

tip   MSN is one of several Microsoft online services. Windows Live Messenger is Microsoft's instant messaging client and part of the Windows Live Essentials suite that "completes" Windows 7.

Games on MSN Games and Games for Windows - LIVE Messenger will typically run in a browser window, accompanied by ads, but they also offer you the opportunity to compete against other people online. A typical MSN Games title, Bubble Town, is shown in Figure 16-18.

Figure 16-18: Most of the MSN Games titles are lighthearted, easy to play, and fun.

Sorting the View

You probably already know that Windows Explorer supports various icon view styles, such as Large Icons, Tiles, and the like. And it's probably no stretch for you to realize then that the Games Explorer also supports all of these view styles, enabling you to customize the window exactly the way you want it. This is Windows 101 stuff, folks.

What may be less obvious, however, is that you can also modify the Games Explorer view in far more useful ways. We mentioned previously that one of the things that Windows 7 will track—if you want it to—is which games you play most frequently, as well as which games you've played most recently. You can use this information—as well as related information, such as which games have been provided updates by their publishers most recently—to display your games in ways that may be more meaningful to you.

The trick, as is the case in any Explorer window, is to utilize right-click and the various Sort By and Group By options. For example, you can sort the game icons in Games Explorer by Last played so that the games you've played most recently are at the top of the window. You can also use the system's grouping options, if desired, to segregate the icons into date-related groups such as Today, Yesterday, Last Week, and the like. In Figure 16-19, you can see that the Games Explorer has been customized to show the most recently played games at the top.

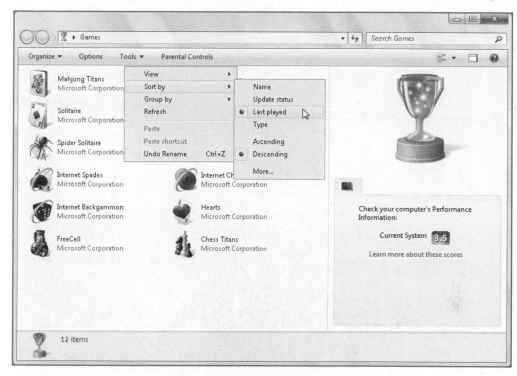

Figure 16-19: Make Games Explorer your own with folder customizations.

Adding and Removing Built-In Games

While the selection of games that come with Windows 7 is pretty decent, you may not want one or more of them installed. Likewise, your PC maker may have chosen to leave some games uninstalled for whatever reason—perhaps to push their own subscription game offerings. In either case, you can customize the games that appear in Games Explorer by installing or uninstalling individual titles so that only the ones you want appear.

To do so, you'll need to access the Windows Programs applet, which is part of the Control Panel. Open the Start menu and select Control Panel. In the Control Panel window, select Programs and then Turn Windows features on or off. (If the Control Panel is displaying an old-school grid of icons, choose Program and Features and then Turn Windows features on or off.)

tip If you're already viewing the Games Explorer, you get to this view more quickly by clicking the Tools toolbar menu item and then Programs and Features.

Either way, you should now see the Windows Features window, shown in Figure 16-20.

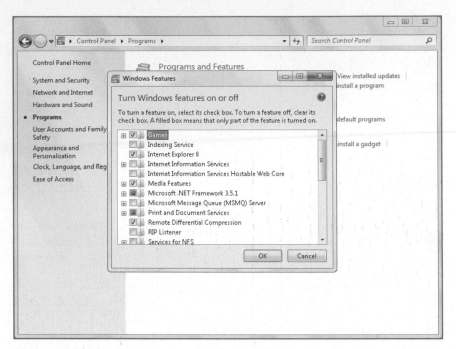

Figure 16-20: Windows Features lets you install and uninstall a subset of Windows features.

Windows Features doesn't let you uninstall (or install) every single Windows feature, but it does provide a far wider range of options in Windows 7 than it has in several previous Windows versions. To see which games are available on your system, expand the Games option. As shown in Figure 16-21, you have a number of options, though what you see here will vary depending on which Windows 7 product edition you're using.

Figure 16-21: Inside of Windows Features, you can uninstall and install various built-in games.

To uninstall a game, uncheck the box next to its name. Likewise, you can install a missing game by checking the box next to its name. Once you've made your choices, click OK and Windows 7 will make the changes. These changes will be reflected in Games Explorer when the process is complete.

While you can install and uninstall any built-in games, you cannot uninstall Games Explorer. Instead, you can choose to hide it from the Start menu, as noted earlier in this chapter.

Users of touch-compatible computers running Windows 7 may see additional games installed, courtesy of Microsoft's Touch Feature Pack for Windows 7. This package of applications is typically provided via your PC maker and includes Microsoft Blackboard, a fun physics-based puzzle game; Microsoft Rebound, an electronic air hockey-type title; and Microsoft Garden Pond, in which you guide origami creatures across a pond by rippling the water via touch-based gestures.

For more information about the Touch Feature Pack for Windows 7, please visit the SuperSite for Windows: Paul has the complete rundown.

`www.winsupersite.com/win7`

Rating Your System's Performance

One of the more interesting features in Windows 7 is the Performance Information and Tools functionality. Using a simple interface, you can let Windows test your system, determine its overall performance rating, or Windows Experience Index (WEI), on a scale from 1 to 7.9, and then get advice about ways to improve performance. This tool isn't just useful for game playing; it should be quite interesting to both gamers and anyone else who wants to ensure that their system is running as efficiently as possible.

In Windows Vista, the Windows Experience Index rated performance on a scale from 1.0 to 5.9. Microsoft raised the scale to 7.9 and made changes to the way it calculates performance in Windows 7 to address new bleeding-edge hardware components such as solid-state disks (SSDs) and the Intel Core i7 microprocessor. You can find out more about changes to the Windows 7 WEI on the SuperSite for Windows. See `www.winsupersite.com/win7/ff_wei.asp`.

In Windows Vista, you could access the Performance Information and Tools directly from the Games Explorer, but this is no longer possible in Windows 7. To access this tool, open the Start menu and type **performance** in the Search box. You'll see Performance Information and Tools in the search results list that appears.

Shown in Figure 16-22, this control panel gives you an idea of how fast your overall system is and rates individual components such as processor, memory, graphics, gaming graphics, and primary hard disk.

Typically, your PC's performance is tested and given a rating during initial setup. However, if you don't see a Windows Experience Index score, or perhaps if you'd like to retest the system because you've made a hardware change, you will see a button titled Rate this computer. Press the button to run the test, which takes a few minutes and then returns a score. If you've already run the test, you can click the link titled Re-run the assessment, at the bottom right of the window, to run the test again at any time.

> **tip**   Be sure not to do anything else with the PC while the test is running: in order to get an accurate score, Windows 7 will need unfettered access to the underlying hardware.

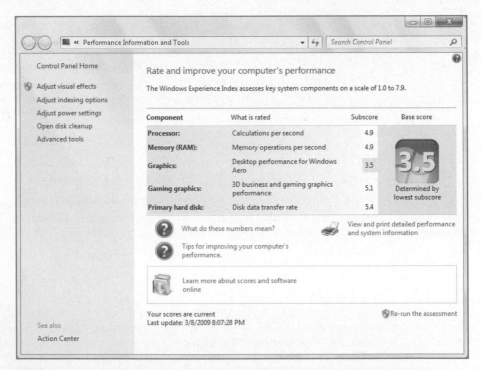

Figure 16-22: Performance Information and Tools puts your system to the test.

> **tip**   Based on the scores your PC and individual components receive, you may want to make some upgrades. For example, a score below 4 in any one category should be a warning sign to any dedicated gamer. You can use the various links in this window to make changes to your system that can help improve overall performance somewhat.

Managing Your Game Controllers and Other Game-Related Hardware

In addition to working with actual games, you can manage your game-related hardware from Games Explorer as well. If you click the Tools menu button in the toolbar, you'll see a number of items in the drop-down menu that are related to hardware gaming:

♦ **Hardware:** This option launches the Hardware and Sound Control Panel, from which you can perform such tasks as accessing configuration information for printers, audio devices, mouse, scanners and cameras, keyboard, and other hardware devices. Hardware and Sound is shown in Figure 16-23.

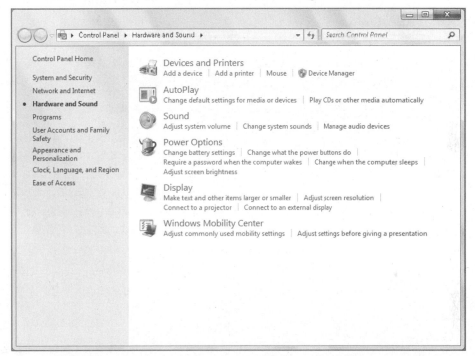

Figure 16-23: Hardware and Sound is a handy front end to all of your hardware devices.

> **tip** This is also a handy place for accessing the Windows Device Manager, which can tell you whether you need updated drivers for any of your hardware devices. You'll see Device Manager in the list of options in the Hardware and Sound Control Panel, under Devices and Printers.

♦ **Display Devices:** This option launches the Screen Resolution window, as shown in Figure 16-24. What you see here varies according to your hardware, but the dialog includes information about the displays and video cards attached to your system, including the screen resolution.

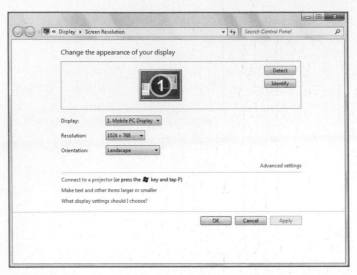

Figure 16-24: From Screen Resolution, you can access configuration information about your display devices, screen resolution, and color depth.

Windows 7 includes a faster way to access this information if you're not already using Games Explorer. Just right-click an empty spot on the Windows desktop and choose Screen Resolution from the pop-up menu that appears.

◆ **Input Devices:** This option launches the Game Controllers dialog, which provides access to configuration information about any game controllers, such as the Microsoft Xbox 360 Controller for Windows, that you may have attached to your PC. The Game Controllers dialog is shown in Figure 16-25.

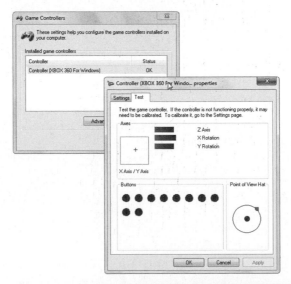

Figure 16-25: The Game Controllers dialog enables you to configure settings for your gaming controllers.

tip Many people play PC-based video games with the mouse and keyboard instead of a joystick or Xbox-style hand controller. You can access the properties for both of these devices from the Devices and Printers window, which is new to Windows 7. To access this window, shown in Figure 16-26, open the Start menu and type devices into the Search box.

Figure 16-26: The new Devices and Printers window provides a friendly front end to the hardware attached to your PC.

♦ **Audio Devices:** This option launches the Sound window, which was significantly updated in Windows Vista and has continued to evolve in Windows 7. As shown in Figure 16-27, this window provides access to all of the sound-related hardware attached to your system and provides separate tabs for Recording, Sounds, and Communications.

Figure 16-27: The Sound window provides access to your audio hardware and sound schemes.

If you double-click an audio device in the list, you can deep-dive into its unique abilities. For example, you can use the Speakers device to configure such properties as levels (volume), various sound enhancements (including virtual surround sound), and more.

New to Windows 7 is the Communications tab, which enables you to configure how Windows reacts when your PC receives or sends a phone call. By default, it will reduce all other sounds in the system by 80 percent. PC-to-phone calling functionality is not part of Windows 7, however. That is a paid optional function of Windows Live Messenger, Microsoft's IM solution.

◆ **Windows Firewall:** This entry is important because some games require specific network ports to be open so that you can play against other people online. Typically, this functionality is, of course, configured by the game in question. However, occasionally games are unable to do so and you will see instructions about making this change manually. In the Windows Firewall application, shown in Figure 16-28, there is a link titled "Allow a program or feature through Windows Firewall." This is the UI you'll need to access if a particular game isn't working online properly.

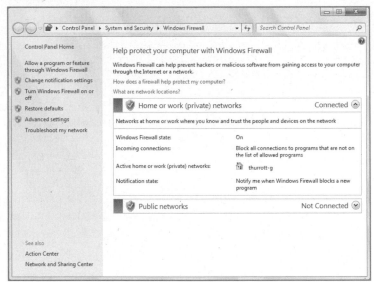

Figure 16-28: Windows Firewall is usually a set it and forget it affair, but if a game isn't communicating online, this is the place to start troubleshooting.

◆ **Programs and Features**: This is the Control Panel applet that is your primary interface for uninstalling or changing applications, and, as it turns out, certain Windows features, including games. We discussed it earlier in this chapter.

Installing and Playing Third-Party Games

Windows 7's built-in games are attractive and even occasionally addictive, but real gamers will want to install their own games. One of the big questions, however, concerns compatibility: how compatible is Windows 7 with the mammoth collection of Windows XP software out there? The question is particularly problematic for gamers, who tend to take more advantage of low-level hardware features that are typically hidden within Windows. And, of course, many of these people skipped right over Windows Vista out of fears—warranted or not—that it would be problematic for gaming.

Secret

The other big gaming-related question, of course, is whether Windows 7 measures up, performance-wise, with Windows XP. We know that with the original shipping version of Vista, the answer was no, though Microsoft fixed most of that system's performance issues by the release of Windows Vista Service Pack 1 (SP1). With the passage of time, most gamer-related hardware drivers had improved to the point where the performance differences between Vista and XP became minimal. With the release of Windows 7, we're seeing even better performance, and Windows 7 runs fantastically well even on low-end netbook computers, a feat that was well beyond the capabilities of Windows Vista. Put simply, performance is no longer an issue, even for gamers.

In our testing of 3D game titles (hey, someone has to do it), we've found Windows 7 to be extremely compatible with everything from so-called legacy game titles to the most modern shooters available. In most cases, there's no work to be done at all: you simply install the game as always—albeit with the occasional User Account Control (UAC) prompt—and things simply work as expected.

Some games, especially older games, will require a bit of prodding. In some cases, Windows 7 includes compatibility information about certain problematic game titles, and in others you'll need to manually set up the game's shortcut to run in Windows XP or Windows Vista compatibility mode before it will run. Figure 16-29 shows the interface for setting the compatibility mode for a poorly behaving application.

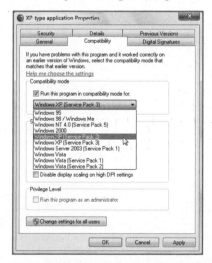

Figure 16-29: Some games expect to run on a certain version of Windows. That's okay; we can fool them into thinking just that.

Secret

Although this isn't documented anywhere, it's quite possible to add games you've installed on your PC to the Games special shell folder, so you can access them as you do the built-in games. Presumably, newer game titles will do this automatically so that they can integrate more closely with the games-related infrastructure Microsoft created in Windows 7. But if they don't, you can make it happen yourself. To do so, simply drag a game shortcut into the Games Explorer. As shown in Figure 16-30, legacy games such as *Ultimate DOOM* can be added directly to Games Explorer. Many games will be added automatically, however, so check before dragging and dropping.

Figure 16-30: You can add your own games to the Games folder, too.

Secret

When Windows Vista first appeared, gamers were advised to avoid x64 versions of the operating system in order to avoid any potential compatibility problems. This is no longer an issue, on either Windows Vista (with Service Pack 2 or higher) or Windows 7. Now, x64 versions of Windows are roughly as compatible as their 32-bit counterparts; and thanks to certain advantages of running on a pure 64-bit OS, including the occasional availability of 64-bit-specific games, x64 versions of Windows 7 are in fact the more desirable platform for gaming. There's no longer any need to be scared of x64.

Games for Windows - LIVE

Separate from its PC gaming initiatives, Microsoft has been promoting its line of Xbox video game consoles since 2001. In late 2005, the company significantly raised the bar with the release of its second-generation Xbox 360 console, featuring unparalleled graphics power and connectivity, and ushering in a new era of high-definition (HD) video gaming. In some ways, the biggest leap forward that Microsoft made with the Xbox 360, however, was the massive set of improvements it made to the system's online service, Xbox Live. This service provides a way for Xbox 360-based gamers to face off in multiplayer matches, of course, but it also offers movie and TV show downloads, instant messaging functionality, and other features. It's the most full-featured online service for any video game console, by far.

Xbox Live has been so successful that is has colored how the company approaches other similar online endeavors. In the years since the launch of the Xbox 360, Microsoft has used its successes with Xbox Live as a model for such things as the Zune Marketplace, an online service that supports Microsoft's digital media players (see Chapter 14) and, more recently, a new initiative called Games for Windows - LIVE.

Secret   As we write this book, there is talk that Microsoft will further integrate its Xbox Live Marketplace and Zune Marketplace with its PC-oriented gaming marketplace endeavors in the future. This makes plenty of sense: if you buy content at, say, the Zune Marketplace, you should be able to access it seamlessly on Zune-compatible devices, the Xbox 360, and a PC.

Games for Windows - LIVE is an attempt to replicate the success of Xbox Live on the PC and, to a much lesser extent, to provide interconnectivity between Windows-based gamers and Xbox 360-based gamers. Since it is both modeled on and tied directly to Xbox Live, it should come as no surprise that Games for Windows - LIVE is very much like Xbox Live from a user experience perspective. That said, Games for Windows - LIVE is still lacking some key Xbox live features. It also has some troubling problems that suggest it will never really take off in the same way that Xbox Live has on Microsoft's consoles.

Here's what's happening.

Xbox Live on Windows?

Xbox Live customers each have a Gamertag, which is associated with a Windows Live ID (formerly called a Passport account; see Chapter 23 for more information). This Gamertag includes a reputation (or Rep, scored from one to five stars), a Gamerscore (the total number of Achievement points collected in all the Xbox 360 games the gamer has played), and other data. You can see this information on the Xbox.com Web site, shown in Figure 16-31.

Figure 16-31: Xbox gamers—and, as it turns out, Games for Windows - LIVE users—can view and modify their Gamertag online

Gamers also can access the list of games they've played, with Achievements broken down by game. (You can of course access other players' Gamertags as well, to compare and contrast experiences or to find potential foes online.) Each Gamertag has associated lists of messages (similar to e-mails), friends (like contacts), and players (other gamers they've faced off against online). Also included are various settings, related to game types, the Dashboard, and other aspects of the Xbox 360 experience.

Secret

It sounds like Microsoft has created a full-fledged e-mail and instant messaging system here, doesn't it? Sure enough, that's exactly what the communications-oriented parts of Xbox Live—and, by extension, Games for Windows - LIVE—provide. You can even do voice and video chat over the service. There's just one thing: all of this communication has to occur over Microsoft's network or, in the case of the e-mail-type messages, on the Web. You can't, for example, access Xbox Live messages via a Windows e-mail application such as Windows Live Mail or an IM solution such as Windows Live Messenger. And that's odd, when you think about it, since the underlying services used by these applications can access e-mail and instant messages sent to the same associated Windows Live ID you may use for gaming. Maybe someday.

The reason the Xbox Live Gamertag system works so well on the Xbox 360 is that Microsoft has made the underlying Xbox Live service so thoroughly integrated across the system. If you're in a game of *Call of Duty World at War* or watching a live or recorded TV show via the Xbox 360's Media Center Extender functionality (see Chapter 15), your friends can see what you're up to, even if they're playing *Gears of War 2* or just browsing the downloadable content on Xbox Live Marketplace, Microsoft's online store.

The trick is bringing this experience to Windows users. Here, Microsoft has been fairly successful. After an initial tepid release, newer versions of Games for Windows - LIVE feature a decent in-game experience and the start of an online marketplace of sorts that may someday be pretty useful.

The Games for Windows - LIVE Experience

Games for Windows - LIVE is available in two places in Windows. The first is a stand-alone Windows application, Games for Windows - LIVE Marketplace, which is shown in Figure 16-32. From this simple but almost useless Dashboard-like UI, you can log on to your Windows Live ID—and thus your Gamertag—but you can't view or update any useful gamer information about that account, as you can from the Xbox 360 Dashboard. Instead, this UI is designed solely to provide access to a fledgling online marketplace.

Figure 16-32: The Games for Windows - LIVE Marketplace client is a curious beast, with no obviously useful functionality.

---

tip From what we can see, only two useful bits of information are available in this interface: your Gamertag, Rep, and Achievement points totals are viewable in the upper-right corner; and on the Marketplace tab, you can see how many Microsoft Points—for making micropayments—are available in your account. That's about it.

The second place is an in-game Dashboard that appears only in Games for Windows - LIVE game titles and works much like the pop-up interface that Xbox 360 gamers see. From this interface, you can view and edit your Gamertag and associated Windows Live ID account, view information about the games you've played, access your Friends list, read and send messages, and engage in private chats. This interface is shown in Figure 16-33.

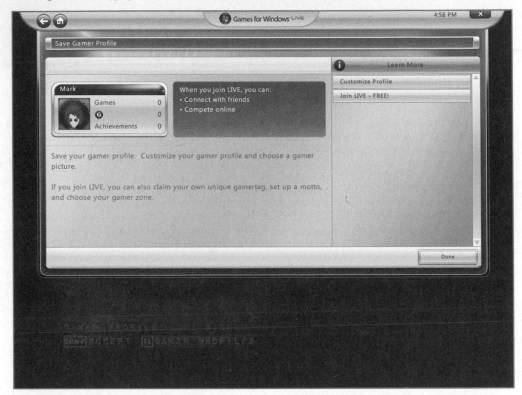

Figure 16-33: Inside of a Games for Windows - LIVE title is a useful Dashboard that works very much like its Xbox 360 relation.

What you can't do from the Dashboard is access the marketplace: that interaction has to occur via the standalone client application.

Using the Games for Windows - LIVE Marketplace

The standalone Games for Windows - LIVE client is single-handedly devoted to the new Games for Windows – LIVE Marketplace, which is an online service and store that provides free and paid game-related content. This content spans the range from game videos and demos to add-on content that you can install into your existing Games for Windows - LIVE games. It's all pretty sparse at this point, and certainly nothing like the similar Xbox Marketplace experience on the Xbox 360. In fact, before you can even access this service, you have to create a Gamertag, and that has to happen on the Web: you can't do it from within the Games for Windows - LIVE standalone client.

That said, it's not a complete loss: in addition to downloading game demos from Games for Windows - LIVE, you can also install these demos from directly in the client. That's handy; though once those game demos are installed, you can't actually run them from Games for Windows - LIVE. Instead, you have to navigate into the Games Explorer or the Start menu to find them.

To browse the marketplace, open the Games for Windows - LIVE client (here, Start Menu Search is your friend, since this application is not automatically added to the Games Explorer for some reason). Then, navigate to the Marketplace tab, shown in Figure 16-34. From here, you can browse game add-ons, demos, videos, games, and other related content.

Figure 16-34: The Games for Windows - LIVE client provides access to a marketplace with a host of game-related downloads.

Some items, like game demos, are free. Others, like some game add-ons, require a fee. As with Xbox Live, you pay for items on the Games for Windows - LIVE Marketplace using Microsoft Points, the software giant's micropayment system.

Secret

Why can't Microsoft simply use local currency like all other online merchants? That's a fair question, and when pressed, Microsoft says the reason is that it would incur a credit card fee on every transaction, even those that were for small amounts of money, thus making local currency transactions prohibitively expensive. With Microsoft Points, you buy points in bulk in amounts like $25 or $50, saving Microsoft money. Of course, the problem with this system is that you often have leftover points that you can't redeem. Did we mention that this was like a free loan to Microsoft, the largest software company on earth? Yeah, it really is.

Microsoft Points do have one redeeming quality, assuming you've bought into the broader Microsoft ecosystem: they work across several services, including Xbox Live, Zune Marketplace, and the Games for Windows - LIVE Marketplace. As a result, you could load up your account with points and purchase an Xbox Live Arcade game on Xbox Live, a Games for Windows - LIVE game title add-on from Games for Windows - LIVE Marketplace, and a digital version of the new U2 album, all in the same day, all using the same account.

Purchased Microsoft Points are associated with your Windows Live ID and, thus, with your Xbox Live Gamertag, your Zune profile, and your Games for Windows - LIVE Gamertag. You can purchase Microsoft Points in various ways, including via the Microsoft Points Web site (http://points.microsoft.com) and with prepaid Xbox Live and Zune Marketplace points cards (found near the register in electronics superstores like Best Buy). If you do need to add points, the Games for Windows - LIVE standalone application has a link, Add Points, that redirects you to the Microsoft Points Web site. Using the client, you can also redeem points using a prepaid card, using the 25-character code it contains.

Beyond this tepid step into e-commerce, the Games for Windows - LIVE client doesn't have much to offer currently. That could change in the future, but for now the real action occurs when you're using an actual Games for Windows - LIVE game title.

Accessing Games for Windows - LIVE from within Compatible Games

You're really only participating in the best of what Games for Windows - LIVE offers when you're playing a compatible game, which still amounts to a pretty small selection of titles. Most game developers today are forgoing the Games for Windows - LIVE program and simply doing their own thing. Or, they're signing up for the less inclusive "Games for Windows" logo program instead. These games supply some of the benefits of Games for Windows - LIVE but none of the online capabilities. That's not to say that you can't play these games online. It means that these games aren't tied into Microsoft's Live network in any way.

> **tip** To see which games are compatible with Games for Windows - LIVE, visit the Games for Windows - LIVE Web site and prepare to be underwhelmed: www.gamesforwindows.com/en-US/Live/Pages/AboutLive.aspx.

Clearly, a better way to handle this would be for Microsoft to create a pervasive Games for Windows - LIVE client, available via Games Explorer and Windows Live Messenger and elsewhere in Windows, which could be accessed both inside and outside of Live-compatible game titles. But since you don't have that kind of seamless experience, we will instead examine what you do get.

Boot up a Live-compatible title like *Quantum of Solace*, *Fallout 3*, or *Grand Theft Auto IV* and you can access the Live service by pressing the Home button on your keyboard, as shown in Figure 16-35.

As you can see, this is a reasonable facsimile of the Xbox Guide, which you access on the Xbox 360 when you press the Xbox button on the controller. From here, you can access your Gamertag's Gamer Profile, as shown in Figure 16-36; your Messages, Friends, and Players lists; a Private Chat area for one-on-one voice conversations; and Settings, which includes Voice, Notifications, and some other features. (The Xbox 360 offers additional functionality, such as Vibration, Themes, Active Downloads, and Shut Down, most of which are specific to the Xbox 360 console.)

Figure 16-35: The Live experience in Windows requires a compatible game and supplies much of the functionality Xbox 360 users are familiar with.

Figure 16-36: Your Gamer Profile provides information about you that is accessible to others on Live.

Unlike with the 360's Xbox Dashboard, you no longer see virtual Xbox 360 controller buttons throughout the UI. Instead, the Games for Windows - LIVE Guide is now more PC-oriented, and designed primarily to work with the keyboard and mouse. That said, you can in fact use an Xbox 360 controller with Windows 7 and with the Games for Windows -LIVE interface, and the controller buttons all work similarly to how they work on the console. (The red "B" button is "Back," for example.) However, on Windows, you can also press the corresponding keyboard key (like the *b* key) to perform the same actions, which is handy and logical, especially for those without Xbox 360 controllers, which is most PC gamers, we'd imagine.

The Games for Windows - LIVE experience provides some interesting functionality, including the following:

◆ **Accessing and modifying information associated with your Gamertag:** You can view your Gamerscore, Rep, and other related info, access overall and individual game Achievements (see Figure 16-37), and so on. Account management occurs outside the client: If you access this option, you'll be presented with an IE browser window.

Figure 16-37: You can look up all of your game Achievements, whether they occurred on the Xbox 360 or on Windows.

◆ **Friends:** This is the list of people with whom you have created online relationships. As with the Xbox 360, this list is ordered with those who are currently online at the top, followed by the remainder of your Friends listed in alphabetical order. You can see what your online Friends are up to (which game they're playing, or other Xbox 360 experiences they're enjoying, such as Windows Media Center or browsing the Xbox Dashboard).

◆ **Messages:** Here, you can access messages sent through the Xbox Live/Games for Windows - LIVE network. These messages are e-mail–like in nature, as shown in Figure 16-38, but can include audio and video messages in addition to normal text messages (the latter of which are limited to 255 characters).You can create new text and audio messages from the client, but not video messages. You can send and approve Friend requests as well.

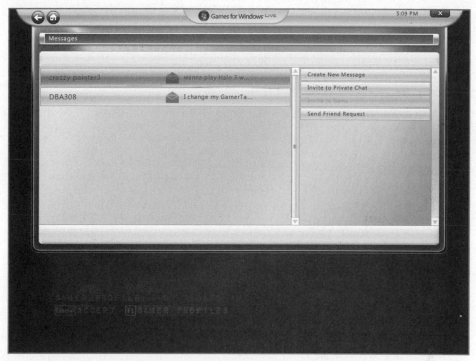

Figure 16-38: It's like e-mail, but you can only access and send these messages from an Xbox 360 or a Games for Windows - LIVE compatible game.

Secret

Okay, you can actually access some of these messages from Microsoft's web-based interface as well, found at www.xbox.com. Note that some messages sent from older Xbox games can only be accessed from within those games. This is less of a problem than it used to be, but some classic Xbox games—notably *Halo 2*—are still quite popular for some reason.

◆ **Players:** This is the list of Xbox Live/Games for Windows - LIVE users with whom you've competed recently online. As with the Friends list, players who are currently online appear at the top of the list. All the normal functions are available, so you can submit a player review, file a complaint, mute them, send a message or invite them to a private chat, or send a Friend Request.

◆ **Private Chat:** Here, you can engage in up to five separate one-on-one audio chats with Friends and other players. This requires an Xbox 360 controller with an attached headset or any Windows-compatible microphone.

◆ **Settings:** In this submenu, you can configure your Voice options (playback and recording volume, plus access to sound hardware and a Mute Microphone option); Notifications (even more limited than on the 360: You can toggle Show Notifications and Play Sound only); and other features, such as the Guide key, which is set to the Home key by default.

While there are two levels of the Xbox Live service, Microsoft no longer requires Games for Windows - LIVE users to subscribe to the higher-end (paid) Xbox Live Gold service in order to compete online against other players. Anyone who plays a Games for Windows - LIVE game title can access a single Gamertag with an associated Gamer Profile, Gamerscore, and Friends list, single-player game Achievements, private text and audio chat, and PC-only multiplayer gaming. You can also access features that Xbox gamers pay for, like TrueSkill Matchmaking for finding players online that better match your own abilities, multiplayer Achievements, and cross-platform game play. At this time, cross-platform game play, whereby an online match can mix and match PC and Xbox 360 gamers, is still limited to a rather lousy title called *Shadowrun*.

If you're an Achievements hound, you may be interested to know that some Xbox 360 games have been ported to Games for Windows - LIVE, enabling you to effectively play the same game twice, once on Xbox 360 and once on Windows, thereby doubling up on the Achievements. As of this writing, games such as *Gears of War*, *Hour of Victory* (EU only), *Kane & Lynch: Dead Men*, *The Club*, *Universe at War*, *Viva Piñata*, and others offer this possibility. Also, an original Xbox blockbuster, *Halo 2*, has been ported to Windows, providing PC gamers with Achievements for the first time. There's never been a better time to rack up Achievements points.

Looking at the big picture, it's hard to escape the conclusion that Microsoft has delivered the absolute minimum here: Games for Windows - LIVE provides a single online identity with a unified contacts list that combines people you communicate with on the Xbox 360 and the PC. So much other obvious functionality is missing in action. For example, there's no way to change a Gamertag picture to any picture you can access from the PC. And you can't access the tremendous Xbox Live Marketplace from the PC at all, though Microsoft is arguably working toward some of this functionality in its related Games for Windows - LIVE Marketplace and Zune Marketplace (see Chapter 14). There are few downloadable games, and certainly nothing like the popular Xbox Live Arcade titles.

In any event, Games for Windows - LIVE is here, and if you're a dedicated gamer, it's still worth looking into, especially if you're an Achievements fanatic.

Summary

There's no doubt about it: Windows 7 is the ultimate operating system for gamers, and arguably a better destination than even the Xbox 360 or Sony's Playstation 3, thanks to the wide variety of compatible game titles, game types, and the never-ending march of PC innovations. With its array of nicely spiffed-up built-in games, parental controls aimed at helping keep children away from inappropriate games, stellar support for gaming hardware, and a handy Games Explorer that works nicely with third-party games, Windows 7 is a great starting point. Add in MSN Games and Games for Windows - LIVE Messenger, and you can play casual games online with others. If you're a hard-core gamer, Microsoft has you covered with its Games for Windows - LIVE service and a growing stable of compatible games. And let's not forget that the largest library of third-party game titles isn't on the Xbox or the PlayStation: it's on Windows. No matter what kind of games you prefer, Windows 7 is the place to be.

Part V

Mobility

Seven to Go: Windows 7 Mobility Features

Chapter
17

◆ ◆

In This Chapter

Managing the Windows 7 user interface settings for optimal performance and battery life

Discovering new power management features

Creating and using your own power plans

Utilizing the Windows Mobility Center

Exploring new features aimed at presentations

Accessing files and folders while disconnected from the network

Using Windows SideShow

Improving performance with ReadyBoost

Windows 7 and netbooks

◆ ◆

Windows 7 is the best version of Windows yet for users on the go. Whether you use a notebook computer, netbook, Tablet PC, or Ultra-Mobile PC, you won't get a better mobile experience than what's available in Microsoft's latest desktop operating system. This time around, Microsoft has fortified Windows 7 with an evolved version of the user interface, power management, and presentation capabilities that debuted in Windows Vista along with dramatically improved performance and a suite of mobile-oriented applications and utilities that tie it all together. You'll learn about each of these features in this chapter.

Windows 7 on the Road

Over the years, Microsoft has steadily improved Windows to better take advantage of the unique hardware features and capabilities offered by portable computers such as notebooks, laptops, Tablet PCs (including a smaller new generation of tablet devices called *Ultra-Mobile Personal Computers*, or *UMPCs*), and, in Windows 7, a new class of low-cost portable PCs called *netbooks*. For the most part, using Windows 7 on a notebook computer or other portable PC is just like using it on a desktop PC. That is, a notebook computer can do anything a desktop PC can, and Windows 7 doesn't have a limited feature set when you're using a portable PC. In fact, if anything, Windows 7 offers more functionality on portable PCs than it does on desktop computers. That's because certain features really only come to life when they're used on a portable PC.

Secret

That said, some PC makers may opt to saddle their netbook computers with the low-end Windows 7 Starter Edition in order to save money. If that's the case with the machine you've purchased, then you actually have a version of Windows 7 that is, in many ways, less capable than more mainstream versions. Check out Chapter 2 for information about using a feature called Windows Anytime Upgrade to upgrade this Windows 7 product edition to a more capable version.

You may want to approach Windows 7 a bit differently when using a notebook computer. Certain operating system features, such as the user interface or power management plan you select, can affect both performance and battery life when you're not connected to power. Windows 7 also includes special presentation, security, and networking features that are often specific to portable computers, or at least work somewhat differently when you're using a portable PC. Windows 7 also includes certain software applications, such as Mobility Center, that are available only on portable computers.

tip

This chapter uses terms such as *portable PC, portable computer, notebook, laptop,* and even, occasionally, *Tablet PC* to describe mobile computers running Windows 7. For the most part, these terms are interchangeable in the context of this chapter unless specifically stated otherwise. This is also true of netbook PCs, though we discuss them separately because their unique form factors and capabilities warrant a separate examination.

Working with the Windows 7 User Interface

One of the most obvious niceties of Windows 7 is the Windows Aero user interface, which is discussed in Chapter 4. Windows Aero offers several unique features compared to the other UI options available in Windows 7, including translucency, various special effects, and even access to certain Windows features (such as the Windows Flip 3D application-switching utility and Aero Peek). Conversely, Windows Aero is more hardware inten-sive than other display modes and can thus drain battery life more quickly than the other user interface options. Your decision whether to use Windows Aero—shown in Figure 17-1—depends on how you feel about battery life, performance, and usability.

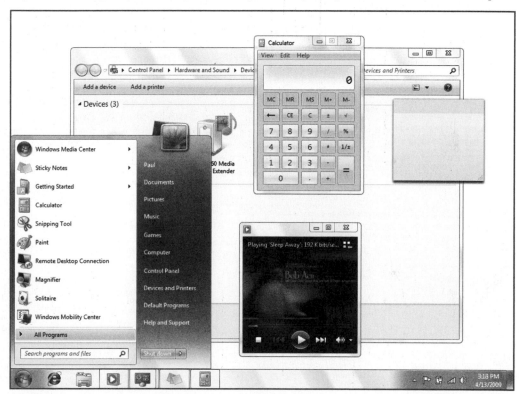

Figure 17-1: Windows Aero is gorgeous-looking but can drain a notebook's battery more quickly than other Windows 7 user interface options.

Before getting to that, however, you should also be aware that many portable computers—especially those made before 2008—simply don't include enough graphical processing power to even run Windows Aero. If this is the case, you will typically see the Windows 7 Basic user interface instead. (On some versions of Windows 7, there's also an option called Windows Standard that offers an enticing middle ground between the beauty of Windows Aero and the power management thriftiness and performance of Windows Classic, the low-end user interface that is designed to resemble the user interface from Windows 2000.)

Depending on your hardware, your choice might already be made: if you install Windows 7 on a portable PC and the user interface is set as Windows 7 Basic and not Windows Aero, then you may be out of luck: your system is most likely not capable of displaying Windows 7's highest-end user interface.

Secret

It *is* possible that your mobile computer can handle Windows Aero even if Windows 7 Basic appears by default. There is a chance that Windows 7 simply didn't install the latest driver for your display hardware. Before sinking into despair, consult the documentation for your notebook, find out exactly which display hardware it uses, and then visit Windows Update via the Start menu to obtain the latest driver and see if that makes a difference. Alternately, visit the hardware maker's Web site; sometimes the vendor offers drivers directly to consumers as well.

Secret

If you're not the kind of person who reads documentation, Windows 7 offers a few utilities that can help you determine which display hardware your system is utilizing. The first is called System Information (type **System Information** in Start Menu Search). Under the System Summary list on the left, choose Components ⇨ Display. You can also try the DirectX Diagnostic Tool (**dxdiag** in Start Menu Search): you'll see information about your display device on the Display tab of this application, shown in Figure 17-2.

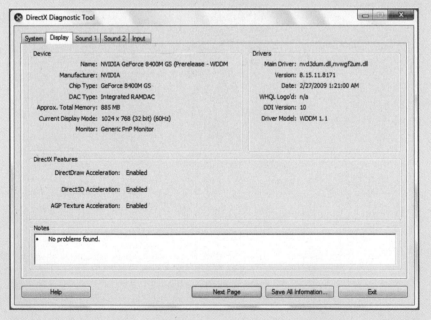

Figure 17-2: You can find out about your display hardware using the DirectX Diagnostic Tool, a hidden Windows feature.

> **tip**
> In order to run Windows Aero, you need a DirectX 9–compatible video card with 64MB or more of discrete graphics RAM, depending on the resolution of your display (64MB is adequate for a 1024 × 768 display, but you need 128MB or more for higher resolutions). Newer integrated graphics chips—the types that share RAM with the system and are more common on notebooks—are now capable of displaying Aero.

Assuming your machine is powerful enough to display Windows Aero, you might still want to opt for the Windows 7 Basic user interface because of its thriftier power management. However, Windows Aero is more stable and reliable than other user interfaces because of the way it interacts with the underlying system and required signed drivers from hardware makers. Like all trade-offs, the decision is not an easy one. Our advice is to test how your particular system behaves on battery power while using both user interfaces. If the battery life difference between the two is negligible, go with Windows Aero.

To change the user interface, right-click the desktop and choose Personalize from the resulting pop-up menu. This displays the Personalization control panel. In the top section, you can choose between various themes, including Aero Themes, which utilize the Windows Aero UI. As shown in Figure 17-3, the Personalization control panel lets you choose between these Aero Themes and other less impressive themes, such as Windows 7 Basic, Windows Classic, and some high-contrast themes aimed at those with vision handicaps.

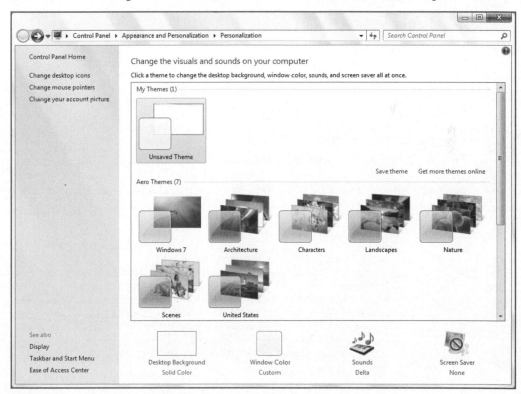

Figure 17-3: Personalization lets you choose between various UI themes.

While using Windows Aero, you can make one change that affects the performance and battery life of Windows 7 while retaining the other features that make Windows Aero worthwhile: you can turn off Windows translucency by clicking Window Color in the bottom of the Personalization control panel and then unchecking the Enable Transparency option that appears in Window Color and Appearance, as shown in Figure 17-4. Translucency is a fun feature, but it doesn't really aid productivity and it's a bit taxing on the battery, so this is an obvious candidate for change.

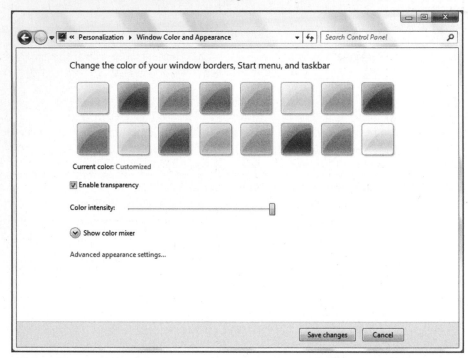

Figure 17-4: From Windows Color and Appearance you can disable transparency.

Alternatively, you could use Windows 7 Basic instead of Aero. To do so, click the Windows 7 Basic theme in Basic and High Contrast Themes.

Secret

Back during Windows Vista's development, Microsoft promised that the OS would seamlessly move between Windows Aero, while attached to power, and Windows Vista Basic, while the machine was untethered and running on battery. This feature, sadly, was never added to the final version of Windows Vista, forcing users to manually switch between user interface modes—and it's missing in Windows 7 as well. But there is one related improvement: now, when you move between Windows Aero and Windows 7 Basic, the transition is much speedier. In Windows Vista, the system would often freeze up for several long seconds, making you wait while it transitioned between themes.

Power Management

Although even desktop-based computers running Windows 7 support various power management features, this functionality is much more relevant on portable computers, which is why we're discussing it in this chapter. Windows 7's power management functionality can be accessed throughout the user interface in various ways, but the easiest way to understand power management in Windows 7 is to realize that it comprises three basic areas: a system notification battery meter icon, a Power Options control panel, and a simplified set of power management plans. This section examines each of these features.

Battery Meter

Mobile computing users are quite familiar with the battery meter that has resided in the tray notification area since Windows 95. This handy icon has been updated yet again in Windows 7 and can appear in various states, each of which changes the look of the icon. The state you see depends on whether the machine is connected to a power source, and how well the battery is charged. Table 17-1 summarizes the various icon types you can expect to see.

Table 17-1: Windows 7 Battery Meter States

Icon	State	What It Means
	Charged, plugged in	The battery is completely charged and the system is plugged into a wall outlet.
	Charging, plugged in	The battery is charging while the system is plugged into a wall outlet. (This icon is animated.)
	On battery power	The battery is discharging because the system is operating on battery power.

Secret

Although the battery meter now offers far more functionality than before, you may find it a bit bewildering. That's because the Windows 7 battery meter offers a completely different experience depending on how you decide to interact with it. Here are the various actions you can perform with the battery meter:

● **Mouse-over:** If you move the mouse cursor over the battery meter, it will display the pop-up window shown in Figure 17-5. This pop-up window summarizes the state of the battery, but unlike Vista, it no longer includes information about the currently used power plan.

Figure 17-5: This pop-up provides you with an at-a-glance look at the state of your battery's charge, but it no longer provides info about your power management plan.

continues

continued

- **Single-click:** If you click the battery meter icon once, you'll see the larger and interactive pop-up window shown in Figure 17-6. This pop-up window provides more information than the mouse-over pop-up, and it enables you to select from one of two preset power plans (Vista offered three), which are discussed in the next section. You can also access other power management–related OS features from this window. (Note that the plans shown in the figure are a subset of Microsoft's defaults: PC makers often replace at least one of these power plans with their own custom plan, so what you see here may vary.)

Figure 17-6: This pop-up offers a wealth of power management functionality in a relatively small space.

- **Right-click:** If you right-click the battery meter, you'll see the pop-up menu shown in Figure 17-7. From this menu, you can adjust the screen brightness, access Power Options (discussed later in this chapter), access Windows Mobility Center (also discussed later in this chapter), or click an option titled "Turn system icons on or off" (It was called "Show System Icons" in Windows Vista), which brings up the new System Icons control panel, from which you can determine which system icons appear by default in the tray.

Figure 17-7: This pop-up menu offers a way to access the Windows 7 mobile and power management features.

If you're running a desktop PC, the Power tray notification icon is unavailable, so there's no obvious way to enable it; but that doesn't mean you can't change the power management settings on a desktop PC. To access Windows 7's Power Options on a desktop PC, just open the Start menu and type **power options** in Start Menu Search. Alternately, you can access the new System Icons control panel directly by typing **system icons** in Start Menu Search.

note Curiously, if you double-click the battery meter, nothing happens.

Power Plans

Microsoft has further simplified the power plans in Windows 7, compared even to the work that began with Windows Vista. These power plans are used to manage your PC's use of its power resources, both while attached to wall power and while running on battery. Three preconfigured power plans are included in a stock installation of Windows 7, though only two of them are available from the Power icon in the tray for some reason. But you can choose any of them, modify each to suit your needs, and even create your own power plans.

tip Confusingly, your PC maker might make its own machine-specific power plans as well, so if you purchased a notebook with Windows 7 preinstalled, you might see additional plans listed. You can edit any plans, however (including those made by Microsoft or your PC maker), and create your own plans. You can also delete plans added by your PC maker, though this isn't necessarily a great idea, as the PC maker probably knows more about the power management characteristics of their hardware than you do.

The three built-in power plans are Balanced (the default on all stock Windows 7 systems), Power Saver, and High Performance. By default, only Balanced and Power saver are available from the Power icon in the system tray, but each is discussed in the following sections.

Balanced

This default plan balances power management between power consumption and performance. It does this based on how you're using the computer at the time. If you begin playing a game or accessing Windows 7's multimedia features, the system automatically ratchets up the processor speed and other hardware features to ensure that you don't experience any slowdowns. Similarly, if you're just browsing the Web or reading text documents, Windows 7 will slow the processor down as much as possible, conserving battery power.

Secret The Windows 7 power management plans are far more aggressive than they were in Windows Vista. The reasoning here is simple: better power management equates to better battery life. But you may be surprised to discover how quickly the screen on your notebook dims, especially when you're running on battery power. Windows 7 is serious about saving the juice.

By default, with the Balanced power plan, your system's microprocessor will be running at about 65 percent of its maximum performance. Based on need, Balanced enables the processor to use as little as 5 percent of its maximum performance and as much as 100 percent. This is true when the system is either running on battery power or plugged in, so don't assume that using Balanced in some way prevents your computer from working at its full potential. If you need the processing power, you'll get it.

While plugged into a power source, the Balanced power plan dims the display after 5 minutes of inactivity and turns it off after 10 minutes of inactivity. However, the computer won't normally go to sleep.

On battery power, it's even more aggressive: 2 minutes to dim the display and 5 minutes to turn it off. The PC goes to sleep after 15 minutes of inactivity.

In our experience, the default Balanced plan is the optimal power plan to use for portable machines of all kinds. Heck, it's even the right plan for desktop machines. This time, Microsoft got it right.

Power Saver

This plan sacrifices performance for better battery life. It should be used only by those with light computing requirements or those who are trying to maximize uptime while on the road. We often switch to Power Saver mode when we're on a flight and need to maximize battery life in order to get some writing done or watch a DVD movie. (Hey, you gotta relax sometimes, too.) However, because Power Saver adversely affects system performance, you won't want to use this mode while performing complex tasks like playing a game or editing video.

By default, with the Power Saver power plan, your system's microprocessor will be running at about 40 percent of its maximum performance. Based on need, Power Saver allows the processor to use as little as 5 percent of its maximum performance; and, as with Balanced, it can actually reach up to 100 percent (whereas in Vista, it topped out at 50 percent.) But unlike Balanced, Power Saver truly is a compromise: in the interests of maximizing battery life, Power Saver forces the processor to work with the lowest possible performance required to get the job done. This is a problem because the system will sometimes struggle to keep up, depending on how much you're doing.

Here's how Power Saver affects your power management settings. Windows 7 aggressively decreases the processor speed and display brightness at all times. On power, Windows 7 dims the display after 2 minutes and turns off the display after 5, and then puts the computer to sleep after just 15 minutes. On battery power, the display dims after 1 minute of inactivity and is turned off after 2 minutes of inactivity, and the computer goes to sleep after just 10 minutes of inactivity.

Secret

Power Saver is also the only power plan to use what Microsoft calls an *adaptive display*. That is, if you've configured your system to use the Windows Aero user interface and you switch to battery power while using the Power Saver plan, Windows automatically switches the display to Windows Standard, removing translucency and other Aero effects. Once you plug in the system again, the Aero effects return automatically. Power Saver does this because certain Aero effects are unduly taxing on the system from a power management perspective.

High Performance

The High Performance plan provides the highest level of performance by maximizing the system's processor speed at the expense of battery life. This plan is aimed at those who spend most of their time playing modern video games or working in graphic-intensive applications. While this used to be the default power plan for all desktop PCs in Windows Vista, that's no longer the case in Windows 7. In fact, High Performance isn't even available as an option from the pop-up menu you see when you click the Power icon in the system tray. To enable this plan, you need to visit the Power Options control panel, which is discussed in the next section.

Secret

Yes, you guessed it: Under the High Performance plan, Windows 7 provides 100 percent of your CPU's processing power, all the time.

Under the High Performance plan, Windows 7 will dim the display after 10 minutes of inactivity when on wall power and turn it off after 15 minutes of inactivity, but never put the PC to sleep. On battery power, you're looking at 5 minutes until the display dims, and 10 minutes until the display is turned off. But again, the computer is never put to sleep.

Secret

Desktop PCs utilize power plans as well, and though you may believe that High Performance has some advantages over Balanced, it may not be the best option, especially if you're concerned about the environment and saving energy. Instead, we recommend leaving even desktop PCs set to Balanced. Windows will be more aggressive about putting the system to sleep and your PC will use less power (and thus draw less energy) in normal use. And, of course, if you need the full power of the processor—for example, when playing a game or using a graphics application—Balanced will provide it. This plan truly is the best of both worlds.

Scanning through the power plans, it's likely that you'll find a plan that at least somewhat matches your expectations, but you don't have to accept Microsoft's default settings. You can easily modify any of the existing plans, and even create your own power plans. You'll look at those possibilities in the next section.

Power Options Control Panel

Windows 7's power options are, go figure, configured via the Power Options control panel, which is available in Control Panel ⇨ Hardware and Sound ⇨ Power Options on any kind of PC. (For some reason, there were different ways to access this control panel in Windows Vista, depending on whether you were using a portable PC or a desktop PC.) As always, Start Menu Search is your friend: just type **power options** into Start Menu Search to get there quickly, regardless of what kind of PC you have.) Shown in Figure 17-8, this control panel initially presents a selection of two of the three power plans mentioned previously. (Again, you may see different options if your PC maker decided to configure its own custom plan.)

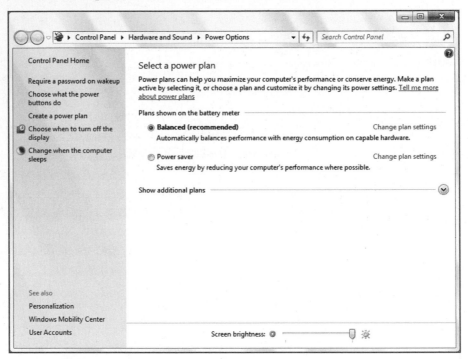

Figure 17-8: Power Options is your central management console for the Windows 7 power management features.

There's a lot more going on here, however, and some things have changed since Windows Vista. On the left side of the window are a number of power management–related tasks. If you're using a mobile computer of any kind, navigate through each of these options to ensure that your system is configured exactly the way you want it. These options are interesting to desktop PC users as well. You can also quickly access the screen brightness settings directly from this window, a new addition in Windows 7.

Requiring a Password on Wakeup

The first option, "Require a password on wakeup," varies a bit according to your system's capabilities and there's a lot more going on here beyond the password option hinted at in the link. On a typical desktop PC, this power plan settings page resembles what is shown in Figure 17-9.

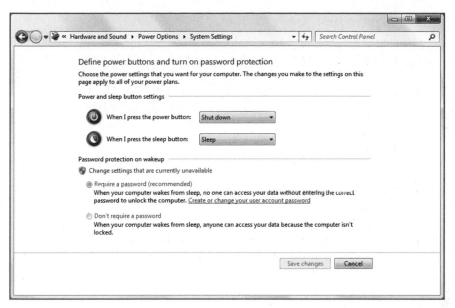

Figure 17-9: Desktop PCs don't have many power management options related to hardware features.

But when you view this page on a typical notebook computer, you'll see the options shown in Figure 17-10. These options are directly related to the additional hardware buttons and features included with mobile computers.

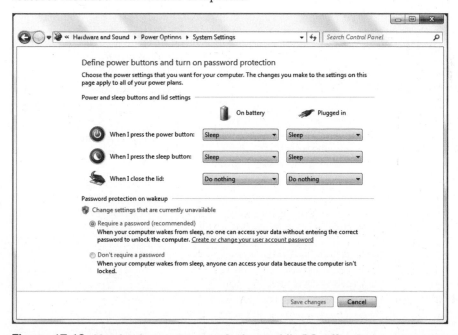

Figure 17-10: Notebook computers and other mobile PCs offer power management options related to the lid and other hardware features.

Here, you can modify how Windows 7 reacts when you press the PC's power button; press the sleep button; or, on portable computers configured with a lid-based display, when you close the lid. Each of these options has different settings for when the system is operating on battery power versus plugged in.

Complementing the "Require a password on wakeup" option described previously, this dialog also includes a single wakeup-related option that determines whether you need to log on again each time the system wakes up after being in the sleep state. By default, Windows 7 does require you to log on again to unlock the computer as a security measure. We strongly advise leaving this feature enabled, especially if you're a mobile computer user who often accesses the PC on the road.

Secret

If you do decide to change the "Require a password on wakeup option," you may very well discover that the options "Require a password (recommended)" and "Don't require a password" are grayed out and thus unavailable for editing. No problem: to change this option, click the link titled "Change settings that are currently unavailable." You'll see a small Windows shield icon next to it, indicating that this choice will trigger a security-oriented User Account Control (UAC) prompt. But, go figure, no UAC prompt actually pops up, unlike with Windows Vista. See? Windows 7 really is less annoying.

Returning to the Power Options display, the following additional options are available on the left side of the window.

Choose What the Power Buttons Do

Humorously, this option triggers the same display described previously. The top half of the dialog relates to this option.

Choose What Closing the Lid Does

This option, which is available only on portable computers with a lid, also brings you to the same dialog described previously. Why three different options all land on the same display is a question best saved for the UI wizards at Microsoft. (And, on a related note, how was this silliness carried over from Windows Vista to Windows 7 with nary a change?)

Create a Power Plan

When you click this option, you're brought to the Create a Power Plan page, a short wizard you can use to create your own power plan:

1. First, choose the preset power plan—Balanced, Power Saver, or High Performance— that you would like to base your plan on (see Figure 17-11). Give the plan a name (ideally, something more inventive than *My Custom Plan 1*, the default) and click the Next button.

2. In this step of the wizard, shown in Figure 17-12, specify when the system will dim the display, turn off the display, and put the system to sleep, on both battery power and when plugged in. (Desktop PC users will see only a single option for each, as these PCs are always plugged in. You may not see a "Dim the display" option on desktop PCs either.)

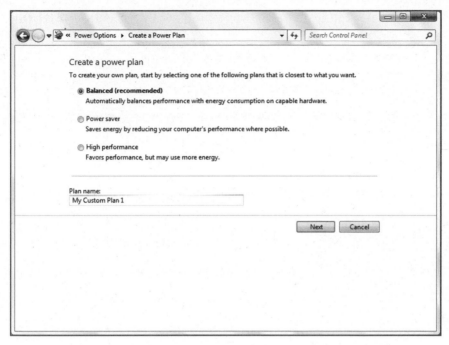

Figure 17-11: New power plans are modeled after one of the existing plans.

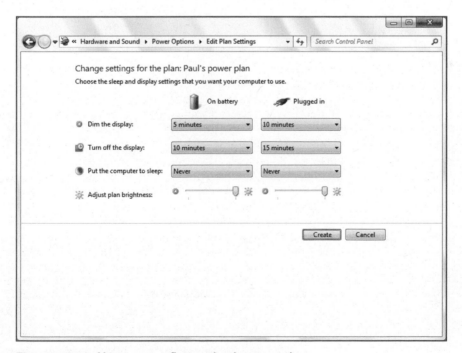

Figure 17-12: Here, you configure what happens when.

3. Click the Create button to create your plan, which will be added to the list of available plans, as shown in Figure 17-13. Annoyingly, it replaces one plan in the so-called Preferred plans list, though that plan is still available in the less impressive-sounding Additional plans section.

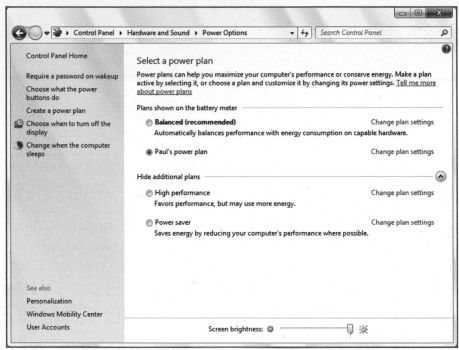

Figure 17-13: Custom power plans replace the plan on which your plan was based, but the old default plan is still available.

This is all well and good, but the short wizard you just used doesn't really provide access to all of the power management options you can configure; and isn't that the point of this exercise—to create a custom power plan that exactly matches your needs and desires?

To modify your custom plan (or an existing preset plan for that matter), click the Change plan settings link next to the plan name in question. This brings you to a dialog that resembles the second phase of the wizard just described, but with one difference: there's now a Change advanced power settings link. Click that link to modify other settings. Doing so opens the Power Options Advanced settings dialog, shown in Figure 17-14.

The Power Options Advanced settings window is, by nature, confusing. The window itself is not resizable, so it provides only a postage-stamp-size view of the many power management features you can customize. More problematic, you have to expand nodes in a tree control—arguably the worst PC user interface element of all time—to find all the options. Nonetheless, it's worth the trouble if you're serious about modifying a power plan.

Figure 17-14: Use this rather complicated dialog to handcraft your power plan using every single power management option available to Windows 7.

Here are the power management options available via this dialog:

♦ **Balanced/Power saver/High performance:** This setting, which is named after the power plan you're changing, lets you configure whether the system requires a password when it wakes from sleep. (Portable PCs divide this option into two sub-options: one for when the system is plugged in and one for when it's attached to a power source.) The default option is Yes for both, and you should leave them alone unless you're interested in playing Russian Roulette with private data stored on your PC.

♦ **Hard disk:** Use this option to configure the hard disk to wind down after a period of time to preserve power. (As with many settings, portable PCs have separate options for battery and plugged in.) On battery, you want this time to be reasonably low, maybe five minutes, but you should also configure a desktop PC or power-attached portable PC to wind down the hard drive after a short period as well, if only to conserve power consumption.

♦ **Desktop background settings:** This setting determines what should happen when you're using a desktop theme with multiple images (in a slide show). There are two settings, one for battery power, and one for plugged in, and two possibilities for both: Available, which leaves background image changing on, and Paused, which prevents the background from changing to save battery power.

♦ **Wireless Adapter Settings:** This option may seem fairly esoteric, but it can affect the performance of your wireless card (a common feature in portable PCs) and the PC. This feature is of interest only to portable PC users. By default, under most power management plans, the wireless adapter is set to run with maximum performance. The only exception is the Power Saver plan, on battery power: in this mode, the wireless adapter is configured to run under maximum power-saving mode, which conserves power by lowering the effectiveness of the wireless radio. You can configure this option as follows: Maximum Performance, Low Power Saving, Medium Power Saving, and Maximum Power Saving. Frankly, this might be too fine-grained for most people, and we've had little success determining what effects each state really has on power management and performance overall. Given this, our recommendation is to leave this setting at its default, based on which power plan you based your own plan on.

◆ **Sleep:** This section supports four options: Sleep after, Allow hybrid sleep, Hibernate after, and, new to Windows 7, Allow wake timers. The first and third are straight-forward, but the second and fourth options might be confusing.

Newer PCs support a new type of Sleep mode called Hybrid Sleep, which enables the machine to appear to turn off and on almost immediately, like a consumer electronics device. If you have a PC manufactured after mid-2006, it might support this feature, so experiment with enabling Hybrid Sleep, especially since it likely won't be enabled by default. If it works well, use this instead of Hibernation, as Hybrid Sleep is essentially a replacement for that older form of power management. Otherwise, you might want to enable Hibernation, which was a major power management feature in Windows XP. Hibernation is faster than turning on and off the PC, but much slower than Sleep or Hybrid Sleep. Although the PC is turned off, it preserves the state of the system so you can get up and running with your applications more quickly.

Allowing the user to configure wake timers is new to Windows 7. Wake timers are used by applications and the OS to wake an idle PC to perform certain tasks that would be impossible if the system were in Sleep mode. By default, wake timers are disabled.

◆ **USB settings:** Your PC can optionally turn off selected USB devices when it enters certain power management states. This can improve battery life, as USB devices, like mice, storage devices, cameras, and other devices, draw power from the PC. However, it also prevents you from using these attached devices. Suspended USB devices will wake up again once the system is plugged in to a power source.

◆ **Power buttons and lid:** What you see here varies according to the hardware capabilities of your PC, but you can usually draw the distinction neatly between desktop PCs and portable PCs. Desktop PCs typically see two options: Power button action and Sleep button action, whereas portable PCs have an additional option: Lid close action. Power button action determines what happens when you press the hardware On/Off switch on the PC (this can be configured separately for battery power and plugged in). Options include Do nothing, Sleep, Hibernate, and Shut Down. Lid close action behaves similarly, but refers to what happens when the lid of a portable computer is shut: you can choose between the same four options. If your PC has a dedicated Sleep button (as do many portable machines), the Sleep button action provides the same configurability, but for that particular button.

◆ **PCI Express:** This option should typically not be changed. On a desktop PC, it should be set to Off so that hardware expansion cards attached via the PCI Express bus are always available. On portable PCs, it is set to Maximum Power Savings or Moderate Power Savings, depending on the power plan and whether the system is running on battery power.

Secret

Windows Vista supported a fourth option here, called Start menu power button. In Windows 7, this option is not related to power management—which makes sense—and is instead available from the Start menu tab of the Taskbar and Start Menu Properties window, shown in Figure 17-15. (You can access this UI by right-clicking the Start button and choosing Properties.)

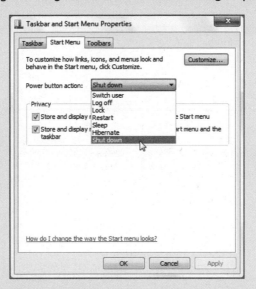

Figure 17-15: The Start menu power button is fully configurable; you just need to know where to look.

- ◆ **Processor power management:** This setting has some of the biggest impact on performance and battery life and should be carefully chosen. Here, you can fine-tune how much processor power is used under certain states. Earlier in this chapter, we described how the default power plans affect processor performance, and you should use that as a guideline. Note, however, that you will likely be disappointed with the system's performance while doing multimedia tasks if 100 percent of the processor's performance isn't available. Note that whereas Windows Vista supported the Minimum processor state and Maximum processor state options, Windows 7 adds a third, new option: System cooling policy. This option is designed for PCs with active cooling systems only and should not be modified unless you know what you're doing.

- ◆ **Display:** Here, you can specify how quickly Windows 7 dims and turns off the display, which is pretty straightforward, and configure the display brightness in both normal and dimmed modes.

- ◆ **Multimedia settings:** One of the nicest features of Windows 7 is that it makes it very easy to share media such as music, videos, and photos from PC to PC and even across the Internet. However, when you're running on battery power, media sharing can be overly resource intensive and thus exacerbate energy consumption, so you may want to curtail media sharing on battery power. Available options include

Allow the computer to sleep, Prevent idling to sleep, and Allow the computer to enter Away mode. The first two are self-explanatory, and portable computers should always be allowed to enter Sleep mode while on battery power. The final option, however, might be confusing. Away mode is a modern power management option (related to media sharing and the Windows Media Center feature) that enables background media tasks, such as Media Center recording of TV shows and media sharing, to occur in the background even while the system otherwise appears to be asleep. This mode thus provides most of the power management benefits of Sleep while still allowing media sharing to occur.

Secret

Away mode first debuted in Windows XP Media Center Edition 2005 Update Rollup 2 (UR2), the last major Media Center update before Vista shipped, but it was enhanced in Windows Vista and 7. The important thing to remember is that Away mode cannot be invoked unless this power management setting is explicitly changed to "Allow the computer to enter Away Mode." In Windows 7, Away mode is used by Windows Media Center Extenders connecting to the PC (see Chapter 15) and media sharing (see Chapter 11).

◆ **Battery:** This option, available only on portable PCs, determines how the system battery is configured to warn you or perform certain actions at specific times, such as when the battery is low or critically low. Options include Critical battery action (what happens when the battery life falls to a "critical" level), Low battery level (at what percentage of full the battery is considered "low"), Critical battery level (at what percentage of full the battery is considered "critical"), Low battery notification (whether the system informs you of the transition into this state), Low battery action (what happens when the battery life falls to a "low" level), and, new to Windows 7, Reserve battery level (an additional warning level between "low" and "critical," kind of like the red area on your car's gas gauge right before true Empty).

◆ **Third-party power management settings:** Many hardware makers have created their own advanced power management settings, which can be exposed to the user via this control panel and configured accordingly. For example, display card maker ATI has an ATI Graphics Power Settings option that helps you configure how ATI Mobility Radeon graphics products impact overall power consumption.

Choose When to Turn Off the Display

This option triggers the same dialog previously described (Edit Plan Settings).

Change When the Computer Sleeps

This option also triggers the same dialog described previously in the "Requiring a Password on Wakeup" section.

Secret

In Windows Vista, you could delete custom power plans in a straightforward manner. Oddly, this capability was removed from the Power Options control panel UI in Windows 7.

Windows Mobility Center

If you've ever owned a mobile PC, you've probably marveled (and not in a good way) at the cruddy utility applications that PC makers seem compelled to ship with their hardware. Microsoft feels your pain. In Windows 7, the software giant continued the work it started in Windows Vista toward creating a centralized management console called Windows Mobility Center for all of this functionality, and it has preloaded this dashboard with all of the utilities a mobile user could want. Best of all, PC makers are free to extend Mobility Center with their own machine-specific mobile utilities. We can't guarantee these products are any good, but at least they're easily located in this new centralized management console.

Shown in Figure 17-16, Windows Mobility Center is available only on mobile computers. You won't see it on desktop PCs.

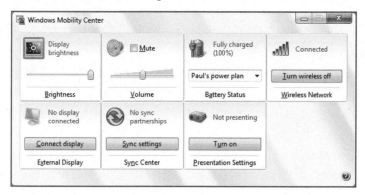

Figure 17-16: Windows Mobility Center looks nothing like most other Windows 7 applications.

The secret keyboard shortcut WinKey+X also starts Mobility Center.

In Windows Vista, you could cause a limited version of Windows Mobility Center to appear on desktop PCs using a registry hack. That hack no longer works in Windows 7, but if we discover a way to implement such a hack, we will write about it on the book's Web site at www.winsupersite.com/book.

You start Mobility Center by finding it in the Start menu or by typing **mobility** into Start Menu Search, which is quite a bit faster.

Curiously, Windows Mobility Center does not really visually resemble any of the other applications that Microsoft bundled with Windows 7. It presents a set of mobile-related options that are arrayed in square tiles across an unadorned window that cannot be resized or formatted in any way. These options, which vary according to the capabilities of your PC, can include Brightness, Volume, Battery Status, Wireless Network, External Display, Sync Center, and Presentation Settings.

Basically, each of these tiles launches a setting that mobile PC users need fairly often, as shown in Figure 17-17. Click the icon in the Volume tile, for example, and the Sound control panel appears. Alternately, you can set or mute the system volume from directly within Mobility Center.

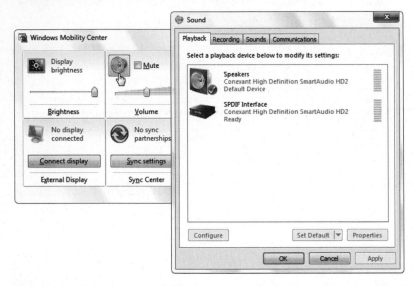

Figure 17-17: Windows Mobility Center is really just a front end to other Windows 7 functionality.

Secret

With one exception, all of the options available in Mobility Center are available elsewhere in the Windows 7 user interface. That one exception is Presentation Settings, covered in the next section.

tip

Remember that you might see additional tiles here that were installed by your PC maker.

Presentations A-Go-Go

Although not a particularly glamorous lifestyle, many mobile users cart their notebooks around the globe, set them up in an unfamiliar location, and attempt to give a presentation using Microsoft PowerPoint or a similar presentation package. Notebooks are perfect companions for such users because of their portability; but until recent versions of Windows, they weren't particularly accommodating if the presentation was conducted on battery power—thanks to various power management settings, the presentation could disappear as the display was shut down or the machine went to sleep. Windows 7 includes three major features related to giving presentations, one of which solves the problem just mentioned.

Presentation Settings

An obscure but useful feature, Presentation Settings enables you to temporarily disable your normal power management settings, ensuring that your system stays awake, with no screen dimming, no hard drive disabling, no screen saver activation, and no system notifications to interrupt you. In other words, with just a few clicks of the mouse, you can set up your mobile PC to behave exactly the way you want it to while giving a presentation.

To enable Presentation Settings, run Mobility Center as described in the previous section and click the projector icon in the Presentation Settings tile. The Presentation Settings dialog is shown in Figure 17-18.

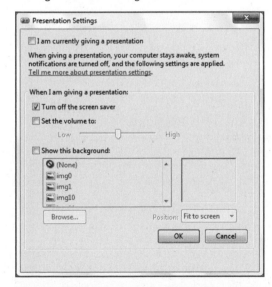

Figure 17-18: Presentation Settings is a boon to anyone who has had to struggle with Windows getting in the way of a presentation.

Select the "I am currently giving a presentation" option to enable Presentation Settings. Optionally, you can turn off the screen saver (the default), turn off the system volume, and temporarily change the desktop background. Presentation Settings also provides a handy way to configure connected displays, including network projectors.

tip You can also enable Presentations with a single click by clicking the Turn On button in the Presentation Settings tile in Windows Mobility Center. Regardless of how you enable this feature, the Presentation Settings tile will change to read Presenting and the projector icon will change to an On state.

Using a Network Projector

If you're going to show a presentation via a modern network-based projector, Windows 7 includes a Connect to a Network Projector utility that automatically configures firewall settings and searches for nearby projectors. To run this utility, find Connect to a Network Project in Start menu ⇨ All Programs ⇨ Accessories. You can search for a projector automatically or enter the projector's IP address.

Secret

Presentation and External Display Options

New to Windows 7 is a secret feature called Presentation and External Display Options that presents yet another new type of window from which you can quickly determine which displays to use. This control panel is nice for anyone with dual displays, but it really comes into its own when you need to give a presentation.

What's so secretive about Presentation and External Display Options? For starters, there's no way to access this feature from the Windows 7 UI. Instead, you have to use the keyboard shortcut WinKey+P to enable it. When you do, you'll see the window shown in Figure 17-19.

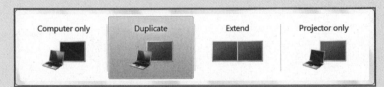

Figure 17-19: Presentation and External Display Options is a secret new feature in Windows 7.

Presentation and External Display Options lets you configure the screen(s) attached to your PC like so:

- **Computer Only:** In this case, only the first display attached to the PC is used and any external display or projector is disabled.
- **Duplicate:** Here, the display in the PC is mirrored to the projector.
- **Extend:** With this setting, the projector is used like a second display and the Windows desktop is extended between the primary display and the projector.
- **Projector Only:** With this setting, the PC's internal display is disabled and the PC desktop is outputted to the projector.

Other Mobile Features

In addition to the major new mobility-related features mentioned previously, Windows 7 ships with a host of other technologies that benefit mobile workers. This section highlights some of these features and explains how you can take advantage of them.

Offline Files and Folders

In Windows XP, Microsoft introduced a feature called Offline Files and Folders that enables mobile users to mark network-based files and folders so that they will be cached (stored) locally, using space on the mobile computer's hard drive. When the mobile PC is connected to the network, the local and remote versions of the files and folders are synchronized so that they are always current. When users work away from the network— which can be a corporate network based on Active Directory or just a simple wireless home network—they can access these remote resources even when in a disconnected state, just as if they were connected.

Offline Files and Folders is a wonderful idea, and it's been made even better in Windows 7. It works almost exactly like it does in Windows Vista, as you'll see here, using Delta Sync technology, first developed by Microsoft's Windows Server team, to speed synchronization. Delta Sync works on the subfile level: if a user changes part of a document, for example, only the changed parts of the document need to be synced to the server. Previously, the entire document would need to be synchronized. This bit of software wizardry is far more efficient than bulk file copies, although we can't really understand how it works under the hood.

To set up Offline Files and Folders for the first time, use the Network Explorer to navigate to a location on your network that contains files or folders you'd like to cache locally. Then, right-click the items you'd like to cache and choose Always available offline. When you do so, the Always Available Offline dialog is displayed (shown in Figure 17-20) and you can synchronize the content to your hard drive.

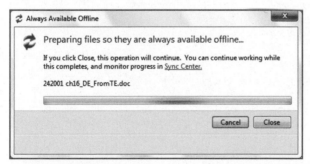

Figure 17-20: You can configure network-based data to be available even when you're not connected to the network.

When the synchronization is complete, you'll see a small sync icon overlay appear on top of the lower-left corner of the folder or file you just synced. This icon overlay indicates that the item is available offline.

In Windows XP, Offline Files and Folders were managed via the Folder Options window. In Windows Vista and Windows 7, you manage these relationships in the Sync Center, which is shown in Figure 17-21. The Sync Center is used to manage relationships between Windows and portable devices (such as PDAs and smartphones), as well as offline files and folders. It does not, however, manage relationships with network-based media devices, such as other PCs, Xbox 360s, and Media Center Extenders. No, we don't know why.

Regardless of how many network-based files and folders you make available offline, you will see only one item, Offline Files, in the main Sync Center display. If you double-click this item, you can dive into the partnership detail and see separate items for each network share that contains shared files and folders. You can also click the Sync button to manually synchronize with the server, or click Schedule to view and manage the sync schedule. The schedule is managed via a simple wizard-based application that enables you to schedule synchronization at specific times or in response to certain events, such as when you log on or lock Windows, or when your computer is idle.

If you take your system on the road and modify network-based files and folders, they will be synchronized with the server when you return. Should there be any conflicts—such as what can occur when a file is edited both on the server and in your local cache—you are given the opportunity to rectify the conflict in a variety of ways, most of which are nondestructive.

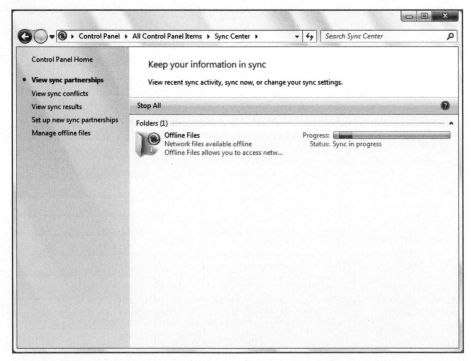

Figure 17-21: Sync Center is an almost one-stop shop for Windows 7's relationships with other devices and network-based files and folders.

Windows SideShow

A new generation of Tablet PCs and notebook computers—and, Microsoft says, even other devices such as TV sets and remote controls—includes a new kind of auxiliary display that enables you to access certain information on the computer even when it's asleep. These auxiliary displays are initially most interesting on mobile computers, and they are available in color and black-and-white versions.

Here's how they work: auxiliary displays access a feature in Windows 7 called SideShow to display small gadgets, similar to Windows Gadgets (see Chapter 4), that provide limited access to various applications and services in Windows. You'll see a Windows Media Player gadget that enables you to play music in your Windows Media Player media library, and an e-mail gadget that helps you read e-mail. All of these gadgets work when the laptop's lid is closed, they require very little power, and they come on instantly. Although Microsoft ships a number of gadgets of its own, you can expect third parties to come up with their own gadgets as well, especially those companies that make and sell SideShow-equipped devices.

The bad news about Windows SideShow is that you need very specific hardware to access this feature. You can't add on an auxiliary display, at least not elegantly, to a mobile PC. Therefore, you need to get a brand-new mobile device with an integrated auxiliary display in order to experience it for yourself. At the time of this writing, years after the feature first shipped in Windows Vista, auxiliary displays are still very rare.

Improved Support for Tablet PC Hardware

If you're using a Tablet PC computer (a notebook computer that typically comes in one of two form factors: a convertible laptop or a true slate-type tablet) or a notebook computer with Tablet PC–like hardware (such as a touch screen, digitizer screen with stylus, or a compatible external writing pad), Windows 7 includes a wide range of functionality related to handwriting recognition, pen-based input, and the like. We discuss these features in the next chapter, which is devoted entirely to Tablet PCs and other computers that have Tablet-like hardware, such as Ultra-Mobile PCs (UMPCs) and the like.

Secret

SyncToy is another other mobility-related Microsoft tool that you may be interested in. According to Microsoft, this fascinating little application helps you quickly and easily copy, move, rename, and delete files between folders and computers. And while that's a very generic description, the beauty of this tool is that it enables you to synchronize the contents of a folder on one computer with the contents of a folder on another computer, so it's a great synchronization tool for people who usually use a desktop PC at home or the office but have to frequently travel with a portable PC as well. You can find out more at www.microsoft.com/downloads/. Just search for **SyncToy**.

Secret

Windows Vista included a peer-to-peer (P2P) collaborative application called Windows Meeting Space that has since been discontinued in Windows 7. Apparently, hardly anyone knew it existed, and those that did know about it had no idea what it was for.

Using Windows 7 with a Netbook

When Microsoft shipped Windows Vista in late 2006, it ushered in an era of next-generation computing that brought with it heady new hardware requirements, rendering certain older PCs immediately obsolete. Microsoft's rationale for this decision was a good one: by taking half-steps in the past, it had held back Windows from a technical perspective in order to include the widest possible audience. With Vista, Microsoft was making a break with the past, and users were expected to upgrade to newer, more powerful PCs in order to take advantage of the new features.

One might debate this strategy indefinitely, but what no one saw coming, not even Microsoft, was the rise of a new class of computers called *netbooks*. (A typical example is shown in Figure 17-22.)

Figure 17-22: Netbooks, like this Lenovo IdeaPad, provide a truly mobile experience in a tiny form factor.

These tiny computers look like miniature versions of regular laptops, with the same clamshell form factor and small screens, keyboards, and trackpads. But there's just one problem with netbooks, from Microsoft's perspective: they're too underpowered to run Windows Vista. And because Windows Vista is relatively expensive compared to the price of a typical netbook—$300 to $400—PC makers originally opted to bypass Windows entirely and install a nearly free version of Linux on the machines instead.

Cue panic in Redmond. Microsoft reacted to the netbook phenomenon by extending the life cycle of Windows XP, Vista's predecessor. It also lowered the price of XP, dramatically, for PC makers that opted to use that system. This pricing tactic worked: in early 2008, over 80 percent of netbooks shipped with some version of Linux instead of Windows. But a year later, Windows was included with 96 percent of all netbooks sold in the U.S. and over 90 percent worldwide.

Success, right? Well, not yet. Microsoft still needed to address the fact that customers were purchasing a relatively ancient version of its flagship OS and skipping Windows Vista, so it architected Windows 7, Vista's successor, so that it would run well on the low-end hardware used by netbooks and a growing generation of low-performance PCs. The result is stunning: Windows 7 runs just as well on netbooks as it does on other mobile computers. But because these netbooks are relatively restrictive compared to full-size and full-featured laptops, we want to address a few of the issues you might run into if you go the netbook route with Windows 7.

◆ **Platform limitations.** Through much of 2009, most netbooks ran on the same basic hardware platform, and featured a dual-core 1.6 GHz Intel Atom processor, 1GB of RAM, a low-end hard drive of some kind, and an 8- to 10-inch wide-screen display. While these systems will be augmented over time with new models based on faster Atom chips (including multi-core and 64-bit versions) or chips from rival companies like NVIDIA, the overall netbook experience won't change: these devices offer cramped quarters and low-end performance compared to other PCs. For that reason, most people currently use netbooks as secondary PCs, but as the lines blur between netbooks and low-end laptops, that may no longer be the case going forward.

Most of today's netbooks feature a resolution of 1024×600, which is sort of an odd-ball resolution that can prove problematic with certain applications and windows. Even the Windows Anytime Upgrade window, shown in Figure 17-23, doesn't quite fit, causing the buttons of the bottom of the window to be hidden.

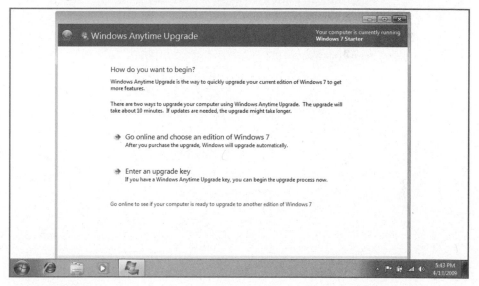

Figure 17-23: Constrained netbook screens will make it hard to use certain applications and windows.

◆ **Windows 7 limitations.** If you tried to save money by getting your netbook with Windows 7 Starter, you may regret it: this low-end version of Windows doesn't support the Aero glass user interface and can only run three applications at a time. See Chapter 1 for our buying advice. But you can also do things like reduce the size of the taskbar and change the desktop and Explorer icons to smaller versions in order to take advantage of the screen real estate you do have. See Chapter 6 for our personalization advice.

While Windows 7 does run just fine on netbooks, you won't be able to play 3D games, edit video, or perform other high-end tasks effectively (or at all) on these systems. Be sure you know what you're getting into.

◆ **Go solid state.** If you can, get a netbook with a solid-state disk (SSD) instead of a traditional hard disk. These drives are more expensive but they perform much better and are more battery friendly.

However you do it, we think you'll be quite satisfied with the Windows 7 experience on a netbook computer. And of course as these low-end devices get more powerful over time, the experience is going to get even better. If you're in the market for a netbook, skip Windows XP and go straight to Windows 7. You won't regret it.

Summary

There's no doubt about it: Windows 7 is the most capable and feature-packed operating system yet created for mobile computers. Thanks to features such as Windows Mobility Center, Presentation Settings, network projector support, Presentation and External Display Options, and integrated power management; Windows 7 will keep any mobile computer humming along nicely with a wide range of new and improved functionality. And if you're lucky enough to be using a low-cost netbook or an innovative Tablet PC or Ultra-Mobile PC (UMPC), your mobility options are even more impressive. You'll take a look at Windows 7's unique support for these tablet-based PC types in the next chapter.

Using Tablet PCs and Ultra-Mobile PCs

Chapter

18

◆ ◆

In This Chapter

Using and configuring Tablet PC features

Entering handwritten text with the Tablet PC Input Panel

Using Flicks and other gestures

Controlling your computer with speech recognition

Understanding Tablet PC–related changes to the Windows shell

Working with Ultra-Mobile PCs

◆ ◆

Duringthelifecycle of Windows XP, Microsoft shipped two versions of that OS that were targeted specifically at Tablet PCs, a different kind of mobile computer based on notebooks that added digitized screens and pens for a more natural style of interaction. Tablet PCs flopped, but Microsoft's software was, for once, widely heralded for its high quality. With Windows Vista and Windows 7, the Tablet PC capabilities have been made available on a far wider range of PCs than was the case with XP, and Microsoft has lifted the restrictions on how users acquire these capabilities. It's now possible to get Tablet PC functionality in all mainstream versions of Windows 7, and on a wide range of hardware types, including unique, tiny mobile devices called Ultra-Mobile PCs, or UMPCs.

A Short History of the Tablet PC

In mid-2002, Microsoft released the first version of Windows XP that was specifically targeted at a new generation of pen-based notebook computers called Tablet PCs. Logically named Windows XP Tablet PC Edition, this software wasn't, of course, the first to try to combine pens (or, really, styluses) with PCs. Indeed, as long ago as the late 1980s, innovative companies such as Go, Apple, and Palm were leading the way to a future of more ergonomic and natural interactions with computers. Even Microsoft got into the game in the early 1990s with a short-lived (and overhyped) product called Pen Windows that, frankly, amounted to nothing.

Tablet PCs, however, were (and still are) different. First, they were mainstream computers with added functionality such as displays with built-in digitizers that could not only sense pen input, but also in many cases even understand when the tip was pressed down harder or lighter. Second, they originally came in two form factors, though more are now available. The first was called a *tablet,* although it's also sometimes referred to as a *slate design.* These machines did not include integrated keyboards and trackpads, but were instead intended to be used primarily via the pen. You could, of course, attach keyboards, mice, and even auxiliary displays to these machines, typically via USB. A typical slate-type Tablet PC is shown in Figure 18-1.

Figure 18-1: Slate-type Tablet PCs do not include integrated keyboards and pointing devices but instead require the use of a pen, or stylus.

The second Tablet PC type, and the one that continues today as the mainstream Tablet PC design, is called a *convertible laptop*. Shown in Figure 18-2, these machines look just like regular laptops, but with one difference: the screen can be swiveled around and rotated back onto the keyboard, giving the machine a temporary slate-like form factor. In this way, a convertible laptop can be used like a regular notebook computer—with a keyboard and trackpad—or like a slate-type Tablet, via the pen.

Figure 18-2: Convertible Tablet PCs have proven to be the most popular design because they can be used like a normal notebook computer when needed.

First-generation Tablet PCs didn't exactly take off in the market. There are many reasons for this, but for once Microsoft wasn't to blame. In fact, the initial version of Windows XP Tablet PC Edition was surprisingly solid. It was based on Windows XP Professional, and thus could do everything that XP Pro could. It supported a variety of screen digitizer types, could perform decent handwriting recognition, could switch the display between landscape and portrait modes on-the-fly (to better simulate writing on a pad of paper), and included some worthwhile software, such as a Windows Journal note-taking application, a Sticky Notes utility, a game, and an add-on pack for Microsoft Office that gave it better Tablet capabilities. All in all, it was an excellent release. Windows XP Tablet PC Edition is shown in Figure 18-3.

Why did Tablet PCs fail in the market? For starters, they were too expensive. Partly to offset research and development costs, and partially to help pay for XP Tablet PC Edition, which carried a premium over other XP editions, PC makers priced first-generation Tablet PCs too high. The machines were also woefully underpowered, with anemic Pentium III Mobile processors. Battery life, too, was horrible, negating the advantages of the platform. Many users who might have otherwise been interested in the ultimate mobile companion gave up given the prices, performance, and battery life.

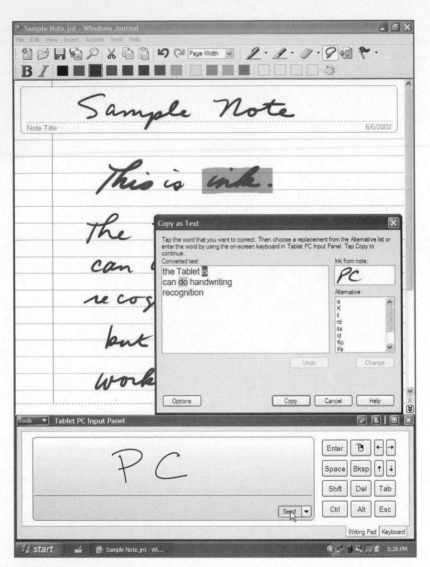

Figure 18-3: Microsoft's original Tablet PC operating system was surprisingly good, but it floundered in the market.

Microsoft trudged on, thanks in part to the backing of Bill Gates, the company's co-founder and then the chairman and chief architect of the software firm. Gates was convinced that Tablet PCs were the future, and in late 2004 the company shipped its second version of Windows XP aimed at Tablet PC hardware. Dubbed Windows XP Tablet PC Edition 2005, this software benefited from the release of Intel's Centrino platform and Pentium-M microprocessors, which offered notebook makers dramatically better performance and battery life. New Tablet PC designs showed up, with both larger and smaller form factors, giving customers more options. In addition, prices came down. (Today, it's possible to get a Tablet PC for little more than a comparable notebook. Some PC makers even include Tablet capabilities as an add-on option.)

Windows XP Tablet PC Edition 2005 added a new version of the Tablet PC Input Panel (TIP), a pop-up window that is used to translate handwriting into non-Tablet-enhanced applications. The new TIP included real-time recognition, so handwriting was translated on-the-fly, giving you the option to correct as you wrote, rather than after a line of text was entered. XP Tablet PC Edition 2005 was also contextually aware, meaning the system could filter its handwriting recognition library based on what you were doing in order to achieve better results. For example, if you entered script into a text field that accepts only numbers, the OS tested your handwriting against numbers, not its entire library of characters. Windows XP Tablet PC Edition 2005 is shown in Figure 18-4.

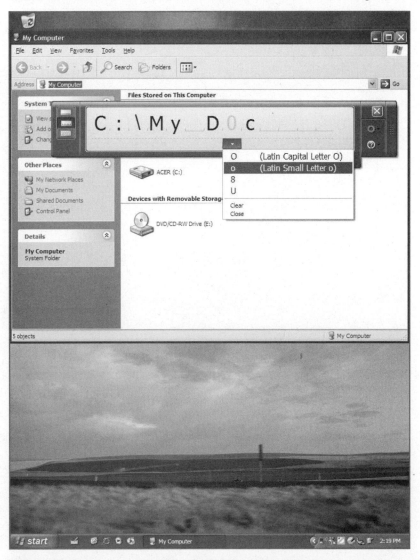

Figure 18-4: Windows XP Tablet PC Edition 2005 offered many improvements over its predecessor, including an enhanced TIP.

Like its predecessor, Windows XP Tablet PC Edition 2005 was technically excellent; unfortunately, also like its predecessor, it failed to make much of a dent in what would seem to be a seemingly endless market, including students, factory floor workers, roaming sales people, doctors, and many others who would benefit from this platform. Part of the reason for this continued lackluster success was that customers couldn't use just any PC with XP Tablet PC Edition 2005: you had to purchase a system with that software preinstalled. You couldn't use any digitizer, like the millions of available pen input systems out there, typically in use by graphic designers. And it didn't support touch-screen interaction: You either interacted with the system via a pen/stylus, or you used the more conventional keyboard and mouse interface common to other PCs.

For Windows Vista, released in late 2006, Microsoft decided to open up the market for Tablet PC functionality dramatically (see Figure 18-5). There was no Windows Vista Tablet PC Edition. Instead, users automatically got Tablet PC functionality if they used Windows Vista Home Premium, Business, Enterprise, or Ultimate editions with a PC that included compatible hardware such as a screen-based digitizer or touch screen.

Figure 18-5: Like Windows 7 after it, Windows Vista featured pervasive Tablet PC capabilities.

Moving forward to Windows 7, Microsoft has evolved the Tablet PC platform yet again. This time around, Tablet PC functionality—identified in the OS as Pen Input capabilities— is available in all mainstream Windows 7 versions, including Windows 7 Home Premium, Professional, Enterprise, and Ultimate. And Microsoft has again evolved its Tablet PC capabilities, making Windows 7 the best OS yet for those interested in accessing the PC with a stylus.

Secret

Microsoft's work on Tablet PC systems has also led to advances in touch-based computing, which in Windows 7 is available pervasively throughout the OS. Indeed, touch and multi-touch capabilities are not limited to mobile computers, as is often the case with Tablet PC pen input capabilities. We look at Windows 7's support for touch and multi-touch in Chapter 4.

Using a Tablet PC

In Windows 7, using the system's integrated Tablet PC functionality is virtually identical to the way it worked in Windows XP Tablet PC Edition and in Windows Vista, but naturally with a few enhancements. Windows Journal, Sticky Notes, and the Tablet PC Input Panel (TIP) all make it over with some functional improvements, as does the Snipping Tool, a favorite Tablet PC download that Microsoft used to provide separately. This section examines how the Tablet PC functionality has improved in Windows 7.

tip   These Tablet PC features also apply, for the most part, to Ultra-Mobile PCs (UMPCs), which are discussed later in this chapter. UMPCs are essentially small form-factor Tablet PCs with touch-screen support.

Configuring Tablet PC Features

Before using your Tablet PC or tablet-equipped PC with a stylus or other pointing device, you should probably take the time to configure the Tablet PC functionality that's built into Windows 7. If you have Tablet hardware, you'll see a few items in the shell that aren't available on non-Tablet hardware, including a handy way to select multiple items with a pen, a few new tray notification icons that appear over time, and the same reordering of Control Panel items that one sees when using Windows 7 with a notebook computer. With the exception of that last item, you'll examine these features throughout this chapter.

Tablet PC features are configured via the Control Panel, through two separate locations, *Tablet PC Settings* and *Pen and Touch*, both of which are available in Hardware and Sound.

tip   If you're used to how these features are configured in Windows Vista, you'll need to get reoriented because Microsoft has moved items around fairly dramatically.

Using Tablet PC Settings

We are going to take a look at Tablet PC Settings first. (You can also access the settings directly by typing **tablet pc settings** in Start Menu Search.) This window, shown in Figure 18-6, includes two tabs that help you configure the system for tablet use.

Figure 18-6: The Tablet PC Settings window is an important first stop for any tablet user.

In the Display tab, you configure which screen is used for both pen (stylus) and touch controls. This interface is extremely simple: just click the Setup button and then tap the screen that will be used for these functions. (You'll see a display like the one shown in Figure 18-7 in each connected display.)

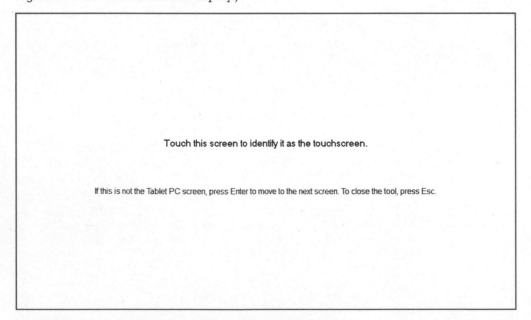

Figure 18-7: Here's a quick way to ID the pen and touch screen.

You can also configure the Tablet PC display's calibration, which lines up pen pushes with onscreen objects, ensuring that the pen hits the screen on target. Anyone who's used a Pocket PC will recognize this tool, shown in Figure 18-8. You launch the tool by clicking the Calibrate button.

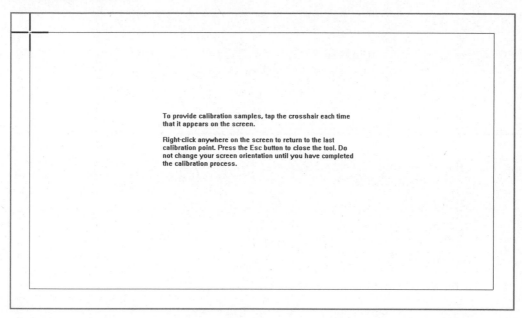

To provide calibration samples, tap the crosshair each time that it appears on the screen.

Right-click anywhere on the screen to return to the last calibration point. Press the Esc button to close the tool. Do not change your screen orientation until you have completed the calibration process.

Figure 18-8: The Digitizer Calibration Tool helps you configure your pen for accuracy.

Secret This Digitizer Calibration Tool only supports calibrating integrated digitizers. It will not work with an external digitizer. If you're using an external digitizer, it should have come with software to help you calibrate the pen.

At the bottom of the Display tab is an innocuous little link titled *Go to orientation.* Clicking this reveals the window shown in Figure 18-9, where you change the order in which the screen orientation changes (primary landscape, secondary portrait, secondary landscape, and primary portrait) when you press the hardware-based screen orientation button that is found on many Tablet PCs.

Consider a typical slate-style Tablet PC device, on which the display takes up most of the surface of the front of the device. On such a machine, you could conceivably view the screen in any of the four configuration options, depending on how you're holding it. The primary landscape and primary portrait modes are the two modes that you'll use most often, based on the button layout on the device, your left- or right-handedness, and the ways that feel most comfortable to you. The secondary portrait and secondary landscape modes are less frequently used modes.

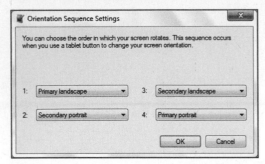

Figure 18-9: Here, you configure which views the system chooses when you push your Tablet's screen orientation button.

Most users will likely just need two screen orientation types, especially if they're using a convertible laptop-style Tablet PC. In normal laptop mode on such a device, when the user is accessing the system through the keyboard and mouse, the screen would be in a horizontal view. This would be primary landscape. But when the screen is rotated so that the system is accessed like a tablet, using the stylus, this would be primary portrait (or perhaps secondary portrait depending on the user and the layout of the device's hardware controls). In this case, you might want to configure primary landscape for the first and third locations in the orientation sequence and primary portrait for positions two and four.

In the Other tab, shown in Figure 18-10, you configure the Tablet PC for right- or left-handed use, and configure Pen and touch and Tablet PC Input Panel (TIP) options. The latter two options open other tools that we examine later in this chapter.

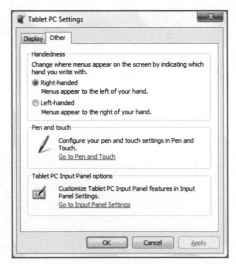

Figure 18-10: The Other tab provides access to other important Tablet PC-related options.

Using Pen and Touch

The Pen and Touch window, shown in Figure 18-11, also offers a variety of tabs, each of which provides configuration options related to the stylus, or pen, you're using with the system, as well as to other options related to Tablet PC and other touch-based systems. This dialog represents the second major entry point in Windows 7 for configuring Tablet PC features.

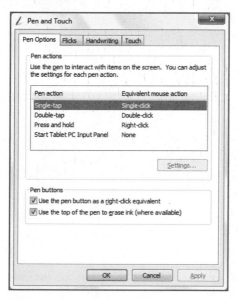

Figure 18-11: Here is where you can configure options related to your stylus and Tablet PC hardware.

The Pen Options tab enables you to configure what different pen actions and Tablet PC buttons do. For example, by default, a single-tap is the equivalent of a single-click with a mouse button, whereas a double-tap, naturally, emulates a mouse double-click. You can also configure press and hold (right-click by default, although some Tablet PC styli actually include a dedicated pen button that acts as a right-click button in conjunction with a tap) and the Start Tablet PC Input Panel button, which is found on some Tablet PCs.

In the Flicks tab, shown in Figure 18-12, you can configure various options related to Flicks, which are discussed later in the chapter. Flicks were one of the major new features in the Windows Vista version of the Tablet PC software, and they've been enhanced in Windows 7 to support touch controls. So hang around—we'll get to that too.

In the Handwriting tab, shown in Figure 18-13, you configure a tool called Automatic Learning that helps you personalize the system's handwriting recognition. Automatic learning is enabled by default—it was an opt-in service in Windows Vista—and it gathers information about the words you use regularly and how you write them, and then skews the system's handwriting recognition so that it can be more accurate and attuned to both your writing style and word usage.

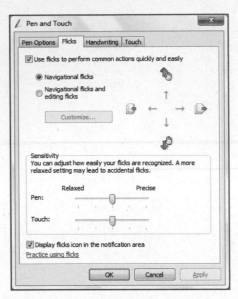

Figure 18-12: In Windows 7, you can be sure
a pen action occurred thanks to dynamic feedback.

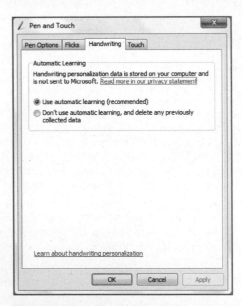

Figure 18-13: The Handwriting tab enables
automatic learning so the system will better
understand how you write over time.

While the personalized recognizer is available on all Windows 7–based PCs, automatic learning is available only on Tablet PCs (including Ultra-Mobile PCs), so if you visit this location on a non-Tablet PC, you'll see a message to that effect, and the Automatic Learning section of the Handwriting Recognition tab is grayed out.

Touch-enabled PCs, like Ultra-Mobile PCs and Multi-Touch PCs, have an extra tab, called Touch, in the Pen and Touch window that's specifically related to touch features. Shown in Figure 18-14, this tab enables you to configure whether you can use your finger as an input device, and how to emulate click and right-click using touch.

Figure 18-14: The Touch tab presents various options related to UMPCs and other touch-enabled systems.

You can also optionally enable the touch pointer, which complements the onscreen keyboard in the TIP (described below) with an onscreen mouse. Shown in Figure 18-15 the touch pointer appears when you tap anywhere on the screen. To emulate a normal mouse click, just tap the left button of the virtual mouse. To emulate a right-click, tap the right button.

Figure 18-15: The touch pointer does for mouse clicks what the TIP does for keyboard input.

Multi-touch PCs will also have a fifth tab, Panning, shown in Figure 18-16. This tab turns on and configures single-figure panning, a special kind of touch gesture.

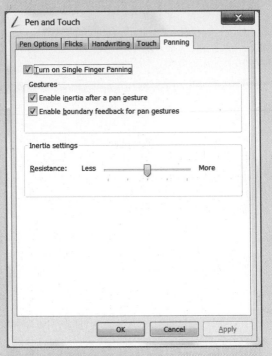

Figure 18-16: Special to multi-touch PCs is the Panning tab.

Using the Tablet PC Input Panel

Back in the original version of Windows XP Tablet PC Edition, the Tablet PC Input Panel, or TIP, was typically docked to the bottom of the screen, just above the taskbar, and you toggled its display by clicking a TIP icon next to the Start button. In Windows XP Tablet PC Edition 2005, Microsoft enhanced the TIP by enabling it to pop up in place, where you needed it. That is, if you wanted to input some text into the address bar of an Internet Explorer window, for example, you could tap the address bar with the pen and the TIP would appear in a floating window right under the tap point. That way, you wouldn't have to move the pen up and down across the entire screen in order to enter text or other characters.

That said, the TIP could still be manually launched by clicking that special icon next to the Start menu; and the TIP in Windows XP Tablet PC Edition 2005 was a pretty big bugger, occupying a large swath of onscreen real estate.

These issues were first fixed in Windows Vista and remain fixed in Windows 7. Instead of a special taskbar button, the TIP is now always accessible, but mostly hidden, on the edge of the screen. As shown in Figure 18-17, only a small portion of the TIP is visible by default.

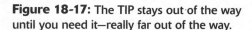

Figure 18-17: The TIP stays out of the way
until you need it—really far out of the way.

Don't see the TIP? Just open the Start menu and type **tablet pc** in Start Menu
Search: the Tablet PC Input Panel will be the first item in the search results.

If you're not even sure you're seeing the TIP, you can mouse over it (using either the
mouse or the pen/stylus). When you do so, the TIP peeks out a bit more, as shown in
Figure 18-18.

Figure 18-18: It's not shy, per se, but the TIP needs
some encouragement before displaying itself completely.

To activate the TIP, simply click it with the pen or stylus. The TIP will then appear in the
center of the screen, as shown in Figure 18-19.

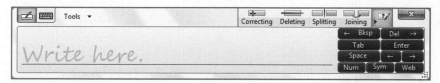

Figure 18-19: An activated TIP is a happy TIP.

So what does the TIP do? The TIP is designed to help you interact with applications that
aren't natively Tablet PC (or Touch) aware. (That is, virtually every single application on
the planet.) Therefore, if you want to enter a URL in the Internet Explorer address bar,
search for an application in Windows 7's Start Menu Search, or perform similar actions,
the TIP does all the work. It enables your pen (or finger) to work with any application.

What's nice about the TIP is that you don't really have to worry about where it is on the desktop, or whether it's enabled. Just tap a text-entry area in any application, even those not made by Microsoft, using the pen or stylus that came with your Tablet. When you do, you'll see a mini-TIP pop-up appear, as shown in Figure 18-20.

Figure 18-20: The TIP is available anytime you need it.

To see (and use) the full TIP, just tap this mini-TIP. You'll then get the full TIP, exactly where you need it.

Compared to the TIP in previous versions of Windows, the Windows 7 TIP offers very similar functionality with a slightly reworked user interface. The Quick Launch icons for the Writing Pad (the default) and Touch Keyboard modes have been moved to the top of the window, next to the Tools and Help menus. (And the Character Pad interface from Windows Vista has been unceremoniously made less accessible: you get to it by tapping Tools and then Write character by character.)

Microsoft has also added new "Show me" buttons to the top right of the TIP button that help you learn how to correct mistyped text, delete text, split text, and join text. Each of these triggers a mini video, like that shown in Figure 18-21, showing you how it's done.

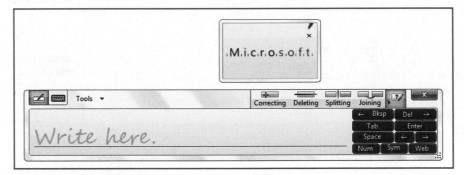

Figure 18-21: Not sure how something is done? TIP will show you the way.

The TIP's three different modes are shown in Figure 18-22.

To close the TIP (which really just returns it to its near-hidden location on the side of the screen), just tap the Close window button.

If you want to return the TIP to its previous behavior of docking at the top or bottom of the screen, click the Tools button and choose the appropriate option: Docking and then Float, Dock at top of screen, or Dock at bottom of screen. Float is the default behavior.

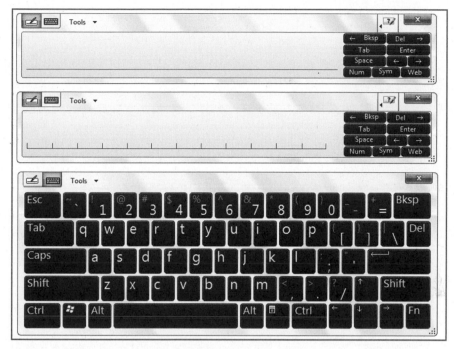

Figure 18-22: The TIP can work like a continuous writing pad, a character-by-character writing pad, or an onscreen keyboard.

Secret

In the previous version of Microsoft's Tablet PC operating system, the TIP included dedicated buttons for Web shortcuts such as http://, www., and so on. These can now be accessed through the Web button, which expands to show these and other related options, as shown in Figure 18-23. Likewise, the Sym button expands to show various symbols (!, @, #, and so on), while the Num button expands to show numbers. The Web button expands automatically when you select the address bar in Internet Explorer.

Figure 18-23: When you tap the Web button, a new menu of Web-oriented shortcuts appears.

Be sure to spend some time meandering around the TIP's Options dialog, shown in Figure 18-24. The TIP supports an amazingly rich collection of configurable options, including such things as to which side of the screen it docks, whether it's configured for left- or right-handed users, and how the Writing Pad and Character Pad recognize handwriting (as you write, the default; or after you pause).

Figure 18-24: The TIP supports a rich array of configurable options.

Finally, while Windows 7 does enable handwriting recognition personalization by default so that the system learns your handwriting style as it goes, you could and probably should take the time to engage in a little handwriting recognition training if you think you're going to be using a pen to interact with Windows 7 regularly. You can open the Handwriting Personalization tool right in the TIP: Click Tools ➪ Personalize handwriting recognition to launch the Handwriting Personalization tool, shown in Figure 18-25.

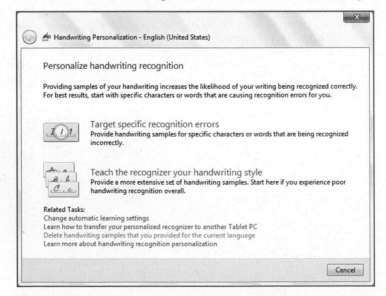

Figure 18-25: Make it your own by teaching Windows 7 how you write.

Flicks and Gestures

Flicks, called "gestures" in other pen-based systems, are special quick movements you can make with a Tablet PC stylus over the digitizer to navigate quickly or launch shortcuts for commonly needed functionality such as copy and paste. With a flick, you literally flick the pen in a certain way to cause an action.

Secret   Windows 7 also supports a related type of gesture called a *touch flick,* which enables you to perform similar actions using your finger on special touch-screen displays.

There are two types of flicks: navigational and editing. Navigational flicks include such things as scroll up, scroll down, back, and forward. Editing flicks include cut, copy, paste, delete, and undo. Flicks occur when you flick the pen in any of eight directions: up, down, left, right, and the diagonal positions between each.

You configure flicks via the Flicks tab of the Pen and Touch window—which can be accessed by typing **pen** in Start Menu Search—as shown in Figure 18-26.

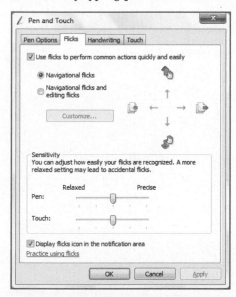

Figure 18-26: Flicks are customized via a lonely tab in an obscure dialog.

Additionally, you can enable the Pen flicks notification icon on any Tablet PC system, as shown in Figure 18-27. This handy icon provides quick access to current Flicks settings when clicked and offers a handy pop-up menu when right-clicked.

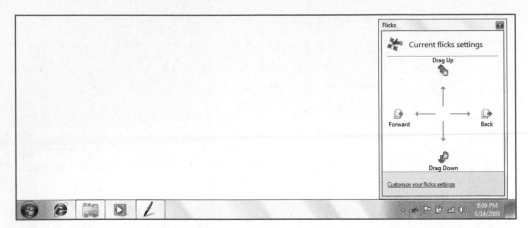

Figure 18-27: The Pen Flicks notification area icon.

Returning to the Flicks tab of the Pen and Touch window, from here you configure whether flicks are available, what types of flicks are available, and how sensitive the digitizer will be to recognizing flicks.

This particular feature varies according to each system, based on the sensitivity of the digitizer and pen combination.

By default, only navigational flicks are available where flicking left and right triggers back and forward actions, respectively, while flicking up and down enables you to scroll within documents. To enable both navigational and editing flicks and then customize the settings, select *Navigational flicks and editing flicks* and then click the Customize button. This launches the somewhat intimidating Customize Flicks window, shown in Figure 18-28.

Figure 18-28: Customize Flicks enables you to specify what each of the eight possible Flicks can do.

The sheer number of options available to each flick can be somewhat daunting, though Microsoft does supply some commonsense defaults. To see which options are available, just click the drop-down box next to any flick, as shown in Figure 18-29.

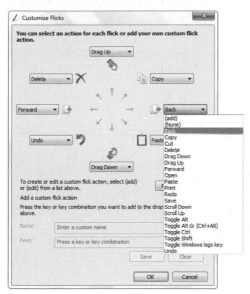

Figure 18-29: If you do find yourself using flicks, you'll have plenty of options to pick from.

> **tip** The *Practice using flicks* link at the bottom of the Flicks tab of the Pen and Touch window provides a link to a handy Flicks Training application, shown in Figure 18-30, that will help get you up to speed with this productivity-enhancing feature pretty quickly.

Figure 18-30: Flicks Training helps you practice and learn how to use flicks.

Password Hiding on Logon with Pen

In the Windows XP Tablet PC Editions, you could log on to the PC using a stylus and the TIP in onscreen keyboard mode: All you had to do was tap your password with the stylus. The problem was that each key in the onscreen keyboard would be highlighted as you tapped, so someone looking over your shoulder could steal your password relatively easily.

In Windows Vista and 7, Microsoft has implemented a small but important security change: as you tap the onscreen keyboard on the TIP during logon, the keys are no longer highlighted. Your password is safe—or at least as safe as it can be—from prying eyes, although it's a little disconcerting to tap the virtual keyboard and not get any feedback at all.

Secret   Microsoft also uses this technique whenever you need to enter a password in a secure Web page.

Shell Changes for Tablet PC Users

One thing you'll probably notice right away is that Windows 7 displays a user interface element by default when it detects Tablet PC hardware on your system. It's a small check box that's available next to virtually every shell item, including the desktop's Recycle Bin and every icon in Computer and the other Explorers that appears when you move the mouse cursor over the item. (It also works in any shell view style.) In addition, it's available in the Start menu.

Shown in Figure 18-31, this check box makes it easier to select multiple items in the shell using a pen. Otherwise, you'd have to drag a selection box around, which can be difficult with a pen.

Secret   Windows 7 users without Tablet PC hardware can turn this feature on if desired. (Conversely, Tablet PC users can turn it off.) To do so, you need to find the Folder Options dialog. (The easiest way is to use Start Menu Search, of course—just open the Start menu and type **folder options**.) Navigate to the View tab and check the *Use check boxes to select items* option.

One of the more disconcerting changes that will affect most users with Tablet PC hardware is that menu items in Explorer and various applications expand to the left of the mouse cursor (see Figure 18-32), instead of to the right, as is usually the case.

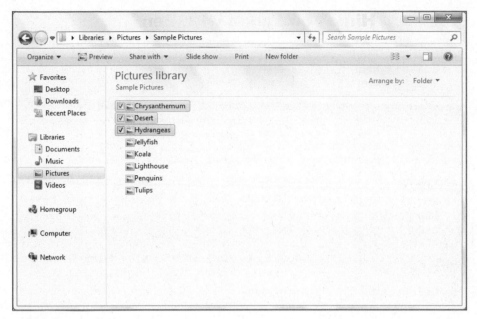

Figure 18-31: Windows 7 offers a fairly elegant way to multi-select items with a pen.

Figure 18-32: Righties will see pop-up menus on the left on Tablet PCs, which can be somewhat disconcerting.

This effect is visible only when you've configured the system's Tablet PC functionality for right-handed use. (If you configured it for left-handed use, the menus appear on the right as usual with other Windows 7 PCs.) This is because users would otherwise cover up the menu with their hand while tapping around with the stylus. By having the menu pop up on the left, Microsoft ensures that your hand won't cover what you need to see.

Working with Ultra-Mobile PCs

In late 2005, Microsoft launched an online viral marketing campaign for something called Origami, which was later revealed to be part of its Ultra-Mobile PC, or UMPC, initiative. UMPCs are basically touch-screen-capable ultra-small form factor mobile computers, sort of sub-sub-notebooks that eschew traditional keyboards and pointing devices in favor of a smaller, highly portable form factor. They're larger than a PDA but smaller than the smallest slate Tablet PC, though they typically incorporate the full feature set of true Tablet PCs as well.

---

tip Don't confuse Ultra-Mobile PCs (UMPCs) with netbooks, a new generation of sub-$500 computers. Netbooks like the Asus EeePC or Lenovo IdeaPad are notebook computers, but they are not UMPCs because they lack touch-screen capabilities.

Origami 1.0

The first generation of UMPC devices ran Windows XP Tablet PC Edition and was criticized for being somewhat pointless, a solution to a problem no one had; but Microsoft had a vision of a very specific portable computing experience that would utilize a seven-inch screen and weigh less than three pounds. With the first-generation UMPC, the company targeted tech enthusiasts—which helps explain the viral marketing campaign—but that proved to be a mistake. The devices sold poorly when they hit the market in early 2006.

The UMPC form factor, not surprisingly, has been at the center of some heated debates. It is too large to place in a typical pocket (like a smartphone or PDA), but too small to contain a usable keyboard (at least by traditional mobile PC standards). And UMPCs cost more than netbooks, which look and behave like regular notebook computers. For these reasons, the UMPC occupies an interesting but perhaps dubious segment of the market. It's just unclear whether customers are really looking for a device that's larger than a cell phone but smaller than a subnotebook.

What Microsoft was doing with the UMPC at a software level, however, was interesting. The company had created a touch-enabled software front end to Windows XP called the Origami Experience, and configured Windows to be optimized for both the capabilities and limitations of the devices at the time. This provided customers with not only the familiar Windows user experience, but also some unique capabilities that were specific to the UMPC platform. Think of it this way: Microsoft was pushing an ultra-mobile touch user interface years before Apple entered the market with the iPhone, and they'll never get any credit for it at all.

A New Origami

For the second go-round, Microsoft fine-tuned the software, based it on Windows Vista, and worked with a new generation of more efficient hardware. It can still be performance-challenged, thanks to the limitations of the ultra-low-voltage (ULV) processors that are typically used to power such devices, but various hardware makers and Microsoft have worked in concert to create more interesting solutions that will appeal to a wider audience. And somewhat surprisingly, UMPCs are heading to the enterprise now as well. It's a potentially compelling solution for those who need to work and connect on the go.

The primary advantage of a UMPC compared to a smartphone or PDA, of course, is that it's a real PC. It runs real Windows software, albeit somewhat slowly, and it can do so in even the most cramped situations, such as a typical aircraft's coach seat. The battery life is fantastic, and much better than anything seen in traditional business notebooks, especially if you're running typical application software. (Battery life during media playback is mediocre, from what we've seen.)

Compared to a Tablet PC, of course, a UMPC is much more compact and portable, which should appeal to a number of user types, including students, soccer moms, and traveling salespeople.

Compared to a netbook, a UMPC is more expensive, but it doesn't need to be opened up for use. And its touch screen makes such devices more natural to use than netbooks, which are often cramped. Because most UMPCs don't look like normal PCs, you don't expect them to act or perform like their bigger siblings.

Thanks to a variety of innovative hardware designs, you'll see interesting keyboard and pointing device solutions. For example, the Samsung Q-Series UMPCs, shown in Figure 18-33, feature an impressive and tiny smartphone-like thumb keyboard, split in half such that there are keys on each side of the screen. Holding the device with two hands, as you would naturally, the keys are right where your thumbs are, and work just like the keyboard on the smartphone you're probably already using. You wouldn't want to type a dissertation on that keyboard, but it's great for e-mail, Web browsing, document editing, and other light editing tasks, and is certainly much better than an onscreen virtual keyboard (which is also available courtesy of the Tablet PC functionality in Windows, of course). When you're back at the office, you can plug into USB keyboards and mice, and even an external screen, and have a desktop-like experience, albeit a fairly slow one.

Figure 18-33: Some UMPCs feature innovative built-in keyboards for typing on the go.

Moving forward to Windows 7, Microsoft hasn't yet updated Origami for its latest operating system, and it's unclear if it ever will. But the existing Origami 2.0 software, originally designed for Windows Vista, works just fine in Windows 7, too. The next section takes a look.

A Tour of the UMPC Software

While the underlying operating system on a UMPC is a stock version of Windows 7 Home Premium, Professional, or Ultimate with full Tablet PC capabilities enabled, Microsoft has added a number of UMPC-specific software solutions to the mix as well, and of course various PC makers also supply their own device-specific utilities. Before we get to that, however, you're probably curious what the UMPC interface looks like. Shown in Figure 18-34, it's basically Windows 7…but on a low-resolution screen, typically 1,024 × 600 or lower.

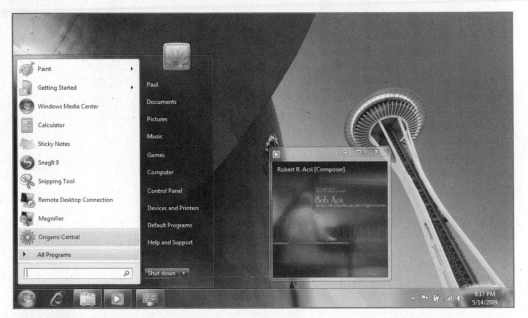

Figure 18-34: UMPCs are immediately familiar, but they generally offer lower-resolution screens than a typical portable computer.

The Origami Experience

The Origami Experience is the poster child of the UMPC world, a unique Microsoft application that combines the simplicity and basic look and feel of Media Center with a touch-enabled interaction scheme. While it's geared primarily toward entertainment— three of the four most prominent options in the initial UI are related to music, video, and pictures—it can also be used as a straightforward program launcher. The Origami Experience is shown in Figure 18-35.

The Origami Experience interface is colorful, obvious, and easy to use. There are quick link buttons on the top for task switching (that is, Windows Flip), battery life, and wireless signal, but most of the screen is occupied by large, colorful icons that are easy to look at and, more important, easy to tap with your finger. Yes, the Origami Experience can be used with a mouse and keyboard, of course, but it's really geared for touch screens.

The Music view offers nice views that include Now Playing (see Figure 18-36) and Library (see Figure 18-37), both of which sport large, finger-friendly icons and controls.

Figure 18-35: It's like Media Center Lite, perfect for small form factor PCs.

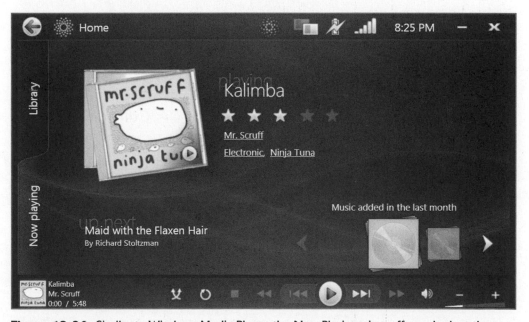

Figure 18-36: Similar to Windows Media Player, the Now Playing view offers a look at the current song.

Figure 18-37: In Library, you can easily access all of the music content stored on the device.

As you might expect, Videos and Pictures offer similar experiences, with both Now Playing and Library views in both.

Aside from Internet, music, video, and pictures, Origami provides another option, Programs, which opens to reveal access to productivity applications on your PC (see Figure 18-38).

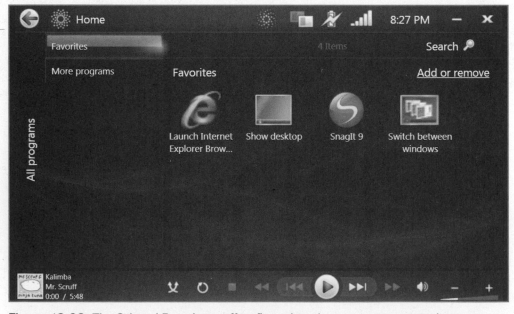

Figure 18-38: The Origami Experience offers finger-based access to non-entertainment applications too.

Of course, once you launch any of the applications displayed within these groups, you're popped out of the Origami Experience. This is somewhat jarring but understandable, as Microsoft couldn't replace the entire Windows UI.

Microsoft says that the Origami Experience isn't just about a new user interface or enabling touch access to most operating system functions. Instead, this environment is optimized for what the company calls *quick interactions*. This is different from the typical Windows user interface paradigm, where you're typically multi-tasking and getting a number of things done in tandem. In the Origami Experience, the expectation is that you're typically doing just one thing, or performing a single task while also playing music. It's a new interaction method that's essentially single-task by design. This makes sense both for the devices that will typically run this system and for the limitations of the underlying hardware.

Another way to view the Origami Experience is via a consumption/management perspective. For example, you won't manage your music collection or import CDs to the hard drive from within the Origami Experience. Instead, you continue using Windows Media Player (or Windows Media Center) for those tasks; but the Origami Experience is a very simple UI for *consuming* content, such as music. In this way, it's very much like the first version of Media Center, which, since then, has evolved to include some management and acquisition functionality, as discussed in Chapter 15.

Summary

As with Windows Media Center, Microsoft has taken the Tablet PC functionality it developed over the course of Windows XP and Vista, enhanced it, and made it available to far more users in Windows 7. Whether you have a traditional Tablet PC, a convertible laptop, a PC with a touch-based screen, an Ultra-Mobile PC (UMPC), or even a normal desktop or notebook computer, there's a Tablet PC feature in Windows 7 that's sure to delight. We hope that as this technology goes more mainstream, more people will become comfortable with this alternative form of computer interaction that could yet change the world.

Windows in Your Pocket—Using a Windows Mobile Smartphone

Chapter
19

In mid-2007, Apple released its iPhone smartphone in the U.S., touching off an explosion in sales of smartphones—cell phones with Internet connectivity and computer-like capabilities. But the iPhone isn't an ordinary smartphone. Instead of targeting the business market, like Microsoft, RIM, and other smartphone OS makers had in the past, Apple went after its bread-and-butter customers, consumers. And just as they did with the company's other wildly successful iPod products, consumers couldn't snap up the iPhone quickly enough.

Apple had created a new market. And existing players, including Microsoft, began to respond with iPhone-like systems of their own. Microsoft, of course, is no stranger to the smartphone market. Devices based on its Windows Mobile system sell in the tens of millions of units per year, or about 12 percent of all smartphones sold worldwide. That's enough to put Microsoft in the top five for this crucial market. But by the time you read this, it's very likely that iPhone market share will surpass that of Windows Mobile, which is astonishing given the short amount of time it has been available.

Microsoft's response has been to bolster Windows Mobile with iPhone-like touch interfaces, free online services that provide capabilities that Apple sells at extra cost, and a continued evolution of a platform that has been around for a surprising amount of time. In this chapter, we'll take a look at Windows Mobile, see how it's evolving to meet the iPhone threat, and explore how you can interact with Windows Mobile devices in Windows 7.

History of Windows Mobile

Windows Mobile has its roots in Windows CE, which originally stood for "consumer electronics," though Microsoft now denies that. The first version of Windows CE, code-named Pegasus, debuted on a new kind of mini portable computing device in 1996, offering users a grayscale Windows 95–like experience that used a pen-type stylus instead of a mouse. Under the covers, however, Windows CE was quite different from the desktop versions of Windows with which most people are familiar. The issue, in the mid-1990s, was that the microprocessors and other hardware that were inside most computers were not yet efficient enough to power the small mobile and embedded devices that Microsoft envisioned for Windows CE, so they created the system that would run on the embedded processors of the day.

Secret   Pegasus wasn't actually Microsoft's first attempt at a pen-based mini-computer system. The company had responded (some say illegally) to news that a company called Go was going to launch pen-based computers in the early 1990s with a project called WinPad that aimed to make Windows 3.x a pen-capable system. WinPad never amounted to anything—though it did succeed in scaring off customers and partners from Go, leading to that company's bankruptcy. Many members of the WinPad team later ended up in the Pegasus project, which of course became Windows CE.

Windows CE 1.0 shipped in late 1996, and the first device, the NEC MobilePro (see Figure 19-1) was typical of first-generation CE devices. Dubbed a Handheld PC (HPC), it featured a laptop-like, clamshell form factor with a small grayscale screen, tiny Chiclet-like keys, a stylus instead of a mouse, and modem connectivity. The UI was just like

Windows 95 for the most part, with a taskbar, Start button, and full-screen version of Windows Explorer. Figures 19-2 and 19-3 show off this early mobile UI.

Figure 19-1: The NEC MobilePro, a first-generation Windows CE device

Figure 19-2: The Windows CE desktop

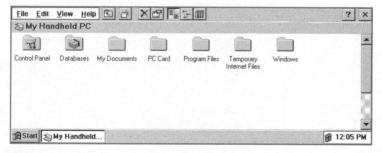

Figure 19-3: A Windows CE Explorer window

Secret

Paul was on the original Pegasus beta test and received pre-production MobilePro hardware for testing. At the end of the test, he returned the hardware to Microsoft in exchange for the final, shipping hardware. But it wasn't a gift: he had to pay to get the hardware in the first place.

Windows CE arrived at a bad time. Just as Microsoft and its partners were prepping these weirdly sized devices that were too small to be computers and too large to be truly portable, Palm shipped its first Palm Pilot personal digital assistant (PDA), setting the world on fire much as the iPhone would a decade later. The Palm Pilot (see Figure 19-4) was small enough to fit in a pocket, also used a stylus, but lacked a hardware keyboard. More important, perhaps, the Palm Pilot was fun to use, inexpensive, and didn't try to warp a PC-based user interface into a device that wasn't designed from the get-go for such a thing. Put simply, it was an instant success.

Figure 19-4: The Palm Pilot was so successful, Microsoft changed tack.

While Microsoft and its partners would continue to peddle HPCs to uninterested business travelers for the next few years, the software giant turned its attention to Palm. Its first PDA product, the Palm PC, was based on a second-generation version of Windows CE. But like the Palm Pilot, the Palm PC was keyboardless and, of course, palm-sized. Palm, however, wasn't amused by the Palm PC, which was very clearly a knock-off. It sued for trademark infringement, and Microsoft responded by changing the name to Palm-sized PC. Over time, some devices even picked up washed-out color displays, but these devices never took off either.

Finally, in 2000, Microsoft unleashed its Pocket PC product line, a new generation of hand-sized PDAs based on Windows CE 3.0. (Also at this time, development of Windows CE and the HPC and PDA products diverged. Windows CE would continue as the underlying platform for HPCs and PDAs, but it would also be used for other embedded devices that would be created and marketed separately.) Pocket PCs, as these devices were simply called, were actually reasonably successful in the market. Like their palm-sized PC predecessors, Pocket PCs could fit in a pocket, had color screens, ran a Windows-like OS, and utilized a stylus, with an onscreen virtual keyboard, as the primary interaction model. The Compaq iPAQ, shown in Figure 19-5, was the quintessential Pocket PC and could be tricked out with expansion sleeves offering storage and connectivity expansion.

Over the first two versions of Pocket PC, Microsoft referred to the underlying Windows CE–based OS as the Pocket PC OS. But in 2003, Microsoft changed the name to Windows Mobile, the brand that continues to this day. The first version of Windows Mobile was Windows Mobile 2003. That was followed by Windows Mobile 2003 5 in 2005, Windows Mobile 6 in 2007, Windows Mobile 6.1 in 2008, and Windows Mobile 6.5 in 2009.

Figure 19-5: The Compaq iPAQ was the most successful Pocket PC.

Over the course of these upgrades, Windows Mobile evolved to meet changing user needs. Originally envisioned as an OS for PDAs only, Windows Mobile evolved to power first-generation phone devices, at first through a special Phone Edition. Eventually, the phone-based OS became the more popular, and if you look at Windows Mobile today, you'll discover that non-phone devices are almost impossible to find outside of niche markets like manufacturing and retail sales. From Windows Mobile 5.0 on, Microsoft's mobile OS has been designed first and foremost for a category of devices that's now called the *smartphone*.

Windows Mobile Today

Windows Mobile 6.x is the modern and, at the time of this writing, current version of Windows Mobile. With Windows 7 debuting on the PC desktop in late 2009, you will see a mix of Windows Mobile 6.1 and 6.5 devices in the market for some time to come, though Microsoft plans to ship a Windows Mobile 7 release in 2010 if all goes well.

Windows Mobile 6, as noted previously, debuted in early 2007, but because of the nature of the device makers and wireless carriers that actually create and then sell Windows Mobile-based devices, it wasn't until late that year that Windows Mobile 6 devices appeared in volume. The system featured a default theme that was visually reminiscent of the Aero UI that was just then debuting with Windows Vista. But Windows Mobile 6 didn't really have anything to do with Vista beyond this look and feel.

Windows Mobile 6 originally shipped in three versions: Windows Mobile 6 Classic (for PDAs), Windows Mobile 6 Standard (for smartphones) and Windows Mobile 6 Professional (for smartphones with touch-screen displays). These versions are in the process of disappearing as Microsoft works toward a single code base for all Windows Mobile devices going forward.

All versions of Windows Mobile 6 got the Pocket Office applications—Word, Excel, Outlook, and PowerPoint—for the first time, and each of these applications was significantly updated for this release. For example, Pocket Word, Excel, and PowerPoint featured more intelligent round-tripping capabilities, whereby you can take a desktop-based document, edit it on the device, and then copy it back to the PC, all while preserving the formatting and styles from the original document. These applications also featured more PC-like features for the first time. And Pocket Outlook's e-mail, calendar, tasks, and contacts modules all supported Direct Push, allowing for automatic and wireless data synchronization with Microsoft's corporate-oriented Exchange Server. Pocket Outlook also added support for HTML e-mail, while the calendar module included a new Calendar Ribbon UI that made it easier to tell at a glance when you were free or busy.

Concurrent with the release of Windows Mobile 6, device makers started shipping a wide range of devices that featured tiny thumb-based keyboards like those popularized on the Palm Treo and RIM Blackberry. Previously, the smartphone market was divided between small keyboardless devices that resembled phones and larger keyboard-enabled devices. With the introduction of keyboard-based devices, the market for smartphones exploded, and device makers responded with me-too devices.

Windows Mobile 6.1

In April 2008, Microsoft shipped Windows Mobile 6.1, though again it wasn't until late in the year that numerous devices based on that update began appearing. The basic Windows Mobile UI didn't change much at all for many users; those who go with the mid-level Standard Edition of the software get a new Home Screen view style called Sliding Panel. This UI is actually quite nice, and while it can't touch the iPhone for simplicity and ease of use, it's certainly a huge improvement over the stock Windows Mobile home screen. (Why it's not available on Windows Mobile Professional is unclear.)

Functionally, the Sliding Panel UI (see Figure 19-6) is very similar to the UIs for Windows Media Center (Chapter 15) and Zune (Chapter 14), if you're familiar with those solutions. You can scroll up and down to select major options—time, communications, appointments, getting started (which can be removed when you're ready), and settings. As you select each major option, you can also scroll left or right within those options to see related options. For example, the communications option includes items such as missed calls, voice mails, text messages, e-mail (with multiple accounts), and, if you've installed Windows Live, Hotmail. Settings includes such things as profile (sound and vibration settings), wireless manager, ringtone, background image, and task manager.

Figure 19-6: The Sliding Panel interface in Windows Mobile 6.1

This UI is logical and easy to use, and you'll be up and running quickly. The only downside, of course, is that it's just a thin veneer over the otherwise ancient Windows Mobile OS. Select most of the aforementioned items, and you'll be brought to an old-school text menu or grid of icons that looks like it was last updated 10 years ago. This is a problem with the proprietary new UIs that Microsoft's partners are also creating on top of Windows Mobile, and it's a reminder that what lies underneath isn't nearly as sophisticated as that top layer.

Another niggling issue with Windows Mobile is that not all phones are created equal from a software perspective. Some come with Mobile Office, including Word, Excel, OneNote, and PowerPoint, and some don't. Some include Windows Live Messenger, while others do not (and you can't download it alongside the other Windows Live applications and services for some reason, which is maddening if you want it).

The version of Internet Explorer that originally shipped with Windows Mobile 6.1 is particularly bad. Microsoft later updated that browser with a new IE 6 product that is available on newer Windows Mobile 6.1 devices (and all Windows Mobile 6.5 devices). As with Messenger, however, this browser only ships with new devices: You cannot download and install it on older Windows Mobile 6.x phones, which severely limits its usefulness.

A number of other software applications round out the Windows Mobile 6.1 experience. These include a simple photo management package for camera-equipped phones (all of them, these days), which is unexceptional but can be integrated with Windows Live Photos online if you're so inclined. There's the ever-present Solitaire, which might just be the most frequently used Windows Mobile application of all time; and there is a decent version of Windows Media Player, which can take advantage of Windows Mobile's PC sync capabilities to play whatever meager collection of music and other content you can fit on such a device.

Windows Mobile 6.5

In early 2009, Microsoft finally admitted that it was working on yet another interim version of Windows Mobile, one that would offer more effective competition for the iPhone. Dubbed Windows Mobile 6.5, this system was completed in May 2009 and began shipping on new phones in late 2009. Compared to previous products in the Windows Mobile 6.x product line, Windows Mobile 6.5 is another interim release, but one that comes with important updates.

First, the home screen has been redesigned yet again (see Figure 19-7) and features a grid-like pattern of big, touchable icons—because Windows Mobile 6.5 targets touch devices primarily. Microsoft has also dramatically changed the lock screen, which you will encounter if you leave the device untouched for a while. Unlike Apple's iPhone, the Windows Mobile lock screen is intelligent about notifications. If you missed a call, for example, you can unlock the device and go right to the message or missed call; if you received an e-mail, you can go right to Pocket Outlook from this screen; and so on. More important, perhaps, if there are two or more notification types, you can pick where to go when unlocking the device, rather than having to remember what happened and navigate there manually as you do on competing devices.

Under the covers, of course, Windows Mobile 6.5 still features the ancient underlying interfaces that have been part of this system since the earliest days of Windows CE. That, Microsoft says, won't change until Windows Mobile 7.

Figure 19-7: Windows Mobile 6.5

Windows Mobile and Windows 7

If you do adopt a Windows Mobile smartphone, you'll find that it's easy to integrate with Windows 7, as well as some other Microsoft software, including Microsoft Office. Windows 7, unlike previous versions of Windows, is Windows Mobile aware, so when you plug in a Windows Mobile device for the first time, the OS will install drivers and then trigger the downloading and installation of a Windows 7 feature called Windows Mobile Device Center (see Figure 19-8). This application controls synchronization between your smartphone and Windows 7.

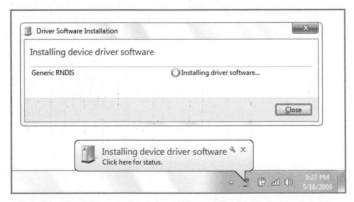

Figure 19-8: When Windows 7 detects and installs drivers for your smartphone, it will then download and install Windows Mobile Device Center.

Secret
Windows Mobile Device Center is also compatible with Windows Vista and comes in different 32-bit and 64-bit (x64) versions. Those with Windows XP will need to use the older (and, in the Windows Mobile world, reviled) ActiveSync software to manage PC-to-device synchronization. Windows Mobile Device Center works with devices dating all the way back to Windows Mobile 2003.

After you've installed Windows Mobile Device Center, the application will appear, as shown in Figure 19-9.

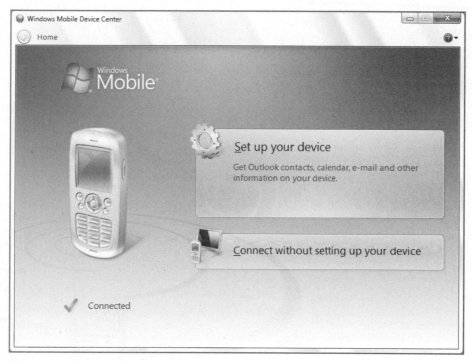

Figure 19-9: Windows Mobile Device Center

At this point, Windows Mobile Device Center will prompt you to establish a partnership between the smartphone and your PC. As shown in Figure 19-10, the application allows syncing between Microsoft Outlook-based contacts, calendar, e-mail, and tasks, as well as Mobile Favorites (between IE on your PC and IE on the device) and files.

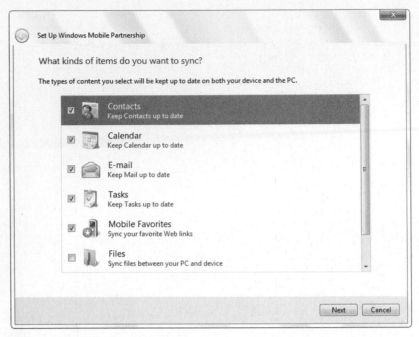

Figure 19-10: It's time to establish a partnership between the smartphone and your PC.

Secret

You must use Microsoft Outlook 2003, 2007, or 2010 to sync e-mail, contacts, tasks, and notes from your PC to a Windows Mobile device using Windows Mobile Device Center. If you don't have Microsoft Outlook, you can utilize Microsoft's free My Phone service, described later in this chapter, in tandem with your device to manage these items. You can sync Mobile Favorites and files regardless of whether you have Outlook.

In the next step, you're asked to name your device and can optionally create a shortcut to Windows Mobile Device Center on your PC. When this is done, Windows Mobile Device Center will sync information between the PC and the device, as shown in Figure 19-11.

Secret

You can create a partnership between your smartphone and up to two PCs. To end a partnership, unplug the smartphone from the PC, run Windows Mobile Device Center, and choose Mobile Device Settings ⇨ End a partnership.

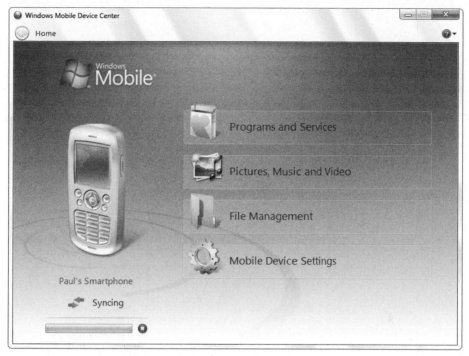

Figure 19-11: Syncing begins . . .

> **tip**   You can manually trigger a sync at any time by clicking the small green sync icon in Windows Mobile Device Center.

Managing the Device Partnership

Once your partnership is established, you can manage various aspects of the device:

- ♦ **Programs and Services:** From here, you can add and remove applications on the device, which is useful, and access various Microsoft Web sites devoted to Windows Mobile (which is passingly useful at best). If you're familiar with the Programs and Features control panel in Windows 7, you'll be right at home with Add/Remove Programs for Windows Mobile (see Figure 19-12).

- ♦ **Pictures, Music, and Video:** Here, you can import photos and video clips you took with your phone (which works identically to image and video acquisition from digital cameras and other similar devices; see Chapter 12) and trigger media sync between the device and Windows Media Player. As you can see in Figure 19-13, Windows Media Player treats a Windows Mobile phone just like any other mobile media device. (See Chapter 11 for more information on Windows Media Player.)

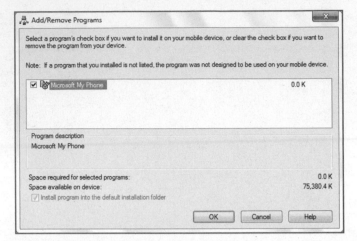

Figure 19-12: Add/Remove Programs enables you to manage the applications installed on your smartphone.

Figure 19-13: You can manage device-based music and video with Windows Media Player in Windows 7.

◆ **File Management:** From this simple interface, you can browse the contents of your device using a standard Windows Explorer window, as shown in Figure 19-14. If your device has integrated memory and a removable memory card, they will appear as separate drives under your smartphone.

Figure 19-14: You can browse your device with Windows Mobile and, if needed, copy files back and forth between your PC and the device.

---

tip You don't need to use Windows Mobile Device Center to access your device's storage with Explorer. That's because your smartphone appears in Computer, right alongside your other storage devices, as shown in Figure 19-15.

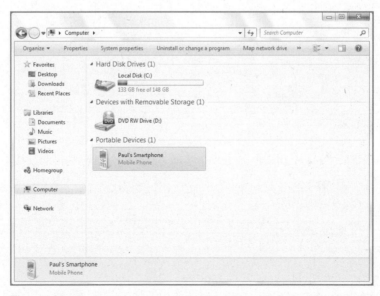

Figure 19-15: A tethered smartphone appears like any other storage device attached to your PC.

◆ **Mobile Device Settings:** This last option in Windows Mobile Device Center provides a number of features. For this reason, we'll examine these options in more depth in the following sections.

Changing Device Settings

From the Mobile Device Settings option in the Windows Mobile Device Center home screen, you are presented with a laundry list of features to configure. Some of these are quite important.

Change Content Sync Settings

The Change content sync settings screen (see Figure 19-16) resembles the initial configuration screen where you choose which items you want to sync between the PC and the device.

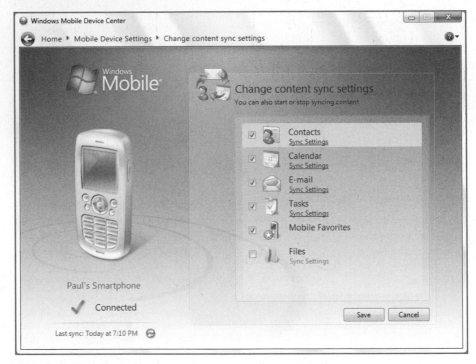

Figure 19-16: This looks familiar but you can actually dig a bit deeper.

But there's much more going on here than just enabling or disabling sync items. Unlike that initial configuration screen, you can use this interface to configure individual item sync settings. To see what this means, click the link Sync Settings under Calendar. As shown in Figure 19-17, you now have some additional settings to fine-tune, including how far in the past to synchronize calendar appointments and, if you've connected the phone to two devices, which PCs to sync this item with. Contacts, Calendar, E-mail, and Tasks all offer additional options in this manner.

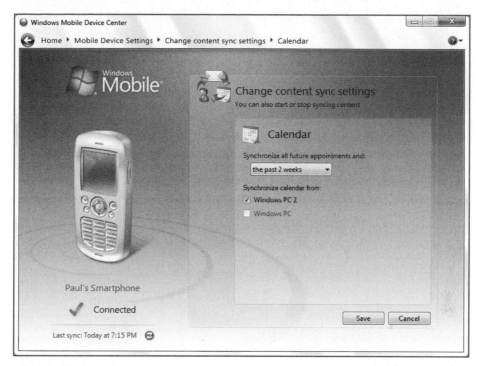

Figure 19-17: Diving into calendar sync, you can determine how many days' worth of scheduled items are synchronized.

> **tip** You can use this interface to configure automatic file sync between your device and the PC too. To do so, click Sync Settings under Files and then click the Add button to add one or more files. From now on, each time you sync, the latest versions of those files are moved between the PC and device.

Sync Wirelessly with Exchange Server

If you use your smartphone to wirelessly synchronize with Exchange-based e-mail, contacts, calendars, and tasks for work, you can use this interface to configure your phone. As shown in Figure 19-18, Exchange configuration is relatively simple because Windows Mobile Device Center can autodiscover all the information it needs.

> **tip** Don't have an Exchange Server handy? No problem: Microsoft offers a free consumer service called My Phone that emulates Exchange but in a friendlier, consumer-oriented package. We take a look at My Phone later in the chapter.

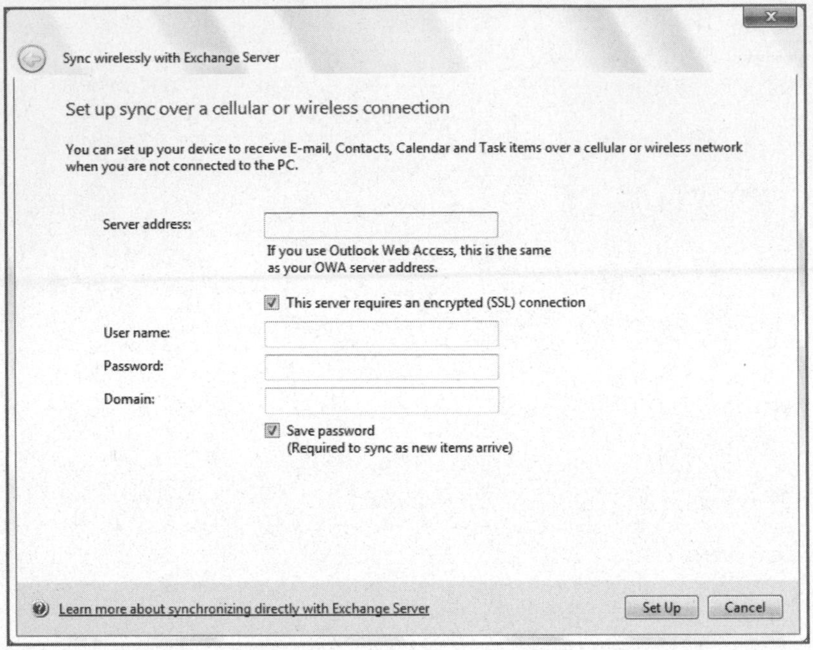

Figure 19-18: You can sync your smartphone wirelessly with Exchange Server and skip out on tethered device sync.

Manage a Partnership

Windows Mobile devices can maintain partnerships with—and, thus, sync between—up to two Windows-based PCs. From this interface, you can provide a name for the current PC only and configure what happens when a sync conflict occurs.

Connection Settings

Old-timers who recall the terrible ActiveSync application from previous versions of Windows will feel right at home with this interface, which helps you configure the ways in which your Windows Mobile device can sync with the PC. As shown in Figure 19-19, your options include USB and Bluetooth wireless sync, but you can also determine how Internet connections work between the PC and device when the two are connected.

Get Device Certificates

In certain corporate settings, you may need to authenticate your device using a digital certificate before you can connect to the company's Wi-Fi network or Exchange Server. If so, your system administrator will provide it and either configure it for you or provide instructions.

End a Partnership

If you'd like to end the partnership between the smartphone and the current PC, this is the place. The one thing you can't do is end a partnership between the smartphone and a different PC. To do that, you'd have to connect the phone to a third computer.

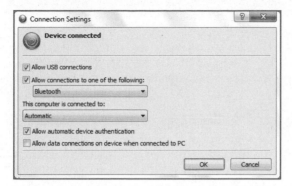

Figure 19-19: Want to use USB for charging only,
but use Bluetooth for sync? This is where you configure it.

tip	Two of these options, Connection settings and End a partnership, are available even when the smartphone is not connected to the PC. The others, however, require the device to be connected.

Windows Mobile in the Cloud: Microsoft's Mobile Web Services

In addition to basic integration between Windows Mobile devices and Windows 7, Microsoft also supports Windows Mobile devices with a number of online services, including My Phone, Windows Live for Windows Mobile, and, coming soon, Windows Marketplace for Windows Mobile. This section describes how you can get the most out of your Windows Mobile smartphone by taking advantage of Microsoft's mobile-oriented online services.

My Phone

When Apple introduced the second-generation iPhone 3G in mid-2008, it also released an associated online service called Mobile Me that provides automatic, wireless ("over the air," or OTA) synchronization of e-mail, contacts, and calendar items, as well as online storage for photo and file sharing. Mobile Me was a disaster when it launched, a rare miscue for the company, and the fact that customers had to pay $99 a year for the privilege just made matters worse.

While Microsoft already offered some Mobile Me functionality through its Windows Live for Windows Mobile services (which we'll examine in just a moment), in 2009 it closed the gap by offering a related and complementary service called Microsoft My Phone. Like Mobile Me, My Phone is designed to sync phone information between the device and a Web site, OTA. And like Mobile Me, My Phone provides Web-based storage for photos so you can share them with others remotely. But My Phone goes beyond Mobile Me in some ways, *way* beyond Mobile Me when you factor in the capabilities that already existed in Windows Live for Windows Mobile. And unlike Mobile Me, My Phone is completely free.

Game, set, match? Maybe.

As with other Microsoft online services, you need a Windows Live ID to take advantage of My Phone. After signing onto the service from the Web on your PC, you need to do so as well from your smartphone. Doing so triggers a download for the My Phone application, which sits on your phone and handles the syncing of information between the device and the Internet cloud.

On the phone, My Phone is pure simplicity: you can view information about the last sync and manually trigger a new sync if you want. You can select which items you wish to sync via this service (it supports contacts, calendar, tasks, text messages, photos, videos, music, and documents; and, if you have a storage card, additional photos, videos, music, and documents that you might have stored there). And you can configure a default sync schedule.

If it works as it should, My Phone will simply work in the background, syncing your data to the My Phone Web site. The rationale here is that people tend to keep important information on their phone, and often only on their phone. And if they lose the phone, or it is stolen, that data is gone for good. With My Phone, it's always backed up, and if you get a different phone in the future—because you upgraded or whatever—you can get that data off the Web site and onto that new device, too.

Viewed from the traditional Web (that is, from a PC), you can see how this works. The My Phone Web site, shown in Figure 19-20, provides a simplified view of the information you've synced from your phone, as well as quick links to common tasks such as viewing and downloading photos, and managing contacts.

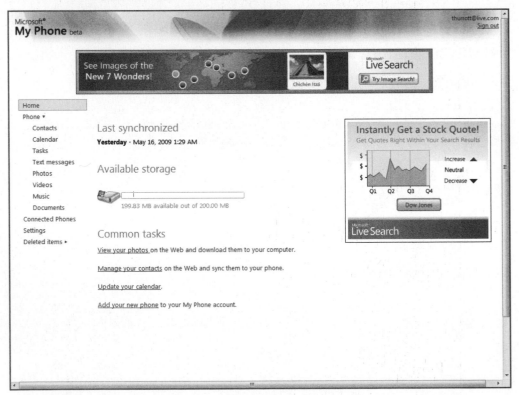

Figure 19-20: Microsoft My Phone, as seen from a PC Web browser

Some of the synced items are interactive, in that they are not trapped in the Web site. For example, if you view your phone-based photos from the My Phone Web site, as shown in Figure 19-21, you can perform in-place management tasks, but you can also multiselect photos and download them to your PC.

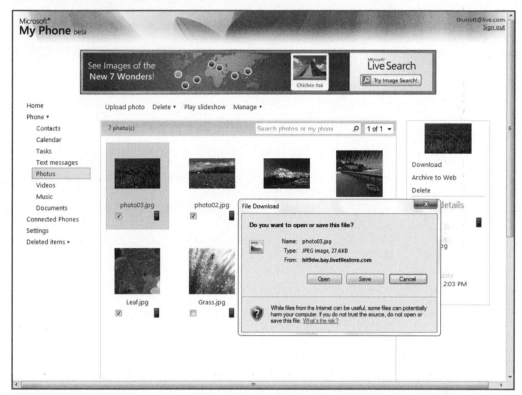

Figure 19-21: My Phone's photos can be managed and downloaded from the Web.

This functionality is useful for a number of reasons, not the least of which is backup. But it's nice to be able to get at your phone-based photos without being required to physically tether it to a particular PC.

Other items, alas, are not so interactive. For example, you can view and manage contacts and calendar items from the My Phone Web site (the Contacts view is shown in Figure 19-22); but there's no way to sync between, say, My Phone and Microsoft Outlook or Windows Live Mail on the PC, or, more interesting, Windows Live Hotmail on the Web.

With My Phone, the presumption is that if you're doing any syncing, you're doing it elsewhere. In the case of Windows Live for Windows Mobile (described later in the chapter), you're generally all set because that service does offer deep integration with Windows Live Hotmail and People with Windows Mobile. But there's no way to sync Windows Live Calendar with Windows Mobile at the time of this writing, and My Phone certainly isn't going to help.

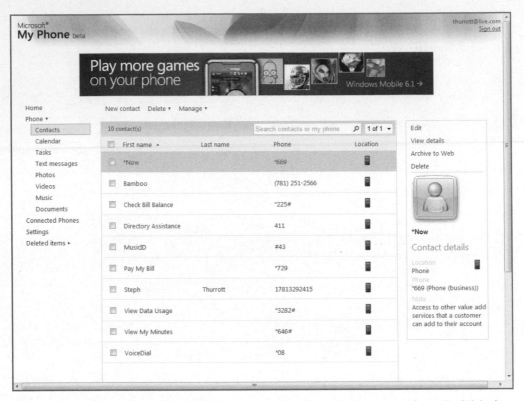

Figure 19-22: Some items, like contacts, can only be viewed and managed from the Web site.

Ultimately, what My Phone is really all about is off-site backup for your phone. And that makes a lot of sense, because it's so easy to misplace these tiny devices. We hope that in the future there will be deeper integration between My Phone and Microsoft's other related PC- and cloud-based solutions.

And to get back to that Mobile Me comparison, let's just say that while Apple's solution is more elegant, it also plays poorly with Windows-based PCs and applications. And did we mention that it costs $99 a year? My Phone may not be pretty, but it is free, and in many ways it provides a much more valuable service than anything Apple offers.

Windows Live for Windows Mobile

Microsoft has offered an integrated set of mobile-oriented Windows Live services for years, and if you're just arriving in the Windows Mobile world you may be surprised how mature they are. Windows Live Hotmail, People, Messenger, Spaces, Search, Events, Photos, and Profile have all been designed to work well within the constraints of these tiny devices, as have related Microsoft online services like MSN Mobile.

You can begin exploring Windows Live for Windows Mobile from the service's home page (www.windowsliveformobile.com). From this page, you can enter your mobile number to get an SMS message on the device, which points you to the mobile version of the site (mobile.live.com), which is of course designed for the tiny screens found on smartphones.

The following types of products and services are available.

Mobile Web

From the Windows Live for Mobile Web site (see Figure 19-23), you can access mobile versions of your Windows Live Home portal, Windows Live Hotmail, Photos, Messenger, Spaces, Search, and more, including MSN Mobile, a more general-purpose home page.

Figure 19-23: Windows Live Home as seen from a mobile device

Mobile Applications

While Web-based applications are interesting, they're limited not just by the physical constraints of the smartphone screen, but also by the subset of Web functionality that is delivered over the mobile Web. For a more complete and integrated Windows Live experience, consider the following native Windows Mobile applications.

Windows Live

This application provides over the air access to your Windows Live Hotmail-based e-mail in Windows Mobile Messaging and Windows Live People-based contacts from the native Contacts application.

Live Search

This application does provide the expected Web search functionality, but more useful to mobile users, perhaps, is access to Local Live Search, which can help you find nearby restaurants, gas stations and other locations, maps, directions, and traffic information.

Live Mesh

Using this application, you can sync between Microsoft's Live Mesh platform (described in Chapter 23) and your mobile phone.

SMS for Windows Live

If you've got a device with a smaller screen or you just prefer not to use a browser, Microsoft offers a pretty amazing set of services over SMS, including the capability to update the personal message on your Windows Live "What's New" list, get new e-mail alerts, get offline instant messages, and more. To register for this service, just visit the mobile version of the Windows Live Home site and enter your cell number in the Set up SMS registration area.

Summary

Windows Mobile is more utilitarian than Apple's exciting iPhone, but if you have such a device, you can integrate it pretty nicely with Windows 7, Microsoft Office, and various Microsoft-oriented online services, including Windows Live, My Phone, and, in the future, Windows Marketplace for Windows Mobile. The most recent versions of Windows Mobile improve the user experience pretty dramatically, and an upcoming Windows Mobile 7 version promises some Windows 7–like innovation on the mobile platform.

Part VI

Windows 7 Online

Browsing the Web

Chapter

20

Windows 7 features a brand-new and much-improved version of the Internet Explorer Web browser called Internet Explorer 8. As with previous Windows versions, Internet Explorer 8 is integrated into Windows 7, although Microsoft offers a free download of Internet Explorer 8 for Windows XP and Vista as well (and for a few Windows Server versions too). This chapter examines Internet Explorer 8.

What Happened

To say that Internet Explorer has an ignoble history is perhaps an understatement. Originally conceived as a minor add-on for Windows 95 and one that did not ship in the initial version of that Windows release, Internet Explorer later became the linchpin of Microsoft's strategy for competing in the dot-com era, and, not surprisingly, the subject of antitrust legal battles that continue to this day.

The problem, legally and technically, is that Microsoft *integrated* Internet Explorer directly into Windows. This co-mingling of Windows and Internet Explorer code began with Windows 98, and Microsoft designed the system in such a way that Internet Explorer could not be easily removed from the operating system. Integrating its immature Web browser with Windows led to years and years of security problems. Some of these were so severe that Microsoft was eventually forced to delay the release of Windows Vista simply so that it could ensure that its Internet Explorer–riddled operating systems were shored up with additional defenses.

Worst of all, after Microsoft won the browser wars in the early 2000s, displacing competitors such as Netscape and Opera, the company lost interest in Internet Explorer and stopped active development of the browser. It even briefly considered removing Internet Explorer from Windows Vista altogether, relegating its Web browsing duties to the Explorer shell, which as you probably know is simply based on Internet Explorer code anyway.

Then a wonderful thing happened. A scrappy group of upstarts from The Mozilla Foundation (since renamed The Mozilla Corporation) took the vestiges of the software code from Netscape's browser and reconstituted it as a small, lean, and powerful browser named Firefox. Roaring out of the gate in 2004, Firefox quickly began seizing market share from Internet Explorer, thanks to its unique new features and functionality. Suddenly, Microsoft was interested in updating Internet Explorer again. It's amazing what a little competition can do.

Starting with the Service Pack 2 (SP2) version of Windows XP, Microsoft reestablished its Internet Explorer team and began working actively on new features. Although the version of Internet Explorer 6 that appeared in Windows XP SP2 was focused largely on security, the next version, Internet Explorer 7, would include a huge number of functional improvements, aimed at closing the gap with Firefox and giving Microsoft's customers reasons not to switch. For the first time in several years, Internet Explorer became a compelling Web browser again.

Shortly after IE 7 was released, Microsoft began work on the next version, Internet Explorer 8. IE 8 had much less ground to make up than with previous versions, so it's an evolution of its predecessor with key new functionality related to Web rendering and compatibility, security, and end user functionality.

In Windows 7 only, Microsoft actually allows users to remove Internet Explorer 8 from the system, the first time it has allowed such a thing in about a decade. The reason? Antitrust regulators in Europe began questioning the bundling of IE with Windows again in 2008 and Microsoft decided to simply nip this one in the bud. To remove IE 8 from Windows 7—after first installing another browser, of course—visit Control Panel ⇨ Programs, and then Turn Windows features on or off. You'll see Internet Explorer 8 is one of the removable features, as shown in Figure 20-1.

Figure 20-1: Now it's possible to remove Internet Explorer from Windows.

Truth be told, we both use, prefer, and recommend Mozilla Firefox over Internet Explorer, although the latest Internet Explorer versions do indeed include a number of new and interesting features that should satisfy the needs of most users. More important, perhaps, IE is no longer dangerous to use. That sounds facetious, but it's not: using IE 6 is like driving without a seatbelt, an accident waiting to happen. IE 8 is safe and quite functional.

Initial Internet Explorer Configuration

When you run Internet Explorer 8 for the first time, the browser displays a Set Up wizard that steps you through a few configuration options. It's worth spending some time understanding what these options mean and how they impact your browser experience. There are two basic sections to the Set Up wizard:

♦ **Suggested Sites:** You are asked whether you would like to discover Web sites that are similar to the sites you visit. The reason you're asked this is because it is a potential privacy issue: In order to match your visited sites against a database of popular Web sites, IE needs to send this information (anonymously) to Microsoft's servers. Suggested Sites is an innocuous feature, however, and we suspect that it will be useful to many IE users.

✦ **Choose Your Settings:** The second step of the Set Up wizard encompasses a wide range of settings, as shown in Figure 20-2. How you configure these settings will dramatically alter your IE experience, and while we understand that Microsoft bundled them into a single step with a Use express settings option, you should at least understand what you're agreeing to.

Figure 20-2: Take the blue pill and trust Microsoft; take the red pill and spend all afternoon answering questions.

In this second step of the wizard, you're asked to gloss over the following actions:

✦ **Choose a default search provider:** By default, IE 8 will utilize your previous search provider during an upgrade or your default search provider, which will be Live Search with retail versions of Windows 7 or whatever search provider your PC maker has chosen. You should explicitly choose the search provider you want and not assume that Microsoft will make the right choice. That said, it's not difficult to change the search provider later.

✦ **Choose whether to download search provider updates:** You can choose whether to always use the soon-to-be-out-of-date version of the default search provider that was available on the day you installed Windows 7, or you can allow IE 8 to download new versions as they are released. You should download updates, as search providers will be making bug and security fixes over time and adding new features (like support for IE 8's cool visual search results feature).

✦ **Choose whether to use Accelerators:** Accelerators are a new feature in IE 8 and they enable you to do things with text you select on Web pages, including getting directions, sending e-mail, translating from foreign languages, and the like. We think this is a useful feature and you should at least try it out. Again, if you find yourself not using Accelerators, you can turn it off later.

✦ **Choose whether to use Compatibility View Updates:** Internet Explorer 8 ships with a new standards mode rendering engine, meaning that it's natively incompatible with a number of Web sites that were written for earlier versions of IE. To overcome this problem, Microsoft has added a feature called Compatibility View Updates into IE 8 that automatically causes the browser to silently switch back to the older IE 7 rendering mode when it encounters an incompatible site. Thus, there's nothing you need to do, and we think you should enable this feature and just browse the Web in peace.

Secret

Even with Compatibility View updates enabled, you may occasionally run into a site that doesn't look right in IE 8. If this happens, click the Compatibility View button in the right of the Address Bar, as shown in Figure 20-3. Problem solved. (This functionality is also available via the Tools command bar menu.)

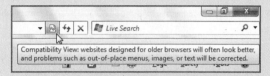

Figure 20-3: You can manually solve compatibility issues with the Compatibility View button.

Once you've stepped through these configuration options, click Finish and IE 8 will run for the first time. Internet Explorer 8 is shown in Figure 20-4.

Figure 20-4: Internet Explorer 8

Core Internet Explorer Usage

Although it's unlikely that *Windows 7 Secrets* readers are unaware of basic Internet Explorer features, many of you have probably moved along to Mozilla Firefox or other browsers over the past few years. If that's the case, this section will serve as a nice refresher.

Starting Internet Explorer

In previous versions of Windows, Microsoft pinned an Internet Explorer shortcut to the top of the Start menu. Now, in Windows 7, that shortcut is pinned to the Windows 7 taskbar instead, as shown in Figure 20-5.

Figure 20-5: Forget the Start menu:
you can launch IE right from the taskbar now.

To pin a shortcut to IE 8 to the Windows 7 Start menu as well, open the Start menu and navigate to All Programs. Then, find the Internet Explorer icon, right-click, and choose Pin to Start Menu.

Secret   In previous versions of Windows you could type a Web address (for example, a URL) in the address bar of any Explorer window and press Enter to change the Explorer window into an instance of Internet Explorer. This no longer works the same way in Windows 7: now, when you type a Web address into an Explorer address bar and press Enter, a new Internet Explorer window opens and loads that page.

Secret   Depending on which version of Windows 7 you're using, you will see two or three different icons for Internet Explorer in the Start menu hierarchy. In 32-bit versions of Windows 7, you will see two icons: one simply labeled *Internet Explorer* and the other named *Internet Explorer (No Add-ons)*. We discuss the differences between these versions later in this chapter. Users of 64-bit/x64 versions of Windows 7 will see a third Internet Explorer icon. This version, *Internet Explorer 64-bit*, is a true 64-bit version of Microsoft's browser. However, it is not the Internet Explorer version you will typically use because the default 32-bit version is more compatible with the wide range of browser add-ons available online. There is no functional advantage to using the 64-bit version of Internet Explorer, but because of the add-on compatibility issues, there are some functional disadvantages. Put simply, there's no really good reason to use the 64-bit version of IE…yet.

New Link, New Window...or New Tab

If you want to open a new window when you jump to a new site, hold down the Shift key when you click the link. (If you prefer, you can right-click the link and then click Open In New Window to do the same thing without using the keyboard.) You'll then be able to see both the target site and the source page in different Internet Explorer windows. You can also choose to use Internet Explorer's tabbed browsing feature instead, which is described in more detail later in the chapter, but you can open links in a new tab by holding down the Ctrl key while clicking the link. (Alternately, you can right-click the link and select Open In New Tab.)

Managing Downloads from the Internet

Like previous versions of Internet Explorer, Internet Explorer 8 does not provide a download manager. Instead, it provides only basic functions for downloading files from Internet servers. Each time you click a link to download a file with Internet Explorer, you get a new download dialog.

Given this limitation, it will come as no surprise that a variety of enterprising developers have created download managers for Internet Explorer. Our favorite comes with a free add-on called IE 7 Pro (www.ie7pro.com) which, among other things, also provides ad blocking facilities. And yes, despite the name, it does work fine with IE 8.

Edit on the Internet Explorer Toolbar

Unlike previous Internet Explorer versions, Internet Explorer 8 doesn't include an Edit button on its command bar by default. (This button is used to open the current page in your text or HTML editor of choice.) If you don't see the Edit button and wish you did, here's how to get it back:

1. Click the Tools button in the Internet Explorer toolbar, which Microsoft has renamed the command bar.
2. Select Toolbars ⇨ Customize.
3. In the Customize Toolbar dialog, shown in Figure 20-6, select Edit from the Available Toolbar Buttons field on the left and then click the Add button.

Figure 20-6: You can customize which buttons Internet Explorer displays in its command bar.

4. Click Close.

This might be a good time to customize the command bar regardless of your interest in the Edit button. You will most likely see a few buttons you'll never use—Research comes to mind—and a few to which you might like ready access (such as Read Mail and Size).

The Complete AutoComplete

Internet Explorer has an autocomplete feature that helps you complete your entry in the address bar as soon as you type in the first few letters. For example, type **www.appl**, pause for a few seconds, and you'll get a drop-down list of sites you have previously visited that start with `www.appl`, including `www.apple.com`, as shown in Figure 20-7. Even if a long list of URLs that start with the same letters that you've typed appears, you can easily use your mouse or arrow keys to scroll to and highlight an entry in the list, and then press Enter or Tab to jump to the site. This feature works much like Start Menu Search.

Figure 20-7: Internet Explorer's address bar includes autocomplete functionality.

If you press Alt+D to select the address bar and then Alt+down arrow (or F4) when the address bar is active, Internet Explorer displays a drop-down list of complete addresses you've recently typed in the address bar. This is a totally different list from the autocomplete drop-down list; it is the same list that appears when you click the down arrow at the right end of the address bar (see Figure 20-8).

To enable or disable autocomplete, choose Tools ⇨ Internet Options, click the Content tab, and click the Settings button in the AutoComplete section. In the AutoComplete Settings dialog, you can choose whether to use AutoComplete for browser history, Favorites, Feeds, Windows Search, forms, or user names and passwords.

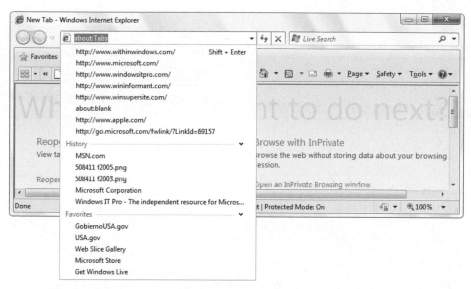

Figure 20-8: You can also view all of the Web addresses you've recently accessed.

---

tip You can save time when typing Web addresses by having Internet Explorer automatically preface your entry with www. and end it with the suffix .com. Just type the domain name in the address bar and then select Ctrl+Enter. For example, type **winsupersite**, select Ctrl+Enter, and you get www.winsupersite.com in a new tab. This is different from actually searching on the Internet for the address; see the "Autosearch for a Web Address" section later in this chapter for more information.

Quickly Searching the Web

Want to find a specific Web site, or text from a specific Web page? Sure, you can use IE 8's integrated Search box, which provides a host of amazing functionality we'll discuss later in the chapter, but did you know you can use the address bar too? Click the address bar, type **find**, **search**, or **?**, type a space, and then type the name of the company or organization whose site you want to find. If the name has a space in it, forget typing the **find**, **search**, or **?**, and just put double quote marks around the name. You can also just type in any word to initiate the search function.

This automatically starts a search for the company, word in a Web page, or organization on Live.com or your configured search provider.

Toggling Internet Explorer between Full-Screen Mode and Restore

Open Internet Explorer and tap the F11 key. You are now in full-screen mode, as shown in Figure 20-9. Pressing F11 again will get you back to the normal, windowed mode. Full-screen mode covers even the taskbar, and features an autohide main toolbar for maximum use of onscreen real estate.

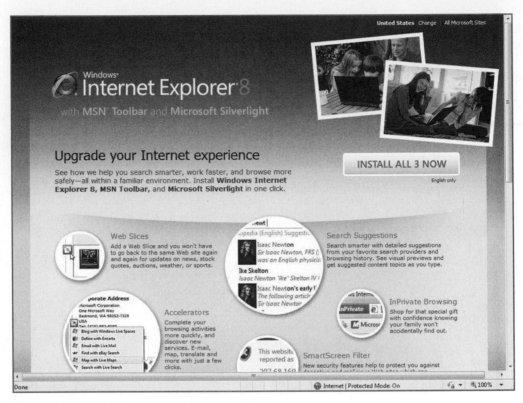

Figure 20-9: IE's full-screen mode

Secret

If you want the main toolbar to always appear while in full-screen mode, right-click the small black area below the Minimize, Restore, and Close window buttons and uncheck Auto-Hide from the menu that appears.

Favorites and Offline Web Pages

A URL (Uniform Resource Locator) is a unique identifier for a Web page or other resource on the Internet. Windows maintains a list of URLs for your favorite sites. Your *Favorites* are actually shortcuts stored in the Favorites folder. And while they used to be accessed from the traditional Favorites menu—it's still there but hidden by default in Internet Explorer 8, along with the rest of the menu bar—you now access Favorites from the Favorites Center, described later in this chapter. (You access Favorites Center by the Favorites button to the left of IE 8's tabs.)

You can store whatever you like in Favorites, but we suggest limiting what you put in these folders to shortcuts (either to URLs or to other folders or documents). You can put copies of URL shortcuts on your desktop and start your Internet Explorer by clicking a shortcut's icon.

To create a shortcut to your favorites, open an Explorer window and navigate to the Favorites folder in your Home folder. Right-drag and drop your Favorites folder onto your desktop. Choose Create Shortcut(s) Here.

Secret

If you use multiple PCs, managing different Favorites lists on each of your PCs might be a bit of a hassle. Microsoft has a solution, albeit it in a non-obvious place. Its Windows Live Toolbar includes a feature that enables you to aggregate your favorites in an online storage area. That way, you can access all of your favorites from any PC, as long as you've installed this toolbar in Internet Explorer. You can find out more about this toolbar in Chapter 23.

Saving Graphics from the Web to Your PC

If you want to save a Web-based graphic that you are viewing in Internet Explorer, right-click it, choose Save Picture As (sometimes you will see Save Background As, as well), and then give it a path and a name.

If you want to turn a graphic in a Web page into wallpaper on your desktop, right-click the graphic and choose Set As Wallpaper.

Saving Complete Web Pages

Saving a Web page as an HTML file in Internet Explorer usually saves only the text and layout of the page—the graphics are saved separately as links. However, Internet Explorer is capable of saving a Web page as a single document. The MIME HTML (.mht) file format incorporates both the graphics and the HTML text on a Web page into one file. The graphics are encoded using MIME (and Uuencoding), so everything is stored in e-mail-capable, 7-bit ASCII text characters, but Internet Explorer can decode the file on-the-fly and display the graphics.

This feature greatly expands the power of the Internet. If a document is displayed as one Web page, you can download it and all of its associated graphic files, and save everything in one very convenient document. If you do this, then you don't have to save the document as an offline page to keep it readily available.

Secret

There's only one problem with MHT-style Web archives: they only work with Internet Explorer. If you choose to utilize an alternative Web browser such as Mozilla Firefox, MHT files will continue to open in Internet Explorer.

To save a Web page in this format, merely tap the Alt key to enable the Internet Explorer menu and then click File ⇨ Save As, and choose Web Archive, Single File in the Save As Type field. This secret isn't hidden, but it sure is powerful. It turns the Web into something that you can actually use as a publishing arena.

Secret

You can see the entire underlying text file if you open a file with an `mht` extension in WordPad. If you click View ⇨ Source in Internet Explorer when viewing an `mht` file, you'll only see the HTML code and not the encoded graphics that are in fact there in the file.

Internet Explorer also enables you to save a document as a complete Web page (click File ⇨ Save As, and choose Web Page ⇨ Complete in the Save As Type field). In this case, the graphic files are not included in the HTML source text. Instead, Internet Explorer creates a subfolder in which it saves the downloaded graphics files. It rewrites the saved Web page to reference the graphics files in this subfolder, and enters the Web page's URL as a comment at the top of the page. These types of documents will typically open fine in other browsers, including Firefox. Indeed, Firefox uses a similar mechanism for saving "complete" Web pages.

Finally, you can also save Web pages as a Web page type, which includes only the text of the page along with links to the online graphics. If you choose this option and view a saved page while offline, you'll see just the text. However, if you are online, the graphics will load as normal.

Turning Your Favorites into a Web Page

The Favorites menu and submenus are fine for starters, but sometimes it is a bit of a drag to search repeatedly through all these menus. How about creating a single Web page of all your favorites? Or separate Web pages for different subsets of favorites?

Internet Explorer includes the Import/Export Wizard, which can export your favorites or cookies. It writes them to your disk in a format that Netscape, Mozilla Firefox, and other browsers can read. You can also use the wizard to import cookies and favorites from other browsers. The wizard writes out your favorites as an HTML file, which makes it easy to look through your favorites with Notepad and edit them if you like. You can also use the HTML file as a page in Internet Explorer, from which you can easily jump to any site on your list.

Choose File ⇨ Import and Export to run the Import/Export Wizard. (Note that you will typically need to tap Alt first to display the menu.) As shown in Figure 20-10, this wizard offers a number of interesting functions, including the aforementioned capability to export Favorites, along with RSS feeds and cookies.

Figure 20-10: The Import/Export Wizard is a vital tool for moving between different Web browsers.

Internet Explorer 8 Is Not Your Father's Web Browser

If you're familiar with Internet Explorer 6 in Windows XP or previous Internet Explorer versions, you might be in for a shock when you first start Internet Explorer 8: gone is the simplicity of the Internet Explorer you know, replaced with a more complicated user interface that mimics the look and feel of the Windows Explorer shell while providing ever-larger areas of onscreen real estate for all its new features. Shown in Figure 20-11, Internet Explorer 8 is similar to IE 7 but quite a bit busier-looking than its older predecessors.

What has changed in the Internet Explorer 8 user interface? First, the menu bar is hidden by default, similar to the Classic Menu in the Explorer shell and many other Windows applications. Microsoft says that it disabled the menu bar to reduce the clutter, but we think you'll agree that the Internet Explorer 8 user interface is still quite a bit more cluttered than that of Internet Explorer 6.

> **tip** If you don't like this design decision, you can temporarily cause the Internet Explorer 8 menu bar to appear by pressing the Alt key once. Alternately, you can simply click the new Tools command bar icon and select Toolbars ⇨ Menu Bar to enable this menu all the time. This is how Internet Explorer 8 is configured if you install it in Windows XP, by the way.

Various user interface elements have also been moved around in IE 8. The Back and Forward buttons are prominently featured in the upper-left corner of the window next to the top-mounted address bar, for example. The main toolbar, now called the *command bar*, is now located way over to the far right of the window, causing the Home button to be located quite far from its original location, which is sure to frustrate those who have committed the location of this commonly needed button to memory. The Refresh and Stop buttons are to the right of the address bar for some reason.

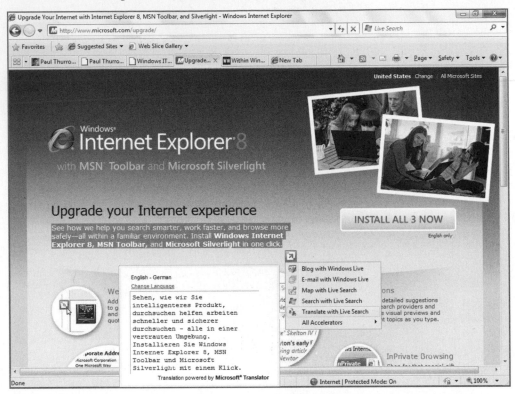

Figure 20-11: Something old, something new: Internet Explorer 8 is clearly a new Internet Explorer, but you may find it difficult to find features you were used to.

---

tip

You can't move the Home button to a more logical location, which is a shame, but you can move the Refresh and Stop buttons back where they belong. Here's how: right-click an empty area of the command bar and choose Customize ⇨ Show Stop and Refresh Buttons Before the Address Bar. In Figure 20-12, you can see a handy before-and-after comparison of this change.

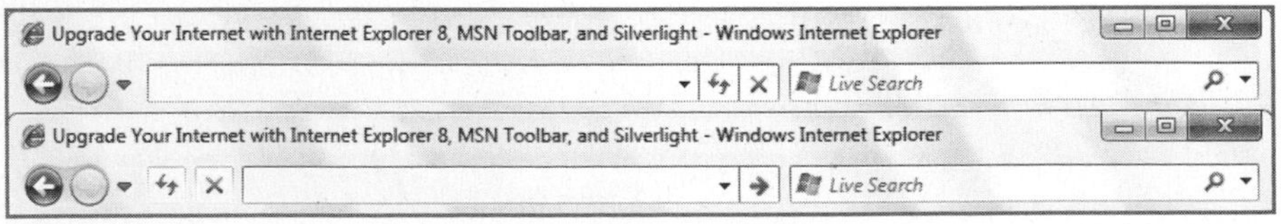

Figure 20-12: You can move the Refresh and Stop buttons back to where God intended.

> tip You can easily resize the command bar if you want in order to see all of its buttons. First, ensure that the toolbars are not locked by navigating to Tools ⇨ Toolbars and unchecking Lock the Toolbars. Then, you can drag the command bar left and right to resize it. If you make the command bar too short, a double chevron will appear at the right, indicating that you can reach the rest of its options via a drop-down menu, as shown in Figure 20-13.

Figure 20-13: Hidden command bar options can be accessed via this handy drop-down menu.

The Command Bar

Love it or hate it, the Internet Explorer command bar houses some of the browser's most commonly needed functionality. Table 20-1 explores the options you'll see, from left to right, in this toolbar by default. All of these features are described in more detail later in this chapter.

Table 20-1: Default Internet Explorer 8 Command Bar Buttons

Command Bar Button	What It Does
Home	Navigates the browser back to your home page (or home pages, as the case may be). This button also includes an optional drop-down menu, which enables you to change your home page(s) and add and remove home page(s). You can also tap Alt+M or Alt+Home to access the home page.
Feeds/Web Slices	Provides access to any RSS feeds or Web Slices that are available in the currently loaded page.
Read Mail	Launches the default e-mail client
Print	Provides printing facilities that are dramatically improved compared to earlier Internet Explorer versions.

continues

Table 20-1: Default Internet Explorer 8 Command Bar Buttons *(continued)*

Command Bar Button	What It Does
Page	This button launches a drop-down menu that provides access to options related to Web pages, such as zoom and text size.
Safety	This button launches a drop-down menu that provides access to options related to IE 8's many security and privacy features.
Tools	Launches a drop-down menu that provides access to options related to the Web browser itself, including Internet options and which tool-bars are displayed. Tools is similar to the Tools menu in the old menu bar but lacks certain options, such as Windows Update.
Help	This button launches a drop-down menu that is similar to the Help menu item in the Classic Menu.

As discussed earlier in this chapter, you can also customize which buttons appear in the Internet Explorer command bar.

Table 20-2 summarizes the optional buttons you can add to the Internet Explorer 8 command bar. As you can see, there are far more possibilities now than in any previous IE version. (For example, IE 7 featured eight optional buttons to add. IE 8 has 25.) You can also add one or more *separators*, which visually separate command bar buttons. Most of these features are described later in this chapter.

Table 20-2: Optional Internet Explorer 8 Command Bar Buttons

Command Bar Button	What It Does
Text Size	Toggles the font size of the text in the current browser window between preset sizes, including Largest, Larger, Medium (the default), Smaller, and Smallest.
Encoding	Provides a drop-down menu that enables you to select from the various language and locale display modes available on your system. Typically, you will leave this at its default value, Unicode (UTF-8), unless you are browsing the Web in an area of the world that uses right-to-left text or other text encoding methods.
Edit	Opens the currently displayed Web page in your default Web page editor application.
Cut	Cuts the currently selected text from the address bar and places it on the Windows clipboard.
Copy	Copies the currently selected text from the address bar or Web page and places it on the Windows clipboard.
Paste	Pastes the contents of the Windows clipboard at the cursor position.
Full Screen	Toggles the Internet Explorer 8 Full-Screen mode.
Developer Tools	Opens IE 8's new Developer Tools window, which enables Web developers to debug problematic Web pages.

Command Bar Button	What It Does
Print Preview	Displays the IE Print Preview window.
Page Setup	Displays the Page Setup window for the default printer.
New Window	Opens a new IE window.
Save As	Opens the IE Save Webpage window, which offers to save the currently loaded Web page to your PC.
Send Page by E-mail	Copies the currently loaded page to a new e-mail message in the default e-mail application so that you can mail it to someone.
Send Link by E-mail	Copies the address (URL) of the currently loaded page to a new e-mail message in the default e-mail application so that you can mail it to someone.
View Source	Displays the source code for the currently loaded Web page in a separate window.
Webpage Privacy Policy	Shows the privacy report for the currently loaded Web page, displaying the address of each site that also displays content on the page (typically advertisement suppliers).
Delete Browsing History	Displays the IE 8 Delete Browsing History window.
Internet Options	Displays the IE 8 Internet Options window.
Online Support	Navigates to the Microsoft Help and Support site at support.microsoft.com.
Manage Add-ons	Displays the IE 8 Manage Add-ons window.
SmartScreen Filter	Provides a pop-down menu with options related to IE 8's SmartScreen Filter feature. (These options are also available via the Safety command bar item.)
Pop-up Blocker	Provides a pop-up menu with options related to IE 8's Pop-up Blocker. (These options are also available via the Tools command bar item.)
Zoom	Provides access to IE 8's zoom controls. Note that these options are also available in the IE status bar, in the bottom-right corner of the window.
InPrivate Browsing	Opens a new InPrivate Browsing IE window.

tip   If you install software that adds a button to the Internet Explorer toolbar, that button is added to the right side of the command bar now. For example, Windows Live Messenger installs a Messenger button, and Microsoft Office (2003 and newer) installs a Research button (and, if you've installed OneNote, a Send to OneNote button). You might see other similar buttons, depending on which software you've installed. Likewise, if you've upgraded from earlier versions of Windows along the way, any buttons that were added to earlier Internet Explorer versions will show up in the Internet Explorer 8 command bar. You can remove these buttons via the Customize Toolbar dialog described previously.

Where Is It Now?

Hundreds of millions of people accustomed to Internet Explorer 6 or 7 may be asking this question. Despite IE's widespread use, Microsoft made a few big changes to the way Internet Explorer 8 works. With that in mind, Table 20-3 should help Internet Explorer 6- and 7-savvy users find their way around the new interface.

Table 20-3: Where Common Internet Explorer Features Moved in Internet Explorer 8

Feature	Where It Is Now
File menu	The menu bar is hidden by default. Press the Alt key to display this menu.
Back button	Now located in the upper-left corner of the browser window.
Forward button	Now located in the upper-left corner of the browser window to the right of the Back button.
Stop button	Moved to the right of the Refresh button.
Refresh button	Moved to the right of the address bar.
Home button	Moved to the command bar.
Search button	Replaced by a new Search box found in the top-right corner of the browser window.
Favorites button	Replaced by the Favorites Center. The icon for Favorites Center is a yellow star and is found to the left of the tabs area.
History button	History is now located in the Favorites Center.
Mail button	Replaced by the Read Mail command bar button.
Print button	Now located in the command bar.
Edit button	Missing in action. To edit a Web page, enable the Classic Menu by pressing Alt and then choose Edit from the File menu.
Go button	Missing in action. To load a Web page whose address you've typed into the address bar, simply press Enter.
Status icon ("throbber")	In previous versions of Internet Explorer, an Internet Explorer E logo or Windows logo in the upper-right corner of the browser indicated progress while a Web page was loading. In Internet Explorer 8 this has been replaced by a standard progress bar, which is located in the middle of the status bar at the bottom of the browser window.
Address bar	Now located in the top row of controls in the browser window to the right of the Forward button.
Information bar	Hidden by default, but still located at the top of the Web page display area.
Status bar	Still located at the bottom of the browser window. The status bar in Internet Explorer 8 behaves similarly to the status bar in previous Internet Explorer versions.

Internet Explorer 8 Features and Functionality

After you get over the new look of Internet Explorer you will discover that Microsoft has added a lot of new functionality as well. This section covers the biggest features Microsoft has added to its browser since 2001.

Playing Favorites

In previous versions of Internet Explorer, the Favorites folder provided a place in the system where you could save links, or shortcuts, to your favorite Web sites. Favorites were typically accessed in Internet Explorer via the Favorites menu. Now, in IE 8, Microsoft provides two places where you can manage Favorites: the Favorites Center, which debuted in IE 7, and the new Favorites Bar.

Managing Favorites with the Favorites Center

The Favorites Center is an Explorer bar that can be triggered to appear on the left side of the browser window. You open the Favorites Center, shown in Figure 20-14, by clicking the Favorites button right below the Back and Forward buttons. (It has a yellow star icon on it as well.)

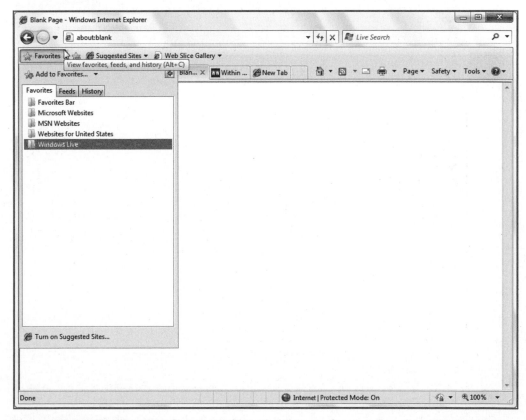

Figure 20-14: The Favorites Center provides a holding pen for your Favorites, browser history, and subscribed RSS feeds.

By default, the Favorites Center appears in Favorites view, which displays your favorite Web sites in a menu-like list; but don't be concerned that Microsoft simply duplicated the functionality of the old Favorites menu and moved it to a new location in order to fool you. The Favorites Center includes far more functionality than the old Favorites menu.

To see what this means, enable the Favorites Center and mouse over the various folders and shortcuts shown in the list. If you mouse over a folder, a small blue arrow appears. If you click this arrow, you will open all of the shortcuts in that folder in their own tabs. (See the next section for more information about tabbed browsing if you don't understand what this means.) Naturally, if you click a shortcut, that shortcut will open in the current browser window; if you click a folder, the view expands to show you the contents of that folder, as shown in Figure 20-15.

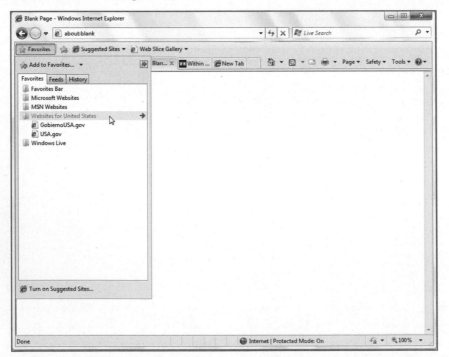

Figure 20-15: The Favorites Center provides a more full-featured hub for your favorite Web sites.

In addition to containing links to your favorite Web sites, the Favorites Center also includes views for History (your browser history) and Feeds (RSS feeds). You might think of the Favorites Center as the front end to the memory of Internet Explorer 8. Here's how these two new buttons work:

* **Feeds:** Contains RSS feeds to which you've subscribed. (You'll examine RSS feeds in detail later in this chapter.)
* **History:** Shows you the Web pages you visited in the past. When you click this button, a drop-down menu enables you to organize the list by various criteria and search your history for a previously viewed page.

To add the Web page you're currently viewing to your Favorites list, click Favorites and then click the Add to Favorites button, which resembles a star with a green plus sign on top of it. This button triggers the dialog shown in Figure 20-16, and from here you can add the current page to Favorites and perform a few other related functions.

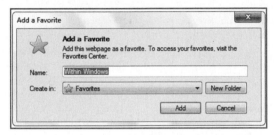

Figure 20-16: Internet Explorer 8 actually makes adding a new favorite a little less obvious.

Managing Favorites with the Favorites Bar

Shown in Figure 20-17, the Favorites Bar is a renamed and improved version of the (reviled) Links bar from previous IE versions. This time around, the Favorites Bar is enabled by default and appears as a toolbar row above the tabs bar and command bar, and below the address bar. The Favorites Bar works like the Bookmarks toolbar in Firefox: it's essentially a secondary (but more visual) place to store Favorites and RSS feeds. But it's also the primary interface for Web Slices, which we'll discuss later in the chapter.

Figure 20-17: The Favorites Bar is another place to store Favorites, but it does so much more than that.

Why have a second place for Favorites? One obvious reason is to give more prominence to certain favorites, like those you may need to access most frequently. Just click the new Add to Favorites Bar button at the left of the Favorites Bar and the currently loaded page will be added to the Favorites bar as a Favorite. (Favorites Bar items are also available in the main Favorites list under a folder called Favorites Bar.)

But the Favorites Bar really comes into its own when you use it with RSS feeds and Web Slices. We'll examine both of these features shortly.

tip Unfortunately, the addition of the Favorites Bar to IE 8 has increased the amount of space utilized by UI at the top of the application window. If you find that you're not using the Favorites Bar, simply remove it: right-click an empty area of the toolbar and uncheck Favorites Bar.

Navigating the Web with Tabs

Tabbed browsing is a feature that optionally enables users to open new Web pages within the frame of a single browser window, and access each individual page via a series of visible tabs. This feature has been available in Web browsers for years, and while Internet Explorer was the last major browser to add the feature, Microsoft has really embraced this functionality. Now, IE 8 has some of the best tabbed browsing features around.

If you haven't had the opportunity to use tabbed browsing, chances are good you'll appreciate the feature, especially if you tend to open a lot of Web documents in different windows. Because you can now optionally open new Web documents in a tab contained within a single browser window, you have fewer windows to manage and less clutter on your desktop.

Here's how tabbed browsing works. By default, Internet Explorer opens with a single document loaded, as before; but now, each document Internet Explorer displays is contained within a tab. The top of the tab—the part that looks like an actual tabbed file folder—is found near the top of the browser window, below the Favorites Bar. If you choose to never deal with tabs per se, Internet Explorer essentially acts as it did before; you will merely see that single tab near the top of the window.

The beauty of tabbed browsing, however, is that you can open multiple tabs, which are essentially child windows of the main browser window. To open a new tab, click the New Tab button, which is the gray square-shaped object to the right of the rightmost tab, as shown in Figure 20-18. When you mouse over this little tab, an icon appears, indicating what will happen if you click it.

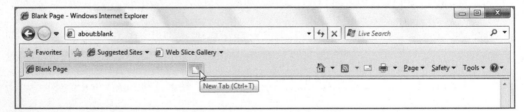

Figure 20-18: To open a new tab, click the New Tab button.

Secret Although it's not documented, you can also open a new tab by double-clicking the blank area to the right of the New Tab button.

By default, the new tab will open to a "What do you want to do next?" page, which provides access to previously browsed pages—perfect if you've closed a browser window or tab by mistake—and other IE 8 features. From here, you can enter a Web address and navigate there, go directly to your home page, or perform any other similar navigational tasks. However, there are better ways to open a new tab. You can use the Ctrl+T keyboard shortcut, for starters. This will open a new tab in a manner similar to clicking the New Tab button.

Alternately, suppose you're doing a Google search and you want to open links to certain search results in new tabs. (This is actually a great use for tabbed browsing.) To open a link in a new tab, you can right-click the link and choose Open in New Tab, or Ctrl+click the link (that is, hold down the Ctrl key on your keyboard while you click it). You can also click the middle mouse button, if your mouse has such a thing, to open a new tab.

This method is particularly effective when you have a list of hyperlinks that you want to open, all at the same time. You can simply move down the list, Ctrl+clicking as you go, and then casually examine each tab in order.

Note, too, that IE 8 automatically colorizes tabs that are Ctrl+clicked from another Web page. In this sense, IE visually groups the pages, which often makes a lot of sense. In the previous Google search example, it stands to reason that those opened tabs are all related.

As for tab navigation, you may recall that you can navigate between open windows in Windows using the Alt+Tab key combination (or, starting in Windows Vista, the new Flip 3D function, which is toggled by using the WinKey+Tab key combination). In Internet Explorer 8, you can select an individual tab by clicking its tab button, but you can also use various key combinations to select tabs. To cycle through the available tabs, use the Ctrl+Tab key combination. To move in reverse order, use Ctrl+Shift+Tab.

IE 8 also integrates with Windows 7 in ways that are not possible on other versions of Windows. One of the integration points revolves around tabs. If you have a single IE window open with multiple tabs and hover over its taskbar icon, as shown in Figure 20-19, the taskbar preview will display each tab separately, as if they were individual IE windows. This lets you navigate to particular IE tabs as if they were separate instances of IE, a feature that is, for now at least, not available with other browsers.

Figure 20-19: The Windows 7 taskbar is savvy about IE tabs and displays a preview for each.

To close a tab, click the Close Tab button, which appears as a small x on the tab button of each tab; or use the Ctrl+W keyboard shortcut. As shown in Figure 20-20, note that Internet Explorer prompts you if you attempt to close the entire browser window if two or more tabs are open: closing down multiple tabs (that is, open documents) with a single mouse click could be disastrous, so this is a nice feature. That said, if you do inadvertently close IE, remember that you can retrieve previously closed tabs from the New Tab page.

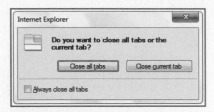

Figure 20-20: Internet Explorer will warn you if you attempt to shut down a browser window with two or more open tabs.

Quick Tabs

Although other browsers have had tabbed browsing functionality for years, Internet Explorer was the first to utilize an innovative new tabbed browsing feature called Quick Tabs. Quick Tabs are a visual way of managing the open tabs you have in any Internet Explorer window, and it's likely that you'll be quite taken with it. In fact, it's so nice-looking that other browser makers rushed to copy it for their own products, an interesting about-face. (Yes, even Apple. *Especially* Apple.)

To understand why Quick Tabs is so cool, you'll have to open a number of Web pages in different tabs in Internet Explorer 8. When you are displaying two or more tabs in an Internet Explorer browser window, you'll notice that a new icon appears next to the Favorites Center and Add to Favorites icons. This icon, resembling four squares, enables you to use Quick Tabs. When you click the Quick Tabs icon, the document contained in each tab is tiled in a thumbnail view within the main browser window, as shown in Figure 20-21.

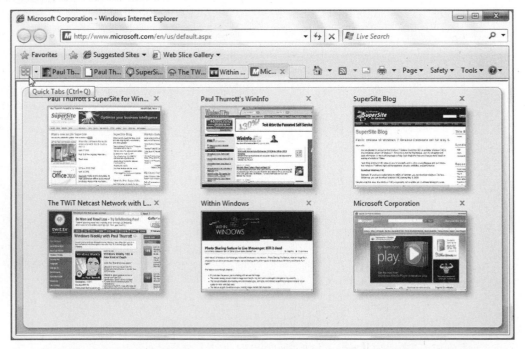

Figure 20-21: Quick Tabs enables you to quickly and visually determine which documents are loaded in each tab.

To select a particular tab from this display, simply click any of the thumbnails. That page will jump to the front and Internet Explorer will return to its normal display. You can also click the Quick Tabs icon again to return to the normal browser display.

Finally, the Quick Tabs icon also provides a drop-down menu. Selecting this menu will display a list of the available documents, as shown in Figure 20-22. You can jump to a particular tab by selecting any of the options, and the currently displayed tab is displayed in bold type.

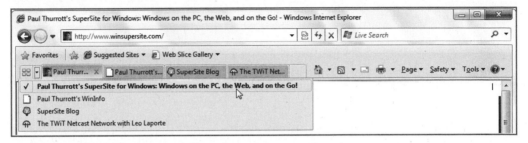

Figure 20-22: The Quick Tabs menu provides yet another way to navigate to particular tabs.

Using Multiple Home Pages

You may recall that older Internet Explorer versions enabled you to specify any Web document as your home page, the page that is displayed when the browser is launched. Now you can now assign multiple documents as your home page, and each document opens in its own tab. This concept is similar to that of a *tab set,* which is portrayed in the Favorites menu or Favorites view of the Favorites Center as a folder full of links. Therefore, your home page can be a single page, like before, or it can be a folder full of links, or a tab set.

There are a number of ways to assign multiple Web documents as your home page, but you will typically first load each of the documents you want into Internet Explorer. Then, perform either of the following actions:

- **Use the Tools button:** Click the Tools button and select Internet Options to display the Internet Options dialog. In the Home page section at the top of the General tab, click the Use Current button. All of the open documents in the current browser window will be added to the list.

- **Use the Home button:** Next to the Home button on the command bar is a small arrow indicating a drop-down menu. Click this arrow and then choose Add or Change Home Page. As shown in Figure 20-23, a new Add or Change Home Page window will appear, with three options.

  Pick "Use the current tab set" as your home page and then click OK.

Figure 20-23: This new window enables you to quickly change your home page.

You can also come back later and add or remove documents from the list. To add a document while keeping all of the other documents, first load the document you want to add. Then, select the complete Web address in the browser's address bar and copy it to the clipboard (by clicking Ctrl+C or right-clicking and choosing Copy). Next, select Tools ⇨ Options, and click inside the list of Web addresses shown in the Home Page section of the General tab. You can edit this list as if it were any text file. Paste the contents of the clipboard into a new line of the list to add it to the list of home pages.

You can delete particular home pages in a similar fashion. Simply open the Internet Options dialog and edit the list, removing the pages you no longer want.

Integrated, Visual Web Search

In older versions of Internet Explorer, Microsoft built very basic Web search features into the address bar, as documented earlier in this chapter; but the company has been busy advancing the state of the art in Web search in other products released since Internet Explorer 6, including a variety of MSN and Windows Live toolbars, its MSN Search and Windows Live Search services, and its index-based Windows Search technologies, which are included in Windows 7. In Internet Explorer 8, Microsoft has taken integrated Web search to a new high. It's pretty obvious, too: a Search box sits prominently in the top-right corner of the browser window, to the right of the address bar and Refresh and Stop buttons. What's not obvious is how powerful this feature is and how easily it can be configured to your needs.

Before getting to that, think about how Web search worked in Internet Explorer 6. Basically, you could navigate to a Web search engine, such as Google (www.google.com) or, if you were savvy enough, you could utilize the autosearch feature to search the Web directly from the address bar. In Internet Explorer 8, you don't have to know about this secret because the Search box is built right into the browser and is displayed by default. To search in Internet Explorer 8, simply select the Search box, type a search query, and tap Enter (or press the Search button, which resembles a magnifying glass). The Search box displays the name of the default search provider—again, Live Search by default—in light-gray text just so you know what it will use.

Secret If you're a keyboard maven, you can also jump directly to the Search box by selecting Ctrl+E. We highlight other IE 8 keyboard shortcuts later in the chapter.

Specifying a Different Search Provider

While I'm sure Microsoft would prefer otherwise, you don't have to use IE's default search engine. If you're a Google fan, for example, you can use Google instead, or any other search engine you prefer. To select Google as the default search provider, click the Search Options button (the small arrow to the right of Search) and select Google if it's available. Now, all of your searches—including autosearch from the Internet Explorer address bar—will use Google instead of MSN Search.

If Google isn't in the list, open the Search Options menu and select Find More Providers. Internet Explorer will navigate to Microsoft's Search Providers Web site (`www.ieaddons.com/en/searchproviders`), where you can pick from a list of search engines, as shown in Figure 20-24.

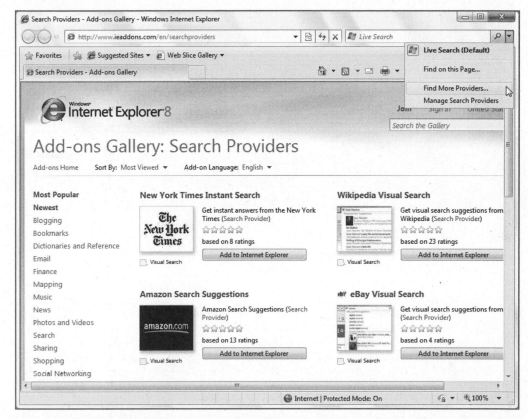

Figure 20-24: Don't get stuck with Live Search. From here you can choose Google, Yahoo!, or any other search engine you prefer.

Once you've selected Google or your search provider of choice, check the option titled "Make this my default search provider" in the Add Search Provider dialog that appears and then click the Add Provider button. The Live Search text in the Web Search box should change to Google. If it doesn't, select Google from the Search Options menu.

Using Visual Search Suggestions

Another cool feature of the IE 8 Search box is that it provides visual search suggestions. With supported search engines—including Google, Live Search, Amazon.com, and several others—you can actually receive visual search results right in a search box drop-down. Obviously, this makes more sense for some queries than others and with some search providers more than others. If you are looking for a specific product, for example, you might configure the search box to use Amazon.com as the provider. As you type the name of the product—like *xbox 360*—a list of Xbox 360–related products appears in the drop-down, complete with images, as shown in Figure 20-25. It's a nice (and useful) effect.

Figure 20-25: Would you like graphics with that search? Of course you would.

The search box also lets you switch search providers on the fly, and it includes matches from your Favorites and History in the bottom part of the search results drop-down box. And thanks to deep integration with search providers, search terms from search engines auto-populate the search box. So if you manually navigate to Google and search for something, that search term will appear in IE's search box, too. Then you can run the same search on Yahoo! Search or any other installed provider. Cool!

Using Find on Page

In addition to searching the Web, the Internet Explorer 8 search functionality also enables you to search the text within a currently loaded document. This is handy when you search the Web for a specific term and then load a page that contains the text, but is quite long. Instead of reading the entire document, you can search within the document for your search string. This feature is called Find on Page.

To access Find on Page, you must first load a Web document. This can be something you searched for, or it can be any Web page anywhere on the Web. Then, tap Ctrl+F to open the Find on Page bar, which appears below the command bar as shown in Figure 20-26.

Enter a search string in the Find box and Find on Page will find it as you type. You can keep tapping Enter repeatedly to find further instances of the search text, or you can simply toggle the Highlight All Matches button (it looks like a tiny highlighter) to highlight all hits. This is shown in Figure 20-27.

Figure 20-26: The Find on Page bar offers in-page searching capabilities.

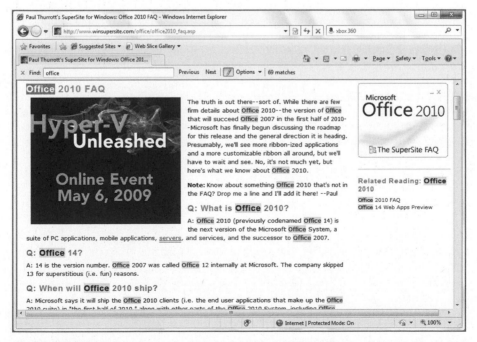

Figure 20-27: Find on Page provides highlighting functionality for finding all instances of your search term in a sea of text.

Working with the Internet Explorer Display

In previous versions of Internet Explorer, the way text was displayed in the browser depended on various factors, including whether you had enabled ClearType (in Windows XP only), a display mode that triples the vertical resolution of text via a technology called *subpixel rendering*. Most people find ClearType to be hugely beneficial on LCD displays, but many complain that it makes text look fuzzy on older CRT-type monitors.

Secret   In Internet Explorer 8, ClearType is always enabled by default; but if you find that the display is blurry on your monitor, you can turn it off. To do so, open Internet Options and navigate to the Advanced tab. In the Settings list, scroll down to the Multimedia section. Then, deselect the option titled Always Use ClearType for HTML and restart the browser. Problem solved.

Configuring Text Size and Page Zoom

Before Internet Explorer 7, Microsoft's browsers offered only rudimentary text-sizing capabilities. Although you would typically view the text in a given Web page at 100 percent magnification, Internet Explorer also offered a Text Size option that enabled you to navigate between options such as Largest, Larger, Medium (the default), Smaller, and Smallest.

Internet Explorer uses a superior Page Zoom feature instead. Unlike the Text Size options, Page Zoom works by retaining the underlying design of the Web page you're viewing. That is, it doesn't just increase or decrease the size of text, which often blows away the underlying layout design. Instead, Page Zoom intelligently zooms the entire page display, including both graphics and text, thereby improving the readability of the text and retaining wonderful graphical image quality as well.

The Page Zoom user interface is located in the bottom-right corner of the browser window, at the far right of the status bar. There, you'll see a small magnifying glass icon with the text 100% next to it (by default). When you click the small arrow to the right of this icon or text, a pop-up menu appears, as shown in Figure 20-28, from which you can choose various zoom amounts.

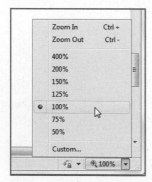

Figure 20-28: Page Zoom enables you to intelligently zoom in on the current Web document.

You can also simply click the Page Zoom icon to jump between preset page zoom values of 100 percent, 125 percent, and 150 percent. The graphics look quite good as they're resized, but the text is simply phenomenal-looking. No matter how much you zoom in, the text looks impressive, as shown in Figure 20-29.

Figure 20-29: People with vision problems will appreciate the way Page Zoom makes text appear crisply and clearly.

Printing

Anyone who has tried to print a Web page with older Internet Explorer versions knows how poorly that feature worked. Well, take heart: Microsoft has fixed IE printing, and in Internet Explorer 8, printing is actually a positive experience. It's been thoroughly overhauled.

You access most printing features directly through the Print button, which is found in the Internet Explorer command bar. If you just click the Print button, Internet Explorer will print the currently displayed Web page using your default printer. There's no warning at all: It just prints. (You can also select Ctrl+P to access the Print dialog and print the current page via a different printer.)

However, the Print button also offers a drop-down menu, shown in Figure 20-30, from which you can access additional functionality, including Print Preview and Page Setup. Both are dramatic improvements over previous Internet Explorer versions.

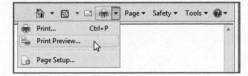

Figure 20-30: IE printing has become a lot more sophisticated.

Using Print Preview

When you select the Print Preview option from the Print button drop-down menu, you'll see the Print Preview display shown in Figure 20-31. From here, you can switch between portrait and landscape display modes, access the Page Setup dialog, and perform other printing-related tasks.

Figure 20-31: The Internet Explorer Print Preview feature is a big improvement over Internet Explorer 6.

The biggest change since Internet Explorer 6 is that you can now easily toggle whether each page includes footer and headers. To see how this works, click the Turn Headers and Footers On or Off button (it's the fifth one from the left) and see how it changes the display in Print Preview. You can also display the pages to print in various ways. For example, you can display an entire page in the window, fit the display to the width of the window, or even display multiple pages, as shown in Figure 20-32.

When you're ready to print, click the Print button at the bottom of the Print Preview window; or click Close to return to Internet Explorer.

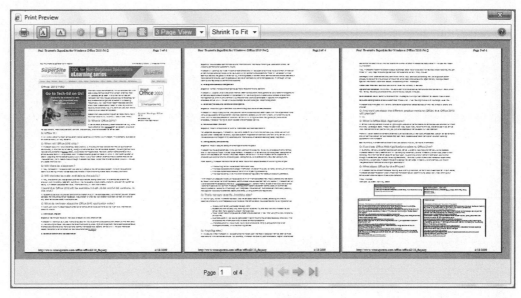

Figure 20-32: A multiple-page preview in Internet Explorer

Secret

Another truly amazing feature is that you can print, and print preview, only the content you've selected in a Web page. That is, you don't have to print an entire Web page. Instead, you can print text that you've selected, or highlighted.

To see how this works, open a Web document and select some text. Then, choose the Print Preview option from the Print button drop-down menu. When the Print Preview window appears, you'll see a new Select Content drop-down menu in the middle top of the window, shown in Figure 20-33. Open the drop-down list and choose As selected on screen. Now, only the selected text is ready to print.

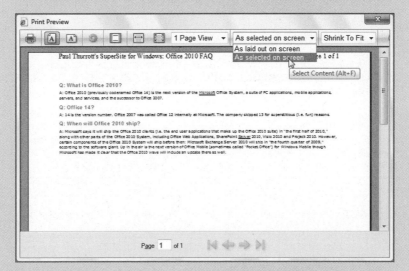

Figure 20-33: You can print only those parts of a Web page you want.

Using Page Setup

If you want even more control over how your Web pages will print, you can use the Page Setup dialog. This dialog can be accessed in two ways: through the Page Setup button in the Print Preview toolbar, or through the Page Setup option in the Print button's drop-down menu. This dialog, shown in Figure 20-34, enables you to configure the paper size and source, the margin sizes, and the header and footer display.

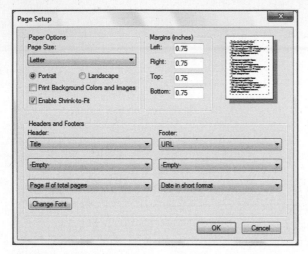

Figure 20-34: Change various printing options through the Page Setup dialog.

> **tip** In older versions of Internet Explorer, you had to use the Page Setup dialog to remove headers and footers from the printout. This method still works, though the Print Preview method described previously is simpler and quicker. To remove the header completely, simply select the Header text box and choose -Empty-.

Covering Your Tracks

Yes, it was possible in previous IE versions to perform housekeeping tasks such as removing temporary Internet files and cookies, and deleting your browser history and saved form data and passwords; but it was also difficult and time-consuming.

In Internet Explorer 8, you can use a special private browsing mode called InPrivate that prevents the browser from storing any personal information, hiding your tracks before they're even made. And if you want to cover tracks you made during normal browsing sessions, you can do so with just two clicks of your mouse button. This latter feature is called Delete Browsing History, and it's also a nifty addition to Microsoft's browser.

Covering Your Tracks with InPrivate Browsing

Internet Explorer 8 can optionally run in a new InPrivate Browsing mode that effectively hides your tracks as you travel around to the more nefarious parts of the Web or, what the heck, secretly shop for a spouse's birthday present online. (That is why you need this feature, right?)

More specifically, InPrivate Browsing turns off IE's ability to locally store or retain browser history, temporary Internet files, form data, cookies, and user names and passwords. It does allow you to download files and add sites to your Favorites. By default, IE add-ons like toolbars are disabled in InPrivate Browsing mode, but you can change that from Internet Settings if desired.

You can start browsing in this mode in a few different ways, but the most obvious are to choose InPrivate Browsing from IE 8's Safety menu or to select Open an InPrivate Browsing Window from the new tab page. In either case, a new browser window will appear with a new dark blue-gray InPrivate badge to the left of the address bar, as shown in Figure 20-35.

Figure 20-35: What happens InPrivate stays InPrivate.

To end an InPrivate session, simply close the browser window.

A related feature, InPrivate Filtering, is a first step in addressing the way in which many Web sites share data with each other. Consider a mainstream Web site like wsj.com, for "*The Wall Street Journal.*" This site is certainly reputable, but it utilizes advertising services that work across multiple non-WSJ Web sites. Once these services have collected information about you on wsj.com, they can track you across other sites that utilize the same services. This is usually innocuous, but it's possible that a malicious site could take advantage of this capability and deliver dangerous content via other sites.

InPrivate Filtering provides basic protection against this potential kind of attack by preventing, by default, over 10 cross-site calls. It's not enabled by default, but once you enable it you have decent control over how it works. For example, you could lower the threshold for cross-site content (down to a minimum of three), choose to allow or block specific sites, and so on. It's interesting to look at just to see what the sites you visit are up to. You might be surprised.

To enable InPrivate Filtering, open the Safety command bar menu and select InPrivate Filtering.

tip InPrivate Filtering has a wonderful and unexpected side use: You can use it to block advertisements from appearing in Web pages. To learn how, please visit Paul's SuperSite blog at `http://tinyurl.com/inprivateads`.

Covering Your Tracks with Delete Browsing History

To access Delete Browsing History, open the Safety command bar menu and choose Delete Browsing History. Shown in Figure 20-36, the resulting window enables you to delete a number of items either individually or all at the same time. It's a one-stop shop for covering your tracks.

Figure 20-36: Delete Browsing History helps you hide your tracks on the fly.

Here's what each of the options means:

♦ **Preserve Favorites website data:** If enabled, cookies and temporary Internet files associated with sites in your Favorites will not be deleted.

♦ **Temporary Internet Files:** These are downloaded files that have been cached in your Temporary Internet Files folder, including Offline Favorites and attachments stored by Microsoft Outlook.

♦ **Cookies:** These are small text files that include data that persists between visits to particular Web sites.

♦ **History:** This is the list of Web sites you've visited with Internet Explorer, and the Web addresses you've typed in the Windows 7 Run dialog.

♦ **Form data:** This is information that has been saved using Internet Explorer's autocomplete form data functionality.

◆ **Passwords:** These are passwords that were saved using Internet Explorer's auto-complete password data functionality.

◆ **InPrivate Filtering data:** This is data related to InPrivate Filtering, which monitors the interaction between sites you visit and sites that monitor your activities. These sites are usually ad-related and innocuous, but they could be a security risk.

Understanding and Using RSS

Although much of the Web is based on a rather passive system whereby users manually browse to the Web sites they would like to visit, a new type of Web technology, alternately named *Really Simple Syndication* or *Rich Site Summary*, but usually referred to by the abbreviation RSS regardless, has turned that paradigm on its head and changed the way many people consume Web-based information. In keeping with this sea change, Internet Explorer 8 supports RSS, enabling Windows 7 users to access Web-based content in both traditional and more leading-edge ways.

RSS is basically a data format, based on XML, designed for distributing news and other Web-based content via the Internet. Content that is available via RSS is said to be published in RSS format, while applications (such as Internet Explorer) that can access RSS content are said to subscribe to that content.

What makes RSS different from traditional Web browsing is that RSS applications periodically poll the content publishers to which you've subscribed, so if you subscribe to the RSS *feed*, as such a link is called, for a particular Web site, that feed will be updated on your local machine periodically, assuming you have an Internet connection. Most good RSS applications, including Internet Explorer 8, enable you to specify how often feeds are updated. Some feeds, obviously, are updated more often than others.

Secret

You won't be surprised to discover that we have a number of RSS feeds for our Web sites. These will be of interest to *Windows 7 Secrets* readers:

Paul Thurrott's SuperSite for Windows: www.winsupersite.com/supersite.xml

Rafael Rivera's Within Windows: feeds2.feedburner.com/WithinWindows

SuperSite Blog: community.winsupersite.com/blogs/paul/rss.aspx

Paul Thurrott's WinInfo: http://feeds2.feedburner.com/windowsitpro/wininfo

The Internet Explorer command bar has a prominent orange Feeds button, which provides an obvious front end to this technology. The Feeds button is grayed out if you are currently visiting a Web page with which no RSS feed is associated, however, so you must visit a site with an RSS feed to discover how it works.

Viewing an RSS Feed

As an example, take a look at Paul's SuperSite for Windows Web site (www.winsupersite .com). Because this site has an RSS feed, the Internet Explorer Feeds button is orange. To view the feed, simply click the button. Internet Explorer will switch to its new Feeds view, which displays the content of the SuperSite for Windows feed (in this case) in the vaguely pleasant, if bland, style shown in Figure 20-37.

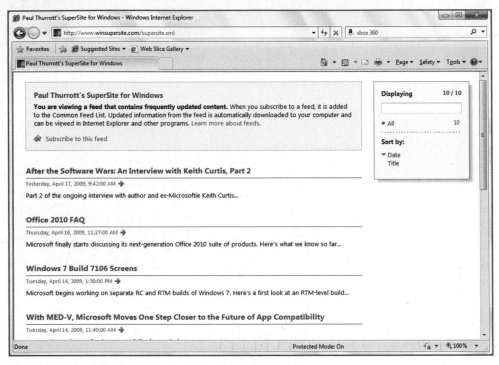

Figure 20-37: Internet Explorer RSS feed reading page

Some Web sites include two or more RSS feeds. If so, you can display the list of available feeds by clicking the small arrow at the right of the Feeds button (see Figure 20-38). Then, simply choose the feed you want. This feature is sometimes visible when sites support different types of feeds too. For example, in addition to RSS, some sites support a similar type of feed called Atom.

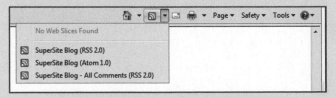

Figure 20-38: Some sites support multiple feeds.

In the Feeds view, you can perform various actions, including searching the feed for specific text using the Search box in the upper-right corner of the page, or sorting by date (the default) or title. The SuperSite for Windows feed publishes only the title and a small abstract for each article it lists; if you want to view a full article, you must click the title of the article you'd like to read. Some feeds publish entire articles directly in the feed, so you don't have to manually visit the main Web site; and some sites, such as the SuperSite Blog, offer categories, so the Feeds view displays those on the right, enabling you to filter the view by category, as shown in Figure 20-39.

Figure 20-39: You can easily sort the Feeds view using a variety of methods.

Subscribing to an RSS Feed

In the Feeds view, you're essentially just browsing the Web as before, albeit through a nonstandard display; but the real power of RSS feeds is realized when you subscribe to feeds. To subscribe to Paul's SuperSite Blog feed, you simply click the Subscribe to this feed link at the top of the page. When you do so, the Subscribe to This Feed dialog appears, shown in Figure 20-40. Here, you can edit the name of the feed (only as it appears in your browser) and where it will be created (the Feeds folder, by default).

When you've subscribed, the Feeds view changes to indicate that you've successfully subscribed to the feed, adding a new View My Feeds link. Additionally, you may see an alert noting that automatic feed updates are turned off. If you see this alert, then your RSS subscriptions will not be updated automatically. To enable this functionality, click the Turn On Automatic Feed Updates link.

Figure 20-40: When you subscribe to an RSS feed, it is stored in a Favorites-like database.

Managing RSS Feeds

Internet Explorer treats RSS subscriptions much like Favorites. However, RSS subscriptions are not stored in your Favorites folder. Instead, they are stored in a special database that is based on the RSS platform technologies built into Windows. They can also easily be added to the new Favorites Bar using a checkbox in the dialog that appears when you subscribe, as shown in Figure 20-40.

You can access all of your subscribed feeds through the Favorites Center. You may recall from the discussion earlier in this chapter that Feeds, like Favorites and History lists, are saved in this browser memory store. If you open the Favorites Center, you'll see that Paul Thurrott's SuperSite for Windows has been added to the Feeds list, as shown in Figure 20-41.

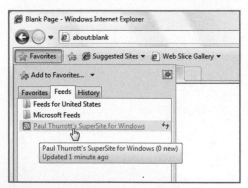

Figure 20-41: The Feeds view in the Favorites Center is like Favorites for Feeds.

As with your Favorites list, you can do a few interesting things with RSS feeds in the Favorites Center. When you mouse over a feed in the list of subscribed feeds, a small refresh icon appears. If you click this icon, the feed is manually updated if there is any new content to download. If you simply click the feed name, the feed will be displayed in the feed reading page as you'd expect.

To configure how an individual feed is updated and archived, you can right-click it in the Feeds list and choose Properties (or, from the Feeds view of an individual feed, click the View Feed Properties link shown on the right side of the window). Either way, you'll see the Feed Properties dialog, shown in Figure 20-42.

Figure 20-42: You can configure individual feed properties from this dialog.

Here, you can configure how often the feed is updated, whether or not to automatically download attached files (disabled by default for security reasons), and when to begin archiving the feed.

You can also view and change feed properties globally. To do so, open the Internet Options dialog and navigate to the Content tab. Then, click the Settings button in the Feeds and Web Slices section. In the Feed and Web Slice Settings dialog, shown in Figure 20-43, you can configure settings that apply globally to Internet Explorer's feeds functionality.

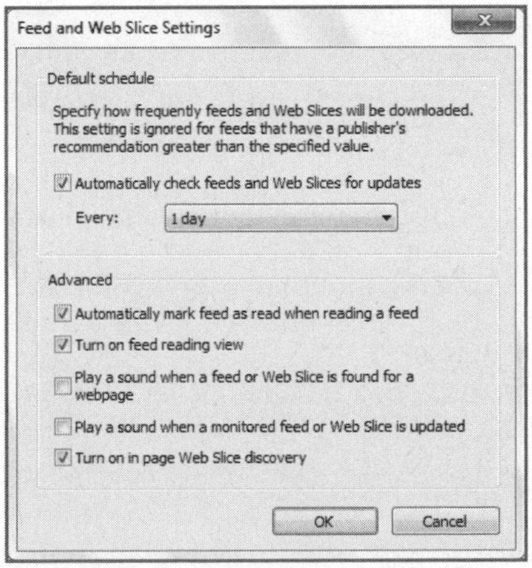

Figure 20-43: Global feeds settings are available via Internet Options.

Using Web Slices

While Internet Explorer 8's use of RSS feeds is nice because of the interoperable nature of that technology, Microsoft's latest browser also includes a similar but more proprietary feature called *Web Slices* that provides "at a glance" access to Web-based information through the Favorites Bar.

Web Slices are literally small pieces, or slices, of Web pages, and they need to be explicitly created by Web site owners. These slices provide a way for readers to peer into a specific part of a site—say, a list of headlines from a news site—or a bit of information in compact form (such as a traffic widget). As with the RSS feed list previously noted, Web Slices are cool because they provide a quick, at-a-glance look at information that is important to you, and they do so without requiring you to open a new tab or otherwise navigate away from the page you're currently viewing. Also, unlike RSS feed lists, Web Slices can be quite graphical.

As with RSS feeds, Web Slices announce themselves by lighting up the Feeds command bar button. When a Web Slice is found on a page, the button turns green, and, as shown in Figure 20-44, when you click this button, you're provided with a pop-up window that lets you add the Slice to your Favorites Bar.

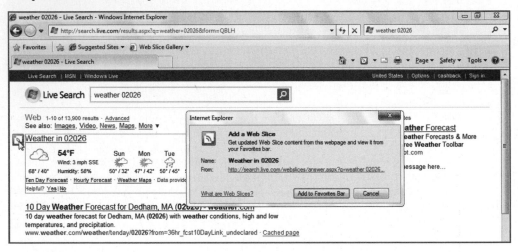

Figure 20-44: Web Slices announce themselves much like RSS feeds, but they will live in your Favorites Bar.

Slices work best with certain types of information, such as e-mail in-boxes, weather reports (see Figure 20-45), traffic updates, sports scores, auction items, and the like. These are exactly the types of things that people need to check throughout the day, but with a typical browser, that would entail manually navigating to a specific site. With Web Slices, you can simply add links to these bits of info directly to the Favorites Bar, so they're always available. And when you click on a Web Slice, you don't navigate to a new page. Instead, a small pop-up appears with the desired info.

Figure 20-45: Web Slices don't require you to navigate away from the current page: Just click the slice, view the information, and go back to what you were doing.

At the time of this writing, third-party support for Web Slices is on the light side, but some of the Microsoft slices—like Live Search Weather and Live Search Traffic—are quite good. But some are horrible: The "Hotmail Service" Web Slice actually throws up a small advertisement, too. Yuck.

You can check out Microsoft's collection of Web Slices on the IE Add-ons Web site at www.ieaddons.com/en/webslices.

Using Accelerators

Accelerators are a new IE 8 feature that address the need that arises after you've found something of interest on a Web page: Often you want to copy that information and then paste it into another Web site so you can perform some action, like look up an address on Yahoo! Maps, search for the term with Google, or e-mail it to another person. Accelerators literally accelerate this process by providing a pop-up menu of options that appears when you highlight text or a graphic in IE 8, and each of these options is related to a Web service of some kind.

Secret

Accelerators were originally called Activities, and while Accelerators are indeed new to IE 8, this isn't the first time Microsoft tried to add this functionality to its browser. Several years ago, Microsoft developed a UI feature called Smart Tags that it planned to incorporate in Office XP and Internet Explorer 6, which shipped as part of Windows XP. Smart Tags were added to Office XP as planned and they still exist today in subsequent versions of that product. But the company's plans to include Smart Tags in IE 6 were scuttled after Web developers and users complained long and hard about the feature, which many saw as anti-competitive and intrusive. So IE 6 shipped without Smart Tags, and the feature, presumably, was dropped for good.

Nope. Smart Tags are back, baby. Only this time they're called Accelerators; and to prove their not exclusionary or anti-competitive, Microsoft is even stocking IE 8 with a number of Tags, er, Accelerators that are made by its competitors. See, they're completely different!

Accelerators provide contextual menus on Web pages that can provide additional information via Web services that will lead readers to new locations. The contents of these contextual menus are determined by what's selected on the page and which Accelerators are available in the user's browser. Put another way, the functionality is not provided by the underlying Web site at all. It is instead provided by the browser via this new feature.

On one level, Accelerators are interesting and useful, as you'll see in a moment. However, they also allow users to completely bypass whatever facilities the Web site itself has provided. For example, you might use the IE 8 Accelerators feature to find a Yahoo! Map for a selected address on a Web page. But that page may supply its own map, one that you have now chosen to bypass.

Okay, so now it's time to see how this feature works. If you select a word or any other text in a Web page, you'll see a small blue Accelerator graphic appear, as shown in Figure 20-46 (though, of course, you can't see the color in this figure).

Figure 20-46: Accelerators pop up when you select something in a Web page.

Click this tag and a menu will appear, loaded with Accelerators that may (or may not) apply to the selected text (see Figure 20-47). What you see, of course, depends on what's selected (that is, it is contextual) and on which Accelerators are loaded in your browser.

Figure 20-47: Via this unique IE 8 feature, you can do things with selected objects in the browser.

By default, IE 8 ships with several Accelerators, including Map with Bing, and Translate with Bing, but you can also visit a Web page to add new Accelerators from Microsoft and companies like eBay, Facebook, and, yes, Yahoo!. The process of adding Accelerators is much like that of adding search providers.

So what might one do with Accelerators? You can highlight an individual word and get a definition. You can select a full address and get a map (see Figure 20-48). You can highlight a word in a foreign language and get a translation. By design, most Accelerators trigger a small pop-up window, but many also provide a link so you can load the information in a separate window or tab.

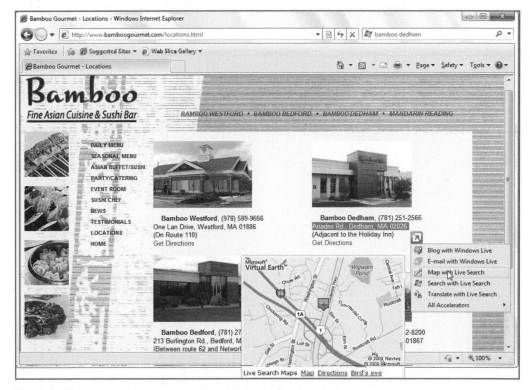

Figure 20-48: Accelerators enable you to quickly access desired information.

You can also use Accelerators to send information from a Web page to another location, triggering a Google search, perhaps, or blogging about the selected text in Windows Live Spaces.

Unlike with Web Slices, however, a huge number of excellent third-party Accelerators are already available. IE 8 ships with several preinstalled, including four Microsoft entries—Blog with Windows Live, E-mail with Windows Live, Map with Live Search, and Translate with Live Search—but you can easily access others, including those related to visual search (for example, Amazon, Google, eBay, New York Times, and many others), mapping (for example, Yahoo!, Live.com), people (for example, Facebook), travel (for example, TripAdvisor, National Geographic), weather (for example, weather.com), and many other categories. There's a lot there.

You can discover more Accelerators on the Internet Explorer Add-ons site at `www.ieaddons`
`.com/en/accelerators`.

Internet Explorer Keyboard Shortcuts

Keyboard shortcuts make it possible to navigate the Internet Explorer user interface without having to move your hand away from the mouse. Internet Explorer 8 supports virtually all of the keyboard shortcuts supported by earlier Internet Explorer versions, but it
also adds a slew of new shortcuts related to new functionality in this version. Table 20-4
summarizes the Internet Explorer 8 keyboard shortcuts.

Table 20-4: Internet Explorer 8 Keyboard Shortcuts

Keyboard Shortcut	What It Does
Alt+left arrow key	Navigate to the previous page.
Alt+right arrow key	Navigate to the next page.
Esc	Stop the current page from loading.
F5 or Ctrl+R or Ctrl+F5	Refresh (reload) the current page.
Alt+Home	Go to your home page.
Alt+D	Select the address bar.
Ctrl+Enter	Automatically add www and .com to what you typed in the address bar.
Spacebar	Scroll down the Web page.
Shift+spacebar	Scroll up the Web page.
Alt+F4	Close the current window.
Ctrl+D	Add the current page to your Favorites list.
Alt+N	Select the information bar.
Shift+F10	Open the context menu for the currently selected item.
Shift+mouse click	Open the link in a new window.
Ctrl+mouse click	Open the link in a new tab but do not select that tab.
Ctrl+Shift+mouse click	Open the link in new tab and navigate to that tab.
Ctrl+T	Open a new tab.
Alt+Enter	Open a new tab from the address bar.
Ctrl+Tab	Switch between available tabs.
Ctrl+Shift+Tab	Switch between available tabs in the opposite direction.
Ctrl+W	Close the current tab (or current window if no tabs are open).

Keyboard Shortcut	What It Does
Ctrl+x (where x represents the number of the tab, as numbered from 1 to 8)	Switch to a particular tab.
Ctrl+9	Switch to the last tab.
Ctrl+Alt+F4	Close other tabs.
Ctrl+Q	Open Quick Tabs.
Ctrl+(+) or Ctrl+(=)	Zoom the page by 10 percent.
Ctrl+(-)	Decrease the page zoom by 10 percent.
Ctrl+0	Zoom to 100 percent (normal view).
Ctrl+E	Navigate to the Toolbar Search box.
Alt+Enter (from the Search box)	Open Search in a new window.
Ctrl+Down Arrow (from the Search box)	Display the search provider menu.
Ctrl+H	Open the Favorites Center to the History view.
Ctrl+I	Open the Favorites Center to the Favorites view.
Ctrl+J	Open the Favorites Center to the Feeds view.

In addition to these handy keyboard shortcuts, Internet Explorer 8 also supports a few helpful mouse actions, which are like shortcuts you can trigger with the mouse. These actions are detailed in Table 20-5.

Table 20-5: Internet Explorer 8 Mouse Actions

Mouse Action	What It Does
Click the middle mouse button	Open the link in a new tab.
Click the middle mouse button on the tab	Close a tab.
Double-click the empty space to the right of the New Tab button	Open a new tab.
Ctrl+mouse wheel up	Zoom the page by 10 percent.
Ctrl+mouse wheel down	Decrease the page zoom by 10 percent.

cross ref
This is Internet Explorer we're talking about, so you might be wondering where you can find a discussion of Internet Explorer 8 security features. Have no fear: Internet Explorer 8 includes a huge number of security-related features, and they're all covered in Chapter 7.

Summary

Internet Explorer 8 is an evolutionary advance over its predecessor, IE 7, but a huge change from IE 6, which shipped with Windows XP. Although one might debate whether the user interface changes make Internet Explorer 8 more difficult to use, it's hard to argue with the other features Microsoft has added—tabbed browsing and Quick Tabs, Favorites Center and the Favorites Bar, integrated and visual Web search, Find on Page, the browser's vastly improved text display and printing functionality, Web Slices, Accelerators, InPrivate Browsing, and its history-hiding techniques are all wonderful advancements. Internet Explorer 8 integration with RSS is also a positive sign: this standards-based Web technology is sweeping across the Internet, enabling everything from blogs to podcasts. For once, Internet Explorer is as capable and usable as its competition, and even more capable and usable in many regards. There's never been a better time to be an IE user.

Managing E-mail and Contacts

Chapter
21

◆ ◆

In This Chapter

Installing and configuring Windows Live Mail

Using Windows Live Mail

Understanding new Windows Live Mail features

Utilizing Web mail and other unique Windows Live Mail features

Managing contacts and contact groups with Windows Live People

◆ ◆

When Microsoft shipped Windows 95, e-mail was a corporate tool but just a curiosity to the wider computer user base. Today, e-mail is a pervasive presence in many people's lives, both personal and professional, and one of the main activities that people perform with computers and other computerized devices, whether they're online or not. For years, Windows has been saddled with an almost universally loathed e-mail client called Outlook Express. That e-mail client carries through to Windows 7, albeit with a new name, Windows Live Mail. Fortunately, Windows Live Mail does address most of the shortcomings of its predecessors. It also integrates nicely with Microsoft's Windows Live People (also known as Windows Live Contacts) contacts management system, providing you with a single solution for e-mail and contacts management.

Secret
While this chapter focuses solely on e-mail and contacts management, Windows Live Mail is actually a multifaceted solution that also handles Usenet newsgroups, RSS feeds, and, oddly, calendar management. We examine Windows Live Mail's calendaring features in Chapter 22.

Introducing Windows Live Mail

In previous versions of Windows, Microsoft offered a bare-bones e-mail and newsgroup client called Outlook Express. (In Windows Vista, it was renamed to Windows Mail but little changed from the version that appeared in Windows XP.) The Outlook Express name suggested that the application was somehow a smaller, less full-featured version of Microsoft's premier e-mail and personal information management (PIM) client, Outlook, although the two applications are in fact not related. Oddly, Outlook Express includes certain functionality that was never included in Outlook—primarily support for Usenet newsgroups—whereas Outlook, of course, includes numerous features not found in Outlook Express, including native Exchange Server support, calendaring and tasks, and more.

tip
We're often asked in which versions of Windows readers can find Outlook or Microsoft Office. These applications are not part of any version of Windows but are instead sold separately. Presumably, this confusion arises because most people obtain new Windows versions with new PCs, and those PCs often come with a version of Office as well. For the record, you can purchase Outlook as a standalone application or as part of various versions of the Microsoft Office suite of applications. Or, you can save a lot of money and simply use Windows Live Mail for e-mail, contacts, and calendar management. These solutions are all free to Windows 7 users, unlike Outlook (or Office).

Shown in Figure 21-1, Windows Live Mail is one of those programs that many people use without ever realizing its full potential. One reason for this is that most people tend to use it as is—without bothering to consider all of the possible configuration options. In the following sections you'll learn how to use Windows Live Mail and make it better fit your needs.

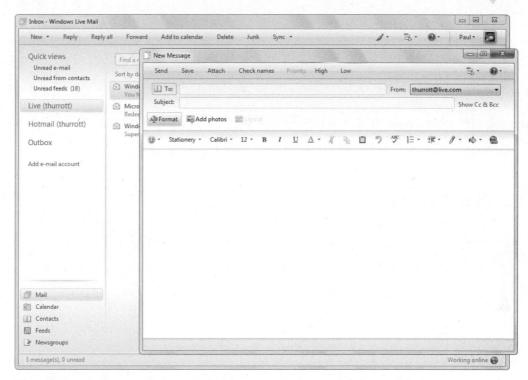

Figure 21-1: Déjà vu—Windows Live Mail is really just a new version of Outlook Express, but it's been updated significantly.

Installing Windows Live Mail

As its name suggests, Windows Live Mail is part of the Windows Live family of products and services and thus may not have been included with your copy of Windows 7. Strictly speaking, Windows Live Mail is part of the Windows Live Essentials product suite, which you can download from `http://download.live.com`. But chances are good you already have it: Microsoft delivers Windows Live Essentials to Windows 7 users via Windows Update, and many PC makers ship the product with their computers as well.

> **tip** If you're not sure whether you have Windows Live Mail installed, open the Start menu and type **windows live mail** into Start Menu Search. If nothing comes up, it's time to download and install the application.

If you don't already have Windows Live Mail, you can download and install the application by visiting the Windows Live Mail Web site (`download.live.com/wlmail/`) or the main Windows Live Essentials Web site listed previously. Once there, simply click the prominent Download button. When you do so, you'll be prompted to run or download the Windows Live Essentials Installer (wl-setup-web.exe), assuming you're using Internet Explorer. (Some other browsers require you to download the file first and then execute it locally.) Choose

Run. Once the install finishes downloading, it will run (after a brief UAC security prompt) and present the simple interface shown in Figure 21-2.

Figure 21-2: The Windows Live Essentials Installer runs directly from the Web.

This installer will present a list of Windows Live Essentials applications you can install. Right now, we're only concerned with Windows Live Mail, which is represented by the Mail option in the list; but you are, of course, free to install any of the other Windows Live Essentials programs if you'd like.

> **tip**
> If you had previously installed one or more Windows Live Essentials programs, the Windows Live Essentials Installer will show green checkmarks next to those applications. You can run this installer repeatedly to add more programs to Windows.

When you're ready to install, click the Install button. The Windows Live Installer begins installing Windows Live Mail (and any other programs you may have selected), as shown in Figure 21-3.

When the Windows Live Essentials Installer is completed, you'll be asked to choose a few simple settings options, click Continue, and then conclude the process. It's time to check out Windows Live Mail.

> **tip**
> As previously discussed, we assume that you have a Windows Live ID, which is Microsoft's online persona management system. If you don't have one, you will need to create one. You can create a Windows Live ID in various ways, but the easiest may be to simply sign up for a Hotmail account (www.hotmail.com). The e-mail account you create during that process will be your Windows Live ID as well. We look at Hotmail in Chapter 23.

Figure 21-3: The Windows Live Essentials Installer will install whatever applications you've selected.

Configuring Windows Mail: A Few Quick Tips for Getting Started

Windows Live Mail is designed to work with Windows Live-type e-mail accounts (that is, Hotmail and MSN), of course, but also industry-standard POP3 and IMAP-type e-mail accounts. The first time you run the application, as shown in Figure 21-4, you'll be asked to configure an account.

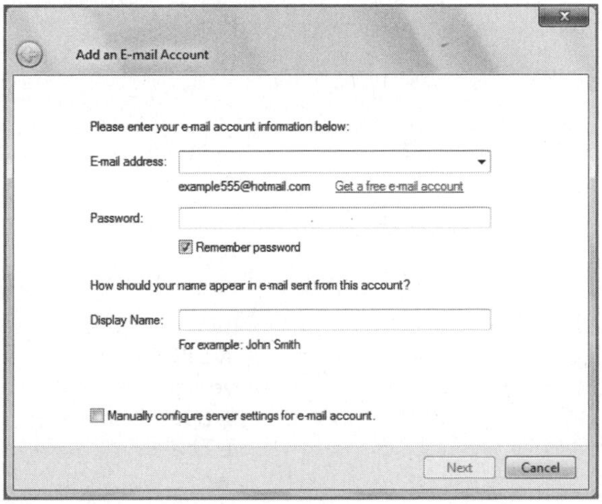

Figure 21-4: Windows Live Mail prompts you to configure an e-mail account on first launch.

To use Windows Live Mail with a Windows Live e-mail account, all you need is your e-mail address, password, and the plain English name that will be shown in the From field when you send e-mail. This type of e-mail account is extremely easy to set up, and when you click Next in that initial wizard, Windows Live Mail will make the appropriate connections and begin downloading the server-side e-mail messages, contacts, and calendaring items that are associated with that account.

Secret   By default, Windows Live accounts are configured such that all of your information is kept on the server and is not downloaded to this one PC. This is the optimal configuration, as using an e-mail account like this means that you can always access your e-mail, contacts, and calendar from any PC or device (including a smart phone). If you download and remove information from the server, that information won't be available elsewhere.

Using Windows Live Mail with a non-Windows Live e-mail account is more complicated. You will need to have the names of the SMTP and POP3/IMAP servers at your Internet service provider (ISP), as well as your e-mail address and e-mail password, your account name (user ID), and your logon password. And you'll need to check the option "Manually configure server settings for e-mail account" in the Add an E-mail Account wizard to do so.

If you need to add a second account (or third, or fourth, or whatever, as Windows Live Mail can handle whatever number of Windows Live or non-Windows Live e-mail accounts you throw at it), or if you've canceled the Add an E-mail Account wizard previously, you can always add e-mail account information later: in the Windows Live Mail window, tap Alt to display the hidden menu and then choose Tools ➪ Accounts, and then Add ➪ E-Mail Account to start configuring your Internet mail account.

Secret   By default, Internet Explorer uses Windows Live Mail as the default mail tool when you click an e-mail address while viewing a Web page. If you want to use another e-mail client (such as Microsoft Outlook or Mozilla Thunderbird), you can change this default behavior. To do so, right-click the Start button, choose Properties, and then click Customize. In the bottom of the Customize Start Menu dialog, click the E-mail link button to pick the default client.

To read the articles (also called *messages* or *postings*) in Usenet newsgroups online, you need to connect to a news server. Your ISP may maintain a news server, but Windows Mail is already preconfigured with a newsgroup account called Microsoft Communities that provides access to Microsoft's public product support newsgroup server. You can also connect to other news servers.

To connect to a news server, choose Newsgroup Account in the New Account wizard.

Changing Windows Mail Options Right Away

Depending on your needs, the default configuration for Windows Live Mail might need to be tweaked. Here are some useful changes you might consider making to the application's configuration before using Windows Live Mail to read or write any e-mail messages:

◆ Tap Alt and then choose Tools ⇨ Options. Click the Read tab, and check the *Automatically expand grouped messages* check box. Now you won't have to click the plus symbol repeatedly to follow a conversation thread, at the slight cost of seeing multiple entries in a thread that you might not bc particularly interested in. Optionally, uncheck the top option *Mark messages read after displaying for 1 second(s)* unless you prefer this behavior.

◆ On the Signatures tab, enter at least a rudimentary signature—your name at least—or other information that you want to appear at the bottom of every e-mail message or newsgroup message you send. You can make additional signatures and get more elaborate, as discussed later in this chapter, but we suggest that you don't get carried away.

◆ To automatically associate a particular signature with a mail or news account, highlight it in the Signatures list and click the Advanced button. In the Advanced Signature Settings dialog, check all the accounts for which this signature is to be the default. For these accounts only, doing so will override the general default signature setting.

◆ In the Send tab, make sure that the *Send messages immediately* check box is checked (as it is by default) if you work online or want to have messages sent as soon as you finish writing them. If you work offline, clear this check box and choose Tools ⇨ Sync all e-mail accounts (or press F5) when you're ready to send your mail. You can also just click the Sync button in the Windows Live Mail toolbar to send mail from your outbox to the mail server.

◆ In the Spelling tab, check the top option, *Always check spelling before sending*. One can only wonder why this isn't checked by default.

Windows Live Mail Basics

Compared to previous versions of Outlook Express and Windows Mail, Windows Live Mail offers a fresher look and feel—and one that is far more customizable to boot—but it also adopts the more modern three-pane view that Microsoft first debuted in its business-oriented Outlook application, and features a Windows 7–like look and feel, as shown in Figure 21-5.

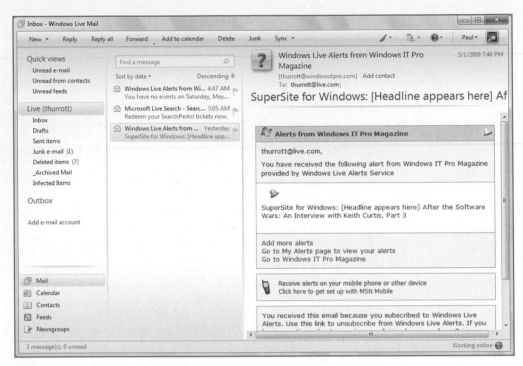

Figure 21-5: Windows Live Mail, like Outlook, presents a three-pane UI.

The Windows Live Mail user interface includes five main areas:

◆ **Menu and toolbar pane:** Windows Live Mail hides its menu bar by default, resulting in a more streamlined look and putting more emphasis on the toolbar. Remember that you can tap the Alt key to temporarily access the Windows Live Mail menu bar. You can also display the menu bar permanently if you so desire.

◆ **Folders pane:** This leftmost pane includes Quick views (essentially prebuilt stored searches that you might frequently need); storage folders, both local and remote, for each of the e-mail accounts you've configured; and Shortcuts, a list of buttons that link to Windows Live Mail experiences such as Mail, Calendar, Contacts, (RSS) Feeds, and (Usenet) Newsgroups.

◆ **Messages pane:** This middle pane includes the instant search box and the message list, which varies according to which e-mail, RSS, or newsgroup folder you're currently viewing.

◆ **Reading pane:** This rightmost pane is shown to the right of the Message list by default, creating the application's three-pane look. However, if you prefer to make Windows Live Mail look more like Outlook Express or Windows Mail, you can move the Reading pane below the message list. To do so, access View ⇨ Layout ⇨ Reading pane (Mail).

Changes to the Toolbar

Aside from the different layout, there are other differences between Windows Live Mail and its predecessors. For example, the menu attached to Windows Live Mail's New button reveals a more diverse set of options. You can create new e-mail and Photo Mail (discussed later in the chapter), but you can also trigger an Event (via the Calendar experience, described in the next chapter), a news message (for the increasingly archaic Usenet newsgroup functionality), a contact, or a folder, the latter of which will be placed within the folder structure of one of your e-mail accounts.

On the Windows Live Mail toolbar, a Junk button is prominently available, enabling you to easily dispatch selected e-mails to the Junk Mail folder. This is much improved over the Junk Mail system in Vista's Windows Mail, which didn't offer a simple way to mark individual messages as junk.

Whereas Windows Mail contained toolbar-based links to Vista applications such as Windows Contacts and Windows Calendar—applications that no longer exist in Windows 7—Windows Live instead offers various links throughout the UI to different Windows Live services. Windows Live Contacts is accessed via the Contacts shortcut in the Folder pane, for example. The more central connection with Windows Live, however, comes via the Windows Live sign-in mechanism in the upper-right corner of the application window. Shown in Figure 21-6, this area varies greatly depending on whether or not you're logged on to your Windows Live ID.

Figure 21-6: If you haven't configured a Windows Live–based e-mail account, this menu doesn't do very much.

There are two other UI options in the Windows Live Mail toolbar worth discussing. At the far right of the toolbar, but to the left of the Windows Live ID button, are two unique buttons. The first, Launch the colorizer, enables you to change the colors of Windows Live Mail, a capability that is present in most downloadable Windows Live applications. The second, Menus, doesn't actually display the classic application menu, but rather presents a short menu of frequently needed options of its own, as shown in Figure 21-7.

Figure 21-7: The Menus button provides a mini-menu of its own.

The Layout option enables you to determine which UI pieces are visible in the Windows Live Mail application, and, in some cases, where they are located. The Layout dialog, shown in Figure 21-8, expands and contracts as you select individual options.

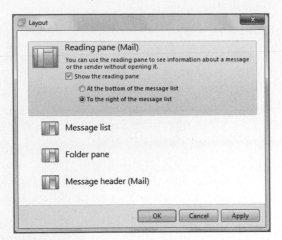

Figure 21-8: Various elements of the Windows Live Mail
UI are highly configurable.

Options, of course, opens the Windows Live Mail Options dialog, previously discussed. That this dialog is almost identical to the Options dialog in Windows Mail is, perhaps, the best indication that these applications share a common heritage. There is one major exception: whereas Windows Mail utilized a Security tab to provide customizable virus protection, image downloading, and secure mail options, Windows Live Mail makes that part of a separate Safety Options dialog (also available via the Menus button). Safety Options, shown in Figure 21-9, include settings related to junk mail filtering, safe and blocked senders, anti-phishing, and more.

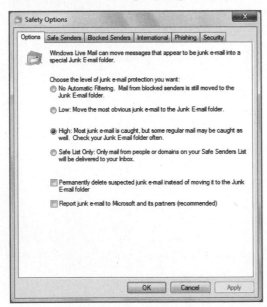

Figure 21-9: The Safety Options dialog replaces the
Junk Mail Settings window from Windows Mail.

Secret

There are some minor differences in the options available to each application as well. Most are related to differences in the focus of each application. For example, Windows Mail contained options that pertained to Windows Contacts, as Windows Mail utilized a separate application for managing contacts, whereas Windows Live Mail has integrated Contacts functionality. Meanwhile, the Windows Live Mail Options dialog presents a number of settings related to Windows Live services integration, as that is a primary feature of this application. Beyond these obvious changes, there are a few hidden gems. Windows Live Mail, for example, sports a custom dictionary, which can be edited and supports as-you-type spell checking.

Finally, you can use the Menus button to customize the Windows Live Mail toolbar and toggle the permanent display of the application's Classic Menu.

Changes in the Folders Pane

In the leftmost pane in the application, called the Folders pane, you'll see a few major improvements. Whereas the Windows Mail Folders List was just that—a literal listing of local and remote folders—the Windows Live Mail Folders pane contains a number of different elements. They're laid out in a more attractive fashion—that is, without using a single tree view as in Windows Mail—but there's also additional functionality.

At the top of the Folders pane is a Quick Views section that includes three custom views by default: Unread e-mail, Unread from contacts, and Unread feeds. These views aggregate all of the e-mail, from all of the accounts you've configured, into a single view—so if you want to see all of your unread e-mail, regardless of the source, that's a great way to do so.

Below that you'll see separate folder structures for your remote e-mail accounts (which vary according to account type and which folders are available on each server) and local folders, which are called *storage folders* in this release. Naturally, you can drag and drop e-mail messages between them, including between different accounts and local folders.

Secret

Be careful when dragging and dropping e-mail messages. Messages you drag are moved, and not copied, to the destination folder. If you'd rather copy messages, perhaps as part of a manual backup, you can instead select the messages, right-click, and choose Copy to Folder from the pop-up menu that appears.

At the bottom of the Folders pane is a new Shortcuts area, which is inspired by a similar UI element in Microsoft Outlook. Basically, it's a box with five buttons, most of which change the view in Windows Live Mail. By default, you're in the Mail view, but other options include Calendar (for Windows Live Calendar interoperability, as described in Chapter 22), Contacts (which opens in its own window and is described later in this chapter), Feeds (for RSS feeds, also covered later in the chapter), and Newsgroups (as with Windows Mail, for Usenet newsgroups).

Changes in the Messages Pane

The central pane has two main sections by default: an instant search box where you can search the contents of your e-mail folders, and a message list, which shows the contents of the currently selected folder.

In Windows Mail, the search box was found in the upper-right corner of the application window, but the Windows Live Mail version works in basically the same way with one major exception: Windows Live Mail enables you to filter search results by account, which is handy when you have several configured accounts.

The Windows Live Mail Messages list works much like the similar feature in Microsoft Outlook, and not like the one in Windows Mail; and that's true even if you configure Windows Mail to work in a three-column view, with the Reading pane next to the Messages list instead of below it. Windows Live Mail looks great configured this way, whereas Windows Mail did not.

Working Online or Offline

If you have a broadband Internet connection, you can work online all the time without thinking about it; but if you want to compose e-mail offline, such as when you're on a plane, you sometimes need a way to use communications applications such as Windows Live Mail and Internet Explorer without them constantly trying to access Internet-based servers.

For example, when you move from your inbox to a news folder, Windows Live Mail attempts to connect to that news server if you are working online. This might also happen when you highlight the header of an e-mail message that links to a Web site. If you just want to look at the messages without connecting, first switch to working offline. This setting is global for all of your applications that use it, so if you are offline in Internet Explorer, you are also offline in Windows Live Mail. (And vice versa: go offline in Windows Live Mail and IE will also be put offline.)

To change your work online/work offline setting manually, choose File ⇨ Work offline. In addition, Windows Live Mail offers two other ways to both see and change your current state. One is an Offline button that you can add to the toolbar. When you are working offline, it appears to be pressed. The button's icon and text show you what will happen if you click it, *not* your current state. Some users might find this confusing.

Secret   More convenient than the toolbar button is the status bar at the bottom of the Windows Live Mail application window. Not only does the status bar clearly indicate the current online/offline state (with text like *Working Offline,* but you can toggle it on and off with a simple double-click. Best of all, it's visible all the time by default.

Handling Multiple E-mail Accounts

If you have multiple e-mail accounts, you can check for new messages on any single account manually. Just choose the Sync button drop-down (in the toolbar) and then choose the account from the submenu that appears. You can choose which e-mail accounts are polled when you click the Sync button too. Just click Tools ⇨ Accounts, highlight a mail account, click the Properties button, and mark or clear the *Include this account when receiving mail or synchronizing* check box. This also works when specifying which accounts Windows Live Mail polls automatically.

Replies to your messages will still go to your specified e-mail address (the reply address you indicate in the General tab of each account's Properties dialog) even though you don't necessarily send your e-mail through the SMTP server at your e-mail address location.

Choosing Which Account to Send Your Messages Through

If you have multiple e-mail accounts configured, the New Message window enables you to choose which account the message will be delivered through via a From drop-down that appears in the upper-right corner of the window (see Figure 21-10). This is true even if you are replying to a message that may have been delivered through a different account. Each account has a specific SMTP outgoing mail server.

If you don't specify an account, then Windows Live Mail sends the message through your default mail server account.

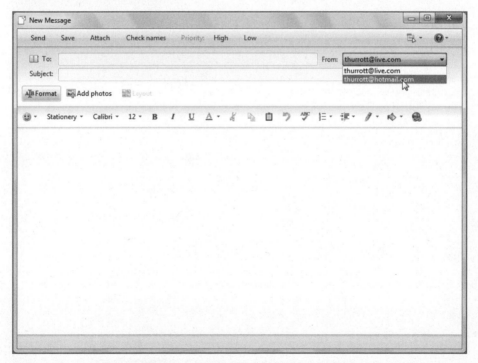

Figure 21-10: Using multiple accounts? Windows Live Mail lets you pick which one to use when sending a mail message.

New Mail Notifications

By default, Windows Live Mail plays a sound when new mail arrives. If this is annoying, you can turn it off. To do this, choose Tools ➪ Options, click the General tab, and deselect the *Play sound when new messages arrive* check box.

Note that Windows Live Mail must be running for the sound to play. If you've configured Windows Live Mail with Windows Live–based e-mail accounts, however, you can also get new mail notifications through Windows Live Messenger, the instant messaging (IM) application that's also included with Windows Live Essentials.

Secret   Maybe you just want to change the sound that plays when new mail arrives. To pick a different new mail sound, right-click the volume icon in the system tray and choose Sounds. Then, in the Program Events list, scroll down to New Mail Notification. Click the Sounds drop-down to pick a default sound, or click the Browse button to find another sound file you'd like to use.

Leaving Mail on the Server

While Windows Live and IMAP mail accounts are typically configured to leave mail on the e-mail server by default, those of you stuck with old-fashioned POP3 e-mail accounts might not be so lucky. To leave mail messages on your mail server, choose Tools ➪ Accounts, highlight your mail server, click the Properties button, select the Advanced tab, and enable the *Leave a copy of messages on server* check box.

Converting Mail

You can import Outlook Express 6, Windows Live Mail, and Windows Mail messages into the latest Windows Live Mail format. Just choose File ➪ Import and then Messages.

No More Identities

Because Outlook Express was first designed to work with Windows 95 and subsequent consumer Windows products that had no real concept of individual user accounts, it used a construct called *identities* to enable users to create two or more pseudo-user accounts within the application. You could use identities in various ways. First, multiple users accessing Outlook Express from the same PC could maintain separate identities so that their e-mail accounts wouldn't co-mingle. Second, individual users could set up multiple identities within Outlook Express in order to keep them separate.

Identities no longer exist in Windows Live Mail. Now, users are expected to maintain their own user accounts, each of which has a separate desktop, separate configuration settings, and, yes, separate configured e-mail accounts.

cross ref   See Chapter 8 for more information about user accounts.

Secret

If you upgrade to Windows 7 from an older computer on which you were using Outlook Express with multiple identities, Windows Live Mail will run a wizard the first time it's launched that enables you to import identities into your user account.

New Mail Storage

Windows Live Mail uses a more modern e-mail storage engine than that used by Outlook Express. (That is, it is more reliable and offers better performance.) Anyone who's been frustrated by Outlook Express's antiquated storage engine—typically noticed when the application slows to a crawl when accessing large e-mail folders or newsgroups—should appreciate this change.

Secret

On a related note, it's much easier to move the Windows Live Mail storage around in the file system because Windows Live Mail keeps everything—its e-mail and newsgroup folders, account information, and settings—in a single, easily accessible folder. Now, when you move the Windows Live Mail storage folder, everything else moves with it. This also makes Windows Live Mail much easier to back up. All of the Windows Live Mail data files can now be found in C:\Users*username*\ AppData\Local\Microsoft\Windows Live Mail by default. To back this up, ensure Windows Live Mail is closed and then simply copy this folder to a different location, such as a rewriteable optical disk or removable hard drive.

Secret

If you do want to move the Windows Live Mail storage folder to a new location, it's actually quite simple:

1. Navigate to Tools ⇨ Options ⇨ Advanced, and click the Maintenance button. The Maintenance dialog will appear (see Figure 21-11).

Figure 21-11: The Maintenance dialog enables you to change the location where you store your Windows Live Mail e-mail.

continues

continued

2. Click the Store Folder button.

3. In the Store Folder dialog, click the Change button and browse to the new location.

The Browse for Folder dialog enables you to create a new folder as well, so you don't have to do that ahead of time as you did in previous Windows versions. Windows Live Mail moves all of your data to the new location automatically after you shut down the application.

tip

Registry buffs should be aware that Windows Live Mail's Registry structure has changed as well, so if you've been using a favorite set of Registry scripts for Outlook Express, beware: they won't work anymore in Windows Live Mail.

Security Features

In keeping with the push for better desktop security in Windows 7, Windows Live Mail includes a few useful features that make it marginally safer than Outlook Express. The first is a Junk Mail filter, which is very similar to the Junk Mail filter found in Microsoft Outlook. You can access Junk Mail options from the Safety Options dialog, shown in Figure 21-12.

Figure 21-12: Finally, Windows Live Mail picks up one of the more useful features of Outlook.

Here, you can choose a level of automatic junk e-mail protection and set up Safe Senders, Safe Recipients, and Blocked Senders lists. There's also an International tab to automatically block mail written in languages you don't understand, and e-mail from certain top-level domain names. If you're familiar with junk e-mail protection in Microsoft Outlook, you'll be right at home here.

Secret

There's one major exception. Junk e-mail protection works only for Windows Live and POP3 accounts, not IMAP accounts.

In addition to its Junk Mail feature, Windows Live Mail also includes a phishing filter, which can prevent certain e-mail-based scams. Here's how a phishing (pronounced like *fishing*) attack works. A malicious user sends random recipients junk e-mail that appears to come from a bank, an online retailer, an auction site, or another trusted institution with which you might do business. These e-mails, which are often written in such a way to suggest that there might be something wrong with an account you have, try to get you to click embedded links and visit malicious Web sites. These Web sites are also masquerading as legitimate locations. They try to get you to provide valid logon information that you might use at the actual institution and then use this information for identity theft. Each year, millions of people fall victim to phishing scams.

To help prevent this, Microsoft includes anti-phishing technology in both Internet Explorer 8 and Windows Live Mail. In Windows Live Mail, the phishing filter is on by default. You can view two phishing filter options from the Phishing tab of the Junk E-Mail Options dialog if you're curious, but the advice here is simple: don't turn this feature off under any circumstances.

Accessing RSS Feeds

Like Windows Vista, Windows 7 includes compatibility with RSS feeds, an automated way of subscribing to frequently updated content online. (RSS is variously expanded to Real Simple Syndication or Rich Site Summary, depending on who you talk to.) This compatibility comes courtesy of technology that's integrated into Internet Explorer 8, Microsoft's Web browser. This makes some sense, because most users typically discover RSS feeds as they browse Web sites online, but there's some debate about whether the browser is really the best place to read, or *consume*, RSS feeds. Some argue, for example, that an e-mail client is the logical place for reading RSS feeds. After all, this application is already used to reading content that is delivered on an ad hoc schedule.

Fair enough. Without picking a winner in this debate, we can at least point out that Microsoft is straddling both sides of the fence, because in addition to the Web-based RSS functionality in Internet Explorer, the company also provides access to RSS feeds in its two best e-mail clients, Microsoft Outlook (part of Office and generally aimed at business users) and Windows Live Mail (which is decidedly consumer oriented).

Secret RSS compatibility in Microsoft Outlook and Windows Live Mail share another similarity: they both require you to be using Internet Explorer 8 (provided as part of Windows 7). That's because IE is still the ideal way to discover new feeds; but now you have a choice regarding where to enjoy that content, depending on your habits: you can do so in the browser, using the IE features discussed in Chapter 20, or you can use your favorite e-mail client.

Any RSS feeds to which you've subscribed in Internet Explorer appear automatically (and immediately, if both applications are open) in Windows Live Mail. RSS feeds are accessed via the Feeds link in the Shortcuts section found in the bottom-left corner of the application window. As shown in Figure 21-13, subscribed feeds look like e-mail messages in Windows Live Mail. This is both familiar and useful, as you can now utilize the application's e-mail-oriented features, like instant search, on subscribed content as well.

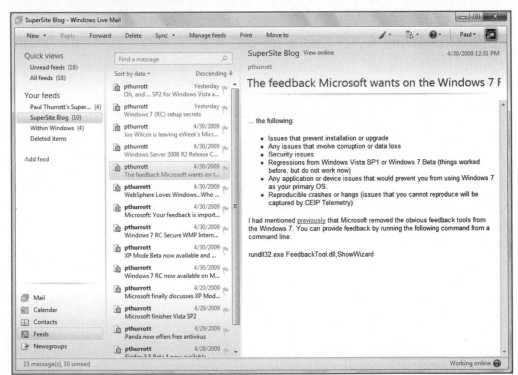

Figure 21-13: In Windows Live Mail, individual posts from RSS feeds resemble e-mail messages.

RSS feeds displayed in Windows Live Messenger provide only the content in each feed, so if the feed you're viewing provides only an abstract of each post and not the entire post, you can click a link in the top of the Reading pane to view the entire post. When you click this link, the post opens in your preferred Web browser.

RSS feeds are managed via a handy Manage Your Feeds dialog, shown in Figure 21-14. You can find this utility by navigating into the Feeds interface in Windows Live Mail and then clicking the Manage feeds toolbar button. (It's also available via the hidden Tools menu.)

Figure 21-14: Manage Your Feeds helps you configure RSS feed settings and manually subscribe to new feeds.

While you will typically find and subscribe to new RSS feeds via Internet Explorer, this window enables you to manually add new feeds via a copy-and-paste mechanism.

Secret

And yes, you guessed it: any RSS feeds you manually subscribe to in Windows Live Mail are visible and accessible via the RSS functionality in Internet Explorer's Favorites Center as well. That's because the underlying RSS storage engine is actually part of IE.

Manually subscribing to RSS feeds isn't particularly enticing, but the real reason you should be interested in this window is that it provides a way to customize how often feeds are updated. The default is daily, which is fine for some feeds, but woefully inadequate for feeds from news sites, blogs, stock updates, and other sources that will update frequently throughout the day. If you're going to use RSS feeds at all, we recommend upping the frequency of feed updates: Set it to update every 15 minutes, which is the shortest possible interval.

Using Photo Mail

While e-mail purists may balk at any talk about HTML e-mail, stationery, emoticons, and any other graphical flourishes that can't easily be transmitted via plain text, we've got a news flash for you—well, two actually. First, a huge segment of the computer-using public is quite taken with these colorfully presented and formatted e-mail messages. Second, and perhaps more important, even if you do consider yourself to be above such silliness, you probably have parents, children, grandparents, or friends who might not share your geeky computer etiquette; and those people may very well enjoy seeing a nicely format-ted e-mail full of family photos or other images.

So we're going to show you how to do it. Deal.

Photo Mail is one of the cooler features of Windows Live Mail. Photo Mail addresses one of the biggest issues with today's e-mail solutions: it's hard to send a bunch of photos to others via e-mail in a way that's attractive and works with virtually any e-mail client on the other end. That's too bad—probably almost everyone you know has e-mail access, and there isn't a better way to send some pictures of the kids to grandma, or vacation photos to friends at work, and so on. Photo Mail is a good idea.

As you might expect given the name, Photo Mail enables you to select one or more pictures, place them attractively in an e-mail—and not as an indecipherable attachment—and then apply other HTML mail elements such as stationery, different layouts, emoticons, and the like. This section describes how it works.

First, click the down arrow next to the New button in the Windows Live Mail toolbar and select Photo e-mail (see Figure 21-15). As it turns out, you can actually construct a Photo Mail out of a normal e-mail message, but choosing this option gets you off on the right foot.

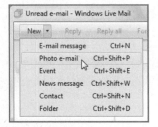

Figure 21-15: You can send a boring old e-mail,
or you can send a new and improved Photo Mail!

A New Message window will open, as with any e-mail message you begin in Windows Live Mail; but on top of this window is an Add Photos dialog (see Figure 21-16). This dialog enables you to select one or more photos (using Ctrl+click or your other selection skills) and then place them in the e-mail using the Add button. What's interesting about this dialog is that you can keep adding photos in batches; it won't close until you click the Done button.

When you do click Done, the Add Photos dialog disappears, and you'll see that Windows Live Mail has formatted the photos into an attractive grid layout like the one shown in Figure 21-17, and provided some room at the top so you can type a message.

Figure 21-16: Photo Mail enables you to choose any number of photographs to send via e-mail.

Figure 21-17: By default, Photo Mail messages are formatted in a simple grid with medium-size thumbnails.

Also showing is an additional Photos pane, which provides access to some interesting capabilities:

♦ **Add more photos:** This will redisplay the Add Photos window so you can add even more photos.

♦ **Borders:** You can choose between seven different photo borders: matting, wood frame, instant photo, metal corners, pushpin, spotlight, and brushed edges. Some of these—including matting, wood frame, metal corners, and pushpin—also let you pick from a selection of customizable colors. As you apply borders and border colors, the photos change to match your selection (see Figure 21-18).

Figure 21-18: Photo Mail supports a wide range of border types and colors.

Secret

It's not obvious, but you can Ctrl+click or otherwise arbitrarily select photos in the e-mail message to apply different borders and/or border colors to different photos. If you want to remove a border, simply select the photo(s) and reclick the border option.

♦ **Photo adjustments:** You can autocorrect the brightness and contrast of the photos, convert them to black-and-white, or rotate them. The first two effects are applied to all photos simultaneously unless you select one or more photos. Rotation can only be applied on a per-photo basis, or to a selection of photos, not to all photos at once.

♦ **Resizing options:** You can opt to send low-quality images (roughly 512K each), medium-quality images (1MB), or high-quality images (5MB or less). Medium is the default, but if you opt for high-quality, only thumbnails are sent via e-mail; the full-size photos are uploaded to Microsoft's servers.

Secret You must be signed into a Windows Live ID to send high-quality photos. That's because the high-quality versions are actually uploaded to your Windows Live Photos account (see Chapter 23) and linked to from the e-mail.

Secret If you do log on to your Windows Live ID account and enable high-quality photos, you are limited to sending 500 photos via Photo Mail per month and to uploading 500MB of photos to your Windows Live Photos account.

On the right side of this Photos pane is some information about the estimated upload time (which can be substantial for big Photo Mail messages) and the total size of the upload.

But wait, there's more. In addition to the photo formatting tools visible in the Photos pane, several other capabilities are present:

♦ **Drag and drop photo layout:** You can actually drag photos around inside the e-mail body, as shown in Figure 21-19, to visually reorder them.

Figure 21-19: Use your desktop skills to move photos around in Photo Mail.

♦ **Replace individual photos:** If you would like to replace an individual photo from the layout, just double-click it. The Add Photos window will appear, where you can choose another.

♦ **Add captions:** To add captions below a photo, just select a photo and then click in the area titled *Click here to add text*.

◆ **Choose different layouts:** The default gridlike layout you're presented with is only one of nine prebuilt layout types. Click the Layout button, shown in Figure 21-20, to view all the potential styles, and experiment.

Figure 21-20: A variety of layout types are also available.

◆ **Use stationery and emoticons:** While we're not positive that graphical emoticons are necessarily the way to go, adding some decent stationery via the Stationery button isn't a bad idea. Each stationery type is a template with a custom background image, unique text fonts and styles, and custom margins. A typical stationery, applied to a Photo Mail message, is shown in Figure 21-21.

You get the idea: Photo Mail is meant to be colorful and fun. Express yourself.

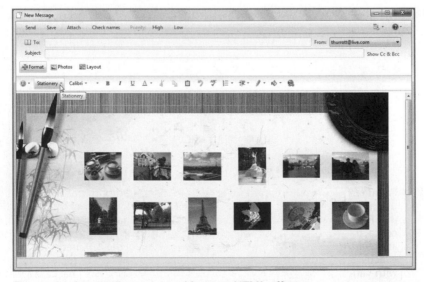

Figure 21-21: Finally, go nuts with some HTML effects.

Managing Contacts

If you're familiar with e-mail, chances are good you're equally at home with the concept of a contacts list or address book. Essentially a database, your own contacts list is a way to store information about the people with whom you regularly correspond, typically by e-mail, but increasingly in other ways, including via instant messaging solutions (such as Windows Live Messenger, discussed in Chapter 23) and social networking services (such as Facebook and MySpace).

This section examines how you can manage Microsoft's consumer-oriented contacts management system, Windows Live People, via Windows Live Mail.

Windows Vista included a dedicated contacts management solution called Windows Contacts. In Windows 7, this solution has been discontinued. Now, you are expected to manage contacts via an online service like Windows Live People or the Windows Live Mail contacts experience. You could also optionally choose to use Microsoft Outlook if you've chosen to purchase that application instead.

There are plenty of online contacts management systems, but because this is a book about Windows 7, this section focuses on Microsoft's solution, called Windows Live People, as its part of the company's Windows Live services efforts to extend Windows. Windows Live People is a true cloud-based service, and of course it integrates with Windows Live Hotmail (or just Hotmail for you old-timers), Microsoft's popular Web mail service. It also happens to work very well with Windows Live Mail, the desktop e-mail client introduced earlier in this chapter. It's time to take a look at how you can use this service online and locally, using Windows Live Mail.

Windows Live People was previously called Windows Live Contacts.

Personally, we think an online contacts service is the way to go. That way, if you use multiple PCs, upgrade your PC, buy a new PC, or do any of the other things that PC users typically do, you never have to worry about blowing away your one contacts list by mistake. Online contacts services, such as Windows Live People, are highly reliable and are managed elsewhere, up in the Internet cloud, which is exactly what most people are looking for; and Windows Live People's integration with various Microsoft products, such as Windows Live Mail, makes it a winner.

Online, Windows Live People is accessed directly via people.live.com. As shown in Figure 21-22, Windows Live People presents a list of the contacts that are associated with your Windows Live ID. By default, you're provided with a list of all your contacts, which are aggregated across both Hotmail (your profile) and Messenger.

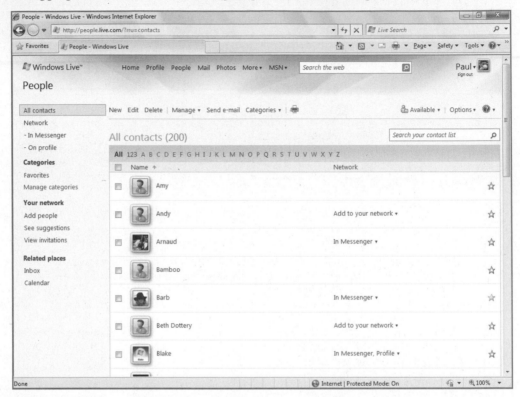

Figure 21-22: The Windows Live People Web service looks and works much like a desktop application.

Secret

One oddity of Windows Live People is that there is quite obviously a place for a photograph or other image in each contact's details view, but there's no way to add a picture. Microsoft tells me this is by design: users of its Windows Live services are free to add their own display picture to their own contacts card, via Windows Live Contacts, Windows Live Messenger, and other entry points to the Windows Live infrastructure. Fair enough; but this doesn't explain why Windows Live People users are unable to use their own images, especially for those contacts that aren't part of Windows Live. We hope that this will change in the future.

For many people, accessing Windows Live People via its Web interface will likely be enough; but Microsoft provides an even nicer interface to this contacts list via Windows Live Mail. You access this functionality via the Contacts button in the Shortcuts list in the lower-left corner of the main Windows Live Mail application window. Shown in Figure 21-23, the local version of Windows Live People (called Windows Live Contacts) is attractive, and looks and works just like Windows Live Mail.

Figure 21-23: Looking for something a little more integrated? Check out Windows Live People in Windows Live Mail.

What's amazing about this application is that what you're seeing is an automatically synchronized version of your online contacts list, so if you make any changes to a contact or group locally, those changes are reflected online immediately and automatically. (The reverse is also true.)

Secret

This means, among other things, that you can work with your master contacts list offline if necessary.

As you might expect of a Windows Live application, one of the hallmarks of Windows Live People is that it integrates with other Windows Live services. When you select a contact who is also in your Windows Live Messenger friends list, you can choose to send that contact an instant message, view their Windows Live Spaces blog, or perform other similar actions.

Secret While Windows Live Mail supports multiple e-mail accounts, you can only manage contacts from a single source at a time. Windows Live Mail uses your default e-mail account as the source for the contacts list it displays when you click the Contacts button.

Summary

Although Windows Live Mail is based on Outlook Express, its predecessor, this application includes numerous improvements such as a phishing filter, automatic spell checking, and better performance, so it's worth a look even if you're a die-hard Outlook Express hater. And thanks to its contacts and RSS management capabilities, integration with Microsoft's online services, and the calendaring functionality discussed in the next chapter, Windows Live Mail might just be an all-in-one e-mail and PIM solution that rivals even the comparatively expensive Microsoft Outlook.

Managing Your Schedule

Chapter
22

♦ ♦

In This Chapter

♦ ♦

Although operating systems such as Linux and Mac OS X have offered calendaring applications for years, Microsoft has historically sold such functionality as part of its Office and Works productivity suites instead of adding it directly to Windows. In Windows Vista, however, the company reversed course, and briefly offered Windows users an application-based calendaring solution as part of their favorite operating system. Sadly, this application, Windows Calendar, was removed from Windows 7. But fear not: in addition to its Windows Live Calendar Web service (part of the company's wider Windows Live efforts), Microsoft also offers an application-based calendaring solution as part of the Windows Live Essentials suite. Oddly enough, it's called Windows Live Mail, and while it can, of course, be used for e-mail and contacts management, as described in Chapter 21, this application also provides attractive and full-featured calendaring options, including tasks functionality, the capability to subscribe to remote calendars, and even a way to publish your own calendars for others to use. This chapter examines this interesting and useful new Windows 7 application and the Web service on which it's based.

Understanding Calendaring

If you've ever used the Calendar component in Microsoft Outlook, shown in Figure 22-1, then you're familiar with the notion of PC-based calendaring and scheduling. Microsoft Outlook is an extremely powerful tool, enabling you to create and manage appointments, meetings, and other events, as well as tasks and other time-based schedules. For all its strengths, however, Microsoft Outlook isn't perfect. First, you must pay a hefty sum for Microsoft Outlook unless you get a version along with other Microsoft Office applications when you purchase a new PC. Second, Outlook is designed to work primarily with Microsoft Exchange–based servers. Although it's possible to use Outlook as an individual, it's not ideal, and even the latest Outlook versions offer only very simple methods for sharing calendaring information with other people.

Meanwhile, standards-based Web calendars have been gaining in popularity for the past few years, and these solutions offer features that are much more applicable to individuals than what Outlook offers. Best of all, most of these Web-based calendars are free. For example, Apple Computer supplies users of its Mac OS X operating system with a calendar application called iCal that integrates very nicely with Web standards for calendaring, making it possible for iCal users to share calendars with family and friends from around the world. The Mozilla Corporation, which makes the popular Firefox Web browser, is developing its own calendar application called Sunbird, offering similar functionality to Windows and Linux users. Alternatively, if you'd prefer to work directly on the Web, you can use a calendaring solution such as Google Calendar, shown in Figure 22-2.

Standards-based calendar applications offer a number of useful features. First, you can create discrete calendars in categories such as Personal, Work, Gym, or any categories you choose and overlay them as needed on the same Calendar view to see how your entire schedule plays out. You can share calendars with others, via a publish and subscribe mechanism that enables you to superimpose your own calendars visually with remote calendars, overlaying these on one another and your own calendars. Using this functionality you could, for example, find a night when both you and your spouse were free to have dinner at a restaurant together, or compare your son's soccer schedule with your own weekend plans to make sure you can get to the game.

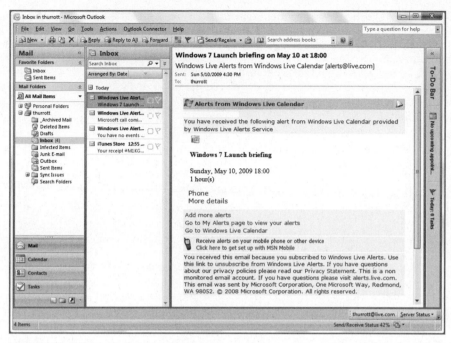

Figure 22-1: Yes, it's full-featured and powerful, but Microsoft Outlook is also expensive.

Figure 22-2: Google Calendar runs via any Web browser but requires you to be online.

More recently, Web-based calendaring solutions have begun interacting and syncing with mobile devices, such as smart phones. So it's easy to freely sync between, say, Google Calendar and Apple's iPhone, two products that are made by different companies with different agendas. The calendaring standards that make this possible have even been adopted by Microsoft, which has added this functionality to its Exchange- and Outlook-based applications, servers, and services, and, more recently, to consumer-oriented offerings as well.

The ramifications of this support are wide-reaching. Because these standards-based calendars are becoming so popular, many organizations and individuals publish their own schedules on the Web so that other individuals can subscribe to them. If you're a fan of the Boston Red Sox or any other sports team, you can subscribe to their schedule and always be alerted when a game is coming up. There are calendars out there for all kinds of events, including regional holidays, concerts, and the like; and these calendars can be superimposed on your own calendars within these calendaring applications.

There's more, of course. Standards-based calendars also typically support lists of tasks, which can be assigned days and times for completion and checked off as they are completed. You can print calendars in attractive styles, and use them as paper-based personal information managers during your work week or on trips. All of this is possible without having to deal with an expensive, centralized server. The Internet's enterprising denizens have gotten their hands on calendaring and rescued it from the proprietary shackles of Microsoft Exchange.

> **tip** When we refer to standards in regard to calendaring, we're referring to the iCal, or iCalendar, standard, which specifies "interoperable calendaring and scheduling services for the Internet." Rather than extend proprietary solutions such as Outlook to the Internet, the iCal standard proposes that all calendars should use a single, open standard for interoperability purposes. It's a great idea and works well in the real world. You can find out more about the iCal format on the IETF Web site (www.ietf.org/rfc/rfc2445.txt).

Exploring Windows Live Calendar

Microsoft isn't blind to this change in how people are interacting online via standards-based calendars. That's why it has added a standards-based calendaring service, Windows Live Calendar, to its ever-expanding set of online services. Windows Live Calendar, shown in Figure 22-3, replaces the company's previous stabs at online calendars, including the horrid calendar component of Hotmail and something called MSN Calendar.

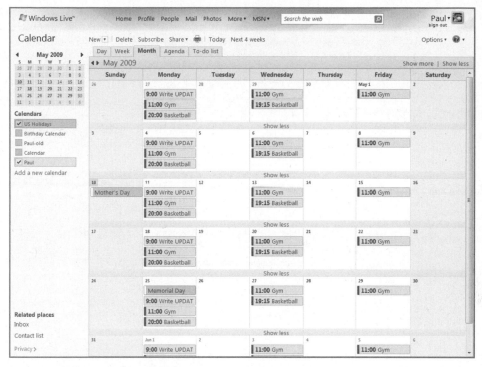

Figure 22-3: Windows Live Calendar

You could pretty much perform all of your schedule-related needs directly from this Web interface if you wanted to, as Windows Live Calendar includes all of the functionality one might expect from an online calendar. Because this book focuses on Windows 7, however, we'll spend most of our time on interacting with Windows Live Calendar from the Calendar component of the Windows Live Mail application, which is part of Windows Live Essentials and, thus, part of Windows 7. That said, there are a few high-level details to understand about Windows Live Calendar first.

◆ **Windows Live Calendar is tied to a Windows Live ID.** As you should expect by now, the calendars and to-do lists you create with Windows Live Calendar need to be associated with a Windows Live ID. This means that you cannot use Windows Live Calendar without first creating such an ID, and that any calendars and to-do lists you create after that will integrate nicely with other Windows Live services and, if you like, be easily shareable with others, especially those who are part of your Windows Live network. Confused by any of these terms? Check out Chapter 23, where we explain the entire Windows Live ecosystem.

◆ **Windows Live Calendar is part of your online persona.** As part of the Windows Live ID integration, Windows Live Calendar becomes one of many Windows Live services you can access through your online persona. But because it's part of your overall Windows Live experience, it can also be themed and customized along the same lines possible with most other Windows Live services. So if you apply a cool theme to your Windows Live Profile, it will show up in Calendar, as shown in Figure 22-4. And if you apply a theme to Windows Live Calendar, it will be applied to the other Windows Live services you visit on the Web.

♦ **Windows Live Calendar supports one or more Web-based calendars.** By default, Windows Live Calendar will provide at least one calendar, My Calendar, but you can add as many other calendars as you'd like. If you've been using other Windows Live services, like Windows Live People, either via the Web or through an application like Windows Live Messenger, you may also see a calendar called Birthday Calendar that provides access to your contacts' birthdays.

tip   You can assign different colors to each calendar, making for a nice, multi-color display.

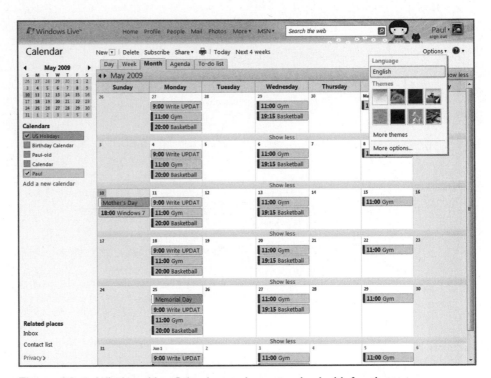

Figure 22-4: Windows Live Calendar can be customized with fun themes.

◆ **Windows Live Calendar provides different views.** Like desktop-based calendars, you can view your schedule via Day, Week, and Month views. But Windows Live Calendar also provides a unique and attractive Agenda view that presents your schedule as a list, as shown in Figure 22-5.

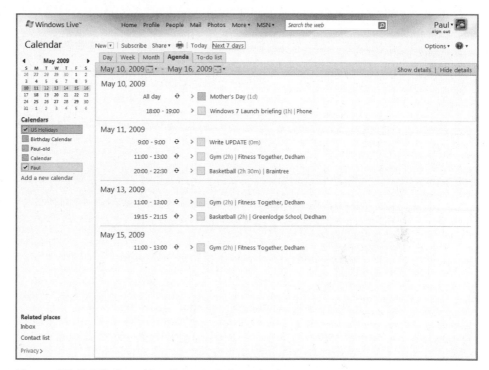

Figure 22-5: Windows Live Calendar's Agenda view

◆ **Windows Live Calendar provides tasks functionality too.** Like Outlook and other desktop calendaring solutions, Windows Live Calendar provides a separate tasks management solution called the To-do list (see Figure 22-6). As with the Agenda view, the To-do list is list-based, but it has provisions for such things as priorities and completion progress. (Because this functionality is not duplicated in the Calendar view of Windows Live Mail, we will look at it more closely later in the chapter.)

Secret

You can rename any calendar, including the default My Calendar. To do so, visit Options ⇨ More Options in the Web interface.

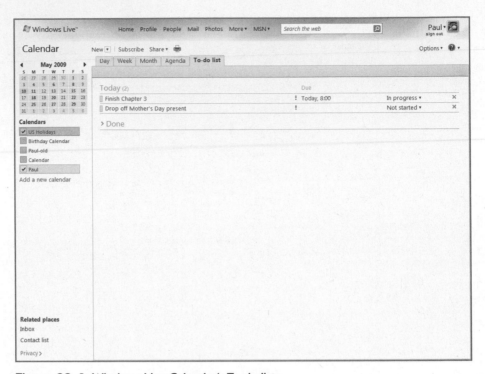

Figure 22-6: Windows Live Calendar's To-do list

◆ **Windows Live Calendar can import and subscribe to other calendars**. Windows Live Calendar allows you to import calendars that have been saved in ICS format. This is handy if you need to import a calendar you've archived from a previous calendaring solution. But if you want to subscribe to an ongoing calendar—one that can change in the future—Windows Live Calendar supports that, too. As with other standards-based calendars, Windows Live Calendar works with iCal-type calendar subscriptions, which we describe in more detail later in this chapter.

◆ **Windows Live Calendar can share and publish to other calendars.** Like other standards-based calendars, Windows Live Calendar can publish your calendars so that they can be consumed, or subscribed to, elsewhere. In addition, Windows Live Calendar supports its own proprietary sharing technology, meaning that you can also share your calendars in other ways. As you can see in Figure 22-7, you can share with others in your Windows Live network, with others in your network via a read-only view, or by making your calendar public (and thus available for view by anyone).

◆ **Windows Live Calendar offers functionality that the Calendar view in Windows Live Mail does not.** Because Windows Live Calendar is a more complete calendaring solution than the Calendar view in Windows Live Mail, you will need to occasionally visit the Web interface, even if you typically prefer to use Windows Live Mail for your calendaring needs. We'll describe these instances in just a bit. But first, let's take a look at Microsoft's new calendaring application for Windows 7.

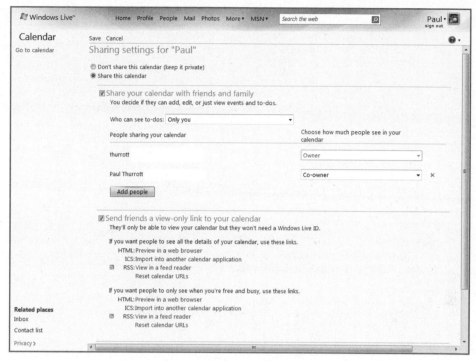

Figure 22-7: Windows Live Calendar provides different ways to share calendars.

Managing Your Schedule with Windows Live Mail

While Windows Vista included a standalone calendaring application called Windows Calendar, that short-lived product was removed from Windows 7. So now, users are expected to manage their schedules via the Web with Windows Live Calendar or locally using the Windows Live Mail application. That's right; you need to think "mail" every time you want to work on your schedule.

That bit of silliness aside, Windows Live Mail offers surprisingly capable calendaring functionality. And if you're familiar with competing calendaring solutions such as Apple iCal or Mozilla Sunbird, the Calendar component in Windows Calendar will seem very familiar. It works with the same standards-based calendaring format, and it can publish and subscribe to the same sources as those solutions.

> **tip** Technically speaking, Windows Live Mail is not included with Windows 7. But if you acquired Windows 7 as part of a new PC, it's highly likely that the PC maker preinstalled this useful software on the machine for you. If not, you can freely download and install Windows Live Essentials (which includes Windows Live Mail and other applications, products, and services) via Windows Update or from the Windows Live Web site (download.live.com). We describe this process in Chapter 21.

tip Obviously, Microsoft isn't giving up on its Exchange Server and Outlook product lines. For a quick understanding of how these solutions are differentiated, think of it this way: Exchange and Outlook are tools for business users, whereas Windows Live Calendar (and Windows Live Mail's Calendar component) are for individuals such as consumers, soccer moms, and your grandparents. Put simply, Windows Live Calendar is for *people,* not businesses. Windows Live Calendar conforms to iCal standards and doesn't integrate at all with Exchange. Even Microsoft is getting the message when it comes to calendaring, albeit slowly.

Understanding the Calendar Interface in Windows Live Mail

To access the Calendar component of Windows Live Mail, launch Windows Live Mail (type **mail** in Start Menu Search). If you haven't done so already, you will need to configure this application for your Windows Live ID, supplying your username, password, and plain English name.

The Calendar view in Windows Live Mail can actually be used without configuring a Windows Live ID (and associated e-mail account). In this case, the application will present a single local calendar, and you'll be able to add multiple additional calendars if you'd like. We don't cover this usage here because it results in stand-alone calendars that are tied to that one PC and not easily sharable or synced elsewhere. To get the full benefits of Calendar, you're going to want to associate your Windows Live ID.

Windows Live Mail launches into the Mail view by default, of course, but you can access the Calendar view by clicking the Calendar link in the Shortcut pane. When you do so, you'll see the one or more calendars that are associated with your Windows Live Calendar (see Figure 22-8).

You can also quickly shift into Calendar view by tapping Ctrl+Shift+X.

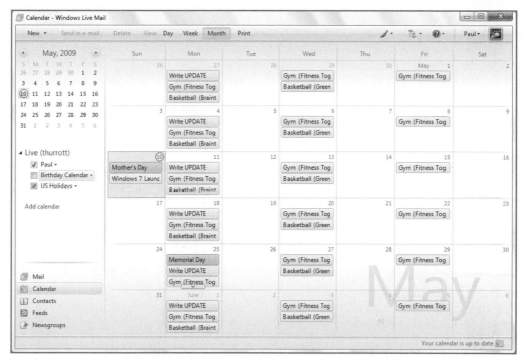

Figure 22-8: Windows Live Mail's Calendar view shares many similarities with other standards-based Internet calendars but is presented in a clean, Windows 7-like user interface.

The Calendar user interface is divided into a number of logical areas. On the top is a toolbar that's customized to the needs of the component's calendaring functionality. Below that are three areas, or panes, all of which are displayed by default, though two are optional. On the left is the Navigation pane, which presents a mini-month view and enables you to select between different calendars that are associated with your Windows Live ID. Below that is the Shortcuts pane, which lets you switch to different Windows Live Mail views, including Mail and Contacts. And on the right side of the application window, taking up most of the display, is the current Calendar view, which is set to Month view by default.

tip | From now on, we'll refer to the Calendar view in Windows Live Mail simply as Calendar.

Understanding Calendar Lingo

Because there are so many calendar applications out there, you might be confused about some of the language Microsoft uses to describe the various items associated with Calendar. Table 22-1 summarizes these items.

Table 22-1: Common Items in Windows Calendar

Windows Calendar Item	Definition
Calendar	A collection of appointments that makes up your schedule. You can have different calendars for different purposes and intermingle or overlay them within the Calendar user interface. Calendars are associated with a Windows Live ID or, if such a thing is not configured, are local to that PC.
Group	A logical grouping of related calendars. Also called a Calendar Group.
Event	A meeting, appointment, or other event. Events can have specific starting and ending times or be all-day or multi-day events. For example, a meeting typically has static start and end times, whereas a vacation could be created as a multi-day event.

Calendar is missing several features that were available in Vista's Windows Calendar, including calendar groups, tasks, and calendar publish and subscribe. In this chapter, we will highlight how you can accomplish most of the missing functionality using the Web-based Windows Live Calendar solution.

Working with Calendars

The first time you enter Calendar, you'll see one or more calendars, depending on which calendars are present in Windows Live Calendar. (Local calendar users instead will see a single calendar named Calendar.) Each calendar gets its own name and color, and you can change either. For some people, a single calendar may be enough, but others may want to create different calendars for the different types of events they confront each day.

In Windows Calendar, Microsoft had added the capability to create calendar groups, called Groups, within which you can collect related calendars if desired. This functionality is missing from both Windows Live Calendar and the Calendar component in Windows Live Mail, so the only way to organize events now is by calendar, not with groups.

That said, Calendar does offer one other interesting possibility here. You can configure two or more Windows Live ID accounts with Windows Live Mail, and each would, of course, have its own associated calendar(s). If you do so, you'll see that the calendars are all segregated by ID in the Navigation pane of Windows Live Mail.

Here are some of the ways in which you might organize your calendars within Calendar. First, because each calendar is assigned a unique color, events for each calendar will stand out visually. Second, because you can arbitrarily hide and show individual calendars, it's possible to simplify the Calendar view as needed, which can especially be handy when printing calendars. The important thing to remember is that Calendar supports a decent level of customization when it comes to calendar management.

For example, you can use Calendar to do any of the following:

◆ **Change the name of the default calendar:** Just select the name of the calendar in the Navigation pane, click Properties in the pop-up menu that appears, and then rename it in the Properties window that appears (Figure 22-9).

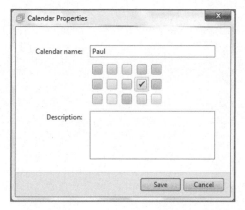

Figure 22-9: Renaming a calendar is simple: just use the Properties window.

◆ **Change the calendar display color:** Using the same method previously described, you can pick from one of 15 colors in the calendar's Properties window.

Secret

In Windows Calendar, you could click a More Colors link to choose from thousands of additional colors. This capability is no longer available in Calendar.

◆ **Create a new calendar:** Click the Add calendar link in the Navigation pane to add a new calendar to the currently selected ID. The Add a Calendar window will appear, as shown in Figure 22-10, letting you pick a name, color, and description for the new calendar.

Figure 22-10: The Add a Calendar window

Secret

Calendars created in Calendar are of course synched back to Windows Live Calendar. Any changes you make in either place will be replicated in the other as well.

Understanding Calendar Views and Navigation

Calendar supports the following three basic view styles:

◆ **Day:** Presents a top-down view of the currently selected day, segregated into 30-minute slices, as shown in Figure 22-11.

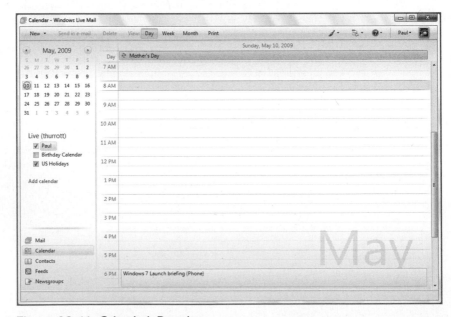

Figure 22-11: Calendar's Day view

◆ **Week:** This view, shown in Figure 22-12, divides the display into seven columns, one for each day of the week. As with Day view, the view is segregated into 30-minute slices of time from top to bottom.

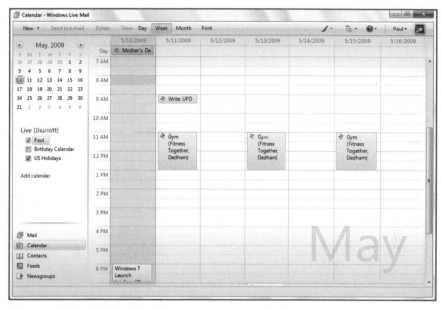

Figure 22-12: Calendar's Week view

> **tip**
>
> Windows Calendar also provided a Work Week view, which, as you might expect, divided the view into five columns, one for each day of the work week (Monday through Friday). This view style is no longer available in Calendar.

◆ **Month:** The Calendar view is presented with a standard monthly calendar view, where each day of the month is denoted by a square shape (see Figure 22-13). This is the default view.

> **tip**
>
> Windows Live Mail will remember the view you were in, so if you exit the application while Calendar is displaying Week view, it will return to that view the next time you run Windows Live Mail and enter the Calendar.

> **tip**
>
> Windows Calendar had a convenient Go to Date function that is no longer available in Calendar. However, you can achieve the same effect by navigating around in the little monthly calendar display located in the top-right corner of Calendar. The current date has a circle around it. Just click it and you're back.

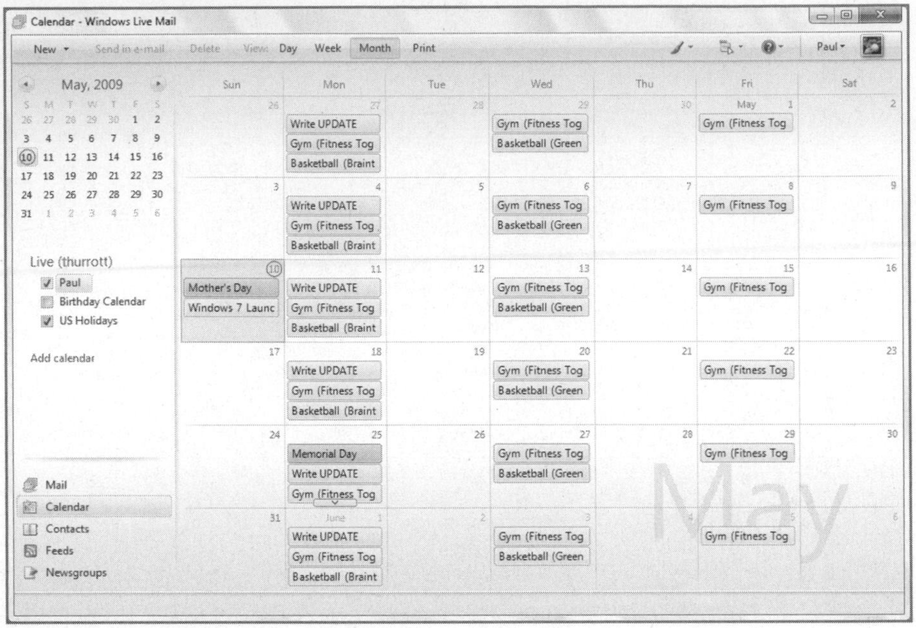

Figure 22-13: Calendar's Month View

Hiding and Viewing Calendars

If you've configured a number of calendars, you may sometimes want to hide certain calendars in the main Calendar view. Notice that each calendar has a check box next to its name in the Navigation pane. When a calendar is checked, events contained within that calendar will display normally within the main Calendar view, using the color that's been assigned to the containing calendar; but when you uncheck a calendar, that item will be hidden.

Configuring Calendar

Calendar doesn't offer much in the way of configuration options. (Indeed, if you visit the application's Options dialog, you will see that none of the options there are related to Calendar at all.) You can resize the Navigation pane, which is actually pretty useful, especially if onscreen real estate is at a premium: if you make this as small as possible, it will revert to a nice icon view, as shown in Figure 22-14.

And while you can indeed edit the Calendar toolbar, it's actually fully populated by default, with its full set of five buttons—New, Send in e-mail, Delete, View (Month, Week, Day), and Print—so all you can really do there is remove items. To do so, right-click any-where in the toolbar and choose Customize toolbar.

Finally, you can configure how reminders are sent: click the Menus toolbar button (it's to the right of the Colorizer's paintbrush-like button) and choose *Deliver my reminders to...* Because this option applies globally to Windows Live Calendar, you're redirected to the Windows Live Calendar Web site, where you can choose between Basic and Custom delivery options, as shown in Figure 22-15. Windows Live Calendar uses the Windows Live Alerts service to deliver schedule reminders via instant messaging (Windows Live Messenger), e-mail, and to Windows Mobile–based smartphones only.

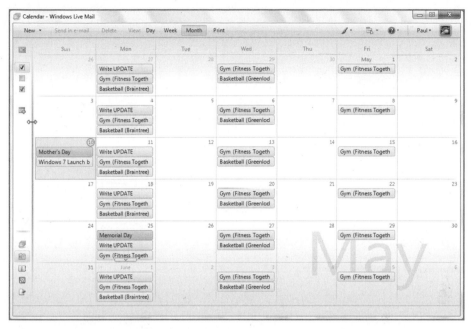

Figure 22-14: The Navigation pane can be reduced to a strip of icons.

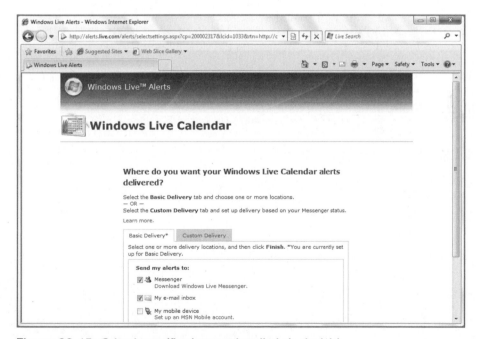

Figure 22-15: Calendar notifications are handled via the Web.

tip If you do use Windows Live Messenger, you can get calendar updates via the application's convenient "toast" pop-ups, as shown in Figure 22-16.

Figure 22-16: Thanks to deep Windows Live integration, you can get notifications on the desktop via Windows Live Messenger.

Working with Events

Within each calendar, you can create various *events*. An event is an appointment or other occasion that occurs on a specific date or over a range of dates. Events can have static beginning and ending times—for example, a meeting that runs from 9:00 a.m. to 10:00 a.m.—or be all-day events. Events also have other characteristics. For example, you might create an event for something that occurs repeatedly, such as a birthday or anniversary.

There are various ways to create a new event in Calendar, but how you do so matters little because you can change any event details during the creation process. For example, suppose you want to schedule a meeting for 9:00 a.m. next Monday. One way to do so would be to select the appropriate calendar and then navigate to the specific date in Day view. Then, position the mouse cursor over the time at which you'd like the appointment to begin, and double-click to start creating the new appointment. As shown in Figure 22-17, the New Event window appears, letting you enter details about the event.

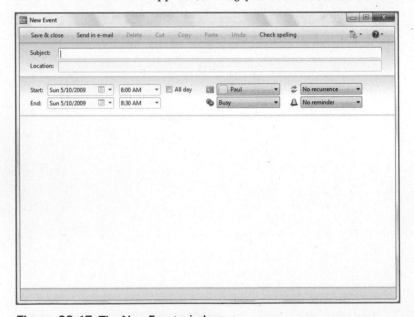

Figure 22-17: The New Event window

Examining Event Properties

You can edit the following characteristics of an event:

♦ **Subject:** This is how you identify an event. You can use any title you'd like, such as *Meeting with Sarah, Paul's birthday,* or *Flight to Paris.*

♦ **Location:** As with the title, this entry can contain any text value (such as *Phone,* for phone calls; *Meeting Room 133; American Airlines Flight 133;* or whatever). Go nuts, it's your calendar. You can even leave it blank.

♦ **Start:** Events start on a particular day and, optionally, at a particular time. All-day events do not have a start (or end) time, so you can click the All day option if that's the case.

♦ **End:** Events also end on a particular day and, optionally, at a particular time.

♦ **Calendar:** This is a drop-down list box where you specify the calendar to which the event will be attached. If you use multiple calendars, you can drop down the list and pick the appropriate calendar.

♦ **Availability:** With this drop-down, you can specify if you will be busy (the default), free, tentative, or away for the duration of the event.

♦ **Recurrence:** This option allows you to specify the frequency with which the event recurs. Many events will be one-time affairs, so you can leave this option on its default value of No recurrence. But Calendar offers a wealth of possibilities for events that do recur, including daily, every weekday, weekly, every two weeks, and many others. Or you can choose the Custom option to view the Event Recurrence window, shown in Figure 22-18. This window enables you to accommodate virtually any recurrence scenario you could imagine.

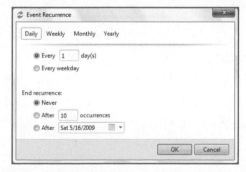

Figure 22-18: The Event Recurrence window lets you customize how events recur.

◆ **Reminder:** If you'd like Calendar to pop up a reminder dialog at a specified interval before an appointment, this drop-down box enables you to configure that. Allowable reminder times include No reminder, as well as 0, 5, 10, 15, 30, and 45 minutes; 1 and 2 hours; 0.5, 1, and 2 days; and 1 and 2 weeks. How reminders are delivered and appear is dictated by the *Deliver my reminders to...* option described in the previous section.

> **tip**
>
> There is a Send in e-mail toolbar button in the New Event window, but don't get too excited: all it does is create a new, plain-text e-mail with the details of the event. Recipients can't use the resulting e-mail to add the event to their own calendars, as you can with a similar function in Microsoft Outlook.

◆ **Notes:** This large text entry area in the bottom two-thirds of the window enables you to write or paste in large blocks of text that may be pertinent to the event.

To save the event, click the Save & close toolbar button. The event will be added to the calendar, as shown in Figure 22-19.

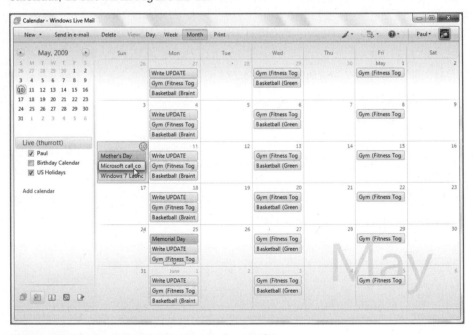

Figure 22-19: A newly added event in the calendar

The display of events varies according to their type. Events with starting and ending times appear as colored rectangles in the Calendar view, but all-day and multi-day events appear in the upper well of the Day and Week views, as shown in Figure 22-20.

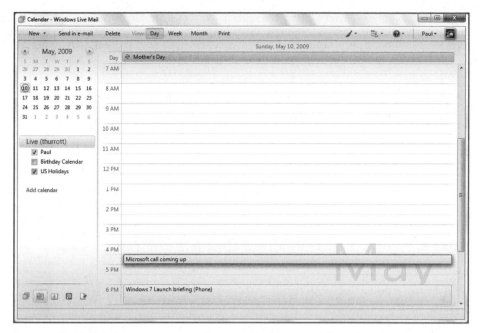

Figure 22-20: All-day events appear in the well at the top of Calendar when in Day or Week view.

In Month view, multi-day events visually expand across all of the applicable days, as shown in Figure 22-21.

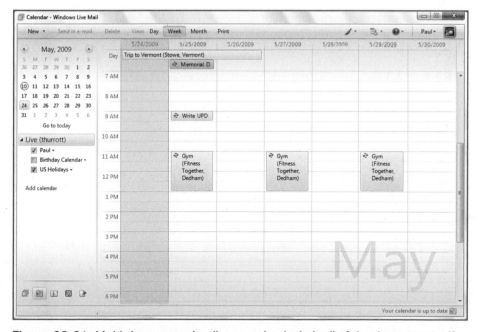

Figure 22-21: Multi-day events visually expand to include all of the days you specify.

If you want to view or edit an event later, just double-click it in the Calendar view. The event window will appear, as you'd expect.

---

tip   If you just need to edit the title of an appointment, slowly double-click it in the Calendar view. The appointment title will be highlighted, enabling you to type a new title. This works much like renaming an icon in Windows Explorer.

Tsk, Tsk: No Tasks

Calendar is a generally full-featured calendaring solution. But it's missing some key functionality that's available in the Web-based Windows Live Calendar service. One of these missing features is tasks. While Calendar offers no way to manage tasks at all, Windows Live Calendar does, through its To-do list functionality. So if you want to manage tasks separately from events, you'll need to use Windows Live Calendar instead.

---

note   Yes, Vista's Windows Calendar application did offer integrated tasks management.

This may seem inconvenient. (And let's be honest, if you want to use Calendar and tasks, it *is* inconvenient.) But because Windows Live Calendar and Calendar each utilizes the same Windows Live Alerts notification system, you can at least rest assured that notifications about your tasks will be delivered in a manner consistent with your events notifications.

Anyway, to manage tasks in the Windows Live ecosystem, you'll need to use Windows Live Calendar. So in this section, that's the tool on which we'll have to focus.

---

tip   It is hoped that a future version of Windows Live Mail will include tasks management capabilities as well.

Like events, to-do's are associated with calendars. This makes sense if you think about it. If you do choose to organize your schedule around various calendars, it's likely you'll want to associate certain to-do's with home, work, or whatever other calendars you may choose to use for other scheduling needs. That said, to-do's are relegated to a separate To-do list tab of the Windows Live Calendar display and are not added to any of the main calendar views. This is actually pretty confusing, as many desktop calendar applications add a task pane at the bottom of certain calendar views.

Creating To-do's

To create a new to-do, click the New button in Windows Live Calendar and then select To-do from the drop-down menu that appears. This displays the Add a to-do window, shown in Figure 22-22.

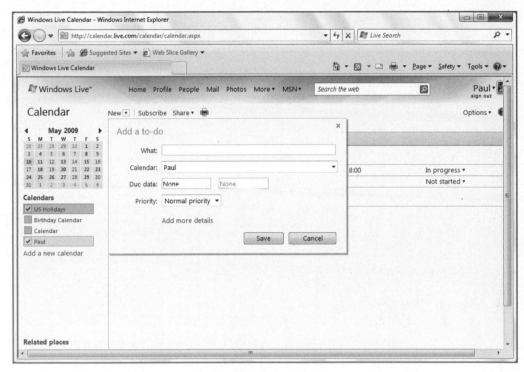

Figure 22-22: Creating a new to-do in Windows Live Calendar

In this window, you'll see a number of options for your newly created to-do:

♦ **What:** This is how you identify the task. You can use any title you'd like.

♦ **Calendar:** This specifies the calendar to which the task is attached. Your default calendar will be selected automatically, but if you have other calendars, you can, of course, change it.

♦ **Due date:** Here, you can specify a date using a pop-up calendar control and, optionally, a time.

♦ **Priority:** Tasks can be marked as Normal, High, or Low priority (Normal is the default).

♦ **More details:** If you click the Add more details link, you'll navigate to a full-page version of the Add a to-do interface (see Figure 22-23), which provides additional options, including Status, Send reminder, and Description fields.

♦ **Status:** To-do items can be marked as not started, in progress, or done.

♦ **Reminder:** As with events, you can configure Windows Live Calendar to remind you when tasks are due. These reminders behave identically to event reminders.

♦ **Description:** This large text entry area enables you to write or paste in large blocks of text that may be pertinent to the task.

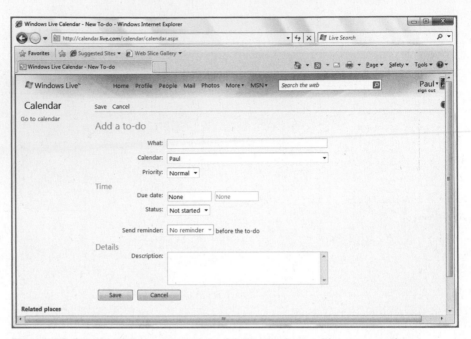

Figure 22-23: The full-screen version of Add a to-do provides more options.

> **tip** What's the difference between a to-do and an event? Events typically come and go at specific times, but to-do's are often more open-ended and have a completion requirement. In addition, events can involve other people. With a to-do, you're on your own. Then again, when a to-do is completed, you don't have to share the glory. Live by the sword, die by the sword.

Click Save to save the to-do. When you do, Windows Live Calendar displays a Web version of the Windows Live Messenger "toast" alert, noting that the to-do item has been created. This is shown in Figure 22-24.

Configuring To-do's

You can configure exactly two to-do-related features from the Options display for Windows Live Calendar. To access this interface, click the Options link near the top-right corner of the window and then choose More options from the pop-up menu that appears. The Calendar options page appears (see Figure 22-25).

Two options are specific to to-do items:

◆ **Select when to delete your completed to-do's:** Here, you can determine whether Windows Live Calendar will delete completed to-do's after a set interval, or never delete them.

◆ **Confirmations:** While this option isn't specific to to-do's, enabling it means that you will see the aforementioned Web-based alert anytime you create a to-do item. (It is enabled by default.)

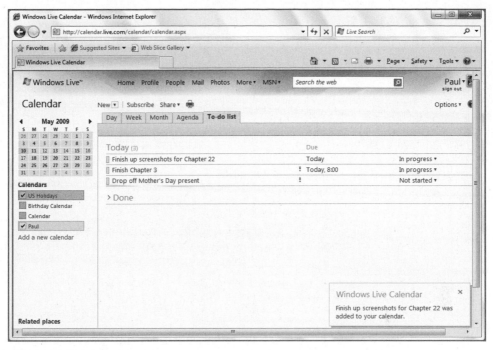

Figure 22-24: Windows Live Calendar provides Web-based alerts too.

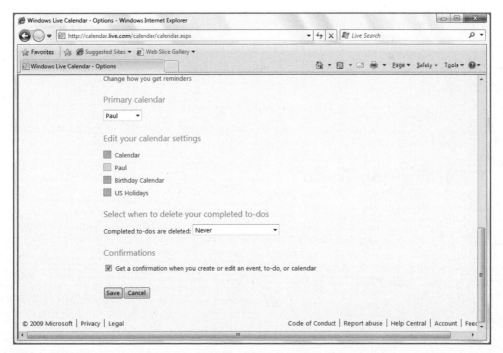

Figure 22-25: Calendar options provides only a few to-do-related options.

Sharing Calendars

Calendar sharing is a second major feature that is not available from Calendar in Windows Live Mail. Again, you will need to utilize Windows Live Calendar on the Web to share calendars.

Importing Calendars

Windows Live Calendar can import only calendars that are formatted in industry-standard ICS (iCalendar) format. This format is supported by applications such as Apple iCal, Mozilla Sunbird, and Microsoft Outlook (2007 or newer).

Follow these steps to import an ICS calendar file into Windows Live Calendar:

1. Click the Subscribe link to display the Import or subscribe to a calendar page.
2. Select Import from an ICS file.
3. You can now import this file into another compatible calendar application. The display will change to accommodate options related to importing, as shown in Figure 22-26.

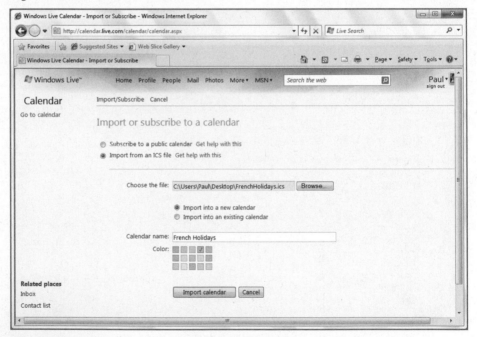

Figure 22-26: From here, you can import static ICS files.

4. Click the Browse button to locate the ICS file and then click Open.
5. Choose either Import into a new calendar or Import into an existing calendar. If you choose the former, you will need to provide a name and color for the new calendar. For the latter, you simply choose the name of the calendar to use, and decide how to handle duplicate events.
6. Click Import calendar.

Obviously, you will need an ICS file to import before you can do this. There are a few ways to get such a file. If you have a calendar application that supports exporting into ICS, then you could use that, of course. But a better method is to download one of the many ICS files out there on the Web. We'll look at this scenario in the next section, and how you should subscribe to, not import, such files.

Subscribing to Calendars

Importing is nice, but this operation is like a slice in time because it can't help you if future changes are made to any of the calendars you've imported. What's needed, of course, is a way to automatically *synchronize* data between remote calendars and Windows Live Calendar so that you can ensure that your calendar is always up-to-date. This, of course, is where the iCal standard comes in. Using the subscribe functionality that's built into Windows Live Calendar, it's possible to subscribe to any number of online calendars and add them to the collection of calendars you view within Microsoft's online service.

---

tip Calendars to which you subscribe with Windows Live Calendar will also show up in the Calendar view of Windows Live Mail.

Before you can subscribe to an online calendar, you need to find one. There are several online calendar resources that you can peruse. One of the best is Apple's iCal Library (www.apple.com/downloads/macosx/calendars) because Apple was one of the first major software companies to embrace the iCal standard. Apple's site includes professional sports schedules, worldwide holidays, movie openings, and much more. Another excellent resource is iCalShare (www.icalshare.com), which lists even more calendars to which you can subscribe, in a bewildering list of categories.

Using either site, or a similar resource, you can browse different calendars until you find one to which you'd like to subscribe. Say you're a Boston Red Sox fan. (I know, who isn't?) If you search for "Red Sox" on iCalShare, you'll see a number of calendars devoted to the schedule of Boston's major league baseball team.

Secret

You might think that you could subscribe to one of these calendars simply by downloading it. Unfortunately, it's not that simple. Instead, you must jump through some hoops.

1. Right-click the link to an online calendar and copy its Web address or URL into the clipboard.
2. Switch to Windows Live Calendar and click the Subscribe button in the toolbar.
3. In the Import or subscribe to a calendar display, paste the URL for the calendar into the Calendar URL text box.
4. Pick a Calendar name and color and click Subscribe to Calendar. Windows Live Calendar will connect to the URL, discover details about the calendar, and subscribe. When that process is complete, you'll receive a message stating that the subscription was successful.
5. Click Done to finish.

continues

continued

Now you will return to the main Calendar view. You will see that the calendar has been added to your list of calendars and that events from that calendar appear in the Calendar view, as shown in Figure 22-27.

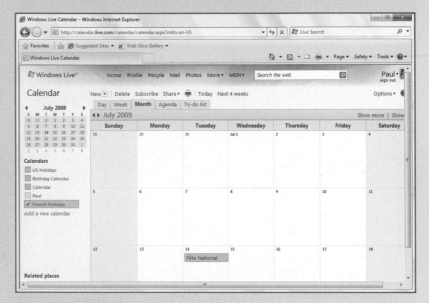

Figure 22-27: Subscribed calendars appear in your Calendar view alongside your own calendars.

There are key differences between subscribed and local calendars as well. Subscribed calendars are read-only, which means you cannot add or change appointments with them. (This is true both on the Web-based Windows Live Calendar and in the Windows Live Mail application.) The people who publish the calendars to which you are subscribing are free to change them, of course. If they do change a calendar you're subscribing to, you will always see the latest changes.

Sharing Your Own Calendars with Others

Windows Live Calendar lets you share your own calendars (that is, calendars you've created; you cannot share subscribed calendars) with others using a proprietary (and, as noted previously, limited) Windows Live Calendar feature or, if you dig deep enough, via standard ICS-based publishing.

To do so, click the Subscribe link in Windows Live Calendar and then choose the appropriate calendar from the pop-up menu that appears. You'll then navigate to the Sharing settings page for the selected calendar. By default, you'll see two options here: "Don't share this calendar (keep it private)" (which will be selected) and "Share this calendar." If you choose the latter option, the display will change to offer various sharing options, as shown in Figure 22-28.

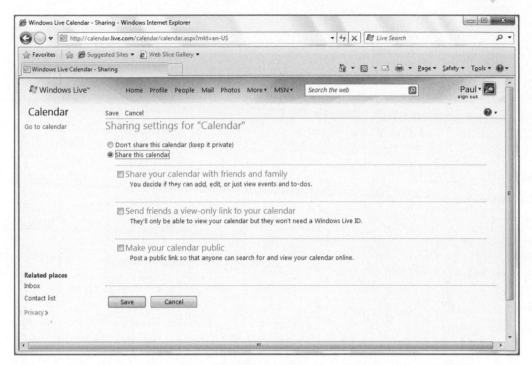

Figure 22-28: You can share, but not publish, Windows Live Calendar–based calendars.

The following options are available from this interface:

◆ **Share your calendar with friends and family:** Here, you can choose to share your calendar with those who are in your contacts list, which is stored in Windows Live People (see Chapter 23); you can also manually add individuals by e-mail address if needed. You add people via the Add people button and then decide, on an individual basis, what sort of access they have. Available access types include co-owner; view, edit, and delete items; view details (the default); view free/busy times, titles, and locations; and view free/busy times. You can also determine which people can see to-do items.

◆ **Send friends a view-only link to your calendar:** In this case, people in your contacts list (and any others you manually add) will be able to view your calendar. You can provide read-only links in various ways, like HTML and RSS, but the one you're most likely going to want is ICS, which provides the Web standards–based publishing functionality we've been talking up.

◆ **Make your calendar public:** If you choose this option, your calendar will be published free and clear on the Web and anyone can view it. We don't recommend this because of the privacy implications. Do you really want the world to know, for example, that you're on vacation and thus your house is empty and unattended for the week?

Secret

People you share calendars with will receive an e-mail-based invitation like the one shown in Figure 22-29.

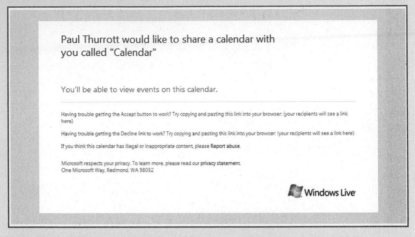

Paul Thurrott would like to share a calendar with you called "Calendar"

You'll be able to view events on this calendar.

Having trouble getting the Accept button to work? Try copying and pasting this link into your browser: (your recipients will see a link here)

Having trouble getting the Decline link to work? Try copying and pasting this link into your browser: (your recipients will see a link here)

If you think this calendar has illegal or inappropriate content, please Report abuse.

Microsoft respects your privacy. To learn more, please read our privacy statement.
One Microsoft Way, Redmond, WA 98052

Windows Live

Figure 22-29: Your friends will receive a formal invitation to view your Calendar.

Secret

Note that this feature requires Windows Live Calendar to create private URLs for your contacts to use. If these URLs got into the hands of others, they'd be able to view your calendar as well. For this reason, Windows Live Calendar provides a link to reset your calendar URLs, which invalidates the old ones.

Secret

If you plan to have your friends subscribe to your Calendar with a non-Microsoft tool (for example, Google Calendar), you may run into problems. This is due to the fact Microsoft prohibits crawling—or access via a search bot—of calendars containing the phrase "/private/" in the URL. The only known workaround is to make your Calendar public.

Printing Calendars

This may seem a bit antiquated in this day of digital tools, but both Windows Live Calendar and the Calendar component of Windows Live Mail include decent printing capabilities, enabling you to print your calendars in various attractive ways. This is handy for people who need a quick printout or haven't otherwise embraced the notion of personal digital assistants (PDAs) or smartphones. Sometimes, a piece of paper just works.

Printing from Windows Live Calendar

To print one or more calendar(s) from Windows Live Calendar, make sure the calendars you want to include are selected. Then, pick the view you want—Day, Week, Month, or Agenda, or To-do list for that matter—from the tabs at the top of the display. Next, click the Print icon. Your Web browser will load a new page, as shown in Figure 22-30, with a rough approximation of the Windows Live Calendar view you selected. If you picked Day, Week, or Month, you can also optionally select the *Include event list* option to add a nice list of the calendar-based events below the Calendar view.

Click the Print link at the top of the window to print the page.

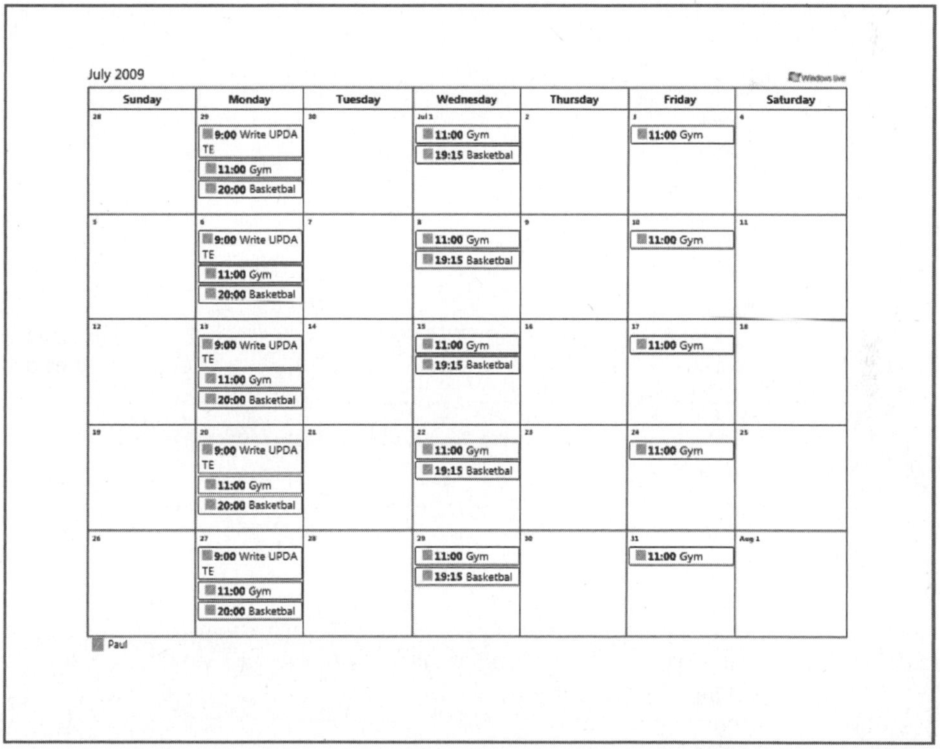

Figure 22-30: Windows Live Calendar offers decent printing capabilities.

Printing from Calendar

To print one or more calendar(s) from the Calendar view in Windows Live Mail, you must again make sure that the calendars you want to include are selected. Then, click the Print toolbar button. In the Print window that appears, select the printer and the Print Style (Day, Week, or Month). The printout, as shown in Figure 22-31, is an exact duplication of the calendar display in Windows Live Mail and is quite attractive.

Figure 22-31: Windows Live Mail offers beautiful calendar printing, though only with a limited range of view styles.

Secret

Because Calendar does not support to-do items, you can print only to-do's with Windows Live Calendar. Also, Windows Live Calendar supports the unique Agenda view.

Secret If Windows Live Calendar has a major limitation in its current state, it's that it does not support syncing with Windows Mobile devices. This will obviously change in the future, quite possibly by the time you read this. But as of this writing, you can sync Windows Live Hotmail and People to Windows Mobile, but not Windows Live Calendar.

Summary

Windows Live Calendar is a decent standards-based Web calendar, and while the Calendar component in Windows Live Mail doesn't provide access to all of its features, it's a great front end for those who prefer local applications. With Windows Live Calendar, you can maintain one or more calendars, subscribe to Web-based calendars, and publish your own calendars so that others can keep up with your activities. It is hoped that this chapter has inspired you to discover this Web service's many and varied features. Unless you require Exchange compatibility or Windows Mobile device integration, this application should meet all of your scheduling needs.

Your Life in Sync—Windows 7 and Live Services

Chapter 23

♦ ♦

In This Chapter

Accessing Windows Live services that Microsoft promotes in Windows 7

Establishing an online persona with Windows Live ID

Utilizing e-mail online with Hotmail

Blogging with Windows Live Spaces

Planning and immortalizing events with Windows Live Events

Storing files online with Windows Live SkyDrive

Downloading and installing Windows Live products with the Windows Live suite

Communicating with others online with Windows Live Messenger

Extending Internet Explorer with the Windows Live Toolbar

Creating a Web portal and searching the Web with Live.com

Taking your first steps toward cloud computing with Live Mesh

♦ ♦

In late 2005, about a year before it completed development of Windows 7, Microsoft announced that it was radically changing its online strategy to better compete with Google, Yahoo!, and other companies. Microsoft's new strategy, called Software + Services (as in "software *plus* services"), is simple: because it already dominates the PC operating system market with Windows, it no longer needs to take the technically dubious (and anti-trust unfriendly) tack of bundling online services directly in Windows, as it did in the past. Instead, Microsoft's online services are combining capabilities from both desktop software and online services to deliver the best possible user experience. More to the point, Microsoft can build off the success of Windows without unnecessarily taking advantage of its market power. Yes, most of its services will work best with Windows, and some will actually require Windows, but none will ship directly in the box with Windows.

It may seem like a subtle distinction; but after a decade of antitrust problems both in the United States and around the world, Microsoft is finally doing the right thing, both for the company itself and its customers. Previously, most of Microsoft's online services were developed through its MSN division, which used to develop the company's Internet access services. Now, however, that work has all been brought into the Windows Division; and not so surprisingly, the online services are now being marketed with the Windows Live brand, along with related Live services that bear brands such as Office Live and, yes, MSN.

Secret

You might not be surprised to discover that the various Windows Live services and desktop products are simply updated or new versions of products and services that were once being developed by MSN and were branded with the MSN name. That is indeed exactly what happened. More surprising, perhaps, is news that brands like "Windows Live" and "Office Live" may actually disappear, as soon as by the time you read this. In early 2009, Microsoft announced that it would merge Windows Live and Office Live into a single family of services that may come with new branding.

note Microsoft's Live services also include a brilliant set of online services for gamers called Xbox Live.

When Microsoft announced its strategy to enhance the Windows product line with a set of online products and services under the Windows Live umbrella, it wasn't clear exactly what form the resulting software would take. Since then, however, Microsoft has shipped an impressive number of Live products and services, almost all of which are updated regularly.

Because the Live services are being updated so frequently, it doesn't make sense to provide an in-depth look at every single one of them. Instead, this chapter covers the Live services that Microsoft is promoting directly in Windows 7, along with those Live products and services that we think are the most interesting and useful to Windows 7 users. You might be surprised by what's out there, both in terms of scope and depth: Microsoft offers a comprehensive line of online products that enhance Windows 7 in various ways. These products and services, in effect, extend the capabilities of Windows 7 and make it a more valuable operating system.

Secret

Microsoft often says that its Live services and other ancillary products, like Zune and Windows Mobile, extend, enhance, and "light up" the Windows 7 experience by completing the picture and providing users with a more cohesive overall environment that extends from the PC desktop to the Web and to mobile devices. This cohesiveness has only deepened with Windows 7 and will no doubt improve again in the future.

Windows Live and Windows 7: What's Included

With previous versions of Windows, Microsoft bundled a few predecessors of its Live services, most notably the Windows Messenger instant messaging client, directly in the OS. With Windows 7, that's not the case. Instead, Microsoft is subtly promoting Windows Live products and services in Windows 7 in two key areas.

First, the Windows Live Essentials suite is advertised in the Windows 7 Getting Started control panel, which is available as both a standalone application and via the Start menu, as shown in Figure 23-1. Because this window is displayed at the top of the Start menu by default when you first use Windows 7, millions of people around the world will be tempted to download and install some of these products. Fortunately, Windows Live Essentials is a collection of free, high-quality products that do indeed enhance Windows 7.

Figure 23-1: There are no Windows Live products or services in the OS, per se, but Microsoft does advertise them so you can "complete" Windows 7.

You might see other offers here as well, as Microsoft allows PC makers to add their own entries in the Welcome Center, just as they do with the Start menu and Windows desktop.

Second, Microsoft offers Windows Live Essentials to users via Windows Update. It's not a critical update, so it won't be installed automatically or behind your back. But it is listed as an important update, and if you do choose to install it, you'll be forced to deal with the Essentials installer, which enables you to choose which applications and services to install.

Going Online and Learning about Windows Live

The shortcut titled *Go online to get Windows Live Essentials* in Getting Started opens Internet Explorer and brings you to the Essentials page in the Windows Live Web site (download.live.com), shown in Figure 23-2.

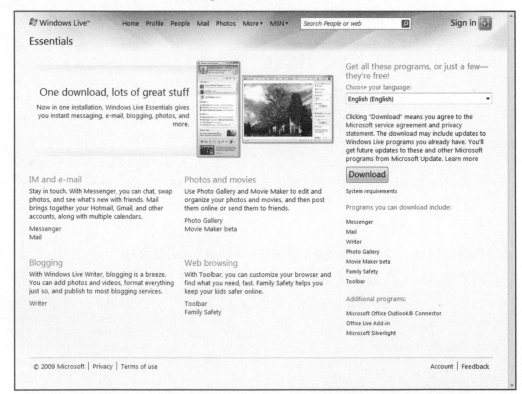

Figure 23-2: The only obvious link to Windows Live in Windows 7 connects you to the Essentials Web site.

But this page is specific to the application suite that you install in Windows 7. If you want to find out more about Microsoft's top-level Windows Live services, including Windows Live Hotmail (Web-based e-mail), Windows Live SkyDrive (Web-based storage), Windows Live People (contacts management), Windows Live Messenger (instant messaging), Windows Live Photos (online photo sharing), and Microsoft's various PC- and smartphone-based downloads, you should visit the main Windows Live Web site at home .live.com. As shown in Figure 23-3, this site also provides a way to sign up for a Windows Live ID, which is a central identity management service that enables you to manage your online persona. We discuss Windows Live ID in just a moment.

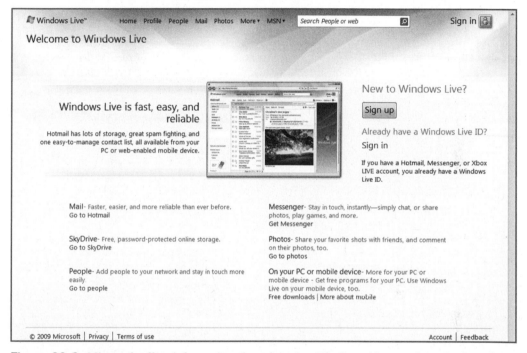

Figure 23-3: Microsoft offers information about its other Windows Live products and services via the main Windows Live site.

Windows Live Services That Make Windows 7 Better

Microsoft promotes its Windows Live offerings specifically as value-added services that enhance your Windows 7 experience with free, familiar, and secure ways to connect and share with others. Marketing baloney aside, there's some truth to this, though Microsoft's lengthy list of available Windows Live products and services—not to mention the products and services that fall under other Live services product families—makes it hard to keep them all straight.

In this section, we focus on a hand-picked list of Windows Live products and services that we believe truly do make Windows 7 better. You're free to pick and choose among them, of course, with one exception: Windows Live ID, which we discuss first, is the "glue" that binds together all of Microsoft's Live products and services, both to each other and, in Windows 7, to the PC desktop as well.

Tying It All Together: Windows Live ID

Why you want it: It's needed to access many other Windows Live products and services.

Type: Online service.

Though Microsoft doesn't explicitly market Windows Live ID, this important service sits at the middle of all of the company's Live products and services—including, yes, its Xbox Live and Zune Marketplace/Zune Social services. That's because Windows Live ID is Microsoft's central single sign-on service, and any Microsoft online product or service that requires a logon of some kind requires a Windows Live ID.

While the name Windows Live ID is unusual, you may be more familiar with the service's previous name, Passport. Microsoft dropped the name Passport when it changed to the Live branding it's now using, but the purpose is still the same. So, too, is the way in which you acquire a Windows Live ID: typically by signing up for a Microsoft online service, such as Hotmail or Windows Live Messenger, which requires a logon. However, you don't have to do it that way. In fact, if you know you're going to be interacting with various Windows Live (and other Microsoft Live) services going forward, you can simply sign up for a Windows Live ID first. Here's how you do it.

Simply navigate to `home.live.com` with Internet Explorer and click the Sign up button. Yes, you're free to use the browser of your choice, but we've found that Microsoft's online services still work best with the company's own browser, so it's best to step through the original sign-up process with IE instead of Firefox or whatever other browser you may use. You can use another browser to access the service after you're signed up.

Your Windows Live ID will be an e-mail address of some kind. Note that you are free to use an existing (non-Microsoft Live) e-mail address as your Windows Live ID (like `paul@thurrott.com`), or you can create a new Windows Live ID using one of Microsoft's domains (typically live.com or hotmail.com in the U.S., but you may see different domains offered in other locales).

Secret When you create a new Windows Live ID using Microsoft's domains, the company will also set up a free Windows Live Hotmail e-mail account for you (see the next section for details). This isn't the case when you use an existing e-mail address, where you're expected to use your existing service's e-mail facilities instead.

Creating a Windows Live ID involves stepping through a basic questionnaire like the one shown in Figure 23-4. You need to find a unique e-mail address if you're going with the Full Meal Deal, enter some information about yourself, and the like.

Because Windows Live Hotmail is one of the more popular services we'll be discussing in this chapter, we will assume you endured the lengthier process of creating a Windows Live ID using one of Microsoft's domains; but the process for adding a Windows Live ID to an existing e-mail account is similar, and simpler. During sign-up, you'll be asked to choose an e-mail address and password, and enter some basic account information.

Once the account is created, you are directed to Windows Live Account Services, where you will see that you are signed in to your new account. At that point you can access any of the Live services described in this chapter: when prompted to log on, do so with your newly created Windows Live ID.

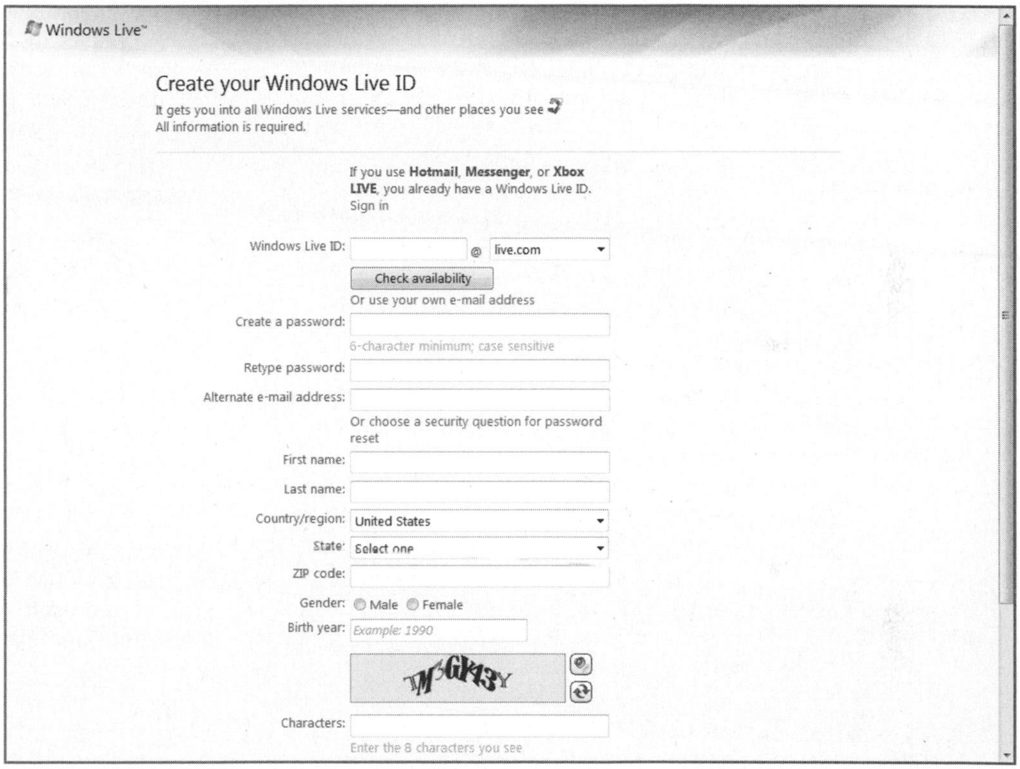

Figure 23-4: The Windows Live ID sign-up process is pretty much standard fare.

Windows Live Home

Why you want it: It provides a single Web page, or portal, that aggregates content from virtually all of the other Windows Live services mentioned in this chapter.

Type: Online service.

Windows Live Home (home.live.com), shown in Figure 23-5, is a dynamic, living front end to your entire life. Okay, that may sound a bit dramatic, but if you configure this page to its full potential, it's hard not to be impressed by how useful it has become. And if you're looking for a single view into how impressive Microsoft's Live services are, look no further.

Microsoft describes Windows Live Home as a dashboard to your network of friends, and this curiously businesslike description is accurate enough. Here, you will find a useful aggregation of what's going on with you and your friends. You will see mail, calendar, and weather information as before, but in a more attractive guise. Favorite photos adorn the header. News headlines and other configurable feeds drive the right side of the display. But the centerpiece, really, is the What's New feed, driven by the activities you and your friends have configured, both within Windows Live and without. This feed lists all of the activities you and others are engaged in, providing a central location for, well, your entire life—again, if you've configured it correctly.

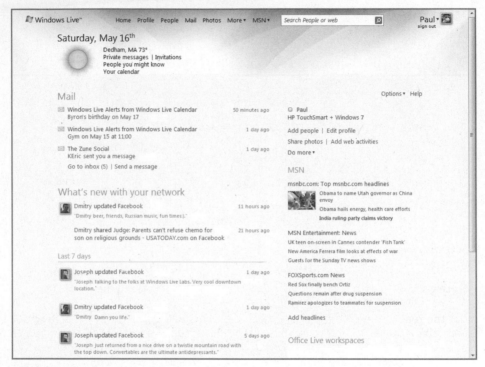

Figure 23-5: Windows Live Home can be a fine Web starting point, especially if you've invested time building out your Windows Live network.

Windows Live Profile

Why you want it: It provides a central location to manage your consolidated online persona, which consists of your Windows Live ID and any associated and shared information as well as an aggregation of numerous third-party services.

Type: Online service.

Where Windows Live Home is about viewing information about your Windows Live network—that is, those people with whom you have some sort of digital relationship, typically via Windows Live People—Windows Live Profile (profile.live.com), shown in Figure 23-6, provides the opposite end of this equation: It is the place you go to broadcast information about yourself to others. Here, you configure which information you'd like to publish about yourself and who you'd like to see it. You can edit all the typical profile information—name, picture, personal message, and the like—and invite people to join your network. On the surface, it's all pretty obvious stuff.

Figure 23-6: Windows Live Profile broadcasts your information to the world.

But the real power of Windows Live Profile lies in its ability to aggregate multiple Web activities—that is, things you're doing on other social networks, Web sites, and services—in a single place, creating an automated "What's New" feed that you can share with others. Microsoft reports that it has partnered with dozens of companies, linking your activities on services like Facebook, iLike, Twitter, WordPress, Yelp, and many others, as well as virtually any custom blog or service that exposes an RSS-type feed, into a single source of information.

So, say you are a Twitter user, a WordPress Blogger, and you upload photos to Windows Live Photos. Without Windows Live Profile, anytime you updated one of these things, you could only share those updates via those specific services. Now, you can share all three—and any number of other activities—via the single Windows Live "What's New" feed that aggregates virtually everything you're doing online. You set up each service from within Windows Live Profile just once and then you're good to go. From then on, everything you do is automatically added to that one What's New feed.

Windows Live Hotmail

Why you want it: This is one of the most pervasive and successful online services ever created; you get a free account with your Windows Live ID.

Type: Online service

Significantly upgraded in 2007, Windows Live Hotmail (`mail.live.com` or `hotmail.com`)—more commonly referred to simply as Hotmail—is now a modern and mature Web mail service. It offers desktop application–like capabilities through its Web-based interface. It features excellent Windows and Windows Mobile integration hooks, and can be accessed from Microsoft's popular Outlook e-mail client.

For hundreds of millions of people worldwide, Hotmail is a big part of what it means to be online, connected, and communicating with other people. Of course, Hotmail also accommodates the various ways and places in which people now want to access e-mail. That is, many people now want to access e-mail constantly, whether they're at work, at home, or, with a new generation of mobile devices, on the go. Microsoft has Hotmail-based solutions for all of these scenarios. Home users can, of course, access the Web-based Hotmail service or access Hotmail through Outlook 2003 and 2007 via free Outlook Live Connector software (part of Windows Live Essentials) or the Windows Live Mail client discussed in Chapter 21.

Here are some features of interest in Windows Live Hotmail.

User Interface

From a look-and-feel perspective, Windows Live Hotmail closely resembles a desktop e-mail application such as Outlook, as shown in Figure 23-7. There's a toolbar at the top, with all the expected options, such as New, Reply, Forward, Delete, Check Mail, and so on. There's also an Outlook-like three-pane view, with a folder list, e-mail list, and Reading pane displayed horizontally as you move your eye from left to right across the page.

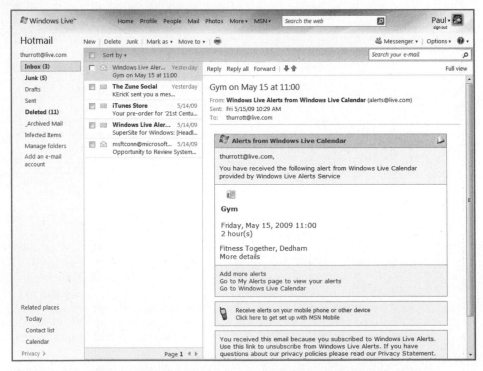

Figure 23-7: Windows Live Hotmail is the dominant Web e-mail service today.

One important part of the Hotmail user interface is the Reading pane, which works like similar features in Microsoft Outlook and Windows Live Mail. This pane, which can be displayed on the right, on the bottom, or disabled altogether, enables you to view e-mail as you navigate from message to message in the e-mail list, without having to open a separate window or, as is more typical with Web mail, navigate to a new page. The result is an e-mail application-like experience.

As part of the wider Windows Live Web experience, Microsoft also provides some stylized themes so you can personalize Hotmail and the other services you access online.

Security Features

If you're familiar with some of the security features Microsoft has added to Windows 7 applications like Internet Explorer and Windows Live Mail, then you won't be surprised by the security advances in Windows Live Hotmail. There's a new safety bar—similar to the information bar debuted in Internet Explorer—that displays color-coded alert flags for e-mails that Hotmail finds suspicious. This provides a nice visual cue about the safety level of the message. For example, you'll see a yellow safety bar if a message with embedded images, links, or attachments arrives from a source that's not in your contacts list or safe senders list; and you'll see a red safety bar when a potentially fraudulent e-mail message, such as a phishing e-mail, arrives.

Hotmail now automatically scans all e-mail attachments. This scanning is free and works regardless of whether you've configured a similar AV scanner on your desktop computer.

Hotmail also sports pervasive junk mail controls with automatic reporting and user-controlled block and allow lists for fine-tuning e-mail filtering. Overall, the level of protection is just about exactly right and what you'd expect from a modern Web mail solution.

Productivity Enhancements

Windows Live Hotmail provides every user with virtually unlimited storage space. Microsoft's policy here is simple: it will increase your storage requirements in the future as needed in order to ensure that storage space is never a differentiator between Hotmail and other services. That's a big deal, because it means that virtually all e-mail users could manage all of their e-mail via Microsoft's servers if they wanted to.

When you compose a new e-mail message, Windows Live Hotmail provides automatic address completion functionality, which is handy. The recommended addresses are drawn from your contacts list as well as the list of e-mail addresses from which you've received e-mail.

In another e-mail application-like feature, Hotmail provides automatic inline spell checking with suggested corrections, just like the desktop-based Windows Live Mail product: you'll see a squiggly red line under potential misspellings, and when you right-click that word, a list of corrections appears. You can also add words to your Hotmail dictionary via this right-click menu, or just choose to ignore the notation. Unfortunately, there's no grammar checker.

You can also drag and drop e-mail items (but not folders, not even for reordering), much like a desktop application. If you want to drag an e-mail message from the Inbox to the Deleted folder, for example, you just click and hold and then and drag it over, as shown in Figure 23-8.

Hotmail also supports multi-selection, so you can select multiple e-mail messages, contiguously or not, and drag them to new locations, or right-click and perform actions such as Mark As Read, Delete, and the like.

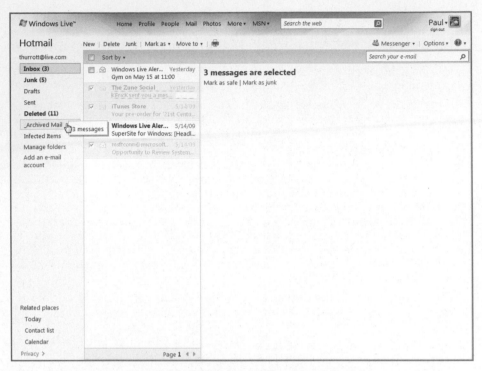

Figure 23-8: Hotmail's drag-and-drop functionality works like a desktop application.

Windows Live Hotmail provides full-text searching of e-mail from a prominent Search box in the toolbar that also enables you to optionally search the Web. E-mail searches are returned in a temporary Search Results folder and appear inline in Windows Live Mail just like the Inbox. (If you do choose to search the Web, Windows Live Mail opens a new browser window and forwards your request to the Live.com search engine.)

E-mail composition includes all the HTML e-mail niceties you'd expect, with various font and font styles, text justification, bulleting, indenting, and so forth. You can easily insert hyperlinks from the toolbar, and note a cool new feature called a Search Link: simply highlight some text in your message, click the Search Link button, and you'll create a hyperlink that will search Live.com for the selected text.

Another hidden feature is the Photo Upload tool: when you are ready to attach a file in an e-mail message in Hotmail, you'll see two options in the pop-down menu: File and Photo. As expected, File displays a Choose File dialog from which you can navigate in your system to find the file you'd like to attach. If you choose Photo, you'll see the Photo Upload tool, which loads in the browser window and enables you to graphically navigate through pictures in a single folder and select the ones you'd like to add, as shown in Figure 23-9.

As you mouse over individual photos in the tool, you can select them for inclusion and rotate them in two directions. If you click a photo, the tool moves into Edit mode, from which you can perform other operations related to contrast, brightness, cropping, and the like. It's no Photoshop, of course, but it's a nice feature.

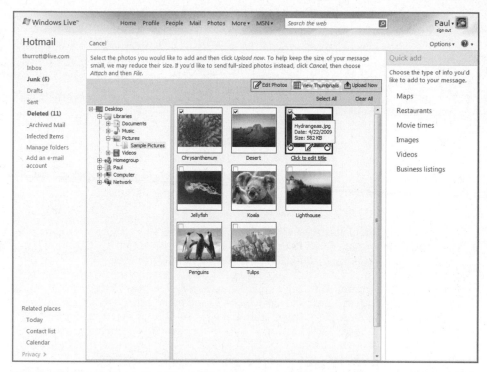

Figure 23-9: Windows Live Hotmail includes a sophisticated photo-attachment system.

Once you've selected all the photos you want, click the Upload Now button and resized versions of the images are added as attachments to your e-mail. By default, larger photos are resized so that they're no more than 600 pixels in the largest dimension. Thumbnail versions in the actual e-mail are no larger than 320 pixels.

Microsoft is also now making industry-standard POP3 access to Hotmail available for the first time. This means that you can use virtually any e-mail application with Hotmail, not just Microsoft Outlook or Windows Live Mail. This functionality previously required a $20 yearly fee.

And speaking of POP3 access, thanks to a new POP aggregation tool, users can also choose to make Hotmail their only e-mail interface. Here's how it works: you can configure Hotmail to receive, send, and respond to e-mail from up to four of your other e-mail accounts, assuming those accounts offer POP3 access. When configured like this, you need only to access Hotmail to get all of your e-mail. When you respond to a message sent to a different account, it will appear to have been sent from that account. You can optionally send new e-mail from any configured account, not just your Hotmail account. POP aggregation is a great idea because it simplifies managing multiple accounts. And if you become a fan of Hotmail, it allows you to stay in the environment you like best, while easing the pain of leaving your old e-mail service.

Finally, a Web Messenger feature provides a little Messenger-like icon in the Hotmail toolbar that indicates your Messenger presence status (online, offline, etc.). New IM-related messages and other notifications appear as Messenger-like "toast" pop-ups in the lower-right corner of the browser window.

Secret The Photo Upload tool requires IE. If you're using Firefox or another full-view-compatible browser, you'll see only the File option, in which case you can simply attach photos as you would any file. Note that these files aren't automatically resized, so be careful if you're sending photos in this way.

Windows Live People

Why you want it: Microsoft's contacts management system aggregates contacts from across all of the other Live services you use, including Hotmail and Messenger.

Type: Online service.

Windows Live People (formerly Windows Live Contacts) was formerly considered a sub-component of Hotmail. It has been upgraded along with Hotmail, while sporting a number of new features of its own. These include contacts searching, one-click contacts addition, and so on. Windows Live People (`people.live.com`), shown in Figure 23-10, integrates with both Hotmail and Windows Live Messenger, Microsoft's instant messaging client, and also with other Windows Live services. If one of your Messenger contacts updates his or her personal information, for example, those changes are reflected across all Windows Live People–compatible products and services, so you'll see the changes in your contacts list in Hotmail as well.

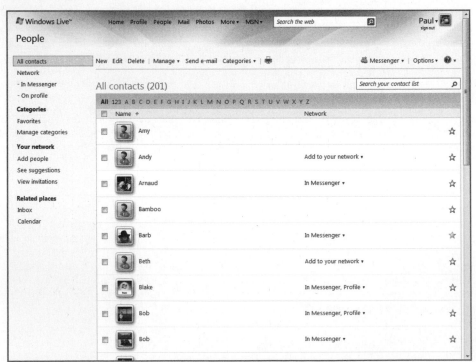

Figure 23-10: Windows Live People provides centralized contacts management.

Windows Live People also integrates nicely with various portable devices, especially Windows Mobile–based smartphones. Here, Microsoft is delivering on its "software plus services" mantra in a major way, because accessing your contacts—and thus their phone numbers—via a mobile device is, of course, the ultimate example of anywhere/anytime information access.

Windows Live Calendar

Why you want it: Microsoft's online calendaring service supports all the expected scheduling features plus tasks management and calendar standards interoperability.

Type: Online service.

Windows Live Calendar, like Windows Live People, was formerly a subcomponent of Windows Live Hotmail. And like Windows Live People, Windows Live Calendar (`calendar .live.com`) is now on a separate development path and has been heavily updated since its inception. Windows Live Calendar is fully described in Chapter 22 because it replaces a previous Windows component called Windows Calendar that is no longer offered in Windows 7. Windows Live Calendar is shown in Figure 23-11.

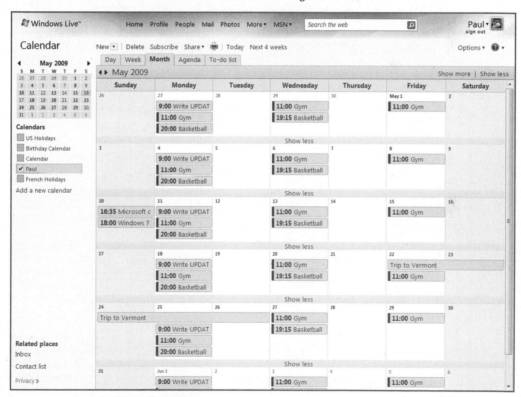

Figure 23-11: Windows Live Calendar

Windows Live Photos

Why you want it: This is a free dedicated photo organization and sharing service.

Type: Online service.

Microsoft's original approach to photo sharing was to integrate this functionality into the Windows Live Spaces blogging service (see below), because most people who want to share photos electronically do so via blogs and personal Web sites. However, Windows Live Spaces isn't an ideal photo-sharing solution for a variety of reasons, and many people simply want to share photos and nothing else. Therefore, Microsoft has created a new service, Windows Live Photos, for photo management and sharing. Windows Live Photos is shown in Figure 23-12.

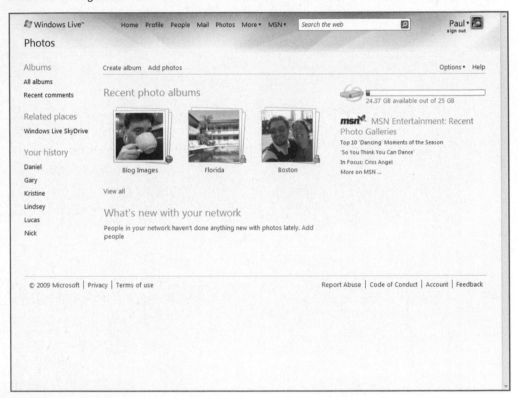

Figure 23-12: Windows Live Photos

Windows Live Photos is perhaps the most deeply integrated of all the Windows Live products and services. Yes, there is, of course, a dedicated site for Windows Live Photos (photos.live.com), and yes, it works with Windows Live Photo Gallery (discussed in Chapter 12) as expected. But you can access your online photo albums from just about anywhere in Windows Live, and that's true of both the services and the Windows Live

Essentials applications. You can share photos and photo albums with friends via Windows Live Messenger, for example, and e-mail them from Windows Live Mail. On the services end, your photos are available from Hotmail (for e-mailing), accessible from Windows Live Profile, can be posted to blogs and Web sites with Windows Live Spaces, and can be shared via Windows Live Events.

Some of the functionality in Windows Live Photos is obvious but welcome: browsing the Windows Live Photos Web site, you can view photo album thumbnails and see animated slide shows. You can push albums to digital photo frames via Windows Live FrameIt (covered later in this chapter). The storage back end? It's all handled by Windows Live SkyDrive. And yes, you can browse your photos there as well.

Looking at the Windows Live Photos site specifically, you'll see mostly basic functionality, so Flickr users won't see any reason to migrate their online photo collections quite yet. You can create and view photo albums, but not subfolders of any kind, which will be problematic for people with large photo collections. You can view photos inside an album by thumbnail (one size only, unfortunately) or via List or Details view.

You can also play slide shows, like that shown in Figure 23-13, which are attractive enough but don't offer much in the way of options.

Figure 23-13: Windows Live Photos offers very simple photo slide shows.

Individual photos cannot be renamed, which is an odd omission, but you can add a caption, tag people in the photo, or add a comment. Others who have permission to do so can also add comments.

As far as protecting photos go, Windows Live Photos offers various sharing options on a per-album basis. You can choose to make albums public (available to one and all) or you can set permissions to your network (view or add, edit, delete) or your extended network. You can also filter permissions based on the groups you've set up in Windows Live People, Windows Live Messenger, and other places; for example, you might set up an album to be viewable only by family members. You can also enter specific e-mail addresses if you'd like.

Windows Live Spaces

Why you want it: This is a super-simple way to create a personalized home page or blog and connect with friends online.

Type: Online service.

Windows Live Spaces (`spaces.live.com`) is Microsoft's blogging solution—software that enables anyone to publish a personal Web site, complete with photos and interactive content, easily and without any technical knowledge. Spaces has proven quite popular—by some metrics it's actually the most popular blogging software in the world—and it certainly does provide a friendly and welcome environment, with professional-looking page design and nice integration with other Windows Live services. A typical Windows Live Spaces blog is shown in Figure 23-14.

Windows Live Spaces provides most of the services that typify blogs. That is, it provides a simplified, nontechnical way to post textual blog entries online, perfect for beginners. It provides syndication services, enabling content from personal Spaces to be subscribed to from news aggregators and other RSS-compatible applications and services such as Internet Explorer 8. It excels at creating lists of items, perfect for a blogroll or similar list of links; and it enables others to post comments to Spaces.

Windows Live Spaces goes beyond stock blogging features, adding functionality that many casual users and consumers are likely to find exciting. It offers a highly customizable user interface, albeit one that exists clearly within the Windows Live site "style." It includes excellent photo uploading and slide show features. It integrates Windows Live Messenger so that you are notified when your friends and other contacts update their own Spaces. In addition, in a nice nod to power users, it even enables you to post blog entries via a mobile phone or e-mail.

If Windows Live Spaces has a weak link, it's that you cannot create one at your own custom Web address, or URL. Instead, you must use Microsoft's more convoluted `spaces.live.com` addressing scheme. We hope that Microsoft will address this issue in a future update.

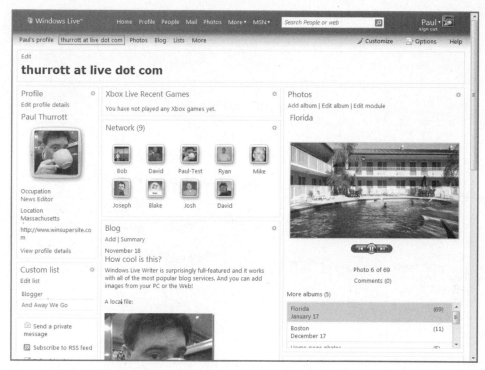

Figure 23-14: Windows Live Spaces enables anyone to create their own Web site.

Windows Live Events

Why you want it: It provides a simple way to plan a party or other event, send electronic invitations, and share memories when it's over.

Type: Online service.

Built as an offshoot of Windows Live Spaces, Windows Live Events (events.live.com) is an Evite competitor that does its inspiration one better: In addition to providing an excellent interface for planning parties and other events and sending electronic invitations to those events, Live Events adds something fairly unique: the capability to enable guests to return to the site after the event is over and share their memories. These memories can take the form of photo galleries and discussion boards. It's a surprisingly personal type of service, one that can turn a one-time event into a gift that keeps on giving.

Shown in Figure 23-15, Windows Live Events provides an interface for inviting guests to an event, sharing photos taken at the event, chatting online with guests both before and after the event, and customizing the event's site in various ways.

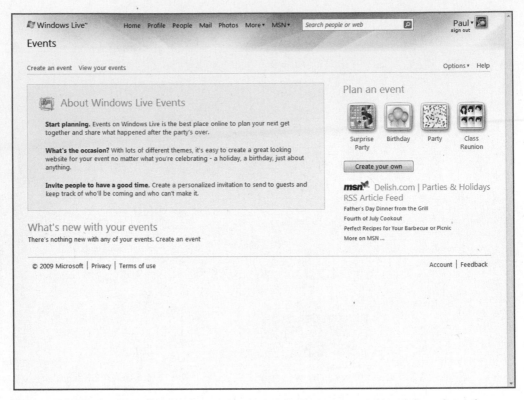

Figure 23-15: Windows Live Events makes it easy to plan events and reminisce about the good times later.

Windows Live SkyDrive

Why you want it: It offers 25GB of free online storage, and drag-and-drop uploading.

Type: Online service.

Windows Live SkyDrive (skydrive.live.com) is Microsoft's first foray into the "storage in the cloud" concept, though the software giant likes to refer to this service as a USB memory key in the sky. However you look at it, SkyDrive is an interesting solution for backing up files that you'll need to access later; and because it's on the Web, you'll be able to access those files from any Internet-connected device.

With SkyDrive, shown in Figure 23-16, you can create public and private folders and files, which you can then lock down or open to others on a per-folder basis.

Integration with other Windows Live services means you can very easily create a folder full of files, for example, which is shared only with specific people in your Windows Live Contacts database. Beyond that, you can also configure individual users as readers or editors, enabling you to specify who can optionally add and change files as well. And SkyDrive is the back-end storage for Windows Live Photos, Microsoft's photo-sharing service.

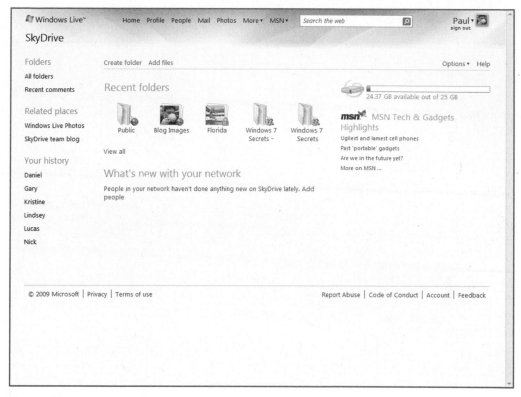

Figure 23-16: Windows Live SkyDrive is an online storage service.

If SkyDrive has a real fault, it's that there is no way to increase the storage allotment or access it easily from Windows 7, perhaps as a shared network drive. Our guess is that Microsoft will eventually move to a yearly subscription fee for more storage as part of a "SkyDrive Pro" service, or perhaps aggregate the storage available across all of its Live services. For now, those with headier storage requirements—such as users who want to back up digital photos—need to look elsewhere, such as Google Picasa Web or Flickr.

Windows Live FrameIt

Why you want it: It delivers photos and other content to digital picture frames.

Type: Online service.

Windows Live FrameIt-compatible digital photo frames are available from a variety of companies, including Aequitas Technologies, Pandigital, PhotoVu, Smartparts, and ViewSonic. The idea is obvious enough: Windows Live FrameIt enables users to publish photo albums (and, curiously, certain non-photo content) to compatible frames over the Internet. The Windows Live FrameIt Web site (frameit.live.com) is shown in Figure 23-17.

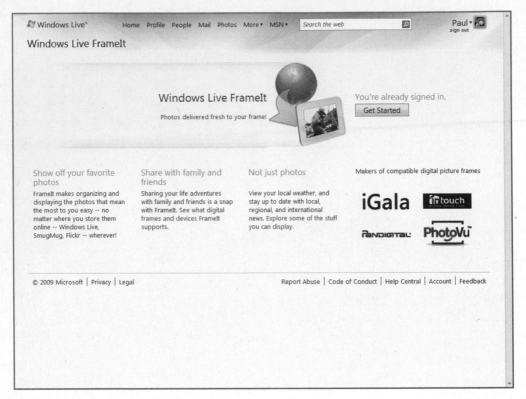

Figure 23-17: Windows Live FrameIt

Whether this is a good idea or not is somewhat debatable. We do like the notion of purchasing a photo frame for grandma and then zapping her updated family photos on a regular basis. But it's unclear whether grandma will know how to use or even want, that benefit. And the availability of non-photo content—such as weather reports, stock prices, traffic, news, and so on—may be superfluous to many users.

Windows Live Groups

Why you want it: It provides a way to collaborate online with groups of people, such as families, sports teams, and the like.

Type: Online service.

Windows Live Groups is an intriguing idea: basically, it's like Microsoft's server-oriented SharePoint for consumers, offering a way for any group of individuals to share things such as documents and other files, calendars, and photos, and a place to connect, discuss things, and discover what's going on. Windows Live Groups (`groups.live.com`) is shown in Figure 23-18.

When you create a group, a group calendar is created for you in Windows Live Calendar and you can optionally overlay your group calendars in your own private calendar if you'd like.

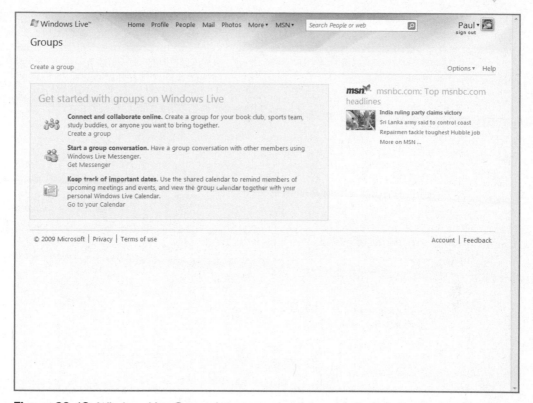

Figure 23-18: Windows Live Groups let you create mini-portals for groups of related people.

Groups also get their own dedicated storage in SkyDrive that is separate from your individual storage, and you can privately share photos among members of a group very easily. Unique to Groups is the ability to start and participate in discussions, which are essentially Web-based newsgroups, but private, of course, to the group.

Windows Live Essentials

Why you want it: It provides a single downloadable version of Microsoft's best Windows Live applications.

Type: Suite of Windows applications, plus some related products and services.

Travel writer Rick Steves likes to refer to a favorite European destination as a "cultural bouillabaisse," and this moniker might equally be applied to Microsoft's Windows Live Essentials, a quirky collection of unique Windows applications that can improve your Windows 7 experience in interesting ways. Windows Live Essentials arose out of a need to aggregate the various downloadable software applications that Microsoft offers via Windows Live. It did this for two reasons. One, these applications are integrated in various ways and thus work better together. (That said, you are free to download only those parts of the suite you actually want or need.) Two, it's simpler to provide access to these applications via a single installer. Otherwise, you'd have to hunt around the Web to find the applications you wanted.

Windows Live Essentials (download.live.com) provides access to five downloadable applications as well as a number of other components. These include Windows Live Mail (an e-mail application that replaces Windows Mail and Outlook Express from previous Windows versions), Windows Live Messenger (an instant messaging and person-to-person communications tool), Windows Live Photo Gallery (a photo management and editing solution that replaces Windows Photo Gallery from Windows Vista), Windows Live Writer (a surprisingly powerful blog editor), and Windows Live Movie Maker, an updated version of the Movie Maker application from previous Windows versions.

Windows Live Essentials also includes Windows Live Toolbar, an Internet Explorer add-on that makes it easy to access Windows Live services from your favorite browser; Windows Live Family Safety, a parental controls solution that augments and improves the built-in Windows 7 parental controls feature; Microsoft Office Live Add-in, a plug-in for Microsoft Outlook 2003 and 2007 that enables users to access Windows Live Mail, Calendar, and People from that popular productivity application; and Silverlight, Microsoft's answer to Adobe Flash.

The suite's integrated installer, shown in Figure 23-19, enables you to choose which Windows Live applications you'd like to install.

Figure 23-19: The various programs in Windows Live Essentials can be installed together or individually via a single installer.

The next sections take a quick look at each of these programs.

Windows Live Mail

Why you want it: This is a surprisingly solid e-mail application that aggregates multiple accounts, including those from Hotmail.

Type: Windows application.

Windows Live Mail is fully discussed in Chapter 21, because it is now the default e-mail application for Windows 7. Figure 23-20 shows Windows Live Mail in action.

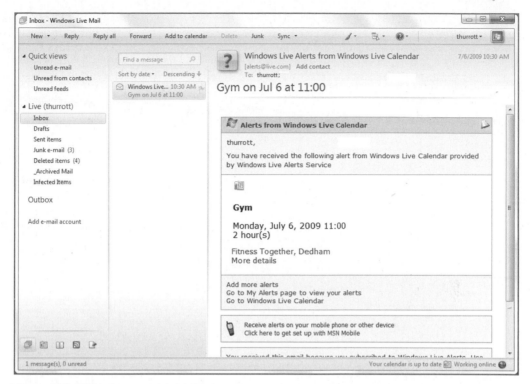

Figure 23-20: Windows Live Mail is based on the same technologies as Windows Mail, but offers many more features.

Windows Live Messenger

Why you want it: It's an excellent way to communicate with others around the world via text, audio, or video chat.

Type: Windows application.

Windows Live Messenger replaces MSN Messenger as Microsoft's mainstream instant messaging (IM) application for consumers. In truth, the term "instant messaging" doesn't really do this application justice. Although it can indeed be used to hold text-, audio-, and video-based chats online with your friends, co-workers, and other contacts, Windows Live Messenger is blurring the line with telephone-like functionality thanks to its integration of Voice over IP (VoIP) technologies. That means you can make long-distance and international phone calls via Windows Live Messenger for a small fraction of what you're probably being charged by the phone company. It might be time to invest in a PC headset. Windows Live Messenger is shown in Figure 23-21.

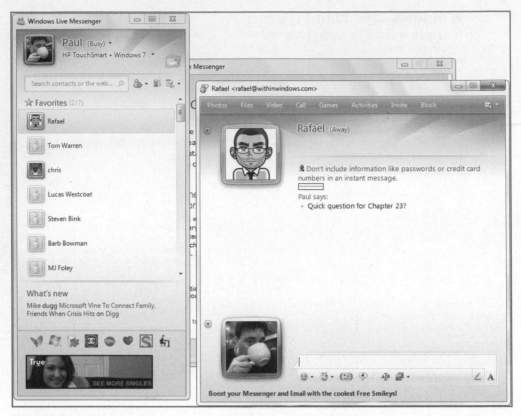

Figure 23-21: Windows Live Messenger offers IM functionality and can be used to make PC-to-phone calls.

The latest version of Windows Live Messenger is the most extensive update yet of Microsoft's popular IM client and it is being refined to form the Windows-based hub for the social features in Windows Live. Windows Live Messenger will integrate with the Favorites and Groups features in Windows Live People. The biggest change, however, is the What's New feed, which works with the consolidated What's New feed that's available across all of your Windows Live and third-party services.

Windows Live Messenger can also be used to communicate with friends using Yahoo! Messenger, a competing instant messaging application.

Windows Live Photo Gallery

Why you want it: It's a superb update to the Windows Photo Gallery application from Windows Vista.

Type: Windows application.

Windows 7 now ships with a basic photo viewing solution, but if you're looking for more advanced features—like photo editing and management—then Microsoft offers Windows Live Photo Gallery, which is shown in Figure 23-22.

Figure 23-22: Windows Live Photo Gallery is a nice upgrade for Windows 7's built-in Windows Photo Gallery.

Windows Live Photo Gallery provides several important improvements to Vista's Windows Photo Gallery and is a must for anyone using Windows 7. These improvements include a dramatically better photo importer, new editing tricks, a cool new photo panorama function, and integration with various online services, including Windows Live Space and even non-Microsoft services such as Flickr. Windows Live Photo Gallery is such a big deal, in fact, that it is covered exhaustively in Chapter 12.

Windows Live Writer

Why you want it: It's the ultimate blog editor.

Type: Windows application.

While every blogging solution available offers a Web form of some sort where aspiring bloggers can post their writings and other blog items, such forms are relatively primitive. Enter Windows Live Writer, a superb blog editor that works with Windows Live Spaces, yes, but also with virtually every other blog service on Earth.

Shown in Figure 23-23, Windows Live Writer features an attractive user interface and an amazingly complete feature set. We've tested Writer with Windows Live Space, Blogger, and Community Server, and the results are fantastic. In fact, we both use it for our own blogs.

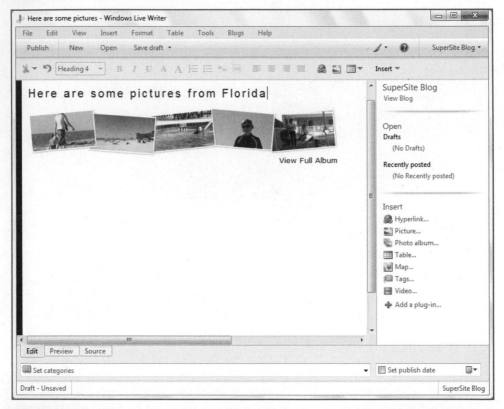

Figure 23-23: Windows Live Writer adopts the look and feel of your blog so it feels like you're editing right on the Web.

Windows Live Writer works with common blog features such as categories, and includes inline spell checking; hyperlink, image, photo, and video insertion capabilities; and awesome text-editing features. You can even upload images to Google's Picasa Web service, in addition to Windows Live Spaces. Writer is an impressive little niche application that many people are going to find quite advantageous. It's that good.

Windows Live Movie Maker

Why you want it: It provides basic video-editing features and Web services integration.

Type: Windows application.

Windows Live Movie Maker includes various editing features, effects, transitions, and themes, as well as numerous ways to share the movies you create via the Internet, optical discs, or your TV, cell phone, or portable video device. Windows Live Movie Maker, shown in Figure 23-24, also supports a new plug-in model, similar to other Windows Live applications, so that third parties can provide other capabilities and format/codec support.

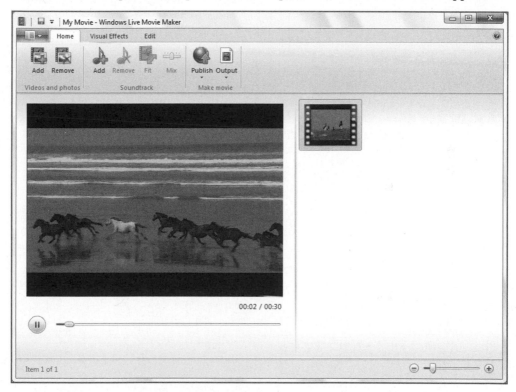

Figure 23-24: Windows Live Movie Maker

Because Windows 7 no longer ships with a video-editing solution, Windows Live Movie Maker is now the preferred application for this need. We cover Windows Live Movie Maker thoroughly in Chapter 13.

Windows Live Toolbar

Why you want it: You're a heavy user of IE and Microsoft's Live services.

Type: Windows application.

Anyone who's used Internet Explorer is probably familiar with the notion of helper toolbars that include such things as integrated search boxes, pop-up blockers, and a variety of other useful features. Given how advanced Internet Explorer is—it includes, by default, both an integrated Search box and a pop-up blocker, for example—you might think that these toolbars would be a thing of the past. That, alas, is not true; and while the Googles and Yahoo!s of the world are still offering their own brands of Internet Explorer–compatible toolbars, Microsoft has one, too. Not surprisingly, it's called Windows Live Toolbar.

Windows Live Toolbar, shown in Figure 23-25, includes numerous potentially useful features, such as smart menus that enable you to find any location on a map simply by highlighting the address on a Web page. There's a form-fill function that saves commonly typed Web form information (name, address, telephone number, and so on), sparing you from having to manually enter that data repeatedly. The toolbar also integrates with a number of useful Windows Live online services, giving you one-click access to such things as Windows Live Spaces (blogging) and Windows Live Mail.

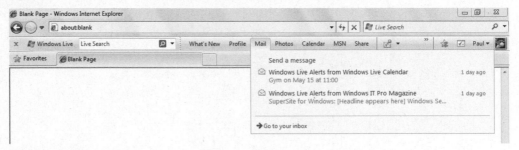

Figure 23-25: The Windows Live Toolbar integrates with Internet Explorer and adds a number of useful features.

Why would you want such a thing? Toolbars like the Windows Live Toolbar are aimed at heavy users of a particular Web services company, so if you have bought into Microsoft's online vision—which is absolutely okay, by the way—the Windows Live toolbar might be useful to you.

The real appeal of the toolbar, frankly, isn't what is installed by default, but rather what you can add to it: Microsoft and its partners offer a wide variety of toolbar buttons that extend the toolbar, and thus the browser itself, in very interesting ways. One excellent example is the Windows Live Favorites button, which enables you to save your Favorites up in the cloud, in a single place, rather than maintain different Favorites collections on each PC. That's a nifty feature. Whether it's worth the download is your call.

Beyond Windows Live: The Mesh

While the name Windows Live can and should suggest a connection with Windows, Microsoft is busy creating a number of other online services and products that it has branded in a curious number of ways. The most interesting is Live Mesh (mesh.com), an evolving new Microsoft platform that encompasses an Internet operating system (exposed as a Web-based desktop), your Windows 7–based PC(s), and your mobile device(s). It enables you to sync documents and other files between the Web-based desktop and your PCs (but only at the folder level). You can also remotely access other PCs using a remote desktop-like experience. Microsoft says it will add other services in the future, and of course developers are racing to take advantage of this new "cloud computing" platform as well.

At a conceptual level, what's most interesting about Live Mesh is that the PC desktop is not at the center of this emerging platform. Instead, Live Mesh is envisioned as a ring or circle, whereby your PC(s), mobile device(s), and Web desktop are all equal partners, like spokes on a wheel (see Figure 23-26).

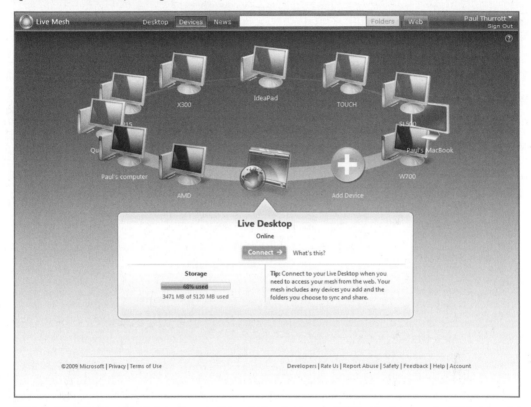

Figure 23-26: Live Mesh is conceptually a circle of connected PCs, devices, and a Web-based desktop.

All of the capabilities of the Live Mesh, today and in the future, will work identically via each entry point. Note, too, that Microsoft also supports non-Microsoft PCs (for example, Macs) and mobile devices (for example, Windows Mobile smartphones) with this platform. The Live Mesh Web-based desktop is shown in Figure 23-27.

In short, Microsoft is creating a cloud computing platform in which the PC is but a component. Like it or not, most computer users today don't typically use just a single device. People increasingly use multiple PCs (and/or Macs), both in the home and at work. They have desktops and laptop computers; they have smartphones, MP3 players, digital cameras, and other mobile devices. In addition, most users have a host of online personas via e-mail and instant messaging services, social networking memberships, e-commerce sites, and other online communities. Users manage these disparate components separately and with great complexity and difficulty.

Figure 23-27: The Live Mesh Web desktop

This situation is similar to what it must have been like being one of the first automobile owners 100 years ago. Back then, you had to have extensive technical knowledge about the vehicle in order to use and maintain it. Today, that market has evolved and matured such that most car owners simply use their vehicles without needing to understand how they work. Computing, too, must mature in the same fashion, and it must do so while meeting the ever-increasing needs of a mobile and interconnected user base.

With Live Mesh, Microsoft seeks to bridge the gap between all the currently disconnected devices, computers, and Web services now used. And though a Web-based desktop sits conceptually on the Live Mesh ring, you use the Web as a hub of sorts for authentication and connections. Naturally, Microsoft utilizes Windows Live ID for this purpose. This provides individual users with a way to collect the list of computers and devices they're using, of course, but it also provides the infrastructure for sharing between users. If you want to do something very simple, such as provide a way for others you trust to access the contents of a shared folder, Live Mesh makes it both possible and seamless.

Live Mesh, alas, is an evolving platform, and much about it will change between the writing and reading of these words. That said, Live Mesh offers two basic features today: document synchronization and remote desktop access. They're worth exploring briefly.

Live Mesh Document Sync

Every time you create a folder in the Web-based Live Mesh Desktop, Live Mesh creates a special blue shortcut to that folder on the desktop of each connected PC. The first time you click this shortcut, you're presented with a Synchronize Folder dialog that enables you to set up synchronization for the folder. The default synchronization option will be changed to *When files are added or modified*. If you accept this option, you can optionally (and preferably) relocate the local version of the folder and move on with life. If, however, you choose to change the sync type back to *Never with this device,* then the shortcut disappears from the PC desktop.

Assuming you do want to sync the folder between your local PC and the Live Desktop (and, potentially, other devices), the icon will change from a special blue shortcut to a special blue folder and the window will open. As with folders viewed from the Live Desktop, locally synced Live Mesh folders also include the Live Mesh Bar on the right, as shown in Figure 23-28. There's one major difference, however: on the PC, you can minimize but not close the Live Mesh Bar if you'd like.

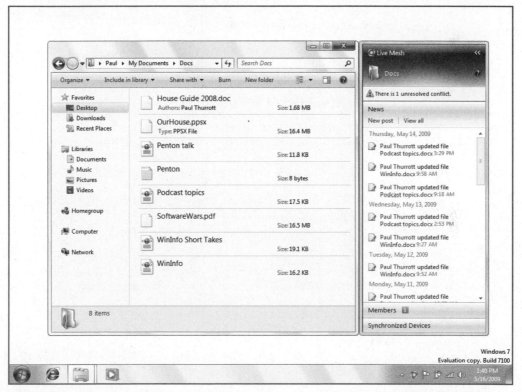

Figure 23-28: Synchronized Live Mesh folders look a bit different from normal Explorer windows.

The most important thing to note about locally accessed synchronized folders, of course, is that you can drag and drop content into them; and because they're automatically synchronized, any files and folders you copy into these folders on your PC are synced back to the Web-based Live Desktop and to any other devices with which you've configured synchronization. Because folder sync occurs on a per-folder basis, you need to manually configure each Live Folder to sync to each device. This can be done via the Live Desktop or individually on each PC.

Secret

Live Mesh folder synchronization has proven to be fast and reliable—so much so, in fact, that we used this mechanism to synchronize the contents of this book between our various PCs, over the Internet. As we worked on the chapters locally, via various desktop PCs and notebook computers, the book files (typically, Word documents and image files) were synchronized automatically, both up to the Internet cloud (the Live Desktop) and to whatever other PCs we both added to our respective Live Mesh. Live Mesh folder sync is an instant backup solution combined with instant access to the very latest versions of files no matter which PC we're using. We relied very much on Live Mesh during the creation of this book, and it never let us down.

Live Mesh Remote Desktop

Live Mesh also includes a handy remote access feature called Live Mesh Remote Desktop. To access this feature, open the Live Mesh menu, either on your local PC or from within Live Desktop, find the PC you'd like to remotely control, and then click the appropriate Connect to Device link. Live Mesh will open a Remote Desktop-type window, complete with a unique Live Mesh Bar that includes remote desktop-oriented functionality such as Send Ctrl+Alt+Delete, Hide desktop on remote device, and Show desktop as actual size. These options are shown in Figure 23-29.

By default, the remote desktop is scaled to fit the confines and resolution of the window, though you can use the aforementioned option to change that and scroll around within a truly windowed view of the remote desktop.

Secret

The Remote Desktop feature in Windows 7 requires Windows 7 Professional, Enterprise, or Ultimate: Home versions need not apply. This is a problem with the remote access feature in Windows Home Server, described in Chapter 10, because that feature relies on Remote Desktop functionality. Thus, Microsoft's "Home" server can't provide remote access to "Home" versions of Windows. Armed with this knowledge, you may assume that Live Mesh Remote Desktop will work only on non-Home versions of Windows, but that's not the case: Live Mesh Remote Desktop works fine with both Windows 7 Home Basic and Starter.

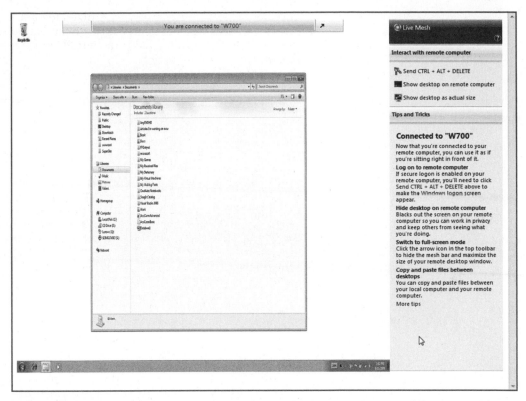

Figure 23-29: Live Mesh Remote Desktop enables you to remotely access PCs connected to your Mesh.

Summary

This chapter examined some of Microsoft's many Live products and services, which extend Windows 7 with a number of useful Web-based capabilities, including instant messaging, PC safety and security, e-mail, and much more. With Windows Live services, you can communicate with friends, co-workers, and loved ones, publish your thoughts and photos to Web sites, and keep your PC running securely and smoothly. Unlike previous Microsoft online services, the Windows Live services integrate with Windows only when you choose to install them: They aren't simply provided for you whether you need or want them or not. Chances are good that if you'd like to do something online, Microsoft has you covered.

Part VII

Windows 7 Power User

Keeping Your
Data Safe: File
and PC Backup

Chapter
24

◆ ◆

In This Chapter

Backing up and restoring data

Utilizing Windows Backup

Creating and restoring data backups

Managing automatic backups with Windows Backup

Backing up an entire PC using system images

Restoring an entire PC using the Windows Recovery Environment

Using the Previous Versions feature to recover old versions of data files

◆ ◆

With Windows 7, Microsoft expands on the pervasive and reliable backup and restore solutions for both data files and the entire computer that it introduced in Windows Vista. You can use Windows Backup to copy your important files and folders to a safe location or create a system image that can be used later to restore a broken PC. There's even a cool new feature that debuted first in Windows Server that helps you recover old versions of data files if you save the wrong version. Windows 7 has everything you need to make sure your data is safe. You may never need to turn to a third-party backup and restore utility again.

Secret

That's right: years before Apple shipped a feature called Time Machine in Mac OS X 10.5 that it promoted with a "go back in time" marketing mantra, Microsoft had this feature in Windows Server and then later in Windows Vista first—and you thought only Microsoft copied features from other operating systems.

Different Backups, Different Goals

Now that you've moved to digital storage for your most valuable data, it's time to start thinking about creating backups, copies of your original data that are ideally kept elsewhere for safekeeping. Many people don't even consider backing up until the unthinkable happens: a hard drive breaks down, literally taking all the data with it, or fire or theft occurs. Whatever the situation, you should be prepared for the worst before it happens. This is all the more important because many people now manage both their professional and private lives on their PCs. It's one thing to lose this week's meeting agenda, but quite another when a hard-drive crash destroys the only copies you had of five years' worth of digital photos. Those are *memories*, for crying out loud.

Given the almost complete lack of decent backup solutions in Windows XP and previous Windows versions, you may be surprised to discover that Windows 7 (like Windows Vista before it) offers an almost mind-boggling array of backup and restore solutions, each aimed at a different need. Best of all, Windows 7 also includes friendly front ends to all these capabilities, so that even the most nontechnical user can get up to speed quickly. Before getting into that, however, consider the various types of data safety facilities that Windows 7 supports.

Data Backup

If you think of your Documents library as the center of your data universe, and keep an elaborate series of folders and files there and in other libraries, then you'll understand the necessity of backing up these crucial files on a regular basis. To this end, Windows 7 supports both automatic and manual data backup options, enabling you to choose which files to back up and when. You can then restore your backups at any time to recover previous versions of documents, or to replace a file you may have accidentally deleted.

System Image

There's nothing worse than discovering that you need to reinstall Windows for some reason. Not only do you have to take the time and make the effort to reinstall the operating system again, you also have to ensure that you have drivers for all your hardware, find and reinstall all the applications you use regularly, reload all your personal data, and reconfigure all of the system's options so that it's exactly the way you used to have it. Rather than go through this rigmarole, you can use a Windows 7 feature called System Image Backup to create what is called a *system image* or *snapshot*. This image—which is essentially a huge backup file—contains the entire contents of your PC as it existed the day you created the image. If you need to recover your entire PC, you can simply restore the system image and get right back to work.

File Recovery

Windows 7 offers the following two excellent ways to recover lost files:

♦ **Previous Versions:** If you want to recover an older version of a document, perhaps because you made an editing error and then saved it, you can use this feature to access previous versions of the file.

♦ **System Restore:** If you make a change to your system that renders the PC unstable, such as installing a bad driver, you can use this feature to return to a previous state in time, or *restore point*. When you reboot, none of your data has been changed, but the rest of your system configuration returns to that of the day and time the restore point was first made. (We cover System Restore in Chapter 25.)

Add all that up, and what you have is the makings of a full-featured data recovery software suite. Amazingly, Microsoft provides all of that functionality in Windows 7, for free.

Secret

Okay, there's gotta be a catch, right? Actually, there is: Microsoft does not offer two kinds of backup that would be useful to have as part of Windows 7. The first is *PC-to-PC data synchronization*, or what we might call *peer-to-peer (P2P) synchronization*. With a such a solution you could, among other things, ensure that all of the files in your home PC's Documents library were always duplicated, automatically, with the Documents library on your laptop; anytime you made a change in either place, it would be replicated in the other. As it turns out, Microsoft does make such a tool, two in fact. They're called Windows Live Sync and Live Mesh, respectively. We cover the superior latter service in Chapter 23.

The second type of backup is online backup, where you back up files to the Internet cloud. Microsoft does have two online storage solutions, Windows Live SkyDrive, which is aimed at general online storage needs, and Office Live Workspace, which is really about document collaboration. (We look at SkyDrive in Chapter 23 as well.) However, neither offers any automated way, perhaps through Windows Backup, to back up files or system images from your PC to the Internet. Maybe in Windows 8.

Available Backup Capabilities in Various Windows 7 Versions

As explained in Chapter 1, different product editions of Windows 7 include support for different features. These differences can be dramatic in some cases—digital media feature support is an obvious example—and subtle in others. In Windows Vista, lower-end versions lacked some of the system's best data and PC reliability features. Fortunately, this is no longer the case in Windows 7: now, all Windows 7 product editions get Windows Backup (with file and system image backup capabilities), Previous Versions, and System Restore. The only exception is network-based backups: Only Windows 7 Professional, Enterprise, and Ultimate support that capability.

As a reminder, Table 24-1 outlines the backup technologies highlighted in this chapter and explains which are available in each mainstream Windows 7 product edition.

Table 24-1: Reliability Features

	Windows 7 Starter	Home Basic	Home Premium	Professional	Enterprise and Ultimate
File backup	Yes	Yes	Yes	Yes	Yes
Backup to network	—	—	—	Yes	Yes
System image backup	Yes	Yes	Yes	Yes	Yes
Previous Versions	Yes	Yes	Yes	Yes	Yes
System Restore	Yes	Yes	Yes	Yes	Yes

One Tool to Rule Them All: Using Backup and Restore

Although various data recovery tools are available scattered through the Windows 7 user interface, a single interface—Backup and Restore—provides a handy front end to most of them. Shown in Figure 24-1, this application helps you backup and restore files on your PC, create and restore complete system image backups as well, and access the System Restore recovery utility.

> **tip** This interface was called Backup and Restore Center in Windows Vista.

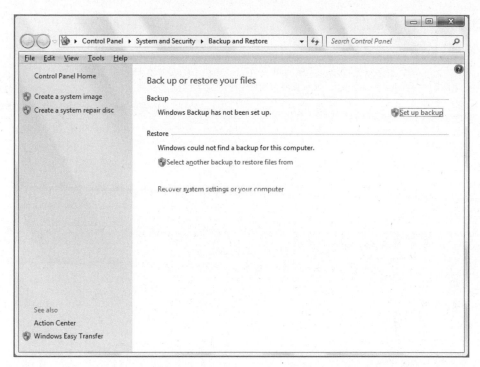

Figure 24-1: Backup and Restore is a one-stop shop for all your data protection needs.

Because Backup and Restore basically sits in front of most of the other data recovery functions included in Windows 7, we will use this as the obvious starting point for most of the data, file, and system backup and restore features discussed in this chapter.

tip Backup and Restore can be found in the Start menu under All Programs ⇨ Maintenance, but the easiest way to find this application, as always, is Start Menu Search: type **backup** and press Enter.

Backing Up Documents, Pictures, and Other Data

If you want to create a data backup, you can use Windows Backup, which is available from Backup and Restore. To do so, launch Backup and Restore and click the Set up backup link. This launches Windows Backup's Setup up backup wizard, as shown in Figure 24-2.

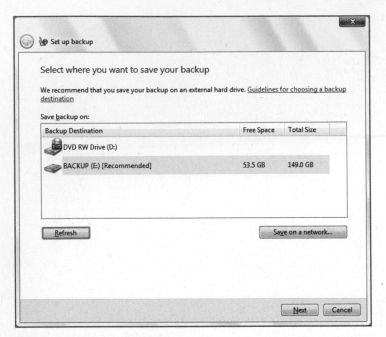

Figure 24-2: Windows Backup helps you manually create a backup of your important data files.

In the first step of the wizard, you must choose a location to store the backup. You can save a backup to an internal or external hard disk or other storage device, a recordable optical disk (typically a writeable CD or DVD), or a network share. (Network backup is not available in Windows 7 Starter, Home Basic, or Home Premium, however.) The amount of space you need, of course, depends on the amount of data you are backing up. The wizard automatically selects the local storage offering the most free space, but you can change this selection, of course.

> **tip** Microsoft does not allow you to back up to the disk or partition you are backing up. That is, if you are backing up data from the C: drive, you cannot save the backup to the C: drive.

In the second step, shown in Figure 24-3, you have two options: *Let Windows choose (recommended)* or *Let me choose*. If you choose the former, Windows Backup will automatically back up data files saved in libraries, on the desktop, and in any folders found in your user folder. (Windows Backup will also create a system image if you choose this option, and then automatically make periodic backups on a schedule going forward.)

If you select *Let me choose*, Windows Backup will present an expandable view of your file system, as shown in Figure 24-4, with some recommended locations already selected for you. From this interface, you can pick and choose exactly what to back up. You can also optionally cause a system image to be made with this type of backup.

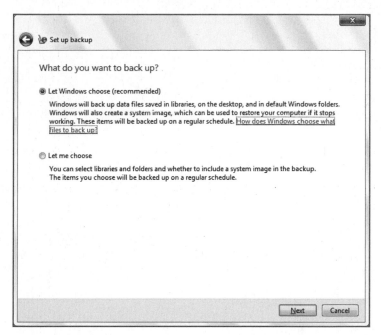

Figure 24-3: Here, it really is best to let Windows choose.

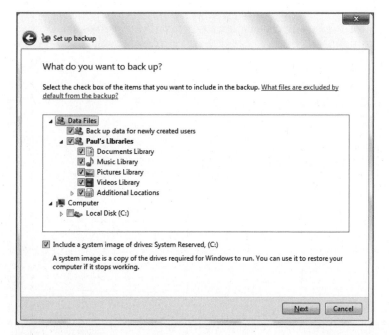

Figure 24-4: If you have specific backup needs, you can micro-manage Windows Backup as well.

In the next step, review what you've chosen. As shown in Figure 24-5, this step is important because you can change the schedule on which Windows Backup backs up your data going forward. Click the Change schedule link to change the default, which is to make a backup every Sunday night at 7:00 p.m.

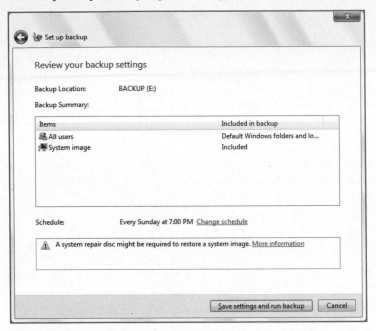

Figure 24-5: This is your last chance to adjust settings before the first backup is created.

Click *Save settings and run backup* to start the backup and establish a backup schedule going forward. As the backup begins, Backup and Restore displays its progress (see Figure 24-6).

> **tip**
>
> If you set up an automatic backup schedule now, Windows 7 will monitor your PC usage and prompt you to perform occasional full backups over time as well.

As the backup runs, the Action Center icon in the notification area of the taskbar changes, adding a small black clock. If you click this icon, you'll see the message shown in Figure 24-7: Backup in progress. This message will occur in the future, when Windows Backup runs in the background.

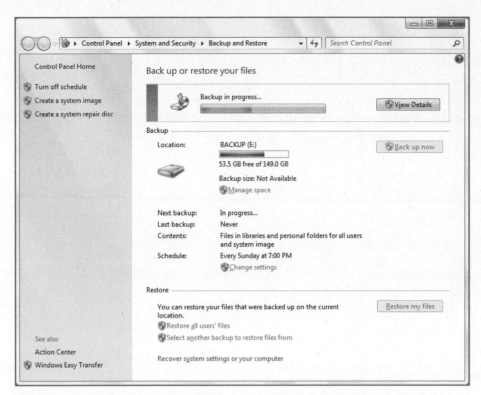

Figure 24-6: You can monitor the backup progress or get on with other work.

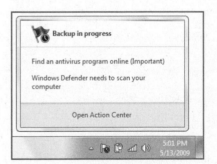

Figure 24-7: Backups trigger a change in
the Action Center notification icon.

---

tip You can create multiple automatic data backup schedules if you want. For example, you may want to back up different drives or data file types at different times or with different regularity.

Managing Backups

Once you have created your first data backup, a few things in the user interface change. First, Backup and Restore indicates that you've configured a backup location, as shown in Figure 24-8, and notes when the last and next backups occur. You can also change the automatic backup settings and restore all of the files for the current user.

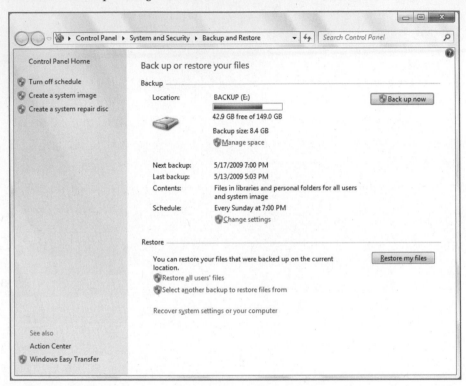

Figure 24-8: Backup and Restore reflects the recent backup.

You can also manage the disk space used on your backup device. When you click the Manage space link in Backup and Restore, the Manage Windows Backup disk space window will appear, displaying information about the currently selected backup device. As shown in Figure 24-9, you can browse the file system of the backup location, view backups stored on that device, and change settings associated with system image backups.

If you do click View backups, you can't actually navigate around inside of the backups you have made so far. Instead, you're provided with the window shown in Figure 24-10. From here, you can view the backups and delete them, but not get into them in any meaningful way.

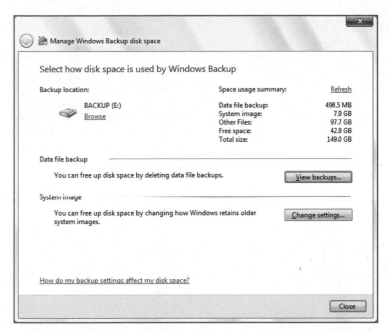

Figure 24-9: From this simple interface, you can manage details associated with your backup device and the backups stored on it.

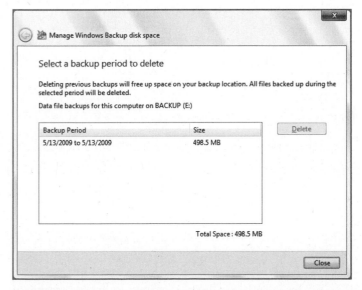

Figure 24-10: Only the simplest of backup management options are available.

tip   Want to see what's in a backup? You can do it, but not from this interface. Instead, go back to the previous window and click Browse. This will open Windows Explorer, pointing at the location of your backup. At this location, you will see a special folder with a Windows Backup icon and the name of your PC. If you try to double-click this folder, a Windows Backup window will appear. Instead, right-click the folder and choose Open. Then, click Continue in the permission folder that appears. You'll be presented with a folder structure representing your various backups. Inside of each of these folders is a number of standard ZIP files (see Figure 24-11) containing your original directory and file structure. If worse comes to worst and you lose everything, at least these files will always be accessible.

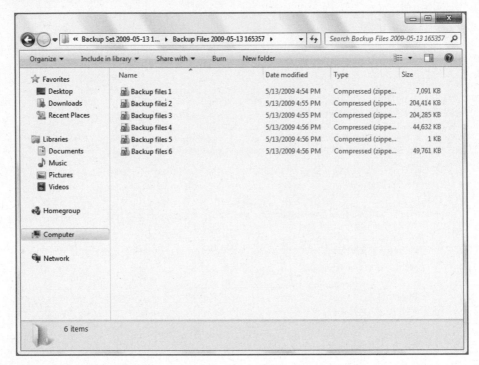

Figure 24-11: Windows Backup uses regular ZIP files under the covers to back up your data.

Restoring Files

Backup and Restore can also be used to restore files you have previously backed up. There are three general file restore methods:

◆ **Restore my files:** Restore your own files and folders.

◆ **Restore all users' files:** Restore your own files and folders as well as those of other users.

◆ **Select another backup to restore files from:** Perform more advanced restoration tasks, such as restoring files from a different PC.

These all work similarly. You can follow these steps to trigger a restore of your own data:

1. Open Backup and Restore and click the Restore my files button.
2. The Restore Files window, shown in Figure 24-12, appears.

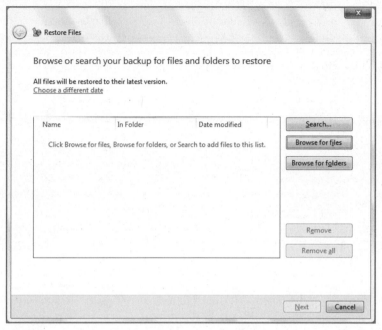

Figure 24-12: Restore Files lets you find the files you'd like to restore.

From here, you have three options:

- **Search:** If you know exactly what you're looking for, and need only one or a handful of files, you can use the Search button to search your existing backup sets.

- **Browse for files:** If you'd like to manually browse around the backup set to find a file or any number of individual files, click Browse for files. You'll be presented with a modified File Open dialog (see Figure 24-13), from which you can browse the various backups you've created, diving into the full backup or just the files in your user account.

- **Browse for folders:** Choose this option to recover entire folders full of files (and other folders).

Whichever method you choose, you can mark files and folders for restoration as you go and then continue looking for more.

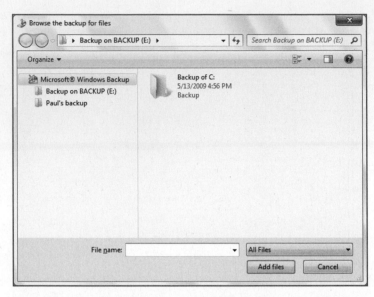

Figure 24-13: With either Browse for files or Browse for folders, you can dig in and root around inside the backup set.

3. When you're ready to go, click the Next button in the Restore Files window. Windows Backup will prompt you to specify where you want to restore the files to: either their original location or a different location (see Figure 24-14).

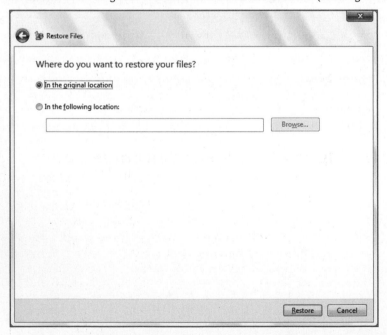

Figure 24-14: While you will often want to simply restore to the original location, sometimes it's a good idea to see what's in the backup before overwriting your files.

Choose one and then click Restore. Windows Backup will begin restoring your files. If any of the backup files will overwrite an existing file, you'll see the normal Copy File window shown in Figure 24-15, which offers you a chance to overwrite, copy but keep both files, or not copy.

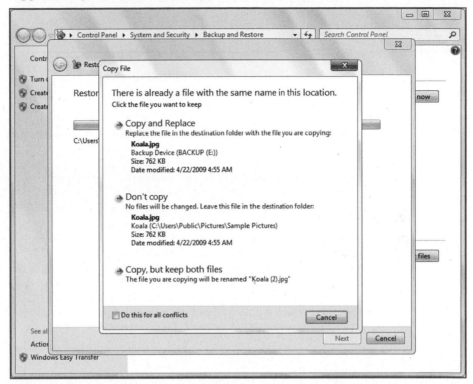

Figure 24-15: Make sure you don't wipe out anything important while restoring files.

When the restore is complete, Windows Backup will let you know that the files have been restored and give you an opportunity to view a list of restored files.

Backing Up the Entire PC: System Image

Backing up and restoring data files is important and should occur on a regular basis; but over the past few years, a new type of backup utility that backs up entire PC systems using *system images* has become quite popular. These types of backups protect against a hardware disaster: if your hard drive completely fails, for example, you can purchase a new drive and use the system image to restore the PC to its previous state.

System imaging utilities aren't actually all that new; corporations have been using them for years. But now that consumer-oriented system imaging utilities have gained in popularity, Microsoft has created its own version, which it includes with Windows 7.

Secret

The system image utility was called Windows Complete PC Backup in Windows Vista.

Secret

System imaging utilities typically compress the data on your hard drives so that the image file takes up a lot less space than the original installation. Various solutions use different compression schemes, but you may be interested to know that Windows 7 uses the tried-and-true Virtual Hard Disk (VHD) format that Microsoft also uses in Windows Virtual PC and its server-based Hyper-V virtualization solutions. That means system images created with Windows 7 will be supported for a long time to come.

caution   System images contain complete PC environments. You can't arbitrarily restore only parts of a system image, as you can with data backups. Instead, when you restore a system image, it restores the entire PC and overwrites any existing operating system you may already have on it. That means you should be careful before restoring a system image: any data you have on the disk will be overwritten. Of course, you're using automatic backups, too, right?

To create a system image, launch Backup and Restore and click the Create a system image link on the left. This launches the Create a system image wizard, shown in Figure 24-16, which walks you through the steps needed to completely back up your PC system. You can save system images to hard disks or optical storage (such as recordable CDs or DVDs), as well as network locations (Windows 7 Professional, Enterprise, or Ultimate only). However, network-based system images cannot be securely protected, as hard drive–based and optical disc–based backups can.

Secret

You can only write a system image to a hard disk that is formatted with the NTFS file system. That's because system images often exceed the 4GB file size limit imposed by the older and less reliable FAT32 file system.

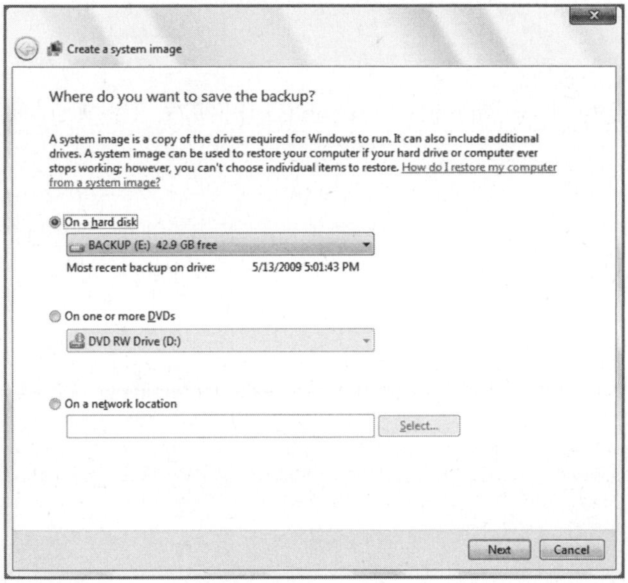

Figure 24-16: System Image is one of the best features in Windows 7.

Click Next. As shown in Figure 24-17, the wizard will give you a chance to confirm the backup settings and remind you which partitions are being imaged. It will also provide an estimate of the amount of space needed to create a system image. The required storage space varies according to the size and usage of the hard disk on your PC.

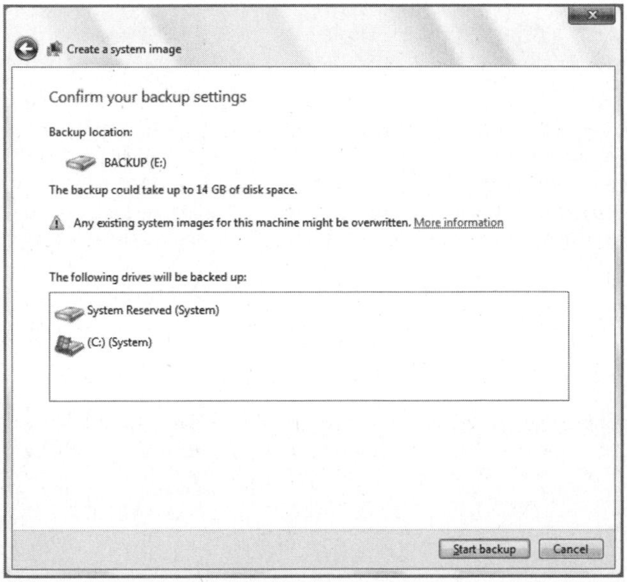

Figure 24-17: System Image is ready to go.

Click Start backup to begin the system image process.

Secret Two file system locations must be included in the system image—what Microsoft refers to as the *boot partition* and the *system partition*. The boot partition is always C:\, whereas the system partition is the drive with the Windows 7 `Windows` directory. This is typically C:, but if you installed Windows 7 in a dual-boot setup with a previous Windows version, the system partition might be in a different location. If you have other drives or partitions, you can optionally choose to include them in the system image as well.

As the image is created, Windows Backup will provide an ongoing progress indicator, as shown in Figure 24-18.

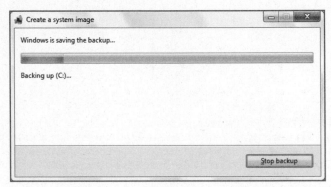

Figure 24-18: Though complete PC backups are huge, they are compressed and therefore much smaller than the actual disk to which you are backing up.

This process could take some time, especially on a heavily used PC. When it's done, Windows Backup will prompt you to create a system repair disc (see Figure 24-19). You should do so: While Windows 7 does install recovery files directly into the boot partition, in some instances, these files will not boot the PC. If that happens, you can use the system repair disc to boot your PC, a requirement for restoring the entire PC with the system image (as you'll see in the next section).

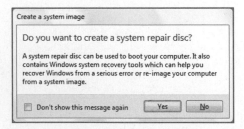

Figure 24-19: If you don't have one already, be sure to create a system repair disc.

You can use any writeable CD or DVD for a system repair disc.

If you have both 32-bit and 64-bit versions of Windows 7 on different PCs, you cannot use the same system repair disc for each. Instead, you must create separate system repair discs for 32-bit and 64-bit systems.

Restoring the Entire PC

If a catastrophic hardware or software failure has rendered your computer untenable, and you simply want to return to a known good system backup, you can use one of the system images you've previously created. Note, however, that you typically need to boot your PC into the Windows Recovery Environment to make this happen, either using the boot files on your PC or using the system repair disc that you previously created. Note, too, that restoring your PC in this fashion will wipe out all of the data and settings changes you've made since the last system image, so this should not be undertaken lightly.

Follow these steps to restore your entire PC using a system image:

1. Reboot the computer.
2. If you are using a system repair disc, boot the PC with that. Otherwise, after your PC has finished its BIOS sequence, hold down the F8 key. Choose Repair Your Computer from the Advanced Boot Options screen (see Figure 24-20) and tap Enter.
3. After the Loading files screen, choose the correct language and keyboard input method and then click Next.
4. If you booted from the hard drive, you will need to choose System Image Recovery from the System Recovery Options window that appears. Otherwise, System Recovery will examine the hard drives attached to your PC and look for Windows installs. When it's done, it will list the install(s) it found and give you the opportunity to use Windows 7's built-in recovery tools to fix problems with Windows (which we cover in Chapter 24) or you can restore your PC to an earlier time using a system image. Choose that latter option and click Next.

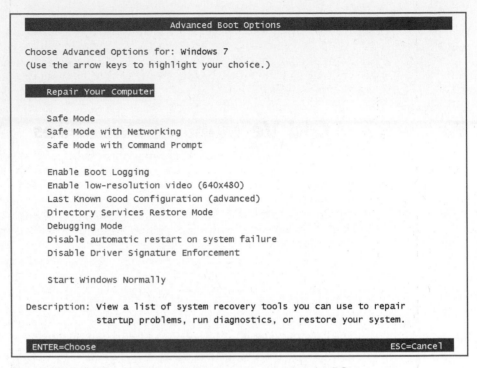

Figure 24-20: Choose the top option to restore your entire PC.

5. The Re-image your computer wizard begins, as shown in Figure 24-21. In the first phase of this wizard, you can choose the latest image available (the default) or you can select a different system image. When you've chosen, click Next.

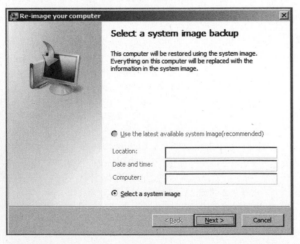

Figure 24-21: This wizard will step you through the process of restoring your PC with a system image.

6. In this step, you can choose to format the PC's hard drive and repartition disks (as Windows 7 Setup would do) to match the layout of the system image. Generally speaking, you should enable this option. Click Next to continue.

7. In the final phase of the wizard, you can verify your selections and click Finish to continue. Note that restoring an entire PC from a system image can be a time-consuming process.

Recovering Old Versions of Data Files

One of the most useful new features for information workers in Windows Server 2003 was *Volume Shadow Copy*, which silently and automatically created tiny backups, called *snapshots*, of data files stored on the server every time a user made any changes. In a managed environment like those based on Windows Server, Volume Shadow Copy is a wonderful feature, because users who save documents on the server can easily recover older document versions without having to summon an administrator to restore an old backup from a tape or a hard drive.

With Windows 7, Microsoft has added Volume Shadow Copy to its client operating system as well, renaming it *Previous Versions*. This means that any Windows 7 user can take advantage of this amazing bit of functionality and recover seemingly lost versions of files they have mistakenly edited. No server operating system is required.

The trade-off, of course, is disk space. Because Windows must store multiple copies of your data files, Previous Versions does eat up a bit of disk space; but because Previous Versions saves only the parts of files that have changed, or what Microsoft calls the *delta changes*, the disk space loss is not as bad as it would be otherwise. In fact, you probably won't even notice it's happening.

Unlike with Windows Server, you can't really manage how much disk space Volume Shadow Copy uses, or even the drives on which it is enabled. Instead, Microsoft enables the service across all drives, folders, and data files on a Windows 7 PC.

Secret   Previous Versions is yet another Windows 7 reliability feature that requires certain Windows 7 product editions. Previous Versions is available on Windows 7 Business, Enterprise, and Ultimate editions only; users with Windows 7 Home Basic and Home Premium need not apply.

To access this feature, find a document that you have changed a lot recently, right-click it, and choose Properties. Then, navigate to the Previous Versions tab. As shown in Figure 24-22, Windows maintains a number of previous versions, each of which you can restore if needed.

Figure 24-22: Previous Versions makes it possible to resurrect old versions of data files.

To restore an older version of a file, select the file version you want and click the Restore button. As with any other file copy operation, you are prompted to replace the existing file, keep the existing file, or keep the existing file and rename the newly recovered version.

Secret

The number of previous versions shown in this dialog depends on a number of factors, including how long your system has been up and running and how many times the document has been edited. In some cases, you may see no previous versions. If so, ensure that the System Restore service is running. We'll show you how in the very next section.

Secret

What happens when you delete a file or folder, either accidentally or otherwise? Can you use Previous Versions to restore that item? Actually, you can. Here's how: using Windows Explorer, navigate to the folder that contained the deleted item, right-click the containing folder, and choose Restore previous versions. (This method does not work with Libraries.) Then, find a previous version of the containing folder; copy it from the Previous Versions tab of the Properties window for that folder to your desktop or some other location. Then, navigate into the folder structure on the desktop (or wherever) and find the folder or file you are looking for.

Summary

Windows 7 includes a surprisingly rich set of features for backing up and restoring documents and other data files, as well as the entire PC. With Windows 7, you get handy file backup and restore wizards, a system imaging utility that enables you to recover completely from almost any PC calamity, and a nice front end from which to manage all of this functionality. It will be interesting to see how the third-party utility market responds to these changes now that virtually all of the most important backup and restore technologies in Windows are available in all product editions.

Troubleshooting and Recovering from Disaster

Chapter
25

◆ ◆

In This Chapter

Using Windows Troubleshooting

Understanding Troubleshooting Packs

Getting help with the Problem Steps Recorder

Using Startup Repair to fix a non-booting PC

Using the Windows Recovery Environment

Restoring Windows to an earlier point in time with System Restore

◆ ◆

W hile Microsoft has made major advances in each Windows version to improve the stability and reliability of the underlying platform, the truth is, sometimes things go wrong. So Windows has always included some kinds of troubleshooting capabilities. In the early days, these tools were fairly esoteric and technical, like the log files that date back to the earliest days of NT. But in Windows 7, we have a wealth of troubleshooting tools at our disposal, and unlike those early NT-based tools, they're designed to be useful to mere mortals.

Windows 7 includes a new troubleshooting platform, a Problem Steps Recorder for telling others what went wrong; a recovery environment that can fix boot-time problems; and of course an updated version of System Restore, which can help restore known good drivers and other system files when an update causes problems.

Using Windows Troubleshooting

In Chapter 7, you learned about the new Windows 7 Action Center, which consolidates system notifications into a single, centralized location. Action Center is a replacement for, and an expansion of, the Windows Security Center feature that first debuted in Windows XP Service Pack 2 (SP2). As such, it notifies you about issues related to the security and maintenance status of your PC when required. You can also manually visit Action Center to configure settings and view previous messages.

In Windows 7, the new Action Center builds off of Security Center in two ways. First, it's far more configurable than its predecessor, and it's now possible to easily control which features deliver notifications through this single UI. Second, Action Center expands into PC maintenance and also provides notifications for Windows Backup and Windows Troubleshooting.

That last bit, too, is new to Windows 7. Windows Troubleshooting is a new software platform that proactively monitors your system and tries to fix any problems that arise. It surfaces through a series of troubleshooters that try to step you through the process of fixing any issues it may have discovered. As with other Action Center functionality, these troubleshooters alert you via the Action Center pop-up window and via the main Action Center control panel. But unlike notifications in previous Windows versions, these alerts won't ever pop up while you're working and disrupt what you're doing.

Secret Some Windows Troubleshooting tasks actually run at periodic intervals in the background. Others pop up automatically when the system discovers that something went wrong. A good example of this latter case is an older application that doesn't install correctly in Windows 7; in such a case, a troubleshooting window will appear automatically and ask if you'd like help reinstalling it.

Accessing Windows Troubleshooting

To access the Windows Troubleshooting interface, load Action Center (from Start Menu Search, type **action**). As shown in Figure 25-1, there is a prominent Troubleshooting link.

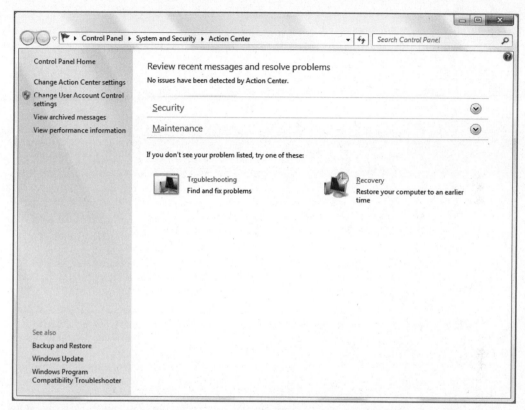

Figure 25-1: Action Center provides a handy front end to Windows 7's new Troubleshooting functionality.

When you click this link, the Windows Troubleshooting control panel appears (see Figure 25-2).

Secret

Actually, you can access Troubleshooting directly from Start Menu Search by typing **trouble**.

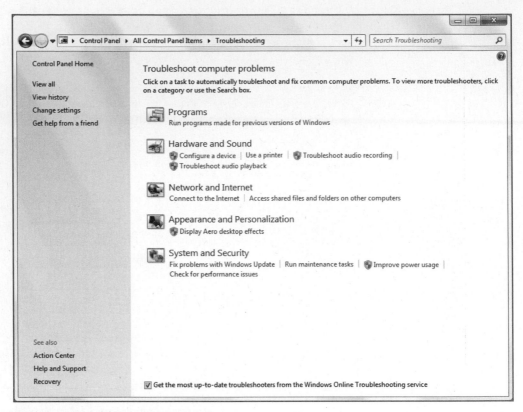

Figure 25-2: Windows Troubleshooting

Configuring Windows Troubleshooting

Before examining Windows Troubleshooting, however, it's time to make sure it's configured correctly. The first thing to look at is in the main Troubleshooting control panel. You will see a link at the bottom of the window called *Get the most up-to-date troubleshooters from the Windows Online Troubleshooting service.* Make sure this option is checked, as Microsoft periodically updates the troubleshooters and releases new troubleshooters.

Now, click the link titled Change settings in the task list on the left. The Change settings interface appears, as shown in Figure 25-3. Here, you can actually disable Windows Troubleshooting, which is not recommended. You can also control whether Windows can find troubleshooters online and whether they should pop up when you interactively run into a problem. Both of these options should be selected as well.

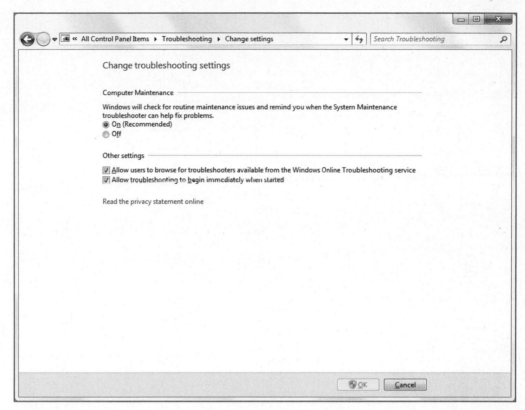

Figure 25-3: There are only a handful of Windows Troubleshooting options. Make sure they're correctly configured.

Examining the Troubleshooters

Back in the Troubleshooting control panel, you will see a list of built-in troubleshooter categories, including Programs, Hardware and Sound, Network and Internet, Appearance and Personalization, and System and Security. Windows Troubleshooting can't solve every problem you could encounter, but it does try to hit the high points. To see how a typical troubleshooter works, you can try out the Programs troubleshooter.

Troubleshooting offers two links around Programs. The first, for the Programs heading itself, will display a Troubleshoot problems – Programs window when clicked, as shown in Figure 25-4. This interface provides links to all of the troubleshooters in the Programs category.

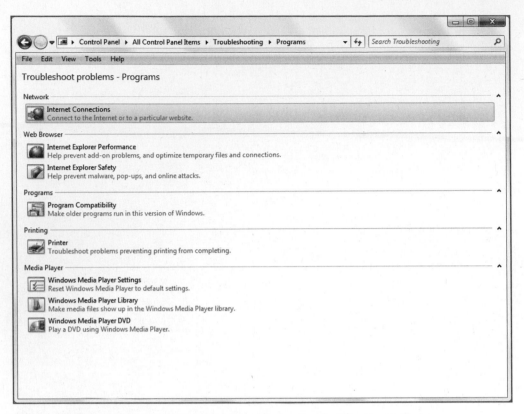

Figure 25-4: Windows 7 includes several troubleshooters just for programs.

Note that not all of the troubleshooters are designed to find or fix issues. Some simply provide you with a way to return an application to its default state. For example, you can troubleshoot issues with media files not appearing in Windows Media Player, which is a pretty obvious issue, but there's also a troubleshooter that returns Windows Media Player to its default settings.

When you click on a specific troubleshooter, a troubleshooter window like the one in Figure 25-5 appears. These troubleshooters are essentially wizard-based applications that step you through the process of fixing a specific problem.

When you click Next, the wizard tries to figure out what has gone wrong. Next, you'll either see a recommendation or a firm message, like that one in Figure 25-6, that explains the issue.

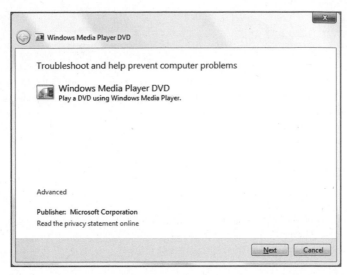

Figure 25-5: We're trying to figure out why DVDs won't play on this PC.

Figure 25-6: Ah, that actually does make sense.

If you do solve the problem, you're told to close the troubleshooter or explore additional options. This brings up the Additional Information view (see Figure 25-7), which provides access to other troubleshooting resources, including Help and Support, Windows Communities (online newsgroups that are populated with snobby Microsoft sycophants and should thus be avoided), and a link to find related troubleshooters. There are also links for Remote Assistance (which debuted back in Windows XP), the new Recovery tools (which we discuss later in this chapter), and online support.

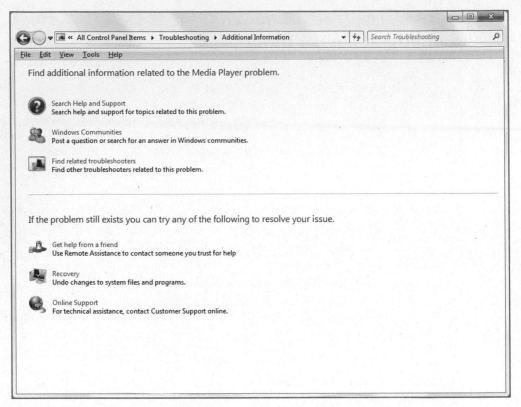

Figure 25-7: Additional Information provides you with other avenues for support.

The Find related troubleshooters link is particularly interesting because it actually searches the available troubleshooters for any that may in fact be related to the issue you just tried to fix. As shown in Figure 25-8, it actually does a pretty good job of finding related issues.

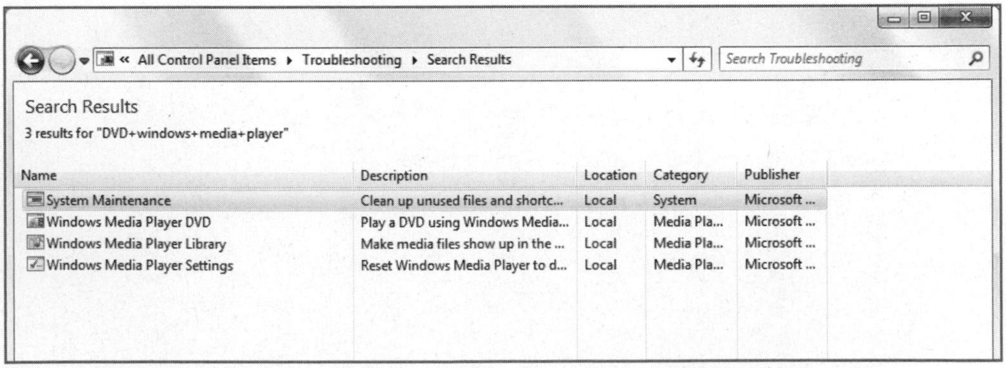

Figure 25-8: Didn't find exactly what you wanted? Troubleshooting tries to help.

Real-World Troubleshooting: What Happens When Something Goes Wrong

Proactively browsing around the available troubleshooters can certainly be instructive, but face it, you're probably not going to spend too much time in there unless something really does go wrong. So what does Windows do in a time of crisis?

To test this, consider what happens when you install Windows 7 for the first time. During Setup, Windows 7 installs as many drivers as it can in a bid to give you a fully working system. But the first thing that happens when you boot into your new desktop is that Windows Update starts and then begins downloading updates. And more often than not, it finds a number of additional drivers that are needed to complete your install. Once you get those installed, you should be all set.

But sometimes you're not. For whatever reason, some PCs simply include a number of devices, often low-level chipset-type devices, that refuse an easy driver fix. These issues often don't result in any perceptible usability issues, and you'd have to manually load Device Manager to even notice that a device or two is unaccounted for. But even if you don't do this, Windows knows. And in the background, periodically, the Windows Troubleshooting platform will fire up, examine the issue, and try to find a fix.

When Troubleshooting does find a fix, it alerts you via the Action Center notification icon, as we discussed previously. Click this icon once and, as you can see in Figure 25-9, it could eventually recommend that you solve a problem, in this case for a chipset driver that never properly installed.

Figure 25-9: Eureka! Windows 7 has solved a problem.

Click the message window and Action Center will load the message details, as shown in Figure 25-10. Here, it recommends downloading a driver directly from the manufacturer, extracting it, and then installing it.

When you click the various links on this Message Details window, the text will expand to provide more information. Under the first link, *Download the driver installation file*, you will discover a direct link to download the correct driver. The second link provides instructions for extracting the ZIP file that contains the driver. The third link provides a roundabout explanation for why Windows 7 was unable to find this driver automatically: it's actually for an older version of Windows. And the troubleshooter provides information on running the driver setup routine in compatibility mode in order to ensure it works properly, as shown in Figure 25-11.

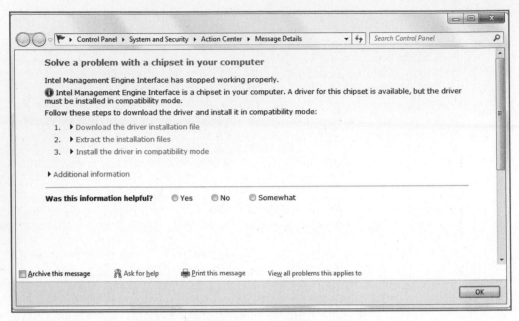

Figure 25-10: Here's what you need to do to make things right.

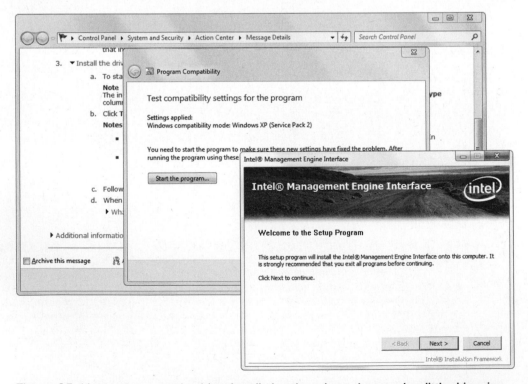

Figure 25-11: In order to get the driver installed, we're going to have to do a little shimming.

Once this process is complete, you can return to Device Manager to ensure that the previous missing driver is now accounted for. Then the Action Center message window should quickly return to its default state, as shown in Figure 25-12. Mission accomplished.

Figure 25-12: And we're done.

While Microsoft provides a number of built-in troubleshooters in Windows 7, it has also created a platform to which others can add their own Troubleshooter Packs to Windows 7 as well, dramatically expanding the capabilities of the OS. PC makers will likely include a number of PC-specific troubleshooters with their own machines, of course, but any developer can create a Troubleshooter Pack. To learn how, visit Rafael's Within Windows Web site: www.withinwindows.com/2009/01/12/crash-course-on-authoring-windows-7-troubleshooting-packs.

Microsoft's troubleshooting efforts extend far beyond Windows. The company is now adding automated "Fix It" tools available on the Web via its Help and Support Web site, instead of just allowing users to search for answers to problems and then read about how to solve them themselves. To see this in action, check out the Microsoft Fix It Solution Center at support.microsoft.com/fixit.

Getting Help with the Problem Steps Recorder

Windows Troubleshooting works well, but sometimes you will run into an issue that isn't covered by the built-in troubleshooters. When that happens, it's time to escalate the issue, either with Microsoft Support or, if you're a corporate customer, with your IT help desk. Either way, Windows 7 includes an excellent new tool that takes the guesswork out of explaining what happened when something went wrong. It's called the *Problem Steps Recorder*, and it enables you to record the steps you took leading up to a problem so you can duplicate it and provide a record of what happened.

Secret

Problem Steps Recorder is hidden in Windows 7, so you have to know it exists before you can access it. To enable this tool, open the Start menu and type **problem steps** in Start Menu Search. You'll see an item called *Record steps to reproduce a problem* in the search results. Click that, and the minimalistic Problem Steps Recorder application, shown in Figure 25-13, appears.

Figure 25-13: Problem Steps Recorder is hidden in the Windows 7 UI and pretty subtle when it's running, too.

Here's how it works. Click the Start Record button in Problem Steps Recorder. When you do, the application interface changes slightly, to indicate that it's recording and provide a few additional options, including Pause Record, Stop Record, and Add Comment (see Figure 25-14).

Figure 25-14: You're on candid camera: duplicate that bug.

Now you step through the things you did that caused the issue you're trying to report. Along the way, as you click on things, you'll see an orange circle appear below the mouse pointer, indicating that Problem Steps Recorder has taken note of that step. If you get to a particularly important part, you can take a manual screenshot and provide a note: just click Add Comment and you'll see something like Figure 25-15.

Figure 25-15: Take a picture and leave a note if you want to explain something further.

When you're done, click Stop Record. Problem Steps Recorder will prompt you to save a ZIP file on your desktop. Give it a name and click Save. At this point, you're supposed to e-mail this to the entity that's going to provide the help. But take a look inside that ZIP file to see what's going on.

Inside the ZIP file, surprisingly, you'll find a single MHTML document, which can be viewed with Internet Explorer. The file, an example of which is shown in Figure 25-16, is actually pretty impressive. It includes a complete walk-through of all the steps you took.

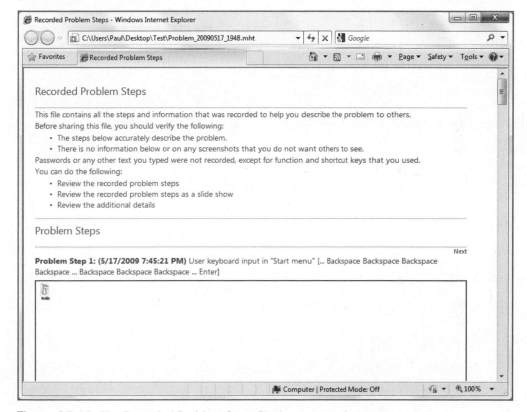

Figure 25-16: The Recorded Problem Steps file documents what went wrong.

But it's even more impressive than that. Each time you clicked anything, the Problem Steps Recorder took a screenshot and highlighted what was clicked. As you can see in Figure 25-17, this can be very specific.

Problem Steps Recorder is so helpful, in fact, that it's not hard to imagine using it as a training tool or for other kinds of documentation. Hmm. . .

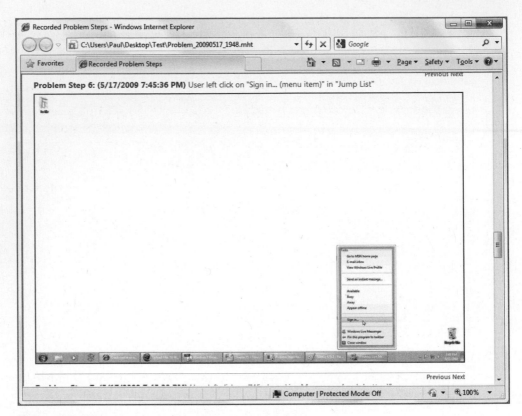

Figure 25-17: Each mouse click triggers a screenshot.

Using the Windows Recovery Environment

Windows Vista included a useful Windows Recovery Environment (Windows RE) that would provide you with a selection of tools for fixing a non-booting PC, accessing System Repair, and the like. There was just one problem: it wasn't installed on the PC hard drive by default, so you had to know to install it or be sure to carry around a copy of the Windows Vista Setup disc with you just in case. (You can also access the Windows RE from the Windows Setup disc.)

In Windows 7, Microsoft turns it up to 11 by preinstalling Windows RE right on the PC's system disk. So anytime there's a problem, you can optionally boot into this environment to fix things.

To access the Windows 7 Recovery Environment, reboot your PC and after the BIOS has completed its thing, press and hold the F8 key. (You must do this before the "Starting Windows" animation appears.) You will see the screen displayed in Figure 25-18.

```
                         Advanced Boot Options

Choose Advanced Options for: Windows 7
(Use the arrow keys to highlight your choice.)

    Repair Your Computer

      Safe Mode
      Safe Mode with Networking
      Safe Mode with Command Prompt

      Enable Boot Logging
      Enable low-resolution video (640x480)
      Last Known Good Configuration (advanced)
      Directory Services Restore Mode
      Debugging Mode
      Disable automatic restart on system failure
      Disable Driver Signature Enforcement

      Start Windows Normally

Description: View a list of system recovery tools you can use to repair
            startup problems, run diagnostics, or restore your system.

ENTER=Choose                                              ESC=Cancel
```

Figure 25-18: Starting the Windows Recovery Environment

Secret

In case it's not obvious, you may occasionally still need to access the Windows RE from the Windows 7 Setup disc. That's because the PC may literally get into a state where even the Recovery Environment can't boot from the hard drive. It's rare but it happens.

Looking at the Repair Tools

You can choose from a variety of system troubleshooting options here, but the first, and selected, option, Repair Your Computer, will get the job done. Select this. After a few "loading" screens (including, curiously, a screen displaying the progress bar that appeared when Windows Vista booted), you are asked to select a keyboard input method (this typically has the correct option pre-selected) and then you are asked to log on with a valid administrator-class account.

Once this is completed, you are presented with the System Recovery Options screen shown in Figure 25-19.

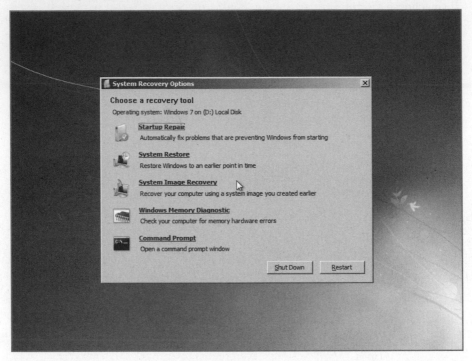

Figure 25-19: The System Recovery Options window provides access to several repair and recovery tools.

From here, you can access the following options.

◆ **Startup Repair:** This tool can help you automatically repair problems that prevent Windows from booting correctly. We examine this tool in the next section.

◆ **System Restore:** This provides a way to access System Restore from outside of Windows. We discuss System Restore later in this chapter.

◆ **System Image Recovery:** This helps you use a previously saved system image to completely reinstall the PC and return it to an earlier state. We discuss Windows 7's system image backup and recovery features in Chapter 24.

◆ **Windows Memory Diagnostic:** This link triggers a reboot so that a special memory diagnostic program can run as the PC boots. This tool is useful if you're worried that some sporadic stability problems may be caused by memory issues.

◆ **Command Prompt.** Advanced users and system administrators can access a standard Windows command prompt to run command-line programs on the PC's hard drive.

Using Startup Repair to Fix a Non-Booting PC

If you choose the option titled Startup Repair, the Startup Repair utility will open and scan your PC for boot-related issues (see Figure 25-20). If it finds any, it fixes them automatically. If not, it simply provides a message to that effect.

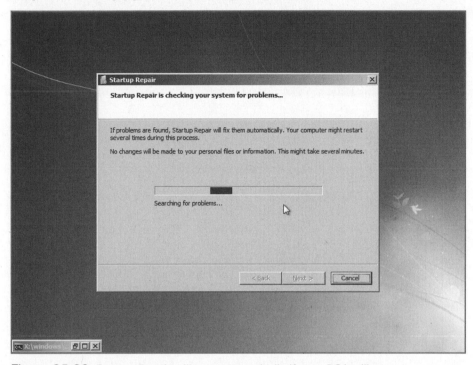

Figure 25-20: Startup Repair will run automatically if your PC is ailing.

And…that's it. That's literally all it does.

Secret

We accessed the Startup Repair tool manually here in order to explain its user interface and functionality, but you won't typically need to do this: if your PC doesn't boot properly for some reason, Startup Repair will run automatically and fix the problem and then boot right into Windows 7. And if you happen to walk away from the computer at that time, you may not even realize it happened.

Using System Restore to Repair Windows

System Restore debuted back in Windows Millennium Edition (Me, which we're all still trying to forget) and it has proven itself to be a life saver over the years. This feature carries forward in slightly improved form in Windows 7. System Restore automatically backs up key system files at opportune times, such as when you're installing a new hardware driver. (Otherwise, an automatic restore occurs once every 24 hours.) That way, if a driver or application wreaks havoc with your PC, you can use System Restore to reload older system file versions and get back up and running again. Microsoft describes this behavior as "restoring Windows to any earlier point in time," but we're pretty sure no actual time travel is involved.

Secret System Restore is the underlying technology that makes Previous Versions, discussed in Chapter 24, possible. Each time System Restore is run, it creates a previous version of files that have changed since the last backup or system restore operation.

System Restore has the following two main interface points:

◆ **System protection:** This is located in the System Properties window, which can be found by opening the Start menu, right-clicking Computer, choosing Properties, clicking Advanced system, and then clicking System protection in the tasks list.

As shown in Figure 25-21, this interface enables you to configure which disks or partitions you will automatically protect (typically only the system volume, which is usually drive C:). You can also manually create a system restore point by clicking the Create button. You need to supply a name for the restore point.

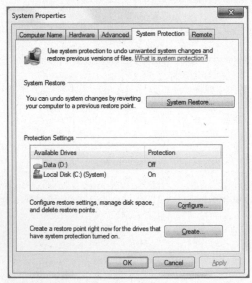

Figure 25-21: From System Protection, you can configure System Restore.

◆ **System Restore wizard:** This wizard restores your PC's key system files to a previous point in time. To launch this wizard, open the Start menu and navigate to All Programs Accessories ⇨ System Tools ⇨ System Restore. (Or just type **system restore** in Start Menu Search.)

In the introductory page of the wizard, shown in Figure 25-22, select *Choose a different restore point* and then click Next to choose a restore point.

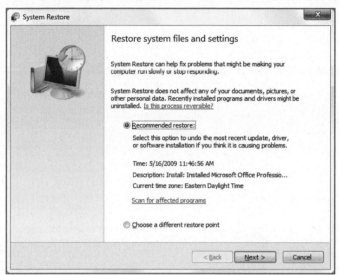

Figure 25-22: Automatic or manual? With System Restore, the choice is yours.

As shown in Figure 25-23, you will now see a list of restore points. Most of these were automatically created by the system and will include a description of what was going on when each restore point was created. If you manually created your own restore points from System Protection, those restore points will have "Manual:" appended to the front of the restore point name.

When you select a restore point, Windows will move into the secure desktop and begin restoring your system to its previous state. This requires the PC to reboot. Note that any applications you have installed since that restore point will almost certainly need to be reinstalled.

You can also access System Restore from the Windows Recovery Environment discussed earlier in the chapter. This is useful when an install has made Windows particularly unstable. As shown in Figure 25-24, accessing System Restore from this environment is similar to doing so from within Windows.

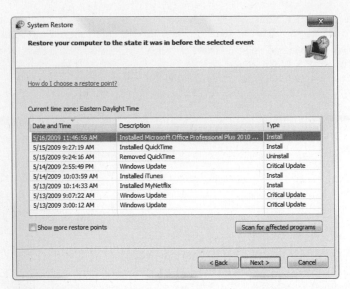

Figure 25-23: Here, you can choose the restore point you'd like to use.

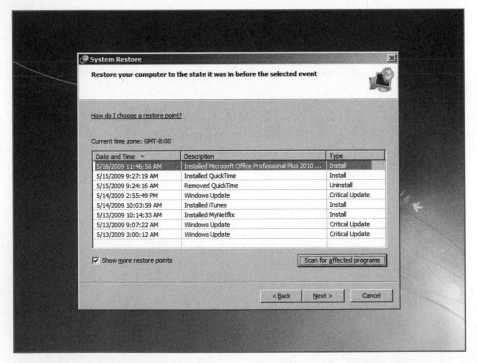

Figure 25-24: System Restore can also be accessed from the Windows Recovery Environment.

Summary

While Windows 7 is more stable and reliable than previous versions of Windows, Microsoft also went the extra mile by ensuring that this latest OS was also imbued with a complete set of troubleshooting and recovery tools. These take the form of the new Windows Troubleshooting infrastructure and its many useful troubleshooters, the Problem Steps Recorder, the Windows Recovery Environment and Startup Repair tools, and of course an updated version of System Restore. Whatever goes wrong in Windows 7, Microsoft can make it right.

IT Pro: Windows 7 at Work

♦ ♦

In This Chapter

Understanding Windows 7's most interesting enterprise features

Understanding which Windows 7 business features are useful on a standalone PC

Using BitLocker and BitLocker To Go to protect hard drives and removable storage devices

Mounting virtual hard disks with Disk Management

Getting started with Windows PowerShell 2.0

♦ ♦

While this book focuses exclusively on you, the end user, the truth is that Windows 7 is a slave to many masters and must serve the needs of hundreds of millions of users, each one of which has different needs and wants. That said, one might easily break down the end user features and functionality in Windows 7 into three core groups: those that serve consumers, those that serve businesses, and those that serve both. That latter category is easily defined. It includes such things as Windows 7's pervasive security features, Tablet PCs, productivity enhancements in the Aero user experience, and networking.

Consumer features, such as Windows Media Player, Media Center, and gaming, are also easily defined and identified. And so it is, too, with Windows 7's business-oriented features. You don't have to understand what features like AppLocker, BranchCache, and PowerShell 2.0 do in order to recognize that they're probably not going to be of interest to your grandmother. But they play a critical role in defining what Windows 7 is, and thus what benefits it offers to different segments of the market.

In this chapter, we look at the most important business-oriented features in Windows 7. But even for the purposes of this discussion, we'll need to break down those features into two broad groups. There are the features aimed at enterprises, those companies that have highly managed network environments, typically controlled by Microsoft's Windows Server-based Active Directory infrastructure; and then there are those business features that can, in many cases, apply to all Windows 7 users, including those who are simply individuals with a single Windows 7 PC. In the case of the former features, we present a high-level overview so that you can at least become conversational in what is possible when Windows 7 is introduced into a managed workplace, and perhaps influence buying and migration decisions down the road.

In the case of those business features that can and often should be implemented at an individual level, we will of course dive a bit deeper and explain how they work in the real world. Ultimately, the goal of this book is to turn Windows 7 users into Windows 7 power users, and we can't think of a better way to leave you than with a discussion of the ultimate power user tools that are available in Windows 7.

Windows 7 for the Enterprise

In the mid-1990s, Paul attended a Microsoft presentation in which a crowded auditorium was stepped through the company's business software of the day. The talk began on a high note, with a discussion of the then-current version of Microsoft Office, which was already killing off competition from Lotus, WordPerfect, and others. After that, the talk turned to something called Microsoft BackOffice, which was an attempt by the software giant to duplicate its desktop success with Office but in the server marketplace. BackOffice consisted of Windows NT Server, SQL Server 4.x (then still based on code created by a company called Sybase), Mail Server 3.x (an unpopular predecessor to today's hugely popular Exchange Server), and...well, some other stuff. He's not entirely sure what else the company discussed that day because he fell asleep.

Since that time, Microsoft's server products have gotten a lot more interesting and, perhaps more important, a lot more capable. (Paul's attention span, alas, is a topic for another day.) From its lowly beginnings as a workgroup server, Windows NT Server has evolved over the years into Windows Server, and that product line alone has exploded into a huge variety of standalone and pre-packed server types that serve virtually every market imaginable. The latest version of Windows Server, called Windows Server 2008 R2, shipped concurrently with Windows 7 in 2009.

The R2 in Windows Server 2008 R2 stands for "Release 2," and as that name suggests, it is indeed the second iteration of the original Windows Server 2008. But R2 didn't just ship concurrently with Windows 7. It was also developed concurrently, marking this product tandem as the first time since Windows 2000 that Microsoft co-developed client and server versions of Windows. This isn't marketing drivel, either. Windows 7 and Windows Server 2008 R2 are really the same product, and share the same code. The difference between the two is that Windows 7 is optimized for running end user applications and comes bundled with solutions that will be of interest to individuals. Server 2008 R2, meanwhile, is optimized for running background services and server applications, and can scale, or grow, to meet the needs of even the biggest corporations in the world. Windows everywhere, indeed.

As Windows Server evolved, Microsoft naturally worked to ensure that it integrated well with its client, or desktop, versions of Windows. So when the Active Directory (AD) directory services technology was added in Windows 2000 Server, Microsoft made sure that Windows 2000 Professional (the desktop version of Windows 2000) was the ultimate AD client. And as you move forward through subsequent versions of both Windows Server and Windows, you can see that all of the business-oriented features in either work best or work exclusively with the other. Every time a set of features is added to Windows, for example, Microsoft updates the capabilities of its Windows Server Group Policy technologies to ensure that system administrators can manage those features from a central location. Put simply, Windows and Windows Server are a team.

Looking at Windows 7 and Windows Server 2008 R2 specifically, some trends emerge, and it's not hard to see that Microsoft is responding to the needs of an ever-evolving market. The workplace has changed a lot since the day Paul feel asleep in that dark auditorium. (And really, why *did* they dim the lights?) Workers often expect to work from home. Or they travel and need instant access to their corporate data, no matter where they are (and, increasingly, not just from PCs, but also from smart phones). Thanks to corporate acquisition and consolidation, employees work in off-site offices that need to be managed remotely because there's little or no on-site IT staff. Security is always an issue—only the details and scope of that challenge have changed over the years—and of course Microsoft has made significant gains in easing the deployment of its technologies over the years.

Generally speaking, Windows 7 does *not* require Windows Server 2008 R2 on the server. It will work fine with Windows Server 2003, Windows Server 2003 R2, and the original version of Windows Server 2008. That is, you can connect to any AD-based domain, and you can access many Group Policy features and the like, regardless of which version of Windows Server is utilized. However, some enterprise-oriented Windows 7 features *do* require Windows Server 2008 R2 on the back end. Most (but not all) of the features mentioned in this section assume Windows 7 on the client and Windows Server 2008 R2 on the server. We'll specify when that's not the case.

Okay, it's time to take a look at some of those features that speak to the deep integration of Windows 7 and Windows Server 2008 R2 in the enterprise.

Search Federation and Enterprise Search Scopes

Windows Search on the desktop was arguably detuned a bit beginning with Windows Vista Service Pack 1 (SP1) and then, subsequently, in Windows 7 as well, thanks to antitrust concerns in the U.S. and elsewhere. But the underlying technology remains in Windows 7 and of course has even been enhanced somewhat.

Secret   That said, you can no longer access Windows Search directly from the Start menu as you could in Windows previous to Vista with SP1. Therefore, you need to access an Explorer-based search box or know to use the F3 keyboard shortcut to display the Windows Search window.

In standalone (non-managed) versions of Windows 7, Windows Search is said to be *scoped* to the local PC. That is, you can search the current folder or Library using Explorer's integrated search box, and if you'd like to search other locations instead, you can use the *Search again in* links at the bottom of the search results to rescope the search to other locations, including your libraries, homegroup, computer, or even the Internet. And by using the Custom link, you can really fine-tune the search to any location in your environment, including network shares, though of course that can be quite inefficient (and thus slow) because those locations may not be indexed.

With Windows 7 and Windows Server 2008 R2, enterprises can dictate that Windows Search is scoped to include enterprise data repositories, such as SharePoint sites, Exchange-based e-mail servers, server-based file shares, and encrypted files. In this way, the search results one receives in a managed environment can include federated results that include multiple locations around the corporate network. This doesn't require a third party or an additional application; instead, users simply continue using the familiar Windows Search. Enterprises can also configure up to five custom search scopes that appear at the bottom of search results so that users can directly access specific data repositories to fine-tune their searches.

VPN Reconnect and DirectAccess

Today, corporate users typically utilize a technology called virtual private network (VPN) to remotely access private business networks across the Internet. VPNs are notable for two reasons:

♦ They provide a secure "tunnel" through which information can be sent between a user's PC outside the network and the servers and other computers that sit behind the corporate firewall.

♦ They are miserable to configure, use, and keep running. For this reason, Windows 7 and Windows Server 2008 include two technologies that take the sting out of using VPNs.

The first, VPN Reconnect, addresses one of the most annoying aspects of using a VPN. That is, you've gone through the rigmarole of buying, installing, and correctly configuring a VPN on your laptop and then you connect to the corporate network from a remote location to get some work done. Then, suddenly, the connection is lost. Maybe the underlying Wi-Fi or broadband wireless connection tripped up for a second. Heck, maybe a butterfly landed on the windowsill. Who knows? Whatever the reason, VPN users frequently find themselves having to reconnect their VPN connections, an annoying and time-consuming process. Thanks to VPN Reconnect, Windows 7 will automatically reestablish a VPN connection anytime you temporarily lose and then regain an Internet connection. The user doesn't have to worry about it all.

Secret VPN Reconnect does not rely on a specific server technology, so it's just a feature of Windows 7. That is, it does not require your servers to be running Windows Server 2008 R2.

If you're ready to give up VPNs all together and have invested in Windows Server 2008 R2 on the server, Microsoft has a better solution for secure tunneled connections between remote clients and the corporate environment. It's called DirectAccess, and it's based on the proven HTTPS (secure HTTP) tunneling technology Microsoft first used with Exchange Server. With DirectAccess, there's no VPN configuring, connecting, and reconnecting. In fact, there's no VPN at all. Instead, DirectAccess-enabled PCs are simply always connected, securely, to the corporate network. As long as you have an Internet connection, you're in. And for the end user, there's nothing to see or configure. You're simply connected.

On the administrative side, IT pros and admins can configure which corporate resources are available to which users, and they can direct Internet-based network traffic as they see fit.

BranchCache

With more and more corporate mergers and acquisitions, and larger companies maintaining separate physical offices in different locales, an IT management issue arises: How does a company centrally manage computing resources when some of their users are in remote, or branch, offices and those offices have little, if anything, in the way of IT pros or administrators?

BranchCache is one attempt to mitigate this problem. When enabled, network (SMB, HTTP, and HTTPS) traffic downloaded by users in the branch office is cached on a branch server or branch PCs. (It can be configured either way.) That way, various types of frequently needed content is cached locally to the branch, freeing up network traffic for better performance. The next time a user in the branch office needs to download a file on the corporate network over a slow WAN connection, Windows 7 will check to ensure that no changes were made since the cached copy was downloaded. If there haven't been changes, the user is given the cached copy, saving time and network bandwidth.

BranchCache requires both Windows 7 on the client and Windows Server 2008 R2 on the server.

Microsoft Desktop Optimization Pack

Microsoft offers a unique set of tools only to companies that take part in the software giant's Software Assurance (SA) volume licensing program. Dubbed the Microsoft Desktop Optimization Pack, or MDOP, this suite of desktop management tools is a must-have collection of valuable utilities—many of which originated as start-ups and were since purchased by Microsoft—and it is an obvious and tangible benefit of Microsoft's subscription-based enterprise licensing programs. If your company is in SA and not taking advantage of MDOP, this should serve as a wake-up call. These tools are excellent, and some are simply awesome.

MDOP is compatible with Windows 7, Vista, and XP-based clients, though certain features are available only in Windows 7 and Vista. In its current incarnation, MDOP 2009, it offers six essential capabilities.

- ◆ PC recovery features
- ◆ Application virtualization
- ◆ Enterprise desktop virtualization
- ◆ Asset inventory
- ◆ Centralized crash and error management
- ◆ Advanced policy-based management

PC Recovery Features

Although Windows 7 does include an excellent Windows Recovery Environment (WinRE) for OS recovery (which we discuss in Chapter 25), MDOP extends this capability with the Microsoft Diagnostics and Recovery Toolset (DaRT), a comprehensive set of recovery tools that includes superior tools such as ERD Commander, Disk Wipe, Hotfix Uninstall, and many others (see Figure 26-1). The latest version of DaRT also includes a standalone system sweeper utility that enables you to detect and remove malware (including rootkits) from a system while it's offline.

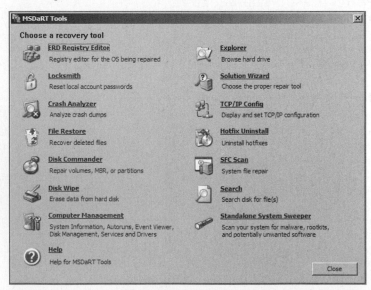

Figure 26-1: The recovery environment in MDOP offers a lot more functionality than the one that's built into Windows 7.

Application Virtualization

Thanks to Microsoft's Application Virtualization (App-V) technologies, MDOP licensees can stream or install individual virtualized application packages, instead of requiring desktop users to access applications via a single virtualized environment. The primary advantage of this scheme is compatibility: you can do such things as install multiple versions of applications, each virtualized and packaged individually with its own specific set of DLLs and prerequisite files.

Enterprise Desktop Virtualization

The most recent addition to MDOP is Microsoft Enterprise Desktop Virtualization (MED-V). This software provides an infrastructure for deploying and managing virtualized applications, using Virtual PC–based technologies, on desktop PCs. You can think of MED-V as the managed server version of XP Mode, which is described later in this chapter.

Asset Inventory

The Asset Inventory Service is delivered as a hosted service with client-installed agents that report to Microsoft servers in the Internet cloud. This has the advantage of not requiring environments to create their own asset management infrastructure, which can help you determine whether you're in compliance with your software licensing.

Centralized Crash and Error Management

Using the Microsoft System Center Desktop Error Monitoring tool, you can redirect crash and error reporting to your own servers and utilize Microsoft's knowledge-resolution database: if Microsoft knows the cause of the problem, it will point you to the appropriate Knowledge Base (KB) article for resolution. You can also optionally choose to continue passing crash and error data along to Microsoft so that it can continue its public reliability improvement efforts.

Advanced Policy-Based Management

Microsoft has added a change control system to Group Policy so that policy changes can be tested in an offline environment before being deployed and can be rolled back more easily. It also includes a more granular level of delegation with different roles, such as admin, editor, reviewer, and so on.

AppLocker

In Windows XP and Windows Server 2003, Microsoft introduced a technology called Software Restriction Policies (SRP) that helped administrators in managed environments specify which end user applications could and could not be installed and run. The goal of such a technology is fairly obvious: for security and productivity reasons, admins want to restrict which applications their users can access, even though such controls may sometimes seem Draconian to users.

With Windows 7 and Windows Server 2008 R2, Microsoft is introducing AppLocker, an updated version of SRP. AppLocker is more flexible and malleable than SRP but offers the same basic functionality: it uses Group Policy–based rules to determine which applications users can access. But it goes deeper than SRP by introducing the concept of *publisher rules*, whereby admins can specify that certain application versions are allowed or disallowed.

For example, say there's a known vulnerability in an out-of-date version of Adobe Reader, the popular PDF viewer utility. With AppLocker, you could specify that users are allowed to install and use only Adobe Reader 8.2 (or whatever) or newer. Problem solved: users retain the ability to view PDFs while you, the administrator, don't need to worry that they're doing so with obsolete and potentially dangerous versions of the software.

Business Features (Almost) Anyone Can Use

There are, of course, many more enterprise-oriented features in Windows 7 (and Windows Server 2008 R2), but we think it makes sense to dedicate more space and time to those business-oriented features that (almost) anyone can use. Just because a feature is designed for a specific scenario or customer type doesn't mean that it can't or shouldn't be taken advantage of in other situations. In fact, we'd argue that the true essence of being a Windows power user involves understanding which of those stuffy and otherwise uninteresting business-oriented features are, in fact, useful to you. Here are our picks of the litter.

BitLocker

In Windows XP and previous NT-based versions of Windows, Microsoft offered a feature called Encrypting File System (EFS) that enabled users to encrypt important folders or files. This prevents thieves from accessing sensitive data should your computer be physically stolen: if the thief removes your hard drive and attaches it to a different computer, any encrypted files cannot be read, even if the thief figures out a way to access the hard drive's file system. EFS has proven to be a popular feature with IT administrators, the security-conscious, and roaming executives with laptops.

---

tip NT-based versions of Windows include Windows NT 3.x and 4, Windows 2000, Windows XP, Windows Server 2003, Windows Vista, Windows 7, Windows Server 2008, and Windows Server 2008 R2. Older versions of Windows, such as Windows 95, 98, and Millennium Edition (Me), were based on less sophisticated and less secure DOS code.

EFS is still present in Windows 7 and works as before, but it's been augmented by a new technology called BitLocker.

Secret While Windows 7 does support per-folder encryption with EFS, as with BitLocker and BitLocker To Go (see below), this feature is limited to Windows 7 Enterprise and Ultimate.

Like EFS, BitLocker enables you to encrypt data on your hard drive to protect it in the event of physical theft. But BitLocker offers a few unique twists:

- ◆ BitLocker is full-disk encryption, not per-file encryption. If you enable BitLocker, it encrypts the entire hard disk on which Windows 7 resides, and all future files added to that drive are silently encrypted as well.
- ◆ BitLocker can also provide full-disk encryption services to nonsystem partitions as well, so in addition to encrypting the entire hard disk on which Windows 7 is installed, you can now optionally encrypt any other partitions.
- ◆ BitLocker protects vital Windows system files during boot-up: if BitLocker discovers a security risk, such as a change to the BIOS or any startup files (which might indicate that the hard drive was stolen and placed in a different machine), it will lock the system until you enter your BitLocker recovery key or password (discussed shortly).
- ◆ BitLocker works in conjunction with new Trusted Platform Module (TPM) security hardware in some modern PCs to provide a more secure solution than is possible with a software-only encryption routine. BitLocker may not be theoretically impregnable, but in most real-world scenarios, no hacker will defeat a BitLocker-protected PC.

There isn't a heck of a lot to configure for BitLocker. It's either on or it's not, and you either have TPM hardware or you don't: if your system does have TPM hardware, BitLocker will use it. Otherwise, you must use a USB memory drive as a startup key. This key is physically required to boot the system. If you don't have the key, or you lose it, you will need to enter a recovery password to access the drive instead. Here's where things get tricky: you can print out the recovery password and store it in a safe place, such as a physical safe or safety deposit box, or you can store it on a different computer in a text file, perhaps in an encrypted folder or encrypting ZIP file. However you store the recovery password, you can't lose it. If you lose both the startup key (either in the TPM hardware or on a USB memory key) and the recovery password, then the data on the BitLocker-protected hard drive is gone forever. There is literally no other recovery option available. Microsoft Support can't help you.

Still undaunted? You enable BitLocker by launching the BitLocker Drive Encryption control panel (as always, Start Menu Search is your friend). Shown in Figure 26-2, BitLocker is straightforward. To enable it, simply click the Turn On BitLocker option.

Secret   When BitLocker debuted in Windows Vista, you had to have previously partitioned your hard disk correctly in order to accommodate the feature. That's no longer true with Windows 7. Here's why: When you install Windows 7, the Setup routine actually creates a secret and hidden 100MB partition at the root of the system drive. This hidden partition is big enough for Windows 7's recovery tools and, yes, BitLocker.

If you have the appropriate TPM hardware, BitLocker will save its encryption and decryption keys in that hardware. Otherwise, you are prompted to insert a USB memory key, which you'll need to insert in the machine every time it boots up. Optionally, you can also create a startup key or PIN to provide an additional layer of protection. The PIN is any number from 4 to 20 digits. The startup key and PIN can be enabled only the first time you enable BitLocker.

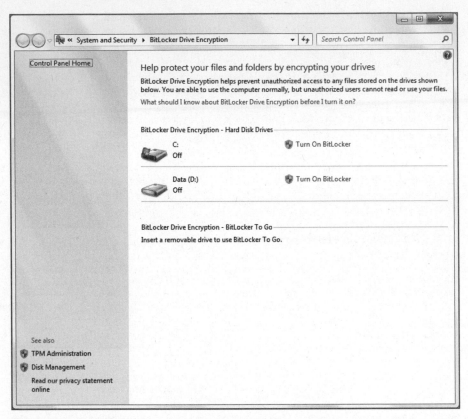

Figure 26-2: BitLocker is an exceedingly easy feature: it's either on or off.

When BitLocker is enabled—a process that takes quite a bit of time, incidentally, because it must encrypt the contents of the drive—you don't have to do much in terms of configuration. You'll see a new Manage Keys link in the BitLocker Drive Encryption control panel, and you can create a recovery password from there. If you choose to print the password, be sure to save it in a safe place. Seriously.

BitLocker To Go

Also new in Windows 7, the BitLocker technologies have been extended with the capability to protect removable storage devices, such as USB-based hard drives, flash devices, and other media. This functionality is called BitLocker To Go, and while the technology is aimed squarely at enterprises, it's quite useful for almost any Windows 7 user.

Secret

BitLocker To Go is available only in Windows 7 Enterprise and Ultimate, which severely limits its availability. But this limitation refers only to the ability to *enable* protection on a removable storage device. Once BitLocker To Go is added to a storage device, that device can be used normally with *any* version of Windows 7. It can also be used in read-only mode in Windows XP and Vista, using a BitLocker Reader application that is silently added to all devices protected by BitLocker To Go.

Put simply, BitLocker To Go is a full-disk encryption protection technology for removable storage devices. Though it is ostensibly based on BitLocker, in reality BitLocker To Go significantly enhances the usability and compatibility of BitLocker by extending it to work with all FAT (FAT32, exFAT, etc.) file systems in addition to NTFS.

BitLocker To Go is designed primarily for enterprises, where there is serious risk of a user bringing an unprotected storage device into the environment, copying important corporate information (inadvertently or not) to it, and then losing the device outside of the workplace. USB memory keys, in particular, are small and convenient, and quite popular, but they're also easily lost. With BitLocker To Go enabled on the device, one can help protect sensitive corporate—or, for that matter, personal—data in the event of loss or theft.

BitLocker To Go works completely independently of BitLocker, so you do not need to enable BitLocker on the PC, or utilize any TPM hardware, in order to use BitLocker To Go. In use, however, it is similar to BitLocker, and can be enabled via a simple right-click menu option.

Installing BitLocker To Go

To enable BitLocker To Go, simply plug in the removable storage device, open Computer, right-click the device, and choose Turn on BitLocker from the pop-up menu that appears, as shown in Figure 26-3.

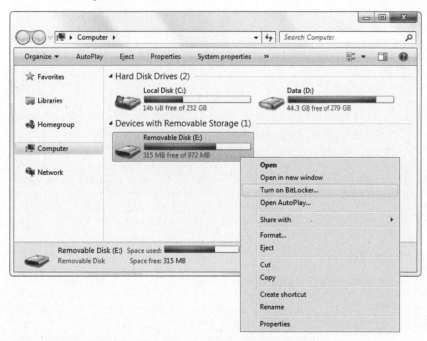

Figure 26-3: Enabling BitLocker To Go couldn't be easier.

Alternatively, you can manually run the BitLocker Drive Encryption control panel (**bitl** in Start Menu Search) to view the status of BitLocker and BitLocker To Go on your various attached drives. From this interface, shown in Figure 26-4, simply click the Turn on BitLocker link next to the appropriate drive.

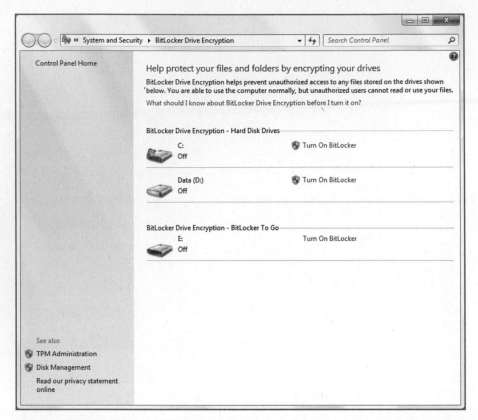

Figure 26-4: The BitLocker Drive Encryption control panel can manage both BitLocker and BitLocker To Go.

Either way, the BitLocker Drive Encryption wizard will start up in a separate window (see Figure 26-5). After a short wait, you'll be asked to choose between password- and smartcard-based locking. Most individuals will need to use a password, but many larger businesses are starting to use smartcards, which allow administrators to centrally manage BitLocker certificates in AD.

In the next step of the wizard, you are asked how you would like to store your recovery key (assuming this hasn't been already configured in a managed AD environment). This key will help you recover the contents of a protected drive should you forget your password, lose your smartcard, or suffer some similar problem. You have two options: save (to a text file) or print. If you do choose to print or save the recovery key, you'll see something like the screen shown in Figure 26-6.

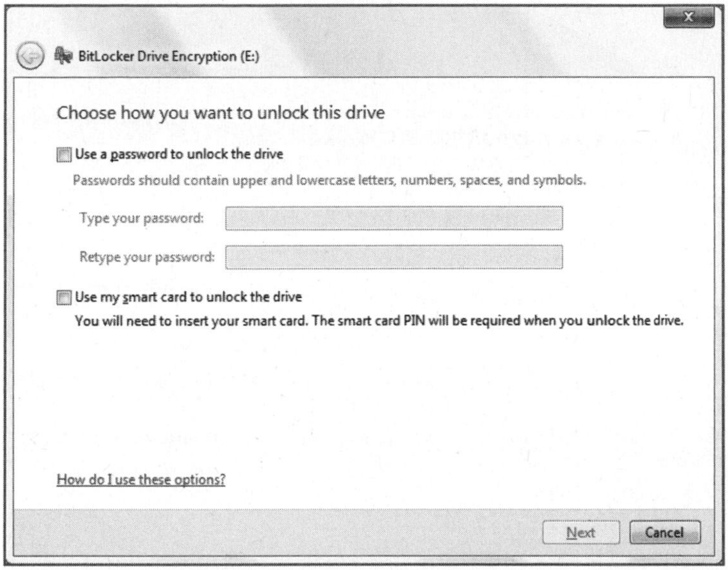

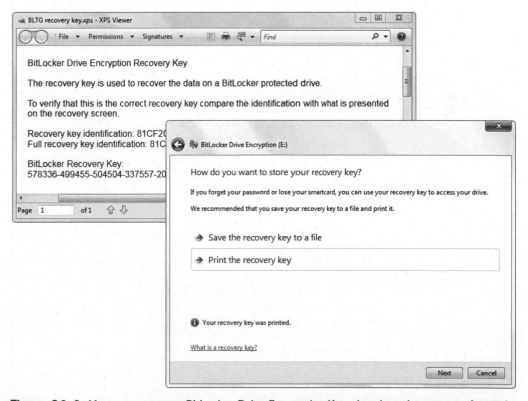

Figure 26-5: This wizard enables BitLocker To Go on a USB-attached storage device.

Figure 26-6: You can save your BitLocker Drive Encryption Key elsewhere in case you forget it.

After that, you're prompted that the encryption is about to start.

Secret

Disk encryption can be agonizingly slow, depending on the size of the storage device. A 2GB USB memory stick takes roughly 20 minutes to be encrypted with BitLocker To Go. In the spirit of "taking one for the team," we encrypted a 320GB USB hard drive using BitLocker To Go. It took all of a work day, or several long hours, to finalize. You've been warned. That said, you can pause the process at any time, use the disk for other purposes, and then restart it. You won't lose any data.

Using BitLocker To Go

Once a storage device is encrypted, you'll notice a few changes. The icon for disks encrypted by BitLocker To Go is different, for starters, and includes a padlock/key overlay, as shown in Figure 26-7.

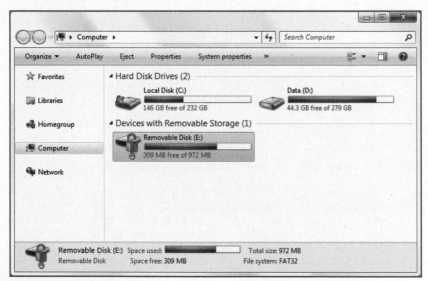

Figure 26-7: BitLocker-protected disks utilize a special icon overlay.

Also, when you remove and then insert a BitLocker-protected storage device, you will be prompted to provide a password to unlock the disk (see Figure 26-8). Once you do so, the normal Auto Run dialog will appear and the device will work normally.

Remember, this prompt will appear when you plug the BitLocker-protected device into any Windows 7–based PC. That is, you do not need Windows 7 Enterprise or Ultimate to use this feature, because once BitLocker To Go protection is added to a device, it is compatible with all Windows 7 versions.

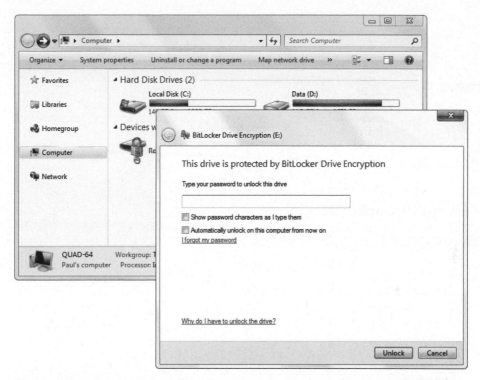

Figure 26-8: BitLocker-protected disks cannot be accessed until you've supplied the magic word.

Secret

You can choose to automatically unlock a BitLocker To Go protected disk on a per-PC basis. This is arguably safe to do if you provide a password when you log on to your PC. And it's certainly more convenient than retyping the device password every time you plug it in. If you do enable this option, it will not affect how BitLocker To Go functions on other PCs.

Configuring BitLocker To Go

You can configure devices protected with BitLocker To Go in various ways. If you right-click a protected device in Explorer, a new Manage BitLocker option appears in the pop-up menu, replacing Turn on BitLocker. (You can also access this functionality from the BitLocker Drive Encryption control panel, of course.) The resulting window, shown in Figure 26-9, provides a number of options, including ways to change and remove the device's password, remove a smart card (if one is configured), add a smart card, resave or print the recovery key, and automatically unlock the drive on the current PC.

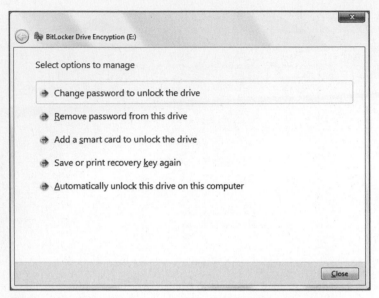

Figure 26-9: Previously protected devices can be configured in various ways.

The BitLocker Drive Encryption control panel provides one unique additional option: The ability to turn off BitLocker, as shown in Figure 26-10. In fact, this is the only place in Windows 7 from which you can remove BitLocker from a device. (Short of formatting the disk, which would of course also delete any data stored on it.)

Secret

> Decrypting devices encrypted by BitLocker To Go also takes an incredibly long time.

Using BitLocker To Go devices on Windows XP and Vista

BitLocker To Go–protected devices work identically on all Windows 7 systems. But you can also use these devices on Windows XP-based and Vista-based PCs. For these systems, Microsoft provides a BitLocker Reader application right on the encrypted device, enabling users of those PCs to access the stored files. However, this Reader application isn't full-featured, as it is read-only. So after you've provided the password to unlock the drive, you can view files on the device and copy them to your PC hard drive, but you cannot save files back to the device.

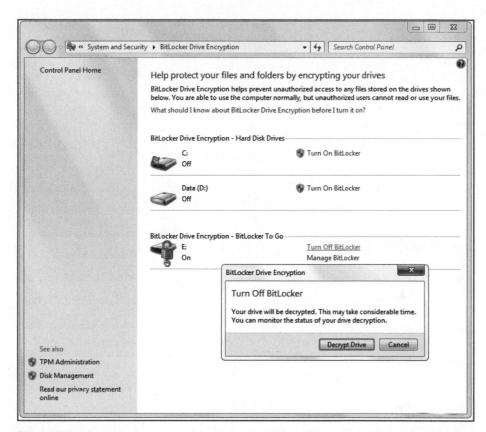

Figure 26-10: You can remove BitLocker To Go protection with the BitLocker Drive Encryption control panel.

Secret

Got a Mac? You're really out of luck, then. You cannot access BitLocker To Go–protected devices from Mac OS X at all.

Windows Virtual PC and Windows XP Mode

Microsoft has provided desktop-oriented virtualization capabilities through its Virtual PC product line since the company purchased the virtualization assets of Connectix in 2003. With Windows 7, Windows Virtual PC, as the latest version of Virtual PC is now known, becomes a feature and benefit of Microsoft's latest operating system. And this time, it offers deep integration features with the Windows 7 Desktop, enabling users to run virtualized Windows XP, Vista, and 7 applications side-by-side with native Windows 7 applications, without forcing users to manage the complexity of dealing with two desktops, one virtualized and one native. Windows Virtual PC is available to users of any Windows 7 product edition; it is not limited to certain versions as was the case with its predecessor, Virtual PC 2007.

Furthermore, as a perk to Windows 7 Professional, Enterprise, and Ultimate users, Microsoft is offering a free, complete, and fully licensed virtualized version of Windows XP with Service Pack 3. This environment, called Windows XP Mode, can be run inside of Windows Virtual PC, providing users with the opportunity to significantly enhance Windows 7's application (and device) compatibility to include most productivity and custom applications that worked with XP. Using this environment, you can run virtualized XP applications side-by-side with native Windows 7 applications, as shown in Figure 26-11.

Windows Virtual PC and Windows XP Mode are fully covered in Chapter 3.

Figure 26-11: Windows XP Mode enables you to run Windows XP and Windows 7 applications side-by-side on the Windows Desktop.

Virtual Hard Drive (VHD) Mounting

Speaking of Windows Virtual PC, the virtual machines (VMs) created and used by this environment—as well as other Microsoft virtualization solutions like the Windows Server-based Hyper-V—utilize a virtual hard drive format that Microsoft creatively calls *virtual hard drive*, or *VHD*. These files are seen as any other files (albeit large ones) by the underlying OS and they can be copied around like any other files, which makes them easily deployable in corporate environments. But in Windows 7, Microsoft has added a few twists to this capability. The biggie is that you can "mount" VHDs using Windows' built-in disk management tools, enabling you to navigate around these virtual disks while the underlying VM is offline, using Windows Explorer. This enables you to copy files in and out of the virtual disks, which can be useful.

Secret Additionally, Windows 7 actually lets you boot your PC using a VHD instead of the native Windows 7 environment you've installed on the physical disk. This capability is obviously more useful in server environments, where you might want a virtual environment to run more efficiently at certain times. But it's an interesting and unique capability on the desktop as well. It requires tools that are available on the Windows Automated Installation Kit (AIK), and it is documented on Paul Thurrott's SuperSite for Windows at www.winsupersite.com/win7.

Mounting a VHD is straightforward. First, run the Windows 7 Disk Management utility, shown in Figure 26-12. You can do so by typing **disk management** in Start Menu Search and then choosing *Create and manage hard disk partitions* from the search results. Alternately, you can open the Start menu, right-click Computer, choose Manage, and then select Disk Management in the Computer Management window that appears.

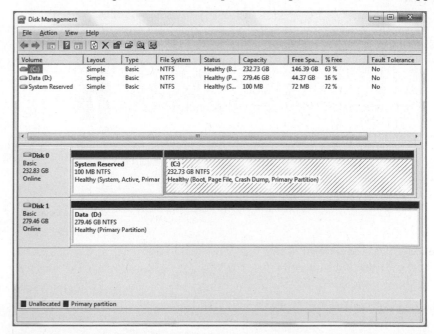

Figure 26-12: The Windows 7 Disk Management utility

This utility hasn't changed much since Windows Vista, with one big exception: when you click the Action menu item, you'll see new Create VHD and Attach VHD options. The first provides a way to create an empty VHD and, as it turns out, automatically mount that VHD in the PC's file system. If you already have a VHD you want to use, you can simply choose Action and then Attach VHD to mount it. When you do so, you'll be prompted to browse the file system to find a VHD file.

Secret

If you're using Windows Virtual PC, VHDs for the virtual machines you've created are found in C:\Users\[*your username*]\AppData\Local\Microsoft\Windows Virtual PC\Virtual Machines by default. Older versions of Virtual PC utilized C:\ Users\[*your username*]\Documents\My Virtual Machines.

Once you've found the VHD you'd like to mount, you can optionally check the Read-only option (if you don't want to inadvertently make any errors) and click OK. If this is the first time you've done this, Windows 7 will automatically install the required VHD host bus adapter (HBA) driver. Then, the selected VHD and any partition(s) it contains will appear in the Disk Management window, as shown in Figure 26-13. You may also see AutoPlay dialog(s) appear for the attached partition(s).

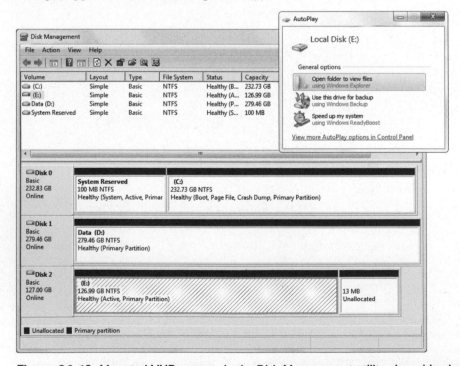

Figure 26-13: Mounted VHDs appear in the Disk Management utility alongside physical disks.

If you navigate to Computer, you'll see that the underlying partition(s) also appear with drive letters alongside your physical disks (see Figure 26-14). You can now navigate inside these drives as you would any physical disks, copying files and making whatever changes you'd like.

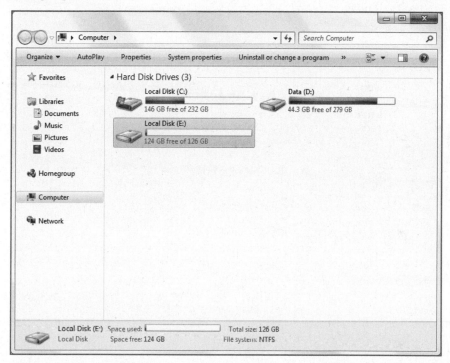

Figure 26-14: Virtual hard disks appear alongside physical disks in Explorer as well.

To unmount a VHD, return to Disk Management, right-click the virtual disk (not one of its partitions), and choose Detach VHD.

Windows PowerShell 2.0

Windows PowerShell is a next-generation command-line and scripting environment with capabilities far beyond the older command interpreters that were included with previous versions of Windows (and, still are, as it turns out). Based on Microsoft's .NET technologies, Windows PowerShell was created because Microsoft wanted to better support the ever-evolving needs of system administrators. For this audience, Windows PowerShell provides an unprecedented level of control, along with a consistent and logical interactive shell that is self-documenting and discoverable. Put more simply, Windows PowerShell makes it easier than ever to automate repetitive tasks; and for power users of all kinds, this new environment points the way to the future.

Today, Microsoft uses PowerShell as the underpinnings of its Exchange Server messaging product, for example, providing a UNIX-like command-line environment on which all of the familiar GUI management tools are actually based. In addition, PowerShell is an integrated part of Windows Server 2008 R2 and forms the basis for some of its management tools as well. Windows 7 is the first version of the Windows client to include a version of PowerShell.

Understanding PowerShell

Originally released around the same time as Windows Vista as a separate add-on, Windows PowerShell 2.0 is now a fully integrated component of Windows 7. It provides an extensive scripting environment that is far richer than the batch language included with the command-line environment in previous versions of Windows. (Though for backward compatibility reasons, Windows 7 continues to include this older command-line environment.) It also comes with an integrated scripting environment, the PowerShell Integrated Scripting Environment, or ISE, which enables you to test and execute scripts.

Secret

PowerShell 2.0 can also be downloaded and run on Windows XP and Windows 2000, as well as earlier versions of Windows Server. This means PowerShell scripts you write can also run on most other Windows PCs in operation today.

As noted previously, PowerShell represents so much capability that Microsoft's Exchange Server 2007 admin console is written in it. You probably won't need to write anything that complex; but regardless of the size of your project, Microsoft has built PowerShell so it has few limitations. It's worlds away from Windows' old batch language, which is run by the `cmd.exe` command interpreter, and is even more powerful—and certainly more consistent—than any UNIX command-line environment.

As just one of the features PowerShell brings to Windows that Microsoft's older command-line environments did not, you can use PowerShell commands to read from and write to hives in the Windows Registry as though they were ordinary drives. For example, you access `HKEY_LOCAL_MACHINE` through a drive named `HKLM`, and `HKEY_CUURENT_USER` via `HKCU`.

It's impossible to adequately document the Windows PowerShell language and environment here—entire books deal with this subject, and we recommend that you study one if you want to become proficient. Instead, this section provides an introduction that will help get you started.

Constructing a PowerShell Command

The Windows PowerShell language draws from several older programming languages. Its grammar is based on POSIX, a character-based command language that's also called a *shell* (because it sits over the operating system *kernel*). POSIX is a subset of the Korn Shell, which is widely used in UNIX environments.

Windows PowerShell, however, is not a copy of POSIX. Instead, it adopts many of the features of the object-oriented Microsoft .NET programming model. In a nutshell, .NET objects have properties and methods, both of which are defined in well-understood ways. For example, a file object has properties such as size (in bytes), a date and time when the file was last modified, a read-only flag (which may be on or off), and so forth.

In creating the commands that would be available in Windows PowerShell, Microsoft's developers used a *verb-noun* naming convention. Some common Windows PowerShell commands are as follows:

```
Get-ChildItem
Get-Content
Remove-Item
```

In each case, the first word is a verb, followed by a hyphen and then a noun on which the verb operates. (Speaking of case, all Windows PowerShell commands are case insensitive. That is, GET-childITEM does the same thing as get-childitem. We're documenting commands here with initial capital letters for the same reason Microsoft does—to improve readability—but you're free to write them in whatever mixed case you wish.)

These commands seem awfully long—and you haven't even done anything yet. Fortunately, shorter versions of Windows PowerShell commands, called *aliases,* are also built into the system for most commands. Additionally, you can define your own aliases. The three Windows PowerShell commands previously shown are equivalent to the following cmd. exe commands that you probably know:

```
dir
type
del
```

That's right—Microsoft has defined long, hard-to-remember commands to replace dir (which shows a directory listing of filenames), type (which displays a file's contents), and del (which erases a file).

Microsoft explains the length of its new PowerShell commands by saying it helps PowerShell developers remember and understand them. It also makes it possible to get a synopsis of a group of commands by using the command get-help, though to be fair, many people will use the command's short, memorable alias instead: help.

For example, you can see a listing of all the Windows PowerShell commands that retrieve, or *get*, some kind of information using the following syntax:

```
help get-*
```

When you enter this at the PowerShell command line or in the PowerShell ISE and press Enter, you'll see the output shown in Figure 26-15.

You can also see those commands that operate on objects:

```
help *-object

Name            Category    Synopsis
ForEach-Object  Cmdlet      Performs an operation against each o...
Where-Object    Cmdlet      Creates a filter that controls which...
Compare-Object  Cmdlet      Compares two sets of objects.
Measure-Object  Cmdlet      Measures characteristics of objects ...
Tee-Object      Cmdlet      Pipes object input to a file or vari...
New-Object      Cmdlet      Creates an instance of a .Net or COM...
Select-Object   Cmdlet      Selects specified properties of an o...
Group-Object    Cmdlet      GrouPowerShell objects that contain the same...
Sort-Object     Cmdlet      Sorts objects by property values.
```

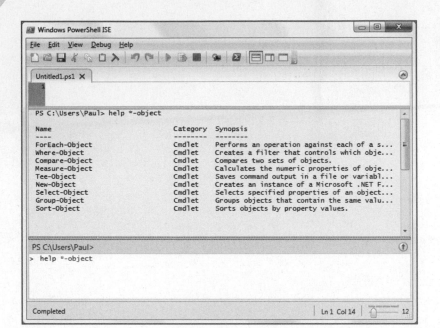

Figure 26-15: The PowerShell ISE is an ideal environment for using PowerShell.

Seeing All the Commands

PowerShell provides a command, known as `Get-Command`, that displays all the built-in commands available. Unlike the old `cmd.exe`, which relies on external, on-disk files for most of its features, PowerShell has a wealth of internal commands. These are known as *cmdlets*, pronounced *commandlets*.

The alias for `Get-Command` is `gcm`. Both the cmdlet and its alias require the addition of a pipe (|) and the `more` command to keep the output from scrolling off the top of the screen. The following lines show how to use the `more` command:

```
gcm | more


CommandType      Name                Definition
-----------      ----                ----------

Function         A:                  Set-Location A:
Cmdlet           Add-Computer        Add-Computer [-DomainName] <Stri...
Cmdlet           Add-Content         Add-Content [-Path] <String[]> [...
Cmdlet           Add-History         Add-History [[-InputObject] <PSO...
...
Function         X:                  Set-Location X:
Function         Y:                  Set-Location Y:
Function         Z:                  Set-Location Z:
```

Getting Help with Commands

To find the syntax and all the parameters of a command, type **help** and the name of the command or its alias. This command automatically pages the output, so no more than one screenful appears at a time:

```
help foreach

NAME
    ForEach-Object

SYNOPSIS
    Performs an operation against each of a set of input objects.


SYNTAX
    ForEach-Object [-Process] <ScriptBlock[]> [-Begin <scriptblock>] [-End
    <scriptblock>] [-InputObject <psobject>] [<CommonParameters>]


DESCRIPTION
    The ForEach-Object cmdlet performs an operation on each of a set of input
    objects. The input objects can be piped to the cmdlet or specified by using
    the InputObject parameter.

    The operation to perform is described within a script block that is provided
    to the cmdlet as the value of the Process parameter. The script block can
    contain any Windows PowerShell script.

    Within the script block, the current input object is represented by the $_
    variable. In addition to using the script block that describes the
    operations to be carried out on each input object, you can provide two
    additional script blocks. One, specified as the value of the Begin
    parameter, runs before the first input object is processed. The other,
    specified as the value of the End parameter, runs after the last input
    object is processed.

    The results of the evaluation of all the script blocks, including the ones
    specified with Begin and End, are passed down the pipeline.


RELATED LINKS
    Online version: http://go.microsoft.com/fwlink/?LinkID=113300

REMARKS
    To see the examples, type: "get-help ForEach-Object -examples".
    For more information, type: "get-help ForEach-Object -detailed".
    For technical information, type: "get-help ForEach-Object -full".
```

Why a New Language?

Windows PowerShell has far more capabilities than the old Windows command prompt, cmd.exe. Take a look at a very simple example to see what you can do with Windows PowerShell.

The dir command, as you probably know, displays a directory listing of the files in the current directory or any specified directory. The output of dir looks the same in both cmd. exe and Windows PowerShell, but PowerShell enables you to do a lot more.

In cmd.exe, the dir command simply outputs the name, size, and other attributes of the files it lists. If you wanted to see whether a particular set of files would fit onto a single CD-R, for example, you might look at the output of a dir command:

```
dir
Mode            LastWriteTime        Length    Name
--------        --------------------  --------  --------
-a---           12/31/2007 10:00 AM  20123456  File1.doc
-a---           12/31/2007 10:30 AM  21234567  File2.doc
-a---           12/31/2007 11:00 AM  22345678  File3.doc
```

You could then add up the length of the files in your head or on a calculator; or you could try to write a batch file that would accept the output of dir, extract the byte sizes, and then somehow add them up and display a total.

With Windows PowerShell, determining the size of a directory in bytes can be accomplished with just three lines of code. First, you define a variable, $bytesize, and set its initial value to zero. Next, you pipe the output of the Windows PowerShell cmdlet alias dir into the foreach alias and add up the bytes. Finally, you display the total. The whole thing looks like this:

```
$bytesize = 0
dir | foreach {$bytesize += $_.length}
$bytesize
```

In response to the third line of code, Windows PowerShell displays the value of $bytesize:

```
63703701
```

Instead of using the third line of this script, which simply outputs the total onscreen, you could feed the number into another process, write the total into a file for later analysis, or any other number of alternatives. For example, if the selected files were too large for a single CD-R, a script you wrote could show you the message "Whoa, boy! You'll need two CDs for those files," or three, or four, or whatever number was calculated.

Notice that we've used the aliases dir and foreach to make the second line of the script concise. If we had used the non-alias name of each cmdlet, the script might look as follows:

```
$bytesize = 0
get-childitem | foreach-object {$bytesize += $_.length}
$bytesize
```

Because a percent sign (%) is also an alias for the for-eachobject cmdlet, you could also make the original script even shorter, at the expense of being less readable:

```
$bytesize = 0
dir | % {$bytesize += $_.length}
$bytesize
```

The percent sign in this case doesn't have anything to do with calculating a percentage. It's just an alias for the command `foreach-object`. This use of symbols may be confusing, but it does reduce the amount of typing developers have to do, which is always a good thing.

Summary

While Windows 7's consumer-oriented features are the flashiest and most often promoted, the truth is that Microsoft serves many different markets and customer types with this versatile desktop solution. And while many of Windows 7's business-oriented features may be snooze-fests for the average individual, understanding what's out there and which business features make sense for you to capitalize on is one of many steps you'll take in your journey toward being a Windows power user. We hope you've found this chapter—and indeed this entire book—useful in achieving that goal. And we look forward to meeting up again in the future, be it online at our respective Web sites, or in the next edition to this book. Windows 8? Bring it on.

Index